MAUI
HANDBOOK
INCLUDING MOLOKAI AND LANAI

D.ASICH

MAUI
HANDBOOK
INCLUDING MOLOKAI AND LANAI

BY J.D. BISIGNANI

UPDATED AND REVISED BY
ROBERT NILSEN

MOON
PUBLICATIONS INC.

MAUI HANDBOOK: INCLUDING MOLOKAI AND LANAI

Please send all comments, corrections, additions, amendments, and critiques to:

J.D. Bisignani
c/o MOON PUBLICATIONS
722 WALL STREET
CHICO, CA 95928 USA

Published by
Moon Publications Inc.
722 Wall Street
Chico, California 95928 USA
tel. (916) 345-5473

Printed by
Colorcraft Ltd., Hong Kong

PRINTING HISTORY

First edition
May 1986
Reprinted
March 1987
April 1988
Second Edition
January 1989
Third Edition
July 1991

Library of Congress Cataloging in Publication Data

Bisignani, J.D., 1947-
  Maui Handbook: Including Molokai and Lanai/J.D. Bisignani — 3rd ed.
    p.   cm.
  Includes bibliographical references.
  ISBN-0-918373-60-3
  1. Maui (Hawaii)—Description and travel—Guide-books. 2. Lanai (Hawaii)—Description
  and travel—Guide-books. 3. Molokai (Hawaii)—Description and travel—Guide-books.
  I. Title
  DU628.M3B57 1991   91-8448
  919.69'2044—dc20   CIP

Printed in Hong Kong

Cover art: Courtesy of Richard Fields Studios, Wailea, Maui

To Sylvester T.,
the best long-distance man
there ever was

ACKNOWLEDGEMENTS

Writing the acknowledgements for a book is supercharged with energy. It's a time when you look forward, hopefully, to a bright future for your work, and a time when you reflect on all that has gone into producing it. Mostly it's a time to say thank you. Thank you for the grace necessary to carry out the task, and thank you to all the wonderful people whose efforts have helped so much along the way. To the following people, I offer my most sincere "thank you."

Firstly, to the Moon staff, professionals every one. As time has passed, and one book has followed another, they've become amazingly adept at their work, to the point where their mastery is a marvel to watch. Mark Morris and Taran March, my editors, whose eagle eyes inspect every page, oftentimes saving me from myself. Christa Jorgensen, who worked in the trenches transcribing over 3,000 pages of travel information. Asha Johnson, a true dynamo, who is typesetter, computer wiz, and "positive vibe person at large." Nancy Kennedy, who fitted all the parts of the giant jigsaw puzzle, matching text with maps, illustrations, photos, graphs, charts, and itsy-bitsy weirdnesses without losing her temper even one time. Hard working Mark Voss, who did the paste-up. Louise Foote, map-maker extraordinaire, and her helper, Alex "Louise Jr." Foote, who did the original maps in this book. Bob Race, who's taken over the map department and who revised each and every map, and whom we all can thank for pointing us in the right direction. Rick Johnson, who knows "where in the world" all the Moon books are, and who is chiefly responsible for keeping them on the bookstore shelves. Donna Galassi, director of sales, and publicist Virginia Michaels who keep the Moon rising with every new order that they bring in the door. Cindy Fahey, bookkeeper, who, with some amazing fancy dancing, robs Peter to pay Paul and somehow makes them like it. My illustrators, Diana Lasich Harper, Louise Foote, Sue Strangio Everett, Mary Ann Abel, Debra Fau, Brian Bardwell, and Robert Race, contributing photographers David Stanley, Howard Lindeman, and R.J. Schallenberger, Bob Nilsen, and cover artist Richard Fields, whose talents grace this book.

California State University at Chico professors Bob Vivian, George Benson, Ed Myles, and Ellen Walker, who provided me with quality interns from their respective departments of Journalism, Tourism, Geography, and English. The following student interns worked in the trenches transcribing, inputting, designing charts and graphs, and generally infusing my surroundings with positive energy: Caroline Schoepp, Maureen Cole, Suzanne Booth, Lee Wilkinson, Sally Price, Elena Wilkinson, Bret Lampman, Rich Zimmerman, Craig Nelson, Pat Presley, Leslie Crouch, Monica Moore, Annie Hikido, and Janeen Thomas.

I would also like to thank the following people for their special help and consideration: Dr. Greg Leo, an adventurer and environmentalist who has done remarkable field research and provided me with invaluable information about the unique flora and fauna of Hawaii; Roger Rose and Elisa Johnston of the Bishop Museum; Lee Wild, Hawaiian Mission Houses Museum; Marilyn Nicholson, State Foundation of Culture and the Arts; the Hawaii Visitors Bureau; Chris Tajeda, Tropical Car Rental; Keoni Wagner, Hawaiian Airlines; Jim and John Costello; Dr. Terry and Nancy Carolan; Sally Proctor of Aston Hotels; Renee Cochran, Carol Wilbur, and Will Titus, Colony Resorts; Linda Darling-Mann, Coco Palms Resort; Glenn Masutani, Hawaiian Pacific Resorts; Barbara Brundage, Dive Hawaii; Donna Jung, Judy Veirck, Patti of Patti Cook Associates, Carol Dawson, Maui Prince Hotel; Sheila Donnelly and Associates, for the Lodge at Koele; Michelle Seto, for the Lahaina Hotel; Blair Shurtleff, Hana Plantation House; and Richard Stancliff, Valley Isle Lodge. To all of you, my deepest *aloha*.

CONTENTS

MAPS

CHARTS

MAP LEGEND

FREEWAY	
MAIN HIGHWAY	
SECONDARY ROAD	
JEEP TRAIL	
FOOT TRAIL	
HIGHWAY NUMBER	
WATER	
MOUNTAIN	

 LARGE TOWN OR CITY

O   TOWN OR VILLAGE

o   POINT OF INTEREST

●   STATE OR BEACH PARK

 HEIAU

 CAMPGROUND

All maps are oriented with north at the top of the map
unless otherwise indicated.

ABBREVIATIONS

Bldg.=Building
4WD=four-wheel drive
HNL=Honolulu
HVB=Hawaii Visitors
    Bureau
mph=miles per hour

NWR=National Wildlife
    Refuge
O/W=one way
p/d=per day
p/h=per hour
P.O.=post office

p/w=per week
Rt.=Route
rm.=room
R/T=round trip
TCs=traveler's checks
YH=youth hostel

IS THIS BOOK OUT OF DATE?

In today's world, things change so rapidly that it's impossible for one person to keep up with everything happening in any one place. This is particularly true in Hawaii, where situations are always in flux. Travel books are like automobiles: they require fine-tuning and frequent overhauls to keep in shape. Help us keep this book in shape! We require input from our readers so that we can continue to provide the best, most current information available. Please write to let us know about any inaccuracies, new information, or misleading suggestions. Although we try to make our maps as accurate as possible, errors do occur. If you have any suggestions for improvement or places that should be included, please let us know about them.

We especially appreciate letters from female travelers, visiting expatriates, local residents, and hikers and outdoor enthusiasts. We also like hearing from experts in the field as well as from local hotel owners and individuals wishing to accommodate visitors from abroad.

As you travel through the islands, keep notes in the margins of this book. Notes written on the spot are always more accurate than those put down on paper later. Send us your copy after your trip, and we'll send you a fresh one as a replacement. If you take a photograph during your trip which you feel could be included in future editions, please send it to us. Send only good slide duplicates or glossy black-and-white prints. Drawings and other artwork are also appreciated. If we use your photo or drawing, you'll be mentioned in the credits and receive a free copy of the book. Keep in mind, however, that the publisher cannot return any materials unless you include a self-addressed, stamped envelope. Moon Publications will own the rights on all material submitted. Address your letters to:

J.D. Bisignani
Moon Publications
722 Wall Street
Chico, CA 95928, U.S.A.

INTRODUCTION

The *Kumulipo,* the ancient genealogical chant of the Hawaiians, sings of the demigod Maui, a half-human mythological sorcerer known and revered throughout Polynesia. Maui was a prankster on a grand scale who used guile and humor to create some of the most amazing feats of derring-do ever recorded. A Polynesian combination of Paul Bunyan and Hercules, Maui's adventures were known as "strifes." He served mankind by fishing up the islands of Hawaii from the ocean floor, securing fire from a tricky mud hen, lifting the sky so humans could walk upright, and slowing down the sun-god by lassoing his genitals with a braided rope of his sister's pubic hair. Maui accomplished this last feat on the summit of the great mountain Haleakala ("House of the Sun"), thus securing more time in the day to fish and to dry tapa. Maui met his just but untimely end between the legs of the great goddess, Hina. This final prank, in which he attempted to crawl into the sleeping goddess's vagina, left his feet and legs dangling out,

causing uproarious laughter among his comrades, a band of warrior birds. The noise awakened Hina, who saw no humor in the situation. She unceremoniously squeezed Maui to death. The island of Maui is the only island in Hawaii and throughout Polynesia named after a god. With such a legacy the island couldn't help but become known as *"Maui no ka oi"* ("Maui is the best!").

AN OVERVIEW

In a land of superlatives, it's quite a claim to call your island *the* best, but Maui has a lot to back it up. Maui has more miles of swimmable beach than any of the other islands. Haleakala, the massive mountain that *is* East Maui, is the largest dormant volcano in the world, and its hardened lava rising over 30,000 feet from the sea floor makes it one of the heaviest concentrated masses on the face of the earth. There are legitimate claims that Maui grows

MAUI

the best onions and potatoes, but the boast of the best *pakololo* may only be a pipe dream, since all islands have great soil, weather, and many enterprising gardeners. Some even claim that Maui gets more sunshine than the other islands, but that's hard to prove.

Maui's Body

If you look at the silhouette of Maui on a map, it looks like the head and torso of a man bent at the waist and contemplating the uninhabited island of Kahoolawe. The head is West Maui. The profile is that of a wizened old man whose wrinkled brow and cheeks are the West Maui Mountains. The highest peak here is **Puu Kukui,** at 5,778 feet, located just about where the ear would be. If you go to the top of the head you'll be at Kapalua, a resort community recently carved from pineapple fields. Fleming Beach begins a string of beaches that continues down over the face, stopping at the neck, and picking up again on the chest, which is Southeast Maui. Kaanapali is the forehead; this massive beach continues almost uninterrupted for four miles. In comparison, this area alone would take in all of Waikiki, from Diamond Head to Ala Moana. Sugar cane fields fringe the mountain side of the road, while condos are strung along the shore. The resorts here are cheek to jowl, but the best are tastefully done with views and access to the beach.

Lahaina would be located at the Hindu "third eye." This town is where it's "happening" on Maui, with concentrations of crafts, museums, historical sites, restaurants, and night spots. Lahaina has always been somewhat of a playground, used in times past by royal Hawaiian *ali'i* and then by Yankee whalers. The good-times mystique still lingers. At the tip of the nose is Olowalu, where a lunatic Yankee trader, Simon Metcalf, decided to slaughter hundreds of curious Hawaiians paddling toward his ship just to show them he was boss. From Olowalu you can see four islands: Molokai, Lanai, Kahoolawe, and a faint hint of Hawaii far to the south. The back of Maui's head is an adventurer's paradise, complete with a tourist-eliminating rugged road posted with over-exaggerated Proceed No Farther signs. Back here are tremendous coastal views, bird sanctuaries, *heiau,* and Kahakuloa, a tiny fishing village reported to be a favorite stomping ground of great Maui himself.

The Isthmus

A low flat isthmus planted primarily in sugar cane is the neck that connects the head of West Maui to the torso of East Maui, which is Haleakala. The Adam's apple is the little port of Maalaea, which has a good assortment of pleasure and fishing boats, and provides an up-close look at a working port not nearly as frenetic as Lahaina. The nape of the neck is

West Maui Mountains
(BOB NILSEN)

made up of the twin cities of Wailuku, the county seat, and Kahului, where visitors arrive at Maui's airport. These towns are where the "people" live. Some say the isthmus, dramatically separating east and west, is the reason Maui is called "The Valley Isle." Head into Iao Valley from Wailuku, where the West Maui Mountains have been worn into incredible peaked monolithic spires. This stunning valley area played a key role in Kamehameha's unification of the Hawaiian Islands, and geologically seems to be a more fitting reason for Maui's nickname.

East Maui/Haleakala

Once you cross the isthmus you're on the immensity of Haleakala. This mountain is a true microcosm and makes up the entire bulging, muscled torso. Its geology encompasses alpine terrain, desert, jungle, pastureland, and wasteland. The temperature, determined by altitude, ranges from subfreezing to subtropical. If you head east along the spine, you'll find world-class sailboarding beaches, artist villages, last-picture-show towns, and a few remaining family farms planted in taro. Route 360, the only coastal road, rocks and rolls you over its more than 600 documented curves, and shows you more waterfalls and pristine pools than you can count. After crossing more than 50 bridges, you come to Hana. Here, the "dream" Hawaii that people seek still lives. Farther along is Oheo Stream and its pools, erroneously known as "The Seven Sacred Pools." However, there is no mistaking the amazing energy vibrations in the area. Close by is where Charles Lindbergh is buried, and many celebrities have chosen the surrounding hillsides as their special retreats and hideaways.

On Haleakala's broad chest are macho cowboy towns complete with Wild West rodeos contrasting with the gentle but riotous colors of carnation and protea farms. Polipoli State Park is here, a thick forest canopy with more varieties of imported trees than anywhere else in Oceania. A weird cosmic joke places Kihei just about where the armpit would be. Kihei is a mega-growth condo area ridiculed as an example of what developers shouldn't be allowed to do. Oddly enough, Wailea, just down the road, exemplifies a reasonable and aesthetic planned community and is highly touted as a "model" development area. Just at the belly button, close to the *kundalini,* is Makena, long renowned as Maui's "alternative beach." It's the island's last "free" beach with no restrictions, no park rangers, almost no amenities, and sometimes, no bathing suits.

Finally, when you pilgrimage to the summit of Haleakala, it'll be as if you've left the planet. It's another world: beautiful, mystical, raw, inspired, and freezing cold. When you're alone on the crater rim with the world below garlanded by the brilliance of sunrise or sunset, you'll know that you have come at last to great Maui's heart.

THE LAND

The modern geological theory concerning the formation of the Hawaiian Islands is no less fanciful than the Polynesian legends sung about their origins. Science maintains that 30 million years ago, while the great continents were being geologically tortured into their rudimentary shapes, the Hawaiian Islands were a mere ooze of bubbling magma 20,000 feet below the surface of the primordial sea. For millions of years this molten rock flowed up from fissures in the sea floor. Slowly, layer upon layer of lava was deposited until an island rose above the surface of the sea. The great weight then sealed the fissure, whose own colossal forces progressively crept in a southwestern direction, then burst out again and again to build the chain. At the same time the entire Pacific plate was afloat on the giant sea of molten magma, and it slowly glided to the northwest carrying the newly formed islands with it.

In the beginning the spewing crack formed Kure and Midway islands in the extreme northwestern sector of the Hawaiian chain. Today, more than 130 islands, islets, and shoals make up the Hawaiian Islands, stretching 1,600 miles across an expanse of the North Pacific. Some geologists maintain that the "hot spot" now primarily under the Big Island remains relatively stationary, and the 1,600-mile spread of the Hawaiian archipelago is only due to a northwest drifting effect of about three

to five inches per year. Still, with the center of activity under the Big Island, Mauna Loa and Kilauea volcanoes regularly add more land to the only state in the Union that is literally still growing. About 30 miles southeast of the Big Island is Loihi Sea Mount, waiting 3,000 feet below the waves. Frequent eruptions bring it closer and closer to the surface until one day it will emerge and become the newest Hawaiian island.

Maui Features

After Hawaii, Maui is the second largest and second youngest of the main Hawaiian Islands. It is made up of two volcanoes: the **West Maui Mountains** and **Haleakala.** The West Maui Mountains are geologically much older than Haleakala, but the two were joined by subsequent lava flows that formed a connecting low, flat isthmus. **Puu Kukui**, at 5,778 feet, is the tallest peak of the West Maui Mountains. It's the lord of a mountain domain whose old weathered face has been scarred by an inhospitable series of deep crags, valleys, and gorges. Haleakala, in comparison, is an adolescent with smooth, rounded features. This precocious kid looms 10,023 feet above sea level, and is four times larger than West Maui. Its incredible mass as it rises over 30,000 feet from the ocean floor is one of the densest on earth. Its gravitational pull is staggering and it was considered a primary power spot in old Hawaii. The two parts of Maui combine to form 728.8 square miles of land with 120 linear miles of coastline. At its widest, Maui is 25 miles from north to south, and 40 miles east to west. The coastline has the largest number of swimmable beaches in Hawaii, and the interior is a miniature continent with almost every conceivable geological feature evident.

Island Builders

The Hawaiians worshiped Madame Pele, the fire-goddess. Her name translates equally as "volcano," "fire pit," or "eruption of lava." When she was angry, she complained by spitting fire which cooled and formed land. Volcanologists say that the islands are huge mounds of cooled basaltic lava surrounded by billions of polyp skeletons which have formed coral reefs. The Hawaiian Islands are shield volcanoes that erupt gently and form an elongated dome much like a turtle shell. Maui, like the rest, is a perfect example of this. Once above the surface of the sea, the tremendous weight of lava seals the fissure below. Eventually the giant tube that carried lava to the surface sinks in on itself and forms a caldera, as evidenced atop Haleakala, whose huge depression could hold all of Manhattan Island. More eruptions occur periodically, and they cover the already existing island like frosting on a titanic cake. Wind and water next take over and relentlessly sculpt the raw lava into deep crevices and cuts that become valleys. The once smooth West Maui Mountains are now more a mini-mountain range due to this process. Great Haleakala is being chiseled, too, as can be seen in the Kaupo Gap and the valleys of Kipahulu and Keanae.

Lava

Lava flows in two distinct types, for which the Hawaiian names have become universal geological terms: *a'a* and *pa'hoehoe*. They're easily distinguished in appearance, but chemically they're the same. *A'a* is extremely rough and spiny, and will quickly tear up your shoes if you do much hiking over it. Also, if you have the misfortune to fall down, you'll immediately know why they call it *a'a*. *Pa'hoehoe* is billowy ropey lava that looks like burned pan-

cake batter which can mold itself into fantastic shapes. Examples of both are frequently encountered on various hikes throughout Maui. Other lava oddities that you may spot on Maui are peridots, green gem-like stones called "Maui Diamonds," clear feldspar, and gray lichens covering the older flows known as "Hawaiian snow."

Rivers And Lakes

Maui has no navigable rivers but there are hundreds of streams. The two largest are Palikea Stream, which runs through Kipahulu Valley forming Oheo Gulch, and Iao Stream, which has sculpted the amazing monoliths in Iao Valley. A few reservoirs dot the island, but

Recent lava flows centered on the Big Island regularly add more land to the state of Hawaii.
(HAWAII VISITOR'S BUREAU)

the only natural body of water is the 41-acre Kanaha Pond, a major bird and wildlife sanctuary on the outskirts of Kahului. Hikers should be aware of the uncountable streams and rivulets that can quickly turn from trickles to torrents, causing flash floods in valleys that were the height of hospitality only minutes before.

Tsunamis

Tsunami is the Japanese word for tidal wave. It ranks up there with the worst of them in causing horror in human beings. But if you were to count up all the people in Hawaii who have been swept away by tidal waves in the last 50 years, the toll wouldn't come close to those killed on bicycles in only a few Mainland cities in just five years. A Hawaiian tsunami is actually a seismic sea wave that has been generated by an earthquake that could easily have had its origins thousands of miles away in South America or Alaska. Some waves have been clocked at speeds up to 500 miles per hour. The safest place, besides high ground well away from beach areas, is out on the open ocean where even an enormous wave is perceived only as a large swell—a tidal wave is only dangerous when it is opposed by land. The worst tsunami to strike Maui in modern times occurred on April 1, 1946. The Hana coast of windward East Maui bore the brunt with a tragic loss of many lives as entire villages were swept away.

Earthquakes

These rumblings are also a concern in Hawaii and offer a double threat because they cause tsunamis. If you ever feel a tremor and are close to a beach, get as far away as fast as possible. The Big Island, because of its active volcanoes, experiences hundreds of technical earthquakes, although 99 percent can only be felt on very delicate equipment. The last major quake occurred on the Big Island in late November 1975, reaching 7.2 on the Richter scale and causing many millions of dollars' worth of damage in the island's southern regions. The only loss of life was when a beach collapsed and two people from a large camping party were drowned. Maui, like the rest of the state, has an elaborate warning system

against natural disasters. You will notice loudspeakers high atop poles along many beaches and coastal areas; these warn of tsunamis, hurricanes, and earthquakes. They are tested at 11 a.m. on the first working day of each month. All island telephone books contain a civil defense warning and procedures section with which you should acquaint yourself. Note the maps showing which areas traditionally have been inundated by tsunamis, and what procedures to follow in case an emergency occurs.

CLIMATE

Maui has similar weather to the rest of the Hawaiian islands, though some aficionados claim that it gets more sunshine than the rest. The weather on Maui depends more on where you are than on what season it is. The average yearly daytime temperature hovers around 80° F and is moderated by the tradewinds. Nights are just a few degrees cooler. Since Haleakala is a main feature on Maui, you should remember that altitude drastically affects the weather. Expect an average drop of three degrees for every 1,000 feet of elevation. The lowest temperature ever recorded in Hawaii was atop Haleakala in 1961, when the mercury dropped well below freezing to a low, low 11°.

Precipitation

Rain on Maui is as much a factor as it is in all of Hawaii. On any day, somewhere on Maui it's raining, while other areas experience drought. A dramatic example of this phenomenon is a comparison of Lahaina with Mount Puu Kukui, both on West Maui and separated by only seven miles. Lahaina, which translates as "Merciless Sun," is hot, arid, and gets only 17 inches of rainfall annually, while Puu Kukui can receive close to 40 *feet* of rain! This rivals Mt. Waialeale on Kauai as the wettest spot on earth. The windward (wet) side of Maui, outlined by the Hana Road, is the perfect natural hothouse. Here, valleys sweetened with blossoms house idyllic waterfalls and pools that visitors treasure when they happen upon them. On the leeward (dry) side are Maui's best beaches: Kapalua, Kaanapali,

Kihei, Wailea, and Makena. They all sit in Haleakala's "rain shadow." If it happens to be raining at one, just move a few miles down the road to the next. Anyway, the rains are mostly gentle and the brooding sky, especially at sundown, is even more spectacular than normal.

When To Go

The prime tourist season starts two weeks before Christmas and lasts until Easter. It picks up again with summer vacation in early June and ends once more in late August. If possible, avoid these times of year. Hotel, airline, and car reservations, which are a must, can be hard to coordinate. Everything is usually booked solid and the prices are inflated. You can save between 10 and 50 percent of the cost and a lot of hassling if you go in the artificially created off-season, from September to early December, and from mid-April (after Easter) until early June. You'll not only find the prices better, but the beaches, hikes, campgrounds, and even restaurants will be less crowded, and the *people* will be happier to see you, too!

AVERAGE MAXIMUM/MINIMUM TEMPERATURE AND RAINFALL

Island	Town		Jan.	Mar.	May	June	Sept.	Nov.
Maui	Lahaina	high	80	81	82	83	84	82
		low	62	63	68	68	70	65
		rain	3	1	0	0	0	1
	Hana	high	79	79	80	80	81	80
		low	60	60	62	63	65	61
		rain	9	7	2	3	5	7
	Kahului	high	80	80	84	86	87	83
		low	64	64	67	69	70	68
		rain	4	3	1	0	0	2

FLORA

Maui's indigenous and endemic trees and flowers are both fascinating and beautiful. Unfortunately, they, like everything else that was native, are quickly disappearing. The majority of flora found interesting by visitors was either introduced by the original Polynesians or later by white settlers. Maui is blessed with state parks, gardens, undisturbed rainforests, private reserves, and commercial nurseries. Combined they offer brilliant and dazzling colors to the landscape.

Silversword

Maui's official flower is a tiny pink rose called a *lokelani*. The island's unofficial symbol, however, is the silversword. The Hawaiian name for silversword is *ahinahina,* which translates as "gray gray," and the English name derives from a silverfish, whose color it's said to resemble. The silversword belongs to a remarkable plant family that claims 28 members, with five in the specific silversword species. It's kin to the common sunflower, and botanists say the entire family evolved from a single ancestral species. The members of the silversword family can all hypothetically interbreed and produce remarkable hybrids. Some plants are shrubs, while others are climbing vines, and

some even become trees. They grow anywhere from desert conditions to steamy jungles. On Maui, the silversword is only found on Haleakala, above the 6,000-foot level, and is especially prolific in the crater. Each plant lives from five to 20 years and ends its life by sprouting a gorgeous stalk of hundreds of purplish-red flowers. It then withers from a majestic six-foot plant to a flat gray skeleton. An endangered species, silverswords are totally protected. They protect themselves, too, from radiation and lack of moisture by growing fuzzy hairs all over their swordlike stalks. You can see them along the Haleakala Park Road at **Kalahaku Overlook,** or by hiking along **Silversword Loop** on the floor of the crater.

Protea

These exotic flowers are from Australia and South Africa. Because they come in almost limitless shapes, sizes, and colors, they captivate everyone who sees them. They are primitive, almost otherworldly in appearance, and they exude a life force more like an animal than a flower. The slopes of leeward Haleakala between 2,000 and 4,000 feet is heaven to protea—the growing conditions could not be more perfect. Here are found the hardiest, highest-quality protea in the world. The days are warm, the nights are cool, and the well-drained volcanic soil has the exact combination of minerals that protea thrive on. Haleakala's crater even helps by creating a natural air flow which produces cloud cover, filters the sun, and protects the flowers. Protea make excellent gifts that can be shipped anywhere. As fresh-cut flowers they are gorgeous, but they have the extra benefit of drying superbly. Just hang them in a dark, dry, well-ventilated area and they do the rest. You can see protea, along with other botanical specialties, at the following: **Kula Botanical Garden** (see "Botanical Gardens" below for more info), **Upcountry Protea Farm** on Upper Kimo Drive one mile off Haleakala Hwy. (Rt. 377), **The Protea Gift Shoppe,** next to Kula Lodge on Haleakala Hwy., **Protea Gardens of Maui,** on Hapapa Road off Rt. 377 not far from Kula Lodge, and **Sunrise Protea Farm** on Haleakala Hwy. above the turnoff from Rt. 377.

Carnations
If protea aren't enough to dazzle you, how about fields of carnations? Most Mainlanders think of carnations stuck in a groom's lapel, or perhaps have seen a table dedicated to them in a hothouse, but not fields full of carnations! The Kula area produces carnations that grow outside nonchalantly, in rows, like cabbages. They fill the air with their unmistakable perfume, and they are without doubt a joy to behold. You can see family and commercial plots throughout the upper Kula area.

Prickly Pear Cactus
Interspersed in countless fields and pastures on the windward slope of Haleakala, adding that final nuance to cattle country, are clusters of prickly pear cactus. The Hawaiians call them *panini,* which translates as "very unfriendly," undoubtedly because of the sharp spines covering the flat thick leaves. These cactus are typical of those found in Mexico and the southwestern U.S. They were introduced to Hawaii before 1810 and established themselves, coincidentally, in conjunction with the cattle being brought in at that time. It's assumed that Don Marin, a Spanish adviser

to Kamehameha I, was responsible for bringing in the cactus. Perhaps the early *paniolo* felt lonely without them. The *panini* can grow to heights of 15 feet and are now considered a pest, but nonetheless look as if they belong. They develop small pear-shaped fruits which are quite delicious. Hikers who decide to pick them should be careful of small yellowish bristles that can burrow under the skin and become very irritating. The fruits turn into beautiful yellow and orange flowers.

Botanical Gardens, Parks, And State Forests
Those interested in the flora of Maui would find a visit to any of the following both educational and entertaining. In the Kula area visit: **Kula Botanical Gardens,** clearly marked along Rt. 377 (Kekaulike Ave.) just a mile from where Rt. 377 joins Rt. 37 at the south end, tel. 878-1715. Five acres of plants and trees include **koa** in their natural settings. Open daily 7 a.m. to 4 p.m., $3 admission, self-guided tour. The **University of Hawaii Experimental Station,** just north of the south junction of Rt. 377 and Rt. 37 off Copp Road is open Mon. to Fri., 7:30 a.m. to 3:30 p.m., closed for lunch, free. The twenty acres of constantly changing plants are quite beautiful even though the grounds are uninspired, scientific, rectangular plots.

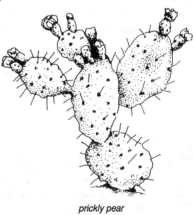

prickly pear
(DIANA LASICH HARPER)

Polipoli Springs State Recreation Area is the finest upcountry camping and trekking area on Maui. At the south end of Rt. 377, turn onto Waipoli Road for 10 miles of bad road. Overnight camping is recommended. Native and introduced birds, magnificent stands of redwoods, conifers, ash, cypress, sugi, cedar and various pines. Known for delicious methley plums that ripen in early June. For more info contact Division of State Parks in Wailuku, tel. 243-5354. **Hosmer Grove,** within Haleakala National Park, is an experimental forest project from the last century. Here are fine examples of introduced trees like cedar, pine, juniper, and sugi that were originally planted in hopes of finding a commercial, economically marketable wood for Hawaii. A short trail now winds through the no longer orderly stands of trees.

Keanae Arboretum, about 15 miles west of Hana on the Hana Hwy. (Rt. 360), is always open, no fee. Native, introduced, and exotic plants, including Hawaiian food plants, are in a natural setting with walkways, identifying markers, tropical trees, and mosquitos. Educational, a must. **Helani Gardens** lie one mile west of Hana, open daily 10 a.m. to 4 p.m., adults $2. These 60 acres of flowerbeds, plots of trees, and winding jeep trails are the lifetime project of Howard Cooper, a lovingly tended, exotic jungle, terrific!

Kahanu Gardens, a branch of the Pacific Tropical Botanical Gardens, is located on the rugged lava coast east of Hana at the site of Piilanihale Heiau. Open Tuesday through Saturday 10 a.m. to 2 p.m. for self-guided tours, there you'll find stands of breadfruit and coconut trees, a pandanus grove, and numerous other tropical plants from throughout the world. One and a half miles down the rough and graveled Ulaine Road, admission is $5. Call 284-8912 for more information.

Maui Zoo and Botanical Garden in Wailuku is easily accessible. Get a basic introduction to flora at this tiny zoo, good for tots, and mildly interesting. In Central Maui try: **Kepaniwai Park,** on Rt. 32 leading to Iao Needle. This tropical setting displays formalized gardens from different nations. Open daily, no fee. Finally, for an extremely civilized treat visit the formal gardens of the **Hyatt Regency Hotel** in Kaanapali, open to the public. The architecture and grounds are impeccable.

silversword
(DIANA LASICH HARPER)

FAUNA

Coral

Whether you're an avid scuba diver or novice snorkeler, you'll become aware of Maui's underwater coral gardens and grottoes whenever you peer at the fantastic seascapes below the waves. Although there is plenty of it, the coral in Hawaii doesn't do as well as in other more equatorial areas because the water is too wild and it's not quite as warm. Coral looks like a plant fashioned from colorful stone, but it's the skeleton of tiny animals, zoophytes, which need algae in order to live. Coral grows best on the west side of Maui where the water is quite still, the days more sunny, and where the algae can thrive. Many of Hawaii's reefs have been dying in the last 20 years, and no one seems to know why. Pesticides, used in agriculture, have been pointed to as a possible cause.

MAUI'S ENDANGERED BIRDS

Maui suffers the same fate as the other islands. Its native birds are disappearing. Maui is the last home of the crested honeycreeper (akohe'kohe). It lives only on the windward slope of Haleakala from 4,500 to 6,500 feet. It once lived on Molokai, but no longer. It's rather a large bird, averaging over seven inches long, and predominantly black. Its throat and breast are tipped with gray feathers, and it has bright orange on its neck and underbelly. A distinctive fluff of feathers forms a crown. It primarily eats ohia flowers and it's believed that the crown feathers gather pollen and help to propagate the ohia. The parrotbill is another endangered bird, found only on the slopes of Haleakala above 5,000 feet. It has an olive-green back and a yellow body. Its most distinctive feature is its parrot-like bill, which it uses to crack branches and pry out larvae.

Two waterbirds found on Maui are the Hawaiian stilt (ae'o) and the Hawaiian coot (alae ke'oke'o). The stilt is about 16 inches tall and lives on Maui at Kanaha and Kealia ponds. Primarily black with a white belly, its sticklike legs are pink. The adults will pretend to be hurt, putting on an excellent performance of the "broken wing" routine, in order to lure predators away from their nests. The Hawaiian coot is a webfooted water bird that resembles a duck. It's found on all the main islands but mostly on Maui and Kauai. Mostly a dull gray, it has a white bill and tail feathers. It builds a large floating nest and vigorously defends its young.

The dark-rumped petrel is slightly different from other primarily marine birds. This petrel is found around the visitor's center at Haleakala Crater about one hour after dusk from May through October. The amakihi and the iiwi are endemic birds that aren't endangered at the moment. The amakihi is one of the most common native birds. It's a yellowish-green, and it frequents the high branches of ohia, koa, and sandalwood looking for insects, nectar, or fruit. It's less specialized than most other Hawaiian birds, the main reason for its continued existence. The iiwi is a bright red bird with a salmon-colored hooked bill. It's found only on Maui, Hawaii, and Kauai in forests above 2,000 feet. It, too, feeds on a variety of insects and flowers. The iiwi is known for its harsh voice that sounds like a squeaking hinge, but is also capable of a melodious song.

Other indigenous birds found on Maui are the wedge-tailed sheerwater, the white-tailed tropic bird, the black noddy, the American plover, and a large variety of escaped exotic birds.

Pueo

This Hawaiian owl is found on all of the main islands, but mostly on Maui, especially in Haleakala Crater. The pueo is one of the oldest examples of an aumakua (family-protecting spirit) in Hawaiian mythology. It was an especially benign and helpful guardian. Old Hawaiian stories abound in which a pueo came to the aid of a warrior in distress or a defeated army, which would head for a tree in which a pueo had alighted. Once there, they were safe from their pursuers and were under the protection of "the wings of an owl." There are many introduced barn owls in Hawaii, easily distinguished from a *pueo* by their distinctive heart-shaped faces. The *pueo* is about 15 inches tall with a mixture of brown and white feathers. The eyes are large, round and yellow and the legs are heavily feathered unlike a barn owl. *Pueo* chicks are a distinct yellow color.

The *Nene*

The *nene,* or Hawaiian goose, deserves special mention because it is Hawaii's state bird and is making a comeback from the edge of extinction. The *nene* is found only on the slopes of Mauna Loa and Mauna Kea on the Big Island, and in Haleakala Crater on Maui. It was extinct on Maui until a few birds were returned there in 1957. *Nenes* are raised at the Wildfowl Trust in Slimbridge, England, which provided the first birds at Haleakala; now they're also raised at the Hawaiian Fish and Game Station at Pohakuloa on Hawaii. By the 1940s there were less than 50 birds living in the wild; now approximately 125 birds are on Haleakala, and 500 on the Big Island. Although the birds can be raised successfully in captivity, their life in the wild is still in ques-

The nene, *the state bird, lives only on Haleakala and on the slopes of Mauna Loa and Mauna Kea on the Big Island.* (MARY ANN ABEL)

tion. Some ornithologists even debate whether the *nene* ever lived on Maui. The *nene* is believed to be a descendant of the Canada goose, which it resembles. Geese are migratory birds that form strong kinship ties, mating for life. It's speculated that a migrating goose became disabled, and along with its loyal mate remained in Hawaii. The *nene* is smaller than its Canadian cousin, has lost a great deal of webbing in its feet, and is perfectly at home away from water, foraging and nesting on rugged and bleak lava flows. The *nene* is a perfect symbol for Hawaii: let it be and it will live!

THE HUMPBACKS OF MAUI

Humpbacks get their name from their style of exposing their dorsal fin when they dive, which gives them a humped appearance. There are about 7,000-8,000 humpback whales alive today, down from an estimated 100,000 at the turn of the century. The remaining whales are divided into three separate global populations: North Atlantic, North Pacific, and South Pacific groups. About 600 North Pacific humpbacks migrate from coastal Alaska starting in November. They reach their peak in February, congregating mostly in the waters off Maui, with a smaller group heading for the waters off Kona on Hawaii. An adult humpback is 45 feet long and weighs in at a svelte 40 tons (80,000 pounds). They come to Hawaii mainly to give birth to a single 2,000-pound, relatively blubberless calf. They nurse their calf for about one year and become impregnated again the next.

While in Hawaiian waters humpbacks generally don't eat. They wait until returning to Alaska, where they gorge themselves on krill. It's estimated that they can live off their blubber without peril for six months. They have an enormous mouth stretching one-third the length of their bodies which is filled with over 600 rows of baleen, a prickly, fingernail-like substance. Humpbacks have been known to blow air underwater to create giant bubble-nets that help to corral krill. They rush in with mouths agape and dine on their catch.

Like all cetaceans they breathe consciously, not involuntarily like humans; like other baleen whales they feed in relatively shallow waters and therefore sound (dive) for periods lasting a maximum of about 25 minutes. In comparison, the sperm whale (a toothed bottom-feeder) can stay down for over an hour. On the surface a humpback will breathe about once every two minutes and will sometimes sleep on the surface or just below it for two hours. A distinctive feature of the humpback is the 15-foot flipper which it can bend over its back. The flippers and tail flukes have white markings that always differ between individuals and are used to recognize the humpbacks from year to year. The humpback is the most aquabatic of all whales and it is a thrilling sight to see one of these playful giants leap from the water and create a monumental splash.

The Humpback's Song

All whales are fascinating, but the humpbacks have a special ability to sing unlike any others. They create their melodies by grunting, shrieking, and moaning. No one knows exactly what the songs represent, but it's clear they're a definite form of communication. The singers appear to be "escort males" that tag along with, and seem to guard, a mother and her calf. Some scientists believe that these are "lone males" and perhaps the song is territorial, or a mating call. The songs are exact renditions that last 20 minutes or more and are repeated over and over again for hours. Amazingly, all the whales know and sing the same song, and the song changes from year to year. The notes are so forceful that they can be heard above and below the water for miles. Some of the deep bass notes will even carry underwater for 100 miles! Scientists devote careers to recording and listening to the humpbacks' songs. As yet they're unexplained, but anyone who hears their eerie tones knows that he is privy to a wonderful secret and that the songs are somehow a key to understanding the consciousness of the great humpback.

The Bark *Carthaginian*

Just to the right of the loading dock in Lahaina Harbor is a restored 19th-century square-rigged ship, the *Carthaginian*. It's a floating museum dedicated to whales and whaling

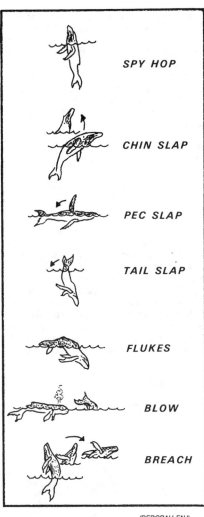

SPY HOP

CHIN SLAP

PEC SLAP

TAIL SLAP

FLUKES

BLOW

BREACH

(DEBORAH FAU)

and features an excellent audio-visual display narrated by actor Richard Widmark. The *Carthaginian* is open daily 9:30 a.m. to 4:30 p.m., admission $3, but to enjoy the entire display allow at least an hour. As you descend into the hold of the ship and bright sunlight fades to cool shadow, you become a visitor in a watery world of the humpback whale. The haunting, mysterious "songs" of the humpback provide the background music and set the mood. Sit on comfortable captain's chairs and watch the display. The excellent photos of whales are by Flip Nicklin, courtesy of the National Geographic Society. The *Carthaginian* is a project of the Lahaina Restoration Foundation, P.O. Box 338, Lahaina, HI 96761, tel. 661-3262. The foundation is a nonprofit organization dedicated to educational and historical restoration in Lahaina.

Whalewatching

If you're in Hawaii from late November to early May, you have an excellent chance of spotting a humpback. You can often see a whale from a vantage point on land but this is nowhere near as thrilling as seeing them close-up from a boat. Either way, binoculars are a must. Telephoto and zoom lenses are also useful and you might even get a nifty photo in the bargain. But don't waste your film unless you have a fairly high-powered zoom: fixed-lens cameras give pictures with a lot of ocean and a tiny black speck. If you're lucky enough to see a whale "breach" (jump clear of the water), keep watching—they often repeat this a number of times. If a whale dives and lifts its fluke high in the air, expect it to be down for quite a while (15 minutes) and not come up in the same spot. Other times they'll dive shallowly, then bob up and down quite often. From shore you're likely to see whales anywhere along

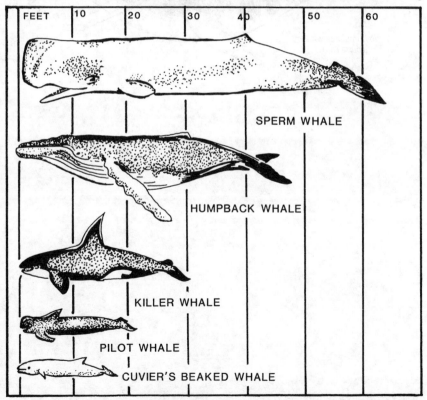

| FEET | 10 | 20 | 30 | 40 | 50 | 60 |

SPERM WHALE

HUMPBACK WHALE

KILLER WHALE

PILOT WHALE

CUVIER'S BEAKED WHALE

(LOUISE FOOTE)

Maui's south coast. If you're staying at any of the hotels or condos along Kaanapali or Kihei and have an ocean view, you can spot them from your lanai or window. A good vantage spot is Papawai Point along Rt. 30 and up the road heading west just before the tunnel. Maalaea Bay is another favorite nursing ground for mothers and their calves; you also get to see a small working harbor up close. An excellent viewpoint is Makena Beach on the spit of land separating Little and Big beaches (local names). If you time your arrival near sunset, even if you don't see a whale you'll have a mind-boggling light show.

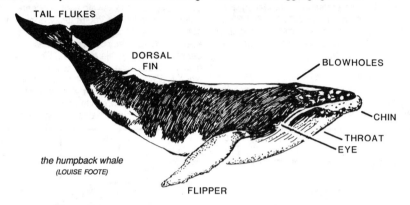

TAIL FLUKES

DORSAL FIN

BLOWHOLES

CHIN

THROAT

EYE

the humpback whale
(LOUISE FOOTE)

FLIPPER

HISTORY

THE ROAD FROM TAHITI

Until the 1820s, when New England missionaries began a phonetic rendering of the Hawaiian language, the past was kept vividly alive only by the sonorous voices of special *kahuna* who chanted the sacred *mele*. The chants were beautiful flowing word pictures that captured the essence of every aspect of life. These *mele* praised the land *(mele aina)*, royalty *(mele ali'i)*, and life's tender aspects *(mele aloha)*. Chants were dedicated to friendship, hardship, and to favorite children. Entire villages sometimes joined together to compose a *mele*—every word was chosen carefully, and the wise old kapuna would decide if the words were lucky or unlucky. Some mele were bawdy or funny on the surface, but contained secret meanings, often with biting sarcasm, that ridiculed an inept or cruel leader. But the most important chants took the listeners back into the dim past, even before people lived in Hawaii. From these genealogies *(ko'ihonua)*, the *ali'i* derived the right to rule since these chants went back to the gods Wakea and Papa, from whom the *ali'i* were directly descended.

The Kumulipo

The great genealogies, finally compiled in the late 1800s by order of King Kalakaua, were collectively known as *The Kumulipo, A Hawaiian Creation Chant,* basically a Polynesian account of Genesis. Other chants related to the beginning of this world, but *The Kumulipo* sums it all up and is generally considered the best. The chant relates that after the beginning of time, there is a period of darkness. The darkness, however, mysteriously brims with spontaneous life; during this period plants and animals are born, as well as Kumulipo, the man, and Po'ele, the woman. In the eighth chant darkness gives way to light and the gods descend to Earth. Wakea is "the sky father" and Papa is "the earth mother," whose union gives birth to the islands of Hawaii. First born is Hawaii, followed by Maui, then Kahoolawe. Apparently, Papa becomes bushed after three consecutive births and decides to vacation in Tahiti. While Papa is away recovering from post-partum depression and working on her tan, Wakea gets lonely, and takes Kaula as his second wife; she bears him the island-child of Lanai. Not fully cheered up, but getting the hang of it, Wakea takes a third wife, Hina, who promptly bears the island of Molokai. Meanwhile, Papa gets wind of these shenanigans, returns from Polynesia, and retaliates by taking up with Lua, a young and virile god, and soon gives birth to the island of Oahu. Papa and Wakea finally decide that they really are meant for each other and reconcile to conceive Kauai, Niihau, Kaula, and Nihoa. These two progenitors are the source to which all the *ali'i* ultimately traced their lineage, and from which they derived their god-ordained power to rule.

Basically, there are two major genealogical families: the **Nana'ulu,** who became the royal *ali'i* of Oahu and Kauai; and the **Ulu,** who provided the royalty of Maui and Hawaii. The best sources of information on Hawaiian myth and legend are Martha Beckwith's *Hawaiian Mythology,* and the monumental three-volume opus *An Account of the Polynesian Race* compiled by Abraham Fornander from 1878 to 1885. Fornander, after settling in Hawaii, married an *ali'i* from Molokai and had an illustrious career as a newspaper man, Maui circuit judge, and finally Supreme Court justice. For years Fornander sent scribes to every corner of the kingdom to listen to the elder *kupuna.* They returned with the first-hand accounts and he dutifully recorded them.

Polynesians
Since prehistory, Polynesians have been seafaring people whose origins cannot be completely traced. They seem to have come from Southeast Asia mostly through the gateway of Indonesia, and their racial strain pulls features from all three dominant races: white, negro, and mongoloid. They learned to navigate on tame narrow waterways along Indonesia and New Guinea, then fanned out eastward into the great Pacific. They sailed northeast to the low islands of Micronesia and southwest to Fiji, the New Hebrides (now called Vanuatu), and New Caledonia. Fiji is regarded as the "cradle of Polynesian culture"; carbon dating places humans there as early as 3,500 B.C. Many races blended on Fiji, until finally the

Negroid became dominant and the Polynesians moved on. Wandering, they discovered and settled Samoa and Tonga, then ranged far east to populate Tahiti, Easter Island, and the Marquesas. Ultimately, they became the masters of the "Polynesian Triangle," which measures more than 5,000 miles on each leg, stretching across both the North and South Pacific studded with islands. The great Maori kingdom of New Zealand is the southern apex of the triangle, with Easter Island marking the point farthest east; Hawaii, farthest north, was the last to be settled.

Migrations And Explorations
Ancient legends common throughout the South Pacific speak of a great Polynesian culture that existed on the island of Raiatea about 150 miles north of Tahiti. Here a powerful priesthood held sway in an enormous *heiau* in the Opoa district called Toputapuatea. Kings from throughout Polynesia came here to worship. Human sacrifice was common, as it was believed that the essence of the spirit could be utilized and controlled in this life; therefore the mana of Toputapuatea was great. Defeated warriors and commoners were used as living rollers to drag canoes up onto the beach, while corpses were dismembered and hung in trees. The power of the priests of Opoa lasted for many generations, evoking trembling fear in even the bravest warrior just by the mention of their name. Finally, their power waned and Polynesians lost their centralized culture, but the constant coming and going from Raiatea for centuries sharpened the Polynesians' already excellent sailing skills and convinced them that the world was vast and unlimited opportunities existed to better their lot.

Now explorers, many left to look for the "heavenly homeland to the north." Samoans called it *Savai'i;* Tongans *Hawai;* Rarotongans *Avaiki;* and Society Islanders *Havai'i.* Others abandoned the small islands throughout Polynesia where population pressures exceeded the limits of natural resources, prompting famine. Furthermore, Polynesians were also very warlike among themselves; power struggles between members of a ruling family were common, as were marauders from other islands. So, driven by hunger or warfare, countless refugee Polynesians headed north. Joining them were a few who undoubtedly went for the purely human reason of wanderlust.

The Great Navigators

No one knows exactly when the first Polynesians arrived in Hawaii, but the great *deliberate migrations* from the southern islands seem to have taken place between A.D. 500 and 800, though anthropologists keep pushing the date backward in time as new evidence becomes available. Even before that, however, it's reasonable to assume that the first people to set foot on Hawaii were probably fishermen, or perhaps defeated warriors whose canoes were blown hopelessly northward into unfamiliar waters arriving by a combination of extraordinary good luck and an uncanny ability to sail and navigate by the seat of their pants. With no instruments they could navigate, using the sun by day and the moon and rising stars by night. They could feel the water and determine direction by swells, tides, and currents. The movements of fish and cloud formations were also utilized to give direction. Since their arrival was probably an accident, they were unprepared to settle on the fertile but barren lands, having no stock animals, plant cuttings, or women. Forced to return southward, undoubtedly many lost their lives at sea, but a few wild-eyed stragglers must have made it home where they told tales of a paradise to the north where land was plentiful and the sea bounteous. This is affirmed by ancient navigational chants from Tahiti, Moorea, and Bora Bora, which passing from father to son revealed how to follow the stars to the "heavenly homeland in the north." Possibly a few migrations followed, but it's known that for centuries there was no real reason for a mass exodus, so the chants alone remained and eventually became shadowy legend.

From Where They Came

It's generally agreed that the first planned migrations were from the violent cannibal islands that Spanish explorers called the Marquesas, 11 islands in extreme eastern Polynesia. The islands themselves are harsh and

inhospitable, breeding a toughness into these people which enabled them to withstand the hardships of long unsure ocean voyages and years of resettlement. Marquesans were a fiercely independent people whose chiefs could rise from the ranks because of bravery or intelligence. They must have also been a savage-looking lot. Both men and women tatooed themselves in complex blue patterns from head to foot. The warriors carried massive, intricately designed ironwood war clubs and wore carved whale teeth in slits in their earlobes which became stretched to the shoulders. They shaved the sides of their heads with sharks' teeth, tied their hair in two topknots that looked like horns, and rubbed their heavily muscled and tattooed bodies with scented coconut oils. Their cults worshiped mummified ancestors; the bodies of warriors of defeated neighboring tribes were consumed. They were masters at building great double-hulled canoes launched from huge canoe sheds. Two hulls were fastened together to form a catamaran, and a hut in the center provided shelter in bad weather. The average voyaging canoe was 60-80 feet long and could comfortably hold an extended family of about 30 people. These small family bands carried all the staples they would need in the new lands.

The New Lands

For five centuries the Marquesans settled and lived peacefully on the new land, as if Hawaii's aloha spirit overcame most of their fierceness. The tribes coexisted in relative harmony, especially since there was no competition for land. Cannibalism died out. There was much coming and going between Hawaii and Polynesia and new people came to settle for hundreds of years. Then, it appears that in the 12th century a deliberate exodus of warlike Tahitians arrived and subjugated the settled islanders. They came to conquer. This incursion had a terrific significance for the Hawaiian religious and social system. Oral tradition relates that a Tahitian priest, Paao, found the mana of the Hawaiian chiefs to be low, signifying that their gods were weak. Paao built the *heiau* at Wahaula on the Big Island, then introduced the warlike god Ku and the rigid

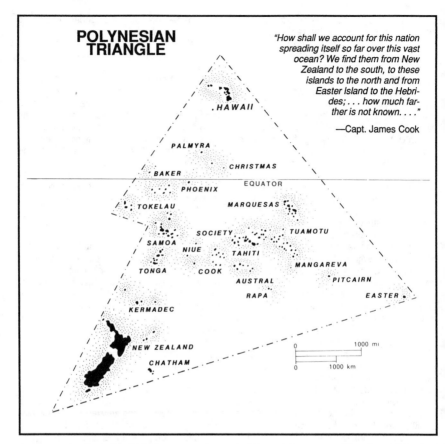

POLYNESIAN TRIANGLE

"How shall we account for this nation spreading itself so far over this vast ocean? We find them from New Zealand to the south, to these islands to the north and from Easter Island to the Hebrides; . . . how much farther is not known. . . ."

—Capt. James Cook

kapu system through which the new rulers became dominant. Voyages between Tahiti and Hawaii continued for about 100 years and Tahitian customs, legends, and language became the Hawaiian way of life.

Then suddenly, for no recorded or apparent reason, the voyages discontinued and Hawaii returned to total isolation. It remained forgotten for almost 500 years until the indomitable English seaman, Capt. James Cook, sighted Oahu on January 18, 1778 and stepped ashore at Waimea on Kauai two days later. At that time Hawaii's isolation was so complete that even the Polynesians had forgotten about

it. On an earlier voyage, Tupaia, a high priest from Raiatea, had accompanied Capt. Cook as he sailed throughout Polynesia. Tupaia's knowledge of existing archipelagos throughout the South Pacific was vast, which he demonstrated by naming over 130 islands and drawing a map that included the Tonga group, the Cook Islands, the Marquesas, even tiny Pitcairn, a rock in far eastern Polynesia, where the mutinous crew of the Bounty found solace. In mentioning the Marquesas Tupaia said, "he ma'a te ka'ata," which equals "food is man" or simply "cannibals!" But remarkably absent from Tupaia's vast knowledge was the existence of Easter Island, New Zealand, and Hawaii. The next waves of people to Hawaii would be white men, and the Hawaiian world would be changed quickly and forever.

THE WORLD DISCOVERS HAWAII

The late 18th century was an extraordinary time in Hawaiian history. Monumental changes seemed to happen all at once. First, Capt. James Cook, a Yorkshire farm boy, fulfilling his destiny as the all-time greatest Pacific explorer, found Hawaii for the rest of the world. For better or worse, it could no longer be an isolated Polynesian homeland. For the first time in Hawaiian history, a charismatic leader named Kamehameha emerged, and after a long civil war united all the islands into one centralized kingdom. The death of Capt. Cook in Hawaii marked the beginning of a long series of tragic misunderstandings between white man and native. When Kamehameha died, the old religious system of *kapu* came to an end, leaving the Hawaiians in a spiritual vortex. Many takers arrived to fill the void: missionaries after souls, whalers after their prey and a good time, traders and planters after profits and a home. The islands were opened and devoured like ripe fruit, as powerful nations including Russia, Great Britain, France, and the United States yearned to bring this strategic Pacific jewel under their own influence.

The 19th century brought the demise of the Hawaiian people as a dominant political force in their own land and with it the end of Hawaii as a sovereign monarchy. An almost bloodless yet bitter military coup followed by a brief period of a Hawaiian Republic ended in annexation by the United States. As the U.S. became completely entrenched politically and militarily, a new social and economic order was founded on the plantation system. Amazingly rapid population growth occurred with the importation of plantation workers from Asia and Europe,which yielded a unique cosmopolitan blend of races like nowhere else on Earth. By the dawning of the 20th century, the face of old Hawaii had been altered forever;

the "sacred homeland in the north" was hurled into the modern age. The attack on Pearl Harbor saw a tremendous loss of life and brought Hawaii closer to the U.S. by a baptism of blood. Finally, on August 21, 1959, after 59 years as a "territory," Hawaii officially became the 50th state of the Union.

Captain Cook Sights Hawaii

In 1776 Captain James Cook set sail for the Pacific from Plymouth, England, on his third and final expedition into this still vastly unexplored region of the world. On a fruitless quest for the fabled Northwest Passage across the North American continent, he sailed down the coast of Africa, rounded the Cape of Good Hope, crossed the Indian Ocean, and traveled past New Zealand, Tasmania, the Friendly Islands (where an unsuccessful plot was hatched by the *friendly* natives to murder him), and finally spotted Hawaii. On January 18, 1778 Capt. Cook's 100-foot flagship HMS Reso*lution* and its 90-foot companion HMS *Discovery* sighted Oahu. Two days later, they sighted Kauai and went ashore at the village of Waimea on January 20, 1778. Though anxious to get on with his mission, Cook decided to make a quick sortie to investigate this new land and reprovision his ships. He did, however, take time to remark in his diary about the close resemblance of these new-found people to others he had encountered as far south as New Zealand, and marveled at their widespread habitation across the Pacific.

The first trade was some brass medals for a mackerel. Cook also stated that he never before met natives so astonished by a ship, and that they had an amazing fascination for iron which they called *toe,* Hawaiian for "adze." There is even some conjecture that a Spanish ship under one Capt. Gaetano had landed in Hawaii as early as the 16th century, trading a few scraps of iron that the Hawaiians valued even more than the Europeans valued gold. It was also noted that the Hawaiian women gave themselves freely to the sailors with the apparent good wishes of the island men. This was actually a ploy by the *kahuna* to test if the white newcomers were gods or men—gods didn't need women. These sailors proved immediately mortal. Cook, who was also a physician, tried valiantly to keep the 66 men (out of 112) who had measurable cases of V.D. away from the women. The task proved impossible as women literally swarmed the ships; when Cook returned less than a year later, it was logged that signs of V.D. were already apparent on some natives' faces.

Cook was impressed with their swimming and with their well-bred manners. They had happy dispositions and sticky fingers, stealing any object made of metal, especially nails. The first item stolen was a butcher's cleaver. An unidentified native grabbed it, plunged overboard, swam to shore, and waved his booty in triumph. The Hawaiians didn't seem to care for beads and were not at all impressed with a mirror. Cook provisioned his ships by trading chisels for hogs, while common sailors gleefully traded nails for sex. Landing parties were sent inland to fill casks with fresh water. On one such excursion a Mr. Williamson, who was eventually drummed out of the Royal Navy for cowardice, unnecessarily shot and killed a native. After a brief stop on Niihau, the ships sailed away, but both groups were indelibly impressed with the memory of each other.

Captain James Cook (HAWAII STATE ARCHIVES)

Cook Returns

Almost a year later, when winter weather forced Cook to return from the coast of Alaska, his discovery began to take on far-reaching significance. Cook had named Hawaii the **Sandwich Islands,** in honor of one of his patrons, John Montague, the Earl of Sandwich. On this return voyage, he spotted Maui on November 26, 1778. After eight weeks of seeking a suitable harbor it was bypassed, but not before the coastline was duly drawn by Lt. William Bligh, one of Cook's finest and most trusted officers. (Bligh would find his own drama almost 10 years later as commander of the infamous HMS *Bounty*.) The *Discovery* and *Resolution* finally found a safe anchorage at Kealakekua on the Kona Coast of the Big Island. It is very lucky for history that on board was Mr. Anderson, ship's chronicler, who left a handwritten record of the strange and tragic events that followed. Even more important were the drawings of John Webber, ship's

artist, who rendered invaluable impressions in superb drawings and etchings. Other noteworthy men aboard were George Vancouver, who would himself lead the first British return to Hawaii after Cook's death and introduce many fruits, vegetables, cattle, sheep, and goats, and James Burney, who would become a longstanding leading authority on the Pacific.

The Great God Lono Returns

By all accounts Cook was a humane and just captain, greatly admired by his men. Unlike many other supremacists of that time, he was known to have a respectful attitude to any people he discovered, treating them as equals and recognizing the significance of their cultures. Not known as a violent man, he would use his superior weapons against natives only in an absolute case of self defense. His hardened crew had been at sea facing untold hardship for almost three years; returning to Hawaii was truly like re-entering paradise.

A strange series of coincidences sailed with Cook into Kealakekua Bay on January 16, 1779. It was *makahiki* time, a period of rejoicing and festivity dedicated to the fertility god of the earth, Lono. Normal *kapu* days were suspended, and willing partners freely enjoyed each other sexually, along with dancing, feasting, and the islands' version of Olympic games. It was long held in Hawaiian legend that the great god Lono would return to Earth. Lono's image was a small wooden figure perched on a tall mast-like crossbeam; hanging from the crossbeam were long white sheets of tapa. Who else could Cook be but Lono, and what else could his ships with their masts and white sails be but his sacred floating *heiau*? This explained the Hawaiians' previous fascination with his ships, but to add to the remarkable coincidence, Kealakekua Harbor happened to be considered Lono's private sacred harbor. Natives from throughout the land prostrated themselves and paid homage to the returning god. Cook was taken ashore and brought to Lono's sacred temple where he was afforded the highest respect. The ships badly needed fresh supplies and the Hawaiians readily gave all they had, stretching their own provisions to the limit. To the sailors delight this included full measures of the aloha spirit.

The Fatal Misunderstandings

After an uproarious welcome and generous hospitality for over a month, it became obvious that the newcomers were beginning to overstay their welcome. During the interim a seaman named William Watman died, convincing the Hawaiians that the *haole* were indeed mortals, not gods. Watman was buried at Hikiau Heiau where a plaque commemorates the event to this day. Incidents of petty theft began to increase dramatically. The lesser chiefs indicated it was time to leave by "rubbing the Englishmen's bellies." Inadvertently many *kapu* were broken by the Englishmen, and once-friendly relations became strained. Finally, the ships sailed away on February 4, 1779. After plying terrible seas for only a week, the foremast on the *Resolution* was badly damaged, and Cook sailed back into Kealekekua Bay dragging the mast ashore on February 13th. The natives, now totally hostile, hurled rocks at the marines. Orders were given to load muskets with ball; firearms had previously only been loaded with shot and a light charge. Confrontations increased when some Hawaiians stole a small boat and marines set after

them capturing the fleeing canoe, which held an *ali'i* named Palea. The Englishmen treated him roughly; to the Hawaiians horror, they even smacked him on the head with a paddle. The Hawaiians then furiously attacked the marines who abandoned the small boat.

Cook Goes Down

Next the Hawaiians stole a small cutter from the *Discovery* that had been moored to a buoy and partially sunk to protect it from the sun. For the first time Capt. Cook became furious. He ordered Capt. Clerk of the *Discovery* to sail to the southeast end of the bay, and to stop any canoe trying to leave Kealekakua. Cook then made a fatal error in judgment. He decided to take nine armed marines ashore in an attempt to convince the venerable King Kalaniopuu to accompany him back aboard ship where he would hold him for ransom in exchange for the cutter. The old king agreed, but his wife prevailed upon him not to trust the *haole*. Kalaniopuu sat down on the beach to think while the tension steadily grew. Meanwhile, a group of marines fired upon a canoe trying to leave the bay and a lesser chief, Nookemai, was killed. The crowd around Cook and his men reached an estimated 20,000, and warriors outraged by the killing of the chief armed themselves with clubs and protective straw-mat armor. One bold warrior advanced on Cook and struck him with his *pahoa*. In retaliation Cook drew a tiny pistol lightly loaded with shot and fired at the warrior. His bullets spent themselves on the straw armor and harmlessly fell to the ground. The Hawaiians went wild. Lt. Molesworth Phillips, in charge of the nine marines, began a withering fire; Cook himself slew two natives. Overpowered by sheer numbers, the marines headed for boats standing offshore, while Lt. Phillips lay wounded. It is believed that Capt. Cook, the greatest seaman ever to enter the Pacific, stood helplessly in knee-deep water instead of making for the boats because he could not swim! Hopelessly surrounded, he was knocked on the head, then countless warriors passed a knife around and hacked and mutilated his lifeless body. A sad Lt. King lamented in his diary, "Thus fell our great and excellent commander."

The Death of Captain Cook by John Webber, ship's artist on Cook's third Pacific exploration, c. 1779
(HAWAII STATE ARCHIVES)

The Final Chapter

Captain Clerk, now in charge, settled his men and prevailed upon the Hawaiians to return Cook's body. On the morning of February 16th a grisly piece of charred meat was brought aboard: the Hawaiians, according to their custom, had afforded Cook the highest honor by baking his body in an underground oven to remove the flesh from the bones. On the 17th a group of Hawaiians in a canoe taunted the marines by brandishing Cook's hat. The Englishmen, strained to the limit and thinking that Cook was being desecrated, finally broke. Foaming with blood-lust, they leveled their cannon and muskets on shore and shot anything that moved. It is believed that Kamehameha the Great was wounded in this flurry, along with four *ali'i* and 25 *maka'ainana* (commoners) killed. Finally on February 21, 1779, the bones of Capt. James Cook's hands, skull, arms, and legs were returned and tearfully buried at sea. A common seaman, one Mr. Zimmerman, summed up the feelings of all who sailed under Cook when he wrote, ". . . he was our leading star." The English sailed next morning after dropping off their Hawaiian girlfriends who were still aboard.

Captain Clerk, in bad health, carried on with the fruitless search for the Northwest Passage. He died and was buried at the Siberian village of Petropavlovisk. England was at war with upstart colonists in America, so the return of the expedition warranted little fanfare. The

Resolution was converted into an army transport to fight the pesky Americans; the once proud *Discovery* was reduced to a convict ship ferrying inmates to Botany Bay, Australia. Mrs. Cook, the great captain's steadfast and chaste wife, lived to the age of 93, surviving all her children. She was given a stipend of 200 pounds per year, and finished her days surrounded by Cook's mementos, observing the anniversary of his death to the very end by fasting and reading from the Bible.

THE UNIFICATION OF OLD HAWAII

Hawaii was already in a state of political turmoil and civil war when Cook arrived. In the 1780s the islands were roughly divided into three kingdoms: venerable Kalaniopuu ruled Hawaii and the Hana district of Maui; wily and ruthless warrior-king Kahekili ruled Maui, Kahoolawe, Lanai, and later Oahu; and Kaeo, Kahekili's brother, ruled Kauai. War ravaged the land until a remarkable chief, Kamehameha, rose and subjugated all the islands under one rule. Kamehameha initiated a dynasty that would last for about 100 years, until the independent monarchy of Hawaii forever ceased to be. To add a zing to this brewing political stew, Westerners and their technology were beginning to come in ever-increasing numbers. In 1786, Capt. La Perouse and his French exploration party landed in what's now La Perouse Bay, near Lahaina, foreshadowing European attention. In 1786 two American captains, Portlock and Dixon, made landfall in Hawaii. Also, it was known that a fortune could be made on the fur trade between the great Northwest and Canton, China; stopping in Hawaii could make it all feasible. After this was reported, the fate of Hawaii was sealed.

Hawaii under Kamehameha was ready to enter its "golden age." The social order was medieval, with the *ali'i* as knights, owing their military allegiance to the king, and the serf-like *makaainana* paying tribute and working the lands. The priesthood of *kahuna* filled the posts of advisors, sorcerers, navigators, doctors, and historians. This was Polynesian Hawaii at its apex. But like the uniquely Hawaiian silversword, the old culture blossomed, and as soon as it did, it began to wither. Ever since, all that was purely Hawaiian has been supplanted by the relentless foreign influences that began bearing down upon it.

Young Kamehameha

Kamehameha was a man noticed by everyone; there was no doubt he was a force to be reckoned with. He had met Capt. Cook when the *Discovery* unsuccessfully tried to land at

Kamehameha I as drawn by Louis Choris, ship's artist for the Von Kotzebue expedition, c. 1816. Supposedly the only time that Kamehameha sat to have his portrait rendered.
(HAWAII STATE ARCHIVES)

Hana on Maui. While aboard, he made a lasting impression, distinguishing himself from the multitude of natives swarming the ships by his royal bearing. Lt. James King, in a diary entry, remarked that Kamehameha was a fierce-looking man, almost ugly, but that he was obviously intelligent, observant, and very good-natured. Kamehameha received his early military training from his uncle Kalaniopuu, the great king of Hawaii and Hana, who fought fierce battles against Alapai, the usurper who stole his hereditary lands. After regaining Hawaii, Kalaniopuu returned to his Hana district and turned his attention to conquering all of Maui. During this period young Kamehameha distinguished himself as a ferocious warrior and earned himself the nickname of "the hard-shelled crab," even though old Kahekili, Maui's king, almost annihilated Kalaniopuu's army at the sand hills of Wailuku.

When the old king neared death he passed on the kingdom to his son Kiwalao. He also, however, empowered Kamehameha as the keeper of the family war god Kukailimoku: Ku of the Bloody Red Mouth, Ku the Destroyer. Oddly enough, Kamehameha had been born not 500 yards from Ku's great *heiau* at Kohala, and had heard the chanting and observed the ceremonies dedicated to this fierce god from his first breath. Soon after Kalaniopuu died, Kamehameha found himself in a bitter war that he did not seek against his two cousins, Kiwalao and his brother Keoua, with the island of Hawaii at stake. The skirmishing lasted nine years until Kamehameha's armies met the two brothers at Mokuohai in an indecisive battle in which Kiwalao was killed. The result was a shaky truce with Keoua, a much embittered enemy. During this fighting, Kahekili of Maui conquered Oahu where he built a house of the skulls and bones of his adversaries as a reminder of his omnipotence. He also extended his will to Kauai by marrying his half brother to a high-ranking chieftess of that island. A new factor would be needed to resolve this stalemate of power—the coming of the *haole*.

The Olowalu Massacre

In 1790 the American merchant ship *Ella Nora,* commanded by Yankee captain Simon Metcalfe, was looking for a harbor after its long voyage from the Pacific Northwest. Following a day behind was the *Fair American,* a tiny ship manned by Metcalfe's son Thomas and a crew of five. Metcalfe, perhaps by necessity, was a stern and humorless man who would broach no interference. While anchored at Olowalu, a beach area about five miles east of Lahaina, some natives slipped close in their canoes and stole a small boat, killing a seaman in the process. Metcalfe decided to trick the Hawaiians by first negotiating a truce and then unleashing full fury upon them. Signaling he was willing to trade, he invited canoes of innocent natives to visit his ship. In the meantime, he ordered that all cannon and muskets be readied with scatter shot. When the canoes were within hailing distance, he ordered his crew to fire at will. Over 100 people were slain; the Hawaiians remembered this killing as "the day of spilled brains." Metcalfe then sailed away to Kealakekua Bay and in an unrelated incident succeeded in insulting Kameiamoku, a ruling chief, who vowed to annihilate the next *haole* ship that he saw.

Fate sent him the *Fair American* and young Thomas Metcalfe. The little ship was entirely overrun by superior forces. In the ensuing battle, the mate, Isaac Davis, so distinguished himself by open acts of bravery that his life alone was spared. While harbored at Kealakekua, Metcalfe sent John Young to reconnoiter. Kamehameha, learning of the capture of the *Fair American,* detained Young so he could not report, and Metcalfe, losing patience, marooned his own man and sailed off to Canton. (Metcalfe never learned of the fate of his son Thomas, and was later killed with another son while trading with the Indians along the Pacific coast.) Kamehameha quickly realized the significance of his two captives and the *Fair American* with its brace of small cannon. He appropriated the ship and made Davis and Young trusted advisors, eventually raising them to the rank of chief. They would all play a significant role in the unification of Hawaii.

Kamehameha The Great

Later in 1790, supported by the savvy of Davis and Young and the cannon from the *Fair American* which he mounted on carts, Kamehameha invaded Maui using Hana as his power-er base. The island defenders under Kalaniekupule, son of Kahekili who was lingering on Oahu, were totally demoralized, then driven back into the death-trap of Iao Valley. There, Kamehameha's forces annihilated them. No mercy was expected and none given, although mostly commoners were slain with no significant *ali'i* falling to the victors. So many were killed in this sheer-walled, inescapable valley that the battle was called *ka pani wai* which means "the damming of the waters". . . literally with dead bodies. While Kamehameha was fighting on Maui, his old nemesis Keoua was busy running amok back on Hawaii, again pillaging Kamehameha's lands. The great warrior returned home flushed with victory, but in two battles could not subdue Keoua. Finally, Kamehameha had a prophetic dream in which he was told that Ku would lead him to victory over all the lands of Hawaii if he would build a *heiau* to the war god at Kawaihae. Even before the temple was finished, old Kahekili attempted to invade Waipio, Kamehameha's stronghold. But Kamehameha summoned Davis and Young, and with the *Fair American* and an enormous fleet of war canoes defeated Kahikili at Waimanu. Kahekili had no choice but to accept the indomitable Kamehameha as the king of Maui, although he himself remained the administrative head until his death in 1794.

Now only Keoua remained in the way and he would be defeated not by war, but by the great *mana* of Ku. While Keoua's armies were crossing the desert on the southern slopes of Kilauea, the fire goddess Pele trumpeted her disapproval and sent a huge cloud of poisonous gas and mud-ash into the air. It descended upon and instantly killed the middle legions of Keoua's armies and their families. The footprints of this ill-fated army remain to this day outlined in the mud-ash as clearly as if they were deliberately encased in wet cement. Keoua's intuition told him that the victorious mana of the gods had swung to Kamehameha and that his own fate was sealed. Kamehameha sent word that he wanted Keoua to meet with him at Ku's newly dedicated temple in Kawaihae. Both knew that Keoua must die. The old nemesis came riding proudly in his canoe, gloriously outfitted in the red and gold feathered cape and helmet signifying his exalted rank. When he stepped ashore he was felled by Kamehameha's warriors and his body was ceremoniously laid upon the altar along with 11 others who were slaughtered and dedicated to Ku, of the Maggot-Dripping Mouth.

Increasing Contact

By the time Kamehameha had won the Big Island, Hawaii was becoming a regular stopover for numerous ships seeking the lucrative sandalwood trade with China. In February 1791, Capt. George Vancouver, still seeking the Northwest Passage, returned to Kealakekua where he was greeted by a throng of 30,000. The captain at once recognized Kamehameha, who was wearing a Chinese dressing gown that he had received in tribute from another chief who in turn had received it directly from the hands of Cook himself. The diary of a crewmember, Thomas Manby, relates that Kamehameha, missing his front teeth, was more fierce-looking than ever as he approached the ship in an elegant double-hulled canoe sporting 46 rowers. The king invited all to a great feast prepared for them on the beach. Kamehameha's appetite matched his tremendous size. It was noted that he ate two sizable fish, a king-size bowl of poi, a small pig, and an entire baked dog. Kamehameha personally entertained the Englishmen by putting on a mock battle in which he deftly avoided spears by rolling, tumbling, and catching them in mid-air, all the while hurling his own a great distance. The English reciprocated by firing cannon bursts into the air, creating an impromptu fireworks display. Kamehameha requested from Vancouver a full table setting with which he was provided, but his request for firearms was prudently denied. The captain did, however, leave beef cattle, fowl, and breeding stock of sheep and goats. The ship's naturalist, Archibald Menzies, was the first *haole* to climb Mauna Kea; he also introduced a large assortment of fruits and vegetables. The Hawaiians were cheerful, outgoing, and showed remorse when they indicated that the remainder of Cook's bones had been buried at a temple close to Kealakekua. John Young, by this time firmly entrenched into Hawaiian society, made no request to sail away with Vancouver. During the next two decades of Kamehameha's rule, the French, Russians, English, and Americans discovered the great whaling waters off Hawaii, and their increasing visits shook and finally tumbled the ancient religion and social order of *kapu*.

Finishing Touches

After Keoua was laid to rest it was only a matter of time till Kamehameha consolidated his power over all of Hawaii. In 1794 the old warrior Kahekili of Maui died, and gave Oahu to his son Kalanikupule, while Kauai and Niihau went to his brother Kaeo. Warring between themselves, Kalanikupule was victorious, though he did not possess the grit of his father nor the great mana of Kamehameha. He had previously murdered a Capt. Brown who had anchored in Honolulu and seized his ship the *Jackall*. With the aid of this ship, Kalanikupule now determined to attack Kamehameha. However, while enroute, the sailors regained control of their ship and cruised to the Big Island to inform and join with Kamehameha. An army of 16,000 was raised and sailed for Maui, where they met only token resistance, destroyed Lahaina, pillaged the countryside, and vanquished Molokai in one bloody battle. The war canoes next sailed for Oahu and the final showdown. The great army landed at Waikiki, and though defenders fought bravely, giving up Oahu by the inch, they were steadily driven into the surrounding mountains. The beleaguered army made its last stand at Nuuanu Pali, a great precipice in the mountains behind present-day Honolulu. Kamehameha's warriors mercilessly drove the enemy into the great abyss. Kalanikupule, who hid in the mountains, was captured after a few months and sacrificed to Ku, The Snatcher of Lands, thereby ending the struggle for power. Kamehameha put down a revolt on Hawaii in 1796 and the king of Kauai, Kaumuali, accepting the inevitable, recognized Kamehameha as supreme ruler without suffering the hopeless ravages of a needless war. Kamehameha, for the first time in Hawaiian history, was the undisputed ruler of all the islands of "the heavenly homeland in the north."

Kamehameha's Rule

Kamehameha was as gentle in victory as he was ferocious in battle. His rule lasted until his death on May 8, 1819, under which Hawaii enjoyed a peace unlike the warring islands had ever known before. The king moved his royal court to Lahaina, where in 1803, he built the "Brick Palace," the first permanent building of Hawaii. And he built a fabulous straw house for his daughter, Princess Nahienaena, that was so well constructed it was later used as the residence of the first U.S. consul. The benevolent tyrant also enacted the "Law of the Splintered Paddle." This law, which protected the weak from the exploitation of the strong, had its origins when, many years before, a brave defender of a small overwhelmed village broke a paddle over Kamehameha's head and taught the chief—literally in one stroke—about the nobility of the common man.

However, just as Old Hawaii reached its "golden age," its demise was at hand. The relentless waves of *haole* both innocently and determinedly battered the old ways into the ground. With the foreign ships came prosperity and fanciful new goods after which the *ali'i* lusted. The *maka'aina* were worked mercilessly to provide sandalwood for the China trade. This was the first "boom" economy to hit the islands, but it set the standard of exploitation that would follow. Kamehameha built an observation tower in Lahaina to watch for ships, many of which were his own, returning laden with riches from the world at large. In the last years of his life Kamehameha returned to his beloved Kona Coast where he enjoyed the excellent fishing renowned to this day. He had taken Hawaii from the darkness of warfare into the light of peace. He died true to the religious and moral *kapu* of his youth, the only ones he had ever known, and with him died a unique way of life. Two loyal retainers buried his bones after the baked flesh had been ceremoniously stripped away. A secret burial cave was chosen so that no one could desecrate the remains of the great chief, thereby absorbing his mana. The tomb's whereabouts remains unknown, and disturbing the dead remains one of the strictest *kapu* to this day. "The Lonely One's" kingdom would pass to his son, Liholiho, but true power would be in the hands of his beloved but feisty wife Kaahumanu. As Kamehameha's spirit drifted from this earth, two forces sailing around Cape Horn would forever change Hawaii: the whalers and the missionaries.

MISSIONARIES AND WHALERS

The year 1819 is of the utmost significance in Hawaiian history. It marked the death of Kamehameha, the overthrow of the ancient *kapu* system, the arrival of the first whaler in Lahaina, and the departure of Calvinist missionaries from New England determined to convert the heathen islanders. Great changes began to rattle the old order to its foundations. With the *kapu* system and all of the ancient gods abandoned (except for the fire goddess Pele of Kilauea), a great void permeated the souls of the Hawaiians. In the coming decades Hawaii, also coveted by Russia, France, and England, was finally consumed by America. The islands had the first American school, printing press, and newspaper *(The Polynesian)* west of the Mississippi. Lahaina, in its heyday, became the world's greatest whaling port, accommodating over 500 ships during its peak years.

The Royal Family

Maui's Hana District provided Hawaii with one of its greatest queens, Kaahumanu, born in 1768 in a cave within walking distance of Hana Harbor. At the age of 17 she became the third of Kamehameha's 21 wives and eventually the love of his life. At first she proved to be totally independent and unmanageable, and was known to openly defy her king by taking numerous lovers. Kamehameha placed a *kapu* on her body and even had her attended by horribly deformed hunchbacks to curb her carnal appetites, but she continued to flaunt his authority. Young Kaahumanu had no love for her great, lumbering, unattractive husband (even Capt. Vancouver was pressed into service as a marriage counselor), but in time she

the great Queen Kaahumanu, by ship's artist Louis Choris, from the Otto Von Kotzebue expedition, c. 1816
(HAWAII STATE ARCHIVES)

learned to love him dearly. She in turn became his favorite wife, although she remained childless throughout her life. Kamehameha's first wife was the supremely royal Keopuolani, who so outranked even him that the king himself had to approach her naked and crawling on his belly. Keopuolani produced the royal children Liholiho and Kauikeaouli, who became King Kamehameha II and III, respectively. When Kamehameha I died in 1819 he appointed Liholiho his successor, but he also had the wisdom to make Kaahumanu the *kuhina nui* or queen regent. Initially, Liholiho was weak and became a drunkard. Later he became a good ruler, but he was always supported by his royal mother Keopuolani and by the ever-formidable Kaahumanu.

Kapu Is Pau
Kaahumanu was greatly loved and respected by the people. On public occasions, she donned Kamehameha's royal cloak and spear: so attired and infused with the king's mana, she demonstrated that she was the real leader of Hawaii. For six months after Kamehameha's death, Kaahumanu counseled Liholiho on what he must do. The wise *kuhina nui* knew that the old ways were *pau* ("finished") and Hawaii could not hope to function in a rapidly changing world under the *kapu* system. In November 1819, Kaahumanu and

Keopuolani prevailed upen Liholiho to break two of the oldest and most sacred *kapu:* to eat together with women and to allow women to eat previously forbidden foods, such as bananas and certain fish. Kaahumanu sat with Liholiho, heavily fortified with strong drink, and attended by other high-ranking chiefs and a handful of foreigners, they ate in public. This feast became known as *Ai Noa* ("free eating"), and as the first morsels passed her lips the ancient gods of Hawaii tumbled. Throughout the land revered *heiau* were burned and abandoned and the idols knocked to the ground. Now the people had nothing but their own weakened inner selves to rely on. Nothing and no one could answer their prayers; their spiritual lives were empty and in shambles.

Missionaries
In October 1819 the *Brig Thaddeus* left Boston carrying 14 missionaries bound for Hawaii. On April 4, 1820 they landed at Kailua on the Big Island where Liholiho had moved the royal court. The Reverends Bingham and Thurston went ashore and were granted a one-year trial missionary period by King Liholiho. They established themselves on Hawaii and Oahu and from there began the transformation of Hawaii. The missionaries were men of God, but also practical-minded Yankees. They brought education, enterprise, and most im-

portantly, unlike the transient seafarers, a commitment to stay and build. In 1823, Rev. Richards established the first mission in Lahaina, a village of about 2,300 inhabitants.

Rapid Conversions

The year 1823 also marked the death of Keopuolani, who was given a Christian burial. Setting the standard by accepting Christianity, a number of the ali'i had followed the queen's lead. Liholiho had sailed off to England, where he and his wife contracted measles and died. Their bodies were returned by the British in 1825, on the HMS *Blonde* captained by Lord Byron, cousin of *the* Lord Byron. During these years, Kaahumanu allied herself with Rev. Richards and together they wrote Hawaii's first code of laws based upon the Ten Commandments. Foremost was the condemnation of murder, theft, brawling, and the desecration of the Sabbath by work or play. The early missionaries had the best of intentions, but like all zealots were blinded by the single-mindedness that was also their greatest ally. The destruction of the native beliefs they felt to be abominations was not surgically selective. *Anything* native was felt to be inferior, and they set about to wipe out all traces of the old ways. In their rampage they reduced the Hawaiian culture to ashes, plucking self-will and determination from the hearts of a once-proud people. More so than the whalers, they terminated the Hawaiian way of life.

The Early Seamen

A good portion of the common seamen of the early 19th century were the dregs of the Western world. Many a whoremongering drunkard had awoken from a stupor and found himself on the pitching deck of a ship, discovering to his dismay that he had been "pressed into naval service." For the most part these sailors were a filthy, uneducated, lawless rabble. Their present situation was dim, their future hopeless, and they would live to be 30 if they were lucky and didn't die from scurvy or a thousand other miserable fates. They snatched brief pleasure in every port, and jumped ship at every opportunity, especially in an easy berth like Lahaina. They displayed the worst elements of Western culture—which the Hawaiians naively mimicked. In exchange for aloha they gave drunkenness, sloth, and insidious death by disease. By the 1850s the population of native Hawaiians tumbled from the estimated 300,000 reported by Capt. Cook in 1778 to barely 60,000. Common conditions such as colds, flu, venereal disease, and sometimes smallpox and cholera decimated the Hawaiians who had no natural immunities to these foreign ailments. By the time the missionaries arrived, *hapahaole* children were common in Lahaina streets. The earliest lawless opportunists had come seeking sandalwood after first filling their holds with furs from the Pacific Northwest. Aided by ali'i hungry for manufactured goods and Western finery, they raped Hawaiian forests of this fragrant wood so coveted in China. Next, droves of sailors came in search of the whales. The whalers, decent men at home, left their morals back in the Atlantic and lived by the slogan "no conscience east of the Cape." The delights of Hawaii were just too tempting for most.

Two Worlds Tragically Collide

The 1820s were a time of confusion and soul-searching for the Hawaiians. When Kamehameha II died the kingdom passed to Kauikeaouli (Kamehameha III), who made his life-long residence in Lahaina. The young king was only nine years old when the title passed to him, but his power was secure because Kaahumanu was still a vibrant *kuhina nui*. The young prince, more so than any other, was raised in the cultural confusion of the times. His childhood was spent during the very cusp of the change from old ways to new, and he was often pulled in two directions by vastly differing beliefs. Since he was royal born, according to age-old Hawaiian tradition, he must mate and produce an heir with the highest ranking ali'i in the kingdom. This natural mate happened to be his younger sister, the Princess Nahienaena. To the old Hawaiian advisors, this arrangement was perfectly acceptable and encouraged. To the increasingly influential missionaries, incest was an unimaginable abomination in the eyes of God. The problem was compounded by the fact that Kamehameha III and Nahienaena were drawn to each other and were deeply in love. The young king could not stand the mental pressure imposed by conflicting worlds. He became a teenage alcoholic too royal to be restrained by anyone in the kingdom, and his bouts of drunkenness and womanizing were both legendary and scandalous. Meanwhile, Nahienaena was even more pressured because she was a favorite of the missionaries, baptized into the church at age 12. She too vacillated between the old and the new. At times a pious Christian, at others she drank all night and took numerous lovers. As the prince and princess grew into their late teens, they became even more attached to each other and hardly made an attempt to keep their relationship from the missionaries. Whenever possible, they lived together in a grass house built for the princess by her father.

In 1832, the great Kaahumanu died, leaving the king on his own. In 1833, at the age of 18, Kamehameha III announced that the "regency" was over and that all the lands in Hawaii were his, personally, and that he alone was

Kamehameha III

the ultimate law. Almost immediately, however, he decreed that his half sister Kinau would be "premier," signifying that he would leave the actual running of the kingdom in her hands. Kamehameha III fell into total drunken confusion, until one night he attempted suicide. After this episode he seemed to straighten up a bit and mostly kept a low profile. In 1836, Princess Nahienaena was convinced by the missionaries to take a husband. She married Leleiohoku, a chief from the Big Island, but continued to sleep with her brother. It is uncertain who fathered the child, but Nahienaena gave birth to a baby boy in September 1836. The young prince survived for only a few hours, and Nahienaena never recovered from her convalescence. She died in December 1836, and was laid to rest in the mausoleum next to her mother, Keopuolani, on the royal island in Mokuhina Pond, still in existence in modern-day Lahaina. After the death of his sister, Kamehameha III became a sober and righteous ruler. Oftentimes seen paying his respects at the royal mausoleum, he ruled longer than any other king until his death in 1854.

The Missionaries Prevail

In 1823, the first mission was established in Lahaina under the pastorage of Rev. William Richards and his wife. Within a few years, many of the notable *ali'i* had been, at least in appearance, converted to Christianity. By 1828 the cornerstones for Wainee Church, the first stone church on the island, were laid just behind the palace of Kamehameha III. The struggle between missionaries and whalers centered around public drunkenness and the servicing of sailors by local native girls. The normally god-fearing whalers had signed on for perilous duty that lasted up to three years, and when they anchored in Lahaina they demanded their pleasure. The missionaries were instrumental in placing a curfew on sailors and prohibiting native girls from boarding ships which had become customary. These measures certainly did not stop the liasons between sailor and *wahine,* but it did impose a modicum of social sanction and tolled the end of the wide open days. The sailors were outraged; in 1825 the crew from the *Daniel* attacked the home of the meddler, Rev. Richards. A year later a similar incident occurred. In 1827, confined and lonely sailors from the whaler *John Palmer* fired their cannon at Rev. Richards' newly built home.

Slowly the tensions eased, and by 1836 many sailors were regulars at the Seamen's Chapel, adjacent to the Baldwin Home. Unfortunately, even the missionaries couldn't stop the pesky mosquito from entering the islands through the port of Lahaina. The mosquitos arrived in 1826, from Mexico, aboard the merchant *Wellington*. They were inadvertently carried as larvae in the water barrels and democratically pestered everyone in the islands from that day forward regardless of race, religion, or creed.

Lahaina Becomes A Cultural Center

By 1831, Lahaina was firmly established as a seat of Western influence in Hawaii. That year marked the founding of Lahainaluna School, the first *real* American school west of the Rockies. Virtually a copy of a New England normal school, it attracted the best students, both native and white, from throughout the kingdom. By 1834, Lahainaluna had an operating printing press publishing the islands' first newspaper, *The Torch of Hawaii*, starting a lucrative printing industry centered in Lahaina that dominated not only the islands but also California for many years.

An early native student was David Malo. He was brilliant and well educated, but more importantly, he remembered the "old ways." One of the first Hawaiians to realize his native land was being swallowed up by the newcomers, Malo compiled the first history of pre-contact Hawaii and the resulting book, *Hawaiian Antiquities,* became a reference masterpiece which has yet to be eclipsed. David Malo insisted that the printing be done in Hawaiian, not English. Malo is buried in the mountains above Lahainaluna where, by his own request, he is "high above the tide of foreign invasion." By the 1840s, Lahaina was firmly established as the "whaling capital of the world"; the peak year 1846 saw 395 whaling ships anchored here. A census in 1846 reported that Lahaina was home to 3,445 natives, 112 permanent *haole,* 600 sailors, and

over 500 dogs. The populace was housed in 882 grass houses, 155 adobe houses, and 59 relatively permanent stone and wooden framed structures. Lahaina would probably have remained the islands' capital, had Kamehameha III not moved the royal capital to the burgeoning port of Honolulu on the island of Oahu.

Foreign Influence

By the 1840s Honolulu was becoming the center of commerce in the islands; when Kamehameha III moved the royal court there from Lahaina the ascendant fate of the new capital was guaranteed. In 1843, Lord Paulet, commander of the warship *Carysfort,* forced Kamehameha III to sign a treaty ceding Hawaii to the British. London, however, repudiated this act and Hawaii's independence was restored within a few months when Queen Victoria sent Admiral Thomas as her personal agent of good intentions. The king memorialized the turn of events by a speech in which he uttered the phrase, *"Ua mau ke ea o ka aina i ka pono,"* ("The life of the land is preserved in righteousness"), now Hawaii's motto. The French used similar bullying tactics to force an unfavorable treaty on the Hawaiians in 1839; as part of these heavy-handed negotiations they exacted a payment of $20,000, and the right for Catholics to enjoy religious freedom in the islands. In 1842 the U.S. recognized and guaranteed Hawaii's independence without a formal treaty, and by 1860 over 80% of the islands' trade was with America.

The Great *Mahele*

In 1840 Kamehameha III ended his autocratic rule and instituted a constitutional monarchy. This brought about the Hawaiian Bill of Rights, but the most far-reaching change was the transition to private ownership of land. Formerly, all land belonged to the ruling chief who gave wedge-shaped parcels called *ahupua'a* to lesser chiefs to be worked for him. The commoners did all the real labor, their produce heavily taxed by the *ali'i.* The fortunes of war, the death of a chief, or the mere whim of a superior could force a commoner off his land. The Hawaiians, however, could not think in terms of "owning" land. No one could *possess* land, one could only *use* land, and its *ownership* was a strange foreign concept. (As a result, naive Hawaiians gave up their lands for a song to unscrupulous traders, which remains an integral unrectified problem to this day.) In 1847 Kamehameha III and his advisors separated the lands of Hawaii into three groupings: crown land (belonging to the king), government land (belonging to the chiefs), and the people's land (the largest parcels). In 1848, 245 *ali'i* entered their land claims in the *Mahele Book,* assuring them ownership. In 1850 the commoners were given title in fee simple to the lands they cultivated and lived on as tenants, not including house lots in towns. Commoners without land could buy small *kuleana* (farms) from the government at 50 cents per acre. In 1850, foreigners were also allowed to purchase land in fee simple, and the ownership of Hawaii from that day forward slipped steadily from the hands of its indigenous people.

KING SUGAR

The sugar industry began at Hana, Maui, in 1849. A whaler named George Wilfong hauled four blubber pots ashore and set them up on a rocky hill in the middle of 60 acres he had planted in sugar. A team of oxen turned "crushing rollers" and the cane juice flowed down an open trough into the pots, under which an attending native kept a roaring fire burning. Wilfong's methods of refining were crude but the resultant high-quality sugar turned a neat profit in Lahaina. The main problem was labor. The Hawaiians, who had made excellent whalers, were basically indentured workers. They became extremely disillusioned with their contracts, which could last up to 10 years. Most of their wages were eaten up by manufactured commodities sold at the company store, and it didn't take long for them to realize that they were little more than slaves. At every opportunity they either left the area or just refused to work.

Claus Spreckles, "King Sugar" himself, had large holdings on Maui; along with his own sugar town, Spreckelsville, he built the Haiku Ditch in 1878. This 30-mile ditch brought 50 million gallons of water a day from Haiku to Puunene so that the "green gold" could flourish. This entrepreneur was able to buy the land for his sugar cheaply. The highly superstitious Hawaiians of the time didn't value this particular plot of land, believing that the souls of those that had not made the leap to heaven were condemned to wandering this wasteland. To them it was obviously cursed, supporting only grasses and scrub bushes, and they felt that they were getting the bargain, offloading it to this unsuspecting *haole.* Moreover, Spreckles was a gambler. In a series of late-night poker games with Kamehameha III he was able to win the water rights to a dozen or so streams in the area, thereby creating the possibility for his Haiku Ditch. Sugar and Maui became one. Then, because of sugar, Lahaina lost its dominance and Paia became the town on Maui during the 1930s, where it housed plantation workers in camps according to nationality.

Imported Labor

The **Masters and Servants Act of 1850,** which allowed importation of laborers under the contract system, ostensibly guaranteed an endless supply of cheap labor for the plantations. Chinese laborers were imported, but were too enterprising to remain in the fields for a meager $3 per month. They left as soon as opportunity permitted, and went into business as small merchants and retailers. In the meantime, Wilfong had sold out, releasing most of the Hawaiians previously held under contract, and his plantation fell into disuse. In 1860 two Danish brothers, August and Oscar Unna, bought land at Hana to raise sugar. They solved the labor problem by importing Japanese laborers who were extremely hard-working and easily managed. The workday lasted 10 hours, six days a week, for a salary of $20 per month with housing and medical care thrown in. Plantation life was very structured with stringent rules governing even bedtimes and lights out. A worker was fined for being late or for smoking on the job. Even the Japanese couldn't function under these circumstances, and improvements in benefits and housing were slowly gained.

Sugar Grows

The demand for "Sandwich Island Sugar" grew as California was populated during the gold rush, and increased dramatically when the American Civil War demanded a constant supply. The first great sugar mill in Hawaii was started by James Campbell in 1861. The only sugar plantations on the Mainland were small plots confined to the Confederate states, whose products would hardly be bought by the Union and whose fields, later in the war, were destroyed. By the 1870s it was clear to the planters, still mainly New Englanders, that the U.S. was their market; they tried often to gain closer ties and favorable tariffs. The Americans also planted rumors that the British were interested in annexing Hawaii; this put pressure on the U.S. Congress to pass the long-desired **Reciprocity Act,** which would exempt sugar from import duty. It finally passed in 1875, in exchange for U.S. long-range rights to the strategic naval port of Pearl Harbor, among other concessions. These agreements gave increased political power to a small group of American planters, whose outlooks were similar to the post-Civil War South where a few powerful whites were the virtual masters of a multitude of dark-skinned laborers. Sugar was now big business and the Hana District alone exported almost 3,000 tons per year. All of Hawaii would have to reckon with the "sugar barons."

Changing Society

The sugar plantation system changed life in Hawaii physically, spiritually, politically, and economically. Now boatloads of workers came not only from Japan, but from Portugal, Germany, and even Russia. The white-skinned workers were most often the field foremen *(luna)*. With the immigrants came new religions, new animals and plants, unique cuisines, and a plantation language known as *pidgin* or better yet, *da kine*. The Orientals mainly, but also portions of all the other groups including the white plantation owners, intermarried with Hawaiian girls. A new class of people properly termed "cosmopolitan" but more familiarly and aptly known as "locals" were emerging. These were the people of multiple race backgrounds who couldn't exactly say *what* they were but it was clear to all just *who* they were. The plantation owners became the new "chiefs" of Hawaii who could carve up the land and dispense favors. The Hawaiian monarchy was soon eliminated.

A KINGDOM PASSES

The fate of Lahaina's Wainee Church through the years has been a symbol of the political and economic climate of the times. Its construction heralded the beginning of missionary dominance in 1828. It was destroyed by a tornado or "ghost wind" in 1858, just when whaling began to falter. The previously dominant missionaries began losing their control to the merchants and planters. In 1894, Wainee Church was burned to the ground by Royalists supporting the besieged Queen Liliuokalani, then was rebuilt with a grant from H.P. Baldwin in 1897 while Hawaii was a Republic ruled by the sugar planters. It wasn't until 1947 that Wainee was finally completed and remodeled.

The Beginning Of The End

Like the Hawaiian people themselves, the Kamehameha dynasty in the mid-1800s was dying from within. King Kamehameha IV (Alexander Liholiho) ruled from 1854 to 1863; his only child died in 1862. He was succeeded by his older brother Kamehameha V (Lot Kamehameha) who ruled until 1872. With his passing the Kamehameha line ended. William Lunalilo, elected king in 1873 by popular vote, was of royal, but not Kamehameha, lineage. He died after only a year in office, and being a bachelor left no heirs. He was succeeded by David Kalakaua, known far and wide as The "Merry Monarch." He made a world tour and was well received wherever he went. He built Iolani Palace in Honolulu and was personally in favor of closer ties with the U.S., helping push through the Reciprocity Act. Kalakaua died in 1891 and was replaced by his sister Lydia Liliuokalani, last of the Hawaiian monarchs.

The Revolution

When Liliuokalani took office in 1891 the native population was at a low of 40,000 and she

Queen Liliuokalani
(HAWAII STATE ARCHIVES)

felt that the U.S. had too much influence over her homeland. She was known to personally favor the English over the Americans. She attempted to replace the liberal constitution of 1887 (adopted by her pro-American brother) with an autocratic mandate in which she would have much more political and economic control of the islands. When the McKinley Tariff of 1890 brought a decline in sugar profits, she made no attempt to improve the situation. Thus, the planters saw her as a political obstacle to their economic growth; most of Hawaii's American planters and merchants were in favor of a rebellion. She would have to go! A central spokesman and firebrand was Lorrin Thurston, a Honolulu publisher who, with a central core of about 30 men, challenged the Hawaiian monarchy. Although Liliuokalani rallied some support and had a small military potential in her personal guard, the coup was ridiculously easy—it took only one casualty. Capt. John Good shot a Hawaiian policeman in the arm and that did it. Naturally, the conspirators could not have succeeded without

some solid assurances from a secret contingent in the U.S. Congress as well as outgoing President Benjamin Harrison, who favored Hawaii's annexation. Marines from the *Boston* went ashore to "protect American lives," and on January 17, 1893, the Hawaiian monarchy came to an end.

The provisional government was headed by Sanford B. Dole who became president of the Hawaiian Republic. Liliuokalani actually surrendered not to the conspirators but to U.S. Ambassador John Stevens. She believed that the U.S. government, which had assured Hawaiian independence, would be outraged by the overthrow and would come to her aid. Actually, incoming President Grover Cleveland *was* outraged and Hawaii wasn't immediately annexed as expected. When queried about what she would do with the conspirators if she were reinstated, Liliuokalani said that they would be hung as traitors. The racist press of the times, which portrayed the Hawaiians as half-civilized blood-thirsty heathens, publicized this widely. Since the conspirators were the leading citizens of the land, the queen's words proved untimely. In January 1895, a small, ill-fated counterrevolution headed by Liliuokalani failed, and she was placed under house arrest in Iolani Palace. Forced to abdicate her throne, officials of the Republic insisted that she use her married name (Mrs. John Dominis) to sign the documents. She was also forced to swear allegiance to the new Republic. Liliuokalani went on to write *Hawaii's Story* and also the lyric ballad "Aloha O'e". She never forgave the conspirators and remained to the Hawaiians "queen" until her death in 1917.

Annexation

The overwhelming majority of Hawaiians opposed annexation and desired to restore the monarchy. But they were prevented from voting by the new Republic because they couldn't meet the imposed property and income qualifications—a transparent ruse by the planters to control the majority. Most *haole* were racist and believed that the "common people" could not be entrusted with the vote because they were childish and incapable of ruling themselves. The fact that the Hawaiians had existed quite well for 1,000 years before the white man even reached Hawaii was never considered. The Philippine theater of the Spanish-American War also prompted annexation. One of the strongest proponents was Alfred Mahon, a brilliant naval strategist who, with support from Theodore Roosevelt, argued that the U.S. military must have Hawaii to be a viable force in the Pacific. In addition, Japan, flushed with victory in its recent war with China, protested the American intention to annex, and in so doing prompted even moderates to support annexation in fear that the Japanese themselves coveted the prize. On July 7, 1898, President McKinley signed the annexation agreement, and this "tropical fruit" was finally put into America's basket.

MODERN TIMES

Hawaii entered the 20th century totally transformed from what it had been. The old Hawaiian language, religion, culture, and leadership were all gone. Western dress, values, education, and recreation were the norm. Native Hawaiians were now unseen citizens who lived in dwindling numbers in remote areas. The plantations, new centers of social order, had a strong Oriental flavor; more than 75% of their work force was Asian. There was a small white middle class, an all-powerful white elite, and a single political party ruled by that elite. Education, however, was always highly prized, and by the turn of the century all racial groups were encouraged to attend school. By 1900, almost 90% of Hawaiians were literate (far above the national norm) and schooling was mandatory for all children between ages 6 and 15. Intermarriage was accepted, and there was a mixing of the races like nowhere else on earth. The military became increasingly important to Hawaii. It brought in money and jobs, dominating the island economy. The Japanese attack on Pearl Harbor, which began U.S. involvement in World War II, bound Hawaii to America forever. Once the islands had been baptized by blood, the average mainlander felt that Hawaii was American soil. A movement among Hawaiians to become part of the Union began to grow. They wanted a real

voice in Washington, not merely a voteless delegate as provided under their territory status. Hawaii became the 50th state in 1959 and the jumbo jet revolution of the 1960s made it easily accessible to growing numbers of tourists from all over the world.

Military History
A few military strategists realized the importance of Hawaii early in the 19th century, but most didn't recognize the advantages until the Spanish-American War. It was clearly an unsinkable ship in the middle of the Pacific from which the U.S. could launch military operations. Troops were stationed at Camp McKinley at the foot of Diamond Head, the main military compound until it became obsolete in 1907. Pearl Harbor was first surveyed in 1872 by General Schofield. Later a military base named in his honor, Schofield Barracks, was a main military post in central Oahu. It first housed the U.S. 5th Cavalry in 1909 and was heavily bombed by the Japanese at the outset of WW II. Pearl Harbor, first dredged in 1908, was officially opened on December 11, 1911. The first warship to enter was the cruiser *California*. Ever since, the military has been a mainstay of island economy. Unfortunately, there has been long-standing bad blood between locals and military personnel. Each group has tended to look down upon the other.

Pearl Harbor Attack
On the morning of December 7, 1941, the Japanese carrier *Akagi,* flying the battle flag of the famed Admiral Togo of the Russo-Japanese War, received and broadcast over its PA system island music from Honolulu station KGMB. Deep in the bowels of the ship a radio man listened for a much different message, coming thousands of miles from the Japanese mainland. When the ironic poetic message "east wind rain" was received, the attack was launched. At the end of the day, 2,325 U.S. servicemen and 57 civilians were dead; 188 planes were destroyed; 18 major warships were sunk or heavily damaged; and the U.S. was in the war. Japanese casualties were ludicrously light and the ignited conflict would rage for four years until Japan, through Nagasaki and Hiroshima, was vaporized into

total submission. At the end of hostilities, Hawaii would never again be considered separate from America.

Statehood

A number of economic and political reasons explain why the ruling elite of Hawaii desired statehood, but simply, the vast majority of people who lived there, especially after WW II, considered themselves Americans. The first serious mention of making "The Sandwich Islands" a state was in the 1850s under President Franklin Pierce, but wasn't taken seriously until the monarchy was overthrown in the 1890s. For the next 50 years statehood proposals were made repeatedly to Congress, but there was stiff opposition, especially from the southern states. With Hawaii a territory, an import quota system beneficial to Mainland producers could be enacted on produce, especially sugar. Also, there was prejudice against creating a state in a place where the majority of the populace was not white. This situation was illuminated by the infamous Massie Rape case of 1931 (see p. 50), which went down as one of the greatest miscarriages of justice in American history. During WW II, Hawaii was placed under martial law, but no serious attempt to intern the Japanese population was made, as in California. There were simply too many Japanese, who went on to gain the respect of the American people by their outstanding fighting record during the war. Hawaii's own 100th Infantry Battalion became the famous 442 Regimental Combat Team which gained notoriety by saving the Lost Texas Battalion during the Battle of the Bulge, and went on to be *the* most decorated battalion in all of WW II. When these GIs returned home, *no one* was going to tell them that they were not loyal Americans. Many of these AJAs (Americans of Japanese Ancestry) took advantage of the GI Bill and received higher education. They were from the common people, not the elite, and they rallied grass-roots support for statehood. When the vote finally occurred, approximately 132,900 voted in favor of statehood with only 7,800 votes against. Congress passed the Hawaii State Bill on March 12, 1959, and on August 21, 1959, President Eisenhower announced that Hawaii was officially the 50th state.

GOVERNMENT

The only difference between the government of the state of Hawaii and other states is that it's "streamlined," and in theory more efficient. There are only two levels of government: the state and the county. With no town or city governments to deal with, considerable bureaucracy is eliminated. Hawaii, in anticipation of becoming a state, drafted a constitution in 1950 and was ready to go when statehood came. Politics and government are taken seriously in the "Aloha State," which consistently turns in the best national voting record per capita. For example, in the first state elections 173,000 of 180,000 registered voters voted—a whopping 94% of the electorate. In the election to ratify statehood, hardly a ballot went uncast, with 95% of the voters opting for statehood. The bill carried every island of Hawaii except for Niihau, where, coincidentally, the majority of people (total population

250 or so) are of relatively pure Hawaiian blood. The U.S. Congress passed the "Hawaii State Bill" on March 12, 1959, and on August 21, 1959, President Eisenhower proclaimed Hawaii the 50th state. The present governor is John Waihee III, first Hawaiian governor in the United States. Mr. Waihee has held this office since 1986.

Maui County

The boundaries of Maui County are a bit oddball, but historically oddball. Maui County encompasses Maui Island, as well as Lanai, Molokai, and the uninhabited island of Kahoolawe. The apparent geographical oddity consists of an arc on East Maui, from Makawao past Hana and along the south coast almost to Kihei, which is a "shared" political area, aligned with the Kohala District of the Big Island since Polynesian times. These two districts were joined with each other, so it's just a traditional carryover. The real strangeness occurs in Maui's 5th Senatorial District and its counterpart, the 9th Representative District. These two political areas include West Maui and the islands of Lanai and Molokai. West Maui, with Kaanapali, Lahaina, and Kapalua, is one of the most developed and financially sound areas in all of Hawaii. It's a favorite area with tourists, and is the darling of developers. On the other hand, Lanai has a tiny population that is totally dependent on a one-company "pineapple economy." Molokai has the largest per capita concentration of native Hawaiians, a "busted economy" with a tremendous share of its population on welfare, and a grass-roots movement determined to preserve the historical integrity of the island and the dignity of the people. You'd have to be a political magician to fairly represent all of the constituents in these widely differing districts.

Maui's Representatives

Hawaii's State Legislature is comprised of 76 members, with the House of Representatives having 51 elected seats, and the State Senate 25. Members serve two- and four-year terms respectively. All officials come from 76 separate electorates based on population. Maui is represented by three state senators,

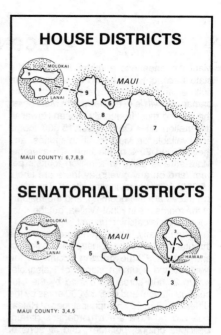

who've usually been Democrats, and five state representatives, who've been Democrats as well.

ECONOMY

Maui's economy is a mirror image of the state's economy: it's based on tourism, agriculture, and government expenditures. The primary growth is in **tourism,** with Maui being the second most frequently chosen Hawaiian destination after Oahu. Over 15,000 rooms are available on Maui in all categories, and they're filled 70% of the time. On average, Maui attracts close to a million tourists per year, and on any given day there are about 15,000 visitors enjoying the island. The building trades are still booming, and the majority of the rooms are in Kihei-Wailea, but the Kaanapali area is catching up fast.

Agriculturally, Maui generates revenue through cattle, sugar, pineapples, *pakololo,* and flowers. **Cattle grazing** occurs on the western and southern slopes of Haleakala, where 20,000 acres are owned by the Ulupalakua Ranch, and over 32,000 acres by the Haleakala Ranch. The upper slopes of Haleakala around Kula are a gardener's dream. Delicious onions, potatoes, and all sorts of garden vegetables are grown, but are secondary to large plots of gorgeous flowers, mainly carnations and the amazing protea.

Sugar, actually in the grass family, is still very important to Maui's economy, but without federal subsidies it wouldn't be a viable cash crop. The largest acreage is in the central isthmus area, which is virtually all owned by the Alexander and Baldwin Company. There are also large sugar tracts along Kaanapali and the west coast that are owned by Amfac and Maui Land and Pineapple. Those lodging in Kaanapali will become vividly aware of the sugar fields when they're burned off just prior to harvesting. Making these unsightly burnings even worse is the fact that the plastic pipe used in the drip irrigation of the fields is left in place. Not cost-efficient to recover, it is burned along with the cane, adding its noxious fumes to the air.

Pineapples grow in central east Maui between Paia and Makawao, where Alexander and Baldwin own most of the land. Another area is the far west coast north of Napili where Maui Land and Pineapple controls most of the holdings. Renegade entrepreneurs grow patches of *pakalolo* wherever they can find a spot that has the right vibes and is away from the prying eyes of the authorities. Deep in the West Maui Mountains and along the Hana coast are favorite areas.

Government expenditures in Maui County are just over $40 million per year. The small military presence on Maui amounts to a tiny Army installation near Kahului and the Navy's ownership of the target island of Kahoolawe. With tourists finding Maui more and more desirable every year, and with agriculture firmly entrenched, Maui's economic future is bright.

The Big Five Corporations
Until statehood, Hawaii was ruled economically by a consortium of corporations known

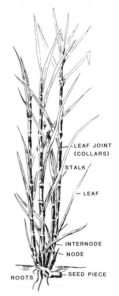

young suger cane (LOUISE FOOTE)

as **The Big Five: C. Brewer and Co.,** sugar, ranching, and chemicals, founded 1826; **Theo. H. Davies & Co.,** sugar, investments, insurance, and transportation, founded 1845; **Amfac Inc.,** originally H. Hackfield Inc. (a German firm that changed its name and ownership during the anti-German sentiment of WW I to American Factors), sugar, insurance, and land development, founded 1849; **Castle and Cooke Inc.,** (Dole) pineapple, food packing, and land development, founded 1851; and, **Alexander and Baldwin Inc.,** shipping, sugar, and pineapple, founded 1895. This economic oligarchy ruled Hawaii with a velvet glove and a steel grip.

With members on all important corporate boards, they controlled all major commerce including banking, shipping, insurance, hotel development, agriculture, utilities, and wholesale and retail merchandising. Anyone trying to buck the system was ground to dust, finding it suddenly impossible to do business in the islands. The Big Five were made up of the islands' oldest and most well-established *haole* families; all included bloodlines from Hawaii's own nobility and *ali'i.* They looked among themselves for suitable husbands and wives, so breaking in from the outside even through marriage was hardly possible. The only time they were successfully challenged prior to statehood was when Sears, Roebuck and Co. opened a store on Oahu. Closing ranks, the Big Five decreed that their steamships would not carry Sears' freight. When Sears threatened to buy its own steamship line, the Big Five relented. Actually, statehood, and more to the point, tourism, broke their oligarchy. After 1960 too much money was at stake for Mainland-based corporations to ignore. Eventually the grip of the Big Five was loosened, but they are still enormously powerful and richer than ever, though unlike before, they don't control everything. Now, their power is land. With only five other major landholders, they control 65 percent of all the privately held land in Hawaii.

Tourism-related Problems

Tourism is both a boon and blight to Hawaii. It is the root cause of two problems: one environmental and the other socioeconomic.

The environmental impact is obvious, and is best described in the lament of songstress Joni Mitchell: "They paved paradise and put up a parking lot." Simply, tourism can draw too many people. In the process, it stresses the very land and destroys the natural beauty that attracted people in the first place. Tourists come to Hawaii for what has been called its "ambient resource"—a balanced collage of indulgent climate, invigorating waters, intoxicating scenery, and exotic people all wrapped up neatly in one area that both soothes and excites. It's in the best interest of Hawaii to preserve this resource. Most point to Waikiki as a prime example of development gone mad. Actually two prime examples of the best and the worst development can be found on Maui's south shore at Kihei and Wailea, less than five miles apart. In the late '60s Kihei experienced a development-inspired "feeding frenzy" that made the real sharks offshore seem about as dangerous as Winnie the Pooh. Condos were slapped up as fast as cement can dry, their architecture reminiscent of a stack of shoeboxes. A coastline renowned for its beauty was overburdened, and the view was wiped out in the process. Anyone who had the bucks built, and now parts of Kihei look like a high-rise, low-income, federally funded housing project. You can bet that those who made a killing building here don't live here.

Conversely, just down the road is Wailea, a model of what development could (and should) be. The architecture is tasteful, low-rise, unobtrusive, and designed with people and the preservation of the scenery in mind. It's obviously more exclusive, but access points to the beaches are open to everyone, and the view is still there for all to enjoy. Wailea points the way for the development of the future.

Land Ownership

Hawaii, landwise, is a small pie, and its slices are not at all well divided. Of 6,425 square miles of land, 98% make up the six main inhabited islands. (This figure does not include Niihau, which is privately owned by the Robinson family and inhabited by the last remaining pure-blooded Hawaiians, nor does it include

Kahoolawe, the uninhabited Navy bombing target just off Maui's south shore.) Of the 4,045,511 acres that make up the inhabited islands, 36% are owned by the state, 10% by the federal government, and the remaining 54% are in private hands. But only 40 owners with 5,000 or more acres own 75% of all private lands. Moreover, only 10 private concerns own two-thirds of these lands. To be more specific, Castle and Cooke Inc. owns 99% of Lanai, while 40-60% of Maui, Oahu, Molokai, Kauai, and Hawaii are owned by less than a dozen private parties. The largest private landowner is the Kamehameha Schools/ Bishop Estate, which recently lost a Supreme Court battle over a ruling that allows the state of Hawaii to acquire privately owned land for "the public good." More than in any other state, Hawaii's landowners tend to lease land instead of selling it, and many private homes are on rented ground. Many feel that with land prices going up all the time, only the very rich land developers will be able to purchase, and the *people* of Hawaii will become even more land-poor.

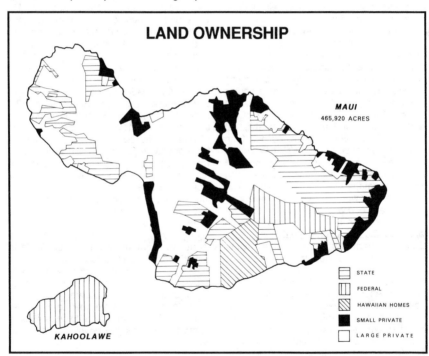

LAND OWNERSHIP

MAUI
465,920 ACRES

STATE

FEDERAL

HAWAIIAN HOMES

SMALL PRIVATE

LARGE PRIVATE

KAHOOLAWE

PEOPLE

Nowhere else on earth can you find such a kaleidoscopic mixture of people. Every major race is accounted for, and over 50 ethnic groups are represented throughout the islands. Hawaii is the most racially integrated state in the Union. Its population of one million includes 120,000 permanently stationed military personnel and their dependents, and it's the only state where whites are not the majority. About 60% of the people living in Hawaii were born there, 25% were born on the mainland U.S., and 15% of the people are foreign born.

The population of Hawaii has been growing steadily in recent times, but it fluctuated wildly in times past. In 1876 it reached its lowest ebb, with only 55,000 permanent residents in the islands. This was the era of large sugar plantations, and their constant demand for labor was the primary cause for the importation of various peoples from around the world, which in turn led to Hawaii's so racially integrated society. WW II saw Hawaii's population swell from 400,000, just prior to the war, to 900,000 during the war. Naturally, 500,000 were military personnel who left at war's end, but many

returned to settle after getting a taste of island living.

Of the one million people in the islands today, 800,000 (80%) live on Oahu, with over half of these living in the Honolulu Metropolitan Area. The rest of the population is distributed as follows: 93,000 (9.3%) on Hawaii, with 36,000 living in Hilo; 63,000 (6.3%) on Maui, with the largest concentration, 23,000, in Wailuku/Kahului; 40,000 on Kauai, including 230 pure-blood Hawaiians on Niihau; Molokai with 6,000; and Lanai with just over 2,000. The population density is 164 people per square mile, equal to California's. The population is not at all evenly distributed, with Honolulu claiming more than 1,400 people per square mile, and Maui the second most densely populated island with only 105 people per square mile. City dwellers outnumber those living in the country by four to one.

THE HAWAIIANS

The study of the native Hawaiians is ultimately a study in tragedy because it ends in their demise as a viable people. When Capt. Cook first sighted Hawaii in 1778, there were an estimated 300,000 natives living in perfect harmony with their ecological surroundings; within 100 years a scant 50,000 demoralized and dejected Hawaiians existed almost as wards of the state. Today, although 115,000 people claim varying degrees of Hawaiian blood, experts say that less than 1,000 are pure Hawaiian, and this is stretching the point. It's easy to see why people of Hawaiian lineage could be bitter over what they have lost, being strangers in their own land now, much like American Indians. The overwhelming majority of "Hawaiians" are of mixed heritage, and the wisest take the best from all worlds. From the Hawaiian side comes simplicity, love of the land, and acceptance of people. It is the Hawaiian legacy of *aloha* that remains immortal and adds that special elusive quality that *is* Hawaii.

Polynesian Roots

The Polynesians' original stock is muddled and remains an anthropological mystery, but it's believed that they were nomadic wanderers who migrated from both the Indian subcontinent and Southeast Asia through Indonesia, where they learned to sail and navigate on protected waterways. As they migrated they honed their sailing skills until they could take on the Pacific, and as they moved, they absorbed people from other cultures and races until they had coalesced into what we now know as Polynesians. Abraham Fornander, still considered a major authority on the subject, wrote in his 1885 *Account of the Polynesian Race* that he believed the Polynesians started as a white (Aryan) race, which had been heavily influenced by contact with the Cushite, Chaldeo-Arabian civilization. He estimated their arrival in Hawaii at A.D. 600, based on Hawaiian genealogical chants. Modern science seems to bear this date out, although it remains skeptical on his other surmises. The intrepid Polynesians who actually settled Hawaii are believed to have come from the Marquesas Islands, 1,000 miles south and a few hundred miles east of Hawaii. The Marquesans were cannibals and known for their tenacity and strength, attributes that would

serve them well. When Capt. Cook stepped ashore on Waimea, Kauai, on the morning of Jan. 20, 1778, he discovered a population of 300,000. Their agrarian society had flourished in the last thousand years.

The Caste System

Hawaiian society was divided into rankings by a strict caste system determined by birth, and from which there was no chance of escaping. The highest rank was the *ali'i,* the chiefs and royalty. The impeccable genealogies of the *ali'i* were traced back to the gods themselves, and the chants *(mo'o ali'i)* were memorized and sung by professionals (called *ku'auhau),* who were themselves *ali'i.* Ranking passed from both father and mother and custom dictated that the first mating of an *ali'i* be with a person of equal status. A *kahuna* was a highly skilled person whose advice was sought before any major project was undertaken, such as building a house, hollowing a canoe log, or even offering a prayer. The *mo'o kahuna* were the priests of Ku and Lono who were in charge of praying and following rituals. They were very powerful *ali'i* and kept strict secrets and laws concerning their various functions.

Besides this priesthood of *kahuna,* there were other *kahuna* who were not *ali'i* but commoners. The two most important were the healers *kahuna lapa'au,* and the black magicians *kahuna ana'ana,* who could pray a person to death. The *kahuna lapa'au* had a mar-

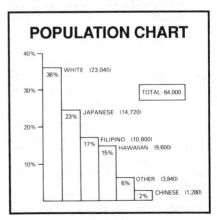

POPULATION CHART

TOTAL: 64,000

- WHITE (23,040) — 36%
- JAPANESE (14,720) — 23%
- FILIPINO (10,800) — 17%
- HAWAIIAN (9,600) — 15%
- OTHER (3,840) — 6%
- CHINESE (1,280) — 2%

The ali'i wore magnificent feathered capes that signified their rank. The noblest colors were red and yellow, provided by specialized hunters who snared and plucked just the right birds. (LOUISE FOOTE)

velous pharmacopeia of herbs and spices that could cure over 250 diseases common to the Hawaiians. The *kahuna ana'ana* could be hired to cast a love spell over a person or cause his untimely death. They seldom had to send out a reminder of payment!

The common people were called the *maka'ainana*, "the people of land"—the farmers, craftsmen, and fishermen. The land that they lived on was owned by the *ali'i*, but they were not bound to it. If the local *ali'i* was cruel or unfair, the *maka'ainana* had the right to leave and reside on another's lands. The maka'ainana mostly loved their local *ali'i* much like a child

loves a parent, and the feeling was reciprocal. All *maka'ainana* formed extended families called *ohana* and they usually lived on the same section of land, called *ahuapua'a*. Those farmers who lived inland would barter their produce with the fishermen who lived on the shore, and thus all shared equally in the bounty of the land and sea.

A special group called *kauwa* was a landless, untouchable caste confined to living on reservations. Their origins were obviously Polynesian, but they appeared to be descendants of castaways who had survived and become perhaps the aboriginals of Hawaii before the main migrations. It was *kapu* for anyone to go onto *kauwa* lands, and doing so meant instant death. If a human sacrifice was needed, the *kahuna* would simply summon a *kauwa*, who had no recourse but to mutely comply. To this day, to call someone *kauwa*, which now supposedly only means servant, is still considered a fight-provoking insult.

Kapu And Day-to-day Life

There were occasional horrible wars, but mostly the people lived a quiet and ordered life based on a strict caste society and the *kapu* (taboo) system. Famine was known but only on a regional level, and the population was kept in check by birth control, crude abortions, and the distasteful practice of infanticide, especially of baby girls. The Hawaiians were absolutely loving and nurturing parents under most circumstances, and would even take in an adopted *hanai* (child or oldster), a lovely practice that lingers to this day. A strict division of labor existed among men and women. Men were the only ones permitted to have anything to do with taro: this foodstuff was so sacred that it had a greater *kapu* than man himself. Men pounded poi and served it to the women. Men also were the fishermen and the builders of houses, canoes, irrigation ditches, and walls. Women tended to other gardens and shoreline fishing, and were responsible for making tapa cloth. The entire family lived in the common house called *hale noa*.

Certain things were kapu between the sexes. Primarily, women could not enter the *mua* (man's house) nor could they eat with men. Certain foods such as pork and bananas were

Punishment of a kapu-breaker was harsh and swift.
(JACQUES ARAGO, HAWAII STATE ARCHIVES)

forbidden to women, and it was *kapu* for a man to have intercourse before going fishing, engaging in battle, or attending a religious ceremony. Young boys lived with the women until they underwent a circumcision rite called *pule ipu*. After this was performed, they were required to keep the *kapu* of men.

Fatal Flaws

Less than 100 years after Capt. Cook's arrival, King Kalaukaua found himself with only 48,000 Hawaiian subjects, down more than 80 percent. Wherever the king went, he would beseech his people, *hooulu lahui*, "increase the race," but it was already too late. It was as if nature herself had turned her back on these once-proud people. Many of their marriages were barren and in 1874, when only 1,400 children were born, a full 75% died in infancy. The Hawaiians sat around and could do nothing as their race faded from existence.

The Causes

The ecological system of Hawaii has always been exceptionally fragile and this included its people. When the white man arrived he found a great people who were large, strong, and virile, but when it came to fighting off the most minor diseases they proved as delicate as

hothouse flowers. To exacerbate the situation, the Hawaiians were totally uninhibited toward sexual intercourse between willing partners, and they engaged in it openly and with abandon. Unfortunately, the sailors who arrived were full of syphilis and gonorrhea. The Hawaiian women brought these diseases home and, given the nature of Hawaiian society at the time, they spread like wildfire. By the time the missionaries came in 1820 and helped to halt the unbridled fornication, they estimated the native population at only 140,000, less than half of what it had been only 40 years since initial contact! In the next 50 years measles, mumps, influenza, and tuberculosis further ravaged the people. Also, Hawaiian men were excellent sailors and it's estimated that during the whaling years, at least 25% of all able-bodied Hawaiian men sailed away, never to return.

But the coup de grace that really ended the Hawaiian race, as such, was the fact that all racial newcomers to the islands were attracted to the Hawaiians and the Hawaiians were in turn attracted to them. With so many interracial marriages, the Hawaiians literally bred themselves out of existence. By 1910, there were still twice as many full-blooded Hawaiians as mixed-bloods, but by 1940 mixed-blooded Hawaiians were the fastest-growing group, and full-blooded the fastest declining.

Hawaiians Today

Many of the Hawaiians who moved to the cities became more and more disenfranchised. Their folk society stressed openness and a giving nature, but downplayed the individual and ownership of private property. These cultural traits made them easy targets for the users and schemers until they finally became either apathetic or angry. Most surveys reveal that although Hawaiians number only 12% (16,000) of the population, they account for almost 50% of the financially destitute families, and similarly, for about half of all arrests and illegitimate births. Niihau, a privately owned island, is home to about 250 pure-blood Hawaiians, representing the largest concentration of them, per capita, in the islands. The Robinson family, who owns the island, restricts visitors to invited guests only.

The second largest concentration is on Molokai, where 2,700 Hawaiians, living mostly on 40-acre *kuleana* of Hawaiian Homes Lands, make up 45% of that island's population. The majority of mixed-blood Hawaiians, 80,000 or so, live on Oahu, where they are particularly strong in the hotel and entertainment fields. People of Hawaiian extraction are still a delight to meet, and anyone so lucky as to be befriended by one long regards this friendship as the highlight of his travels. The Hawaiians have always given their aloha free-

aloha still shows (J.D.BISIGNANI)

ly to all the peoples of the world, and it is we who must acknowledge this precious gift.

THE CHINESE

Next to Yankees from New England, the Chinese are the oldest migrant group in Hawaii, and their influence has far outshone their meager numbers. They brought to Hawaii, along with their individuality, Confucianism, Taoism, and Buddhism, although many have long since become Christians. The Chinese population at 57,000 makes up only six percent of the state's total, and the majority (52,000) reside on Oahu. As an ethnic group they account for the least amount of crime, the highest per capita income, and a disproportionate number of professionals.

The First Chinese

No one knows his name, but an unknown Chinese man is credited with being the first person in Hawaii to refine sugar. This Oriental wanderer tried his hand at crude refining on Lanai in 1802. Fifty years later the sugar plantations desperately needed workers, and the first Chinese brought to Hawaii under the newly passed Masters and Servants Act were 195 coolies from Amoy who arrived in 1852. These conscripts were contracted for three to five years and given $3 per month plus room and board. This was for 12 hours a day, six days a week, and even in 1852 these wages were the pits. The Chinese almost always left the plantations the minute their contracts expired. They went into business for themselves and promptly monopolized the restaurant and small shop trades.

The Chinese Niche

Although almost all people in Hawaii considered all Chinese the same, they were actually quite different. The majority came from Kwangtung Province in southern China. They were two distinct ethnic groups: the Punti made up 75% of the immigrants, and the Hakka made up the remainder. In China, they remained separate from each other, never mixing; in Hawaii, they mixed out of necessity. Hardly any Chinese women came over at first, and the ones who followed were at a premium and gladly accepted as wives, regardless of ethnic background. The Chinese were also one of the first groups who willingly inter-married with the Hawaiians, from whom they gained a reputation for being exceptionally caring husbands. The Chinese accepted the social order and kept a low profile. For ex-ample, during the turbulent labor movements of the 1930s and '40s in Hawaii, the Chinese community produced not one labor leader, radical intellectual, or left-wing politician. When Hawaii became a state, one of the two senators elected was Hiram Fong, a racially mixed Chinese. Since statehood, the Chinese community has carried on business as usual as they continue to rise both economically and socially.

THE JAPANESE

Most scholars believe that (inevitably) a few Japanese castaways floated to Hawaii long before Capt. Cook arrived, and might have introduced iron, which the islanders seemed to be familiar with before white men arrived. The first official arrivals were ambassadors sent by the shogun to negotiate in Washing-ton; they stopped en route at Honolulu in March, 1860. But it was as plantation workers that the Japanese were brought to the islands. A small group arrived in 1868, and mass mi-gration started in 1885. In 1886, because of famine, the Japanese government allowed farmers mainly from southern Honshu, Ky-ushu, and Okinawa to emigrate. Among these were members of Japan's little-talked-about untouchable caste, called *eta* or *burakumin* in Japan and *chorinbo* in Hawaii. They gratefully seized this opportunity to better their lot, an impossibility in Japan. The first Japanese mi-grants were almost all men. Between 1897 and 1908 migration was steady, with about 70% men and 30% women arriving. After-wards, migration slowed because of a "gentle-men's agreement," a euphemism for racism against the "yellow peril." By 1900 there were over 60,000 Japanese in the islands, consti-tuting the largest ethnic group.

AJAs, Americans Of Japanese Ancestry

Parents of most Japanese children born be-fore WW II were *issei* (first generation), who considered themselves apart from other Americans and clung to the notion of "We Japanese." Their children, the *nisei* or second generation, were a different matter altogether. In one generation they had become Ameri-cans, and they put into practice the high Ja-panese virtues of obligation, duty, and loyalty to the homeland, and that homeland was now unquestionably America. After Pearl Harbor was bombed, the FBI kept close tabs on the Japanese community, and the menace of the "enemy within" prompted the decision to place Hawaii under martial law for the duration of the war. It has since been noted that not a single charge of espionage or sabotage was ever reported against the Japanese community in Hawaii during the war.

AJAs As GIs

Although Japanese had formed a battalion during WW I, they were insulted by being considered unacceptable as American sol-diers in WW II. Some American-Japanese volunteered to serve in labor battalions, and because of their flawless work and loyalty, it was decided to put out a call for a few hundred volunteers to form a combat unit. Over 10,000 signed up! AJAs formed two distinguished units in WW II: the 100th Infantry Battalion, and later the 442nd Regimental Combat Team. They landed in Italy at Salerno and even fought from Guadalcanal to Okinawa. They distinguished themselves by becoming *the* most decorated unit in American military history.

The AJAs Return

Many returning AJAs took advantage of the G.I. Bill and received college educations. The "Big Five" Corporations (see p. 40) for the first time accepted former AJA officers as execu-tives and the old order was changed. Many Japanese became involved with Hawaiian politics and the first elected to Congress was Daniel Inouye, who had lost an arm fighting in WW II. Hawaii's past governor, George Ariyo-shi, elected in 1974, was the country's first

The Japanese GIs returned as "our boys."

not without blemish; true to their custom of family loyalty, they do stick together. There are now 240,000 people in Hawaii of Japanese ancestry, 25% of the state's population. They are the least likely of any ethnic person to marry outside of their group—especially the men—and they enjoy a higher-than- average standard of living.

CAUCASIANS

White people have a distinction from all other ethnic groups in Hawaii: they are all lumped together as one. You can be anything from a Protestant Norwegian dock worker to a Greek Orthodox shipping tycoon, but if your skin is white, in Hawaii, you're a *haole*. What's more, you could have arrived at Waikiki from Missoula, Montana, in the last 24 hours, or your *kamaaina* family can go back five generations, but again, if you're white, you're a *haole*. The word *haole* has a floating connotation that depends upon the spirit in which it's used. It can mean everything from a derisive "honky" or "cracker" to nothing more than "white person." The exact Hawaiian meaning is clouded, but some say it meant "a man of no background," because white men couldn't chant a genealogical *kanaenae* telling the Hawaiians who they were. *Haole* then became euphemised into "foreign white man" and today, simply "white person."

White History

Next to the Hawaiians themselves, white people have the oldest stake in Hawaii. They've been there as settlers in earnest since the missionaries of the 1820s, and were established long before any other migrant group. From last century until statehood, old *haole* families owned and controlled everything, and although they were benevolent, philanthropic, and paternalistic, they were also racist. They were established *kamaaina* families, many of whom made up the boards of the "Big Five" corporations or owned huge plantations, and formed an inner social circle that was closed to the outside. Many managed to find mates from among close family acquaintances. Their paternalism, which they accepted with grave

Japanese-American ever to reach such a high office. Most Japanese, even as they climb the economic ladder, tend to remain Democrats. Today, one out of every two political offices in Hawaii is held by a Japanese-American. In one of those weird quirks of fate, it is now the Hawaiian Japanese who are accused by other ethnic groups of engaging in unfair political practices—nepotism and reverse discrimination. Many of these accusations against AJAs are undoubtedly motivated by jealousy, but the AJAs' record with social fairness issues is responsibility, at first only extended to the Hawaiians, who saw them as replacing their own *ali'i.* Orientals were considered "primarily as instruments of production." These supremacist attitudes tended to drag on in Hawaii until quite recent times. They are today responsible for the sometimes sour relations between white and non-white people in the islands. Today, all individual white people are resented to a certain degree because of these past acts, even though they personally were in no way involved.

White Plantation Workers

In the 1880s the white land-owners looked around and felt surrounded and outnumbered by Orientals, so they tried to import white people for plantation work. None of their schemes seemed to work out. Europeans were accustomed to a much higher wage scale and better living conditions than what was provided on the plantations. Although only workers and not considered the equals of the ruling elite, they still were expected to act like a special class. They were treated preferentially, which meant higher wages for the same job performed by an Oriental. Some of the imported workers included: 600 Scandinavians in 1881; 1,400 Germans from 1881-85; 400 Poles from 1897-98; and 2,400 Russians from 1909-12. Many proved troublesome, like the Poles and Russians who staged strikes after only months on the job. Many quickly moved to the Mainland. A contingency of Scots, who first came as mule skinners, did become successful plantation managers and supervisors. The Germans and Scandinavians were well received and climbed the social ladder rapidly, becoming professionals and skilled workers.

The Depression years, not as economically bad in Hawaii as in the continental U.S., brought many Mainland whites seeking opportunity, mostly from the South and the West. These new people were even more racist toward brown-skinned people and Orientals than the *kamaaina haole,* and they made matters worse. They also competed more intensely for jobs. The racial tension generated during this period came to a head in 1932 with the infamous "Massie Rape Case."

The Massie Rape Case

Thomas Massie, a naval officer, and his young wife Thalia attended a party at the Officers Club. After drinking and dancing all evening, they got into a row and Thalia rushed out in a huff. A few hours later, Thalia was at home, confused and hysterical, claiming to have been raped by some local men. On the most circumstantial evidence, Joseph Kahahawai and four friends of mixed ethnic background were accused. In a highly controversial trial rife with racial tensions, the verdict ended in a hung jury. While a new trial was being set, Kahahawai and his friends were out on bail. Seeking revenge, Thomas Massie and Grace Fortescue, Thalia's mother, kidnapped Joseph Kahahawai with a plan of extracting a confession from him. They were aided by two enlisted men assigned to guard Thalia. While questioning Joseph, they killed him and attempted to dump his body in the sea but were apprehended. Another controversial trial—this time for Mrs. Fortescue, Massie, and the accomplices—followed. Clarence Darrow, the famous lawyer, sailed to Hawaii to defend them. For killing Kahahawai, these people served *one hour* of imprisonment in the judge's private chambers. The other four, acquitted with Joseph Kahahawai, maintain innocence of the rape to this day. Later, the Massies divorced, and Thalia went on to become a depressed alcoholic who took her own life.

The Portuguese

The last time anyone looked, Portugal was still attached to the European continent, but for some anomalous reason the Portuguese weren't considered *haole* in Hawaii for the longest time. About 12,000 arrived from 1878 to 1887 and another 6,000 came between 1906 and 1913. Accompanied during this period by 8,000 Spanish, they were considered one and the same. Most of the Portuguese were illiterate peasants from Madeira and the Azores, and the Spanish hailed from Andalusia. They were very well received, and because they were white but not *haole* they made a perfect "buffer" ethnic group. Committed to staying in Hawaii, they rose to be skilled workers—the *"luna* class" on the plan-

Portuguese plantation workers maintained their own ethnic identity. (MARY ANN ABEL)

tations. They, however, spent the least amount on education and became very racist toward Orientals, regarding them as a threat to their job security. By 1920 the 27,000 Portuguese made up 11% of the population. After that they tended to blend with the other ethnic groups and weren't counted separately. Portuguese men tended to marry within their ethnic group, but a good portion of Portuguese women married other white men and became closer to the *haole* group, while another large portion chose Hawaiian mates and grew further away. Although they didn't originate pidgin English (see "Language"), the unique melodious quality of their native tongue did give pidgin that certain lilt it has today. Also, the ukulele ("jumping flea") was closely patterned after the *cavaquinho,* a Portuguese stringed folk instrument.

The White Population

Today all white people together make up the largest racial, if not ethnic, group in the islands at 33% (about 330,000) of the population. There are heavy white concentrations on the Kihei and Kaanapali coast of Maui. The white population is the fastest growing in the islands, because most people resettling in Hawaii are white Americans predominently from the West Coast.

FILIPINOS AND OTHERS

The Filipinos who came to Hawaii brought high hopes of making a fortune and returning home as rich heroes: for most it was a dream that never came true. Filipinos had been American nationals ever since the Spanish-American War of 1898, and as such weren't subject to immigration laws that curtailed the importation of Oriental workers at the turn of this century. The first to arrive were 15 families in 1906, but a large number came in 1924 as strikebreakers. The majority were illiterate peasants called Ilocanos from the northern Philippines, with about 10% Visayans from the central cities. The Visayans were not as hardworking or thrifty, but were much more sophisticated. From the first, they were looked down upon by all the other immigrant groups and were considered particularly uncouth by the Japanese. They put the least amount of value on education of any group, and even by 1930 only about half could speak rudimentary English, the majority remaining illiterate. They were billeted in the worst housing, performed the most menial jobs, and were the last hired and first fired.

One big difference with Filipinos was that they had no women to marry, so they clung to the idea of returning home. In 1930 there were 30,000 men and only 360 women. This hopeless situation led to a great deal of prostitution and homosexuality; many of these terribly lonely bachelors would feast and drink on weekends and engage in their gruesome but exciting pastime of cockfighting on Sundays. When some did manage to find wives, their mates were inevitably part Hawaiian. Today, there are still plenty of old Filipino bachelors who never managed to get home, and the Sunday cockfights remain a way of life. The Filipinos constitute 14% of Hawaii's population (140,000) with almost 90% living on Oahu. Many visitors to Hawaii mistake Filipinos for Hawaiians because of their dark skin, and this is a minor irritant to both groups. Some streetwise Filipinos even claim to be Hawaiians, because being Hawaiian is "in" and goes over well with the tourists, especially the young women tourists. For the most part, these people are hardworking, dependable laborers who do tough work for little recognition. They still remain low man on the social totem pole and have not yet organized politically to stand up for their rights.

Minor Groups

About 10% of Hawaii's population is made up of a conglomerate of small ethnic groups. Of these, the largest is Korean with 14,000 people. About 8,000 Koreans came to Hawaii from 1903 until 1905, when their own government halted emigration. During the same period about 6,000 Puerto Ricans arrived, but they have become so assimilated that only 4,000 people in Hawaii today consider themselves Puerto Rican. There were also two attempts made last century to import other Polynesians to strengthen the dying Hawaiian race, but they were failures. In 1869 only 126 Central Polynesian natives could be lured to Hawaii, and from 1878 to 1885 2,500 Gilbert Islanders arrived. Both groups became immediately disenchanted with Hawaii. They pined away for their own islands and departed for home as soon as possible.

Today, however, 12,000 Samoans have settled in Hawaii, and with more on the way they are the fastest growing minority in the state. For unexplainable reasons, Samoans and native Hawaiians get along extremely poorly and have the worst racial tensions and animosity of any groups. The Samoans ostensibly should represent the archetypical Polynesians that the Hawaiians are seeking, but it doesn't work that way. Samoans are criticized by Hawaiians for their hot tempers, lingering feuds, and petty jealousies. They're clannish and often are the butt of "dumb" jokes. This racism seems especially ridiculous, but that's the way it is. Just to add a bit of exotic spice to the stew, there are about 10,000 Afro-Americans, a few thousand American Indians, and a smattering of Vietnamese refugees.

LANGUAGE

Hawaii is part of America and people speak English there, but that's not the whole story. If you turn on the TV to catch the evening news, you'll hear "Walter Cronkite" English, unless of course you happen to tune in a Japanese-language broadcast designed for tourists from that country. You can easily pick up a Chinese-language newspaper, or groove to the music on a Filipino radio station, but let's not confuse the issue. All your needs and requests at airports, car rental agencies, restaurants, hotels, or wherever you happen to travel will be completely understood, as well as answered, in English.

However, when you happen to overhear "islanders" speaking, what they're saying will sound somewhat familiar, but you won't be able to pick up all the words, and the beat and melody of the language will be noticeably different. Hawaii, like New England, the Deep South, and the Midwest, has its own unmistakable linguistic regionalism. All the ethnic peoples who make up Hawaii have enriched the English spoken there with words, expressions, and subtle shades of meaning that are commonly used and understood throughout the islands. The greatest influence on English has come from the Hawaiian language itself, and words such as aloha, *kapu,* and muumuu are familiarly used and understood by most Americans. Other migrant peoples, especially the Chinese, Japanese, and Portuguese, influenced the local dialect to such an extent that the simplified plantation lingo that they spoke has become known as "pidgin." A fun and enriching part of the "island experience" is picking up a few words of Hawaiian and pidgin. English is the official language of the state, business, education, and perhaps even the mind; but pidgin is the language of the people, the emotions, and life, while Hawaiian remains the language of the heart and the soul.

PIDGIN

The dictionary definition of pidgin is: a simplified language with a rudimentary grammar used as a means of communication between people speaking different languages. Hawaiian pidgin is a little more complicated than that. It had its roots during the plantation days of last century when white owners and *luna* had to communicate with recently arrived Chinese, Japanese, and Portuguese laborers. It was designed as a simple language of the here and now, and was primarily concerned with the necessary functions of working, eating, and sleeping. It has an economical noun-verb-object structure (not necessarily in that order). Hawaiian words make up most of pidgin's non-English vocabulary. There is a good smattering of Chinese, Japanese, Samoan, and the distinctive rising inflection is provided by the melodious Mediterranean lilt of the Portuguese. Pidgin is not a stagnant language. It's kept alive by hip new words introduced by people who are "so radical," or especially by slang words introduced by teenagers. It's a colorful English, like "jive" or "ghettoese" spoken by American blacks, and is as regionally unique as the speech of Cajuns from Louisiana's bayous. *Maka'ainana* of all socio-ethnic backgrounds can at least understand pidgin. Most islanders are proud of it, while some consider it low-class jargon. The Hawaiian House of Representatives has given pidgin an official sanction, and most people feel that it adds a real local style and should be preserved.

Pidgin Lives

Pidgin is first learned at school where all students, regardless of background, are exposed to it. The pidgin spoken by young people today is "fo' real" different from that of their parents. It's no longer only plantation talk, but has moved to the streets and picked up some sophistication. At one time there was an academic movement to exterminate it, but that idea died away with the same thinking that insisted on making left-handed people write with their right hand. It is strange, however, that pidgin has become the unofficial language of Hawaii's grass-roots movement, when it actually began as a white owners' language which was used to supplant Ha-

CAPSULE PIDGIN

The following are a few commonly used words and expressions that should give you an idea of pidgin. It really can't be written properly, merely approximated, but for now, *"Brah, study da kine an' bimbye you be hele on, brah! O.K.? Lesgo."*

an' den—and then?; big deal; so what's next; how boring

bimbye—after a while; bye and bye. "Bimbye, you learn pidgin"

blalah—brother, but actually only refers to a large, heavy-set, good-natured Hawaiian man

brah—all the bro's in Hawaii are brahs; brother; pal. Used to call someone's attention. One of the most common words used even among people who are not acquainted. After a fill-up at a gas station, a person would say "Tanks, brah."

cockaroach—steal; rip off. If you really want to find out what *cockaroach* means, just leave your camera on your beach blanket when you take a little dip.

da' kine—a catch-all word of many meanings that epitomizes the essence of pidgin. *Da' kine* is easily used as a euphemism for pidgin and is substituted whenever the speaker is at a loss for a word or just wants to generalize. It can mean: you know?; watchamacallit; of that type.

geev um—give it to them; give them hell; go for it. Can be used as an encouragement. If a surfer is riding a great wave, the people on the beach might yell, "Geev um, brah!"

hana ho—again; especially after a concert the audience shouts "hana ho" (one more!)

hele on—right on!; hip; with it; groovy

howzit?—as in "howzit brah?"; what's happening?; how is it going? The most common greeting, used in place of the more formal "How do you do?"

hu hu—angry! "You put the make on the wrong da' kine wahine brah, and you in da' kine trouble, if you get one big Hawaiian blalah plenty hu hu."

kapu—a Hawaiian word meaning forbidden. If *kapu* is written on a gate or posted on a tree it means "No trespassing." *Kapu*-breakers are still very unpopular in the islands.

li'dis an' li'dat—like this or that; a catchall grouping especially if you want to avoid details; like, ya' know?

lesgo—Let's go! Do it!

lolo buggah—stupid or crazy guy (person). Words to a tropical island song go, "I want to find the lolo who stole my pakalolo" (marijuana).

mo' bettah—real good!; great idea. An island sentiment used to be, "mo' bettah you *come* Hawaii." Now it has subtly changed to, "mo' bettah you *visit* Hawaii."

ono—number one! delicious; great; groovy. "Hawaii is ono, brah!"

pakalolo—literally "crazy smoke"; marijuana; grass; reefer "Hey, brah! Maui-wowie da' kine ono pakalolo."

pakiki head—stubborn; bull-headed

pau—a Hawaiian word meaning finished; done; over and done with. *Pau hana* means end of work or quitting time. Once used by plantation workers, now used by everyone.

stink face—basically frowning at someone; using facial expression to show displeasure. Hard looks. What you'll get if you give local people a hard time.

swell head—burned up; angry

talk story—spinning yarns; shooting the breeze; throwing the bull; a rap session. If you're lucky enough to be around to hear *kapuna* (elders) "talk story," you can hear some fantastic tales in the tradition of old Hawaii.

tita—sister, but only used to describe a fun- loving, down-to-earth country girl

waddascoops—what's the scoop?; what's up?; what's happening?

Opposite page: Kihei is one of Hawaii's sailboarding meccas. (ROBERT NILSEN)

waiian and all other languages brought to the islands. Although hip young *haole* use it all the time, it has gained some of the connotation of a language of the non-white local, and is part of the "us against them" way of thinking. All local people, *haole* or not, do consider pidgin their own island language, and don't really like it when it's used by *malihini* (newcomers). If you're in the islands long enough, you don't have to bother learning pidgin; it'll learn you. There's a book sold all over the islands called *Pidgin to da Max*, written by (you guessed it) a *haole* from Nebraska named Doug Simonson. You might not be able to understand what's being said by locals speaking pidgin (that's usually the idea), but you should be able to *feel* what's being meant.

HAWAIIAN

The Hawaiian language sways like a palm tree in a gentle wind. Its words are as melodious as a love song. Linguists say that you can learn a lot about people through their language: when you hear Hawaiian you think of gentleness and love, and it's hard to imagine the ferocious side so evident in Hawaii's past. With many Polynesian root words that are easily traced to Indonesian and Malayan, it's evident that Hawaiian is from this same stock. The Hawaiian spoken today is very different from old Hawaiian. Its greatest metamorphosis occurred when the missionaries began to write it down in the 1820s. There is a movement to re-establish the Hawaiian language, and courses in it are offered at the University of Hawaii. Many scholars have put forth translations of Hawaiian, but there are endless, volatile disagreements in the academic sector about the real meanings of Hawaiian words. Hawaiian is no longer spoken as a language except on Niihau, and the closest tourists will come to it is in place names, street names, and in words that have become part of common usage, such as aloha and *mahalo*. A few old Hawaiians still speak it at home and there are sermons in Hawaiian at some local churches. Kawaiahao Church in downtown Honolulu is the most famous of these. (See

THE ALPHABET.

VOWELS.

	Names.	Ex. in Eng.	Ex. in Hawaii.
A a	â	as in *father*,	la—sun.
E e	a	— *tete*,	hemo—cast off.
I i	e	— *marine*,	marie—quiet.
O o	o	— *over*,	ono—sweet.
U u	oo	— *rule*,	nui—large.

CONSONANTS.	Names.	CONSONANTS.	Names.
B b	be	**N n**	nu
D d	de	**P p**	pi
H h	he	**R r**	ro
K k	ke	**T t**	ti
L l	la	**V v**	vi
M m	mu	**W w**	we

The following are used in spelling foreign words:

F f	fe		S s	se	
G g	ge		Y y	yi	

cover page of the first hawaiian primer

glossary for lists of commonly used Hawaiian words.)

Wiki Wiki Hawaiian

Thanks to the missionaries, the Hawaiian language is rendered phonetically using only 12 letters. They are the five vowels, a-e-i-o-u, sounded as they are in Italian, and seven consonants, h-k-l-m-n-p-w, sounded exactly as they are in English. Sometimes "w" is pronounced as "v," but this only occurs in the middle of a word and always follows a vowel. A consonant is always followed by a vowel, forming two-letter syllables, but vowels are often found in pairs or even triplets. A slight oddity about Hawaiian is the glottal stop. This is merely an abrupt break in sound in the middle of a word such as "oh-oh" in English, and is denoted with an apostrophe ('). A good example is *ali'i* or even better, the Oahu town

Opposite page (top): The verdant Halawa Valley was one of the first places populated by the early Polynesians. (ROBERT NILSEN); (bottom left): Wailua Falls, one of Hana's many tropical delights (ROBERT NILSEN) ; (bottom right):The path to Waimoku Falls at Oheo takes you into a rainforest. (ROBERT NILSEN) of **Ha'iku**, which actually means "abrupt break."

Pronunciation Key

For those unfamiliar with the sounds of Italian or other Romance languages, the vowels are sounded as follows:

A—in stressed syllables, long **a** as in **A**h (that feels good!). For example, Haleakala (Hah lay ah kah lah.) Unstressed syllables get a short **a** as in **a**gain or **a**bove. For example, Kamehameha (**Ka**mehameha).

E—short **e** as in p**e**n or d**e**nt (H**a**le). Long **e** sounded as "ay" as in sw**ay** or d**ay**. For example the Hawaiian goose (**Nene**) is a "nay nay," not a "knee knee."

I—a long **i** as in "**see**" or "**we**" (Hawa**ii** or p**a**li).

O—round **o** as in n**o** or **o**h (*koa,* or **o**no).

U—round **u** like "d**o**" or "st**ew**." (ka**pu,** or **pu**na).

Diphthongs

There are also eight vowel pairs known as "diphthongs" (ae-ai-ao-au-ei-eu-oi-ou). These are the sounds made by gliding from one vowel to another within a syllable. The stress is placed on the first vowel. In English, examples would be soil and euphoria. Common examples in Hawaiian are lei (lay) and heiau.

Stress

The best way to learn which syllables are stressed in Hawaiian is just by listening closely. It becomes obvious after a while. There are also some vowel sounds that are held longer than others and these can occur at the beginning of a word such as the first "a" in *aina* or in the middle of a word like the first "a" in *lanai*. Again, it's a matter of tuning your ear and paying attention. No one is going to give you a hard time if you mispronounce a word. It's good, however, to pay close attention to the pronunciation of street and place names because many Hawaiian words sound alike and a misplaced vowel here or there could be the difference in getting to where you want to go and getting lost.

CAPSULE HAWAIIAN

The lists on the following pages are merely designed to give you a "taste" of Hawaiian and to provide a basic vocabulary of words in common usage which you are likely to hear. Becoming familiar with them is not a strict necessity, but they will definitely enhance your experience and make it more congenial when talking with local people. You'll soon notice that many islanders spice their speech with certain words especially when they're speaking "pidgin," and you too can use them just as soon as you feel comfortable. You might even discover some Hawaiian words that are so perfectly expressive that they'll become a regular part of your vocabulary. Many Hawaiian words have actually made it into the English dictionary. Place names, historical names, and descriptive terms used throughout the text may not appear in the lists below, but will be sited in the Glossary at the back of the book. Also see "Pidgin," "Food," and "Getting Around" for applicable Hawaiian words and phrases in these categories. The definitions given are not exhaustive, but are generally considered the most common.

BASIC VOCABULARY

a'a—rough clinker lava. *A'a* has become the correct geological term to describe this type of lava found anywhere in the world.

ae—yes

akamai—smart; clever; wise

ali'i—a Hawaiian chief or nobleman

aloha—the most common greeting in the islands. Can mean both hello and goodbye, welcome or farewell. It also can mean romantic love, affection or best wishes.

aole—no

hale—house or building; often combined with other words to name a specific place such as Haleakala ("House of the Sun"), or Hale Pai at Lahainaluna, meaning "printing house"

hana—work; combined with *pau* means end of work or quitting time

haole—a word that at one time meant foreigner, but now means a white person or Caucasian. Many etymological definitions have been put forth, but none satisfy everyone. Some feel that it signified a person without a background, because the first white men could not chant their genealogies as was common to Hawaiians.

hapa—half, as in a mixed-blooded person being refered to as *hapa haole*

hapai—pregnant. Used by all ethnic groups when a *keiki* is on the way.

heiau—a traditional Hawaiian temple. A platform made of skillfully fitted rocks, upon which structures were built and offerings made to the gods

holomuu—an ankle-length dress that is much more fitted than a muumuu, and which is often worn on formal occasions

hoolaulea—any happy event, but especially a family outing or picnic

hoomalimali—sweet talk; flattery

huhu—angry; irritated; mad

hui—a group; meeting; society. Often used to refer to Chinese businessmen or familiy members who pool their money to get businesses started.

hula—a native Hawaiian dance where the rhythm of the islands is captured in swaying hips and the stories told by lyrically moving hands

huli huli—barbecue, as in *huli huli* chicken

imu—underground oven filled with hot rocks and used for baking. The main cooking feature at a luau, used to steambake the pork and other succulent dishes. Traditionally the tending of the *imu* was for men only.

ipo—sweetheart; lover; girl or boyfriend

kahuna—priest; sorcerer; doctor; skillful person. *Kahuna* had tremendous power in old Hawaii which they used for both good and evil. The *kahuna 'ana'ana* was a feared individual because he practiced "black magic" and could pray a person to death, while a *kahuna lapa'au* was medical practitioner bringing aid and comfort to the people.

kalua—means roasted underground in an *imu*. A favorite island food is *kalua* pork.

kamaaina—a child of the land; an old-timer; a longtime island resident of any ethnic background; a resident of Hawaii or native son. Oftentimes, hotels and airlines offer discounts called *"kamaaina* rates" to anyone who can prove island residency.

kane—means man, but is actually used to signify a husband or boyfriend. Written on a door, it means "Men's Room."

kapu—forbidden; taboo; keep out; do not touch

kapuna—a grandparent or old-timer; usually means someone who has gained wisdom. The statewide school system now invites *kapuna* to talk to the children about the old ways and methods.

kaukau—slang word meaning food or chow; grub. Some of the best eating in Hawaii is from *"kaukau* wagons," which are trucks from which plate lunches and other morsels are sold.

keiki—child or children; used by all ethnic groups. "Have you hugged your *keiki* today?"

kokua—help. As in "Your *kokua* is needed to keep Hawaii free from litter."

kona wind—a muggy subtropical wind that blows from the south and hits the leeward side of the islands. It usually brings sticky hot weather, and is one of the few times when air-conditioning will be appreciated.

lanai—veranda or porch. You'll pay more for a hotel room if it has a lanai with an ocean view.

lei—a traditional garland of flowers or vines. One of Hawaii's most beautiful customs. Given at any auspicious occasion, but especially when arriving or leaving Hawaii.

limu—varieties of edible seaweed gathered from the shoreline. It makes an excellent salad, and is used to garnish many island dishes—a favorite at luaus.

lomilomi—traditional Hawaiian massage; also, a vinegared salad made up of raw salmon, chopped onions, and spices

lua—the toilet; the head; the bathroom

luau—a Hawaiian feast featuring poi, *imu* baked pork and other traditional foods. A good luau provides some of the best gastronomical delights in the world.

mahalo—thanks; thank you. *Mahalo nui* means big thanks or thank you very much.

mahu—a homosexual; often used derisively like "fag" or "queer"

makai—toward the sea; used by most islanders when giving directions

malihini—what you are if you have just arrived: a newcomer; a tenderfoot; a recent arrival

manauahi—free; gratis; extra

manini—stingy; tight. A Hawaiianized word taken from the name of Don Francisco *Marin,* who was instrumental in bringing many fruits and plants to Hawaii. He was known for never sharing any of the bounty from his substantial gardens on Vineyard Street in Honolulu, therefore his name came to mean stingy.

mauka—toward the mountains; used by most islanders when giving directions

mauna—mountain. Often combined with other words to be more descriptive, as in Mauna Kea ("White Mountain").

moana—the ocean; the sea. Many businesses and hotels as well as place names have *moana* as part of their name.

muumuu—the garment introduced by the missionaries to cover the nakedness of the Hawaiians. A "Mother Hubbard," a long dress with a high neckline that has become fashionable attire for almost any occasion in Hawaii.

ohana—a family; the fundamental social division; extended family. Now used to denote a social organization with "grass roots," as in the "Save Kahoolawe Ohana."

okolehau—literally "iron bottom"; a traditional booze made from *ti* root; *okole* means your "rear end" and *hau* means iron, which was descriptive of the huge blubber pots that it was made in. Also, if you drink too much it'll surely knock you on your *okole*.

ono—delicious; delightful; the best. *Ono ono* means "extra or absolutely" delicious.

opu—belly; stomach

pa'hoehoe—smooth ropey lava that looks like burnt pancake batter. *Pa'hoehoe* is now the correct geological term used to describe this type of lava found anywhere in the world.

pakalolo—"crazy smoke"; marijuana; grass; smoke; dope

pali—a cliff; precipice. Hawaii's geology makes them quite common. The most famous are the *pali* of Oahu where a major battle was fought.

paniolo—a Hawaiian cowboy. Derived from the Spanish *espaniola*. The first cowboys brought in during the early 19th century were Mexicans from California.

pau—finished; done; completed. Often combined into *pau hana,* which means end of work or quitting time.

pilau—stink; smells bad; stench

pilikia—trouble of any kind, big or small; bad times

poi—a glutinous paste made from the pounded corn of taro which, slightly fermented, has a light sour taste. Purplish in color, it is a staple at luaus, where it is called one-, two-, or three-finger poi, depending upon its thickness.

pono—righteous or excellent

puka—a hole of any size. *Puka* is used by all island residents and can be employed when talking about a tiny *puka* in a rubber boat or a *puka* (tunnel) through a mountain.

punee—bed; narrow couch. Used by all ethnic groups. To recline on a *punee* on a breezy lanai is a true island treat.

pu pu—an appetizer; a snack; hors d'oeuvres; can be anything from cheese and crackers to sushi. Oftentimes, bars or nightclubs offer them free.

pupule—crazy; nuts; out of your mind

tapa—a traditional paper cloth made from beaten bark. Intricate designs were stamped in using beaters, and color was added with natural dyes. The tradition was lost in Hawaii, but is now making a comeback, and provides some of the most beautiful folk art in the islands.

tutu—grandmother; granny; older woman. Used by all as a term of respect and endearment.

ukulele—*uku* means "flea" and **lele** means "jumping," thus ukelele means "jumping flea," which was the way the Hawaiians perceived the quick finger movements on the banjo-type Portuguese folk instrument called a *cavaquinho*. The ukulele quickly became synonymous with the islands.

wahine—young woman; female; girl; wife. Used by all ethnic groups. When written on a door means "Women's Room."

wai—fresh water; drinking water

wela—hot. *Wela kahao* is a "hot time" or "making whoopee."

wiki—quickly; fast; in a hurry. Often seen as *wiki wiki* ("very fast"), as in "Wiki wiki Messenger Service."

USEFUL PHRASES

Aloha ahiahi—Good evening.
Aloha au ia oe—I love you!
Aloha kakahiaka—Good morning.
aloha nui loa—much love; fondest regards
Hauoli la hanau—Happy Birthday.

Hauoli makahiki hau—Happy New Year.
Komo mai—Please come in; enter; welcome
Mele kalikimaka—Merry Christmas.
okole maluna—bottoms up; salute; cheers; kampai

RELIGION

The Lord saw fit to keep His island paradise secret from mankind for a few million years, but once we finally arrived we were awfully thankful. Hawaii sometimes appears like a floating tabernacle; everywhere you look there's a church, temple, shrine, or *heiau*. The islands are either a very holy place, or there's a powerful lot of sinning going on that would require so many houses of prayer. Actually, it's just America's "right to worship" concept fully employed . . . in microcosm. All the peoples who came to Hawaii brought their own form of devotion. The Polynesian Hawaiians praised the primordial creators, Wakea and Papa, from whom their pantheon of animistically inspired gods sprang. Obviously to a modern world these old gods would never do. Unfortunately for the old gods, there were simply too many of them, and belief in them was looked upon as mere superstition, the folly of semi-civilized pagans. So the famous missionaries of the 1820s brought Congregational Christianity and the true path to heaven.

Inconveniently, the Catholics, Mormons, Reformed Mormons, Adventists, Episcopalians, Unitarians, Christian Scientists, Lutherans, Baptists, Jehovah's Witnesses, Salvation Army, and every other major and minor denomination of Christianity that followed in their wake brought their own brand of enlightenment and never quite agreed with each other. The Chinese and Japanese migrants came and established all the major sects of Buddhism, Confucianism, Taoism, and Shintoism. Allah is praised, the Torah is chanted in Jewish synagogues, and nirvana is available at a variety of Hindu temples. If the spirit moves you, a Hare Krishna devotee will be glad to point you in the right direction and give you a free flower for only a dollar or two. If the world is still too much with you, you might find peace at a Church of Scientology, or meditation at a Kundalini Yoga institute, or you may perhaps find relief at a local assembly of Baha'i. Anyway, rejoice, because in Hawaii you'll not only find paradise, but you might even find salvation.

THE WATERS OF KANE

The Polynesian Hawaiians worshipped nature. They saw its forces manifested in a multiplicity of forms to which they ascribed god-like powers, and daily life was based on this animistic philosophy. Hand-picked and specially trained storytellers chanted the exploits of the gods. These ancient tales, kept alive in a special oral tradition called *moolelo,* were recited only by day. Entranced listeners encircled the chanter; in respect for the gods and in fear of their wrath, they were forbidden to move once the tale was begun. This was serious business where a man's life could be at stake. It was not like the telling of *kaao,* which were simple fictions, tall tales, and yarns of ancient heroes, merely related for amusement and to pass the long nights. Any object, animate or inanimate, could be a god. All could be infused with mana, especially a dead body or a respected ancestor.

Ohana had personal family gods called *aumakua* whom they called on in times of danger or strife. There were children of gods called *kupua* who were thought to live among men and were distinguished either for their beauty and strength or for their ugliness and terror. It was told that processions of dead *ali'i,* called "Marchers of the Night," wandered through the land of the living and unless you were properly protected it could mean death if they looked upon you. There were simple ghosts known as *akua lapu* who merely frightened people. Forests, waterfalls, trees, springs, and a thousand forms of nature were the manifestations of *akua li'i,* "little spirits" who could be invoked at any time for help or protection.

Behind all of these beliefs was an innate sense of natural balance and order. It can be interpreted as positive-negative, yin-yang, plus-minus, life-death, light-dark, whatever, but the main idea was that everything had its opposite. The time of darkness when only the gods lived was *po.* When the great gods descended to the earth and created light, this was *ao* and man was born. All of these *moolelo* are part of the *Kumulipo,* the great chant that records the Hawaiian version of creation. From the time the gods descended and touched earth at Ku Moku on Lanai, the genealogies were kept. Unlike the Bible, these included the noble families of female *ali'i* as well as males.

THE STRIFES OF MAUI

Of all the heroes and mythological figures of Polynesia, Maui is the best known. His "strifes" are like the great Greek epics, and they make excellent tales of daring that elders loved to relate to youngsters around the evening fire. Maui was abandoned by his mother, Hina of Fire, when he was an infant. She wrapped him in her hair and cast him upon the sea where she expected him to die, but in heroic fashion he lived and returned home to become her favorite. She knew then that he was a born hero and had strength far beyond that of ordinary mortals. His first exploit was to lift the sky. In those days the sky hung so low that men had to crawl around on all fours. Then a seductive young woman approached Maui and asked him to use his great strength to lift the sky. In fine heroic fashion, the big boy agreed, if the beautiful woman would euphemistically "give him a drink from her gourd." He then obliged her by lifting the sky, and he might

Ku (DIANA LASICH HARPER)

even have made the earth move for her once or twice.

More Land

The territory of man was small at that time. Maui decided that more land was needed, so he conspired to "fish up islands." He descended into the land of the dead and petitioned an ancestress to fashion him a hook out of her jawbone. She obliged, and created the mythical hook, *Manai ikalani*. Maui then secured a sacred *alae* bird that he intended to use for bait and bid his brothers to paddle him far out to sea. When he arrived at the deepest spot, he lowered *Manai ikalani* baited with the sacred bird, and his sister, Hina of the Sea, placed it into the mouth of Old One Tooth, who held the land fast to the bottom of the waters. Maui then exhorted his brothers to row, but warned them not to look back. They strained at the oars with all their might and slowly a great land mass arose. One brother, overcome by curiosity, looked back, and when he did so, the land shattered into all of the islands of Polynesia.

Further Exploits

Maui still desired to serve mankind. People were without fire, whose secret was held by the sacred *alae* birds which learned it from Maui's far-distant mother. Hina of Fire gave Maui her burning fingernails, but he oafishly kept dropping them into streams until all had fizzled out and he had totally irritated his generous progenitor. She pursued him, trying to burn him to a cinder; Maui chanted for rain to put out her scorching fires. When she saw that they were all being quenched, she hid her fire in the barks of special trees and informed the mud hens where they could be found, but first made them promise never to tell men. Maui knew of this and captured a mud hen, threatening to wring its scrawny, traitorous neck unless it gave up the secret. The bird tried trickery and told Maui first to rub together the stems of sugar cane, then banana and even taro. None worked, and Maui's determined rubbing is why these plants have hollow roots today. Finally, with Maui's hands tightening around the mud hen's gizzard, the bird confessed that fire could be found in the *hau* tree

and also the sandalwood, which Maui named *ili aha* ("fire bark") in its honor. He then rubbed all the feathers off the mud hen's head for being so deceitful, which is why their crowns are featherless today.

The Sun Is Snared

Maui's greatest deed, however, was snaring the sun and exacting a promise that it would go slower across the heavens. The people complained that there were not enough daylight hours to fish or farm. Maui's mother could not dry her tapa cloth because the sun rose and set so quickly. She asked her son to help. Maui went to his blind grandmother, who lived on the slopes of Haleakala and was responsible for cooking the sun's bananas, which he ate every day in passing. She told him to personally weave 16 strong ropes with nooses out of his sister's hair. Some say these came from her head, but other versions insist that it was no doubt Hina's pubic hair that had the power to hold the sungod. Maui positioned himself with the rope, and as each of the 16 rays of the sun came across Haleakala, he snared them until the sun was defenseless and had to bargain for his life. Maui agreed to free him if he promised to go more slowly. From that time forward the sun agreed to move slowly and Haleakala ("The House of the Sun") became his home.

ANCIENT WORSHIP

Heiau And Idols

A *heiau* is a Hawaiian temple. The basic *heiau* was a masterly built and fitted rectangular stone wall that varied in size from as large as a basketball court to the size of a football field. Once the restraining outer walls were built, the interior was backfilled with smaller stones and the top dressing was expertly laid and then rolled, perhaps with a log, to form a pavement-like surface. All that remains of Hawaii's many *heiau* are the stone platforms. The buildings upon them, made from perishable wood, leaves, and grass, have long since disappeared. Some *heiau* were dreaded temples where human sacrifices were made. Tradition says that this barbaric custom began at Wahaula Heiau on the Big Island in the 12th century and was introduced by a ferocious Tahitian priest named Paao. Other *heiau,* such as Puuhonua O Honaunau, also on the Big Island, were temples of refuge where the weak, widowed, orphaned, and vanquished could find safety and sanctuary.

Idols

All the people worshipped gods who took the form of idols fashioned from wood, feathers, or stone. The eyes were made from shells and until these were inlaid, the idol was dormant. The hair used was often human hair, and the arms and legs were usually flexed. The mouth was either gaping or formed a wide figure eight lying on its side, and more likely than not, it was lined with glistening dog teeth. There were small figures made of woven basketry that were expertly covered with feathers. Red and yellow were favorite colors which were taken from specific birds by men whose only work was to roam the forests in search of them. It made no difference who or what you were in old Hawaii; the gods were ever-present and they took a direct and active role in your life.

MISSIONARIES ONE AND ALL

In Hawaii, when you say "missionaries," it's taken for granted you're referring to the small and determined band of Congregationalists who arrived aboard the brig *Thaddeus* in 1820, and the follow-up groups called "companies" or "packets" that reinforced them. They were sent from Boston by the American Board of Commissioners for Foreign Missions (ABCFM), which learned of the supposed sad and godless plight of the Hawaiian people through returning sailors and especially by the few Hawaiians who had come to America to study. The person most instrumental in bringing the missionaries to Hawaii was a young man named Henry Opukahaia. He was an orphan befriended by a ship's captain and taken to New England, where he studied theology. Obsessed with the desire to return home and save his people from certain damnation, his accounts of life in Hawaii were published and widely read. These accounts were directly

Henry Opukahaia (MISSION HOUSES MUSEUM)

responsible for the formation of the Pioneer Company to the Sandwich Islands Missions in 1819. Unfortunately, Opukahaia died in New England from typhus the year before they left.

"Civilizing" Hawaii

The first missionaries had the straightforward task of bringing the Hawaiians out of paganism and into Christianity and civilization. They met with terrible hostility—not from the natives, but from the sea captains and traders who were very happy with the open debauchery and wanton whoremongering that was status quo in the Hawaii of 1820. Many direct confrontations between these two factions even included the cannonading of missionaries' homes by American sea captains, who were denied the customary visits of island women, thanks to meddlesome "do-gooders." The most memorable of these incidents involved "Mad Jack" Percival, the captain of the USS *Dolphin*. In actuality, the truth of the situation was much closer to the sentiments of James Jarves who wrote, "The missionary was a far more useful and agreeable man than his Catholicism would indicate; and the trader was not so bad a man as the missionary would make him out to be." The missionaries' primary aim might have been conversion, but the most fortuitous byproduct was education, which raised the consciousness of every Hawaiian, regardless of his religious affiliation. In 40 short years Hawaii was considered a civilized nation well on its way into the modern world, and the American Board of Missions officially ended its support in 1863.

Non-Christians

By the turn of the century, both Shintoism and Buddhism, brought by the Japanese and Chinese, were firmly established in Hawaii. The first official Buddhist temple was Hongpa Hongwanji, established on Oahu in 1889. All the denominations of Buddhism account for 17% (170,000 parishioners) of the island's religious total, and there are about 50,000 Shintoists. The Hindu religion has perhaps 2,000 adherents, and about the same number of Jewish people live throughout Hawaii with only one synagogue, Temple Emanuel, on Oahu. The largest number of people in Hawaii (300,000) remain unaffiliated, and about 10,000 people are in new religious movements and lesser-known faiths such as Baha'i and Unitarianism.

ARTS AND CRAFTS

Wild Hawaiian shirts or bright muumuus, especially when worn on the Mainland, have the magical effect of making wearers "feel" like they're in Hawaii, while at the same time eliciting spontaneous smiles from passers-by. Maybe it's the colors, or perhaps it's just the "vibe" that signifies "party time" or "hang loose," but nothing says Hawaii like alohawear does. There are more than a dozen fabric houses in Hawaii turning out distinctive patterns, and many dozens of factories creating their own personalized designs. Oftentimes these factories have attached retail outlets, but in any case you can find hundreds of shops selling alohawear. Aloha shirts were the brilliant idea of a Chinese merchant in Honolulu, who used to hand-tailor them and then sell them to the tourists who arrived by ship in the glory days before WW II. They were an instant success. Muumuus or "Mother Hubbards" were the idea of missionaries, who

were appalled by Hawaiian women running about au naturel and insisted on covering their new Christian converts from head to foot. Now the roles are reversed, and it's Mainlanders who come to Hawaii and immediately strip down to as little clothing as possible.

Alohawear

At one time alohawear was exclusively made of cotton, or from manmade yet naturally based rayon; these materials were and still are the best for any tropical clothing. Beware, however: polyester has slowly crept into the market! No material could possibly be worse than polyester for the island climate, so when buying your alohawear make sure to check the label for material content. Muumuus now come in various styles and can be worn for the entire spectrum of social occasions in Hawaii. Aloha shirts are still basically cut the same, but the patterns have undergone changes, and apart from the original flowers and ferns, modern shirts might depict an island scene giving the impression of a silkscreen painting. A basic good-quality muumuu or aloha shirt starts at about $25 and is guaranteed to be worth its price in good times and happy smiles. The connoisseur might want to purchase *The Hawaiian Shirt: Its Art and History,* by R. Thomas Steele. It's illustrated with more than 150 shirts that are now considered works of art by collectors the world over.

Scrimshaw

This art of etching and carving on bone and ivory has become an island tradition handed down from the times of the old whaling ships.

scrimshaw (DIANA LASICH HARPER)

Although scrimshaw can be found throughout Hawaii, the center remains in the old whaling capital of Lahaina. Here along Front Street are numerous shops specializing in scrimshaw. Today, pieces are carved on fossilized walrus ivory that is gathered by Eskimos and shipped to Hawaii. It comes in a variety of shades from pure white to mocha, depending upon the mineral content of the earth in which it was buried. Elephant ivory or whalebone is no longer used because of ecological considerations, but there is a "gray market" in Pacific walrus tusks. Eskimos can legally hunt the walrus. They then make a few minimal scratches on the tusks which technically qualifies them to be "Native American art," and free of most governmental restrictions. The tusks are then sent to Hawaii as art objects, but the superficial scratches are immediately removed and the ivory is reworked by artisans. Scrimshaw is made into everything from belt buckles to delicate earrings and even into coffee-table centerpieces. The prices can go from a few dollars up into the thousands.

Woodcarvings

One Hawaiian art that has not died out is woodcarving. This art was extremely well developed among the old Hawaiians and they almost exclusively used *koa* because of its density, strength, and natural luster. It was turned into canoes, woodware, and furniture used by the *ali'i. Koa* is becoming increasingly scarce, but many items are still available, though costly. Milo and monkeypod are also excellent woods for carving and have largely replaced *koa*. You can buy tikis, bowls, and furniture at numerous shops. Countless inexpensive carved items are sold at variety stores, such as little hula girls or salad servers, but most of these are imported from Asia or the Philippines and can be bought at any variety store.

Weaving

The minute you arrive in Hawaii you should shell out $2 for a woven beach mat. This is a necessity, not a frivolous purchase, but it definitely won't be made in Hawaii. What is made in Hawaii is *lau hala*. This is traditional Hawaiian weaving from the leaves *(lau)* of the pandanus *(hala)* tree. These leaves vary greatly in length, with the largest over 6 feet, and they have a thorny spine that must be removed before they can be worked. The color ranges from light tan to dark brown. The leaves are cut into strips from one-eighth to one inch wide and are then employed in weaving. Any variety of items can be made or at least covered in *lau hala*. It makes great purses, mats, baskets, and table mats.

Woven into a hat, it's absolutely superb but should not be confused with a palm-frond hat. A *lau hala* hat is amazingly supple and even when squashed will pop back into shape. A good one is expensive ($25) and with proper care will last for years. All *lau hala* should be given a light application of mineral oil on a monthly basis, especially if it's exposed to the sun. For flat items, iron over a damp cloth and keep purses and baskets stuffed with paper when not in use. Palm fronds also are widely used in weaving. They, too, are a great natural raw material, but not as good as *lau hala*. Almost any item, such as a beach bag woven from palm, makes a good, authentic yet inexpensive gift or souvenir, and a wide selection of woven art is available in countless shops.

Gift Items

Jewelry is always an appreciated gift, especially if it's distinctive, and Hawaii has some of the most original. The sea provides the basic raw materials of pink, gold, and black coral, and it's so beautiful that it holds the same fascination as gemstones. Harvesting the coral is very dangerous work. The Lahaina beds off Maui have one of the best black coral lodes in the islands, but unlike reef coral these trees grow at depths bordering the outer limits of a scuba diver's capabilities. Only the best can dive 180 feet after the black coral, and about one diver per year dies in pursuit of it. Conservationists have placed great pressure on the harvesters of these deep corals, and the state of Hawaii has placed strict limits and guidelines on the firms and divers involved.

Pink coral has long been treasured by man. The Greeks considered it a talisman for good health, and there's even evidence that it has been coveted since the Stone Age. Coral jewelry is on sale at many shops throughout Hawaii and the value comes from the color of the coral and the workmanship. *Puka* (shells with little naturally occurring holes) and *opihi* shells are also made into jewelry. Many times these items are very inexpensive, yet they are authentic and great purchases for the price. Hanging macrame planters festooned with seashells are usually quite affordable and sold at roadside stands along with shells.

Hawaii produces some unique food items that are appreciated by most people. Varioussized jars of macadamia nuts and butters are great gifts, as are tins of rich, gourmet-quality Kona coffee, the only coffee produced in the U.S. Guava, pineapple, passion fruit, and

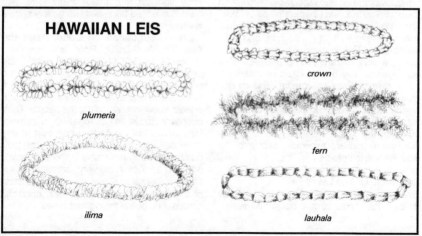

HAWAIIAN LEIS

plumeria

ilima

crown

fern

lauhala

(LOUISE FOOTE)

mango are often gift-boxed into assortments of jams, jellies, and spicy chutneys. And for that special person in your life, you can bring home island fragrances in bottles of perfumes and colognes in the exotic odors of gardenia, plumeria, and even ginger. All of the above items are reasonably priced, lightweight, and easy to carry.

HULA AND LEIS

Hawaiian hula was never performed in grass skirts; tapa or *ti*-leaf skirts were worn. Grass skirts came to Hawaii from the Gilbert Islands, so if you see grass or cellophane skirts in a "hula revue," you'll know that it's not traditional. Hula, like all artforms, has its own highly specialized techniques. A dancer has to learn how to control every part of his or her body, including the facial expressions, which become very important and help to set the mood. The hands are extremely important and provide instant background scenery. For example, if the hands are thrust outwardly in an aggressive manner, this can be a battle; if they sway gently overhead, they refer to the gods or the early time of creation. They can easily become rain or clouds or the sun, sea, or moon. You must watch the hands to get the gist of the story, but the best comeback to this advice was the classic wisecrack, "You watch the parts you like, and I'll watch the parts I like." Swaying hips, depending upon their motion, can be a long walk, a canoe ride, or sexual intercourse. The foot motion can portray a battle, a walk, or any kind of movement or conveyance. The overall effect is multidirectional synchronized movement. The correct chanting of the *mele* is an integral part of the performance. These story-chants, combined with the various musical instruments that accompany the dance, make the hula very much like opera, and are especially similar in the way the tale is unfolded.

Language Of The Lei

Every major island of Hawaii is symbolized by its own lei, made from a distinctive flower, shell, or fern. Each island has its own official color as well, which doesn't necessarily correspond to the color of the island's lei. Maui is the pink island and its lei is the corresponding small pink rose called the *lokelani*. These flowers are not native, but were imported and widely cultivated at one time. In recent years they've fallen prey to a rose beetle and sometimes when they're scarce, a *roselani* is substituted for Maui's leis.

ART INFORMATION

Arts Council of Hawaii, P.O. Box 50225, Honolulu, HI 96850, tel. 524- 7120, Karl Ichida, Executive Director. This is a citizens' advocacy group for the arts, which provides technical assistance and information to individuals and groups. It publishes the *Cultural Climate,* a newsletter that covers what's happening in the arts of Hawaii. It includes a calendar of events, feature articles, and editorials. Anyone interested in Hawaiian arts can become a member of ACH for only $15, which entitles you to receive the *Cultural Climate.* Nonmembers can pick it up for 50 cents an issue.

Pacific Handcrafters Guild, P.O. Box 15491, Honolulu, HI 96818, tel. 923-5726. The guild's focus is on developing and preserving handicrafts in Hawaii and the Pacific. They sponsor four major crafts fairs, two guild-sponsored fairs, and two gallery shows annually.

State Foundation on Culture and the Arts, 335 Merchant St., Room 202, Honolulu, HI 96813, tel. 548-4145. Begun by the State Legislature in 1965, its goals are to preserve Hawaii's diverse cultural heritage, promote the arts and artists, and to make cultural and artistic programs available to the people. Their budget includes the purchasing of artwork (one percent of the construction cost of any state building goes for art). Many of their purchases hang for a time in the governor's office. They publish the very complete *Hawaii Cultural Resource Directory,* which lists most of the art organizations, galleries, councils, co-ops, and guilds throughout Hawaii.

SHOPPING

This chapter will provide general information about shopping on Maui for general merchandise, books, arts, crafts, and specialty items. Specific shops are listed in the "Shopping" section of each travel chapter. Here, you should get an overview of what's available and where, with enough information to get your pockets twitching and your credit cards smoldering! Happy bargain hunting!

SHOPPING MALLS

Those who enjoy one-stop shopping will be happy with the choices in Maui's various malls. You'll find regularly known department stores as well as small shops featuring island-made goods. The following are Maui's main shopping malls. For food markets and health food stores see "Food And Drink."

Kahului/Wailuku

Along Kaahumanu Avenue, you'll find **Kaahumanu Shopping Center,** tel. 877- 3369, the largest on the island. Here's everything from **Sears** and **Liberty House** to **Sew Special,** a tiny store featuring island fabrics. The mall is full service with apparel stores, shoe stores, computer centers, art shops, music stores, gourmet coffee shop, and **Waldenbooks.** You can eat at numerous restaurants, buy ice cream cones, or enjoy a movie at **Holiday Theaters.**

Down the road is **Maui Mall,** tel. 877-5523, featuring photo centers, **Longs** for everything from aspirin to film, **Woolworth's, J.C. Penney, Waldenbooks,** sports and swimwear shops, and numerous restaurants and food outlets. Sandwiched between these two modern facilities is **Kahului Shopping Center,** tel. 877-5527. It's definitely "downhome" with old-timers sitting around outside. The shops here aren't fancy, but they are authentic and you can make some offbeat purchases by strolling through.

Across the street from Maui Mall is the **Old Kahului Store,** a refurbished mini-mall with apparel shops, a restaurant, deli, surf shop, video store, and other specialty shops.

Lahaina And Vicinity

You can't beat Lahaina's Front Street for the best, worst, most artistic, and tackiest shopping on Maui. This is where the tourists are, so this is where the shops are . . . shoulder to shoulder. The list is endless, but you'll find art studios, galleries, kites, T-shirts galore, scrimshaw, jewelry, silks, boutiques, leathers, souvenir junk, eelskins, and even a permament tattoo memory of Maui. No wimps allowed! Lahaina also has the best special-interest shopping on Maui in various little shops strung out along Front Street (see "Shopping" in the Lahaina section).

The following are the local malls: **The Wharf,** tel. 661-8748, on Front St. has a multitude of eating establishments, as well as stores and boutiques in its multilevel shopping facility. When you need a break, get a coffee and browse the fine selections at The Whaler's Book Shoppe—great selections and a top-notch snack bar. **Lahaina Market Place,** tel. 667-2636, tucked away on Front St., features established shops along with open-air stalls. **Lahaina Square Shopping Center,** tel. 242-4400, **Lahaina Shopping Center,** and **Lahaina Business Center** all between Rt. 30 and Front St., have various shops, and are probably the most *local* of the Lahaina malls. The **505 Front Street Mall,** tel. 667-2514, is at the south end of Front St. and offers distinctive and quiet shopping away from the frenetic activity.

The **Lahaina Cannery Shopping Mall,** tel. 661-5304, is a newly opened center on Lahaina's west end, featuring restaurants, boutiques, specialty shops, fast food, and plenty of bargains. It's the largest mall on West Maui and has some of the best shopping under one roof on the island. The newest center, and potentially the largest, is the **Lahaina Center,** located along Front Street at Papalaua Street. While not yet full, stores include Hillo Hatties, Lahaina Licks, and a Hard Rock Cafe.

Kaanapali
Whaler's Village, tel. 661-4567, is a Kaanapali mall, set right on the ocean, which features a decent self-guided museum. There are various eateries, bottle shops, boutiques, galleries, a **Liberty House,** and a **Waldenbooks.** It's a great place to stroll, buy, and learn a few things about Maui's past. The **Sheraton, Marriott, Westin Maui,** and **Royal Lahaina** hotels all have shopping arcades, but the best is at the **Hyatt Regency.** You'll need a suitcase stuffed with money to buy anything there, but it's a blast just walking around the grounds and checking out the big-ticket items.

Kihei And Wailea
Azeka Place, tel. 874-8400, is along Kihei Road. Here there's food shopping, a **Liberty House,** a dive shop, and an activities center, among many other specialty shops. Strung along Kihei Road, one after another, are **Kukui Mall, Kihei Town Center, Dolphin Shopping Center, Kamaole Beach Center, ABC Shopping Center, Kamaole Shopping Center,** and **Rainbow Mall** where restaurants, food outlets, boutiques, and gift shops can be found. The exclusive **Wailea Shopping Village,** tel. 879-4474, has an assortment of both chic and affordable boutiques near the Intercontinental, Stouffer's, The Four Seasons, and Grand Hyatt hotels, all of which have shopping arcades of their own.

SPECIALTY STORES, ITEMS, AND NEAT THINGS

Some truly nifty and distinctive stores are wedged in among Maui's run-of-the-mill shopping centers, but for real treasures you'll find the solitary little shop the best. Lahaina's Front Street has the greatest concentration of top-notch boutiques, but others are dottted here and there around the island. The following is only a sampling of the best; many more are listed in the individual chapters.

Tattered sails on a rotted mast, tattooed sea-dogs in wide-striped jerseys, grim-faced Yankee captains squinting at the horizon, ex-

shell macrame (J.D. BISIGNANI)

otic, probably extinct, birds on the wing, flowers and weather-bent trees, and the beautiful, simple faces of Polynesians staring out from ancient days are faithfully preserved at **Lahaina Printsellers Ltd.** Here is one of the newest and most unusual purveyors of art on Maui. Their shops, like mini-museums, are hung with original engravings, drawings, maps, charts, and naturalist sketches ranging in age from 150 to 400 years. Each, marked with an authenticity label, can come from anywhere in the world, but the Hawaiiana collection is amazing in its depth. Many works feature a nautical theme, reminiscent of the daring explorers who opened the Pacific. The Lahaina Printsellers have been collecting for over 15 years, and are the largest collectors of material relating to Capt. Cook in the entire Pacific Basin. Prices range from $25 for the smallest antique print, up to $15,000 for a rare museum-quality work.

The Lahaina Printsellers keep Maui's art alive by representing modern artists as well, like Richard Fields, whose works are destined to become classics. The production end of the Lahaina Printsellers is located at the historic Hale Aloha, an old-time meeting house, at 636 Luakini St., Lahaina, tel. 661-5120. Two shops are in malls, one at the Whaler's Village in Kaanapali, tel. 667-7617, and the other at the Wailea Shopping Village, tel. 879-1567. Perhaps their most interesting shop is at the historic Seamen's Hospital, tel. 667-8177, along Lahaina's Front Street. Here, some of the sailors who opened the Pacific, and whose exploits are commemorated on the walls, lay sick and dying, never to return home.

For a unique memento of Maui have your photo taken along Front Street near Pioneer Square. Here, you'll become the human perch for macaws and cockatoos. The birds are very tame, natural hams, and the only thing on Maui guaranteed to be more colorful than your Hawaiian shirt. For $15-$20 they'll take your picture and the next day deliver your photos. You also might run across "Bud the Birdman."

Strolling the streets of Lahaina, with birds perched on his shoulders or hanging from his fingers, he will take photos of you with his birds and deliver the pictures the next day.

Paia is quickly becoming the unofficial art center of Maui, along with being the windsurfing capital of Hawaii. Lahaina has slicker galleries, but you come much closer to the source in Paia. The **Maui Crafts Guild** is an exemplary crafts shop that displays the best in local island art. All artists must be selected by active members before their works can be displayed. All materials used must be natural, with an emphasis on those found only in Hawaii. Quickly comes **Paia Gallery**, hung with distinctive island works; **Exotic Maui Woods;** and the workshop of Eddie Flotte, a modern Maui master. A few miles past Paia, you turn up an old road to the **Old Pauwela Cannery,** where artists like Piero Resta have honeycombed studios into this massive old building.

Upcountry's Makawao is a wonderful and crazy combination of old-time paniolo, matured hippies who now worry about drugs and their kids, and sushi-munching yuppies. This hodgepodge makes for a town with tack shops, hardware stores, exclusive boutiques, art shops, gourmet coffee shops, and non-dairy, guaranteed-to-be-good-for-you ice cream stores. All are strung along two Dodge City-like streets.

Near Kahului airport visit the **Pink and Black Coral Factory**. Local craftsmen make distinctive coral jewelry from the amazing corals found under Maui's seas. Each year some divers lose their lives while harvesting these fantastic corals. **Maui Swap Meet** at Maui County Fairgrounds, in Kahului off Puunene Avenue (Hwy. 35) is open every Sat. 8 a.m to 1 p.m.; admission 50 cents. Great junk! **Wailuku** is Maui's attic turned out on the street. About five odd little shops on Market Street display every kind of knickknack, curio, art treasure, white elephant, grotesque and sublime piece of furniture, jewelry, stuffed toy, game, or oddity that ever floated, sailed, flew, or washed up on Maui's beaches.

MUSEUMS, GARDENS, ET CETERA

Alexander & Baldwin Sugar Museum, 3957 Hansen Rd., Lahaina, tel. 871- 8058.

Baldwin Home, Front St., Lahaina. Open daily from 9:30 a.m. to 5 p.m., $2, tel. 661-3262. Two-story home of medical missionary Dwight Baldwin.

Brig Carthaginian Floating Museum, Lahaina Harbor, Lahaina. Open daily 9 a.m. to 5 p.m., $3. Replica of a 19th-century brig. Features whaling artifacts and exhibits on the humpback whale.

Hale Hoikeike, 2375-A Main Street, Wailuku, tel. 244-3326. Also known as the Bailey House Museum, it is a repository of Hawaiian historical objects, artifacts from Kahoolawe, and the renowned paintings of Edward Bailey.

Hale Pa'i Printshop Museum, P.O. Box 338, Lahaina, tel. 667-7040. Located on the grounds of Lahainaluna school. Operational relics of original printing press, original Lahainaluna press publications, and an exhibit of Lahainaluna school past and present. Open by appointment only—contact the Lahaina Restoration Foundation or the Baldwin Home.

Hana Cultural Center, Box 27, Hana, tel. 248-8622. Preserves and restores historical sites, artifacts, photos, documents, etc.

Helani Gardens, privately owned, 70-acre drive-through garden on the western outskirts of Hana, well marked. Self-guided tours. Open daily, 10 a.m. to 4 p.m., $2.

Kahanu Gardens, on Ulaina Road in Hana. This 20-acre garden, part of the National Tropical Botanical Garden, contains commercial and decorative varieties of tropical plants, as well as **Piilanihale Heiau,** one of the largest in all of Hawaii. Open Tues.-Sat. 10 a.m. to 2 p.m., $5.

Kula Botanical Gardens, Hwy. 377 to Upper Kula Road, tel. 878-1715. Open daily 7 a.m. to 4 p.m. Excellent arrangements of tropical plants and flowers in upcountry Maui.

Lahaina Arts Society, P.O. Box 991, Lahaina, tel. 661-0111. Established to perpetuate and further Hawaiian culture, the arts, and crafts. Sponsors two galleries, an annual scholarship, traveling exhibitions, and helps maintain Lahaina district courthouse.

Lahaina Restoration Foundation, P.O. Box 991, Lahaina, HI 96761, tel. 661-3262. James C. Luckey, director. Open Mon. to Sat. 10 a.m. to 4 p.m. Organization dedicated to the preservation of historical Lahaina. Sponsors restorations, archaeological digs, and renovation of cultural and historical sites. Operates Baldwin Home, Brig *Carthaginian,* among others.

Maui Historical Society, 2375 A Main, Wailuku, tel. 244-3326. Open 25 hours per week. Housed in the Bailey House Museum. Promotes interest in and knowledge of history of Hawaii and Maui County. Free lectures during the year.

Whaler's Village Museum, Whaler's Village Shopping Center, Kaanapali, tel. 661-5992. Whaling artifacts, and a 30-foot sperm whale skeleton set among gift shops. Self-guided learning experience while you shop.

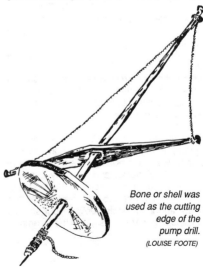

Bone or shell was used as the cutting edge of the pump drill.
(LOUISE FOOTE)

EVENTS

National holidays and Hawaiian state events are all celebrated and commemorated in Maui County, but several other unique happenings occur only on the Valley Isle, Molokai, and Lanai. If you happen to be visiting when any of the following are in progress, be sure to attend!

January

The **Molokai Challenge,** a new biathlon, is held along Molokai's amazing north coast. Watch a three-mile run and a kayak race against time and the power of the sea.

The grueling **Maui Triathlon,** Kaanapali, Maui, is a very competitive sporting event with world-class athletes running for top prizes.

February

The **Carole Kai Bed Race** is a fund-raising race of crazies, pushing decorated beds down Front Street in Lahaina.

March

This is the month for marathons. The Valley Island Runners sponsor the **Maui Marathon** in early March from Wailuku to Lahaina. Later

the **Kukini Run** follows an ancient trail through Kahakuloa Valley on Maui's coast.

The **LPGA Womens Kemper Open** is a world-class match at Kaanapali Golf Course, and mid-month features another type of feminine beauty, grace, and athletic ability at the **Miss Maui Pageant** at Baldwin High School, Wailuku.

May

Costumed pageants, canoe races, and a beard-judging contest commemorate times past at the **Lahaina Whaling Spree,** Lahaina.

June

The **Annual Upcountry Fun Fair** at the Eddie Tam Center, Makawao, Maui, is an old-fashioned farm fair right in the heart of Maui's *paniolo* country. Crafts, food, and competitions are part of the fair.

July

Head for the coolness of upcountry Makawao for the annual 4th of July rodeo. *Paniolo* are an old and very important tradition in Hawaiian life. Held at the Oskie Rice Arena, this old-time upcountry rodeo can't be beat for fun and entertainment anywhere in the country.

August

Late July or early August offers *the* most difficult marathon in the world. **The Run to the Sun** takes runners from sea level to the top of Haleakala (10,023 feet), over 37 long grueling miles. Also, a good-time music festival featuring local entertainers is held in Kapalua.

September

Head back up to Makawao for another excellent **Maui County Rodeo** as well as plenty of good happenings during the statewide **Aloha Week.**

The **Molokai To Oahu Canoe Race** for women (men in October) takes off at the end of September in Hawaiian-style canoes from a remote beach on Molokai to Fort DeRussy in Honolulu. In crossing, the teams must navigate the always rough Kaiwi Channel.

October

The **Molokai To Oahu Canoe Race** for men.

The **Kapalua International Championship of Golf,** at Kapalua, Maui, is one of the best pro tournaments, drawing the world's best golfers for one of the world's largest purses. Runs to early November.

Visit the Maui County Fair held at the fairgrounds in Kahului, an old-fashioned fair with Western and homespun flavor. Wild costumes and outlandish behavior set the mood islandwide for Halloween. Lahaina's Pioneer Inn is HQ for the **Lahaina Jackpot Fishing Tournament,** where the biggest marlin landed can bring prize money of $50,000.

November

This month remembers Maui of old with the **Na Mele O Maui** festival in Lahaina and Kaanapali. Hawaiian music, dance, arts, and crafts are featured.

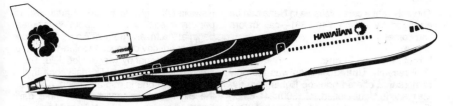

GETTING THERE

Maui, the Hawaiian destination second only to Oahu, attracts over a million visitors per year. A limited number of direct flights from the Mainland are offered, but most airlines servicing Hawaii, both domestic and foreign, land at Honolulu International Airport and then carry on to Maui or offer connecting flights on "inter-island carriers" from there; in most cases they're part of the original ticket price with no extra charge. Different airlines have "interline" agreements with different Hawaiian carriers so check with your travel agent. All major and most smaller inter-island carriers service Maui from throughout Hawaii with over 100 flights per day in and out of Kahului Airport and several dozen a day to Kapalua-West Maui airport.

Note: Airlines usually adjust their flight schedules about every three months to account for seasonal differences in travel and route changes. Before planning a trip to and around the islands, be sure to contact the airlines directly or go through your travel agent for the most current information on routes and flying times.

Maui's Airports

There are three commercial airports on Maui, but the vast majority of travelers will be concerned with **Kahului Airport,** which accommodates 95% of the flights in and out of Maui. Kahului Airport is only minutes from Kahului city center, on the north central coast of Maui. A full-service facility with most amenities, it has car rental agencies, information booths, and limited public and private transportation. This airport is currently undergoing a major expansion—opposed by many island residents—that will allow it to land the biggest commercial planes and handle a great increase in traffic, including direct international flights. The first phase was completed in 1990 and work will continue for the next several years, causing only minor inconvenience to travelers. Major roads lead from Kahului Airport to all primary destinations on Maui.

Hawaiian Airlines opened **Kapulua-West Maui Airport** in early 1987. This brand-new facility is conveniently located between Kaanapali and the Kapalua resort areas, on the *mauka* side of the Honoapiilani Hwy. at Mahinahina just a few minutes from the major Kaanapali Hotels. This is definitely the airport that you want to use if you are staying anywhere on West Maui, if possible. Besides Hawaiian Air, which operates 22 daily flights connecting West Maui with the rest of Hawaii, seven other commuter airlines have contracted to use the facility, but for now only Aloha Island Air and Panorama Air Tours have a booth. The facility opens West Maui to its first-ever service to all the Hawaiian Islands, the South Pacific, and the Mainland's West Coast. The brand-new facility is very user-friendly with a snack bar, sundries, and car rental agencies or courtesy phones for car rental pick up. A free trolley bus connects you with major Kaanapali hotels.

The third airstrip is **Hana Airport,** an isolated runway with a tiny terminal on the northeast coast just west of Hana. It has no amenities and transportation is available only to the Hotel Hana Maui via the hotel shuttle. People flying into Hana Airport generally plan to vacation in Hana for an extended period and have made prior arrangements for being picked up.

The only rental cars available in Hana can be arranged by calling 248-8391—call before you come!

Direct Mainland Flights

Until recently, **United Airlines** was the only carriers that offered nonstop flights from the Mainland to Maui. United, tel. (800) 241-6522, flies one daily nonstop to Maui from both San Francisco and Los Angeles. Denver, Portland, and Seattle passengers fly via San Francisco or Los Angeles. Now, **Delta Airlines**, tel. (800) 221-1212, flies once daily direct from Los Angeles, with other flights originating in Los Angeles and San Francisco going through Honolulu at no extra charge. **Hawaiian Air,** tel. (800) 367-5320, offers daily flights via San Francisco and Los Angeles through Honolulu.

INTER-ISLAND CARRIERS

Hawaiian Air, tel. (800) 367-5320, Maui 244-9111, offers more flights to Maui than any other inter-island carrier. The majority of flights are to and from Honolulu (average flight time 30 minutes), with over 30 per day in each direction. Hawaiian Air flights to Kahului Maui from Honolulu begin at 5:30 a.m., with flights thereafter about every 30 minutes until 8 p.m. Flights from Kahului to Honolulu begin at 6:30 a.m. and go all day until 9 p.m. In addition, there are over 20 flights daily connecting Kapalua-West Maui airport to Honolulu starting at 7:24 a.m. (6:30 a.m. from Honolulu) and running until 6:10 p.m. (5:15 from Honolulu).

Hawaiian Air flights to and from Kauai (over 15 per day in each direction, about 35 minutes) begin at 7 a.m. and go until 7 p.m. Four more flights every day connect Kapalua-West Maui airport and Kauai by way of Honolulu. There are two flights to/from Hilo daily, one in the morning and one in mid-afternoon. Kona, on the Big Island, is serviced with three daily flights from Kahului. Flights from Maui begin at 9 a.m. with the last at 4:05 p.m.; from Kona at 9:50 a.m. with the last at 4:55 p.m. There is one direct flight between Maui and Molokai, leaving Maui at 10:20 a.m. and Molokai at 12:30 p.m. on Dash 7 prop planes. Molokai and Lanai are connected by twice-weekly flights, both going through Honolulu.

Aloha Airlines, tel. (800) 367-5250, Maui 244-9071, with its all-jet fleet of 737s, flies from Honolulu to Maui over 30 times per day beginning at 5:40 a.m. with the last flight at 8:12 p.m.; to Honolulu at 6:35 a.m., last at 9 p.m. Multiple flights throughout the day from Kauai begin at 6:35 a.m. until 7:15 p.m.; to Kauai at 6:35 a.m. and throughout the day until 7:20 p.m. From Hilo, three flights depart in mid-morning and the last at 7:05 p.m.; to Hilo four flights are interspersed from 8:25 a.m. until 6:10 p.m. From Kona six flights leave from 9:25 a.m. until 6:55 p.m.; to Kona five flights from 7:10 a.m. until 4:30 p.m.

Commuter Airlines

Aloha Island Air, tel. (800) 323-3345 Mainland, (800) 652-6541 statewide, 833-3219 Oahu, offers daily flights connecting Maui with all the major islands. Along with only two of the state's main airports (Honolulu and Kahului), they service the smaller and sometimes more convenient airports of Kapalua and Hana on Maui, Princeville on Kauai, Kalaupapa on Molokai, and Kamuela on the Big Island. Over a dozen flights a day connect Honolulu to Kahului (most via Molokai, Lanai, or Kapalua West Maui) beginning at 7:30 a.m. (6:10 from Honolulu) and run until 6:20 p.m., with two late night flights at 11 p.m. and 1 a.m.; from there four carry on to Princeville.

Five daily flights run from Molokai to Kahului (6:50 a.m. to 3 p.m.), with four from Lanai (7:05 a.m. to 3:45 p.m.). There are four daily

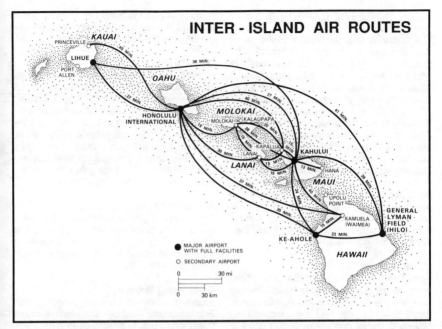

INTER - ISLAND AIR ROUTES

flights to/from Hana from 7:55 a.m. (8:25 a.m. from Hana) to 3 p.m. (5:55 p.m. from Hana), and one flight a day to Kamuela at 12:50 p.m. From Kapalua West Maui, direct flights go to Kahului three times a day (7:30 a.m., 10:25 a.m., and 2:35 p.m.), Lanai once daily at 4:50 p.m., Molokai twice daily at 8:25 a.m. and 12:45 p.m., and six to Honolulu from 9:10 a.m. to 5:10 p.m. In addition, flights to Princeville go through Honolulu and to Hana and Kamuela through Kahului. All four daily flights to Hana come from Kahului. There is one daily flight from Molokai to Lanai at 6:45 a.m. and two from Lanai to Molokai at 9:25 a.m. and 5:20 p.m., with additional flights on Monday morning and Friday evening to accommodate workers. There are flights to Kalaupapa from Kahului, Molokai, and Honolulu, but only with a reservation on one of the organized tours (see pp. 338-339 for more information).

Panorama Air, tel. (800) 367-2671, 836-2122 on Oahu, 669-0205 on Maui, runs a commuter schedule between Honolulu, Kapa-

lua-West Maui, and Molokai, and two scenic tours, a Volcano Tour and an Eight-Island Tour, leaving both from Oahu and Kapalua-West Maui airport.

Air Molokai, tel. 521-0090 on Oahu, 877-0026 Maui, has flights connecting Oahu, Molokai, Maui, and Lanai. There are four interspersed throughout the day between Oahu and Molokai, $83 RT adults, $58.25 children. Twice daily flights connect Molokai and Kahului Maui, same rates as above. The Lanai station was opened in Sept 1990; rates for the flights connecting Maui and Lanai are also the same as above, but those for the Molokai to Lanai route are $78 RT adults, $54.60 children. Reduced *kamaaina* rates are available for residents.

Charter Airlines

If you've got the bucks or just need to go when there's no regularly scheduled flight, try either **Paragon Air,** tel. 244-3356, or **Trans Air,** tel. 833-5557, for island-wide service.

DOMESTIC CARRIERS

The following is a description of the major domestic carriers to and from Hawaii. The planes used are primarily DC-10s and 747s with a smaller 727 thrown in here and there. A list of the "gateway" cities from which they fly "direct and nonstop" is given, but "connecting" cities are not. All flights by all carriers land at Honolulu International Airport except for **Delta Airlines**, which has limited direct flights to Maui, and **United**, which flies direct to Maui and the Big Island. The following lists only the established companies; entrepreneurial small airlines such as the now-defunct Hawaii Express pop up now and again and specialize in dirt-cheap fares. There is a hectic frenzy to buy their tickets, business is great for a while, then the established companies lower their fares and the gamblers fold.

United Airlines

Since their first island flight in 1947, United has become "top dog" in flights to Hawaii. Having bought all of Pan American's Pacific routes, they'll dominate the field even more. Their Mainland routes connect over 100 cities to Honolulu. The main gateways include direct flights from San Francisco, Los Angeles, Seattle, Chicago, and Denver. They also offer direct flights from San Francisco and Los Angeles to Maui, and from San Francisco to Kona on the Big Island. Call (800) 241-6522 for information and reservations. United offers a number of packages ranging from first-class to more moderate deals, which include air fares, hotels, and some sights. They also interline with **Aloha Airlines** and offer special deals with **National Car Rental** among others. United's Vacation Planning Center can be reached by calling tel. (800) 328-6877. They're the "big guys" and they intend to stay that way—their packages are hard to beat.

Hawaiian Air

One of Hawaii's own domestic airlines has entered the Mainland market with daily flights from Los Angeles, San Francisco, Seattle, and a weekly flight to Las Vegas. The "common fare" ticket price includes an ongoing flight to any of the Neighbor Islands, and if leaving from Hawaii, a free flight from a Neighbor Island to the link-up in Honolulu.

Delta Airlines

In 1985, Delta entered the Hawaiian market with nonstop flights to Honolulu from Atlanta and Dallas/Ft. Worth. In 1987 they purchased Western Airlines and added numerous connecting flights from all over the country. Currently, their gateway cities to Honolulu are Los Angeles, San Francisco, and San Diego. They offer one direct morning flight from Los Angeles to Maui, with others going through Honolulu. For information call (800) 221-1212.

American Airlines

Offers direct flights to Honolulu from Los Angeles, San Francisco, San Jose, Dallas, and Chicago. They also fly from Los Angeles to Maui via Honolulu with no change of plane. Call (800) 433-7300.

Continental Airlines

Flights to Honolulu from Los Angeles, San Francisco, and Houston. International routes from Honolulu go to several cities in Australia, Auckland, New Zealand, and Tokyo, with connections through Air Micronesia to Guam. Call (800) 525-0280.

Northwest Airlines

Direct flights to Honolulu from Los Angeles, San Francisco, and Seattle. Northwest has an inter-island agreement with Aloha Airlines to connect to Neighbor Islands. Onward flights travel to numerous cities in Asia. Call (800) 225-2525.

TWA

One daily direct flight to Honolulu from Los Angeles. Call (800) 221-2000.

American West Airlines

The most recent arrival in the Hawaiian market is worker-owned America West Airlines. Starting service in Nov. 1989, they currently have direct daily flights only from Phoenix to Honolulu with direct return flights to both Phoenix and Las Vegas. Call (800) 247-5692.

FOREIGN CARRIERS

The following carriers operate throughout Oceania but have no U.S. flying rights. This means that in order to vacation in Hawaii using one of these carriers, your flight must originate or terminate in a foreign city. You can stop over in Honolulu with a connecting flight to a Neighbor Island. For example, if you've purchased a flight on Japan Airlines from San Francisco to Tokyo, you can stop in Hawaii, but you then must carry on to Tokyo. Failure to do so will result in a stiff fine, and the balance of your ticket will not be refunded.

Canadian Airlines International
Flights from Canada to Honolulu originate in Vancouver and Toronto. Canadian Airlines International flights continue on to Fiji, Australia, and New Zealand. Call (800) 426-7007.

Air New Zealand
Flights link New Zealand, Australia, and Fiji with Los Angeles via Honolulu. There is also a remarkable advance-purchase fare (APEX) offered at a very reasonable price which takes you from Los Angeles to Honolulu, then continues on with 11 stopovers throughout Oceania before deplaning in New Zealand. Call (800) 262-1234.

Japan Air Lines
The Japanese are the second largest group, next to our fellow Americans, to visit Hawaii. Daily JAL flights to Honolulu originate from Tokyo and Osaka, with flights five times a week from Nagoya. There are no JAL flights between the U.S. Mainland and Hawaii. Call (800) 232-2517 in Hawaii and (800) 525-3663 on the Mainland.

Philippine Airlines
Daily flights depart Los Angeles and San Francisco to Manila via Honolulu. Connections in Manila are available to most Asian cities. Call (800) 435-9725.

Qantas
Multiple weekly flights from San Francisco and Los Angeles to Sydney via Honolulu. Stopovers are possible in New Zealand, Fiji, and Tahiti before arriving in Australia. Call (800) 227-4500.

Korean Air
Offers some of the least expensive flights to Asia. Free stopovers from Los Angeles in both Honolulu and Tokyo are possible on a round-trip ticket; a one-way ticket each way allows only one stopover. Connections are available to many Asian cities. Call (800) 421-8200.

Singapore Airlines
Flights to and from Los Angeles to Singapore and/or Taipei via Honolulu. Free stopover on some fares; call (800) 742-3333.

Air Nauru
The South Pacific's richest island offers flights throughout Polynesia including most major islands, with connections to Japan, Taipei, Hong Kong, Manila, Singapore, and Australia. In Hawaii, call (808) 531-9766.

Hawaiian Air
This domestic carrier flies to the South Pacific, with flights one to four times a week to Guam, Tahiti, Western Samoa, American Samoa, Tonga, and Rarotonga. For information call (800) 367-5320, (808) 537-5100 on Oahu, and (800) 882-8811 on the Neighboring Islands.

TRAVEL BY SHIP

At one time Hawaiians lined the pier in Honolulu waiting to greet the cruise ships bringing visitors. It was the only way to get to Hawaii, but those days are long gone. Now only one American company and a few foreign lines make the crossing.

American Hawaii Cruises
This American cruise ship company operates two 800-passenger ships, the SS *Independence* and the SS *Constitution*. Primarily, these ships offer similar seven-day itineraries that circumnavigate and call at the four main islands. Their price ranges from an inside "thrifty cabin" at $1095 to a luxury suite for $3695. Children under 16 are often given special rates, and cruise free from June to

September if they share a cabin with their parents. You come aboard in Honolulu after arriving by plane arranged by American Hawaii Cruises. Each ship is a luxury seagoing hotel and gourmet restaurant; swimming pools, driving ranges, tennis courts, health clubs, theaters, and nightclubs are all part of the amenities. For details contact: American Hawaii Cruises, 550 Kearny St., San Francisco, CA 94108, tel. (800) 227-3666; from Canada call (415) 392-9400.

Alternatives

Other companies offering varied cruises are **P&O Lines,** which operates the Sea Princess through the South Pacific, making port at Honolulu on its way from the West Coast once a year.

Royal Cruise Line out of Los Angeles, or Auckland alternatively, sails the *Royal Odyssey,* which docks in Honolulu on its South Pacific and Orient cruise, from $2200 to $4000.

The **Nauru Pacific Line** offers freighter/passenger service from San Francisco to Micronesia via Honolulu, six-week intervals year-round.

The **Holland America Line** sails the *Rotterdam* on its 108-day Grande Circle cruise, departing Fort Lauderdale, passing around South America, and calling at Honolulu as it heads for Asia. Prices are from $20,000 to $70,000. Call (800) 426-0327.

Society Expeditions offers a 42-day cruise thoughout the South Paciic departing fom Honolulu. Fares are from $3000 to $9000. Call (800) 426-0327.

Information

Most travel agents can provide information on the above cruise lines. If you're really interested in traveling by ship cntact: **Freighter Travel Club of America,** Box 12693, Salem Oregon U.S.A. 97305; or **Ford's Freighter Travel Guide** Box 505, 22151 Clarendon St., Woodland Hills, CA U.S.A. 91302.

TOUR COMPANIES

Many tour companies offering packages to Hawaii appear in large city newspapers every week. They advertise very reasonable air fares, car rentals, and accommodations. Without trying, you can get roundtrip airfare from the West Coast and a week in Hawaii for $400 using one of these companies. The following are tour companies that offer great deals and have excellent reputations. Others that cover only specific Hawaiian islands are listed in the appropriate chapters. This list is by no means exhaustive.

Pacific Outdoor Adventures

This truly remarkable tour company, formerly Adventure Kayaking International, operated by John Gray and Bob Wilson offers the best in nature tours. The emphasis is on the outdoors with hiking, camping, snorkeling, and kayaking central. The professional guides go out of their way to make your trip totally enjoyable and safe. Their specially designed kayaks are seaworthy in all conditions and for all ability levels. They focus on giving you a fun-filled "edutainment" adventure, where you can immerse yourself in the local culture, geography, and natural wonder of the areas visited. Although based on Oahu with a full schedule of trips to various locations on Oahu, Molokai, and the Big Island, Pacific Outdoor Adventures also heads for fantastic and little-visited kayaking destinations in Fiji and Thailand. The totally-inclusive prices for their regular tours are absolutely unbeatable for the experience offered and arrangements for charter group packages can be made when requested. Itineraries vary from a 2½ hour paddle around Kahana Bay on Oahu for $45 to a five day-four night trip on Molokai for $750. For a full list of itineraries contact Pacific Outdor Adventures at P.O. Box 61609, Honolulu, HI 96839, tel. (808) 924-8898, toll-free (800) 52-KAYAK. If an unforgettable outdoor adventure is your goal, you can't go wrong!

STA Travel

This company is known by most travelers as Student Travel Network, but you don't have to be a student to avail yourself of their services. There is no longer an office in Honolulu, but an L.A. office can be reached from Hawaii by dialing tollfree tel. (800) 777-0112. Their West Hollywood office address is 7202 Melrose Ave., Los Angeles, CA 90046, tel. (213) 934-

8722. STA also maintains ten other offices in the USA, including New York, San Diego, San Francisco, and Boston, as well as nearly 100 throughout the Pacific, Southeast Asia, and Europe. It's focus is on young and/or independent travelers.

Nature Expeditions International

These quality tours have wildlife and natural history as the theme. Their guides are experts in their fields and give personable and attentive service. The company has 30 destinations throughout the world and runs one tour to Hawaii with scheduled trips year round. The Hawaii tour is 15 days in length and stops on each of the four biggest island. Contact Nature Expeditions International at 474 Willamette, P.O. Box 11496, Eugene, Oregon 97440, tel. (503) 484-6529, or (800) 869-0639.

SunTrips

This California-based tour and charter company sells vacations all over the world. They're primarily a wholesale company, but will work with the general public. They consistently offer the cheapest fares from the West Coast to Hawaii, using American Trans Air as their chartered airline to Hawaii and Aloha Airlines inter-island. They also arrange rental cars and air/car packages. Contact SunTrips, 2350 Paragon Dr. San Jose, CA 95131, or P.O. Box 611690, San Jose CA 95161, tel. (800) 444-7866.

Pleasant Hawaiian Holidays

A California-based company specializing in Hawaii, located at 2404 Townsgate Rd., Westlake Village, CA 91361, tel. (800) 242-9244.

Island Holiday Tours

An established Hawaiian-based company that offers flights with United and rental cars through Budget. Aside from arranging for transportation to and accomodations in Hawaii, they also arrange optional tours to tourist sites on all the islands. Contact Island Holiday Tours, 2222 Kalakaua Ave., Suite 1100, Honolulu, HI 96815, tel. (800) 448-6877.

Hawaiian Holidays

A Hawaiian-based company with plenty of experience, Hawaiian Holidays, offers flights with United and Hawaiian Air, and cars from National Car Rental. Contact Hawaiian Holidays at 2222 Kalakaua Ave., Honolulu, HI 96815, tel. (800) 367-5040; in Hawaii (808) 923-6548.

Others

Tradewind Tours, tel. (800) 645-2000; **Aloha Hawaii Travel,** tel. (800) 367-5300; **Macenzie Hawaii,** tel. (800) 367-5190; **Ask Mr. Foster,** tel. (800) 544-1322; **Hawaii Leisure,** tel. (800) 426-4116; **Condo Resorts,** tel. (800) 854-3823.

GETTING AROUND

If it's your intention to *see* Maui when you visit, and not just to lie on the beach in front of your hotel, the only efficient way is to rent a car. Limited public transportation, a few free shuttles, taxis, and the good old thumb are available, but all these are flawed in one way or another. Other unique and fun-filled ways to tour the island include renting a bike or moped, or hopping on a helicopter, but these conveyances are highly specialized and are more in the realm of sports than touring.

Public Transportation
The **Grayline** airporter, tel. 877-5507, makes daily scheduled runs from the Kahului Airport to Kaanapali (reservations for pick-up *to* the airport are a must!). Departure from the airport is every hour on the hour from 7 a.m. to 5 p.m., returning from Kaanapali every hour on the half hour from 8:30 a.m. to 6:30 p.m. The airporter services all major resorts in Kaanapali, running as far as the Royal Lahaina Resort, and makes three stops in Lahaina at Pioneer Inn, the Maui Islander, and Lahaina Shores hotels. It's a slightly expensive but

no-hassle way to deal with arrival and departure, but out of the question for every-day transportation. One-way fares are $9.50 adults and $4.75 children. Grayline also offers numerous bus tours throughout Maui. It has a booth at the Kahului Airport car rental building.

The **Akina** Bus Service, tel. 879-2828, runs a similar schedule to East Maui. They leave every hour on the half hour from from 7:30 a.m. to 7:30 p.m. from the Kahului Airport and from 7 a.m. to 7 p.m. on the hour from Makena, Wailea, and Kihei to the airport. One-way fares to Kihei and Wailea are $10 single, $8 per person for two or more; to Makena fares are $10 per person. Children under seven accompanied by an adult travel free. Reservations are a must. Use the free direct-line courtesy phone at Kahului Airport or visit their booth in the rental car building.

The free **Kaanapali Trolley** runs along the Kaanapali strip about every half hour throughout the day, stopping at all major resorts, the golf course, Whaler's Village Shopping Center, and the train station. Look for the green jitneys. Service starts at 7 a.m. and runs until

11 p.m. About a dozen of these buses run to Kapalua-West Maui airport from 8:25 a.m. to 4:05 p.m., while those from the airport run from 8:15 a.m. to 5:15 p.m. Pick up free printed tourist literature or ask at any hotel desk for the schedule.

Also free is the **Lahaina Express** shuttle which runs between 9:10 a.m. and 9:45 p.m. connecting various stops in Lahaina to Kaanapali. The major pick-up point in Lahaina is at the rear of the Wharf Cinema Center along Front Street.

Transportation to the new Lahaina Cannery Mall is provided by the free **Lahaina Cannery Shuttle** from major hotels and the Whaler's Village shopping center in Kaanapali and from Honokowai.

For those riding the Sugar Cane Train, free transportation aboard the **Suger Cane Trolley** is available from Front Street and the Lahaina Harbor to the Lahaina Station.

For those in the Wailea area the **Wailea Resorts Shuttle** is free and stops at all Wailea Beach hotels and condos, the Wailea Shopping Center, golf course, and tennis courts throughout the day.

Taxis

About 18 taxi companies on Maui more or less operate in a fixed area. Most, besides providing normal taxi service, also run tours all over the island. Taxis are expensive and metered by the distance traveled. For example, a ride from Kahului Airport to Kaanapali is $39 and about $24 to Wailea. Try Yellow Cab of Maui (the only concessionaire allowed to pick up at the airport) from the airport, tel. 877-7000; Kahului Taxi Service at tel. 877-5681; Alii Cabs in Lahaina at tel. 661-3688; Kaanapali Taxi, tel. 661-5258; Wailea Taxi, tel. 874-5000; Kihei Taxi, tel. 879-3000.

Hitchhiking

The old tried-and-true method of hitchhiking—with thumb out, facing traffic, a smile on your interesting face—is "out" on Maui! It's illegal, and if a policeman sees you, you'll be hassled, if not outright arrested. You've got to play the game. Simply stand on the side of the road facing traffic with a smile on your interesting face, but put away the old thumb. In other words, you can't actively solicit a ride. People know what you're doing; just stand there. You can get around quite well by thumb, if you're not on a schedule. The success rate of getting a ride to the number of cars that go by isn't that great, but you will get picked up. Locals and the average tourist with family will generally pass you by. Recent residents and single tourists will most often pick you up, and 90% of the time these will be white males. Hitching short hops along the resort beaches is easy. People can tell by the way you're dressed that you're not going far and will give you a lift. Catching longer rides to Hana or up to Haleakala can be done, but it'll be tougher because the driver will know that you'll be with him or her for the duration of the ride. Women under no circumstances should hitch alone.

BY BOAT

Inter-island Ferry

From time to time ferry companies have operated in Hawaii, but very stiff competition generated by the airline industry and the notoriously rough waters of the Hawaiian channels have combined to scuttle their opportunity for success. However, a new company has opened, making daily runs between Molokai

MAUI PRINCESS SAILING SCHEDULE

For information and reservations:
on Molokai call 553-5736
on Maui call 661-5857
Mainland toll-free (800) 533-5800

Depart:	Kaunakakai, Molokai	5:45 a.m.
Arrive:	Lahaina, Maui slip 3	7:15 a.m.
Depart:	Lahaina, Maui slip 3	7:30 a.m.
Arrive:	Kaunakakai, Molokai	8:45 a.m.
Depart:	Kaunakakai, Molokai	3:45 p.m.
Arrive:	Lahaina, Maui slip 3	4:45 p.m.
Depart:	Lahaina, Maui slip 3	5:00 p.m.
Arrive:	Kaunakakai, Molokai	6:45 p.m.

(Kaunakakai) and Maui (Lahaina) aboard their 118-foot vessel, **The Maui Princess.** The boat, a converted oil-platform-personnel carrier from Louisiana, has been re-outfitted for Hawaii and includes a sun deck and hydraulic stabilizers which take some of the roll out of the rocky crossing. In effect, it's still a work boat, carrying workers from Molokai to Lahaina, along with some light cargo. As beautiful as the Hawaiian Islands are from the air, this is a wonderful opportunity to experience them from sea level. The cabin is comfortable with air-conditioning, and the crew, all local people, play guitar, ukulele, and sing old island tunes, helping to raise everyone's spirits. The majority of the people riding the shuttle are islanders, so if you're looking for a colorful and cultural experience, this is one of the best opportunities. The snack bar serves soft drinks and snacks for under $2 but no alcohol.

In Lahaina you are met about 300 yards offshore by the *Lin Wa,* a sister ship usually used as a local tourist cruiser. Since Lahaina Harbor is so small, the *Maui Princess* cannot enter. Passengers and luggage are offloaded *at sea* as the crew performs some amazing feats of balance, handling all manner of cargo between the pitching, yawing boats. Upon arrival in Lahaina, prearrange a pick-up by the car companies (most have offices in nearby Kaanapali) or you'll be stranded. The *Maui Princess* is often late and some car companies close early, another logistical problem. The trip is tough, but adds a realness to island arrival that you don't get from a plane. Fares are $42 RT, children half price, $21 one way. Bicyclists will be especially happy because there is no extra fee charged to transport your wheels. The *Maui Princess* makes the 1½-hour roundtrip twice a day, leaving Molokai at 5:45 a.m. and 4 p.m. and Lahaina at 7 a.m. and 5 p.m. For information and reservations call (800) 833- 5800, on Molokai tel. 553-5736, on Maui tel. 661-8397.

To Lanai

A new passenger ferry, *Expeditions,* now plies between Lahaina and Manele Bay on Lanai. This shuttle service is not luxury travel but offers a speedy, efficient, and convenient transportation alternative to the Pineapple Island. You are allowed to take luggage free of charge, but there's an extra $10 fee for a bicycle. The one-hour crossing leaves Lahaina's public launch pier daily at 6:45 a.m., 9:15 a.m., and 3:45 p.m., and from Manele Bay at 8 a.m., 10:30 a.m., and 4:30 p.m., with late departures on Thur., Fri., and Sun. evenings; adults pay $25 one way, and children below 11 pay $20. This shuttle takes only 24 passengers so it is best to reserve your place. For information and reservations call (808) 661-3756 or write P.O. Box 1763, Lahaina, Maui, HI 96767.

RENTAL CARS

Maui has about 40 car rental agencies that can put you behind the wheel of anything from a Mercedes convertible to a used station wagon with chipped paint and torn upholstery. There are national companies, inter-island firms, good local companies, and a few fly-by-nights that'll rent you a clunker. Eleven companies are clustered in little booths at the Kahului Airport, a few at Kapalua-West Maui Airport, and none at Hana Airport, but the Hana Hotel can arrange a car for you or you can do it yourself by calling Purdee's at 248-8391. The rest are scattered around the island, with a heavy concentration on Dairy Road in Kahului, at the Kaanapali Transportation Center, and along S. Kihei Road. Those without an airport booth either have a courtesy phone or a number to call; they'll pick you up and shuttle you to their lots. Stiff competition tends to keep the prices more or less reasonable. Good deals are offered off-season, with price wars flaring at anytime and making for real savings, but these unfortunately can't be predicted. Even with all these companies, it's best to book ahead. You might not save money, but you can save youself headaches.

Tips

The best cars to rent on Maui happen to be the cheapest: subcompacts with standard shift. (If you can drive a standard!) Maui's main highways are broad and well paved, just like major roads on the Mainland, but the back roads, where all the fun is, are narrow twisty affairs. You'll appreciate the downshifting ability of standard transmissions on curves and steep inclines. If you get a big fatso luxury car, it'll be great for "puttin' on the ritz" at the resort areas, but you'll feel like a hippopotamus in the backcountry. If you've got that much money to burn, rent two cars! Try to get a car with cloth seats. Vinyl is too sticky, but sitting on your towel will help. Air-conditioning is nice, especially if you plan on being in Lahaina a lot.

The mile markers on back roads are great for pinpointing sites and beaches. The lower number on these signs is the highway number, so you can always make sure that you're on the right road. The car rental agencies prohibit travel past Seven Sacred Pools on the other side of Hana, or around the top of the head of Maui. These roads are indeed rugged, but passable; the locals do it all the time. The car companies will warn you that your insurance "might" not cover you on these roads. They're really protecting their cars from being banged around. Traveling these roads is not recommended . . . for the fainthearted. Be careful, drive slowly, and have fun.

Nationally Known Companies

The following are major firms that have booths at Kahului Airport. **National Car Rental** (Kaanapali office services Kaanapali area and Kapalua-West Maui Airport with a free shuttle), is one of the best of the nationally known firms. They have GMs, Nissans, Toyotas, Datsuns, vans, jeeps, and station wagons. National offers excellent weekly rates, especially on standard subcompacts. All major credit cards are accepted. On Maui, call 871-8851, or nationwide at (800) 227-7368. **Avis** is also located in Kaanapali. They feature late-model GM cars as well as most imports and convertibles. Call Avis at 871-7575 or in Kaanapali at tel. 661-4588, toll-free (800) 831-8000. **Budget** offers competitive rates on a variety of late-model cars. In Kahului call 871-8811, in Kaanapali 661-8721, or nationwide (800) 527-7000. **Hertz,** perhaps the best-known company, offers a wide variety of vehicles with some special weekly rates. Hertz has locations at Kaanapali and Wailea. Call 661-3195 and request the location nearest you; call

(800) 654-3131 for nationwide service. **Dollar** rents all kinds of cars as well as jeeps and convertibles. At Kahului, call 877-2731, Kaanapali, 669-7400, or toll-free (800) 342-7398. **Alamo** has good weekly rates. Call (800) 327-9633, 871-6235 in Kahului, and 661-7181 in Kaanapali.

Island Companies

The following companies are based in Hawaii and either have a booth at the airport or pick-up service through courtesy phones. A Hawaii-based company with an excellent reputation is **Tropical Rent A Car.** Being based in Hawaii, they can take care of any problem on the spot without hassle. Tropical 's personnel go out of their way to make your rental go smoothly by adding that "aloha touch." Prices are very competitive, and they can put you into anything from an economy car to a sporty Pontiac convertible or Cadillac. Free shuttle from the Kahului Airport. Also located at Kaanapali, call 877-0002, 661-0061, or toll-free (800) 367-5140 Mainland, (800) 352-3923 in Hawaii. **Word of Mouth Rent a Used Car,** at 607 Haleakala Hwy., tel. 877-2436, pick-up van provided, offers some fantastic deals on their used but not abused cars. All cars, standard shift or automatic, go for $90 per week with a three-day minimum or $17 per day. Office open 8 a.m. to 5 p.m., but they will leave a car at the airport at earlier or later hours with prior arrangement. **Roberts** also has a good reputation, call 871-6226. Others include: **Sunshine,** tel. 871-6222 at Kahului Airport; **Trans Maui,** tel. 877-5222; **Andres,** tel. 877-5378;

HAWAII'S *Tropical* SM RENT A CAR

Klunkers, variable rates at tel. 877-3197; **Rainbow Rent A Car,** tel. 661-8734 in Lahaina; and **Kihei Rent A Car,** tel. 879-7257. **Encore Autos, Rock and Roll Rentals,** tel. 874-6936, along S. Kihei Road will put you in the seat of a '50s model reproduction Porsche, Sebring, or T-bird for $85-125 a day.

Four-wheel Drive

Though much more expensive than cars, some people might feel safer in them for completely circling Maui. Also unlike cars, the rental companies offering 4WDs put no restrictions on driving past the Seven Sacred Pools or around the head of West Maui (roads subject to closure, check!). 4WDs can be had from **Maui Rent Ahh Jeep,** tel. 877-6626; **Hertz,** tel. 877-5167, **Sunshine,** tel. 871-6222, and a few others. Variable rates, mostly from $60-70 per day, from company to company depend on availability and length of rental.

Camper Rentals

These offer a good alternative to staying in hotels or condos. You might also want to rent a camper for an overnight trip to Hana. The convenience will offset the extra cost and might even save money over staying in a hotel. Unlike cars, campers carry a per-mile charge. The only outfit renting campers is **Hawaiian Custom Campers,** tel. 877-4522, at 180 D E. Wakea Ave., Kahului, HI 96732.

Mopeds

Just for running around town or to the beach mopeds are great. Expect to pay about $5-10 an hour, $25-35 for the day, or up to $125 for the week. For mopeds: **Go Go Bikes** at the Kaanapali Transportation Center, call 661-3063 or 669-6669; **A & B Mopeds** at Honokowai, tel. 669-0027; **Fun Rentals** in Lahaina at tel. 661-3053; and **Rainbow Rent A Car,** also in Lahaina, at tel. 661-8734.

BICYCLES

Bicycle enthusiasts should be thrilled with Maui, but the few flaws might flatten your spirits as well as your tires. The countryside is great, the weather is perfect, but the roads are heavily trafficked and the most interesting ones are narrow and have bad shoulders. Peddling to Hana will give you an up-close personal experience, but for bicycle safety this road is one of the worst. Haleakala is stupendous, but with a rise of more than 10,000 feet in less than 40 miles it is considered one of the most grueling rides in the world. A paved bike path runs from Lahaina to Kaanapali that's tame enough for everyone and you can even arrange a bicycle tour of Lahaina. In short, cycling on Maui as your primary means of transportation is not for the neophyte; because of safety considerations and the tough rides, only experienced riders should consider it.

Getting your bike to Maui from one of the Neighbor Islands is no problem. All of the inter-island and commuter carriers will fly it for you for $20-25 on the same flight as you take—just check it in as baggage. If you plan ahead, you can send your bike the previous day by air freight. Aloha Airlines has an excellent system promising 24-hour delivery. You don't have to box or disassemble your bike, but you must sign a damage waiver. This is usually OK because the awkwardness of a bike almost ensures that it will be placed on the top of the baggage out of harm's way. The freight terminal at Kahului is just a few minutes' walk from the passenger terminal and opens at 7 a.m. You can also take your bike free on the inter-island ferry, the *Maui Princess* (see p. 83).

Getting your bike to Hawaii from the Mainland will depend upon which airlines you take. Some will accept bicycles as baggage traveling with you (approximate additional charge of $30) if the bikes are properly broken down and boxed in a bicycle box, while others will only take them as air freight, in which case the rates are exorbitant. Check with the airlines well before you plan to go or explore the possibility of shipping it by sea through a freight company.

For bike rentals, try: **Fun Rentals** in Lahaina, tel. 661-30-53; **Go Go Bikes Hawaii** in Kaanapali, tel. 661-3063; and **Paradise Pedaling, Inc.,** tel. 874-5303 in Kihei. **Fun Rentals,** at 193 Lahainaluna Rd., Lahaina, open daily 8 a.m. to 6 p.m., is a semi-benign bike and bike rental shop. Semi-benign because their prices are high, but they could be higher,

Opposite page (top): A late afternoon rainbow over the West Maui Mountains (ROBERT NILSEN); (bottom): rainbow over Kaanapali (ROBERT NILSEN)

and they have the best selection. This full-service bike shop sells and rents everything from clunkers for around town, up to world-class Tomasso racing bikes ($200 per week). Prices vary considerably but a good mid-range example is a 15-speed mountain bike that rents from $20 for eight hours, $25 for 24 hours, $40 for two days, and up to $85 for one week. One- and five-speed town bikes go for $60 per week. They'll tell you that the Park Service does not allow you to take your bike up to Haleakala National Park—bull droppings! You *cannot* ride the bike on the hiking paths, but going up the road (40 miles uphill) is OK if you have the steam. You are given this misinformation because they don't want the wear and tear on their bikes, but for the prices they charge, they shouldn't squawk.

Bicycle Tours

An adventure on Maui that's become famous is riding a specially equipped bike from the summit of Mt. Haleakala for 40 miles to the bottom at Paia. A pioneer in this field is **Maui Downhill**, 199 Dairy Rd., Kahului, tel. 871-2155, toll-free (800) 535-BIKE. Included in the bike ride at $93 you get two meals (continental breakfast and an all-you-can-eat brunch or a gourmet picnic lunch) and windbreakers, gloves, and helmets.

To drench yourself in the beauty of a Haleakala sunrise, you have to pay your dues. You arrive at the base yard in Kahului at about 3:30 a.m. after being picked up at your condo by the courtesy van. Here, you'll muster with other bleary-eyed but hopeful adventurers, and munch donuts and coffee, which at this time of the morning is more like a transfusion. Up the mountain through the chilly night air takes about 1½ hours, with singing and story-telling along the way. Once atop, find your spot for the *best* natural light show in the world: the sun goes wild with colors as it paints the sky and drips into Haleakala Crater (see p. 240). This is your first reward. Next comes your bicycle environmental cruise down the mountain with vistas and thrills every inch of the way. For the not-so-early risers, an afternoon ride down the mountain to Pukalani for $82 is also available one meal provided. **Cruiser Bob's,** at 505 Front St., Lahaina, tel. 667-7717 or (800) 654-7717, offers a variation on the same theme. Essentially you get a similar experience for about the same amount of money, and their breakfast is an all-you-can-eat buffet at the Kula Lodge. A picnic ride from 7 a.m. to 3 p.m. is also available. Cruiser Bob's limits their groups to 13 people. **Maui Mountain Cruiser** of Makawao, tel. 572-0195, is the newest of the three companies. They offer basically the same services.

For downhilling you have to be a fair rider; those under 16 require parental release. All riders must be at least five feet tall, pregnant

Experienced guides will lead you on your "environmental cruise" down the face of Haleakala.
(J.D. BISIGNANI)

women are not allowed, and proper clothing, shoes, and glasses must be worn. The rides are popular so reserve well in advance. These outfits offer tamer tours of Lahaina and the beach resorts with admissions into historical sites and museums included. There's no gripe with the Haleakala experience; it's guaranteed thrills, and since they have you for eight hours with two meals and pick-up service, the price isn't too hard to take.

For those who like to strike out on their own, two routes can be suggested. One takes you for a 50-mile loop from Wailuku (or Lahaina) up the Kaanapali coast and around the head of Maui back to Wailuku. The road starts out in good repair but the traffic will be heavy until you pass Kapalua. Here the road begins to wind along the north coast. The road surface eventually turns to gravel making a mountain bike with wide tires a *necessity.* Traffic around the north end is almost nonexistent so the road will be yours—but there is no place to get service either. Go prepared.

The second route is from Kahului up to Kula or Pukalani via Pulehu Road and back down the mountainside via Paia, Haiku, or Ulumalu, taking you through irrigated cane fields, the cool upcountry region, the lush, sculpted north slope of Haleakala, and along the back of Maui.

SIGHTSEEING TOURS

Tours are offered that will literally let you cover Maui from head to foot; you can walk it, drive it, sail around it, fly over it, or see it from below the water. Almost every major hotel has a tour desk from which you can book.

Booking Agencies

The biggest, **Ocean Activities Center,** happens to be the best agency for booking any and all kinds of activities on Maui. For much of the fun events like snorkeling, scuba diving, whalewatching, sunset cruises, and deep sea fishing, teh center has its own facilities and equipment, which means they not only provide you with an excellent outing, but offer very competitive prices. Ocean Activities can also book you on helicopters, parasails, land tours,

and rent and sell boogie boards, snorkel equipment, sailboards, and surfboards. They have sun and surf stores/booking agencies in the Kihei/Wailea area at: the Maui Intercontinental Wailea Hotel, tel. 879-7466; the Maui Prince Hotel, tel. 879-7218; Stoufers Wailea Beach Hotel, tel. 879-0181; Mana Kai Hotel, tel. 879-6704; Maui Hill Hotel, tel. 879-0180; Azekas Shopping Center, tel. 879-0083; the Lahaina Cannery Mall, tel. 661-5309; the Maui Marriot in Kaanapali, tel. 661-3631; and at the Embassy Suites in Honokowai, tel. 667-7116. Ocean Activities also runs a boat from the beach at the Maui Prince Hotel to the underwater fantasy of Molokini Crater. Prices on all of their activities are very reasonable, and the service is excellent. If you had to choose one agency for all your fun needs, this would be your best bet!

And for some personalized attention by a very knowledgeable Maui resident, check out **Donya** at the Maui Hill Condominium, tel. 879-0180. She's got the inside scoop on many of the activities, and can book you on the best and save you some money at the same time.

One of the easiest ways to book an activity and sightsee at the same time is to walk along the Lahaina Wharf—there's an information booth here as well operated by many of the companies who rent slips at the harbor. Check it out first, and then plan to be there when the tour boats return. Asking the passengers, right on the spot, if they've had a good time is about the best you can do. You can also check out the boats and do some comparative pricing of your own.

In Lahaina along Front Street try any of the **Fantasy Island Activities and Tours** kiosks or call 661-5333, the **Visitor Info & Ticket Center** in the Wharf Shopping Complex at tel. 661-5151, or **Tom Barefoot's Cashback Tours,** tel. 661-8889. You will find a whole horde of other activities desks up and down Front Street; you almost don't have to search for them—they'll find you. **Maui Beach Center**, at 505 Front St., tel. 667-4355, open daily 8:30 a.m. to 5 p.m., does it all. Rentals for 24 hours are: surfboards $8, snorkel equipment $6, boogie boards $5, and the best surf lessons on Maui, with guaranteed results. They can also arrange a wide variety of activities like parasailing and a Zodiac trip. Another organization with a solid reputation is **Activities Information Center,** tel. 667-7777, at 888 Wainee St. in the Lahaina Business Center.

For boats and a full range of activities out of quiet Maalaea Harbor, contact Jerome at **Maalaea Activities,** tel. 242-6982. They do it all, from helicopters to horseback. They specialize in the boats berthed at Maalaea.

To get information about these tours, other activities, and general information on Maui, a convenient telephone service has been set up to assist you. For specific information about Maui activities, simply call **Teleguide Information Service** at tel. 877-4266 and punch in a four- digit code for the specific activity of interest or wait for an operator. For a list of the codes, pick up a brochure from any printed-information stand around the island.

Land Tours

It's easy to book tours to Maui's famous areas such as Lahaina, Hana, Kula, Iao Valley, and Haleakala. Normally they're run on either half- or full-day schedules (Hana is always a full day) and range anywhere from $20 to $80 with hotel pick-up included. Big bus tours are run by **Grayline,** tel. 877- 5507, and **Roberts,** tel. 871-6226. These tours are quite antiseptic as you sit behind tinted glass in an air-conditioned bus. You get more personalized tours in the smaller vans, such as **Akamai Tours,** tel. 871-9551. Among other destinations they'll take you to Hana for $45. **Aloha Nui Loa Tours** tel. 669-0000, goes to Hana for $65, breakfast and lunch included, or to Haleakala for the sunrise for $36. **No Kai Oi Tours** hits all the high spots and has competitive prices, tel. 871-9008; **Ekahi Tours** specializes in all-day, catered trips to Hana for $60, tel. 572-9775. Both **Temptation Tours,** tel. 877-8888 and **Tropical Excursions,** tel. 877-7887, offer guided tours to Hana in truly deluxe vans with six passengers maximum— filling breakfast and lunch served. Tropical also goes to Haleakala, Upcountry, and to Iao Valley. **Polynesian Adventure Tours,** tel. 877-4242, offers tours to Hana, $605, or a Haleakala, Central Maui, and Iao Valley tour

for $42. For a truly wonderful hiking tour with Maui's foremost naturalist, see **Hike Maui** p. 116. If photography and hiking are your interests, see **Locations with Marianne** p. 95.

For those who desire a go-at-your-own pace alternative to van tours, yet want the convenience of an escort, **Best of Maui Cassette Tours** may be for you. Your choice of quality tapes to the Hana Highway or the road to Haleakala comes with a cassette player, a small guidebook of sights, history, and legends, bird and flower handbooks, a route map, and a free T-shirt. Rental is $25, and you can pick up cassettes from 6:30 a.m.-12:30 p.m.; reservations are appreciated. Call Best of Maui at 871-1555 or stop by their office at 333 Dairy Rd., Kahului, Maui 96732.

Air Tours

Maui is a spectacular sight from the air. A few small charter airlines, a handful of helicopter companies, and one sailplane outfit swoop you around the island. These joy rides are literally the highlight of many people's experiences on Maui, but they are expensive. The excursions vary, but expect to spend at least $100 for a basic half-hour tour. The most spectacular ones take you over Haleakala crater, or perhaps to the remote West Maui Mountains, where inaccessible gorges lie at your feet. Other tours are civilized; expect a champagne brunch after you visit Hana. Still others take you to nearby Lanai or Molokai to view some of the world's most spectacular sea cliffs and remote beaches. Know, however, that many hikers and trekkers have a beef with the air tours: after they've spent hours, or maybe days, hiking into remote valleys in search of peace and quiet, out of the sky comes the mechanical whir of a chopper to spoil the solitude.

Helicopters

Kenai Helicopter, tel. 871-6463, is one of the better and more experienced companies. All their rides are smoothly professional. **Papillon Helicopters,** tel. 669-4884, (800) 562-5641 Maui, (800) 367-7095 Mainland, is also one of the larger and more experienced firms. Flights from $95 for a 30-minute West Maui excursion to $245 for 1½- hour flights to Hana or Molokai. However, you'll be perfectly safe and can make some better deals with local Maui companies. **Maui Helicopter,** tel. 879-1601 or (800) 367-8003 has an excellent reputation as a locally owned outfit, and they offer preferred seating. The chopper is purely utilitarian, but with only four passengers, two front and two rear, everyone is assured of a good view. **Hawaii Helicopter,** tel. 877-3900, has plush interiors for your comfort, but they squeeze four people in the back, so the two middle ones don't get a good view. **Sunshine Helicopter,** tel. 871-0722, is another local, family-run outfit with one chopper. The inside is bare-bones, but the seating is two by two, and they go out of their way to give you a good ride. They sometimes offer a 20-minute "special" for only $49. Others are: **Blue Hawaiian Helicopters,** tel. 871-8844, and **Alex Air,** tel. 871-0792.

For all, tours are narrated over specially designed earphones, and some companies offer a video of a helicopter tour of Maui as a souvenir at the end of the flight. On certain flights the craft will touch down for a short interlude, and on some flights a complimentary lunch will be served. Most companies will make special arrangements to drop off and pick up campers in remote areas, or design a package especially for you. Chopper companies are competitively priced, with tours of West or East Maui at around $100. Circle-island tours are approximately $175, but the best would be to include a trip to Molokai at approximately $200 in order to experience the world's tallest sea cliffs along the isolated windward coast. All flights leave from the heliport at the back side of Kahului Airport.

Airplane Excursions

For a slightly different thrill, experience a Maui joy ride out of Kahului Airport with **Paragon Airlines,** tel. 244-3356. **Scenic Air Tours,** tel. 871-2555 or (800) 352-3722 toll-free, has five all-day tours leaving daily from the Kahului Airport commuter terminal. All tours are narrated and conducted in 10-seat Beachcraft planes so everyone has good viewing. Prices range from the $109 Kalaupapa tour to the $190 seven-island tour. From Kapalua-West Maui Airport, try **Panorama Air Tours,** tel. 669-0205, (800) 367-2671 Mainland, for their full-day fly/drive tours of Maui, Molokai, and Oahu for $69 or $89.

Sailplanes

For a quieter, but not totally silent, means of seeing the mountains of East Maui, try a glider flight with **Soar Maui.** These smooth, motorless craft lift you with amazing agility and give you a birds-eye view of the immensity of Haleakala and its incredibly sculpted north coast. Located at the Hana Airport, Soar Maui is the sole glider company on Maui. Their four flights are: "Introduction Scenic Flight," a 20-minute swoop over Hana for $75 ($90 for two); "Mile High Scenic Flight," 40-minute over the coastline as far as the Seven Sacred Pools for $125-150; "Aerobic Flight," a $175 thrill ride only for the real adventurous with a steady stomach; and the 1¼-hour "Haleakala Crater Flight," $225-250. Open 9 a.m. to 5 p.m. year round, they also give flight instruction. For more information and reservations (preferred), call 284-7433.

OCEAN TOURS

You haven't really seen Maui unless you've seen it from the sea. Tour boats operating out of Maui's Lahaina and Maalaea harbors take you fishing, sailing, whalewatching, dining, diving, and snorkeling. You can find boats that offer all of these or just sail you around for pure pleasure—Maui presents one of the premier sailing venues in the Pacific. Many take day trips to Lanai or to Molokai, with a visit to Kalaupapa included. Others visit Molokini, a submerged volcano with only half the crater rim above water that's been designated a Marine Life Conservation District. The vast majority of Maui's pleasure boats are berthed in Lahaina Harbor and most have a booth right there on the wharf where you can sign up. Other boats come out of Maalaea with a few companies based in Kihei. The following are basically limited to sailing/dining/touring activities, with snorkeling often part of the experience. If you're interested in other ocean activi-

The Trilogy II *prepares to leave Lahaina Harbor at dawn.*
(J.D. BISIGNANI)

ties such as scuba and fishing, see "Sports And Recreation." That chapter also includes activities such as water or jet-skiing, parasailing, sailboarding, and surfing.

Excursions/Dinner Sails

Sunset cruises are very romantic, and very popular. They last for about two hours and cost $25-35 for the basic cruise. A cocktail sail can be as little as $20, but for a dinner sail expect to spend $40-50. Remember, too, that the larger established companies are usually on Maui to stay, but that smaller companies come and go with the tide! The following are general tour boats that offer a variety of cruises.

Trilogy Excursions, tel. 661-4743, (800) 874-2666, was founded and is operated by the Coon Family. A success in many ways, their Lanai Cruise is the best on Maui. Although the handpicked crews have made the journey countless times, they never forget that it's your first time. They run trimarans and catamarans, including the 54-foot Trilogy II which carries up to 50 passengers to Lanai. Once aboard you're served a mug of steaming Kona coffee, fresh juice, and Mama Coon's famous cinnamon rolls. After anchoring in Manele Bay, a tour van picks you up and you're driven to Lanai City. Along the way, the driver, a Lanai resident, tells stories, history, and anecdotes concerning the Pineapple Island.

After the tour, you return to frolic at Hulopoe Bay, which is beautiful for swimming, boogie boarding, and renowned as an excellent snorkeling area. All gear is provided. While you play, the crew is busy at work preparing a barbecue at the picnic facilities at Manele Harbor. The meal is delicious: marinated chicken, Hong Kong stir-fry noodles, green salad with Mama's secret dressing, the sweetest island-fresh pineapple, and a beverage. An all-day affair, you couldn't have a more memorable or enjoyable experience than sailing with Trilogy. But don't spoil your day; be sure to bring along (and use!) a wide-brim hat, sunglasses, sunscreen, a long-sleeve shirt, and a towel. For this full day's experience, adults pay $125, children half price.

Captain Nemo's Emporium, tel. (800) 367-8088 Mainland or 661-5555 in Hawaii, located at 150 Dickenson Street, sails *Seasmoke,* a 58-foot catamaran (built for James Arness and reported to be the fastest "cat" on the island), to Lanai on a snorkel and diving run Mon. through Sat. They leave from Kaanapali Beach at 8 a.m. and return at 2 p.m. and serve a fine continental breakfast of hot coffee, fresh juice, hot pastry, and sweet island fruits. A lunch of fresh vegatables, chips, sandwich fixings, homemade cookies, and all the beverages that you can drink are also provided. On the way to Lanai, you'll be given an orientation to the crew, boat safety, what's happening on the sail, and an introduction to the marinelife in the sea below.

While anchored in a small bay on Lanai's south side, those who snorkle or scuba will be treated to a fabulous show of colorful fish and coral—the water here is clear to a depth of many dozen feet. When the conditions are right, as they are most afternoons, the *Seasmoke* hoists its sails and rides the wind back to Lahaina. Capt. Nemo's is one of the finest outfits operating on Maui and has a well deserved reputation for an outing filled with fun, safety, and excitement. You can't go wrong! For those along to snorkle the fare is $66, $79 for certified divers, and $89 if you are getting an introduction to scuba. Capt. Nemo's also offers a sunset sail departing every day from Kaanapali Beach aboard the Seasmoke. Watch the sun set into the ocean as you sip your wine, fill up on munchies, and are seranaded by live Hawaiian music, all for $29. Owned and operated by John Palmer and his wife Lynn, both are excellant divers and concientious about understanding and preserving the ecology of Hawaii.

Windjammer Cruises, tel. 667-6834, offers twice-daily trips aboard their 65-foot, three-masted schooner. They pack in over 100 passengers and provide snacks on board. They also do a dinner cruise on the *Spirit of Windjammer.* Departing from slip #1 at 5 p.m., the two-hour trip takes you up and down the West Maui coast as the sun sets. A double entree is served, an open bar is available, and live entertainment is provided throughout the ride; $54 adults, children half price. Their newly refurbished *Coral Sea* is a glass bottom boat that runs a snorkel/picnic tour of Molokini. For $54 (children half price) they provide equipment, continental breakfast, lunch, and an open bar. Free transportation is given from Kaanapali aboard their double decker buses. **Scotch Mist,** tel. 661-0386, has two racing yachts, *Scotch Mist I* and *II.* They are the oldest sailing charters on Maui (since 1970) and claim to be the fastest sailboats in the harbor: boasting the lightest boat, the biggest sail, and the best crew. They'll cruise/snorkle West Maui for $40, sail and snorkle Lanai for half a day for $50, or take their 16 passengers

on a sunset sail complete with champagne for $30. When the time is right, a moonlight starlight sail and a whalewatching sail are offered, both for $30.

One of the most respected sunset dinner cruises is aboard the 80-foot schooner *Machias.* Free drinks, a Hawaiian-style dinner cooked on board, and live entertainment are all part of the sail. A five-hour Sunday brunch sail ($59) is a gastronome's delight. Cruises from Lahaina Harbor. Call Aloha Voyages at 667-6284.

The *Lin Wa* is a glass-bottom boat that's a facsimile of a Chinese junk. One of the tamest and least expensive tours out of Lahaina Harbor, it departs four times a day from slip #3 for the 1½-hour tour and charges $17.50 adults and $8.75 children. It gives you a tour just off Maui's shore and even offers whalewatching in season. It's little more than a seagoing carnival ride. Call the *Lin Wa* at 661-3392, and remember that it's very popular.

One of the least expensive cruises ($25) is a cocktail sail aboard the 44-foot catamaran *Frogman,* tel. 667-7622. It departs from Maalaea Harbor and serves *pu pu,* mai tais, and beer on its tradewind sail. From Maalaea Harbor is the champagne sunset dinner sail offered by *Ocean Activities Center,* tel. 879-4485, aboard their 65-foot catamaran *Wailea Kai.* They sail Mon., Wed., Fri., and Saturday. Also out of Maalaea Harbor is the *Mahana Maia,* tel. 871-8636, a 58-foot cat that'll carry 50 passengers out to Molokini.

The *Prince Kuhio* is a different kind of trip altogether. The comfort, luxury, and stability of this 92-foot long ship is perhaps for those who don't want quite as adventurous a trip as one on a smaller boat. Departing from Maalaea Harbor, it makes a three-hour shoreline cruise along Maui, Molokini, Kahoolawe, and Lanai, as well as a dinner cruise. Call Maui-Molokai Sea Cruises at (800) 468-1287 or 242-8777 on Maui.

Out of Kihei you might try the **Maui Sailing Center,** tel. 874-0332, which takes a limited number of passengers on its Santa Cruz 50 ocean racer for a full-day snorkel sail to Molokini or a sunset sail. It departs from Kealia Beach along N. Kihei Road in Kihei. Perhaps the quickest way to Molokini, which means more time in the water, is aboard the catamaran *Kai Kanani,* which departs from Makena Beach in front of the Maui Prince Hotel. Equipment and food are provided. Call 879-7218. From Kaanapali the *Sea Sails* makes an evening dinner sail from its anchorage at the Sheraton Beach. Contact **Sea Sport Activities Center,** tel. 667-2759.

Some of the above companies offer a variety of cocktail sails and whale-watches for much cheaper prices, but many tend to pack people in so tightly that they're known derisively as "cattle boats." Don't expect the personal attention you'd receive on smaller boats (always check number of passengers when booking). However, all the boats going to Molokai or Lanai will take passengers for the one-way trip. You won't participate in the snorkeling or the food, but the prices (negotiable) are considerably cheaper. This extra service is offered only if there's room. Talk to the individual captains.

sailing the Lahaina Roads (BOB NILSEN)

Unique Ocean Tours

For a totally different experience try **Captain Zodiac**, located at 115 Dickenson St., Lahaina, tel. 667-5351. A Zodiac is a highly maneuverable, totally seaworthy high-tech motorized raft. Its main feature is speed and an ability to get intimate with the sea as its supple form bends with the undulations of the water. Simply, it can go where other craft cannot. Captain Zodiac pioneered the field starting as a one-man operation on Kauai. They've now come to Maui and offer their unique experience daily. Schedules change, but basically they offer a full day (7:30 a.m. to 2:30 p.m.) and half day (9 a.m. to 12:30 p.m., and again in the afternoon) for $95 and $53 respectively, children less; snacks, drinks, lunch (full day only), and snorkel gear included. A whale-watch during the season is also offered. Departing from Mala Wharf, they cross the Lahaina Roads heading for the hidden spots of Lanai. En route, the knowledgeable crew tells tales, legends, and the natural history of the area. Once Lanai is reached, you snorkel along its amazing coastline in pristine spots like Five Needles, a virtually untouched wonderland of tropical fish and underwater grottoes.

Two other companies that offer similar experiences in their oceangoing rafts are: **Blue Water Rafting,** tel. 879-7238, P.O. Box 10172, Lahaina, HI 96761. They depart from the Kihei Boat Ramp and primarily offer snorkel trips to Molokini (whalewatching in season); and Ocean Riders, tel. 661-3586, departing from Mala Wharf in Lahaina for trips to Lanai and Molokini.

If you've had enough of Front Street Lahaina, **Club Lanai**, tel. 871-1144, is a Maui-based company that runs day excursions to its developed facilities on the east side of Lanai. (Besides Trilogy Excursions, Club Lanai is the only company with permission to land on Lanai.) You board one of two catamarans at Lahaina Harbor, leaving at 7:30 a.m. En route you're served a continental breakfast of Danish pastry, juices, and coffee. The boats cruise to Club Lanai's private beach just near old Halepaloa Landing, between the deserted villages of Keomoku and Naha, on Lanai's very secluded eastern shore. Awaiting you is

Researchers at the Pacific Whale Foundation are happy to share their research findings with visitors.
(J.D. BISIGNANI)

an oasis of green landscaped beach. Palm trees provided shade over manmade lagoons, and hammocks wait for true relaxation. The club provides you with snorkel gear, boogie boards, kayaks with instruction, a glass-bottom boat, bicycles for your personal exploration of the area, horseshoes, volleyball, and even a guided tour. On the grounds are a gift shop and a Hawaiian village where you can learn handicrafts from a sparkling Lanai *kapuna,* Auntie Elaine. She keeps alive the oral traditions of storytelling and will be happy to tell you about the history, legends, and myths of Lanai. Mika, also a longtime Lanai resident, goes out of his way to ensure that you have a good time. The bar serves exotic drinks and is open all day. Lunch is a delicious buffet featuring Korean short ribs, barbecued chicken, *mahi mahi,* juices, fresh fruit, and salads. The entire day including sail, meals, and use of facilities is reasonably priced under $69, children 5-12 pay $35. Generally oriented toward the younger crowd, with plenty of activities for children. Club Lanai is the type of experience in which you set your own pace . . . do it all, or do nothing at all!

Whalewatching
Anyone on Maui from November to April gets the added treat of watching humpback whales as they frolic in their feeding grounds just off Lahaina, one of the world's major wintering areas for the humpback. Almost every boat in the harbor runs a special whale-watch during this time of year. A highly educational whale-watch is sponsored by the **Pacific Whale Foundation,** located at Kealia Beach Plaza, Suite 25, 101 N. Kihei Rd., Kihei, HI 96753, tel. 879-8811, open daily 9 a.m. to 5 p.m. A nonprofit organization founded in 1980, it is dedicated to research, education, and conservation, and is one of the only research organizations that has been able to survive by generating their own funds through membership, donations, and their excellent whale-watch cruises. They have the best whale-watch on the island aboard their own two ships, the *Whale I* and *II,* because actual scientists and researchers make up the crew. They rotate and come out on the whale-watch when they're not out in the Lahaina Roads getting up close to identify, and make scientific observations of, the whales. Most of the information that the other whale-watches dispense to the tourists is generated by the Pacific Whale Foundation. Departures from Maalaea Harbor are four times daily from 7 a.m. to 4:30 p.m.; adults $34. The foundation also offers an "Adopt-a-whale Program," and various reef and snorkel cruises that run throughout the year.

Since Lahaina Harbor is an attraction in itself, just go there and stroll along to handpick your own boat. Many times the whale-watch is combined with a snorkel and picnic sail so prices vary accordingly. Two of the cheapest are aboard the *Lin Wa* and the *Coral See*. Another is the *Kamehameha,* a 40-foot catamaran for snorkeling or whalewatching at $24-34, in slip #67, tel. 661-4522. **Ocean Activities Center,** tel. 879-4485, can book you on a variety of whalewatch sails. Call for competitive prices. If Lahaina is too frenetic for your tastes, head for Kihei where you can get a boat out of Maalaea. Get all the information you need from Jerome at the **Maalaea Activities** booth on the wharf in Maalaea or try booking through **The Dive Shop,** tel. 879-5172. For further information on whales, see "Flora And Fauna."

OTHER TOURS

The Sugar Cane Train
The old steam engine puffs along from Lahaina to Kaanapali pulling old-style passenger cars through cane fields and the Kaanapali golf course. The six miles of narrow-gauge track are covered in 25 minutes (each way) and the cost is $6 one way and $9 roundtrip adults, $3 and $4.50, respectively, for children 3-12. A free double-decker bus shuttles between Lahaina Station and the waterfront to accommodate the most popular tour on Maui. The train runs throughout the day from 8:55 a.m. to 4:40 p.m. It's very popular so book in advance. All rides are narrated and there may even be a singing conductor. It's not only great fun for children; everybody has a good time. All kinds of combination tours are offered as well: some feature lunch, a tour of Lahaina with admission into the Baldwin House and the *Carthaginian,* and even a cruise on a glass-bottom boat. They're tame, touristy, and fun. The price is right. Call the Lahaina Kaanapali and Pacific Railroad at tel. 661-0089.

Locations With Marianne
If you like photography, Maui's natural outdoors, and short hikes, these tours are for you. Day tours include a hike into the Iao or Waihee valleys ($150), up to Haleakala for the sunrise

and a walk through a redwood forest ($200), the Keanae Peninsula ($180), and a full-day fly/drive/hike to Maui's east coast ($250). Seven-day two-island and 10-day three-island intensive tours ($1300-1650) are also offered. Custom-designed tours can be arranged. These excursions will bring you memorable picture taking opportunities and a chance to experience the varied nature of Hawaii.

The group leader is a profesional photographer and former teacher who provides workshop instruction before you go out and on-the-spot instruction while on the trail. Full of energy and a passion for photography, Marianne will teach you much about the islands and photographing in a tropical setting. You'll discover picturesque locations which you might not have had an opportunity to explore otherwise. Locations With Marianne is associated with Rainforest Action Network. Tours require a minimum of two and maximum of eight persons. All prices are inclusive of photo instruction, food, entrance fees, specialty clothes (when needed), ground transportation, accommodations, and air transportation (if applicable). For information and reservations, write to Marianne Pool, Locations With Marianne, P.O. Box 2250, Kihei, Maui, HI 96743, or call (808) 874-3797.

Private Tour Guides
These are individualized tours arranged with your needs and desires in mind. You provide the rental car, they drive and provide the knowledge and expertise about the island. Try **Personal Maui** for a half-day ($60), full-day ($110), or two-day Hana overnight ($200); add $10 for each additional passenger. For one or two people the prices are a bit steep, but for three or more fares become more competitive with other tour companies. Contact Dan Kuehn, P.O. Box 1834, Makawao, Maui, HI 96768, or call (800) 367-8047, ext. 474, or 572-1589 in Hawaii. Another reputable company offering similar services is **Guides of Maui.** Call (800) 228-6284, 877-4042 in Hawaii, or write 333 Dairy Road, Suite 104-B, Kahului, Maui, HI 96732.

ACCOMMODATIONS

With over 16,000 rooms available, and more being built every day, Maui is second only to Oahu in the number of visitors it can accommodate. There's a tremendous concentration of condos on Maui (approximately 10,000 units—predominating in the Kihei area), plenty of hotels (the majority in Kaanapali), and a growing number of bed and breakfasts. Camping is limited to a handful of parks, but what it lacks in number it easily makes up for in quality.

Tips

Maui has an **off-season** like all of Hawaii, which runs from after Labor Day to just before Christmas, with the fall months being particularly beautiful. During this period you can save 25% or more on accommodations. If you'll be staying for over a week, get a condo with cooking facilities or a room with at least a refrigerator; you can save a bundle on food costs. You'll pay more for an ocean view, but along Maui's entire south shore from Kapalua to Wailea, you'll have a cheaper and cooler room if you're mountainside, away from the sun.

Your Choices

Over 80 hotels and condos have sprouted on West Maui, from Kapalua to Lahaina. The most expensive are in **Kaanapali** and include the Hyatt Regency, Marriott, Westin Maui, and Sheraton, strung along some of Maui's best beaches. The older condos just west in Honokowai are cheaper, with a mixture of expensive and moderate as you head toward Kapalua. **Lahaina** itself offers only a handful of places to stay: condos at both ends of town, the famous nonluxury Pioneer Inn, and four hotels. Most people find the pace a little too hectic, but you couldn't get more in the middle of *it* if you tried. **Maalaea Bay,** between Lahaina and Kihei, has 11 quiet condos. Prices are reasonable, the beaches are fair, and you're within striking distance of the action in either direction.

Kihei is "condo row," with well over 50 of them along the six miles of Kihei Avenue, plus a few hotels. This is where you'll find topnotch beaches and the best deals on Maui. **Wailea** just up the road is expensive, but the hotels here are world class and the secluded

*Relax and enjoy
la dolce vita.*
(J.D. BISIGNANI)

beaches are gorgeous. **Kahului** often takes the rap for being an unattractive place to stay on Maui. It isn't all that bad. You're smack in the middle of striking out to the best of Maui's sights, and the airport is minutes away for people staying only a short time. Prices are cheaper and Kanaha Beach is a sleeper, with great sand, surf, and few visitors. **Hana** is an experience in itself. You can camp, rent a cabin, or stay at an exclusive hotel. Always reserve in advance and consider splitting your stay on Maui, spending your last few nights in Hana. You can really soak up this wonderful area, and you won't have to worry about rushing back along the Hana Highway.

Amenities

All hotels have some of them, and some hotels have all of them. Air-conditioning is available in most, but under normal circumstances you won't need it. Balmy tradewinds provide plenty of breezes, which flow through louvered windows and doors in many hotels. Casablanca room fans are better. TVs are often included in the rate, but not always. In-room phones are provided, but a service charge is usually tacked on, even for local calls. Swimming pools are very common, even though the hotel may sit right on the beach. There is always a restaurant of some sort, a coffee shop or two, a bar, cocktail lounge, and some-

times a sundries shop. Some hotels also offer tennis courts or golf courses either as part of the premises or affiliated with the hotel; usually an activities desk can book you into a variety of daily outings. Plenty of hotels offer laundromats on the premises, and hotel towels can be used at the beach.

Bellhops get about $1 per bag, and maid service is free, though maids are customarily tipped $1-2 per day and a bit more if kitchenettes are involved. Parking is free. Hotels can often arrange special services like babysitters, all kinds of lessons, and often special entertainment activities. A few even have bicycles and some snorkeling equipment to lend. They'll receive and send mail for you, cash your traveler's checks, and take messages.

Condominiums

The method of paying for and reserving a condo is just about the same as for a hotel. However, requirements for deposits, final payments, and cancellation charges are much stiffer than in hotels. Make absolutely sure you fully understand all of these requirements when you make your reservations. The main qualitative difference between a condo and a hotel is in amenities. At a condo, you're more on your own. You're temporarily renting an apartment, so there won't be any bellhops and rarely a bar, restaurant, or lounge on the premises, though many times you'll find a sundries store. The main lobby, instead of having that grand entrance feel of many hotels, is more like an apartment house entrance, although there might be a front desk. Condos can be efficiencies (one big room), but mostly they are one- or multiple-bedroom affairs with a complete kitchen. Reasonable housekeeping items should be provided: linens, all furniture, and a fully equipped kitchen. Most have TVs and phones, but remember that the furnishings provided are all up to the owner. You can find brand-new furnishings that are top of the line, right down to garage sale bargains. Inquire about the furnishings when you make your reservations. Maid service might be included on a limited basis (for example, once weekly), or you might have to pay extra for it.

Condos usually require a minimum stay, although some will rent on a daily basis, like hotels. Minimum stays when applicable are often three days, but seven is also commonplace, and during peak season, two weeks isn't unheard of. Swimming pools are common, and depending on the "theme" of the condo, you can find saunas, weight rooms, jacuzzis, and tennis courts. Rates are about 10-15% higher than comparable hotels, with hardly any difference between doubles and singles. A nominal extra is charged for more than two people, and condos can normally accommodate four to six guests. You can find clean, decent condos for as little as $200 per week, all the way up to exclusive apartments for well over $1000. Their real advantage is for families, friends who want to share, and especially long-term stays where you will always get a special rate. The kitchen facilities save a great deal on dining costs, and it's common to find units with their own mini-washers and dryers. Parking space is ample for guests, and like hotels, plenty of stay/drive deals are offered. You'll find condos all over Hawaii, but they're particularly prevalent on Maui.

Hotel/Condominium Information
The best source of hotel/condo information is the **Hawaii Visitor's Bureau**. While planning your trip, either visit one nearby or write to them in Hawaii. (Addresses are given in the "Information" section in this Introduction.) Re-

quest a copy of their free and current *Member Accommodation Guide*. This handy booklet lists all the hotel/condo members of the HVB, with addresses, phone numbers, facilities, and rates. General tips are also given.

BED AND BREAKFAST

Bed and breakfasts are hardly a new idea. The Bible talks of the hospitable hosts who opened the gates of their homes and invited the wayfarer in to spend the night. Bed and breakfasts (B&Bs) have a long tradition in Europe, and were commonplace in Revolutionary America. Now, lodging in a private home called a bed and breakfast is becoming increasingly fashionable throughout America, and Hawaii is no exception. Not only can you visit Maui, you can "live" there for a time with a host family and share an intimate experience of daily life.

Points To Consider
The primary feature of bed and breakfast homes is that every one is privately owned, and therefore uniquely different from every other. The range of B&Bs is as wide as the living standards in America. You'll find everything from semi-mansions in the most fashionable residential areas to little shacks offered by a downhome fisherman and his family. This means that it's particularly important for the guest to choose a host family with whom their lifestyle is compatible. Unlike a hotel or a condo, you'll be living *with* a host and most likely their family, although your room will be private, with private baths and separate entranceways being quite common. You don't just "check in" to a bed and breakfast. In Hawaii you usually go through agencies (listed below) which act as a go-between, matching host and guest. Write to them and they'll send you a booklet with a complete description of the bed and breakfast, its general location, the fees charged, and a good idea of the lifestyle of your host family. With the reservations application they'll include a questionnaire that will basically determine your profile: are you single? children? smoker? etc., as well as arrival and departure dates and all pertinent particulars.

Since bed and breakfasts are run by individual families, the times that they will accept guests can vary according to what's happening in their lives. This makes it imperative to write well in advance: three months is good; earlier is too long and too many things can change. Four weeks is about the minimum time required to make all necessary arrangements. Expect a minimum stay (three days is common) and a maximum stay. Bed and breakfasts are not long-term housing, although it's hoped that guest and host will develop a friendship and future stays can be as long as both desire.

B&B Agencies

One of the most experienced agencies, **Bed And Breakfast Honolulu Statewide**, at 3242 Kaohininai Dr., Honolulu, HI 96817, tel. 595-7533, or (800) 288-4666, owned and operated by Marylee and Gene Bridges, began in 1982. Since then, they've become masters at finding visitors the perfect accommodation to match their desires, needs, and pocketbook. Their repertoire of guest homes offers more than 400 rooms, with half on Oahu, and the other half scattered around the state. Accommodations from Marylee and Gene are more personally tailored than a hotel room. When you phone, they'll match your needs to their computerized in-house guidelines. B&B Honolulu Statewide also features bargain package deals for inter-island fly/car rentals. If you have special needs and are coming during the peak season, reserve up to four months in advance; normal bookings are perfect with two-month's lead time. But, don't count them out if you just show up at the airport. Rooms can't be guaranteed, but they'll do their best to find you a place to stay.

Another top notch B&B agency is **Bed and Breakfast Hawaii,** operated by Evelyn Warner and Al Davis. They've been running this service since 1979. Bed and Breakfast Hawaii has about 50 host homes throughout Maui. Write for guest applications and other information. If you wish, for $10.95 they will mail you their "Bed and Breakfast Goes Hawaiian," an all-islands listing of homes and their periodic "hot sheet" of new listings. Write Bed and Breakfast Hawaii, Box 449, Kapaa, HI 96746. Phone info and reservations at tel. (808) 822-7771, or (800) 733-1632.

Bed and Breakfast "Maui Style" is the oldest B&B agency operating on Maui. The friendly host, Leslie, can arrange a stay on Maui as well as on any of the other islands including Molokai. Accommodations range from a room in a private home to one bedroom apartments. Write Bed and Breakfast "Maui Style", P.O. Box 98, Puunene, HI 96784, tel. 879-7865, (800) 848-5567 from the Mainland.

Another agency is **Pacific Hawaii Bed and Breakfast,** 970 N. Kalahei Ave., Suite A218, Kailua, HI 96734, tel. 262-6026, toll-free (800) 999-6026.

Two specializing in beachfront and more exclusive homes are **Premier Connections of Hawaii,** tel. 879-6496, 1993 S. Kihei Rd., Suite 209, Kihei, Maui, HI 96753; and **Vacation Locations Hawaii,** tel. 874-0077 or (800) 522-2757 toll-free, P.O. Box 1689, Kihei, HI 96753.

Information on B&Bs can also be obtained from the **American Bed and Breakfast Assn.,** 16 Village Green, Suite 203, Crafton, MD 21114, tel. (301) 261-0180; or from the **National Bed and Breakfast Assoc.,** P.O. Box 332, Norwalk, CT 06852, tel. (203) 847-6196. Both organizations publish directories of member homes and disseminate information about the B&B movement.

HOME EXCHANGES

One other method of staying in Hawaii, open to homeowners, is to offer the use of their home for use of a home in Hawaii. This is done by listing your home with an agency that facilitates the exchange and publishes a descriptive directory. To list your home and to find out what is available, write **Vacation Exchange Club,** 12006 111th Ave., Youngtown, AZ 85363, tel. (602) 972-2186; or **Interval International,** 6262 Sunset Dr., Penthouse #1, South Miami, FL 33143, tel. (305) 666-1861 for those who desire to exchange their time-share homes.

FOOD AND DRINK

Hawaii is a gastronome's Shangri-la, a sumptuous smorgasbord in every sense of the word. The considerable array of ethnic groups that have come to Hawaii in the last 200 years have brought their own special enthusiasm and culture, and lucky for all, they didn't forget their cook pots, hearty appetites, and exotic taste buds. The Polynesians who first arrived found a fertile but barren land. Immediately they set about growing their taro, coconuts, and bananas, and raising chickens, pigs, fish, and even dogs, though these were reserved for the nobility. The harvests were bountiful and the islanders thanked the gods with the traditional feast called the luau. The underground oven, the *imu,* baked most of the dishes, and participants were encouraged to feast while relaxing on straw mats and enjoying the hula and various entertainments. The luau is as popular as ever, and a treat that's guaranteed to delight anyone with a sense of eating adventure.

The missionaries and sailors came next and their ships' holds carried barrels of ingre-

dients for puddings, pies, dumplings, gravies, and roasts—the sustaining "American foods" of New England farms. The mid-1800s saw the arrival of boatloads of Chinese and Japanese peasants, who wasted no time making rice instead of bread the staple of the islands. The Chinese added their exotic spices, creating complex Szechuan dishes, as well as workingmen's basics like chop suey. The Japanese introduced *shoyu,* sashimi, boxed *(bento)* lunches, delicate tempura, and rich, filling noodle soups. The Portuguese brought their luscious Mediterranean dishes with tomatoes and peppers surrounding plump spicy sausages, nutritious bean soups, and mouthwatering sweet treats like *malasadas* and *pao dolce* (sweet bread). Koreans carried crocks of zesty *kimchi,* and quickly fired up barbecue pits for *pulgogi,* a traditional marinated beef cooked over an open fire. Filipinos served up their rich *adobo* stews of fish, meat, or chicken in a sauce of vinegar and garlic.

Recently, Thai and Vietnamese restaurants have been offering their irresistible dishes side by side with fiery burritos from Mexico and elegant marsala cream sauces from France. The ocean breezes of Hawaii not only cool the skin, but on them waft some of the most delectable aromas on earth, to make the taste buds thrill and the spirit soar.

THE CUISINES OF HAWAII

Hawaiian foods, oldest of all island dishes, are wholesome, well prepared, and delicious. All you have to do on arrival is notice the size of some of the local boys (and women) to know immediately that food to them is indeed a happy and serious business. An oft-heard island joke is that "local men don't eat until they're full; they eat until they're tired." Many Hawaiian dishes have become standard fare at a variety of restaurants, eaten one time or another by anyone who spends time in the islands. Hawaiian food in general is called *kaukau,* cooked food is *kapahaki,* and something broiled is called *kaola.* Any of these prefixes on a menu will let you know that Hawaiian food is served. Usually inexpensive, they'll definitely fill you and keep you going.

Traditional Favorites
In old Hawaii, although the sea meant life, many more people were involved with cultivat-

ing beautifully tended garden plots of taro, sugar cane, breadfruit, and various sweet potatoes *(uala)* than fished. They husbanded pigs and barkless dogs *(ilio),* and prized *moa* (chicken) for their feathers and meat, but found eating the eggs repulsive. Their only farming implement was the *o'o,* a sharpened hardwood digging stick. The Hawaiians were the best farmers of Polynesia, and the first thing they planted was taro, a tuberous root that was created by the gods at the same time as man. This main staple of the old Hawaiians was made into poi. Every luau will have poi, a glutinous purple paste made from pounded taro root. It comes in liquid consistencies referred to as "one- , two-, or three-finger poi." The fewer fingers you need to eat it, the thicker it is. Poi is one of the most nutritious carbohydrates known, but people unaccustomed to it find it bland and tasteless, although some of the best, fermented for a day or so, has an acidy bite. Poi is made to be eaten *with* something, but locals who love it pop it in their mouths and smack their lips. However, those unaccustomed to it will suffer constipation if they eat too much.

A favorite popular desert is *haupia,* a custard made from coconut. *Limu* is a generic term for edible seaweed, which many people still gather from the shoreline and eat as a

Hawaiian family
eating poi, by A.
Plum, c. 1846
(HAWAII STATE ARCHIVES)

salad, or mix with ground *kukui* nuts and salt as a relish. A favorite Hawaiian snack is *opihi*, small shellfish (limpets) that clings to rocks. People gather them, always leaving some on the rocks for the future. Cut from the shell and eaten raw by all peoples of Hawaii, as testament to their popularity they sell for $150 per gallon in Honolulu. A general term that has come to mean *hors d'oeuvres* in Hawaii is *pu pu*. Originally the name of a small shellfish, now everyone uses it for any "munchy" that's considered a finger food. A traditional liquor made from *ti* root is *okolehao*. It literally means "iron bottom," reminiscent of the iron blubber pots used to ferment it.

TROPICAL FRUITS AND VEGETABLES

Some of the most memorable taste treats from the islands require no cooking at all: the luscious tropical and exotic fruits and vegetables sold in markets and roadside stands, or found just hanging on trees, waiting to be picked. Make sure to experience as many as possible. The general rule in Hawaii is that you are allowed to pick fruit on public lands, but it should be limited to personal consumption. The following is a sampling of some of Hawaii's best produce.

common banana
(DIANA LASICH HARPER)

Bananas
No tropical island is complete without them. There are over 70 species in Hawaii, with hundreds of variations. Some are for peeling and eating while others are cooked. A "hand" of bananas is great for munching, back packing, or just picnicking. Available everywhere—and cheap.

Avocados
Brought from South America, avocados were originally cultivated by the Aztecs. They have a buttery consistency and a nutty flavor. Hundreds of varieties in all shapes and colors are available fresh year-round. They have the highest fat content of any fruit next to the olive.

Coconuts
What tropical paradise would be complete without coconuts? Indeed, these were some of the first plants brought by the Polynesians. When children are born, coconut trees were planted for them so they'd have fruit throughout their lifetime. Truly tropical fruits, they know no season. Drinking nuts are large and green, and when shaken you can hear the milk inside. You get about a quart of fluid from each. It takes skill to open one, but a machete can handle anything. Cut the stem end flat so that it will stand, then bore a hole into the pointed end and put in a straw or hollow bamboo. Coconut water is slightly acidic and helps to balance alkaline foods. Spoon meat is a custard-like gel on the inside of drinking nuts. Sprouted coconut meat is also an excellent food. Split open a sprouted nut, and inside is the yellow fruit, like a moist sponge cake. "Millionaire's salad" is made from the heart of a coconut palm. At one time an entire tree was cut down to get to the heart, which is just inside the trunk below the fronds and is like an artichoke heart except that it's about the size of a watermelon. In a downed tree, the heart stays good for about two weeks.

Breadfruit
This is a staple of the islands that provides a great deal of carbohydrates, but many people find the baked, boiled, or fried fruit bland. It grows all over the islands and is really thou-

breadfruit
(Diana Lasich Harper)

sands of little fruits growing together to form a ball.

Mangos

These are some of the most delicious fruits known to humans. They grow wild all over the islands; the ones on the leeward sides of the islands ripen from April to June, while the ones on the windward sides can last until October. They're found in the wild on trees up to 60 feet tall, and the problem is to stop eating them once you start!

Papayas

This truly tropical fruit has no real season but is mostly available in the summer. They grow on branchless trees and are ready to pick as soon as any yellow appears. Of the many varieties, the "solo papaya," meant to be eaten by one person, is the best. Split them in half, scrape out the seeds, and have at them with a spoon.

Passionfruit

Known by their island name of *lilikoi*, they make excellent juice and pies. They're a small yellow fruit (similar to lemons but smooth-skinned) mostly available in summer and fall, and many wild ones grow on vines, waiting to be picked. Slice off the stem end, scoop the seedy pulp out with your tongue, and you'll know why they're called "passionfruit."

Guavas

These small round yellow fruits are abundant in the wild where they are ripe from early summer to late fall. Considered a pest—so pick all you want. A good source of vitamin C, they're great for juice, jellies, and desserts.

Macadamia Nuts

The king of nuts was brought from Australia in 1892. Now it's the state's fourth largest agricultural product. Available roasted, candied, or buttered.

Litchis

Called nuts but they're really a small fruit with a thin red shell. They have a sweet and juicy white flesh when fresh, and appear like nuts when dried.

Potpourri

Beside the above, you'll find pineapples, oranges, limes, kumquats, thimbleberries, and blackberries, as well as carambolas, wild cherry tomatoes, and tamarinds.

FISH AND SEAFOOD

Anyone who loves fresh fish and seafood has come to the right place. Island restaurants specialize in seafood, and it's available everywhere. Pound for pound, seafood is one of the best dining bargains on Maui. You'll find it served in every kind of restaurant, and often the fresh catch-of-the-day is proudly displayed on ice in a glass case. The following is a sampling of the best.

Mahi Mahi

This excellent eating fish is one of the most common and least expensive in Hawaii. It's referred to as a "dolphin," but is definitely a fish and not a mammal at all. *Mahi mahi* can weigh 10-65 pounds; the flesh is light and moist. This fish is broadest at the head. When caught it's a dark olive color, but after a while the skin turns iridescent—blue, green, and yellow. It can be served as a main course, or as a patty in a fish sandwich.

A'u

This true island delicacy is a broadbill swordfish or marlin. It's expensive even in Hawaii because the damn thing's so hard to catch. The meat is moist and white and truly superb.

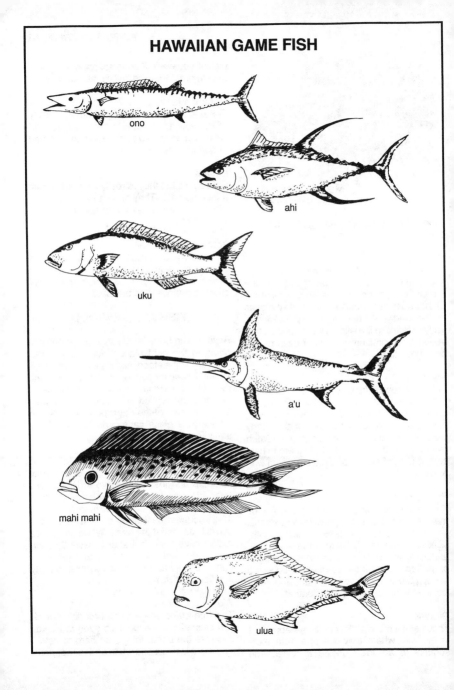

HAWAIIAN GAME FISH

ono

ahi

uku

a'u

mahi mahi

ulua

If it's offered on the menu, order it. It'll cost a bit more, but you won't be disappointed.

Ono

Ono means "delicious" in Hawaiian so that should tip you off to the taste of this wahoo, or king mackerel. *Ono* is regarded as one of the finest eating fishes in the ocean, and its white flakey meat lives up to its name.

Manini

These five-inch fish are some of the most abundant in Hawaii and live in about 10 feet of water. They school and won't bite a hook but are easily taken with spear or net. Not often on a menu, but they're favorites with local people who know best.

Ulua

This member of the jack crevalle family ranges between 15 and 100 pounds. Its flesh is white and has a steak-like texture. Delicious and often found on the menu.

Uku

This is a gray snapper that's a favorite with local people. The meat is light and firm and grills well.

Ahi

A yellowfin tuna with distinctive pinkish meat. A great favorite cooked, or uncooked in sushi bars.

Moi

This is the Hawaiian word for "king." This fish has large eyes and a shark-like head. Considered one of the finest eating fishes in Hawaii, it's best during the autumn months.

Seafood Potpourri

Some other island seafood found on the menu include *limu,* edible seaweed; *opihi,* a small shellfish (limpets) that clings to rocks and is considered one of the best island delicacies, eaten raw; *aloalo,* like tiny lobsters; crawfish, plentiful in taro fields and irrigation ditches; *ahipalaka,* albacore tuna; various octopuses (squid or calamari); and sharks of various types.

EXOTIC ISLAND DRINKS

To complement the fine dining in the islands, the bartenders have been busy creating their own tasty concoctions. The full range of beers, wines, and standard drinks is served in Hawaii, but for a real treat you should try some mixed drinks inspired by the islands. Kona coffee is the only coffee grown in America. It comes from the Kona District of the Big Island and it is a rich, aromatic, truly fine coffee. If it's offered on the menu, have a cup.

Drinking Laws

There are no state-run liquor stores; all kinds of spirits, wines, and beers are available in markets and shops, generally open during normal business hours, seven days a week. The drinking age is 21, and no towns are "dry." Legal hours for serving drinks depend on the type of establishment. Hours generally are: hotels, 6 a.m. to 4 a.m.; discos, and nightclubs where there is dancing, 10 a.m. to 4 a.m.; bars, lounges where there is no dancing, 6 a.m. to 2 a.m. Most restaurants serve alcohol, and in many that don't, you can bring your own.

Exotic Drinks

To make your experience complete, you must order one of these colorful island drinks. Most look very innocent because they come in pineapples, coconut shells, or tall frosted glasses. They're often garnished with little umbrellas or sparklers, and most have enough fruit in them to give you your vitamins for the day. Rum is used as the basis of many of them. It's been an island favorite since it was introduced by the whalers of last century. Here are some of the most famous: mai tai, a mixture of light and dark rum, orange curaçao, orange and almond flavoring and lemon juice; chi chi, a simple concoction of vodka, pineapple juice, and coconut syrup, a real sleeper because it tastes like a milk shake; Blue Hawaii, vodka and blue curaçao; Planter's Punch, light rum, grenadine, bitters, and lemon juice—great thirst quencher. A Singapore Sling is a sparkling mixture of gin, cherry, brandy and lemon juice.

Beers

A locally brewed beer is **Primo.** At one time brewed only in Hawaii, it's also made on the Mainland now. It's a serviceable American brew in the German style, but like others, it lacks that full, hearty flavor of the European beers.

Maui Lager is a new, premium, all-natural beer brewed in Wailuku at the Pacific Brewing Company by brothers Klaus and Aloysius Klink. The non-pasteurized beer follows the strict German *Reinheitsgebot* ("Purity Law") which calls for only water, hops, and malted barley.

MUNCHIES AND ISLAND TREATS

Certain "finger foods," fast foods, and island treats are unique to Hawaii. Some are a meal in themselves, but others are just snacks. Here are some of the best and most popular.

Pu Pu

Pronounced as in "Winnie the Pooh Pooh," these are little finger foods and hors d'oeuvres. They're everything from crackers to cracked crab. Often, they're given free at lounges and bars and can even include chicken drumettes, fish kebabs, and tempura. With a good display of them you can have a free meal.

Crackseed

A sweet of Chinese origin, these are preserved and seasoned fruits and seeds. Some favorites include coconut, watermelon, pumpkin seeds, mango, and papaya. Different tasting, they take some getting used to, but make great "trail snacks." Available in all island markets. Also look for dried fish (cuttlefish) on racks, usually near the crackseed. These are nutritious and delicious and make a great snack.

Shave Ice

This real island institution makes the mainland "snow cone" melt into insignificance. Special machines literally shave ice to a fluffy consistency. It's mounded into a paper cone and you choose from dozens of exotic island syrups that are generously poured over it. You're given a straw and a spoon, and just slurp away.

Malasadas And Pao Dolce

Two sweets from the Portuguese. *Malasadas* are holeless donuts and *pao dolce* is sweet bread. They're sold in island bakeries and they're great for breakfast or just as a treat.

Lomi Lomi Salmon

This is a salad of salmon, tomatoes, and onions with garnish and seasonings. It often accompanies "plate lunches" and is featured at buffets and luaus.

MONEYSAVERS

Only one thing is better than a great meal: a great meal at a reasonable price. The following are island institutions and favorites that will help you to eat well and keep prices down.

Kaukau Wagons

These are lunch wagons, but instead of being slick stainless-steel jobs, most are old delivery trucks converted into portable kitchens. Some say they're a remnant of WW II, when workers had to be fed on the job; others say the meals they serve took their inspiration from the Japanese *bento,* a boxed lunch. You'll see them parked along beaches, in city parking lots, or on busy streets. Usually a line of local people will be placing their orders, especially at lunchtime, a tip-off that they serve a delicious, nutritious island dish for a reasonable price. They might have a few tables, but basically they serve food to go. Most of their filling meals are $3.50-4.50, and they specialize in the "plate lunch."

Plate Lunch

This is one of the best island standards. These lunches give you a sampling of authentic island food and can include teriyaki chicken, *mahi mahi, lau lau,* and *lomi* salmon, among others. They're served on paper or styrofoam plates, are packed to go, and usually cost less than $3.50. Standard with a plate lunch is "two-scoop rice," a generous dollop of macaroni salad, or some other salad. A full meal, they're great for keeping down food costs and for making an instant picnic. Available everywhere, from *kaukau* wagons to restaurants.

Saimin

Special "saimin shops," as well as restaurants, serve this hearty Japanese-inspired noodle soup on their menu. Saimin is a word unique to Hawaii. In Japan, these soups would either be called *ramin* or *soba,* and it's as if the two were combined into saimin. These are large bowls of noodle soup, in a light broth with meat, chicken, fish, or vegetables stirred in. They cost only a few dollars and are big enough for an evening meal. The best place to eat saimin is in a little local hole-in-the-wall shop, run by a family.

Tips

Even some of the island's best restaurants in the fanciest hotels offer "early bird specials"— the regular-menu dinners offered to diners who come in before the usual dinner hour, which is approximately 6 p.m. You pay as little as half the normal price, and can dine in luxury on some of the best foods. Often advertised in the "free" tourist books, coupons for reduced meals might also be included: two for one, or limited dinners at a much lower price. Great early bird specials are offered at the **Moana Terrace** at Kaanapali's Marriott, the two **Island Fish Houses** in Kahului and Kihei, and at **Leilani's** in the Whaler's Village. Also, **Kihei Prime Rib House** offers some dandy specials. Buffets are also quite common in Hawaii, and like luaus (see below) they're all-you-can-eat affairs. Offered at a variety of restaurants and hotels, buffets usually cost $10-15 and up. The food, however, ranges from quite good to only passable. At lunchtime, they're even cheaper, and they're always advertised in the free tourist literature, which often includes a discount coupon.

"Happy hour" is another time not only to save on drinks but to sample light fare for free or at greatly reduced prices. Many bars offer their happy hours in conjunction with free *pu pu.* At some places the *pu pu* are only light snacks, but at others, like Stouffer's Sunset Terrace, they're a mini-buffet with gourmet tidbits.

Maui also has the full contingent of American fast-food chains including Jack in the Box, McDonald's, Shakey's Pizza, Kentucky Fried Chicken, and all the rest.

RESTAURANTS

If you love to eat you'll love Maui. Besides great fish, there's fresh beef from Maui's ranches and fresh vegetables from Kula. The cuisines offered are as cosmopolitan as the people: Polynesian, Hawaiian, Italian, French, Mexican, Filipino, and Oriental. The following are just hors d'oeuvres. Check the "Food" sections of the travel chapters for full descriptions.

Classy Dining

Five-star restaurants on Maui include: **Raffles** at Stouffer's Wailea Resort, **The Planatation Veranda** at the Kapalua Bay Hotel, **The Swan Court** at the Hyatt Regency, **La Perouse** at the Maui Intercontinental Wailea, and the **Prince Court** at the Maui Prince Hotel. You won't be able to afford these every day, but for that one-time blowout, take your choice.

Fill 'Er Up

For more moderate fare, try these no-atmosphere restaurants that'll fill you up with good food for "at home" prices: **Ma Chan's** in the Kaahumanu Shopping Center; **Kitada's** in Makawao for the best bowl of saimin on the island; and both restaurants at the **Silversword** and **Makena golf courses.** For great sandwiches try the snack bars at all of the island's health food stores, especially **Paradise Fruit Co.** in Kihei, and **Picnics** in Paia. The best inexpensive dining is in Kahului/ Wailuku. Look in the "Food" sections of those chapters for a complete list.

Can't Go Wrong

Great Mexican food (some vegetarian, no lard) at **Polli's Restaurant** in Kihei and Makawao, and **La Familia's** in Kihei include a happy hour, complete with free chips and salsa. **Longhi's** in Lahaina is well established as a gourmet cosmopolitan/Italian restaurant. Also do yourself a flavor and dine in Lahaina at **Avalon,** or **Gerard's**—both out of this world! **Mama's Fish House** in Paia receives the highest compliment of being a favorite with the locals, and **The Grill and Bar** at the Kapalua Golf Course is extraordinarily good and always consistent. **Erik's Seafood Grotto** in Kahana is good value, and **Leilani's** is an up-and-comer in the Whaler's Village. The Sunday brunches at **Raffles Restaurant** at Stouffer's in Wailea and the **Maui Prince** in Makena are legendary. If you had to choose just one blowout, these would make an excellent choice.

LUAUS AND BUFFETS

The luau is an island institution. For a fixed price of about $40, you get to gorge yourself on a tremendous variety of island foods, and have a night of entertainment as well. On your luau day, eat a light breakfast, skip lunch, and do belly-stretching exercises! Only a few are listed below.

Old Lahaina Luau has an excellent reputation because it is as close to authentic as you can get. Seating is Tuesday through Saturday, from 5:30 to 8:30 p.m., but reserve at least three days in advance to avoid disappointment. It's held on the beach at Lahaina's south end fronting 505 Front Street Mall. All-you-can-eat buffet and all-you-can-drink bar, tel. 667-1998, $42 adults, childen 3-12, $21. The hula dancers use *ti*-leaf skirts, and the music is *fo' real*. A favorite with local people.

Stouffer's Wailea Beach Resort, tel. 879-4900, recounts tales of old Hawaii with its very authentic and professional hula show and luau every Thursday at 6 p.m. Host Rod Guerrero spins yarns and tales of Maui's past, and then bursts into song with his intriguing falsetto voice. Dramatically, a fire dancer appears, and the show moves on into the evening as you dine on a wonderful assortment of foods expertly prepared by Stouffer's chefs. Price includes open bar at $38 adults, $21 children 12 and under. Reservations are required.

The Aloha Luau, tel. 661-5828, every night 5 p.m. to 8 p.m. at the Sheraton Maui, is a fun time of feasting and entertainment on one of the most beautiful sunset beaches on Maui. Prices, including full buffet, bar, and entertainment, are $39.50; children under 12 pay $17.

The **Royal Lahaina Resort,** tel. 661-3611, has been offering a nightly luau and entertainment for years in their Luau Gardens. The show is still spectacular and the food offered is authentic and good. Prices are $39.95 adults, children $19.95, reservations suggested.

Others include **Maui's Merriest Luau,** tel. 879-1922, 5:30 Tuesdays, $39 adults, children 6-10 $19.50, at the Maui Intercontinental Wailea; Hyatt Regency Maui's **Polynesian Light Show,** tel. 661-1234, every evening but Sunday and Thursday at 5:30 p.m., $42 adults, $34 for children 6-12; and **Aloha Friday Luau,** tel. 661-0011, 5:30 p.m. at Kaanapali Beach Hotel, adults $37.50, children 5-12 $18.75.

For something a little different try the **Hawaiian Country Revue** at Maui Tropical Plantation, tel. 242-8605, in Waikapu near Wailuku (see p. 157). Here you get a *yippee yai yo kai yeah* good time complete with hula and square dancing! The grill is fired up and sizzles with savory steaks, and there's a big pot of chili and all the fixin's. The price is $38, and the fun happens every Mon., Wed., and Fri. from 5:30 p.m. Host is Uncle Buddy Fo, who lassoes everyone into the good time with his singing, dancing, and drumming.

New on the scene is the Pioneers Inn's **Whaling Party,** tel. 661- 3636. This show will take you back to the days of historic Lahaina town, where you will be entertained by cancan girls on stage, sailors in the crowd, and bar girls from the balcony. And of course the missionaries are there as well to try to keep you from being lead astray. The evening is rounded out by a buffet dinner and open bar. Every Sun. and Mon. at 6 p.m., $39.50 adults, children 6-12 $18.95.

MARKETS

If you're shopping for general food supplies and are not interested in gourmet, specialty items, or organic foods, you'll save money by shopping at the big-name supermarkets, located in Lahaina, Kahului, and Kihei, often in malls. Smaller towns have general stores which are adequate, but a bit more expensive. You can also find convenience items at com-

Some of the best island treats come from small roadside stands.
(J.D. BISIGNANI)

missaries in many condos and hotels, but these should be used only for snack foods or when absolutely necessary, because the prices are just too high.

Kahului

The greatest number of supermarkets is found in Kahului. They're all conveniently located along Rt. 32 (Kaahumanu Avenue) in or adjacent to the three malls, one right after the other. **Foodland,** open 7 days 8:30 a.m. to 10 p.m., is in the **Kaahumanu Shopping Center.** Just down the road in the **Kahului Shopping Center** is the ethnic **Ah Fooks** (open 7 days, 8 a.m. to 7 p.m., closes early Sat. and Sun.), specializing in Japanese, Chinese, and Hawaiian foods. Farther along in the **Maui Mall** is **Star Market,** open 7 days, 8:30 a.m. to 9 p.m., until 7 p.m. Sunday. Just behind the Maui Mall on E. Kamehameha Ave. is a **Safeway.** Wailuku doesn't have shopping malls, but if you're taking an excursion around the top of West Maui, make a "last chance" stop at **T.K. Supermarket** at the end of N. Market St. in the Happy Valley area. They're open 7 days, but close early on Sunday afternoons. **Ooka Supermarket,** just off Main St., is the biggest and most well-stocked in town. Its hours are 7:30 a.m. to 8 p.m. Mon.-Wed. and Sat., until 9 p.m. Thurs. and Fri., and to 6 p.m. on Sunday.

Kihei

In Kihei you've got a choice of three markets, all strung along S. Kihei Road., the main drag. **Foodland** in the Kihei Town Center, and **Star Market** just down the road, offer standard shopping. The most interesting is **Azeka's Market** in Azeka Plaza. This market is an institution, and is very famous for its specially prepared (uncooked) ribs, perfect for a barbecue. In Wailea you'll find **Wailea Pantry** in the Wailea Shopping Village, open seven days a week, 8 a.m. to 7 p.m., but it's an exclusive area and the prices will make you sob.

Lahaina And Vicinity

In Lahaina you can shop at **Foodland** in Lahaina Square, just off Rt. 30. More interesting is **Nagasako's** in the Lahaina Shopping Center, just off Front Street. They've got all you need, plus a huge selection of Chinese and Japanese items. Nagasako's is open daily, 7 a.m to 9 p.m., till 7 p.m. Sunday. If you're staying at a condo and doing your own cooking the largest and generally least expensive supermarket on West Maui is the **Safeway,** open daily, 24 hours, in The Cannery Shopping Mall. Just west of Lahaina in Honokowai, you'll find the **Food Pantry**. Although there are a few sundry stores in various hotels in Kaanapali, this is the only real place to shop. It's open daily, 8 a.m. to 9 p.m. In Napili, pick up supplies at **Napili Village Store,** a bit expensive, but well stocked and convenient. In Olowalu, east of Lahaina, you can pick up some limited items at the **Olowalu General Store.**

Hana

In Hana is the **Hana Store,** which carries all the necessities and even has a selection of health foods and imported beers. Open daily 7:30 a.m. to 6:30 p.m.

Around And About

Other stores where you might pick up supplies are: **Komoda's** in Makawao. They're famous throughout Hawaii for their cream buns, which are sold out by 8 a.m. At **Pukalani Superette** in Pukalani, open seven days a week, you can pick up supplies and food to go, including sushi. In Paia try **Nagata's** or **Paia General Store** on the main drag.

HEALTH FOOD

Those into organic foods, fresh vegetables, natural vitamins, and take-out snack bars have it made on Maui. At many fine health food stores you can have most of your needs met. Try the following: in Wailuku, **Down to Earth** is an excellent health food store complete with vitamins, bulk foods and a snack bar. This Krishna-oriented market, on the corner of Central and Vineyard, is open seven days, 8 a.m. to 6 p.m., to 5 p.m. Sat., 4 p.m. Sunday. Formerly Lahaina Natural Foods, **Westside Natural Food** is now relocated on Dickenson Street. Open daily, they're a full-service health food store, featuring baked goods and Herbalife vitamins. **Paradise Fruit**

Company on S. Kihei Rd. is terrific. It's not strictly a health food store, but does have plenty of wholesome items. Their food bar is the best. They're open 24 hours every day. You can't go wrong! In Paia is **Mana Natural Foods,** open daily 8 a.m. to 8 p.m., and possibly the best health food store on Maui. You can pick up whatever you need for your trip to Hana. **Maui Natural Foods,** tel. 877-3018, in the Maui Mall in Kahului is open daily and has a fair selection of fresh foods with a big emphasis on vitamins.

Fresh Fruit And Fish

What's Hawaii without its fruits, both from the vine and from the sea? For fresh fish try the **Fresh Island Fish Co.** in Maalaea. They get their fish right from the boats, but they do have a retail counter. In Wailuku, both **Nagasako Fishery** on Lower Main and **Wakamatsu Fish Market** on Market Street also have a great selection of fresh fish daily. In Kihei, **Azeka's Market** is the place to go; however, some enterprising fishermen set up a roadside stand along S. Kihei just west of Azeka's whenever they have a good day. Look for their coolers propping up a sign. For the best and freshest fruits, vegies, cheese, and breads search out **The Farmers' Market.** Gardeners bring their fresh Kula vegetables to roadside stands on Mon. and Thurs. 7:30 a.m. to 1:30 p.m. in Honokawai near Fat Boy's Restaurant, and every Tues. and Fri. 2-5 p.m. in north Kihei by Suda's Store. Be early for the best selections. All along the road to Hana are several little fruit stands tucked away. Many times no one is in attendance and the very reasonably priced fruit is paid for on the honor system.

CAMPING AND HIKING

A major aspect of the "Maui experience" is found in the simple beauty of nature and the outdoors. Visitors come to Maui to luxuriate at resorts and dine in fine restaurants, but everyone heads for the sand and surf, and most are captivated by the lush mountainous interior. What better way to savor this natural beauty than by hiking slowly through it or pitching a tent in the middle of it? Maui offers a full range of hiking and camping, and what's more, most of it is easily accessible and free. Camping facilities are located near many choice beaches and amid the most scenic areas of the island. They range in amenities from full-housekeeping cabins to primitive "hike-in" sites. Some restrictions to hiking apply because much of the land is privately owned, so you may require advance permission to hike. But plenty of public access trails along the coast and deep into the interior would fill the itineraries of even the most intrepid trekkers. If you enjoy the great outdoors on the Mainland, you'll be thrilled by these "mini-continents," where in one day you can go from the frosty summits of alpine wonderlands down into baking cactus-covered deserts and emerge through jungle foliage onto a sun-soaked subtropical shore.

Note
Descriptions of individual state parks, county beach parks, and Haleakala National Park, along with directions on how to get there, are given under "Sights" in the respective travel chapters.

HALEAKALA NATIONAL PARK

Camping at Haleakala National Park is free, but there is an automobile entrance fee of $3, with a senior citizen discount. Permits are not needed to camp at Hosmer Grove, just a short drive from Park Headquarters, or at Oheo Stream Campground (Seven Sacred Pools) near Kipahulu, along the coastal road 10 miles south of Hana. Camping is on a first-come, first-served basis, and there's an official three-day stay limit, but it's a loose count, especially at Oheo, which is almost always empty. The case is much different at the campsites located inside Haleakala Crater proper. On the floor of the crater are two primitive tenting campsites, one at Paliku on the east side and the other at Holua on the north rim. For these you'll need a wilderness permit from Park Headquarters. Because of ecological considerations, only 25 campers per night can stay at each site, and a three-night, four-day per month maximum stay is strictly enforced, with tenting allowed at any one site for only two consecutive nights. However, because of the strenuous hike involved, campsites are open most of the time. You must be totally self-sufficient, and equipped for cold-weather camping to be comfortable at these two sites.

Also, Paliku, Holua, and another site at Kapalaoa on the south rim offer cabins. Fully self-contained with stoves, water, and nearby pit toilets, they can handle a maximum of 12 campers each. Cots are provided, but you must have your own warm bedding. The same maximum-stay limits apply as in the campgrounds. Staying at these cabins is at a premium—they're popular with visitors and residents alike. They're geared toward the group, with rates at $5 per person, but there is a $6 minimum for a single. To have a chance at getting a cabin you must make reservations, so write well in advance for complete information to: Haleakala National Park, Box 369, Makawao, HI 96768, tel. 572-9306. For general information write: National Park Serv-ice, 300 Ala Moana Blvd., Honolulu, HI 96850, tel. 546-7584.

STATE PARKS

There are 10 state parks on Maui, managed by the Department of Land and Natural Resources through their Division of State Parks. These facilities include everything from historical sites to wildland parks accessible only by trail. Some are only for looking at, some are restricted to day use, and two of them have overnight camping. Poli Poli and Wainapanapa offer free tenting, and self-contained cabins are available on a sliding fee; reservations highly necessary. Permits are required at each, and RVs technically are not allowed.

Park Rules

Tent camping permits are free and good for a maximum stay of five nights at any one park. A permit to the same person for the same park is again available only after 30 days have elapsed. Campgrounds are open every day.

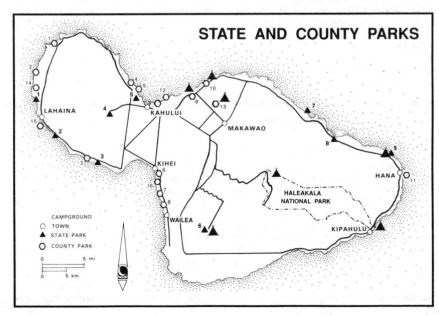

STATE AND COUNTY PARKS

STATE PARKS

CODE NUMBER	PARK NAME	RESTROOMS	OVERLOOKS	PICNIC TABLES	OUTDOOR STOVES	DRINKING WATER	SWIMMING	SHELTERS	TENT CAMPING	CABINS	SHOWERS
1.	Wahikuli State Wayside	•		•	•	•	•	•			•
2.	Launiupoko State Wayside	•		•	•	•	•				•
3.	Papalaua State Wayside						•				
4.	Iao Valley State Park	•	•			•		•			
5.	Halekii-Pihana Heiau St. Hist. Mon.		•								
6.	Polipoli Spring St. Recreation Area	•		•	•	•			•	•	
7.	Kaumahina State Wayside	•	•	•	•	•			•		
8.	Puaa Kaa State Wayside	•		•	•	•	•		•		
9..	Waianapanapa State Park	•	•	•	•	•	•		•	•	•

COUNTY PARKS

CODE NUMBER	PARK NAME	RESTROOMS	OVERLOOKS	PICNIC TABLES	OUTDOOR STOVES	DRINKING WATER	SWIMMING	SHELTERS	TENT CAMPING	CABINS	SHOWERS
1.	D.T. Fleming	•		•			•	•			•
2.	Honokowai	•		•			•				•
3.	Ukumehame						•				
4.	Waihee	•		•	•	•					
5.	Waiehu										
6.	Mai Poina Oe Iau	•		•	•	•	•	•			•
7.	Kalama	•		•	•	•	•	•			•
8.	Kamaole	•					•				
9.	H.A. Baldwin	•		•	•	•	•	•	•		•
10.	Hookipa	•	•	•	•	•		•			•
11.	Hana Bay	•		•	•	•	•	•			•
12.	Kanaha	•		•	•	•	•	•			•
13.	Rainbow	•		•	•	•		•	•		
14.	Hanakaoo						•				
15.	Puamana						•				
16.	Kaonoulu	•		•	•	•					

You can arrive after 2 p.m. and you should check out by 11 a.m. The minimum age for park permits is 18, and anyone under that age must be accompanied by an adult. Alcoholic beverages are prohibited, as is nude sunbathing. Plants and wildlife are protected, but reasonable amounts of fruits and seeds may be gathered for personal consumption.

Fires on cookstoves or in designated pits only. Dogs and other pets must be under control at all times and are not permitted to run around unleashed. Hunting and freshwater fishing are allowed in season and only with a license, but ocean fishing is permitted, unless prohibited by posting. Permits are required for certain trails, so check at the state parks office.

Cabins And Shelters

Housekeeping cabins are available as indicated on the accompanying chart. As with camping, permits are required with the same five-day maximum stay. Reservations are absolutely necessary, especially at Wainapanapa, and a 50% deposit at time of confirmation is required. There's a three-day cancellation requirement for refunds, and payment is to be made in cash, money order, certified check, or personal check, the latter only if it's received 30 days before arrival so that cashing procedures are possible. The balance is due on date of arrival. Cabins are on a sliding scale of $10 single, $14 double, and about $5 for each person thereafter. These are completely furnished down to the utensils, with heaters for cold weather and private baths.

Permit-issuing Office

Permits can be reserved up to one year in advance but at least seven days prior to arrival by writing a letter including your name, address, phone number, number of persons in your party, type of permit requested, and duration of your stay. They can be picked up on arrival with proof of identification. Office hours are 8 a.m. to 4:15 p.m., Mon. through Friday. Usually, tent camping permits are no problem to secure on the day you arrive, but reserving ensures you a space and alleviates anxiety. The permits are available from the Maui (Molokai also) Division of State Parks, 54 High St., Wailuku, HI 96793, tel. 243-5354; or write Box 1049 Wailuku, HI 96793.

COUNTY PARKS

There are 16 county parks scattered primarily along Maui's coastline, and because of their locations, they're generally referred to as **beach parks**. Most are for day use only,

where visitors fish, swim, snorkel, surf, picnic, and sunbathe, but two have overnight camping. The rules governing use of these parks are just about the same as those for state parks. The main difference is that along with a use permit, county beach parks charge a fee for overnight use. Again, the differences between individual parks are too numerous to mention, but the majority have a central pavilion for cooking, restrooms, and cold-water showers, individual fire pits and picnic tables, with electricity usually only at the central pavilion. RVs are allowed to park in appropriate spaces. One safety point to consider is that beach parks are open to the general public and most are used with regularity. This means that quite a few people pass through, and your chances of encountering a hassle or running into a rip-off are slightly higher in beach parks.

Fees And Permits

The fees are quite reasonable at $3 per night per person, children $.50. No more than three consecutive nights at any park. To get a permit and pay your fees for use of a county beach park, either write in advance or visit the following issuing office, open 9 a.m. to 5 p.m., Mon. through Friday: Dept. of Parks and Recreation, Recreation Division, 1580 Kaahumanu Ave., (in the War Memorial Gym) Wailuku, HI 96793, tel. 243-7389.

HIKING

The hiking on Maui is excellent; most times you have the trails to yourself, and the wide possibility of hikes range from a family saunter to a strenuous trek. The trails are mostly on public lands with some crossing private property. With the latter, the more established routes cause no problem, but for others you'll need special permission.

Haleakala Hikes

The most spectacular hikes on Maui are through Haleakala Crater's 30 miles of trail. **Halemauu Trail** is 10 miles long, beginning three miles up the mountain from park headquarters. It quickly winds down a switchback descending 1,400 feet to the crater floor. It passes Holua Cabin and goes six more miles

Enjoy some of the world's unique landscapes hiking the trails of Haleakala.
(J.D. BISIGNANI)

to Paliku Cabin, offering expansive views of Koolau Gap along the way. A spur leads to Sliding Sands Trail with a short walk to the Visitors Center. This trail passes Silversword Loop and the Bottomless Pit, two attractions in the crater. **Sliding Sands Trail** might be considered the main trail, beginning from the Visitor's Center at the summit and leading 10 miles over the crater floor to Paliku Cabin. It passes Kapalaoa Cabin en route and offers the best walk through the crater, with up-close views of cinder cones, lava flows, and unique vegetation. **Kaupo Gap Trail** begins at Paliku Cabin and descends rapidly through the Kaupo Gap, depositing you in the semi-ghost town of Kaupo. Below 4,000 feet the lava is rough and the vegetation thick. You pass through the private lands of the Kaupo Ranch along well-marked trails. Without a pick-up arranged at the end, this is a tough one because the hitching is scanty.

West Maui Trails
The most frequented trails on West Maui are at Iao Needle. From the parking area you can follow the **Tableland Trail** for two miles, giving you beautiful panoramas of Iao Valley as you steadily climb to the tableland above, or you can descend to the valley floor and follow Iao Stream for a series of small but secluded swimming holes. **Waihee Ridge Trail** is a three-mile trek leading up the windward slopes of the West Maui Mountains. Follow Rt. 34 around the backside to Maluhia Road and turn up it to the Boy Scout camp. From here the trail rises swiftly to 2,560 feet. The views of Waihee Gorge are spectacular. The **Waihee Trail** runs into this narrow valley. North of the town of Waihee turn left at the Oki Place road sign. Proceed as far as you are able to drive, park your car, and walk up along the flume. This level track takes you over two suspension foot bridges, through a bamboo forest, and under huge banyon trees until you reach the head dam. By crossing the river here, you can follow a smaller trail farther up the valley. **Kahakuloa Valley Trail** begins from this tiny forgotten fishing village on Maui's backside along Rt. 34. Start from the schoolhouse, passing burial caves and old terraced agricultural sites. Fruit trees line the way to trails ending two miles above the town.

Kula And Upcountry Trails
Most of these trails form a network through and around Poli Poli State Park. **Redwood Trail,** 1.7 miles, passes through a magnificent stand of redwoods, past the ranger station and down to an old CCC camp where there's a rough old shelter. **Tie Trail,** one-half mile, joins Redwood Trail with **Plum Trail,** so named because of its numerous plum trees, which bear during the summer. **Skyline Trail,** 6½ miles, starts atop Haleakala at 9,750 feet,

passing through the southwest rift and eventually joining the **Haleakala Ridge Trail,** 1.6 miles, at the 6,500-foot level, then descends through a series of switchbacks. You can join with the Plum Trail or continue to the shelter at the end. Both the Skyline and Ridge trails offer superb vistas of Maui.

Others throughout the area include: **Poli Poli,** .6 miles, passing through the famous forests of the area; **Boundary Trail,** four miles, leading from the Kula Forest Reserve to the ranger's cabin, passing numerous gulches still supporting native trees and shrubs; **Waiohuli Trail** descends the mountain to join Boundary Trail and overlooks Keokea and Kihei with a shelter at the end; **Waiakoa Trail,** seven miles, begins at the Kula Forest Reserve Access Road. It ascends Haleakala to the 7,800-foot level and then descends through a series of switchbacks, covering rugged territory and passing a natural cave shelter. It eventually meets up with the three-mile **Waiakoa Loop Trail.** All of these trails offer intimate views of forests of native and introduced trees, and breathtaking views of the Maui coastline far below.

Coastal Trails

Along Maui's southernmost tip the **King's Highway Coastal Trail,** 5½ miles, leads from La Perouse Bay through the rugged and desolate lava flow of 1790, the time of Maui's last volcanic eruption. Kihei Road leading to the trail gets extremely rugged past La Perouse and should not be attempted by car, but is easy on foot. It leads over smooth stepping stones that were at one time trudged by royal tax collectors. The trail heads inland and passes many ancient Hawaiian stone walls and stone foundation sites. Spur trails lead down to the sea, including an overview of Cape Hanamanioa and its Coast Guard lighthouse. The trail eventually ends at private land. **Hana Wainapanapa Coastal Trail,** three miles, is at the opposite side of East Maui. You start from Wainapanapa State Park or from a gravel road near Hana Bay and again you follow the flat, laid stones of the "King's Highway." The trail is well maintained but fairly rugged due to lava and cinders. You pass natural arches, a string of heiau, blowholes, and caves. The vegetation

Ken Schmitt (J.D. BISIGNANI)

is lush, and long fingers of black lava stretch out into cobalt-blue waters.

Hiking Tour

This special Maui tour is a one-man show operated by an extraordinary man. It's called **Hike Maui,** and as its name implies, it offers walking tours to Maui's best scenic areas accompanied by Ken Schmitt, a professional nature guide. Ken has dedicated years to hiking Maui and has accumulated an unbelievable amount of knowledge about this awesome island. He's proficient in Maui archaeology, botany, geology, anthropology, zoology, history, oceanography, and ancient Hawaiian cosmology. Moreover, he is a man of dynamic and gracious spirit who has tuned in to the soul of Maui. He hikes every day and is superbly fit, but will tailor his hikes for anyone, though good physical conditioning is essential. Ken's hikes are actually workshops in Maui's natural history. As you walk along, Ken imparts his knowledge but he never seems to intrude on the beauty of the site itself.

His hikes require a minimum of two people and a maximum of six. He offers gourmet breakfasts, lunches, and snacks with an emphasis on natural health foods. All special equipment, including snorkel gear and camping gear for overnighters, is provided. His hikes take in sights from Hana to West Maui and to the summit of Haleakala, and range from the moderate to the hardy ability level. Half-day hikes last about five hours and all-day hikes go for at least 12 hours. The rates vary from $60 (about half for children) to $100. By special arrangement, overnighters can be arranged with prices quoted upon request. A day with Ken Schmitt is a classic outdoor experience. Don't miss it! Contact Hike Maui at tel. 879-5270, P.O. Box 330969, Kahului, Maui, HI 96733.

EQUIPMENT, INFORMATION, AND SAFETY

Camping And Hiking Equipment

Like everything else you take to Maui, your camping and hiking equipment should be lightweight and durable. Size and weight should not cause a problem with baggage requirements on airlines: if it does, it's a tip-off that you're hauling too much. One odd luggage consideration you might make is to bring along a small **styrofoam cooler** packed with equipment. Exchange these for food items when you get to Hawaii; if you intend to car-camp successfully and keep food prices down, you'll definitely need a cooler. You can also buy one on arrival for only a few dollars. You'll need a lightweight **tent,** preferably with a rainfly and a sewn-in floor. This will save you from getting wet and miserable, and will keep out mosquitos, cockroaches, ants, and the few stinging insects on Maui. In Haleakala Crater, where you can expect cold and wind, a tent is a must; in fact you won't be allowed to camp without one.

Sleeping bags are a good idea, although you can get along at sea level with only a blanket. Down-filled bags are necessary for Haleakala—you'll freeze without one. **Camp-stoves** are needed because there's very little

wood in some volcanic areas, it's often wet in the deep forest, and open fires are often prohibited. If you'll be car-camping, take along a multi-burner stove, and for trekking, a backpacker's stove will be necessary. The grills found only at some campgrounds are popular with many families that go often to the beach parks for an open-air dinner. You can buy a very inexpensive charcoal grill at many variety stores throughout Maui. It's a great idea to take along a **lantern**. This will give added safety for car-campers. Definitely take a **flashlight,** replacement batteries, and a few small **candles**. A complete **first-aid kit** can mean the difference between life and death, and is worth the extra bulk. Hikers, especially those leaving the coastal areas, should take rain gear, a plastic ground cloth, utility knife, compass, safety whistle, mess kit, water purification tablets, canteen, nylon twine, and waterproof matches. You can find plenty of stores that sell, and a few that rent, camping equipment. A good one is **Maui Expedition** in Wailuku. For others, see the Yellow Pages under "Camping Equipment" and "Sporting Goods Dealers."

Safety

There are two things on Maui that you must keep your eye on to remain safe: humans and nature. The general rule is, the farther you get away from towns, the safer you'll be from human-induced hassles. If possible, don't hike or camp alone, especially if you're a woman. Don't leave your valuables in your tent, and always carry your money, papers, and camera with you. (See "Theft" below.) Don't tempt the locals by being overly friendly or unfriendly, and make yourself scarce if they're drinking. While hiking, remember that many trails are well maintained, but trailhead markers are often missing. The trails themselves can be muddy, which can make them treacherously slippery and knee-deep. Always bring food because you cannot, in most cases, forage from the land. Water in most streams is biologically polluted and will give you bad stomach problems if you drink it without purifying it first, either through boiling or with tablets. For your part, please don't use the streams as a toilet.

Precautions

Always tell a ranger or official of your hiking intentions. Supply an itinerary and your expected route, then stick to it. Twilight is short in the islands, and night sets in rapidly. In June sunrise and sunset are around 6 a.m. and 7 p.m.; in December these occur at 7 a.m. and 6 p.m. If you become lost at night, stay put, light a fire if possible, and stay as dry as you can. Hawaii is made of volcanic rock which is brittle and crumbly. Never attempt to climb steep *pali* (cliffs). Every year people are stranded and fatalities have occurred. If lost, walk on ridges and avoid the gulches, which have more obstacles and make it harder for rescuers to spot you. Be careful of elevation sickness, especially on Haleakala. The best cure is to head down as soon and as quickly as possible.

Heat can cause you to lose water and salt. If you become woozy or weak, rest, take salt, and drink water as you need it. Remember, it takes much more water to restore a dehydrated person; take small frequent sips. Be mindful of flash floods. Small creeks can turn into raging torrents with upland rains. Never camp in a dry creek bed. Fog is only encountered at the 1,500- to 5,000-foot level, but be careful of disorientation. Generally, stay within your limits, be careful, and enjoy yourself.

Guidebooks

For a well-written and detailed hiking guide complete with maps, check out *Hiking Maui* by Robert Smith, published by Wilderness Press, 2440 Bancroft Way, Berkeley, CA 94704. Another book by the same company is *Hawaiian Camping* by Shirley Rizzuto. Geared toward family camping, it's adequate for basic information and listing necessary addresses, but at times it's limited in scope.

Helpful Departments And Organizations

The following will be helpful in providing trail maps, accessibility information, hunting and fishing regulations, and general forest rules. Write to the Dept. of Land and Natural Resources, Division of Forestry and Wildlife, 1151 Punchbowl St., Honolulu, HI 96813, tel. 548-2861. Their "Maui Recreation Map" is excellent and free. The following organizations can provide general information on wildlife, conservation, and organized hiking trips although they are not based on Maui: Hawaiian Trail and Mountain Club, P.O. Box 2238, Honolulu, HI 96804; Hawaiian Audubon Society, Box 22832, Honolulu, HI 96822; Sierra Club, 1212 University Ave., Honolulu, HI 96826, tel. 946-8494.

Topographical And Nautical Charts

For in-depth topographical maps, write U.S. Geological Survey, Federal Center, Denver, CO 80225. In Hawaii, a wide range of topographical maps can be purchased at Trans-Pacific Instrument Co., 1406 Colburn St., Honolulu, HI 96817, tel. 841-7538. For nautical charts, write National Ocean Survey, Riverdale, MD 20240.

SPORTS AND RECREATION

Maui won't let you down when you want to go outside and play. More than just a giant sandbox for big kids, its beaches and surf are warm and inviting, and there are all sorts of water sports from scuba diving to parasailing. You can fish, hunt, camp, or indulge yourself in golf or tennis to your heart's content. The hiking is marvelous and the horseback riding on Haleakala is some of the most exciting in the world. The information offered in this chapter is merely an overview to let you know what's available. Specific areas are covered in the travel sections. Have fun!

Note
You can book most of the following through "activity centers." Please see "Sightseeing Tours" p. 88, and also check p. 90 for sailing boats and charters that may also offer other activities such as snorkeling and scuba.

BEACHES AND PARKS

Since your island is blessed with 150 miles of coastline, over 32 of which are wonderful beach, your biggest problem is to choose which one you'll grace with your presence. The following should help you choose just where you'd like to romp about. But before you romp, pick up and read the brochure *Maui Beach Safety Tips* by the American Red Cross.

Southwest Maui Beaches
The most plentiful and best beaches for swimming and sunbathing are on the south coast of West Maui, strung along 18 glorious miles from Kapalua to Olowalu. For an all-purpose beach you can't beat **Kapalua Beach** (Fleming Beach) on Maui's western tip. It has everything: safe surf (except in winter), great swimming, snorkeling, and bodysurfing in a first-class, family-oriented area. Then comes the Kaanapali beaches along Rt. 30, bordered by the hotels and condos. All are open to the public and "rights of way" pass just along hotel grounds. **Black Rock** at the Sheraton is the best for snorkeling. Just east and west of Lahaina are **Lahaina Beach,** convenient but not private; **Launiupoko and Puamana waysides** have only fair swimming, but great views and grassy beaches. **Olowalu** has very good swimming beaches just across from the General Store, and **Papalaua Wayside** offers seclusion on a narrow beach fringed by *kiawe* trees that surround tiny patches of white sand.

Kihei And Wailea Beaches

The 10 miles stretching from the west end of Kihei to Wailea are dotted with beaches that range from poor to excellent. **Maalaea** and **Kealia** beachs extend for miles from Maalaea to Kihei. Excellent for walking, windsurfing, and enjoying the view, but little else. **Kamaole Beach Parks I, II,** and **III** are at the east end of Kihei. Top-notch beaches, they have it all—swimming, snorkeling, and safety. **Keawaka-pu** is more of the same. Then come the great little beaches of Wailea, that get more secluded as you head east: **Mokapu, Ulua, Wailea** and **Polo.** All are surrounded by the picture-perfect hotels of Wailea and all have public access. **Makena Beach,** down an unpaved road east from Wailea, is very special. It's one of the island's best beaches. At one time, alternative people made Makena a haven and it still attracts free-spirited souls. There's nude bathing here in secluded coves, unofficial camping, and freedom. It gets the highest compliment when locals, and those staying at hotels and condos around Maui, come here to enjoy themselves.

Wailuku And Kahului

Poor ugly ducklings! There are shallow, unattractive beaches in both towns and no one spends any time there. However, **Kanaha Beach** between Kahului and the airport isn't bad at all. **Baldwin Beach Park** has a reputation for hostile locals protecting their turf, but the beach is good and you won't be hassled if you "live and let live." **Hookipa Beach** just west of Paia isn't good for the average swimmer but it is the "sailboarding capital" of Hawaii, and you should visit here just to see the exciting, colorful spectacle of people skipping over the ocean with bright sails.

Hana Beaches

Everything about Hana is heavenly, including its beaches. There's **Red Sand Beach,** almost too pretty to be real. **Wainapanapa** is surrounded by the state park and good for swimming and snorkeling, even providing a legendary cave whose waters turn blood red. **Hana Bay** is well protected and safe for swimming. Farther along at **Oheo Stream** (Seven Sacred Pools) you'll find the paradise you've been searching for—gorgeous freshwater pools at the base of wispy waterfalls and fronted by a tremendous sea of pounding surf only a few yards away.

Freshwater Swimming

The best place for swimming is in various stream pools on the road to Hana. One of the very best is **Twin Falls,** up a short trail from Hoolawa Bridge. **Helio's Grave** is another good swimming spot between Hana and O-heo Stream, which are excellent themselves, especially the upper pools. Also, you can take a refreshing dip at Iao Valley stream when you visit Iao Needle or in the nest valley north in Waihee stream.

SNORKELING AND SCUBA

Maui is as beautiful from under the waves as it is above. There is world-class snorkeling and diving at many coral reefs and beds surrounding the island. You'll find the best, coincidentally, just where the best beaches are: mainly from Kihei to Makena, up around Napili Bay and especially from Olowalu to Lahaina. Backside Maui is great (but mostly for experts), and for a total thrill, try diving Molokini, the submerged volcano, just peeking above the waves and designated a Marine Life Conservation District.

Great Underwater Spots

These are some of the best on Maui, but there are plenty more (see "Sights" in individual chapters). Use the same caution when scuba diving or snorkeling as when swimming. Be mindful of currents. It's generally safer to enter the water in the center of a bay than at the sides where rips are more likely to occur. The following sites are suitable for beginners to intermediates: on Maui's western tip **Honolua Bay,** a Marine Life Conservation District; nearby **Mokuleia Bay,** known as "Slaughterhouse," but gentle; Napili Bay for usually good, and safe conditions; in Kaanapali you'll enjoy **Black Rock** at the Sheraton Hotel; at **Olowalu,** the ocean is very gentle with plenty to see; also try **Kamaole Parks II** and **III** in Kihei; and **Ulua, Polo** and **Wailea** beaches in Wailea. On the windward side **Baldwin Beach**

Park in Paia, and **Wainapanapa State Park** near Hana are both generally good. Under no circumstances should you miss taking a boat out to Molokini. It's worth every penny!

For **scuba divers,** there are underwater caves at **Nahuna** ("Five Graves") **Point** between Wailea and Makena, great diving at Molokini, magnificent caves out at the **Lanai Cathedrals,** and a sunken Navy sub, the USS *Bluegill,* to explore. Advanced divers *only* should attempt the backside of West Maui, the Seven Sacred Pools, and beyond Pu'uiki Island in Hana Bay.

Equipment

Sometimes condos and hotels have snorkeling equipment free for their guests, but if you have to rent it, don't do it from a hotel or condo, but go to a dive shop where it's much cheaper. Expect to spend $5-7 a day for mask, fins, and snorkel. One of the best snorkel deals is through **Snorkel Bob's,** tel. 879-7449 Kihei, or 669-9603 Napili. Old Snorkel Bob will dispense info and full snorkel gear for only $15 weekly. Scuba divers can rent gear for about $40 from most shops. In Lahaina rent from: **Lahaina Divers,** tel. 667-7496, at 710 Front St., one of the best all-around shops/schools on Maui; **Dive Maui,** Lahaina Market Place, tel. 667-2080; **Central Pacific Divers,** 780 Front, tel. 661-8718; **Hawaii Reef Divers,** 129 Lahainaluna, tel. 667-7647, offer good instruction, and can arrange a reasonably priced snorkel/sail to Lanai; **Capt. Nemo's Emporium,** 150 Dickenson, tel. 661-5555. In Kihei an excellent all-around shop is **The Dive Shop,** 2411 S. Kihei Rd., Suite 2-A, tel. 879-5172; **Maui Dive Shop,** Azeka Pl., tel. 879-3388; and **Molokini Divers,** at 1993 S. Kihei Road, tel. 879-0055. You might also consider renting an underwater camera. Expect to spend $15-20, including film.

Scuba Certification

A number of Maui companies take you from your first dive to PADI, NAUI, or NASDS certification. Prices range from $50 for a quickie refresher dive up to around $350 for a four- to five-day certification course. Courses or arrangements can be made with any of the dive shops listed above or following: **Ocean Activities Center,** tel. 879-4485; **Beach Activities of Maui,** tel. 661-5500; **Destination Pacific,** tel. 874-0305; **Aquatic Charters,** tel. 879-0976.

Snorkel And Scuba Excursions

Many boats will take you out snorkeling or diving. Prices range from $30 (half day, four hours) to $60 (full day, eight hours) for a snorkeling adventure, and from $50 to $80 for scuba diving. Check "Getting Around—Ocean Tours" for many of the boats that do it all, from deep-sea fishing to moonlight cruises. All of the "activities centers" can arrange these excursions for no extra charge; check "Getting Around—Sightseeing Tours" for names and numbers.

The best all-around snorkel/scuba excursions/lessons are offered by a cooperative of dive shops that have joined to become part of **Dive Hawaii,** tel. 922-0975, P.O. Box 90295, Honolulu, HI 96835. All operators associated with Dive Hawaii have been thoroughly checked by their peers for safety, fair prices, reliable service, and know-how. Send $3 for the association's 24-page full-color *Dive Hawaii Guide* by writing or phoning the above address. Most of the shops/operations listed above are members. Dive Hawaii is a self-regulatory body interested in giving you a safe and worthwhile diving experience. Simply, they're the best!

Capt. Nemo's is one of Maui's premier scuba and snorkle shops. Lessons are given for everyone from the rank beginner to instructor certification. Their shop sells and rents all equipment, and carries accessories, clothes, and books.

Others that you might try are **Sea Safari Travel,** 2770 Highland Ave., Manhattan Beach, CA 90266, which offers a seven-night package for scuba divers to Maui; **Mike Severns,** tel. 879-6596, is one of the most experienced and respected divers on Maui. As a marine scientist/explorer, he is extremely knowledgeable about Maui both above and below the waves. Mike has his own boat and accepts both beginning and advanced divers. Diving with Mike is an extraordinary educational experience.

REEF FISH

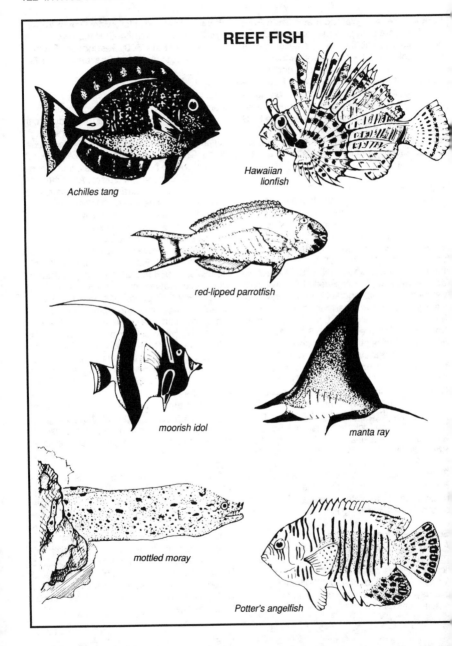

Achilles tang

Hawaiian lionfish

red-lipped parrotfish

moorish idol

manta ray

mottled moray

Potter's angelfish

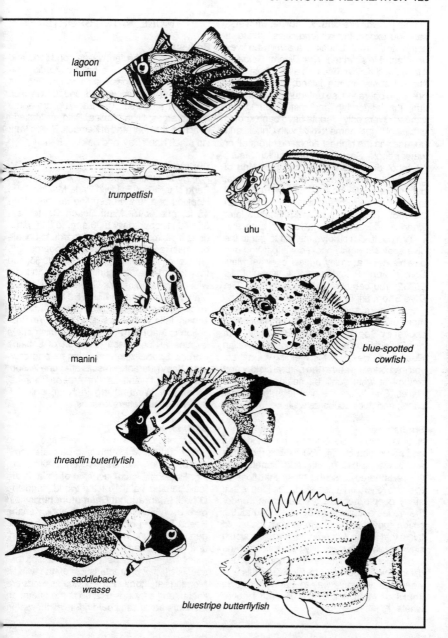

lagoon humu

trumpetfish

uhu

manini

blue-spotted cowfish

threadfin butterflyfish

saddleback wrasse

bluestripe butterflyfish

With a name like **Chuck Thorne,** what else can you expect but a world-class athlete of some kind? Well, Chuck is a diver who lives on Maui. He's written *The Divers' Guide to Maui,* the definitive book on all the best dive/snorkel spots on the island. Chuck has a one-man operation, so unfortunately, he must limit his leadership and instruction to advanced divers only. People have been known to cancel flights home to dive with Chuck, and he receives the highest accolades from other water people. Some feel that Chuck is Maui's "Rambo" diver. He's a no-nonsense kind of guy who's out to show you some great spots, but never forgets about safety first. He'll arrive in a pickup truck, oftentimes with ladders on the roof. These might come in handy later when he drives you to a remote area and you've got to climb down the cliff to get to the dive spot. No pencil-necked wimps! You can buy his book at many outlets or write: Maui Dive Guide, P.O. Box 1461, Kahului, HI 96732. You can contact Chuck through **The Dive Shop,** tel. 879-5172, or at 879-7068.

For a pure snorkeling adventure besides those offered by the dive shops and tour boats above, try **Snorkel Maui,** tel. 572-8437, with Ann Fielding, the naturalist author of *Hawaiian Reefs and Tide Pools.* Ms. Fielding will instruct you in snorkeling and in the natural history and biology of what you'll be seeing below the waves. She tailors the dive to fit the participants, and does scuba as well.

Snuba
No, that's not a typo. Snuba is half snorkeling and half scuba diving. You have a regulator, and a weight belt, mask, and flippers, and you're tethered to scuba tanks that float 20 feet above you on a sea-sled. The idea is that many people become anxious diving under the waves encumbered by tanks and all the scuba apparatus. Snuba frees you. You would think that being tethered to the sled would slow you down, but actually you're sleeker and can make better time than a normal scuba diver. If you would like to try diving, this is a wonderful and easy way to start. Try **Snuba Tours of Maui,** tel. 874-1001, 485 Hoohalahala, Kihei, HI 96753.

MORE WATER SPORTS

Bodysurfing
All you need are the right waves, conditions, and ocean bottom to have a ball bodysurfing. Always check conditions first as bodysurfing has led to some very serious neck and back injuries for the ill prepared. The following are some decent areas: Ulua, Wailea, Polo, or Makena beaches, the north end of Kamaole Beach Park I in Kihei, Napili Bay, and Baldwin Park.

Surfing
For good surfing beaches try: Lower Paia Park, Napili Bay, Baldwin Park, Maalaea and Hookipa beaches. For surfing lessons ($35-45 for one hour): **Maui Beach Center,** tel. 661-4941, open daily 8:30 a.m. to 5:30 p.m., does it all from rental of surfboards to boogie boards. Rentals for 24 hours: surfboards $28, snorkel equipment $6, boogie boards $5, and they feature the *best* surfing lessons on Maui with guaranteed results. The owner is a local Maui waterman named Eric. He takes a hand in all the activities and most times will personally take you on a surfing safari. Another option is **Maui Surfing School,** which offers lessons at the beach just east of Lahaina Harbor. Specializing in "beginners and cowards," they guarantee results after one lesson. Call 877-8811 and ask for Andrea Thomas. **Kaanapali Windsurfing** in Kaanapali, tel. 667-1964, also offers lessons.

Sailboarding
This is one of the world's newest sports, and unlike surfing, which tends to be male-dominated, women, too, are excellent at sailboarding. Hookipa Beach, just east of Paia, is the "sailboarding capital of the world," and the **O'Neill International Championship** is held here every year in March and April. Kanaha Beach Park, in nearby Kahului, has perfect, gentle winds and waves for learning the sport, and Kealia Beach in Kihei is the choice of many. Summer is best for windsurfing because of the characteristics of the winds. Mornings are good for the novice as winds are lighter, and as winds pick up in the afternoon the more advanced board riders hit the water.

Any sailboard shop will point you in the right direction for location and gear according to your skill level.

To rent boards and to take instructions, try **Maui Sailing Center** at Kealia Beach Center, N. Kihei Rd., tel. 879-5935. You can rent equipment here for $15 an hour; lessons are extra. Other possibilities include **Sailboards Maui**, 430 Alamaha, Suite 103, Kahului, tel. 871-7954, $25 half day, $35 full; and **Kaanapali Windsurfing School,** tel. 667-1964. Also check the **Maui Windsurfing Company,** tel. 877-4816 or (800) 872-0999. They have rentals from $40 to $460 for three weeks, and lessons for about $55. Remember—start with a big board and a small sail! Take lessons to save time and energy.

Note

A recent controversy has focused on what has been called "thrill craft." Usually this refers to jet-skis, water-skiing boats, speed boats, and even by some to sailboards. The feeling among conservationists is that these craft disturb others, and during whale season disturb the whales that come to nest in the rather small Lahaina Roads. This is definitely a case of "one man's pleasure is another man's poison." Recently, a law was passed that resticts the use of these moter-powered craft during the time when whales are in the Lahaina Roads.

Parasailing

If you've ever wanted to soar like an eagle, here's your chance with no prior experience necessary. Basically a parasail is a parachute tethered to a speed boat. And away we go! **Lahaina Parasail,** tel. 661-4887, located in downtown Lahaina on the south end of the breakwater, is a family-run business that was the first of its kind on Maui. These folks know what they're doing and have taken tens of thousands of people aloft on their thrill-of-a-lifetime ride. The most dangerous part, according to the crew, is getting in and out of the shuttle boat that takes you to the floating platform about 1,000 yards offshore from where you take off. Awaiting you is a power

boat with special harness attached to a parachute. You're put in a life vest, and strapped to the harness that forms a cradle upon which you sit while aloft. Make sure, once you're up, to pull the cradle as far under your thighs as you can. It's much more comfortable. Don't be afraid to loosen your steel grip on the guide ropes because that's not what's holding you anyway. In the air, you are as free as a bird and the unique view is phenomenal. You don't have time to fret about going up. The boat revs and you're airborne almost immediately. Once up, the feeling is very secure. The technology is simple, straightforward, and safe. Relax and have a ball. Cost is $48 for this eight- to 10-minute joy ride.

Other companies include **West Maui Parasail,** tel. 661-4060; **UFO Parasail,** tel. 661-7UFO; **Para-Sail Hawaii,** tel. 661-5322.

Jet-skiing

To try this exciting sport, contact: **Kaanapali Jet Ski,** at Whaler's Village, tel. 667-7851; **Jammin Jet Skis,** in Kihei at tel. 879-6662, with rates from $30 to $60, seasonal prices, Kawasakis, and Yamaha Wave Runners.

Water-skiing

Kaanapali Water Skiing, tel. 661-3324, can arrange an outing with lessons. Another is **Lahaina Water Ski,** tel. 661-5988, with professional instructors and a wide range of equipment.

Sailing/Boating

The most popular day sails are from Maui to Molokai or Lanai (fully discussed in "Getting Around—Ocean Tours"). Your basic half-day snorkel and swim sail will be $50. For serious sailors, some top-notch boats in Lahaina and Maalaea harbors are open for lengthy charters. Try: **Alihilani Yacht Charters,** tel. 871-1156; **Scotch Mist Sailing Charters,** tel. 661-0368; **Seabern Yachts,** tel. 661-8110; or **Genesis Yacht Charters,** tel. 667-5667, at Lahaina Harbor; or **Lavengro,** tel. 879-8188, at Maalaea Harbor.

For **kayaking** see p. 80. And see "Ocean Tours" for more alternatives, p. 90.

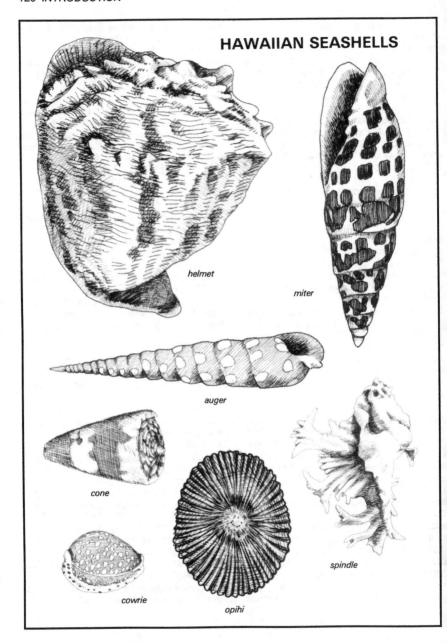

HAWAIIAN SEASHELLS

helmet

miter

auger

cone

spindle

cowrie

opihi

HORSEBACK RIDING

Those who love sightseeing from the back of a horse are in for a big treat on Maui. Stables dot the island, so you have a choice of terrain for your trail ride: a breathtaking ride through Haleakala Crater, or a backwoods ride out at the Seven Sacred Pools. Unfortunately, none of this comes cheap. In comparison, a bale of alfalfa, which goes for under $5 on the Mainland, fetches $18-22 on Maui. If you plan to do some serious riding, it's advisable to bring jeans (jogging suit bottoms will do) and a pair of boots, or at least jogging shoes.

The Rainbow Ranch

The Rainbow Ranch is operated by Kimo Harlacher and his top hands. You'll have your choice of rides: beginners ride daily at 9 a.m., $25, gentle horses; sunset, mountain, pineapple field, and extended rides for experienced riders, $35-50; The West Maui Adventure, $45 for two hours, runs through the foothills of the mountains; picnic rides (bring your own) depart at 10 and return at 1 p.m., $50. No dress code, but long pants and close-toed shoes required. Rainbow Ranch, P.O. Box 10066, Lahaina, HI 96761, tel. 669-4991, is located at mile marker 29 along Rt. 30 toward Kapalua.

Holo Lio And Makena Stables

Recently opened, these stables provide unique overnight camping at La Perouse Bay. Located just past Polo Beach in Wailea on the road to Makena, you can't go wrong with these local cowpokes who have an old-fashioned love and respect for the land, tel. 879-1085.

Makena Stables, tel. 879-0244, is nearby on Old Makena Road, where Helaine and Pat Borge will take you on a 2½-hour ride through low-elevation rangeland, lava flows, and along the mountain trails of Ulupalakua Ranch.

Haleakala And Environs

A few Upcountry companies offer trail rides through the crater or over the mountain. Wear *warm* clothes! Here are some of the best: **Charley's Trailride and Pack Trips** takes you overnight camping in Haleakala, arranging for cabins and supplying all meals. Run by

Charles Aki, c/o Kaupo Store, Hana, HI 96713, tel. 248-8209. **Pony Express Tours** offers Maui's only trail rides into Haleakala crater. Full day $123, partial day $98; lunch provided. One- and two-hour rides ($25 and $45 respectively) are also offered across private ranch land high on the slope of this volcanic mountain. Write Pony Express Tours, P.O. Box 535, Kula, HI 96790, tel. 667-2200. **Thompson Ranch Riding Stables** guides you over the slopes of Haleakala on one of Maui's oldest cattle ranches. Write Thompson Stables, Thompson Rd., Kula, HI 96790, tel. 878-1910.

Adventures On Horseback offers waterfall rides along the north coast for $125, maximum six riders. Call 242-7445 for reservations and information, or write P.O. Box 1771, Makawai, Maui, HI 96768.

Kau Lio Stables

Just near Lahaina, they offer two-hour rides leaving at 9 a.m., 10 a.m., and at 1:15 p.m., $53-67, and a sunset ride leaving at 4:15 p.m., $67. They're located on private land, so they'll pick you up in Kaanapali. Write P.O. Box 16056, Kaanapali Beach, HI 96761, tel. 667-7896.

Hotel Hana-Maui Stables

The hotel guests are given priority for use of the horses, but you can call ahead to arrange a trail ride on this truly magnificent end of the island. For information call 248-7238.

TENNIS AND GOLF

Maui specializes in these two sports. The two high-class resort areas of Kaanapali and Wailea are built around golf courses, with tennis courts available all over the island. See the charts on pp. 128 and 129 for more information.

HUNTING

Most people don't think of Hawaii as a place to hunt, but actually it's quite good. Seven species of introduced game animals and 16 species of game birds are regularly hunted, 12 each on Maui, Molokai, and Lanai. Some species of game animals are restricted on all islands, but every island offers hunting.

TENNIS COURTS OF MAUI

COUNTY COURTS

Under jurisdiction of the
Department of Parks & Recreation
200 High St., Wailuku, Maui.
Phone: 244-7750
Courts listed are in or near visitor areas.
There are Three additional locations around the island.

Name	Location	No. of Courts	Lighted
Hana	Hana Ball Park	2	Yes
Kahului	Kahului Community Center	2	Yes
Kihei	Kalami Park	4	Yes
Kihei	Seaside of Maui Sunset Condo	4	Yes
Lahaina	Lahaina Civic Center	8	Yes
Lahaina	Malu-ulu-olele Park	4	Yes
Makawao	Eddie Tam Memorial Center	2	Yes
Pukalani	Pukalani community Center	2	Yes
Wailuku	Maui Community College Tel. 244-9181 Courts available after school hours	4	No
Wailuku	Wailuku Community Center	7	Yes
Wailuku	Wailuku War Memorial	4	Yes

HOTEL AND PRIVATE COURTS
OPEN TO THE PUBLIC (fees vary)

Kaanapali	Maui Marriott Resort	5	No
Napili Bay	Napili Kai Beach Club	2	No
Kaanapali	Royal Lahaina Hotel	11	6 are
Kaanapali	Sheraton Maui Hotel	3	Yes
Kapalua	Tennis Club	10	4 Yes
Wailea	Wailea Tennis Club	14	3 are
Makena	Makena Tennis Club	6	No

General Hunting Rules

Hunting licenses are mandatory to hunt on public, private, or military land anywhere in Hawaii. They're good for one year beginning July 1. Hunting licenses cost $7.50 residents, $15 nonresidents, senior citizens free. Licenses are available from sporting goods stores and the various offices of the Division of Forestry

GOLF COURSES OF MAUI

* = Weekday and special twilight rates in effect. Call for details.

Course	Holes	Par	Yards	Rates	Cart
* Kapalua Golf Club, Bay Course	18	72	6,761	$70	Incl.
Villa Course	18	71	6,632	$70	Incl.
Kapalua, HI 96791 669-8044					
* Makena Golf Course	18	72	6,739	$90	Incl.
Kinei, HI 96753 879-3344					
Maui Country Club, Front Course	9	37	3,148	$35	Incl.
Back Course	9	37	3,247	$35	Incl.
Paia, HI 96779 877-0616 (Monday only for visitors)					
Pukalani Country Club	18	72	6,945	$34	$11
Pukalani, HI 96788 572-1314					
* Royal Kaanapali North Course	18	70	6,734	$90	Incl.
South Course	18	72	6,758	$90	Incl.
Kaanapali, HI 96761 661-3691					
Waiehu Municipal Golf Course	18	72	6,330	$25	$12.50
Waiehu, HI 96793 243-7300					
Wailea Golf, Blue Course	18	72	6,743	$105	Incl.
Orange Course	18	72	6,810	$105	Incl.
Wailea, HI 96753 879-2966					
* Silversword Golf Course	18	71	6,6801	$50	Incl.
Kihei, HI 96753 874-0777					

and Wildlife (see below), which also sets and enforces the rules, so contact them with any questions. Generally hunting hours are from a half-hour before to a half-hour after sunset. At times there are "checking stations" where the hunter must check in before and after hunting.

Rifles must have greater than a 1,200-foot-pound muzzle velocity. Shot-guns larger than .20 gauge are allowed, and muzzleloaders must have a .45 caliber bore or larger. Bows must have a minimum draw of 45 pounds for straight bows and 30 pounds for compounds. Arrows must be broadheads. Dogs are permitted only with some birds and game, and smaller caliber rifles and shotguns are permitted with their use, along with spears and knives. Hunters must wear orange safety cloth on their chest and backs no smaller than a 12-inch square. Certain big game species are hunted only by lottery selection; contact the Division of Forestry and Wildlife two months in advance. Guide service is not mandatory, but is advised if you're unfamiliar with hunting in Hawaii. You can hunt on private land only with permission, and you must possess a valid hunting license. Guns and ammunition brought into Hawaii must be registered with the chief of police of the corresponding county within 48 hours of arrival.

Information

Hunting rules and regulations are always subject to change. Also, environmental considerations often change bag limits and seasons. Make sure to check with the Division of Forestry and Wildlife for the most current information. Request "Rules Regulating Game Bird Hunting, Field Trails and Commercial Shooting Preserves," "Rules Regulating Game Mammal

feral pig (LOUISE FOOTE)

Hunting," and "Hunting in Hawaii." Direct inquiries to: Dept. of Land and Natural Resources, Division of Forestry and Wildlife Office, 1151 Punchbowl St., Honolulu, HI 96813, tel. 548-2861; on Maui, 54 S. High St., P.O. Box 1015, Wailuku, HI 96793, tel. 243-5352.

Game Animals

All game animals in Hawaii have been introduced. Some are adapting admirably and becoming well entrenched, while the survival of others is still precarious. **Axis deer** originated in India and were brought to Lanai and Molokai, where they're doing well. The small herd on Maui is holding its own. Their unique flavor makes them one of the best wild meats; they're hunted on Molokai and Lanai in March and April by public lottery. **Feral pigs** are escaped domestic pigs and are found on all islands except Lanai. The stock is a mixture of

gray francolin (LOUISE FOOTE)

original Polynesian pigs and all that came later. Hunted with dogs and usually killed with a spear or long knife, pig hunting is not recommended for the timid or tender-hearted. These beasts' four-inch tusks and fighting spirits make them tough and dangerous. Feral goats come in a variety of colors. Found on all islands except Lanai, they have been known to cause erosion and are considered a pest in some areas, especially on Haleakala. Openly hunted on all islands, their meat when properly cooked is considered delicious.

Game Birds

A number of game birds are found on most of the islands. Bag limits and hunting seasons vary, so check with the Division of Forestry and Wildlife for details. **Ring-necked pheasants** are one of the best game birds, and found on all the islands. **Green pheasants** are found on Maui. **Francolins,** gray and black, from India and the Sudan, are similar to partridges. They are hunted with dogs and taste great roasted. There are also **chukar** from Tibet, found on the slopes of all islands; **quails**, including the Japanese and California varieties; **doves;** and the wild Rio Grande **turkey.**

GONE FISHING

Surrounding Maui are some of the most exciting and productive "blue waters" in all the oceans and seas of the world. Here you can find the "sport-fishing fleet," made up of skippers and crews who are experienced professional anglers. You can also fish from jetties, piers, rocks, and from shore. If rod and reel don't strike your fancy, try the old-fashioned "throw net," or take along a spear when you go snorkeling or scuba diving. There's nighttime torch fishing that requires special skills and equipment, and freshwater fishing in public areas. Streams and irrigation ditches yield introduced trout, bass, and catfish. While you're at it, you might want to try crabbing for Kona and Samoan crabs, or working low-tide areas after sundown hunting squid (really octopus), a long-time island delicacy.

The Game Fish

The most thrilling game fish in Hawaiian waters is marlin. These are generically known as "billfish" or *a'u* to the locals. The king of them is the blue marlin, with record catches well over 1,000 pounds. There's also striped marlin and sailfish, which often go over 200 pounds. The best times for marlin are during spring, summer, and fall. The fishing tapers off in January and picks up again by late February. "Blues" can be caught year-round, but, oddly enough, when they stop biting it seems as though the striped marlin pick up. Second to the marlin are tuna. *Ahi* (yellowfin tuna) are caught in Hawaiian waters at depths of 100-1,000 fathoms. They can weigh 300 pounds, but between 25 and 100 pounds is common. There are also *aku*, skipjack tuna, and the delicious *ono*, which averages between 20 and 40 pounds.

Mahi mahi is another strong, fighting, deep-water game fish abundant in Hawaii. These delicious eating fish can weigh up to 70 pounds. Shorefishing and baitcasting yield *papio*, a jack tuna. *Akule*, a scad (locally called *halalu*,) is a smallish schooling fish that comes close to shore and is great to catch on light tackle. *Ulua* are shore fish and can be found in tidepools. They're excellent eating, average two to three pounds, and are taken at night or with spears. *O'io* are bonefish that come close to shore to spawn. They're caught baitcasting and bottomfishing with cut bait. They're bony, but they're a favorite for fish cakes and *poki*. *Awa* is a schooling fish that loves brackish water. It can get up to three feet long, and is a good fighter. A favorite for "throw-netters," it's even raised commercially in fishponds. Besides these there are plenty of goatfish, mullet, mackerel, snapper, various sharks, and even salmon (see p. 104).

Deep-sea Fishing

Most game-fishing boats work the blue waters on the calmer leeward sides of the islands. Some skippers, carrying anglers who are accustomed to the sea, will also work the much rougher windward coasts and island channels where the fish bite just as well. Trolling is the preferred method of deep-sea fishing; this is

The Salty Dog *takes passengers in search of "the big one."* (BOB NILSEN)

done usually in waters of between 1,000-2,000 fathoms. The skipper will either "area fish," which means running in a crisscrossing pattern over a known productive area, or "ledge fish," which involves trolling over submerged ledges where the game fish are known to feed. The most advanced marine technology, available on many boats, sends sonar bleeps searching for fish. On deck, the crew and anglers scan the horizon in the age-old Hawaiian tradition. They're searching for seabirds clustered in an area, feeding on baitfish which have been pursued to the surface by the huge and aggressive game fish. Some "still fishing" or bottomfishing, with hand lines, yields some tremendous fish.

Deep-sea Fishing Boats

Deep-sea fishing on a **share basis** costs approximately $65-80 half day (four hours) and

$110-145 full day. On a **private basis,** expect $300-350 half day, $500-600 full day. Some of the best boats at Maalaea Harbor include: **Salty Dog,** with Capt. Joe; **Excel,** tel. 877-3333; **Excaliber,** the largest boat in the harbor; **Carol Ann,** tel. 877-2181; and **No Ka Oi III,** tel. 879-4485, run by Ocean Activities Center. In Lahaina you can't go wrong with the **Judy Ann,** tel. 667-6672, or **Aerial Sportfishing,** tel. 667-9089.

Freshwater Fish

Hawaii has only one native freshwater game fish, the *o'opu.* This goby is an oddball with fused ventral fins. They grow to be 12 inches and are found on all islands, especially Kauai. Introduced species include largemouth and smallmouth bass, bluegills, catfish, tucunare, oscar, carp, and tilapia. The only trout to survive is the rainbow, found only in the streams of Kauai. The tucunare is a tough, fighting, good-tasting game fish introduced from South America, similar to the oscar, from the same region. Both have been compared to bass, but are of a different family. Tilapia are from Africa and have become common in Hawaii's irrigation ditches. They're "mouth breeders" and the young will take refuge there even a few weeks after hatching. Snakehead are eel-like fish that inhabit the reservoirs and are great fighters. Channel catfish can grow to over 20 pounds and bite best after sundown. There are also carp, and with their broad tail and tremendous strength, they are the poor man's game fish. All of these species are best caught with light spinning tackle, or with a bamboo pole and a trusty old worm.

Fishing Licenses

Hawaiian fishing licenses are good from July 1 to June 30. Licenses cost $7.50 for nonresidents, $3.75 for tourists (good for 30 days), $3.75 for residents and military personnel, $1.50 for children between nine and 15 years old, and free to senior citizens. Licenses are obtained from the Division of Conservation and Resources Enforcement (on Oahu, tel. 548-8766) or from most sporting goods stores. For free booklets and information write Division of Aquatic Resources, 1151 Punchbowl St., Honolulu, HI 96813. All game fish may be taken year-round, except for trout, which may be taken for 16 days commencing on the first Saturday of August. Thereafter, for the remainder of August and September, trout can be taken only on Saturdays, Sundays, and state holidays.

As there is no freshwater fishing on Maui (Molokai or Lanai), no licenses are issued. Shoreline and recreational fishing is permitted without a license. For additional information, contact the Division of Aquatic Resources, Kahului, at tel. 244-2072.

HEALTH AND WELL-BEING

In a recent survey published by *Science Digest,* Hawaii was cited as the healthiest state in the Union to live in. Indeed, Hawaiian citizens live longer than anywhere else in America: men to 74 years and women to 78. Lifestyle, heredity, and diet help with these figures, but Hawaii is still an oasis in the middle of the ocean, and germs just have a tougher time getting there. There are no cases of malaria, cholera, or yellow fever. Because of a strict quarantine law, rabies is also nonexistent. On the other hand, tooth decay, perhaps because of a wide use of sugar and the enzymes present in certain tropical fruits, is 30% above the national average. With the perfect weather, a multitude of fresh-air activities, soothing negative ionization from the sea, and a generally relaxed and carefree lifestyle, everyone feels better there. Hawaii is just what the doctor ordered: a beautiful natural health spa. That's one of the main drawing cards. The food and water are per-

fectly safe, and the air quality is the best in the country.

Handling The Sun

Don't become a victim of your own exuberance. People can't wait to strip down and lie on the sand like a beached whale, but the tropical sun will burn you to a cinder if you're silly. The burning rays come through easier in Hawaii because of the sun's angle, and you don't feel them as much because there's always a cool breeze. The worst part of the day is from 11 a.m. until 3 p.m. You'll just have to force yourself to go slowly. Don't worry; you'll be able to flaunt your best souvenir, your golden Hawaiian tan, to your green-with-envy friends when you get home. It's better than showing them a boiled lobster body with peeling skin! If your skin is snowflake white, 15 minutes per side on the first day is plenty. Increase by 15-minute intervals every day, which will allow you a full hour per side by the fourth day. Have faith; this is enough to give you a deep golden uniform tan.

Haole Rot

A peculiar condition caused by the sun is referred to locally as *haole* rot. It's called this because it supposedly affects only white people, but you'll notice some dark-skinned people with the same condition. Basically, the skin becomes mottled with white spots that refuse to tan. You get a blotchy effect, mostly on the shoulders and back. Dermatologists have a fancy name for it, and they'll give you a fancy prescription with an even fancier price tag to cure it. It's common knowledge throughout the islands that Selsun Blue shampoo has some ingredient that stops the white mottling effect. Just wash your hair with it and then make sure to rub the lather over the affected areas, and it should clear up.

Bugs

Everyone, in varying degrees, has an aversion to vermin and creepy crawlers. Hawaii isn't infested with a wide variety, but it does have its share. Mosquitos were unknown in the islands until their larvae stowed away in the water barrels of the *Wellington* in 1826 and were introduced at Lahaina. They bred in the tropical climate and rapidly spread to all the islands. They are a particular nuisance in the rainforests. Be prepared, and bring a natural repellent like citronella oil, available in most health stores on the islands, or a commercial product available in all groceries or drugstores. Campers will be happy to have mosquito coils to burn at night as well.

Cockroaches are very democratic insects. They hassle all strata of society equally. They breed well in Hawaii and most hotels are at war with them, trying desperately to keep them from being spotted by guests. One comforting thought is that in Hawaii they aren't a sign of filth or dirty housekeeping. They love the climate like everyone else, and it's a real problem keeping them under control.

WATER SAFETY

Hawaii has one very sad claim to fame: more people drown here than anywhere else in the world. Moreover, there are dozens of yearly victims of broken necks, backs, and scuba and snorkeling accidents. These statistics shouldn't keep you out of the sea, because it is indeed beautiful, benevolent in most cases, and a main reason to go to Hawaii. But if you're foolish, the sea will bounce you like a basketball and suck you away for good. The best remedy is to avoid situations you can't handle. Don't let anyone dare you into a situation that makes you uncomfortable. "Macho men" who know nothing about the power of the sea will be tumbled into a Cabbage Patch doll in short order. Ask lifeguards or beach attendants about conditions, and follow their advice. If local people refuse to go in, there's a good reason. Even experts get in trouble in Hawaiian waters. Some beaches, such as Waikiki, are as gentle as a lamb and you would have to tie an anchor around your neck to drown there. Others, especially on the north coasts during the winter months, are frothing giants.

While beachcombing, or especially when walking out on rocks, never turn your back to the sea. Be aware of undertows (the waves drawing back into the sea). They can knock you off your feet. Before entering the water, study it for rocks, breakers, reefs, and riptides. Riptides are powerful currents, like rivers in the sea, that can drag you out. Mostly they peter out not too far from shore, and you can often see their choppy waters on the surface. If caught in a "rip," don't fight to swim directly against it; you'll lose and only exhaust yourself. Swim diagonally across it, while going along with it, and try to stay parallel to the shore. Don't waste all your lung power yelling, and rest by floating.

When bodysurfing, never ride straight in; come to shore at a 45-degree angle. Remember, waves come in sets. Little ones can be followed by giants, so watch the action awhile instead of plunging right in. Standard procedure is to duck under a breaking wave. You can even survive thunderous oceans using this technique. Don't try to swim through a heavy froth and never turn your back and let it smash you. Don't swim alone if possible, and obey all warning signs. Hawaiians want to entertain you and they don't put up signs just

This "denizen of the deep" is much more afraid of you than you are of him.
(HOWARD LENDEMAN)

to waste money. The last rule is, "If in doubt, stay out."

Yikes!

Sharks live in all the oceans of the world. Most mind their own business and stay away from shore. Hawaiian sharks are well fed—on fish —and don't usually bother with unsavory humans. If you encounter a shark, don't panic! Never thrash around because this will trigger their attack instinct. If they come close, scream loudly. Portuguese men-o-war put out long floating tentacles that sting if they touch you. Don't wash it off with fresh water, as this will only aggravate it. Hot salt water will take away the sting, as will alcohol, the drinking or rubbing kind, after-shave lotion, and meat tenderizer (MSG), which can be found in any supermarket or Chinese restaurant. Coral can give you a nasty cut, and it's known for causing infections because it's a living organism. Wash it immediately and apply an antiseptic. Keep it clean and covered, and watch for infection.

Poisonous sea urchins, such as the lacquer-black *wana,* can be beautiful creatures. They are found in shallow tidepools and can only hurt you if you step on them. Their spines will break off, enter your foot, and burn like blazes. There are cures. Vinegar and wine poured on the wound will stop the burning. If not available, the Hawaiian method is urine. It might be ignominious to have someone pee on your foot, but it'll put the fire out. The spines will disintegrate in a few days, and there are generally no long-term effects. Hawaiian reefs also have their share of moray eels. These creatures are ferocious in appearance, but will never initiate an attack. You'll have to poke around in their holes while snorkeling or scuba diving to get them to attack. Sometimes this is inadvertent on the diver's part, so be careful where you stick your hand while underwater.

HAWAIIAN
FOLK MEDICINE AND CURES

Hawaiian folk medicine is well developed, and its cures for common ailments have been used effectively for centuries. Hawaiian *kahuna* were highly regarded for their medicinal skills, and Hawaiians were by far some of the healthiest people in the world until the coming of the Europeans. Many folk remedies and cures are used to this day and, what's more, they work. Some of the most common plants and fruits that you'll encounter provide some of the best remedies. When roots and seeds and special exotic plants are used, the preparation of the medicine is as painstaking as in a modern pharmacy. These prescriptions are exact and take an expert to prepare. They should never be prepared or administered by an amateur.

Common Curative Plants

Arrowroot, for diarrhea, is a powerful narcotic used in rituals and medicines. The pepper plant *(Piper methisticum)* is chewed and the juice is spat into a container for fermenting. Used as a medicine in urinary tract infections, rheumatism, and asthma, it also induces sleep and cures headaches. A poultice for wounds is made from the skins of ripe bananas. Peelings have a powerful antibiotic quality and contain vitamins A, B, and C, phosphorous, calcium, and iron. The nectar from the plant was fed to babies as a vitamin juice. Breadfruit sap is used for healing cuts and as a moisturizing lotion. Coconut is used to make moisturizing oil, and the juice was chewed, spat into the hand, and used as a shampoo. Guava is a source of vitamins A, B, and C. Hibiscus has been used as a laxative. *Kukui* nut oil is a gargle for sore throats, a laxative, and the flowers are used to cure diarrhea. *Noni* reduces tumors, diabetes, high blood pressure, and the juice is good for diarrhea. Sugar cane sweetens many concoctions, and the juice of toasted cane was a tonic for sick babies. Sweet potato is used as a tonic during pregnancy, and juiced as a gargle for phlegm. Tamarind is a natural laxative, and contains the most acid and sugar of any fruit on earth. Taro has been used for lung infections, thrush, and as suppositories. Yams are good for coughs, vomiting, constipation, and appendicitis.

HELP FOR THE DISABLED

A physically disabled person can have a wonderful time in Hawaii; all that's needed is a little pre-planning. The following is general advice that should help with your planning.

Commission On The Handicapped

This commission is a source of invaluable information and distributes self-help booklets free of charge. Any handicapped person heading to Hawaii should write first or visit their offices on arrival. For a *Handicapped Travelers Guide* to each of the four islands, write or visit the head office at Commission on the Handicapped, Old Federal Bldg., 335 Merchant St., no. 215, Honolulu, HI 96813, tel.

KUKUI (CANDLENUT)

Reaching heights of 80 feet, the kukui (candlenut) was a veritable department store to the Hawaiians, who made use of almost every part of this utilitarian giant. Used as a cure-all, its nuts, bark, or flowers were ground into potions and salves and taken as a general tonic, applied to ulcers and cuts as an effective antibiotic, or administered internally as a cure for constipation or asthma attacks. The bark was mixed with water and the resulting juice was used as a dye in tattooing, tapa cloth making, canoe painting, and as a preservative for fishnets. The oily nuts were burned as a light source in stone holders, and ground and eaten as a condiment called inamona. Polished nuts took on a beautiful sheen and were strung as leis. Lastly, the wood itself was hollowed into canoes and used as fishnet floats.

(808) 548-7606; on Maui, 54 High St., Wailuku, HI 96793, tel. 243-5441.

General Information

The key for a smooth trip is to make as many arrangements ahead of time as possible. Here are some tips concerning transportation and accommodations. Tell the companies concerned of the nature of your handicap in advance so that they can make arrangements to accommodate you. Bring your medical records and notify medical establishments of your arrival if you'll be needing their services. Travel with a friend or make ar-

rangements for an aide on arrival (see below). Bring your own wheelchair if possible and let airlines know if it is battery powered; boarding inter-island carriers requires steps. No problem. They'll board you early on special lifts, but they must know that you're coming. Many hotels and restaurants accommodate disabled persons, but always call ahead just to make sure.

Maui Services
On arrival at Kahului Airport, parking spaces are directly in front of the main terminal. The restaurant here has steps, so food will be brought to you in the cocktail lounge. There are no special emergency medical services,

but visitor information is available at tel. 877-6431. There is no centralized medical service, but Maui Memorial Hospital in Wailuku will refer, tel. 244-9056. Getting around can be tough because there is no public transportaion on Maui, and no tours or companies to accommodate non-ambulatory persons. However, both Hertz and Avis rent cars with hand controls. Health care is provided by **Maui Center for Independent Living,** tel. 242-4966. Medical equipment is available at Hawaiian Rentals, 877-7684, and Maui Rents, tel. 877-5827. Special recreation activities referrals are made by Easter Seal Society, tel. 877-4443, or by the Commission on Persons with Disabilities, tel. 244-4441.

CONDUCT

ILLEGAL DRUGS

The use and availability of illegal, controlled, and recreational drugs are about the same in Hawaii as throughout the rest of America. Cocaine constitutes the fastest growing recreational drug, and it's available on the streets of the main cities, especially Honolulu. Although most dealers are small-time, the drug is brought in by organized crime. The underworld here is mostly populated by men of Asian descent, and the Japanese *yakuza* is said recently to be displaying a heightened involvement in Hawaiian organized crime. Cocaine trafficking fans out from Honolulu.

A new drug menace hitting the streets is known as "ice." Ice is smokable methamphetamine that will wire a user for up to 24 hours. The high lasts longer, and is cheaper, than cocaine or its derivative, "crack." Users become quickly dependent, despondent, and violent because ice robs them of their sleep, along with their dignity. Its use is particulairly prevalent among late-night workers. Many of the violent deaths in Honolulu have been linked to the growing use of ice. Not as prevalant as on Oahu, ice is making inroads onto the streets of Maui.

However, the main drug available and commonly used in Hawaii is marijuana, which is locally called *pakalolo*. There are also three

varieties of psychoactive mushrooms that contain the hallucinogen psilocybin. They grow wild, but are considered illegal controlled substances.

Pakalolo Growing

About 20 years ago, mostly *haole* hippies from the Mainland began growing pot in the more remote sections of the islands, such as Puna on Hawaii and around Hana on Maui. They discovered what legitimate planters had known for 200 years: plant a broomstick in Hawaii, treat it right, and it'll grow. *Pakalolo,* after all, is only a weed, and it grows in Hawaii like wildfire. The locals quickly got into the act when they realized that they, too, could grow a "money tree." As a matter of fact, they began resenting the *haole* usurpers, and a quiet and sometimes dangerous feud has been going on ever since. Much is made of the viciousness of the backcountry "growers" of Hawaii. There are tales of booby traps and armed patrols guarding their plants in the hills, but mostly it's a cat and mouse game between the authorities and the growers. If you, as a tourist, are tramping about in the forest and happen upon someone's "patch," don't touch anything. Just back off and you'll be OK. Pot has the largest monetary turnover of any crop in the islands, and as such, is now considered a major source of agricultural revenue.

There are all kinds of local names for pot in Hawaii, the most potent being "Kona Gold," "Puna Butter," and "Maui Wowie." Actually, these names are all becoming passe. Today the generic term for the best pot is "buds." You can ask a likely person for pot, but mostly dealers will approach you. Their normal technique is to stroll by, and in a barely audible whisper say, "Buds?"

Hawaiian *pakalolo* is sold slightly differently than on the Mainland. The dealers all seem to package it in those heat-sealed "Seal-a-Meal" plastic bags. The glory days are over, and many deals are rip-offs.

THEFT AND HASSLES

From the minute you sit behind the wheel of your rental car, you'll be warned about not leaving valuables unattended and locking your car up tighter than a drum. Signs warning about theft at most major tourist attractions help to fuel your paranoia. Many hotel rooms offer coin-operated safes, so you can lock your valuables away and be able to relax while getting sunburned. Stories abound about purse snatchings and surly locals who are just itching to give you a hard time. Well, they're all true to a degree, but Hawaii's reputation is much worse than the reality. In Hawaii you'll have to observe two golden laws: if you look for trouble, you'll find it; and, a fool and his camera are soon parted.

Theft

The majority of theft in Hawaii is of the "sneak thief" variety. If you leave your hotel door unlocked, a camera sitting on the seat of your rental car, or valuables on your beach towel, you'll be inviting a very obliging thief to pad away with your stuff. You have to learn to take precautions, but they won't be anything like those employed in rougher areas like South America or Southeast Asia; just normal American precautions.

If you must walk alone at night, stay on the main streets in well-lit areas. Always lock your hotel door and windows and place all valuable jewelry in the hotel safe. When you leave your hotel for the beach, there is absolutely no reason to carry all your traveler's checks,

credit cards, or a big wad of money. Just take what you'll need for drinks and lunch. If you're uptight about leaving any money in your beach bag, just stick it in your bathing suit or bikini. American money is just as negotiable if it is damp. Don't leave your camera or portable stereo on the beach unattended. Ask a person nearby to watch them for you while you go for a dip. Most people won't mind at all, and you can repay the favor.

While sightseeing in your shiny new rental car, which immediately brands you as a tourist, again, don't take more than what you'll need for the day. Why people leave a camera sitting on the seat of their car is a mystery! Many people lock valuables away in the trunk, but remember most good car thieves can "jimmy" it as quickly as you can open it with your key. If you must, for some reason, leave your camera or valuables in your car, lock them in the trunk or consider putting them under the hood. Thieves usually don't look there and on most modern cars, you can only pop the hood with a lever on the inside of the car. It's not failsafe, but it's worth a try.

Campers face special problems because their entire scene is open to thievery. Most campgrounds don't have any real security, but

who, after all, wants to fence an old tent or a used sleeping bag? Many tents have zippers that can be secured with a small padlock. If you want to go trekking and are afraid to leave your gear in the campgrounds, take a large green garbage bag with you. Transport your gear down the trail and then walk off through some thick brush. Put your gear in the garbage bag and bury it under leaves and other light camouflage. That's about as safe as you can be. You can also use a variation on this technique instead of leaving your valuables in your rental car.

Hassles

Another self-perpetuating myth about Hawaii is that "the natives are restless." An undeniable animosity exists between locals, especially those with some Hawaiian blood, and *haole*. Fortunately, this prejudice is directed mostly at the group and not at the individual. The locals are resentful against those *haole* who came, took their land, and relegated them to second-class citizenship. They realize that this is not the average tourist and they can tell what you are at a glance. Tourists usually are treated with understanding and are given a type of immunity. Besides, Hawaiians are still among the most friendly, giving, and understanding people on earth.

Haole who live in Hawaii might tell you stories of their children having trouble at school. They could even mention an unhappy situation at some schools called "beat-up-a-*haole*" day, and you might hear that if you're a *haole* it's not a matter of "if" you'll be beaten up, but "when." Truthfully, most of this depends upon your attitude and your sensitivity. The locals feel infringed upon, so don't fuel these feelings. If you're at a beach park and there is a group of local people in one area, don't crowd them. If you go into a local bar and you're the only one of your ethnic group in sight, you shouldn't have to be told to leave. Much of the hassle involves drinking. Booze brings out the worst prejudice on all sides. If you're invited to a beach party, and the local guys start getting drunk, make this your exit call. Don't wait until it's too late.

Most trouble seems to be directed toward white men. White women are mostly immune from being beaten up, but they have to beware of the violence of sexual abuse and rape. Although plenty of local women marry white men, it's not a good idea to try to pick up a local girl. If you're known in the area and have been properly introduced, that's another story. Also, girls out for the night in bars or discos can be approached if they're not in the company of local guys. If you are with your bikini-clad girlfriend, and a bunch of local guys are, say, drinking beer at a beach park, don't go over and try to be friendly and ask, "What's up?" You, and especially your girlfriend, just might find out. Maintain your own dignity and self-respect by treating others with dignity and respect. Most times you'll reap what you sow.

WHAT TO TAKE

It's a snap to pack for a visit to Maui. Everything is on your side. The weather is moderate and uniform on the whole, and the style of dress is delightfully casual. The rule of thumb is to pack lightly: few items, and light clothing both in color and weight. What you'll need will depend largely on your itinerary and your desires. Are you drawn to the nightlife, the outdoors, or both? If you forget something at home, it won't be a disaster. You can buy everything you'll need in Hawaii. As a matter of fact, Hawaiian clothing, such as muumuus and aloha shirts, are some of the best purchases you can make, both in comfort and style. It's quite feasible to bring only one or two changes of clothing with the express purpose of outfitting yourself while there. Prices on bathing suits, bikinis, and summer wear in general are quite reasonable.

Matters Of Taste

A grand conspiracy in Hawaii adhered to by everyone—tourist, traveler, and resident—is to "hang loose" and dress casually. Best of all, alohawear is just about all you'll need for virtually every occasion, and for comfort. The classic muumuu is large and billowy, and aloha shirts are made to be worn outside of the pants. The best of both are made of cool cotton. Rayon is a natural fiber that isn't too bad, but polyester is hot, sticky, and not authentic. Not all muumuus are of the "tent persuasion." Some are very fashionable and form-fitted with peek-a-boo slits up the side, down the front, or around the back. *Holomuus* are muumuus fitted at the waist with a flowing skirt to the ankles. They are not only elegant, but perfect for "stepping out."

In The Cold And Rain

Two occasions for which you'll have to consider dressing warmly are visiting the top of mountains, and going for boat rides where wind and ocean sprays are a factor. You can conquer both with a jogging suit (sweat suit) and a featherweight, water-resistant windbreaker. If you're intending to visit Haleakala, it'll be downright chilly. Your jogging suit with a hooded windbreaker/raincoat will do the trick for all occasions. If you're going to camp or trek, you should add another layer, the best being a woollen sweater. Wool is the only fiber that retains most of its warmth-giving properties even if it gets wet. If your hands get cold, put a pair of socks over them. Tropical rain showers can happen at any time, so you might consider a fold-up umbrella; but the sun quickly breaks through and the warming winds blow.

Shoes

Dressing your feet is hardly a problem. You'll most often wear zoris (rubber thongs) for going to and from the beach, leather sandals for strolling and dining, and jogging shoes for trekking and sightseeing. A few discos require leather shoes, but it's hardly worth bringing them just for that. If you plan on heavy-duty trekking, you'll definitely want your hiking boots. Lava, especially *a'a,* is murderous on shoes. Most backcountry trails are rugged and muddy, and you'll need those good old lug soles for traction. If you plan moderate hikes, you might want to consider bringing rubberized ankle supports to complement your jogging shoes. Most drug stores sell them, and the best are a rubberized sock with toe and heel cut out.

Specialty Items

Following is a list of specialty items that you might consider bringing along. They're not necessities but most will definitely come in handy. A pair of binoculars really enhances sightseeing—great for watching birds, sweeping panoramas, and almost a necessity if you're going whalewatching. A folding Teflon-bottomed travel iron makes up for cotton's one major shortcoming, wrinkles, and you can't always count on hotels having irons. Consider also nylon twine and miniature clothespins for drying garments, especially bathing suits. Commercial and hotel laundromats abound, but many times you'll get by with hand washing a few items in the sink. A transistor radio/tape recorder provides news, weather, entertainment, and can be used to record impres-

sions, island music, and a running commentary for your slide show. Hair dryer: although the wind can be relied on to dry, it leaves a bit to be desired in the styling department. An inflatable raft for riding waves, along with flippers, mask and snorkel, can easily be bought in Hawaii, but don't really weigh that much or take up much space in your luggage. If you'll be camping, trekking, or boating with only sea water available for bathing, take along "Sea Saver Soap," available from good sporting goods stores. This special soap will lather in sea water and rinse away the sticky salt residue with it.

For The Camper

If you don't want to take it with you, all necessary camping gear can be purchased or rented while in Hawaii. Besides the above, you should consider taking the following: framed backpack or the convertible packs that turn into suitcases; daypack; matches in a waterproof container; all-purpose knife; mess kit; eating utensils; flashlight (remove batteries); candle; nylon cord; and sewing kit (dental floss works as thread). Take a first-aid kit containing Band-aids, all-purpose antiseptic cream, alcohol swabs, tourniquet string, cotton balls, an elastic bandage, razor blade, Telfa pads, and a small mirror for viewing private nooks and crannies. A light sleeping bag is good, although your fleecy jogging suit with a ground pad and covering of a light blanket or even your rain poncho will be sufficient. Definitely bring a down bag for Haleakala or mountainous areas, and in a film container pack a few nails, safety pins, fish hooks, line, and bendable wire. Nothing else does what these do and they're all handy for a million and one uses. (See also p. 117.)

Basic Necessities

As previously mentioned, you really have to consider only two "modes" of dressing in Hawaii: beachwear and casual clothing. The following is designed for the mid-range traveler carrying one suitcase or a backpack. Remember there are laundromats and you'll be spending a considerable amount of time in your bathing suit. Consider the following: one or two pairs of light cotton slacks for going out and about, and one pair of jeans for trekking, or better yet, corduroys which can serve both purposes; two or three casual sundresses—muumuus are great; three or four pairs of shorts for beachwear and for sightseeing; four to five short-sleeved shirts or blouses and one long-sleeved; three or four colored and printed T-shirts that can be worn anytime from trekking to strolling; a beach cover-up with the short terrycloth-type being the best; a brimmed hat for rain and sun—the crushable floppy type is great for purse or daypack; two or three pairs of socks are sufficient, nylons you won't need; two bathing suits, nylon ones dry quickest; plastic bags to hold wet bathing suits and laundry; five to six pair of underwear; towels (optional, because hotels provide them, even for the beach); a first-aid kit, pocket size is sufficient; suntan lotion, insect repellent; a daypack or large beach purse; and don't forget your windbreaker, perhaps a shawl for the evening, and a universal jogging suit.

INFORMATION

Emergency
To summon the police, fire department, or ambulance to any part of Maui, dial 911. This help number is available throughout the island. **Helpline,** the island's crisis center, is tel. 244-7407. **Maui Memorial Hospital,** Mahalani St., Wailuku, tel. 244-9056. **Pharmacies:** Kahului, tel. 877-0041; Kihei, tel. 879-8499; Lahaina, tel. 661-3119; Pukalani, tel. 572-8244.

Information
The state operates two **visitors' kiosks** at Kahului Airport. Open daily, 6 a.m. to 9 p.m., tel. 877-6431, plenty of practical brochures. **Hawaii Visitor's Bureau,** 380 Dairy Road, Kahului, tel. 871-8691 is open Mon. to Fri., 8 a.m. to 4:30 p.m. **Teleguide,** tel. 877-3324, is a 24-hour telephone activities information service. Use a touch-tone phone to enter a four-digit code for particular tourist information desired. Brochures listing codes can be picked up at any tourist literature stand. **On Call,** tel. 244-8934, offers free service also using touch-tone codes (see front of telephone book) to access community service, entertainment, shopping, news, sports, and cultural information. The **Maui Chamber of Commerce** is located at 26 Puunene Ave., Kahului, tel. 871-7711; for **consumer complaints,** call 243-5387. For **time,** call 242-0212.

Before you leave for the islands, information can be accessed from the *Official Recreation Guide* through travel agents who have a Sabre hookup. Among other items, information can be garnered on transportation, travel activities, and cultural events, and reservations can be made.

Reading Material
For bookstores try **Waldenbooks,** at Maui Mall, Kahului, tel. 877-0181, Kaahumanu Shopping Center, tel. 871-6112, Lahaina Cannery Shopping Center, tel. 667-6172, at Whaler's Village, tel. 661-8638, and at the Kukui Mall, tel. 874-3688. There's also **The Whalers Book Shoppe** at The Wharf, Front St., Lahaina, tel. 667-9544.

Libraries: main branch at 251 High St., Wailuku, tel. 243-5945, other branches in Kahului, Lahaina, Makawao, Kihei, and Hana. A hodgepodge of hours through the week, usually closed Fri. or Saturday.

Free tourist literature is well done and loaded with tips, discounts, maps, happenings, etc. Found in hotels, restaurants, and street stands. They include: *This Week Maui,* every Friday; *Guide to Maui* on Thursdays; *Maui Beach Press,* newspaper format and in-depth articles, every Friday; *Maui Gold,* one for each season; *Drive Guide,* excellent

The "HVB Warrior" is posted alongside the roadway, marking sites of cultural and historical importance.

maps and tips, given out free by all car rental agencies, bi-monthly; **TV Maui,** a weekly television and entertainment guide with feature articles and local events; and **A Taste of Maui,** all about food. Newspapers include the **Maui News,** a local newspaper for 25 cents, good "Datebook" listings of local events, published Mon. to Fri., tel. 244-3981. **The Gold Coast News** has local-interest stories; **Lahaina News** is a community paper of news, feature stories, and entertainment listings; **Island Living** specializes in dining and entertainment; the **Island Calendar of Events** is an alternative "event and networking newsletter;" **ECO Report** is an environmental paper with local and global focus; and to keep abreast of what's happening on the local scene read the **Kama'aina News.**

Parks And Recreation
State Parks in Wailuku, tel. 243-5354; County Parks in Wailuku, tel. 243-7230; Haleakala National Park HQ, tel. 527-7749.

Weather And Whales
For all Maui weather, tel. 877-5111; for recreational areas, tel. 877-5054; for Haleakala, tel. 571-5054; for marine weather, tel. 877-3477; for whale sighting and reports in season, tel. 661-8527.

Post Offices
In Wailuku, tel. 244-4815; in Kahului, tel. 871-4710; in Kihei, tel. 879- 2403; in Lahaina, tel. 667-6611. Other branch offices are scattered around the island.

Legal Help
For any legal problems, or advice while on Maui, contact **Padgett and Henry,** at 2099 Wells St., Wailuku, tel. 244-5514. They specialize in personal injury, and are well versed in the special problems that a tourist can have if they're involved in an accident. Husband-and-wife team Matthew and Elizabeth have a good and solid reputation.

Maui Facts
Maui is the second youngest and second largest Hawaiian island after Hawaii. Its nickname is the Valley Island. Its color is pink and its flower is the *lokelani,* a small rose.

HAWAII VISITOR'S BUREAU OFFICES
Hawaii
The main HVB administration office is at Waikiki Business Plaza, 2270 Kalakaua Ave., Suite 801, Honolulu, HI 96815, tel. 923-1811. On Maui, 380 Dairy Rd., Kahului, HI 96732, tel. 871-8691. On Kauai, 3016 Umi St., Lihue HI 96799, tel. 245-3971. Hawaii has two branches: Hilo Plaza, 180 Kinoole St., Suite 104, Hilo HI 96720, tel. 961-5797, and 75-5719 W. Alii Dr., Kailua-Kona, HI 96740, tel. 329-7787.

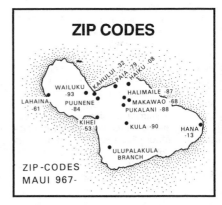

ZIP CODES

ZIP-CODES
MAUI 967-

North America
441 Lexington Ave., Room 1407, New York, N.Y. 10017, tel. (212) 986-9203. 1511 K St. N.W., Suite 415, Washington, D.C. 20005, tel. (202) 393-6752. 180 N. Michigan Ave. Suite 1031, Chicago, IL 60601, tel. (312) 236-0632. Central Plaza, 3440 Wilshire Blvd. Room 502, Los Angeles, CA 90010, tel. (213) 385-5301. Suite 450, 50 California St., San Francisco, CA 94111, tel. (415) 392-8173.

Canada
4915 Cedar Crescent, Delta, B.C., Canada V4M 1J9, tel. (604) 943-8555.

United Kingdom
c/o First Public Relations Ltd., 16 Bedford Sq., London WC 1B 3JH, England.

Australia
c/o Walshes World, 92 Pitt St., Sydney, N.S.W. 2000.

Asian Offices
Japan, 129 Kokusai Bldg., 1-1 Marunouchi 3-chome, Chiyoda-ku, Tokyo 100; **Indonesia,** c/o Pacific Leisure, Jalan Prapatan 32, Jakarta; **Hong Kong,** c/o Pacific Leisure, Suite 1001, Tung Ming Bldg., 40 Des Voeux Rd., Central Hong Kong; **Philippines,** c/o Philippine Leisure Inc., Interbank Bldg., 111 Paseo de Roxas, Makati, Metro Manila; **Korea,** c/o Bando Air, Room 1510, Ankuk Insurance Bldg., 87, 1-ka, Eulchi-ro, Chung Ku, Seoul 100; **Singapore,** c/o Pacific Leisure, #03-01 UOL Bldg., 96 Somerset Rd., Singapore 0923; **Thailand,** c/o Pacific Leisure, 542/1 Ploenchit Rd., Bangkok; other offices are found through Pacific Leisure in **Kuala Lumpur, Penang,** and **Taipei.**

MONEY AND FINANCES

Currency
U.S. currency is among the drabbest in the world. It's all the same size and color; those unfamiliar with it should spend some time getting acquainted so that they don't make costly mistakes. U.S. coinage in use is: $.01, $.05, $.10, $.25, $.50, and $1 (uncommon); paper currency is $1, $2 (uncommon), $5, $10, $20, $50, $100. Bills larger than $100 are not in common usage.

Banks
Full-service banks tend to open slightly earlier than Mainland banks, at 8:30 a.m. Mon. through Friday. Closing is at 3 p.m., except for late hours on Fri. when most banks remain open until 6 p.m. Of most value to travelers, banks sell and cash traveler's checks, give cash advances on credit cards, and exchange and sell foreign currency.

Traveler's Checks
Traveler's checks are accepted throughout Hawaii at hotels, restaurants, car rental agencies, and in most stores and shops. However, to be readily acceptable they should be in American currency. Some larger hotels that often deal with Japanese and Canadians will accept their currency. Banks accept foreign-currency traveler's checks, but it'll mean an extra trip and inconvenience.

Credit Cards
More and more business is transacted in Hawaii using credit cards. Almost every form of accommodation, shop, restaurant, and amusement accepts them. For renting a car they're almost a must. With "credit card insurance" readily available, they're as safe as traveler's checks and sometimes even more convenient. Don't rely on them completely because there are some establishments that won't accept them, or perhaps won't accept the kind that you carry.

OTHER PRACTICALITIES

Telephone: All-Hawaii Area Code 808
Like everywhere else in the U.S., long-distance rates go down at 5 p.m. and again at 11 p.m. until 8 a.m. the next morning. From Fri. at 5 p.m. until Mon. morning at 8 a.m. rates are cheapest. Local calls from public telephones (anywhere on the same island is a local call) cost 25 cents. Calling between islands is a toll call, and the price depends on when and from where you call and for how long you speak. Emergency calls are always free. The area code for the entire state of

MEASUREMENTS

Distance, weights, and measures: Hawaii, like all of the U.S., employs the "English method" of measuring weights and distances. Basically, dry weights are in ounces and pounds; liquid measures are in ounces, quarts and gallons; and distances are measured in inches, feet, yards, and miles. The metric system, based on units of 10, is known but is not in general use. The following conversion charts should be helpful.

1 inch = 2.54 centimeters (cm)
1 foot = .304 meters (m)
1 mile = 1.6093 kilometers (km)
1 km = .6214 miles
1 fathom = 1.8288 m
1 chain = 20.1168 m
1 furlong = 201.168
1 acre = .4047 hectares (ha)
1 sq km = 100 ha
1 sq mile = 59 sq km
1 ounce = 28.35 grams
1 pound = .4536 kilograms (kg)
1 short ton = .90718 metric ton
1 short ton = 2000 pounds
1 long ton = 1.016 metric tons
1 long ton = 2240 pounds
1 metric ton = 1000 kg
1 quart = .94635 liters
1 US gallon = 3.7854 liters
1 Imperial gallon = 4.5459 liters
1 nautical mile = 1.852 km

To compute centigrade temperatures, subtract 32 from Fahrenheit and divide by 1.8. To go the other way, multiply centigrade by 1.8 and add 32.

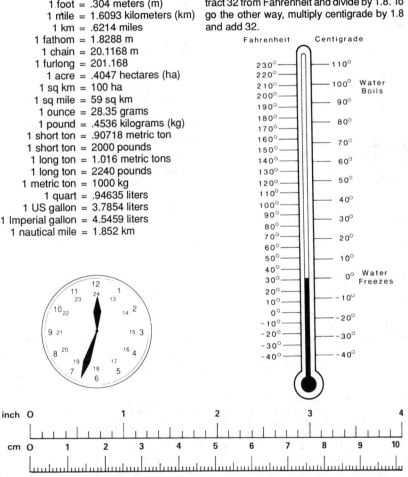

Hawaii is 808. For directory assistance: local, 1-411; inter-island, 1-555-1212; Mainland, 1-area code-555-1212; toll free, (800) 555-1212.

Time Zones

There is no "daylight saving time" observed in Hawaii. When daylight saving time is not observed on the Mainland, Hawaii is two hours behind the West Coast, four hours behind the Midwest, and five hours behind the East Coast. Hawaii, being just east of the International Date Line, is almost a full day behind most Asian and Oceanic cities. Hours behind these countries and cities are: Japan, 19 hours; Singapore, 18 hours; Sydney, 20 hours; New Zealand 22 hours; Fiji 22 hours.

Electricity

The same electrical current applies in Hawaii as on the U.S. Mainland and is uniform throughout the islands. The system functions on 110 volts, 60 cycles of alternating current (AC). Appliances from Japan will work, but there is some danger of burnout, while those requiring the normal European current of 220 will not work.

Distance, Weights, And Measures

Hawaii, like all of the U.S., employs the "English method" of measuring weights and distances. Basically, dry weights are in ounces and pounds; liquid measures are in ounces, quarts, and gallons; and distances are measured in inches, feet, yards, and miles. The metric system, based on units of 10, is known but is not in general use. The accompanying conversion charts should be helpful.

Storage

As there are no storage facilities at the Kahului Airport, private storage companies must be used. Try **Store and Lock,** tel. 871-4240, in Kahului for various-sized lockers—daily, weekly, or monthly rates. Others can be found through the phonebook. For guests of the Northshore Inn and Valley Isla Lodge in Wailuku, an alternative is to use the on-site storage rooms for everything from backpacks to surfboards and bicycles.

CENTRAL MAUI: THE ISTHMUS

KAHULUI

It is generally believed that Kahului means "The Winning," but perhaps it should be "The Survivor." Kahului suffered attack by Kamehameha I in the 1790s, when he landed his war canoes here in preparation for battle at Iao Valley. In 1900 it was purposely burned to thwart the plague, then rebuilt. Combined with Wailuku, the county seat just down the road, this area is home to 22,000 Mauians, over one-third of the island population. Here's where the people live. It's a practical, homey town, the only deep-water port from which Maui's sugar and pineapples are shipped. Although Kahului was an established sugar town by 1880, it's really only grown up in the last 20 years. In the 1960s, Hawaiian Commercial and Sugar Co. began building low-cost housing for its workers which became a model development for the whole of the U.S. Most people land at the airport, blast through for Lahaina or Kihei, and never give Kahului a second look. It's in no way a resort community, but it has the best general-purpose shopping on the island, a few noteworthy sites, and a convenient location to the airport.

SIGHTS

Kanaha Pond Wildlife Sanctuary
This one-time royal fishpond is 1½ miles southwest of the airport at the junctions of Routes 36 and 37. It's on the migratory route of various ducks and Canada geese, but most importantly it is home to the endangered Hawaiian stilt *(ae'o)* and the Hawaiian coot *(alae ke'oke'o)*. The stilt is a slender, 16-inch bird with a black back, white belly, and stick-like pink legs. The coot is a gray-black duck-like bird, which builds large floating nests. An observation shelter is maintained along Route 37. Kanaha Pond is always open and free of charge. Bring binoculars.

Maui Community College
Just across the street from the Kaahumanu Shopping Center on Route 32, the college is a good place to check out the many bulletin boards for various activities, items for sale, and cheaper long-term housing. The **Student Center** is conspicuous as you drive in, and is

a good place to get most information. The library is adequate.

Maui Zoo And Botanical Gardens

These grounds are more aptly described as a children's park. Plenty of young families enjoy themselves in this fenced-in area. The zoo houses various colorful birds such as cockatoos, peacocks, and macaws, as well as monkeys, baboons, and a giant tortoise that looks like a slow-moving boulder. The chickens, ducks, and swans are run-of-the-mill, but the ostriches, over seven feet tall, are excellent specimens. With pygmy goats and plenty of sheep, the atmosphere is like a kiddies' petting zoo. It's open daily 9 a.m. to 4 p.m., free. Turn at the red light onto Kanaloa Avenue off Route 32 about midway between Kahului and Wailuku.

Also at this turn is **Wailuku War Memorial Park and Center.** Here you'll find a stadium, gymnasium, swimming pool, and free hot showers. To the left, at the entrance to the gym, you can pick up county camping permits (see p. 114).

Alexander And Baldwin Sugar Mill Museum

The museum is located at the intersection of Puunene Ave. (Rt. 350) and Hanson Rd., about one-half mile from Dairy Rd. (Rt. 380), tel. 871-8058, open Mon.-Sat. 9:30 a.m. to 4 p.m., admission $2 adults, children $1, 5 and under admitted free. (Avoid the area around 3 p.m. when the still-working mill changes shifts.) This small but highly informative museum could easily be your first stop after arriving at Kahului Airport only 15 minutes away (especially if you're heading to Kihei). Once you get off the plane, you'll realize that you're in the midst of sugar cane fields, and if you want to know the history of this crop and the people who worked and developed it, visit the museum. The vintage building was the home of the sugar mill supervisor, who literally lived surrounded by his work. Inside is a small but well-stocked bookstore and shop featuring Hawaiiana and handmade clothing and artifacts, with goodies like passionfruit syrup and raw sugar. One of the unique items for sale are *waraji*, Japanese sandals fashioned from bulrushes by a 92-year-old *sensei*, Kinichi

Hawaiian stilt
(LOUISE FOOTE)

Tasaka from Kauai. These sandals are traditional in Japan, often used by pilgrims to the 88 Sacred Temples of Shikoku, and for making the climb up Mt. Fuji. This is a dying handicraft even in Japan, so take the opportunity to see and to buy these distinctive gifts from days gone by.

As you begin your tour, notice the ancient refrigerator in the corner that the staff still uses. In the first room, you are given a brief description of the natural history of Maui, along with a rendition of the legends of the demigod Maui. Display cases explain Maui's rainfall and use of irrigation for a productive sugar cane yield. There is an old-fashioned copper rain gauge along with pragmatic artifacts from the building of the Haiku Ditch. A collection of vintage photos feature the Baldwin and Alexander families, while a historical plaque recalls when workers lived in ethnic camps, each with its own euphemistic name (Chinese at Ah Fong, Japanese at Nashiwa,

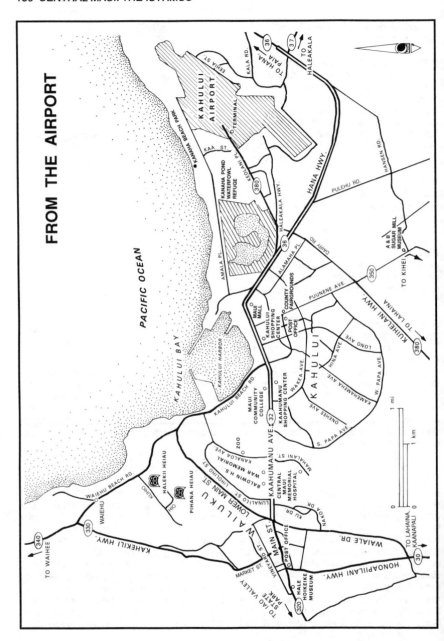

FROM THE AIRPORT

Portuguese at Cod Fish). This setup was designed to discourage competition (or cooperation) between the ethnic groups during labor disputes, and to ease the transition to the new land. These people are represented by everything from stuffed fighting cocks to baseball mitts from the '30s. The museum is in the shadow of the mill, and you can hear the wheels turning and the mill grinding. It's not an antiseptic remembrance, but a vital one where the history still continues.

Kanaha Beach Park

This is the only beach worth visiting in the area. Good for a swim and a picnic. Follow Route 380 toward the airport and turn left on Kaa Street. Alternately, from Kaahumanu Avenue, turn left onto Hobron Avenue, and then immediately right onto Amala Street, and follow the signs to the park. It's also *the* best place to begin learning sailboarding. The wind is steady but not too strong, and the wave action is gentle.

ACCOMMODATIONS

Kahului features motel/hotels because most people are short-term visitors, heading to or from the airport. These accommodations are all bunched together across from the Kahului Shopping Center on the harbor side of Kaahumanu Avenue (Rt. 32). The best are the **Maui Beach Hotel,** tel. 877-0051, and just across a parking lot, its sister hotel, **The Maui Palms,** tel. 877- 0071. The Maui Beach has a pool on the second floor, and its daily buffet is good value. The central courtyard, tastefully landscaped, is off the main foyer, which has a Polynesian flavor. The Red Dragon Room provides the only disco (Fri. and Sat. nights) on this part of the island. Rates for the Maui Beach are $79-138, and $61-74 at the Maui Palms ($10 less in the off season). For reservations, call (800) 367-5004, inter-island (800) 272-5275. The one other hotel, 100 yards to the east, is the **Maui Seaside,** (now combined with the Maui Hukilau) tel. 877-3311, part of the Sand and Seaside Hotels, an island-owned chain. Rates are $55-79, $71-95 with rental car. For reservations, call (800) 367-7000.

FOOD

The Kahului area has some elegant dining spots as well as an assortment of inexpensive yet good eating establishments. Many are found in the shopping malls. Here are some of the best.

Inexpensive

Ma Chan's, tel. 877-7818, is a terrific little "no atmosphere" restaurant in the **Kaahumanu Shopping Center** (Kaahumanu Ave.) offering Hawaiian, American, and Asian food—breakfast, lunch, or dinner. Order the specials, such as the shrimp dinner, and for under $5 you get soup, salad, grilled shrimp, rice, and garnish. No credit cards, but friendly island waitresses, and good quality. Also in the center, **The Coffee Store,** tel. 871-6860, is open daily 7:30 a.m. to 6 p.m., till 9 p.m. on Thurs. and Friday, Sat. 8 a.m. to 6 p.m. and Sun. 10 a.m. to 4 p.m. Follow your nose to the delightful smell of coffee and you'll find a bright and airy new shop. Light lunch includes savories like a hot croissant at $1.40 to a spinach roll pastry puff for $3.95. Coffees by the cup under $2.25, refills 35 cents. The coffees, roasted on the premises, are from 40 gourmet varieties hand-picked in Africa, South America, and Indonesia, and include exotic beans like Jamaican Blue Mountain. Gifts and giftwear too! Or try the **Original Maui Sweet Baked Ham** deli for any of their filling sandwiches, deli salads, soup, or lunch baskets (great for the trip to Hana). Their gift shop has "hog" motif items in keeping with their motto: "Maui No Ka Oink." Located in the Old Kahului Store.

The **Maui Mall** has a terrific selection of inexpensive eateries. **Matsu Restaurant,** tel. 877-0822, is a quick-food Japanese restaurant with an assortment of daily specials for under $4, or a steaming bowl of various types of saimin for $3.80. Very authentic, like a *sobaya* in Japan, nothing great but downhome. Japanese standards include *katsu don buri,* tempura, or curry rice, all for under $5. Adjacent is **Siu's Chinese Kitchen**: most of their typical Chinese dishes are under $4. **Sir Wilfred's,** tel. 877-3711, is another gourmet coffee shop that offers a commodious setting for sipping a hot brew and eating their gourmet sandwiches, like hot pastrami, for under $5. A good place for an inexpensive lunch with some atmosphere. **Luigi's Pizza Factory** serves up decent pizza.

At counter seating in the back of **Toda Drugs,** locals enjoy daily specials of Hawaiian and other ethnic foods. Better than you'd think! Daily special under $5. In the Kahului Mall, open daily 8:30 a.m. to 4 p.m., tel. 877-4550. Next door you'll find **Ichiban,** another authentic and inexpensive Japanese restaurant.

Others worth trying include **Shirley's** and **Dairy Queen,** near each other on Lono Avenue. Both serve good and inexpensive plate lunches and sandwiches, and Shirley's is open early mornings.

Finally, for those who need their weekly fix of something fried and wrapped in styrofoam, Kahului's main streets are dotted with McDonald's (Puunene Ave.), Pizza Hut (Kamehameha Ave.), Burger King (Kaahumanu Ave.), and Kentucky Fried Chicken (Wakea Ave.); there are more at Maui and Kaahumanu malls.

Moderate

The Maui Beach Hotel's **Rainbow Dining Room** serves food in the second-floor dining room. You can fill up here at their lunch buffet from 11 a.m to 2 p.m., $6.50 ($5.50 salad bar only), or come for dinner from 6 to 9 p.m. (except Mon.) to the **Red Dragon Restaurant** for their "Cantoneese Buffet Dinner," offered for a very reasonable $9.95 ($5.25 children under 11). Prime rib and seafood dinners are also served. Breakfast (from 7 a.m.) features fresh-baked goods from $5.75. For reservations, call 877-0051.

Maui Palms Hotel's **East-West Dining Room,** offers an "Imperial Tepanyaki Japanese Buffet," every day from 5:30 to 8:30 p.m. for $15. The food, although plentiful, is prepared for the undiscerning conventioneer, and is either fried to death or a generic mish-mash of Japanese cuisine. All-you-can-eat salad bar daily for lunch, 11 a.m to 1 p.m., $6, tel. 877-0071.

Across from the Maui Mall is **Aurelio's,** tel. 871-7656, that presents a selection of Italian dishes, with most pasta priced around $5.50,

plate lunches like shrimp marinade, $6.75, hamburger steak, $5.50. Early-bird specials Mon.-Sat. from 5 to 6:30 p.m. offer New York steak at $9.95, or chicken teriyaki, $8.95.

At **Ming Yuen,** tel. 871-7787, for under $9 you can dine on Chinese treats such as braised oysters with ginger and scallions. The hot-and-sour soup ($5.25) is almost a meal in itself. Inexpensive lunch from 11 a.m to 5 p.m. except Sun., dinner 5 to 9 p.m. daily. Behind the Maui Mall at 162 Alamaha St., off E. Kamehameha Avenue. Cantonese and Sichuan specialties. Reservations suggested, take out also available.

Across the street from Ming Yuen is **Lopaka's Bar and Grill,** tel. 871-1135. Open for lunch and dinner Mon.-Sat. 11 a.m. to closing, there is entertainment nightly—no cover. Lunches are mostly burgers, salads, plate lunches, sandwiches for less than $7.75, and full steak, seafood, or chicken dinners for up to $10.95

Vi's Restaurant, tel. 877-3311, is at the Maui Seaside Hotel. Breakfast from 7 to 9:30 a.m., dinner 6 to 8 p.m. Vi's offers over 20 dinners for under $10. Breakfast includes omelettes, hot cakes, and other island favorites.

Expensive

The Chart House, on Kahului Bay at 500 N. Puunene Ave. (also in Lahaina), is a steak and seafood house that's not really expensive. This is a favorite with businesspeople and travelers in transit to or from the airport. The quality is good and the atmosphere is soothing. Open for dinner daily 5:30 to 10 p.m., tel. 877-2476.

Mickey's, tel. 871-7555, is the only really elegant restaurant in Kahului. Located in the Kahului Building at 33 Lono Ave., they specialize in island fish, prepared seven different ways. Open for lunch with slightly cheaper prices. Expect to spend $17 and up per person for dinner.

Liquor

Maui Wine and Liquor at 333 Dairy Road (out near the airport), tel. 871-7006, is an excellent liquor store. They have an enormous wine selection, over 80 different types of imported beer, and even delivery service. For a quick

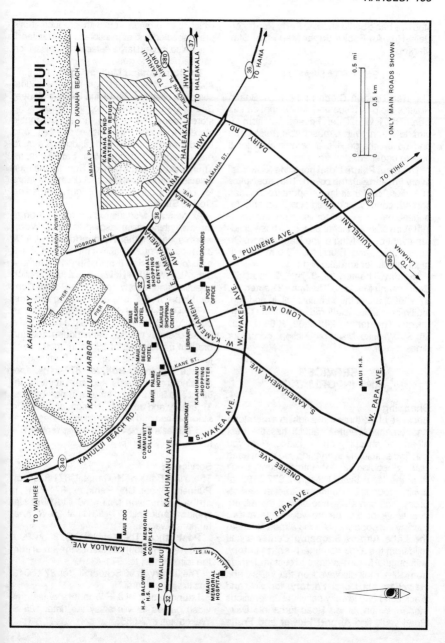

stop at a basic bottle shop try **Party Pantry** on Dairy Rd., **Ah Fooks Super Market,** or **Star Market.**

ENTERTAINMENT

The **Red Dragon Disco** at the Maui Beach Hotel is the only disco and dance spot on this side of the island. Open Fri. and Sat. from 10 p.m. to 2 a.m. With a reasonable dress code and cover charge, it's a favorite with local people under 25.

The **Maui Palms Hotel** hosts the "Sakuras" every Fri. and Sat. (no cover). They specialize in "oldies," and their large repertoire includes Top 40, country, and even Hawaiian and Japanese ballads. Good for listening and dancing! A favorite with local people, whose children might be partying at the Red Dragon. On Tues., Wed., and Thurs. from 8 p.m. to midnight stop in for karoake night.

Holiday Theater, tel. 877-6622, is at the Kaahumanu Mall, and **The Maui Theater,** tel. 877-3560, are at the Kahului Mall. In addition, legitimate theater is offered by the **Maui Community Theater,** tel. 242-6969, at 68 N. Market St., Wailuku. Major productions occur four times a year.

SERVICES AND INFORMATION

Shopping

Because of the three malls right in a row along Kaahumanu Avenue, Kahului has the best all-around shopping on the island. Here you can find absolutely everything you might need (see "Shopping" in the Introduction). Don't miss the **Maui Swap Meet,** tel. 877-3100, at the fairgrounds on Puunene Street every Saturday. You can also shop almost the minute you arrive or just before you leave at two touristy but good shops along Airport Road. At the **Little Airport Shopping Center** a half mile from the airport are the **T- shirt Factory,** with original Maui designs and custom T-shirts from $7-19 (all displayed on the walls), and **Hawaiian Alii Coral Factory,** for pink and black coral and jewelry set with semiprecious stones. When Airport Road turns into Dairy Road you'll find **Airport Flower and Fruits** which can provide you with produce that's pre-inspected and admissible to the Mainland. They also have a large selection of leis which can be packed to go.

The **Kaahumanu Mall,** along Kaahumanu Avenue, is the largest and has the widest selection of stores. You'll find **Liberty House, Sears, Ben Franklin's,** apparel stores, shoe stores, computer centers, art shops, music stores, a dozen inexpensive eateries, and **Waldenbooks,** tel. 871-6112, open 9 a.m. to mall closing at 5:30 p.m. Mon.-Sat., 9 p.m. on Thur. and Fri., and 3 p.m. on Sun. for the best selection of books on Maui. A great new store for a relaxing cup of coffee or light lunch is **The Coffee Store.**

At the **Maui Mall** just up the road is **Longs** for everything from aspirin to film, **Woolworth's,** and another **Waldenbooks,** tel. 877-0181, open Mon.-Thurs. 9 a.m. to 6 p.m., Fri. 9 a.m. to 9 p.m., Sat. 9-5:30, Sun. 10 a.m. to 4 p.m. Also, **Wow! of Hawaii** has a full selection of action and resortwear, and a **Postal Center,** Mon.-Fri., 9-5, offers full mailing services.

The **Old Kahului Store Mall** is just that, an old building from 1916 that held a bank and a series of shops that has been modernized and brought back to life, at 55 Kaahumanu Ave., just across from the Maui Mall. Some shops include **Lightning Bolt,** tel. 877-3484, specializing in surfboards and surf attire by Instinct and Billy Long; women's apparel stores, **Tiger Lily** and **Jazzed; Tropica,** another surf store; a futon and furniture shop; a video store; and **Tester's Shoe Repair,** which repairs Birkenstocks ($21.50!).

Services

There is a **Bank of Hawaii,** tel. 871-8250, on Puunene Street. **City Bank,** tel. 871-7761, is at the Kaahumanu Mall. And find **First Hawaiian Bank,** tel. 877- 2311, at 20 W. Kaahumanu Avenue.

Post office: The Kahului P.O. is on Puunene Ave. (Rt. 350) just across the street from the fairgrounds, tel. 871-4710.

The library, at 90 School St., tel. 877-5048, has irregular hours.

Laundromat: W & F Washerette features video games to wile away the time, 125 S. Wakea, tel. 877-0353.

WAILUKU

Often, historical towns maintain a certain aura long after their time of importance has passed. Wailuku is one of these. Today Maui's county seat, the town has the feel of one that has been important for a long time. Wailuku earned its name, "Bloody Waters," from a ferocious battle fought by Kamehameha I against Maui warriors just up the road in Iao Valley. The slaughter was so intense that over four miles of the local stream literally ran red with blood. Last century the missionaries settled in Wailuku, and their architectural influences, such as a white-steepled church and the courthouse at the top of the main street, give an impression of a New England town.

Wailuku is a pretty town, especially in the back streets. Built on the rolling foothills of the West Maui Mountains, this adds some character—unlike the often flat layout of many other Hawaiian towns. You can "do" Wailuku in only an hour, though most people don't even give it this much time. They just pass through on their way to Iao Needle, where everyone goes, or to Happy Valley and on to Kahakuloa, around the backside, where the car companies hope that no one goes. You *can* see Wailuku's sights from the window of your car, but don't short-change yourself this way. Definitely visit the Bailey House, now called **Hale Hoikeike,** and while you're out, walk the grounds of **Kaahumanu Church.** Market Street, just off Main, has a clutch of intriguing shops that you can peek into while you're at it. With new restaurants, art galleries, community theater, and a cultural center, Wailuku is starting to take on the trappings of a cultural center.

SIGHTS

Kaahumanu Church

It's fitting that Maui's oldest existing stone church is named after the resolute but loving Queen Kaahumanu. This rock-willed woman is the "Saint Peter" of Hawaii, upon whom Christianity in the islands was built. She was *the* most important early convert, often attending services in Kahului's humble grass hut chapel. In 1832 an adobe church was built on the same spot and named in her honor. Rain and time washed it away, to be replaced by the island's first stone structure in 1837. In 1876 the church was reduced to about half its original size, and what remained is the white and green structure we know today. Oddly enough, the steeple was repaired in 1984 by Skyline Engineers, who hail from Massachusetts, the same place from which the missionaries came 150 years earlier! You can see the church sitting there on High Street (Rt. 30), but it's usually closed during the week. Sunday services are at 9 a.m., when the Hawaiian congregation sings the Lord's praise in their native language. An excellent cultural and religious event to attend!

Kaahumanu Church (J.D. BISIGNANI)

Hale Hoikeike

This is the old **Bailey House,** built from 1833-50, with various rooms added throughout the years. In the 1840s it housed the "Wailuku Female Seminary," of which Edward Bailey was principal until it closed in 1849. Bailey then went on to manage the Wailuku Sugar Company. More important for posterity, he became a prolific landscape painter of various areas around the island. Most of his paintings record the period from 1866 through 1896 and are now displayed in the "annex," known as the Bailey Gallery. This one-time seminary dining room was his actual studio. In July 1957 this old missionary homestead formally became the Maui Historical Society Museum, at which time it acquired its new name of Hale Hoikeike, "House of Display." It closed in 1973, then was refurbished and reopened in July 1975.

You'll be amazed at the two-foot-thick walls the missionaries taught the Hawaiians to build, using goat hair as the binding agent. Years of whitewashing make them resemble new-fallen snow. The rooms inside are given over to various themes. **The Hawaiian Room** houses excellent examples of the often practical artifacts of pre-contact Hawaii; especially notice the fine displays of tapa cloth and calabashes. Hawaiian tapa, now a lost art, was considered Polynesia's finest and most advanced. Upstairs is the bedroom. It's quite large and dominated by a canopied bed.

There's a dresser with a jewelry box and fine lace gloves. Peek behind the wooden gate in the rear of the bedroom to see swords, dolls, walking canes, toys, and muskets—now only a jumble, one day they'll be a display. Upstairs at the front of the house is the old office. Here you'll find roll-top desks, ledgers, and excellent examples of old-time wicker furniture, prototypes of examples you still see today. Downstairs you'll discover the sitting room and kitchen, heart of the house: the "feelings" are strongest here. There are excellent examples of Hawaiian adzes, old silverware, and plenty of photos. The lintel over the doorway is as stout as the spirits of the people who once lived here. The stonework on the floor is well laid and the fireplace is totally homey.

Go outside! The lanai runs across the entire front and down the side. Around back is the canoe shed, housing accurate replicas of Hawaiian-sewn sennit outrigger canoes, as well as Duke Kahanamoku's redwood surfboard. On the grounds you'll also see exhibits of sugar cane, sugar pots, *konane* boards, and various Hawaiian artifacts. Hale Hoikeike is open daily 10 a.m. to 4:30 p.m., on Main Street (Rt. 320) on your left, just as you begin heading for Iao Valley. Admission is well worth $2 (children 50 cents). Usually self-guided, but tour guides are available free if arrangements are made in advance. The bookstore/gift shop has a terrific selection of souvenirs and Hawaiiana at better-than-average prices. The office of the Maui Historical Society is in the basement.

Kepaniwai Park

As you head up Route 320 to Iao Valley, you're in for a real treat. Two miles after leaving Wailuku, you come across Kepaniwai Park and Heritage Gardens. Here the architect, Richard C. Tongg, envisioned and created a park dedicated to all of Hawaii's people. See the Portuguese villa and garden complete with an outdoor oven, a thatch-roofed Hawaiian grass shack, a New England "salt box," a Chinese pagoda, a Japanese teahouse with authentic garden, and a bamboo house, the little "sugar shack" that songs and dreams are made of. Admission is free and there are

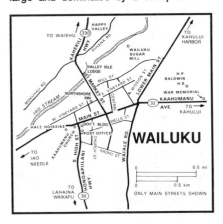

TO WAIEHU (330)

HAPPY VALLEY

KANEHA HWY.

PIIHANA RD.

TO KAHULUI HARBOR

WAILUKU SUGAR MILL

VALLEY ISLE LODGE

MILL ST.

VINEYARD ST.

H.P. BALDWIN H.S.

MOKUHAU RD.

MARKET ST.

NORTHSHORE INN

MISSION ST.

LOWER MAIN ST.

HIGH ST.

W. VINEYARD ST.

WAR MEMORIAL

KAAHUMANU (32) AVE.

TO KAHULUI

IAO STREAM

MAIN ST.

WELLS ST.

HALE HOIKEIKE

GOV'T. BLDG.

KAAHUMANU CHURCH

POST OFFICE

S. HIGH ST.

KAOHU ST.

WAIALE RD.

WAILUKU

TO IAO NEEDLE

HONOAPIILANI HWY.

TO LAHAINA WAIKAPU (30)

0   0.5 mi

0   0.5 km

ONLY MAIN STREETS SHOWN

a Japanese pagoda at Kepaniwai (J.D. BISIGNANI)

Maui Tropical Plantation

This new attraction is somewhat out of the ordinary. The Maui Tropical Plantation presents a model of a working plantation which you can tour by small tram. Most interesting is an up-close look at Maui's agricultural abundance. Displays of each of these products are situated around the taro patches at the plantation village. An $8 ($3 for children), 45-minute tram ride (optional) takes you through fields of cane, banana, mango, papaya, pineapple, and macadamia nuts; flowers here and there add exotic color. The plantation, with a restaurant, gift shop, and tropical flower nursery, is in Waikapu, a small village along Route 30 between Wailuku and Lahaina. Open daily 9 a.m. to 5 p.m., tel. 244-7643. As an added attraction, have your photo taken with a brightly feathered parakeet or cockatiel and transformed into a picture postcard (overnight service) by **Birds of Paradise.** Buddy Fo's **Hawaiian Country Show** is put on here Mon., Wed., and Fri. evenings, 5-9 p.m. (see "Luaus" in the general Introduction for more information).

pavilions with picnic tables. This now tranquil spot is where the Maui warriors fell to the invincible Kamehameha and his merciless patron war-god, Ku. *Kepaniwai* means "Damming of the Waters"—literally with corpses. Kepaniwai is now a monument to man's higher nature: harmony and beauty.

John F. Kennedy Profile

Up the road toward Iao Valley you come to a scenic area long known as Pali Ele'ele, or Black Gorge. This stream-eroded amphitheater canyon has attracted attention for centuries. Amazingly, after President Kennedy was assassinated, people noticed his likeness portrayed there by a series of large boulders; mention of a profile had never been noted or recorded there before. A pipe stuck in the ground serves as a rudimentary telescope. Squint through it and there he is, with eyes closed in deep repose. The likeness is uncanny, and easily seen, unlike most of these formations, where you have to stretch your imagination to the breaking point.

Tropical Gardens Of Maui

This private garden of tropical flowers and fruits is located on the way to Iao Valley, tel. 244-3085, open 9 a.m. to 5 p.m., admission $4 to the gardens. The gift shop has a good display of flowers, certified for mailing to the Mainland, also a deli counter for sandwiches, burgers, ice cream, and beverages.

IAO VALLEY STATE PARK

This valley has been a sacred spot and a place of pilgrimage since ancient times. Before Westerners arrived, the people of Maui, who came here to pay homage to the "Eternal Creator," named this valley *Iao,* "Supreme Light." In the center of this velvety green valley is a pillar of stone rising over 1,200 feet (actual height above sea level is 2,250 feet), that was at one time a natural altar. Now commonly called "The Needle," it's a tough basaltic core that remained after water swirled away the weaker stone surrounding it. Iao Valley is actually the remnant of the volcanic caldera of the West Maui Mountains, whose grooved walls have been smoothed and enlarged by the restlessness of mountain streams. Robert Louis Stevenson had to stretch poetic license to create a word for Iao when he called it "viridescent."

The road here ends in a parking lot, where signs point you to a myriad of paths that crisscross the valley. The paths are tame and well maintained, some even paved, with plenty of vantage points for photographers. If you take the lower path to the river below, you'll find a good-sized and popular swimming hole; but remember, these are the West Maui Mountains, and it can rain at any time! You can escape the crowds even in this heavily touristed area by following the path toward The Needle until you come to the pavilion at the top. As you head back, take the paved path that bears to the right. It soon becomes dirt, skirting the river, and the tourists magically disappear. Here are a number of pint-sized pools where you can take a refreshing dip.

Iao is for day use only. On your way back to Wailuku you might take a five-minute side excursion up to Wailuku Heights. Look for the road on your right. There's little here besides a housing development, but the view of the bay below is tops!

PRACTICALITIES

Accommodations

Visitors to Wailuku mostly stay elsewhere on Maui because there really isn't any place to lodge in town except for two very specialized and very humble hotels. The newest and most pleasant is the **Northshore Inn**, tel. 242-8999, at 2080 Vineyard St., above Hazel's Cafe. After several months of cleaning and painting (it was previously the fleabag, drug-infested Wailuku Grand Hotel), this clean, light, and comfortable inn caters mostly to young independent travelers and surfers. Skylights brighten the upstairs; potted plants add color to the beige walls; the homey sitting room offers a place for the guests (from many countries of the world) to get together and talk, share information, listen to music, or watch television; the balcony is a fine place to catch the evening air; and a bulletin board is filled with great information about Maui and the other islands. Bunk rooms go for $15 a bed,

single rooms $29, and double rooms $39. The 25 rooms all have small refrigerators. Ask about their deal with Word of Mouth Rental Cars for low daily rates. The four shared bathrooms are spotless.

Not only is this an easy-going, well-cared for place, the owners, who live on the premises, are environmentally conscious and are recycling, using low-wattage light bulbs, solar-heated water, and low-flow shower heads. They also will store sailboards, bicycles, backpacks, and other luggage. There are laundry facilities on the premises, and a small garden with an 80-year-old banyon tree and tropical fruit trees in the back. The owners have won the respect of the community for transforming this inn into a viable business and dealing equitably with the local citizenry.

The **Banana Bungalow** is at 310 N. Market St., Wailuku, HI 96793 (in Happy Valley across from Aki's Restaurant), tel. 244-5090, and costs $29 s or $35 d, or $13 for bunk rooms sleeping 3-4 persons. Until very recently, it was a flophouse for locals who were down on their luck. Now, it's a clean, plain, and spartan hotel, with a fresh coat of paint and new bathrooms up and down, that's a draw for avid sailboarders, cyclists, and students. Typically, you're liable to hear languages from a dozen countries, and if you're into sailboarding or just after a cross-cultural experience, this is the spot. The Happy Valley Inn offers basic accommodations, and if you care more about wind and surf conditions than what your bedroom looks like, it's the place for you. Call to reserve. Check in and office hours are only 4 to 6 p.m. If you leave a message, they *will* return your call anywhere in the world. Make sure to give international area codes, etc.

Molina's Bar and Rooms, at 197 Market St., offers utilitarian rooms at $350/month, $25/night, $125/week, with private bath and room service. Bogart playing a character with a five-day-old beard and a hangover would be comfortable waking up at this basic, clean, and friendly fleabag.

Food

The establishments listed below are all in the bargain or reasonable range. The decor in most is basic and homey, with the emphasis

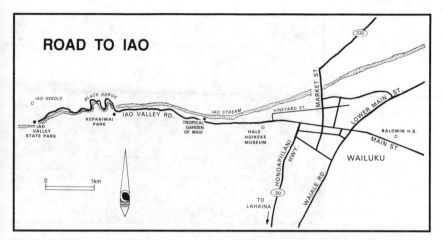

ROAD TO IAO

placed on the food. Wailuku has the best and the most inexpensive restaurants on Maui.

Sam Sato's is at 318 N. Market St., open Mon.-Sat. (closed Thurs.) 8 a.m. to 4 p.m. (Happy Valley). Sato's is famous for *manju,* a puff-like pastry from Japan usually filled with sweets, meats, or *adzuki* beans. One of those places that, if you are a local resident, you *must* bring Sato's *manju* when visiting friends or relatives off-island. Lunch is served only until 2 p.m. A highly specialized place, but worth the effort.

Hazel's Cafe, 2080 Vineyard St., tel. 244-7278, open Tues. to Fri. for lunch (10-2) and dinner (5-9), Sat. and Sun. for breakfast (7-11), lunch (11-2), and dinner (5-9). One of the finest arrays of local foods at unbeatable prices. Daily specials like roast beef and mushrooms, $5.75, grilled butterfish, $5.50, pork tofu, $4.50. It's difficult to spend over $6. Very clean and friendly. This is where the *people* of Wailuku go to eat. Oxtail soup on Mon. and Thurs., pig's feet soup on Friday. Bright and airy with ceiling fans.

Maui Boy Restaurant, tel. 244-7243, open daily 6:30 a.m. to 9 p.m., is just up the street from Hazel's at 2102 Vineyard Street. Another downhome place with excellent local foods for under $6. Sandwiches, *miso,* and Portuguese bean soup, Maui omelettes, $4.50. Dishes like teri-beef and *katsu don* are under $5, but the real specialties are Hawaiian foods like *kalua*

pork or *lau lau* under $9. Good island food at reasonable prices.

Across the street is the new **Canto's Creative Cuisine,** tel. 242-9758. Open 8 a.m. to 8 p.m., except Sun., this restaurant specializes in sandwiches, pastries, fresh-baked bread, and pies; there are several lunch and dinner specials daily.

Siam Thai is a small restaurant painted black and white at 123 N. Market, tel. 244-3817. Excellent Thai food with an emphasis on vegetarian cuisine. Maybe the best deal in Wailuku! Open Mon.-Fri. 11 a.m. to 2:30 p.m., and again from 5-9:30 p.m., Sat. and Sun. dinner only.

Almost next door to Siam Thai at 133 N. Market is **Fujiya's,** tel. 244-0206, offering a full range of Japanese food and sushi. Open 11 a.m. to 5 p.m. The *miso* soup and tempura are inexpensive and quite good.

A second Thai restaurant is **Saeng's,** tel. 244-1567, at 2119 Vineyard. Open daily for lunch and dinner (dinner only Sat.), this new establishment serves all varieties of Thai food, most for under $7.50.

Just up the street is the **Vineyard Tavern,** tel. 242-9938, with dynamite burgers.

The **Maui Grill Restaurant** on the corner of Main and Market streets is now open for American and Mexican food with prices under $7.

If you get off the main highway and take Mill Street and Lower Main, the beachside roads

The "aloha Santa" waves from Wailuku's "antique row."
(J.D. BISIGNANI)

connecting Kahului and Wailuku, you'll be rewarded with some the *most* local and *least* expensive restaurants on West Maui. They are totally unpretentious, and serve hefty portions of tasty, homemade local foods. If your aim is to *eat,* search out one of these. **Tasty Crust Restaurant,** at 1770 Mill St., tel. 244-0845, opens daily from 5:30 a.m. to 1:30 p.m., and again from 5-10 p.m., closed Monday night. If you have to carbo-load for a full day of sailing, snorkeling, or windsurfing, order their famous giant homemade hotcakes for only $.80. Or try **Nazo's Restaurant,** at 1063 Lower Main St., second floor of the Puuone Plaza, an older yellowish two-story building, tel. 244-0529. Park underneath and walk upstairs. Daily specials under $6, but they're renowned for their oxtail soup, $5.50, a clear-consommé broth with peanuts and water chestnuts floating around, a delicious combination of East and West. **Tokyo Tei,** in the same complex, tel. 242-9630, open daily 11 a.m. to 1:30 p.m. for lunch, 5 to 8:30 p.m. dinner, open Sunday for dinner only, is another institution that has been around for decades serving Japanese dishes to a devoted clientele. Eating here is as consistent as eating at grandma's kitchen, with traditional Japanese dishes like tempura, various *don buri,* and seafood platters.

If you want to sample real Japanese food at affordable prices, come here!

Hale Lava is a little cafe/lodge serving Japanese and American food. For under $7, you can get a full meal. Located at 740 Lower Main, tel. 244-0871. Opens from 5:30 a.m. to 1:30 p.m., closed Monday.

A favorite with locals, **Archie's Place** serves full meals for $6, specializing in Japanese. Located at 1440 Lower Main, tel. 244-9401. Open daily 10:30 a.m. to 2 p.m., 5 to 8 p.m., closed Sunday.

Moon Hoe Seafood Restaurant at 752 Lower Main St., tel. 242-7778, offers delicacies from the sea at a fair price. They're open on Sunday evenings when many other places are closed, daily (except Sun.) 11 a.m. to 2 p.m., and every day from 5-9 p.m.

Down To Earth sells natural and health foods and has an excellent snack bar—basically a little window around back with a few tables available. Really filling! Located at 1910 Vineyard, tel. 242- 6821. Open Mon. to Sat. until to 6:30 p.m.

And, for a different taste treat, try the *mochi* made fresh daily at Wailuku's **Shishido Bakery,** next door to the Moon Hoe Restaurant. Nearby on Lower Main Street are **Maui Coffee Roasters**—stop in for a variety of the world's best beans roasted on the spot—and **Tropical Chocolate.**

Both **Nakamatsu** on Market Street and **Nagasako Fish Market** on Lower Main have a wide variety of fresh fish.

Shopping

Most shopping in this area is done in Kahului at the three big malls. But for an interesting diversion try one of these, all on or around Main or Market Street. **T-Shirt Factory Outlet** can save you money on T-shirts that you'll see all over the island. For better clothes and accessories vist **Tropical Emporium. St. Anthony's Thrift Shop** on lower Main is open Wed. and Fri. from 8 a.m. to 1 p.m., where you'll find used articles from irons to aloha shirts. **Maui Wholesale Gold,** sells gold, jewelry, and eel-skin items; **Treasure Imports** sells just about the same type of articles, as does **Take's. Miracles Unlimited,** on Central Street, has what you need in the way of crystals, metaphysical books, and jewelry. **New Maui Fishing Supply** has all you need to land the big ones.

Wailuku's attic closets are overflowing. Several discovery shops in a row hang like promnight tuxedos, limp with old memories. Each has its own style. Look for the aloha Santa Claus waving to you on the elevated portion of N. Market as you head toward Happy Valley. Here, you'll find **Things From The Past,** tel. 244-8177, with antiques, collectibles and jewelry, old mirrors, contemporary paintings, carvings, glass floats, old china, crystal, and Oriental curios. Next door is **Ali'i Antiques,** tel. 244-8012, open daily 9 a.m. to 8 p.m., offering Depression glass, dolls, china, photos, chandeliers, 200-year-old kimonos, and a menagerie of teddy bears. **Traders of the Lost Art** specializes in carvings from the Pacific, especially from New Guinea. Here as well are **Memory Lane** for curios and collectibles and **Able Antiques** with its many pieces of furniture, glassware, and artwork; **Wailuku Gallery** is next door.

Services

There's a **Bank of Hawaii,** at 2105 Main, tel. 871-8200; **First Interstate,** 2005 Main, tel. 244-3951. The **post office** is on High St., next to the state office building, and the **library** is at 251 High St., tel. 244-3945.

For conventional health care, go to **Maui Memorial Hospital,** off Route 32, tel. 244-9056, or **Kaiser Permanente, Wailuku Clinic** near the hospital. On Vineyard, next to Saeng's Thai Restaurant, are the **Healing Light Health Center** and **East West Clinic.**

Camping permits for county parks are available at the War Memorial Gym, Room 102, Route 32, tel. 244-9018. They cost $3 for adult, 50 cents for children, per person, per night. State park permits can be had at the State Building, High St., tel. 243-5354 (see p. 114).

KAHAKULOA—WEST MAUI'S BACKSIDE

To get around to the backside of West Maui you can head northeast from Kaanapali, but the majority of those few who defy the car companies and brave the bad road strike out northwest from Wailuku. (Note: The dirt road portion of Route 340 is rugged and a sign warns that it is closed to all but local residents. Although the ordinance is not enforced, be extremely cautious on this road, especially during or just after bad weather.) Before you start this rugged 18-mile stretch, make sure you have adequate gas, water, and food. It'll take you a full three hours to go from Wailuku to Kapalua. Start heading north on Market Street, down toward the area of Wailuku called **Happy Valley** (good restaurants—see "Food," above). At the end of Market Street (Rt. 330) you'll find **T.K. Supermarket,** your best place to buy supplies (open seven days). At mile 2, Route 330 turns into Route 340, which you'll follow toward Kahakuloa Bay and all the way around. In a few minutes, just when you come to the bridge over Iao Stream, will be Kuhio Place on your left. Turn here to **Halekii and Pihana Heiaus.** Although uninspiring, this area is historical and totally unvisited.

Back on Route 340 you come shortly to **Waihee** ("Slippery Water"). There's a little store here, but even if it's open it's probably understocked. On the right, a sign points you to **Waiehu Golf Course,** tel. 243-7400. Mostly local people golf here; fees are $25 for nonresidents, $12.50 club rental. The fairways, strung along the sea, are beautiful to play. **Par Five Restaurant** is an adequate little eatery at the golf course. Also here are two county beach parks: **Waiehu** and **Waihee.** They're secluded and frequented mostly by local people. Some come here to spear fish inside the reef. Although for day use only, they'd probably be OK for an unofficial overnight stay. For Waihee, turn at the Kiwanis Park (softball on Sat.) and go left just before the golf course parking

Kahakuloa is the only village on the rugged north coast of Maui. (BOB NILSEN)

lot along the fence; for Waiehu take Lower Waiehu Road, off Rt. 340, at the north end of Wailuku—follow the "shoreline access" signs.

At mile 11 the pavement begins to deteriorate. The road hugs the coastline and gains elevation quickly; the undisturbed valleys are resplendent. At mile 11, just past the Boy Scout camp, you'll see a metal gate and two enormous carved tikis. No explanation, just sitting there. You next enter the fishing village of **Kahakuloa** ("Tall Hill") with its dozen weatherworn houses and tiny white church. Here the road is at its absolute roughest and narrowest! The valley is very steep-sided and beautiful. Supposedly, great Maui himself loved this area. Two miles past Kahakuloa, you come to **Pohaku Kani,** the bell stone. It's about six feet tall and the same in diameter, but graffiti spoil it. Here the seascapes are tremendous. The surf pounds along the coast below and sends spumes skyward, roaring through a natural blowhole. The road once again becomes wide and well paved and you're soon at **Fleming Beach Park.** Civilization comes again too quickly.

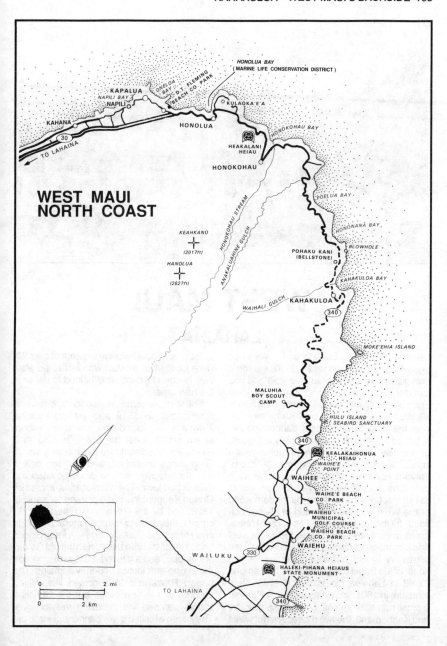

HONOLUA BAY
(MARINE LIFE CONSERVATION DISTRICT)

KAPALUA
NAPILI BAY
NAPILI
ONELOA BAY
D.T. FLEMING BEACH CO. PARK
KULAOKA'E'A

KAHANA
HONOLUA
HONOKOHAU BAY
30
TO LAHAINA

HEAKALANI HEIAU

HONOKOHAU

WEST MAUI NORTH COAST

POELUA BAY

KEAHKANO
+
(2017ft)

HONONANA BAY

HANOLUA
+
(2627ft)

POHAKU KANI
(BELLSTONE)
BLOWHOLE

KAHAKULOA BAY

WAIHALI GULCH
KAHAKULOA
340

MOKE'EHIA ISLAND

MALUHIA
BOY SCOUT
CAMP

*HULU ISLAND
SEABIRD SANCTUARY*

340
KEALAKAIHONUA
HEIAU
WAIHEE POINT

WAIHEE

WAIHE'E BEACH
CO. PARK

WAIEHU
MUNICIPAL
GOLF COURSE

WAIEHU BEACH
CO. PARK

WAILUKU
330
WAIEHU

HALEKI-PIHANA HEIAUS
STATE MONUMENT

TO LAHAINA
340

0   2 mi
0   2 km

WEST MAUI

LAHAINA

Lahaina ("Merciless Sun") is and always has been the premier town on Maui. It's the most energized town on the island as well, and you can feel it from the first moment you walk down Front Street. Maui's famed warrior- king Kahekili lived here and ruled until Kamehameha, with the help of new-found cannon power, subdued Kahekili's son in Iao Valley at the turn of the 19th century. When Kamehameha I consolidated the island kingdom, he chose Lahaina as his seat of power. It served as such until Kamehameha III moved to Honolulu in the 1840s. Lahaina is where the modern world of the West and the old world of Hawaii collided, for better or worse. The *ali'i* of Hawaii loved to be entertained here; the **royal surf spot,** mentioned numerous times as an area of revelry in old missionary diaries, is just south of the Small Boat Harbor. Kamehameha I built in Lahaina the islands' first Western structure in 1801, known as the **Brick Palace;** a small ruin still remains. Queens Keopuolani and Kaahumanu, the two most powerful wives

of the great Kamehameha's harem of over 20, were local Maui women who remained after their husband's death and helped to usher in the new order.

The whalers came preying for "sperms and humpbacks" in 1819 and set old Lahaina Town a-reelin'. Island girls, naked and willing, swam out to meet the ships, trading their favors for baubles from the modern world. Grog shops flourished, and drunken sailors with their brown-skinned doxies owned the debauched town. The missionaries, invited by Queen Keopuolani, came praying for souls in 1823. Led by the Reverends Stuart and Richards, they tried to harpoon moral chaos. In short order, there was a curfew, a *kapu* placed on the ships by wise but ineffectual old Governor Hoapili, and a jail and a fort to discourage the strong-arm tactics of unruly captains. The pagan Hawaiians transformed like willing children to the new order, but the Christian sailors damned the meddling missionaries. They even whistled a few cannonballs into the

Lahaina homestead of Rev. Richards, hoping to send him speedily to his eternal reward. Time, a new breed of sailor, and the slow death of the whaling industry eased the tension.

Meanwhile, the missionaries built the first school and printing press west of the Rockies at **Lahainaluna,** in the mountains just above the town, along with downtown's **Wainee Church,** the first stone church on the island. Lahaina's glory days slipped by and it became a sleepy "sugar town" dominated by the Pioneer Sugar Mill that has operated since the 1860s. In 1901, the **Pioneer Inn** was built to accommodate inter-island ferry passengers, but no one *came* to Lahaina. In the 1960s, AMFAC had a brilliant idea. They turned Kaanapali, a magnificent stretch of beach just west, into one of the most beautifully planned and executed resorts in the world. The Pioneer Sugar Mill had long used the area as a refuse heap, but now the ugly duckling became a swan, and Lahaina flushed with new life. With superb farsightedness, the **Lahaina Restoration Foundation** was begun in those years and almost the entire town was made a national historical landmark. Lahaina, subdued but never tamed, throbs with its special energy once again.

SIGHTS

In short, strolling around Lahaina offers the best of both worlds. It's busy, but it's bite-sized. It's engrossing enough, but you can "see" it in half a day. The main attractions are mainly downtown within a few blocks of each other. Lahaina technically stretches, long and narrow, along the coast for about four miles, but you'll only be interested in the central core, a mere mile or so. All along Front Street, the main drag, and the side streets running off it are innumerable shops, restaurants, and hideaways where you can browse, recoup your energy, or just wistfully watch the sun set. Go slow and savor, and you'll feel the dynamism of Lahaina past and present all around you. Enjoy!

Parking
Traffic congestion is a problem that needs to be addressed. Stay away from town from 4:30

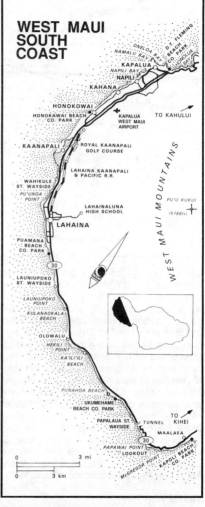

to 5:30 p.m., when traffic is heaviest. While there still are no traffic lights on Front Street, a spree of construction in the last several years has increased the number of lights on the highway from two to over half a dozen. The other thing to know to make your visit carefree is where to stash your car. The parking lot on the corner of Wainee and Dickenson street

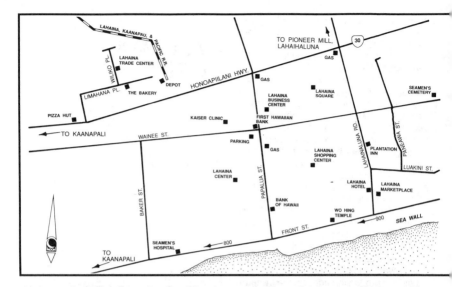

charges only $5 for the entire day. There's another large lot on Prison Street, just up from Front (free three-hour limit), two smallish lots along Luakini Street ($5), and small lots ($8) behind the Baldwin House, the Lahaina Hotel, and Burger King on Front Street. The Lahaina Shopping Center has three-hour parking. Most of the meters in town are a mere one hour, and the most efficient people on Maui are the "meter patrol!" Your car will wind up in the pound if you're not careful! The best place to find a spot is down at the end of Front Street past the Kamehameha School and along Shaw. You'll have to walk a few minutes, but it's worth it. For those staying in Kaanapali, leave your car at your hotel and take the Lahaina Express for the day. (See "Getting Around" in the main Introduction for details.)

The Banyan Tree

The best place to start your tour of Lahaina is at this magnificent tree at the corner of Hotel and Front. You can't miss it as it spreads its shading boughs over almost an entire acre. Use the benches to sit and reconnoiter while the sun, for which Lahaina is infamous, is kept at bay. Children love it, and it seems to bring

out the Tarzan in everyone. Old-timers sit here chatting, and you might be lucky enough to hear Ben Victorino, a tour guide who comes here frequently, entertain people with his ukulele and endless repertoire of Hawaiian tunes. The tree was planted in April 1873 by Sheriff Bill Smith in commemoration of the Congregationalist Missions' golden anniversary. One hundred years later, a ceremony was held here and over 500 people were accommodated under this natural canopy. Just left of the banyan, down the lane toward the harbor, was a canal and the Government Market. All kinds of commodities, manufactured and human, were sold here during the whaling days, and it was given the apt name of "Rotten Row."

The Courthouse

Behind the banyan on Wharf Street is the Courthouse. Built in the 1850s from coral blocks recycled from Kamehameha III's ill-fated palace, Hale Piula ("House of Iron"), it also served as the police station, complete with a jail in the basement. Today, the jail is home to the **Lahaina Art Society,** where paintings and artifacts are kept behind bars, waiting for patrons to liberate them. Adjacent is **The Fort,**

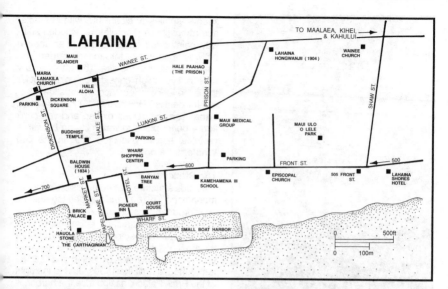

built in the 1830s to show the sailors that they couldn't run amok in Lahaina. It was more for show than for force, though. When it was torn down, the blocks were hauled over to Prison Street to build the real jail, **Hale Pa'ahao.** A corner battlement of the fort was restored, but that's it, because restoring the entire structure means mutilating the banyan.

Small Boat Harbor

Walking along the harbor stimulates the imagination and the senses. The boats waiting at anchor sway in confused syncopation. Hawser ropes groan and there's a feeling of anticipation and adventure in the air. Here you can board for all kinds of seagoing excursions. In the days of whaling there was no harbor; the boats tied up one to the other in the "roads," at times forming an impromptu floating bridge. The whalers came ashore in their chase boats; with the winds always up, departure could be made at a moment's notice. The activity here is still dominated by the sea.

The *Carthaginian II*

The masts and square rigging of this replica of the enterprising freighters that braved the Pacific tower over Lahaina Harbor. You'll be drawn to it . . . go! It's the only truly square-rigged ship left afloat on the seas. It replaced the *Carthaginian I* when that ship went a-ground in 1972 while being hauled to Honolulu for repairs. The Lahaina Restoration Foundation found this steel-hulled ship in Denmark; built in Germany in 1920 as a two- masted schooner, it tramped around the Baltic under converted diesel power. The foundation had it sailed 12,000 miles to Lahaina, where it underwent extensive conversion until it became the beautiful replica that you see today. The sails have yet to be made for lack of funds.

The *Carthaginian* is a floating museum dedicated to whaling and to whales. Richard Widmark, the actor, narrates a superb film documenting the life of humpbacks. Below-decks is the museum containing artifacts and implements from the whaling days. There's even a whaling boat which was found intact in Alaska in the 1970s. The light below decks is subdued, and while you sit in the little "captains' chairs" the humpbacks chant their peaceful hymns in the background. Flip Nicklin's sensitive photos adorn the bulkheads. It's open daily 9:30 a.m. to 4:30 p.m., but arrive

Carthaginian II *(BOB NILSEN)*

no later than 3:45 to see all the exhibits and videos. Admission is $3.

Pioneer Inn

This vintage inn, situated at the corner of Hotel and Wharf streets, is just exactly where it belongs. Stand on its veranda with the honky-tonk piano playing in the open bar behind you and gaze at the *Carthaginian*. Presto . . . it's magic time! You'll see. It was even a favorite spot for actors like Errol Flynn and later Spencer Tracy, when he was in Lahaina filming *Devil at Four O'clock*. The green and white inn was built in 1901 to accommodate inter-island ferry passengers, but its style seems much older. If ironwork had been used on the veranda, you'd think you were in New Orleans. A new wing was built behind it in 1965 and the two form a courtyard. Make sure to read the hilarious rules governing behavior that are posted in the main lobby. The inn is still functional. The rooms in the old wing are colorfully

seedy—spotlessly clean, but with character and atmosphere. The off-level wooden stairway, painted red, leads upstairs to an uneven hallway lined with a threadbare carpet. The interior smells like the sea. There's no luxury here, but you might consider one night just for the experience. (See "Accommodations" below for details.) Downstairs the **Harpooner's Lanai Terrace** serves dinner, and you can't find a better place to watch life go by with a beautiful sunset backdrop than in the **Old Whaler's Saloon**.

The Brick Palace

This rude structure was commissioned by Kamehameha I in 1801 and slapped together by two forgotten Australian ex-convicts. It was the first Western structure in Hawaii, but unfortunately the substandard materials have for the most part disintegrated. Kamehameha never lived in it, but it was occupied and used as a storehouse until the 1850s. Just to the right of the Brick Palace, as you face the harbor, is **Hauola Stone,** marked by an HVB Warrior. Formed like a chair, it was believed by the Hawaiians to have curative powers if you sat on it and let the ocean bathe you. Best view at low tide.

Baldwin Home

One of the best attractions in Lahaina is the Baldwin Home, on the corner of Front and Dickenson. It was occupied by Doctor/Reverend Dwight Baldwin, his wife Charlotte, and their eight children. He was a trained teacher, as well as the first doctor/dentist in Hawaii. The building served from the 1830s to 1868 as a dispensary, meeting room, and boarding home for anyone in need. The two-foot-thick walls are of cut lava, and the mortar made of crushed coral over which plaster was applied. As you enter, notice how low the doorway is, and that the doors inside are "Christian doors" —with a cross forming the upper panels and an open Bible at the bottom. The Steinway piano that dominates the entrance was built in 1859. In the bedroom to the right, along with all of the period furniture, is a wooden commode. Also notice the lack of closets; all items were kept in chests. Upstairs was a large dormitory where guests slept.

The doctor's fees are posted and are hilarious. Payment was by "size" of sickness: very big $50, diagnosis $3, refusal to pay $10! The Rev. Baldwin was 41 when he arrived in Hawaii from New England and his wife was 25. She was supposedly sickly (eight children!) and he had heart trouble, so they moved to Honolulu in 1868 to receive better health care. The home became a community center, housing the library and meeting rooms. Today, the Baldwin Home is a showcase museum of the Lahaina Restoration Society. It's open daily 9:30 a.m. to 5 p.m., admission $2, kids free accompanied by a parent.

Master's Reading Room

Originally a missionaries' storeroom, the Master's Reading Room was converted to an officers' club in 1834. Located next door to the Baldwin Home, these two venerable buildings constitute the oldest Western structures on Maui, and fittingly, this uniquely constructed coral stone building is home to the Lahaina Restoration Foundation. The building is not really open to the public, but you can visit to pick up maps, brochures, and information about Lahaina.

The **Lahaina Restoration Foundation,** begun in 1962, is headed by Jim Luckey, a historian in his own right who knows a great deal about Lahaina and the whaling era. The main purpose of the foundation is to preserve the flavor and authenticity of Lahaina without stifling progress—especially tourism. The foundation is privately funded and has managed to purchase many of the important historical sites in Lahaina. They own the two buildings mentioned, the restored Wo Hing Temple, the land under the U.S. Seamen's Hospital, and they'll own the plantation house next door in 18 years. The 42 people on the board of directors come from all socio-economic backgrounds. You don't get on the board by how much money you give but by how much effort and time you are willing to invest in the foundation; the members are extremely dedicated. Merchants approach the foundation with new ideas for business and ask how they can best comply with the building codes. The townspeople know that their future is best served if they preserve the feeling of old La-

haina rather than rush headlong into frenzied growth. The historic village of Williamsburg, Virginia, is often cited as Lahaina's model, except that Lahaina wishes to remain a "real" living, working town.

Hale Pa'ahao

This is Lahaina's old prison, located mid-block on Prison Street, and its name literally means "Stuck-in-Irons House." It was constructed by prisoners in the 1850s from blocks of stone salvaged from the old defunct Fort. It had a catwalk for an armed guard, and cells complete with shackles for hardened criminals, but most were drunks who yahooed around town on the Sabbath, wildly spurring their horses. The cells were rebuilt in 1959, the gatehouse in 1988, and the structure is maintained by the Lahaina Restoration Foundation. The cells, curiously, are made of wood, which shows that the inmates weren't that interested in busting out. It's open daily, admission free.

Maluuluolele Park

This nondescript area at the corner of Shaw and Front was at one time the most important spot in Lahaina. Here was a small pond with a diminutive island in the center. The pond, Mokuhinia, was home to a *moo*, a lizard spirit. The tiny island, Mokuula, was the home of the Maui chiefs, and the Kamehamehas, when they were in residence. It became a royal mausoleum, but later all the remains were taken away and the pond was filled and the ground leveled. King Kamehameha III and his sister Princess Nahienaena were raised together in Lahaina. They fell in love, but the new ways caused turmoil and tragedy. Instead of marrying and producing royal children, a favored practice only 20 years earlier, they were wrenched apart by the new religion. He, for a time, numbed himself with alcohol, while she died woefully from a broken heart. She was buried here, and for many years Kamehameha III could frequently be found at her grave, quietly sitting and meditating.

Wainee Church And Cemetery

The church itself is not impressive, but its history is. This is the spot where the first Christian services were held in Hawaii, in

1823. A church was built here in 1832 which could hold 3,000 people, but it was razed by a freak hurricane in 1858. Rebuilt, it survived until 1894, when it was deliberately burned by an angry mob, upset with the abolition of the monarchy in Hawaii and the islands' annexation by the United States. Another church was built, but it too was hit not only by a hurricane but by fire as well. The present structure was built in 1953. In the cemetery is a large part of Maui's history: buried here are Hawaiian royalty. Lying near each other are Queen Keopuolani, her star-crossed daughter, Princess Nahienaena, and old Governor Hoapili, their royal tomb marked by two large headstones surrounded by a wrought-iron fence. Other graves hold missionaries such as William Richards and many infants and children.

Churches And Temples
You may wish to stop for a moment at Lahaina's churches and temples dotted around town. They are reminders of the mixture of faiths and peoples that populated this village and added their particular cultural styles. **The Episcopal Cemetery** on Wainee Street shows the English influence in the islands. Many of the royal family, including King Kalakaua, became Anglicans. This cemetery holds the remains of many early Maui families, and of Walter Murray Gibson, the notorious settler, politician, and firebrand of the 1880s. Just behind is **Hale Aloha,** "House of Love," a small structure built by Maui residents in thanksgiving for being saved from a terrible smallpox epidemic that ravaged Oahu but bypassed Maui in 1858. The structure was restored in 1974. Also on Wainee is **Maria Lanakila Church,** the site of the first Roman Catholic Mass in Lahaina, celebrated in 1841. The present structure dates from 1928. Next to the church's cemetery is the **Seamen's Cemetery** where many infirm from the ships that came to Lahaina were buried. Most stones have been obliterated by time and only a few remain. Herman Melville came here to pay his last respects to a cousin buried in this yard. **Hongwanjii Temple** is also on Wainee, between Prison and Shaw. It's a Buddhist temple with the largest congregation in Lahaina and

The Wo Hing Temple was restored by the Lahaina Restoration Foundation. (BOB NILSEN)

dates from 1910, though the present structure was raised in 1927.

The **Wo Hing Temple** on Front Street is the Lahaina Restoration Foundation's newest reconstruction. It was opened to the public in 1984 and shows the Chinese influence in Lahaina. Downstairs are displays, upstairs is the altar. In the cookhouse next door, you can see film clips of Hawaii taken by the Edison Company in 1899 and 1906. It's open 9 a.m. to 4 p.m. daily, from 10 a.m. Sunday, admission $1.00. **Holy Innocents Episcopal Church,** built in 1927, is also on Front Street, near Kamehameha III school. Known for its "Hawaiian Madonna," its altar is resplendent with fruits, plants, and birds of the islands.

The **Lahaina Jodo Mission** is at the opposite end of Front Street, near Mala Wharf on Ala Moana Street. When heading west, you'll leave the main section of town and keep going until you see a sign over a building that reads Jesus is Coming Soon. Turn left toward the beach and you'll immediately spot the three-storied pagoda. Here the giant bronze Buddha sits exposed to the elements. The largest outside of Asia, it was dedicated in 1968 in commemoration of the centennial of the Japanese arrival as workers in Hawaii. The grounds are impeccable and serenely quiet. You may stroll around, but the buildings are closed to the public. If you climb the steps to peek into the temple, kindly remove your shoes. A striking cemetery is across the street along the beach. It seems incongruous to see tombstones set in sand. The entire area is quiet and a perfect spot for lunch or solitary meditation if you've had enough of frenetic Lahaina.

U.S. Seamen's Hospital

This notorious hospital was reconstructed by the Lahaina Restoration Foundation in 1982. Here is where sick seamen were cared for under the auspices of the U.S. State Department. Allegations during the late 1850s claimed that the care here extended past the grave! Unscrupulous medicos supposedly charged the U.S. government for care of seamen who had long since died. The hospital is located at Front and Baker, heading toward Kaanapali, near the Jodo Mission. The hospital now houses a Lahaina Printsellers Shop, specializing in vintage art of Hawaii and the Pacific. (See p. 71.) In the front yard is a 10,000 pound, swivel-end Porter anchor, found off Black Rock in Kaanapali.

Lahainaluna

Head up the mountain behind Lahaina on Lahainaluna Road for approximately two miles. On your left you'll pass the **Pioneer Sugar Mill,** in operation since 1860. Once at Lahainaluna ("Above Lahaina") you'll find the oldest school west of the Rockies, opened by the Congregationalist missionaries in 1831. Children from all over the islands, and many from California, came here if their parents could afford to send them away to boarding school. Today, the school is West Maui's public high school, but many children still come here to board. The first students were not only

given a top-notch academic education, but a practical one as well. They built the school buildings, and many were also apprentices in the famous **Hale Pa'i** ("Printing House") that turned out Hawaii's first newspaper and made Lahaina famous as a printing center.

One look at Hale Pa'i and you think of New England. It's a white stucco building with blue trim and a wood-shake roof. It was restored in 1982 and is open by appointment only (contact the Lahaina Restoration Foundation or the Baldwin Home). If you visit the campus when school is in session, you may go to Hale Pa'i, but if you want to walk around, please sign in at the vice-principal's office. Lahainaluna High School is still dedicated to the preservation of Hawaiian culture. Every year, in April, they celebrate the anniversary of death of one of their most famous students, David Malo. Considered Hawaii's first scholar, he authored the definitive *Hawaiian Antiquities.* His final wish was to be buried "high above the tide of foreign invasion" and his grave is close to the giant "L" atop Mount Ball, behind Lahainaluna. On the way back down to Lahaina, you get a wide, impressive panorama of the port and the sea.

Heading East

Five miles east of Lahaina along the coastal road (Rt. 30) is the little village of Olowalu. Today, little more than a general store and a French restaurant are here. This was the place of the Olowalu Massacre perpetrated by Capt. Metcalf. Its results were far-reaching, greatly influencing Hawaiian history. Two seamen, Young and Davis, were connected with this incident, and with their help Kamehameha I subdued all of Hawaii. Behind the store are petroglyphs. Follow the dirt track behind the store for about one-half mile; make sure you pass a water tower within the first few hundred yards because there are three similar roads here. You'll come to the remains of a wooden stairway going up a hill. There once was an HVB Warrior here, but he might be gone. Claw your way up the hill to the petroglyphs, which are believed to be 300 years old.

If you continue east on Route 30, you'll pass **Papawai** and **McGregor Point,** both noted for

Hale Pa'i, the oldest printing house west of the Rocky Mountains
(BOB NILSEN)

their vistas and as excellent locations to spot migrating whales in season. The road sign merely indicates a scenic lookout.

BEACHES

The best beaches around Lahaina are just west of town in Kaanapali, or just east toward Olowalu. A couple of adequate places to spread your towel are right in Lahaina, but they're not quite on a par with the beaches just a few miles away.

Maluulu O Lele Park

"The Breadfruit Shelter of Lele" is in town and basically parallels Front Street. It's crowded at times and there's plenty of "wash up" on this beach. It's cleaner and quieter at the east end down by Lahaina Shores Hotel, a one-time favorite with the *ali'i*. There are restrooms, the swimming is fair, and the snorkeling acceptable past the reef. **Lahaina Beach** is at the west end of town near Mala Wharf. Follow Front to Puunoa Place and turn down to the beach. This is a good place for families with tots because the water is clear, safe, and shallow.

Puamana Beach County Park

About two miles before you enter Lahaina from the east along Route 30, you'll see signs for this beach park, a narrow strip between the road and the sea. The swimming and snorkeling are only fair. The setting, however, is quite nice with picnic tables shaded by ironwood trees. The views are terrific and this is a great spot to eat your plate lunch only minutes from town. **Launiupoko State Park**, a mile farther east, has restrooms and showers, but no beach. This is more of a pit stop than anything else, although many come to sunbathe on the grass below the coconut trees.

Wahikuli State Wayside

Along Route 30 between Lahaina and Kaanapali, the park is a favorite with local people and excellent for a picnic and swim. Restrooms and tennis courts are just across the street. The park is very clean and well maintained. Just up the highway, as if connected to this wayside park, is **Hanakaoo Beach County Park.** This beach runs north past some of the most exclusive hotels on the island. Often the local canoe club will put their canoes in the water here and at certain times of the year paddling events will be held at this beach.

ACCOMMODATIONS

Lodging in Lahaina is limited, surprisingly inexpensive, and an experience . . . of sorts. Most visitors head for Kaanapali, because Lahaina tends to be hot and hot to trot, especially at night. But you can find good bargains here, and if you want to be in the thick of the "action," you're in the right spot.

Pioneer Inn

This is the oldest hotel on Maui still accommodating guests, located at 658 Wharf St., Lahaina, HI 96761, tel. 661-3636, or (800) 657-7890. Absolutely no luxury whatsoever, but a double scoop of atmosphere: this is the place to come if you want to save money and be the star of your own movie with the Pioneer Inn as the stage set. Enter the tiny lobby full of memorabilia, and follow the creaking stairway up to a wooden hallway painted green on green. This is the old wing. Screen doors cover inner doors to clean but basic rooms which open out onto the building-long lanai, overlooking the harbor, and have ceiling fans. Rates are about $30 with shared bath, private bath (showers) a few dollars extra. Music and the sounds of life from the bar below late in the evening at no extra charge. The "new wing," basic modern, circa 1966, is attached. Starting at $60, it's no bargain. It offers a private lanai, bath, a/c, and overlooks the central courtyard. The old section is fun; the new section is only adequate. The Pioneer Inn is planning a major renovation during 1991-92 (after a change of ownership in 1990) so in the years to come expect changes and, undoubtedly, higher room rates.

The Plantation Inn

If Agatha Christie were seeking inspiration for *the* perfect setting for one of her mysteries, this is where she would come. The neo-Victorian building is appointed with posted verandas, hardwood floors, natural wood trim around windows and doors, and counterpointed by floral wall coverings and bedspreads. Rays of sunlight are diffused through stained-glass windows and wide double doors. Each room is comfortable, with overstuffed couches, four-poster beds, and private tiled baths with bold brass fixtures. The complete illusion is turn of the century, but the modern amenities of a/c, remote TV and VCR, a hidden fridge, daily maid service, and a soothing spa and pool are included. A new addition in the back brings the total room count to 17. Most of the 10 new units have lanais overlooking the garden, pool, spa, and guest pavilion. Prices are a reasonable $99 standard, $109 deluxe, $129 superior deluxe, $159 suite, and all include breakfast at Gerard's, the fine French restaurant on the first floor (see following). The Plantation Inn also has money-saving options for dinner at Gerard's, and air, car, and dive package deals. For full information contact the inn at 174 Lahainaluna Rd., Lahaina, HI 96761, tel. 667-9225 or (800) 433-6815 U.S.A.; they will accept collect calls from Canada. Set on a side street away from the bustle, it's simply the best accommodation that Lahaina has to offer.

Lahaina Hotel

Is nothing sacred? Will Birkenstocks be on *every* foot, quiche on *every* table, and a sensible Volvo in *every* driveway? The old, down-at-the-heels, traveler's classic, Lahainaluna Hotel, has been completely renovated and remodeled. Gone from this cockroach paradise are the weather-beaten linoleum floors, bare-bulbed musty rooms, and rusted dripping faucets. In their place are antique-stuffed, neo-Victorian, tastefully appointed rooms that transport you back to the late 1800s. If you aren't overcome by a feeling of the last century while staying here you never will be! Period pieces include everything from wardrobes to nightstands, rugs, ceramic bowls, mirrors, pictures, lamps, and books. The only deference to modernity are the bathrooms with their new but mostly old-style fixtures, the air-conditioning, telephone, and safes—no TV. You can still peer from the balcony of this vintage hotel—each room has a lanai with two hardwood rocking shairs and a table—or observe the masses below from behind heavy drapes and lace curtains. The thirteen units include three spacious suites. Rates are $110-170, and include a complimentary continental breakfast, served every morning from about 7:30 a.m. at the sideboard at the end of the hall. After new clothes and much-needed primping, this doughty orphan has had her coming out and been transformed into a lovely lady. The Lahaiana Hotel's only drawback is the complete lack of parking facilities. You must either park in a lot (one to the rear charges $8 overnight) or find a place on the street. Overnight parking

The Pioneer Inn has graced Lahaina Harbor since 1901. (BOB NILSEN)

in downtown Lahaina is officially prohibited, but the fine of $5—if any ticket is issued—is less than the cost of most parking lots. The Lahaina Hotel is located at 127 Lahainaluna Rd., Lahaina, HI 96761, tel. 661-0577, or (800) 669-3444.

David Paul's Lahaina Cafe, a trendy restaurant serving new American cuisine, is on the first floor. Remodeled at the same time as the hotel, it's under different ownership and management.

Maui Islander

Located a few blocks away from the hubbub, at 660 Wainee St., Lahaina, HI 96761, tel. 667-9766, (800) 367-5226, the Maui Islander is a very adequate hotel offering rooms with kitchenettes, studios, and suites of up to three bedrooms for seven guests or more. All with a/c and TV, plus pool and tennis courts. Homey atmosphere with daily planned activities. Basic hotel rooms start at $81, studios $93, $105 one bedroom; two and three bedroom suites are also available.

Lahaina Shores

This six-story condo was built before the Lahaina building code limited the height of new construction. It's located at the east end of town, at 475 Front St., Lahaina, HI 96761, tel. 661-4835, or (800) 628-6699. The tallest structure in town, it's become a landmark for

incoming craft. It offers a swimming pool and spa and is located on the only beach in town. From a distance, the Southern mansion facade is striking: up close, though, it becomes painted cement blocks and false colonnades. The rooms, however, are good value for the money. The basic contains a full bathroom, powder room, large color TV, and equipped kitchen. They're all light and airy, and the backside views of the harbor or frontside of the mountains are the best in town. Studios begin at $99, one bedroom suites $130, penthouse $165, $8 for additional guests; reduced rates of about 10% for the low season.

Lahaina Roads

This condo/apartment is at the far west end of town at 1403 Front St., Lahaina, HI 96761, tel. 661-3166, (800) 624-8203. All units have fully equipped kitchens, TV, and maid service on request. One-bedroom units (for two) run $75 ($95 high season), two-bedroom units (for four) $105-150 ($125-200 high season); $10 for each additional guest. There is a three-night minimum stay. Two nights' deposit required for reservations. Select credit cards are honored except for the week or longer stay discounts. There is no beach as it sits right along the seawall, but there is a pool, and you couldn't have a better view, with all the units being ocean-view deluxe at a standard price.

Puamana

A private community of condos, located one mile southeast of town on the ocean, Puamana is a quiet hideaway away from the hustle and bustle of town. One-bedroom units (fully equipped) begin at $105 in the low season, up to four people, $140 garden, $170 ocean, $155-210 for two-bedroom units, and $260 for three-bedroom townhouses; rates are higher from mid-Dec. to mid-April. Discounts for long stays. Puamana features an oceanside swimming pool, tennis, badminton, volleyball courts, and a sauna. Write Box 515, Lahaina, HI 96767, tel. 667-2551, (800) 367-5630 U.S.A., (800) 423-8733, ext. 255 in Canada. Check in at the clubhouse, the local sugar plantation's former manager's house.

Tony's Place

A less expensive alternative for your stay in Lahaina is this newly opened bed and breakfast at 13 Kanaula Road, off Front Street near downtown Lahaina. Rooms are $50 single and $55 double, with a two-night minimum stay. Call 661-8040 for reservations.

FOOD

Lahaina's menu of restaurants is gigantic; all palates and pocketbooks can easily be satisfied: there's fast food, sandwiches, sushi, happy hours, and elegant cosmopolitan restaurants. Because Lahaina is a dynamic tourist spot, restaurants and eateries come and go with regularity. The following is not an exhaustive list of Lahaina's food spots—it couldn't be. But there is plenty listed here to feed everyone at breakfast, lunch, and dinner. *Bon appetit!*

Inexpensive

Seaside Inn, 1307 Front St., tel. 661-7195, serves local plate lunches and Japanese *bento* during the day for about $5, hot-table style with teriyaki chicken, beef tomatoes, and chicken curry. The evening menu offers American and Asian selections like rib-eye steak for $7.50, tempura, *tonkatsu,* or various tofu dishes for under $5; for a complete dinner add $2 and receive *miso* soup, salad, and *tsukemono.* This is where local people and those in the know come for a very good but no-frills meal.

If eating hearty without caring about the ambience (actually the sunset view couldn't be better) is your aim, come here. An added attraction is the Karaoke sing-along on Fri. and Sat. from 8 p.m.

The **Thai Chef,** tel. 667-2814, will please any Thai food lover who wants a savory meal at a good price. Search for this restaurant stuck in a corner at the Lahaina Shopping Center, open Mon.-Sat. 11:30 a.m. to 2 p.m. for lunch, dinner nightly 5 to 10 p.m. As in most Thai restaurants vegetarians are well taken care of with plenty of spicy tofu and vegetable dishes. The extensive menu offers everything from scrumptious Thai soups with ginger and coconut for $7.25 (enough for two) to curries and seafood. Most entrees are under $8 with a good selection under $6. It's not fancy, but food-wise you won't be disappointed.

Zushi's is a hole-in-the-wall, very reasonably priced Japanese restaurant selling sushi and various other Japanese dishes at the Lahaina Business Plaza, across the street from McDonald's. It's stuck away in the corner, so look for it around the back. They serve lunch (takeout too) 11 a.m. to 2 p.m., and dinner 5 to 9 p.m. Authentic with most items under $5. Also in the plaza next to the Activities Information Center is a small takeout window with the imaginative name of **Local Food** which sells local food in the form of plate lunches. Basic, cheap, filling, and good.

Sunrise Cafe, open from 5:30 a.m. to 10 p.m. at 693 Front, tel. 661-3326, is the kind of place that locals keep secret. It's a tiny little place where you can have excellent coffee or a sandwich on whole wheat or pita bread. The food is provided by the excellent La Bretagne French Restaurant. You get gourmet quality for downhome prices. Seafood chowder is only $2.95, Micronesian chicken only $5.95. The most scrumptious deals, however, are the pastries, which La Bretagne is known for. The fine coffee selections are always freshly brewed, and they're complemented by a good selection of herbal teas. The Sunrise Cafe is just down the side street from **Lappert's Ice Cream,** which not only has ice cream, shave ice, and cookies, but also serves "fat-free" yogurt, about the only thing on Maui that is fat-free!

The open-air **Cheeseburger in Paradise** has the perfect location, overlooking the bay and Front Street, on the second floor of the oceanside building at the end of Lahainaluna street. Served are burgers, fries, sandwiches, soft drinks, and other inexpensive foods.

The tiny **Sushiya Deli** is a local plate lunch, bento, and saimen place on Prison Street just after you turn toward the mountains off Front Street. Look for it across the street from the public parking lot. Open weekdays 7 a.m. to 4 p.m. Very reasonable prices.

Your sweet tooth will begin to sing the moment you walk into **The Bakery** at 911 Limahana, near the Sugar Cane Train Depot off Honoapiilani Road (Hwy. 30) as you head toward Kaanapali. You can't beat their stuffed croissants for under $2, or their sandwiches for under $4! Coffee is a mere $.40 and their pastries, breads, and pasta are gooood! Open daily 7 a.m. to 5 p.m., until noon on Sun., tel. 667-9062.

Happy Days, tel. 661-3235, is a theme restaurant along Lahainaluna Road just a block from Front Street. Inside they've done a good job with bent-back chairs and juke box that make you feel like you're in a soda shop from the '50s. The menu has all-American offerings like hot dogs, burgers, hot roast beef, and full breakfast selections. Actually Happy Days has good vibes, and good food if you want pure American.

Lahaina Coolers in the Dickenson Plaza serves breakfast, lunch, and dinner. Lunch specials daily, and the bar has happy hour from 4-6 p.m. and 10-midnight "eight days a week." The most expensive item on the menu is about $10. Bright and breezy, tables are also set out on the courtyard.

Wiki Wiki Pizza across from the Cannery Mall, at 1285 Front, tel. 661-5686, has a takeout window featuring an eight-inch lunch pizza for only $3.95, 12-inch $8.95, 16-inch $11.95, toppings extra, and sandwiches from $5.99. A deck-patio on the premises gives you a quiet nook to eat in as you overlook Mala Wharf and the Lahaina Roads. If you're in a nearby condo, they'll deliver free.

The Wharf Shopping Center includes the inexpensive **Blue Lagoon Saloon**, selling steak and seafood on the ground floor. The offerings are hot-table counter style, but the surroundings in the courtyard are pleasant. Clam basket, $5.95, daily special of soup and sandwich for under $5, sandwiches under $4. **Orange Julius** dispenses its famous drinks, along with hot dogs and sandwiches for a quick cheap meal. **Pancho and Lefty's** is a very passable Mexican restaurant stuck away in the corner where you can get a full meal for around $6.95. To the rear on the opposite side is **Song's Oriental Kitchen.** This unpretentious restaurant is of the precooked hot plate variety, but you can stuff yourself on meals like beef stew for $3.95 or barbecued chicken, $3.85, all with two-scoop rice and macaroni salad. **Lani's Pancake Cottage** will carboload you with pancakes, waffles, omelettes, or even burgers for under $5. **The Fisherman's Wharf** is a moderately priced restaurant on the second floor of The Wharf Shopping Center. You can perch here and watch life go by on Front Street below. The menu presents *mahi mahi* for $6.50, deep-fried scallops, $8.50, or cold combination seafood plate for $9.75, with most entrees under $13.

A good one for a quick snack is **Mr. Sub,** tel. 667-5683, at 129 Lahainaluna Road. They feature double-fisted sandwiches and packed picnic lunches. **Take Home Maui** has sandwiches, soups, plate lunches, and a variety of fruit drinks. Eat on the veranda or take it along. From here you can mail a Maui pineapple back home.

Blackie's Bar is on Route 30 across from the Lahaina Cannery Shopping Center. Look for the orange roof. Open daily 10 a.m. to 10 p.m., tel. 667-7979. An institution, sort of, selling Mexican food and hamburgers! It's also known for its jazz on Sun., Mon., Wed., and Fri. evenings from 5 to 8 p.m.

Aside from the full range of produce, vitamins, and health foods, the **Westside Natural Food and Deli** on Dickenson has some reasonably priced and healthy prepared foods and fruit drinks.

Fast Food

Fanatics can get their fix at: **Burger King,** on Front Sreet near the banyan tree; **Pizza Hut** at 127 Hinau Street; or across the street at **Chris's Smokehouse.** The Lahaina Shopping Center has **Jack in the Box, McDonald's, Kentucky Fried Chicken,** and **Denny's** across the street.

Moderate

Musahi's is a Japanese restaurant and sushi bar in the Lahaina Shopping Center, tel. 667-6207, open daily for lunch 11 a.m. to 2 p.m., dinner 5 to 9:45. p.m. A wonderful assortment of Japanese dishes for lunch, like *tonkatsu* and sukiyaki, all cost under $9; for dinner add about $6. The best deal however is all-you-can-eat sushi at lunchtime for only $12.50, a mere pittance for true sushi fanatics. The interior is modern American with enough natural wood around and shoji screens to give a Japanese feel. This restaurant is tops for what it serves, and the prices are right.

Kobe Japanese Steak House is at 136 Dickenson at the corner of Luakini, tel. 667-5555, open daily for dinner from 5:30 p.m. Service is *teppan yaki*-style, which means that the chef comes to you. His sharp blade flashes through the air and thumps the table, keeping the culinary beat as it slices, dices, and minces faster than any Veg-o-matic you've ever seen. The delectables of marinated meat, chicken, and vegetables are then expertly flash-fried at your own grill, oftentimes with aplomb in a ball of sake- induced flame. The experience is fun, the food very good, and the interior authentic Japanese. *Teppan* meals come complete with soup, tea, and dessert. Expect to spend at least $15 for an entree, $10 for an appetizer, or have sake or beer while munching at the sushi bar.

New on the restaurant scene is the **Tigar Restaurant,** upstairs at 730 Front Street, tel. 661-0112. Here you'll find good sushi, three full-course Korean meals, and vegetable, chicken, seafood, and meat dishes cooked in the traditional manner by a Korean chef. With its black-lacquer furniture, potted plants, and modern architecture, it has a formal yet comfortable feel. Dowstairs is the Tigar's Den for plate lunches, quick food, and live evening entertainment.

The **Harbor Front Restaurant** on the second floor at The Wharf Shopping Center on Front Street, tel. 667-8212, has a logo that reads "Established a long time ago." Lunch up

to $10, $6.50 sandwiches, $19 dinners. A display case at the entrance holds the fresh catch-of-the-day. The interior is surprisingly well done with many hanging plants in distinctive planters, high-backed wicker chairs, and white tables and bright orange table settings.

Lahaina Steak 'n' Lobster is at 1312 Front St., way at the west end near the Cannery Shopping Center, tel. 667-5558. They offer $8.95 early-bird specials like *mahi mahi,* prime rib, or teriyaki chicken from 5 to 6:30 p.m. The bar opens at 3 p.m. Nothing fancy, but a straightforward filler-up at a good price.

The **Whale's Tail** is next door to The Wharf Shopping Plaza, second level, at 666 Front St., tel. 661-3676. Daily lunch 11:30 a.m. to 2:30 p.m., dinner from 5 p.m. They usually offer a guitarist, or sometimes an entire band for afternoon and evening entertainment. Lobster and filet mignon, $17.95, fresh catch in mango and butter, $19.95, or *mahi mahi* tempura $15.95. Lunch specials for only $3.95, a good centrally located place to "perve" on the action. Children's menu.

Harpooner's Lanai is in the Pionner Inn, tel. 661-3636. Daily breakfast from 7 a.m., lunch from 11:30 a.m. Basic but good foods including pancakes and butter, and Portuguese bean soup. Most dishes and sandwiches under $8.

Kimo's, 845 Front St., tel. 661-4811, is friendly and has great harbor and sunset views on the lower level. If you're in Lahaina around 6 p.m. and need a break, head here to relax with some "Kimo therapy." Popular, but no reservations taken. They offer seafood from $12, with most entrees between $15 and $25, and are known for their catch-of-the-day, usually the best offering on the menu; limited menu for children. The downstairs bar has top-notch well drinks featuring brand-name liquors.

Moose McGillycuddy's, 844 Front Street, tel. 667-7758, is almost an institution. A wild and zany place, there is music nightly (live on Fri. and Sat.), daily specials, early-bird specials (both breakfast and dinner), and a happy hour from 4-8 p.m. Their large portions are filling, and the menu reads like a book.

Bettino's, 505 Front Street Mall, tel. 661-8810, is open daily from 7 a.m. It's off the beaten track and a favorite with locals. Italian food, including fettucine from $9.95. Also featured are steaks and seafood, and they're renowned for their enormous salads. Worth the trip, and when others are overcrowded you can usually find a good table here.

Sam's Beachside Grill, at 505 Front Street Mall, tel. 667-4341, is open daily for lunch 11 a.m. to 4 p.m., dinner 5 to 10 p.m., Sunday brunch 9 a.m. to 2 p.m. This is one of the newest additions to the Lahaina food scene. Away from the central action, it's a great bet for always finding a table. The sunset view and classic interior of Italian marble floors and triton shell chandelier as you mount the circular staircase add that special touch for a great evening. Prices on the full menu are moderate, from an assortment of *pu pu* for under $6 to full-course meals from $15 to $20. Popular with restaurant workers and other late-night people, Sam's cuts meal prices in half by about 10 p.m.

Tree House Restaurant in the Maui Marketplace off Front Street serves dinners from 5 to 9 p.m. Keeping with their name, there is a second floor surrounded by trees where you can perch and eat. Most entrees are only $12.95, with appetizers around $7. Lunch from $5.95 to $7.95 and afternoon *pu pu* are also served. An open-air restaurant away from the action and where you can always get a good seat, the Tree House has a full bar. Expect a reasonable meal, but not gourmet.

The **Chart House** at the far west end of Lahaina at 1450 Front St., tel. 661-0937, serves daily dinner 5 to 9:30 p.m. No reservations, and a wait is common. They have another, less crowded restaurant in Kahului; both offer a good selection of seafood and beef. It's reasonably priced with a decent salad bar, and though the food is usually very good, it can slip to mediocre, depending upon the daily chef. There's no way of telling, so you just have to take a chance.

Gourmet Dining
When you feel like putting a major dent in your budget and satisfying your desire for gourmet food, you should be pleased with one of the following.

Avalon: Whoever said "East is East and West is West" would have whistled a different tune if only they had had the pleasure of dining at this terrific restaurant first. Owner/chefs Andy Leeds and Mark Ellman have put together a uniquely blended menu that they've dubbed "Pacific Basin cuisine." Here are dishes from Sausalito to Saigon, and from Mexico City to Tokyo, with a bit of Nebraska and Hong Kong thrown in for good measure. Moreover, they've spiced, herbed, and garnished their delectables by mixing and matching the finest and most refined tastes from all the geographical areas, creating a culinary extravaganza.

If you're tired of the same old appetizers, try Maui onion rings with tamarind-chipotle catsup, or don't resist the combination platter with a selction of the best appetizers for $11.95 (enough for two). Move on to mixed greens and crispy noodles tempting in a ginger sesame dressing, or *gado-gado* on a bed of brown rice turned sumptuous by a Balinese peanut sauce. Drift the Pacific through their grill selections like wok-fried veal in a picante salsa, or savor the juices of succulent Asian prawns with *shitake* mushrooms, or served in a sun-dried tomato and basil cream sauce. If you need more convincing, try the house specialty of whole Dungeness crab and clams in a garlic black bean sauce ($50 for two), or the mouthwatering Asian pasta like mama san wished she could make. If only people could get along together as well as this food! Lunch or late nights are special too with sandwiches at the bar. The Avalon is at 844 Front St., Lahaina, HI 96761, tel. 667-5559, just below Moose McGillycuddy's.

Gerard's: Everyone knows that to qualify as a *real* Frenchman you must be an artist. Gerard Reversade, trained in the finest French culinary tradition since age 14, creates masterpieces. He feels that eating is not *an* experience, but *the* experience of life, around which everything else that is enjoyable revolves. He is aided by his friend Pierre, the hospitable wine steward, who intimately understands the magical blend of wine and food, bringing out the best in both. The menu changes, but it's always gourmet. Breakfast and lunch are actually quite reasonable, with many portions being large enough for two to share. Some superb choices are the island greens with raspberry vinaigrette dressing, and crusty French bread. Appetizers feature mouthwatering choices like *shitake* and wild mushrooms in a puff pastry. Full entrees like herbed rack of lamb, or savory veal in a light tomato sauce and a side of spinach-and cheese-filled ravioli, titillate the palate. Gerard also insists that the people working as waiters and waitresses share his philosophy, so along with the excellent food comes excellent service.

This elegant restaurant is in the **Plantation Inn** (see above), the epitome of neo-Victorian charm. The comfortable, puff-pillowed wicker chairs, fine linen and table settings, along with the glass-topped tables on the dining veranda couldn't be more perfect. Fronting the building is a small dining garden, and inside the interior is rich with hardwood floors and a full oak bar. If you want a truly memorable dining experience go to Gerard's, at 174 Lahainaluna Rd., tel. 661-8939. Breakfast is for hotel guests only, but dinner is served from 6-10 p.m. daily, with lunch on Friday only from 11:30 a.m to 2 p.m. Parking and validated free parking nearby.

Alex's Hole-in-the-Wall, down an alleyway at 834 Front, tel. 661-3197, will put a small hole in your wallet and a big smile on your face. The food is Italian with delights like veal parmigiana for $23, and chicken marsala for $16. The pasta is locally made and fresh. Open for dinner daily except Sun., from 6 to 10 p.m. Lunch from Mon. to Fri. from 11 a.m. to 2:30 p.m. has less expensive salads, sandwiches, and pasta.

Longhi's, 888 Front St., tel. 667-2288, serves daily from 7:30 a.m. to 10 p.m. Longhi owns the joint and he's a character. He feels that his place has "healing vibes" and that man's basic food is air. Prices at Longhi's may seem expensive but the portions are enormous and can fill two. Better yet is ordering a half-order for half-price, which is really just a little less than a full order. With all meals and salads comes a wonderful basket of jalapeno and pizza breads which are delicious and filling in themselves. Sometimes people complain about the service. It is different! No written menu, so when you sit down and aren't handed one, you might feel ignored, especially when they're busy. Don't! The waiter or waitress will come around and explain the menu to you. This is an attempt to make the dining experience richer, and it does with the added benefit of personal attention if you just wait and relax. Mornings you can order *frittatas,* like spinach, ham, and bacon, $5.50, easily enough for two. A good lunch choice is pasta Siciliana with calamari, spicy with marinara sauce; for dinner, the prawns amaretto and shrimp Longhi are good. Save room for the fabulous desserts that circulate on a tray, from which you may choose. It's hard not to have a fine meal here; there's always a line, no reservations, no dress code, and complimentary valet parking! There's also entertainment in the upstairs bar, which is open nightly, with live dance music Fri. and Sat. from 10:30 p.m.

Tasca, at 608 Front Street, is the new kid on the block and is carving out an epicurean niche for itself in Lahaina. Operated by three Frenchmen, Tasca's serves "tapas", which are snacks or hors d'oeuvers-like food, and most items on the menu can be ordered in small, medium, or large portions. Rather than ordering an ordinary meal, sample several of the dishes here like red potatoes, pan-fried oysters, prawns Mediteranean, paella (spicy saffron rice with shellfish, seafood, and chicken), or ratatouille, and top it off with a rich sinful dessert like creme caramel, chocolate mousse, or fresh strawberries and Grand Marnier. You won't be disappointed. Open Mon. to Sat. 11:30 a.m. to midnight (from 5:30 p.m. to midnight on Sun.), Tapas is a gathering place for the late-night crowd.

La Bretagne, at the east end town on Mokuhinia Place, is in a vintage historical house surrounded by a tamed jungle of greenery. Open daily for dinner from 6 p.m., tel. 661-8966. Reservations. French, and a touch pretentious? But of course, *ma chere!* Meals run $20 and up. Elegant dining with exemplary desserts. The menu changes daily, but a great standby is bouillabaisse in puff pastry. A small place and very leisurely, expect to spend two hours dining and lounging. Among the best on the island.

Chez Paul, five miles east of Lahaina in Olowalu, tel. 661-3843, is secluded, romantic, very popular, and French—what else! Local folks into elegant dining give it two thumbs up. The wine list is tops, the desserts fantastic, and the food, *magnifique!* Prices start at $22. There are two seatings daily at 6:30 and 8:30 p.m., reservations only, credit cards accepted.

ENTERTAINMENT

Lahaina is one of those places where the real entertainment is the town itself. The best thing to do here is to stroll along Front Street and people-watch. As you walk along, it feels like a block party with the action going on all around you—as it does on Halloween. Some people duck into one of the many establishments along the south side of Front Street for a breather, a drink, or just to watch the sunset. It's all free, enjoyable, and safe.

Art Night
Friday night is Art Night in Lahaiana. In keeping with its status as the cultural center of Maui, Lahaina opens the doors of its galleries, throws out the welcome mat, sets out food and drink, provides entertainment, and usually hosts a well-known artist or two for this weekly party. It's a fine social get-together where the emphasis is upon gathering people together to appreciate the arts and not necessarily on making sales. Take your time and stroll Front Street from one gallery to the next. Stop and chat with shopkeepers, munch the goodies, sip the wine, look at the pieces on display, corner the featured artist for comment on his/her work, soak in the music of the strolling musicians, and strike up a conversation with the person next to you who is eyeing that same piece of art with the same respect and admiration. It's a party. People dress up, but don't be afraid to come casually. Take your time and immerse yourself in the immense variety and high quality of art on display in Lahaina.

Halloween
This is one of the big nonofficial events of the year. It seems that everyone dresses in costume, strolls Front Street, parties around town, and gets into the spirit of the evening. It is a party in the street with lots of people, dance, music, color, and activities. In fact, it's becoming so popular with some that they fly in from Honolulu just for the night.

Night Spots/Discos
All of the evening entertainment in Lahaina are in restaurants and lounges (see corresponding restaurants in "Food" for details). The following should provide you with a few laughs.

Jazz is featured at **Blackie's** Sun., Mon., Wed., and Fri. evenings from 5 to 8 p.m.; there's free Hawaiian music and dance at the **Wharf Shopping Mall** courtyard as announced in the free tourist literature, and jam sessions and popular combos at the **Whale's Tale**.

An old standby with yet another new name (formerly The Keg, Blue Max) is **The Tiger Den** at 730 Front St., tel. 667-7003. Besides all-day videos on their big-screen TV, they rock nightly with various bands, singers, and combos. A Korean fine-dining restaurant is upstairs. Live music is performed from 9:30 p.m. to closing. Still a good place to groove.

You, too, can be a disco king or queen on Longhi's black-and-white chessboard dance floor every weekend (see "Food" above). **Moose McGillycuddy's** (just listen for the loud music on Front Street) is still a happening place with nightly music though it's becoming more of a cruise joint for post-adolescents. Those that have been around Lahaina for a while usually give it a miss, but if you want to feast your eyes on prime American two-legged beef on the hoof, this place is for you.

The new experience in town is *Stardancer,* the floating, art-deco dinner and disco nightclub, associated with Club Lanai. The *Stardancer* is anchored a short distance from shore and a shuttle ferries you out for an enchanting evening. There are two seatings for the dinner cruise, at 5 p.m. and 7:30 p.m., with Sun. brunch at 9 a.m. For those making the scene on the black-and-white dance floor, shuttles start at 10 p.m. and run every half hour until 2 a.m. from pier 4. Dress code. Reservations required; call tel. 871-1144.

Hawaii Experience Omni Theater at 824 Front has continuous showings on the hour from 10 a.m. to 10 p.m. (45-min. duration), adults $5.95, children 12 and under $3.95. The idea is to give you a total sensory experience by means of the giant, specially designed concave screen. You sit surrounded by it. You will tour the islands as if you were sitting in a helicopter or diving below the waves. And you'll be amazed at how well the illusion works. You'll soar over Kauai's Waimea Canyon, dip low to frolic with humpbacks, and rise with the sun over Haleakala. If you can't afford the real thing, this is about as close as you can get. The lobby of the theater doubles as a gift shop where you can pick up souvenirs like carved whales, T-shirts, and a variety of inexpensive mementos, including Maui chips.

Cinema

Lahaina Cinemas, the only multi-plex theater on West Maui, are located on the third floor of the Wharf Shopping Center. Showing only first-run features, movies start at about 12 noon and run throughout the day. Adults $5, kids 12-16 $3.50, seniors and children $2.50; all seats $2.50 until 5 p.m.

Drugs

Like everywhere else in Hawaii, the main street drug is *pakalolo.* You might pass guys on Front Street, especially around the seawall, who'll make a distinctive "joint sucking" sound or whisper, "Buds?" It's usually vacuum-packed in Seal-a-Meal plastic bags; the tendency is to push the crops out as fast as possible, creating plenty of immature smoke. Most growers save all the best buds for personal use and pawn off the inferior stuff on the tourists. Some even go to the trouble of wrapping leaf tightly with thread to make it look good. It's a gamble, but most deals are usually straight, although inflated, business transactions.

Hookers

Lahaina had more than its share last century, and thankfully they haven't had a great resurgence, as in Waikiki. In the words of one long-time resident, "There's no prostitution in Lahaina. People come as couples. For single people, there's so much free stuff around that the pros would go hungry." Skin merchants in Honolulu, operating under the thin guise of escort services or masseuses, will fly their practitioners to Maui, but anyone going to this length would be better off at home on their knees praying for any kind of a clue to life!

SHOPPING

Once learned, everybody loves to do the "Lahaina Stroll." It's easy. Just act cool, nonchalant, and give it your best strut as you walk the gauntlet of Front Street's exclusive shops and exotic boutiques. The fun is just in being here. If you begin in the evening, go to the east end of town and park down by Prison Street; it's much easier to find a spot and you walk westward, catching the sunset.

The Lahaina Stroll

On Prison, check out **Dan's Green House,** specializing in birds, and *fukubonsai.* These miniatures were originated by David Fukumoto. They're mailable (except to Australia and Japan), and when you get them home, just plop them in water and presto . . . a great little plant, from $16-27.

The **505 Front Street Mall** offers a barrel full of shops, stores, and restaurants at the south end of Front Street, away from the heavier foot traffic. The mall is like a New England village, and the shopping is good and unhurried with free underground parking for customers. Some shops include **Maui Scrim-**

Dan and friends (J.D. BISIGNANI)

shaw and Nautical Co., selling carved ivory and neat items for the sailor, **The Bikini Center** for swimwear, **Cruiser Bob's** for a Haleakala downhill experience, **Maui Beach Center** for all your surf and sand needs, and **Panama Jack's** for men's clothes. Also at the mall, **Sea Level Trading Co.,** open all week, Mon. through Sat. 10 a.m. to 9 p.m., till 6 p.m. on Sun., has affodable hand-painted cotton clothing from $7.50 to $60, with a design emphasis on Hawaiian flowers and marinelife.

Lee Sands Eelskins, open daily 9:30 a.m. to 9:30 p.m., is filled with accessories, clothing, handbags, briefcases, purses, and belts made from reptile and other unique animal skins. If "you are what you wear," set your own standards by adorning yourself in something made from pig skin, cobra, shark, stingray, peacock, and even chicken skin.

As you head west on Front **Pearls of Tahiti** will make you swoon with its assortment of fine jewelry and beads. **Shibumi Leather** has bags, purses, belts, etc. that you'll be proud to take home. Visit the "pin and ink" artist upstairs at **Skin Deep Tatooing,** tel. 661-8531, where you can get a permanent memento of your tip to Maui. They feature "new age primal, tribal tattoos," Japanese-style intricate beauties, with women artists for shy women clientele. The walls are hung with sample photos and Harley-Davidson T-shirts that say Maui or Hawaii. No wimps allowed! **Cammellia** is a treasure chest laden with gifts and jewelry made from gold, silver, and ivory. **Pricilla's Maui** sells T-shirts, towels, beach blankets, sunglasses, and other assorted items, and **Alexia** features natural clothing with supernatural price tags. **Cotton Comfort, Maui Style** may be cheaper, with lovely cotton clothing and hats that can be hand-painted, unique gifts for someone back home.

The Wharf Shopping Center at 658 Front offers three floors of eateries and shops. Browse **Lahaina Shirt Gallery** for fine aloha shirts. **Seeger People,** on the ground floor, tel. 661-1084, is a shop with a new concept—you create your own photo souvenir of Maui. A series of photos is mounted on a quarter-inch acrylic backing, and then cut out to form a multiple-image sculpture of you and/or your family. Costs $150, prepaid, mailed to you

within four weeks. **The Whaler's Book Shoppe** on the third floor is well stocked with books, everything from Hawaiiana to bestsellers. There's a coffee bar where you can relax and read. The **Mad Hatter** has an unbelievable variety of straw (and a few cloth) hats. If you can't find something here to fit your head, your style, and your pocketbook, you won't find it anywhere. **Island Coins and Stamps** on the second floor is a shop as frayed as an old photo album. They specialize in philatelic supplies. For postal needs and gifts stop by the **Lahaina Mail Depot** on the lower level at the rear. Across the walk is a free exhibit about the lighthouses of Hawaii, a project of the Lahaina Restoration Foundation. The Fresnel lens on display was once in the lighthouse at Kalaupapa on Molokai. Next door to this display is **Island Sandals,** a small shop run in the honest old-style way that produces fully adjustable, tie sandals, styled from the days of Solomon. As the gregarious sandalmaker says, he creates the right sandal for $85 and gives you the left as a gift. Stop in and have him trace your feet for an order (or mail in tracings). As he works, he'll readily talk about political, social, or island local issues.

More Front Street Shopping
Claire the Ring Lady, with rings for every finger and occasion, is open 9:30 a.m. to 9:30 p.m., tel. 667-9288. Featured are gems from all over the world that Claire collects herself; 14-karat gold settings start at $95. Nearby, **Luana's** features contemporary resortwear, hand-painted accessories, and jewelry. **Seabreeze Ltd.** is a souvenir store with junk, like fake leis or generic muumuus that are no better or worse than others you'll find along Front Street, but their prices are good, especially for film. **The South Seas Trading Post** is just across from the Wo Hing Temple, at 851 Front St., tel. 661-3168, open daily 8:30 a.m. to 10 p.m., and is the second oldest shop open in modern Lahaina, dating back to 1871. They indeed have artifacts from the South Pacific, like tapa cloth from Tonga, but also colorful rugs from India, primitive carvings from Papua New Guinea, and Burmese *kalaga* wall hangings with their beautiful and intricate stitching from $30 to $300. You can pick up a one-of-a-

kind bead necklace for only a few dollars, or a real treasure that would adorn any home, for a decent price. Sold are antiques and reproductions; the bona fide antiques have authenticating dates on the back or bottom sides. **Maui Clothing Co.** has racks of hand-screened men's, women's, and kids' apparel; nice stuff. **Crazy Shirts** also has a great assortment of T-shirts and other clothes. Also in this store at 865 Front Street is the tiny but intriguing **Lahaina Whaling Museum** (free) that displays antiques, nautical instruments, scrimshaw, harpoons, and other whaling artifacts. Open 9 a.m. to 10 p.m. Mon. to Sat., until 9 p.m. on Sunday.

The **Lahaina Shopping Center**, just behind Longhi's, has a few inexpensive shops, a drugstore, and **Nagasako's Market**, known for its good selection of local and Oriental food. Across the street are the **Lahaina Square Shopping Center**, with a **Foodland**, and the **Lahaina Business Plaza** with many more shops. Across Papalaua Street is the new **Lahaina Center** with **Hilo Hatties, Hard Rock Cafe,** and other shops yet to be determined.

Golden Reef is at 695 Front St., tel. 667-6633, open daily 10 to 10. Inside is all manner of jewelry from heirloom quality to costume baubles made from black, gold, red, and pink coral, malachite, lapis, and mother of pearl. All designs are created on the premises. Everyone will be happy shopping here because prices range from $1 to $1000 and more. Golden Reef is also very happy to create individual one-of-a-kind work for you and you alone.

In the **Old Poi Factory**, **Pacific Visions** sells hand-painted local garments done at Haiku, and art-deco items from Los Angeles, San Francisco, and New York. Or pick up a plumeria lei fashioned by a local girl sitting in an old chair for only $3. **Fox Photo** one-hour lab is on Front Street just across the street.

Off The Main Drag

Just off Front Street and Lahainaluna is **The Lahaina Market Place**, a collection of semi-open-air stalls, open daily 9-9. Some buskers have roll-up stands and sell trinkets and baubles like hanging crystals and ivory *netsuke*.

It's junk, but it's neat junk. An interesting shop is **Donna's Designs**, where Donna has tie-dyed T-shirts and sweatshirts with wild colors. For only $15 they make distinctive beachwear that will dazzle the eyes. **Crystal Creations** has fine examples of Austrian crystal and pewterwear, and **Annie's Candle Shop** deals in hand-dipped candles. **Kula Bay**, tel. 667-5852, open 9 to 9, sells distinctive, 100% cotton tropical clothing that has been fabric washed. Not ordinary tourist quality, they have special prints exclusive to Kula Bay, reprints from the '40s and '50s.

Nagamine Camera at 139 Lahainaluna Rd., tel. 667-6255, open daily 8:30 a.m. to 8:30 p.m., is a full-service, one-hour-developing camera store. They're the best on West Maui for any specialized photo needs. Prices on film, however, could be better.

To save some money try **991 Limahana Place** just near the Sugar Cane Train Depot off Hwy. 30. Here you'll find **Posters Maui**, which features a wide selection of posters that you'll spot on Front Street, but at a more reasonable price; **J.R.'s Music Shop** has a great selection of music from "Beyond the Reef" to new age, but the prices aren't much cheaper than elsewhere.

The **Salvation Army Thrift Shop** on Shaw Street just up from Front Street has the usual collection of inexpensive used goods but occasionally some great buys on older aloha shirts. Open Mon. through Sat., regular business hours.

Arts, Crafts, And Photos

At The Wharf Shopping Mall check out the **The Royal Art Gallery,** with distinctive paintings of island dream scenes of superimposed faces in the clouds. Make sure to visit the **Lahaina Art Society** in the basement of the old jail in the courthouse. The artists here are up and coming, and the prices for sometimes remarkable works are reasonable. The **Waterfront Gallery and Gifts** will tickle big kids with their fine ships, models, and imported sheep skins.

The vintage open-beamed stone building of the Seamen's Hospital (see pp. 71 and 171) is the perfect setting for **Lahaina Printsellers**, tel. 667-7843. It is much more poignant looking at the antique prints and charts hung on the plaster walls because the seamen who used them, or whose lives depended upon them, may have actually lain ill in these very rooms. The building itself is a monument to the days of the great explorations, and the great hardships involved in opening the Pacific.

Provenance Gallery of Hawaii, at 122 Lahainaluna Rd., tel. 667-6222 or (800) 367-8047, ext. 555, advertise themselves as world-class art, and they are. Inside is artwork by Dali, Picasso, and Chagall. Others include Joseph Venus, an American Indian who has captured the breath of the Great Spirit in his distinctive works; Guillaume Azoulay, one of only three living artists displayed at the Louvre; a wonderful collection of seascapes, often in panels like Japanese paintings, by Gary Fenske; Robert Blue's *Vogue*-like high-fashion women that are the rage in Japan; Eyvind Earle, the genius, famous for illustrating the Disney movies *Sleeping Beauty, Fantasia,* and *Snow White*; Frederic Remington's cowboys and Indians are here locked in fluid bronze; and Brian Davis brightens the walls with his famous flowers.

Lahaina Cannery Shopping Center

As practical looking as its name on the outside, the center's bright and well-appointed interior features some of the best and most convenient shopping on West Maui, open 9:30 a.m. to 9:30 p.m. If you'll be staying at a condo and doing your own cooking, the largest and generally least expensive supermarket on West Maui is **Safeway,** open daily 24 hours. To book any activities, from a whale-watch to a dinner cruise, you'll find the **Ocean Activities Center** offers the most activities on Maui for the right price. Quickies can be picked up at the **ABC Sundry Store,** and you can beat the sun's glare by stopping into **Shades of Hawaii.** Chocoholics will be happy to discover the **Rocky Mountain Chocolate Factory,** where they even have sugarless chocolates for diabetics. **Dolphin Galleries** is an art shop specializing in whales and other mammals of the sea. Fast food is available at **Orange Julius** and **Burger King.** Although the mall is new, don't let that fool you because some of Lahaina's oldest and best shops, like the **Scrim-**

shaw Factory and **Gem Creations,** are here. You can take care of all your needs with shops like **Superwhale** for the kids, or **The Maui Dive Shop, Crazy Shirtz,** and the **Footlocker. Waldenbooks** has one of its excellent, well-stocked stores in the mall. Open daily 9:30 a.m. to 9:30 p.m., tel. 667-6172. One of the most unusual shops is **The Kite Fantasy,** featuring kites, windsocks, and toys for kids of all ages. You can buy kites like a six-foot flexifoil for $105 or a simple triangular plastic kite for only $2.50. Cloth kites are made from nylon with nice designs for a reasonable $15.95.

If you're into designer coffees come to **Sir Wilfred's.** They also feature lunches like roast beef on a baguette for $4.25 and quiche for $2.50. Their great selection of roasted coffees also make a terrific gift. **Longs Drugs** is one of the cheapest places to buy and develop film. You can also find a selection of everything from aspirin to boogie boards.

Local Motion, at 1295 Front, tel. 661-7873, across from the Cannery Shopping Center, open Mon.-Sat. 9 a.m. to 9 p.m., Sun. 9 a.m. to 6 p.m., tel. 661-7873, specializes in cotton T-shirts and lycra sportswear, most bearing the "Local Motion" logo. T-shirts are priced around $12; they're beauties and make great souvenirs. Also surfboards, boogie boards, skateboards, and skim boards for sale and rent.

All those dreams of past and present kids "wished upon a star" come to life in the **Maui Mouse House** across from the Cannery Shopping Center, at 1287 Front St., tel. 661-5758, open daily 9 to 9. Owner/dreamer Martha Hughes has collected amazing gifts of licensed Disney merchandise. All the characters are here—Donald Duck and the boys, Mickey, Minnie, Pluto, and those whacky, wild Looney Toons. The shop is a stuffed toy of apparel, jewelry, stationery, educational materials, T-shirts, sweatshirts, umbrellas, and more. "Tha-that's all folks."

SERVICES AND INFORMATION

Emergency: For fire, police, or ambulance, dial 911 throughout the Lahaina area. **Banks:** In Lahaina during normal banking hours try **Bank of Hawaii** in the Lahaina Shopping

Center, tel. 661-8781; **First Interstate** at 135 Papalaua St., tel. 667-9714; or **First Hawaiian,** Papalaua St., tel. 661-3655.

Post Office

The post office is on the west edge of town towards Kaanapali, well marked, tel. 667-6611. **Lahaina Mail Depot** is a post office contract station located at The Wharf Shopping Plaza, 658 Front St., tel. 667-2000. They're open 10 a.m. to 5 p.m. (until 1 p.m. Sat.) and along with the normal stamps, etc., they specialize in sending packages home. They've got mailing boxes, tape, and packaging materials. They also sell souvenir packs of coffee, nuts, candies, and teas which might serve as a last-minute purchase, but are expensive. In the Lahaina Shopping Center you'll find the **Mail Room** for shipping and packaging services. Hours 9:30 a.m. to 6 p.m. Mon. to Fri, Sat until 3:30 p.m.; closed for lunch.

Medical Treatment

A concentration of all types of specialists is found at **Lahaina Medical Group,** located at Lahaina Square, tel. 667-2534. Look also at the **Maui Medical Group,** tel 661-0051, on Prison Street. Open Mon. to Fri 8 a.m. to 5 p.m. and Sat. 8 a.m. to 12 noon; call for emergency hours. Professional medical care can also be had at the **Kaiser Permanente Clinic** on Wainee Street, tel. 661-0081. Alternatively, the **Lahaina Health Center,** 180 Dickenson St. at Dickenson Square, Suite 205, tel. 667-6268, offers acupuncture, chiropractic, therapeutic massage, and podiatry. Most practitioners charge approximately $30 for their services. In Suite 218 of the Dickenson Square are **Doctors On Call,** tel. 667-7676. They see patients in the office or will make house or hotel calls from 7 a.m. to 11 p.m. daily. Pharmacies in Lahaina include: **Lahaina Pharmacy** at the Lahaina Shopping Center, tel. 661-3119, and **Valley Isle** at 130 Prison, tel. 661-4747.

Next door to Lahaina Health Center is **Lahaina Nautilus Center,** tel. 667-6100, that has exercise machines, free weights, and massage by appointment. Open Mon. to Fri. 6:30 a.m. to 10 p.m., Sat. 8-8, and Sun. 9-2. Daily, weekly, and monthly (from $50 for one month to $499 for one year) rates available. One-hour massages run $32 members and $47 for nonmembers.

Laundromats

Try **Fabritek Cleaners,** Lahaina Shopping Center, tel. 661-5660. For self-service try **Cabanilla Kwik'n Kleen,** also at the Lahaina Shopping Center, or the 24-hour **First Hawaiian Laundry** on Limahula Street, behind Pizza Hut, tel. 661-3061.

Information

The following groups and organizations should prove helpful: **Lahaina Restoration Foundation,** Box 338, Lahaina, HI 96761, tel. 661-3262, or in the "Master's Reading Room" along Front Street. They are a storehouse of information about historical Maui; make sure to pick up their brochure, *Lahaina, A Walking Tour of Historic and Cultural Sites.* **The library** is at 680 Wharf St., tel. 661-0566, open Mon. through Thursday. Stop in at **Whaler's Book Shoppe** in the upper level of The Wharf Mall along Front Street. They have an excellent book selection as well as a gourmet coffee and sandwich shop if you get tired browsing. See also "Information" in the main Introduction for general information sources.

KAANAPALI AND VICINITY

Five lush valleys, nourished by streams from the West Maui Mountains, stretch luxuriously for 10 miles from Kaanapali northwest to Kapalua. All along the connecting **Honoapiilani Highway** (Rt. 30), the dazzle and glimmer of beaches is offset by black volcanic rock. Two sensitively planned and beautifully executed resorts are at each end of this drive. Kaanapali Resort is 500 acres of fun and relaxation at the east end. It houses six luxury hotels, six beautifully appointed condos, a shopping mall and museum, 36 holes of world-class golf, tennis courts galore, and epicurean dining in a chef's salad of cuisines. Two of the hotels, the **Hyatt Regency** and **Westin Maui**, are inspired architectural showcases that blend harmoniously with Maui's most beautiful seashore surroundings. At the western end is another gem, the **Kapalua Resort,** 750 of Maui's most beautifully sculpted acres with its own showcase, the **Kapalua Bay Hotel.** Here, too, is prime golf, **Fleming Beach,** plus exclusive shopping, horseback riding, and tennis aplenty.

Kaanapali, with its four miles of glorious beach, is Maui's westernmost point. In general, it begins where Lahaina ends, and continues west along Route 30 until a mile or so

before the village of Honokowai. Adjacent at the west end are the villages of Honokowai and Kahana, which service the condos tucked away here and there along the coast and mountainsides. Both are practical stops where you can buy food, gas, and all necessary supplies to keep your vacation rolling. The accommodations are not as grand, but the beaches and vistas are. Along this entire southwestern shore, Maui flashes its most captivating pearly white smile. The sights all along this coast are either natural or manmade, but not historical. This is where you come to gaze from mountain to sea and bathe yourself in natural beauty. Then, after a day of surf and sunshine, you repair to one of the gorgeous hotels or restaurants for a drink or dining, or just to promenade around the grounds.

History

Southwestern Maui was a mixture of scrub and precious *lo'i* land, reserved for taro, the highest life-sustaining plant given by the gods. The farms stretched to Kapalua, skirting the numerous bays all along the way. The area was important enough for a "royal highway" to be built by Chief Piilani, and it still bears his name. Westerners used the lands surrounding Kaanapali to grow sugar cane, and **The Lahaina, Kaanapali, and Pacific Railroad,** known today as the "Sugar Cane Train," chugged to Kaanapali Beach to unburden itself onto barges that carried the cane to waiting ships. Kaanapali, until the 1960s, was a blemished beauty where the Pioneer Sugar Mill dumped its rubbish. Then AMFAC, one of the "Big Five," decided to put the land to better use. In creating Hawaii's first planned resort, they outdid themselves. Robert Trent Jones was hired to mold the golf course along this spectacular coast, while the Hyatt Regency and its grounds became an architectural marvel. The Sheraton-Maui was built atop, and integrated with, Puu Kekaa, "Black Rock." This area is a wave-eroded cinder cone, and the Sheraton architects used its sea cliffs as part of the walls of the resort. Here, on a deep underwater shelf, daring divers descend to harvest Maui's famous black coral trees. The Hawaiians believed that Puu Kekaa was a very holy place where the spirits of the dead left this earth and migrated into the spirit world. Kahekili, Maui's most famous 18th-century chief, often came here to leap into the sea below. This old-time daredevil was fond of the heart-stopping activity, and made famous "Kahekili's Leap," an even more treacherous sea cliff on nearby Lanai. Today, the Sheraton puts on a sunset show where this "leap" is reenacted.

Unfortunately, developers picked up on AMFAC's great idea and built condos up the road starting in Honokowai. Interested in profit, not beauty, they earned that area the dubious title of "condo ghetto." Fortunately, the Maui Land and Pineapple Co. owned the land surrounding the idyllic Kapalua Bay, and Colin Cameron, one of the heirs to this holding, had visions of developing 750 acres of the plantation's 20,000 into the extraordinary **Kapalua Bay Resort**. He teamed up with Rockresort Management, headed by Laurence Rockefeller, and the complex was opened in 1979.

Transportation
Kaanapali is serviced by the **Kaanapali Trolley** and by the **Lahaina Cannery Shuttle** as far as that center. The Sugar Cane Train offers a day of fun for the entire family. The Kapalua-

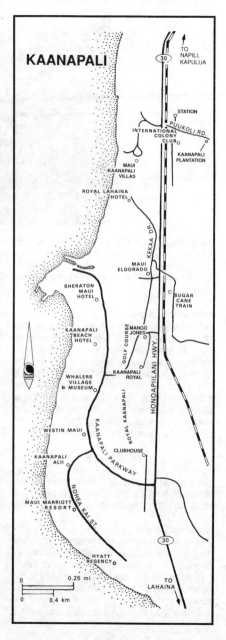

*Burning cane fields
create "Kaanapali
incense."*
(J.D. BISIGNANI)

West Maui Airport is the most convenient for air travel to this end of the island. For details see "Getting There—Airports" and "Getting Around—Public Transportation" in the general Introduction.

Kaanapali Extras

Two situations in and around Kaanapali mar its outstanding beauty—you might refer to them as "Kaanapali Perfume." There are still plenty of sugar cane fields in the area, and when they're being burned off, the smoke is heavy in the air; the soot which falls at this time is called "black snow" by locals. Also, the sewage treatment plant is inadequate, and even the constantly blowing trade winds are insufficient to push this stench out to sea.

BEACHES

The four-mile stretch of pristine sand at Kaanapali is what people come to expect from Maui, and they are never disappointed.

Hanakoo Beach

This is an uninterrupted stretch of sand running from the Hyatt Regency to the Sheraton. Although these are some of the most exclusive hotels on the island, public access to the beach is guaranteed in the state's constitution. There are "rights of way," but parking your car is definitely a hassle. A good idea is to park at

Wahikuli State Park and walk westward along the beach. You can park (10 cars) in the Hyatt's lower lot and enter along a right of way. There's access between the Hyatt and the Marriott (pay parking ramp) and between the Marriott and the Kaanapali Alii, which also has limited parking. There is also some parking near the Sheraton and at the Whaler's Shopping Center parking ramp, but you must pass through the gauntlet of shops.

Black Rock

One of the most easily accessible and visually engaging snorkeling spots on Maui is located at the Sheraton's Black Rock. Follow the main road past the Sheraton until it climbs the hill around back. Walk up the hill and through the hotel grounds until you come to a white metal fence. Follow the fence down toward the sea. You'll come to a spur of rock jutting out, and that's it. The entire area is like an underwater marine park. Enter at the beach area and snorkel west around the rock, staying close to the cinder cone. There are schools of reef fish, rays, and even a lonely turtle. If you want to play it safe, park at the small parking lot at the far west end of Kaanapali near the Aston Kaanapali Villas. It's only a 10-minute walk away.

Sports

For a full listing of the sporting facilities and possibilities in the Kaanapali area, contact the information center in the Whaler's Village or any of the activity desks at the hotels on the strip. **Golf** at the Royal Kaanapali North/South costs $90, par 72, tel. 661-3691. For **tennis,** the most famous is the Royal Lahaina Tennis Ranch with 11 courts, tennis clinics, and tournaments. The Hyatt and Marriott have five courts each, the Whaler three courts, and there's one at the Kaanapali Royal. For **water sports,** catamarans are available twice a day from Kaanapali Beach. Contact any major hotel activities desk in the resort area, or **Maui Beach Center** at the Whaler's Village, tel. 667-4355.

ACCOMMODATIONS

The Kaanapali Resort offers accommodations ranging from "moderate deluxe" to "luxury." There are no budget accommodations here, but just northwest toward Honokowai are plenty of reasonably priced condos. As usual, they're more of a bargain the longer you stay, especially if you can share costs with a few people by renting a larger unit. And as always, you'll save money on food costs. The following should give you an idea of what's available.

Hyatt Regency
Located at Kaanapali's eastern extremity, at 200 Nohea Kai Drive, Lahaina, HI 96761. Reservations are made at tel. (800) 228-9000, or on Maui at tel. 661-1234. The least expensive room in this truly luxury hotel is $195 a day; they go as high as $2000 for the Presidential Suite. Of course, like many Hyatts, you don't have to stay there to appreciate its beauty. If you visit, valet parking is in front of the hotel. Cost is $4.50, or complimentary if you validate your ticket by dining at Spats or the Palm Court, or spend $25 in one of the shops. Around back is a self-parking lot with 160 spaces for guests (disregard numbered spaces; parking here is OK).

The moment you enter the main lobby the magic begins. A multi-tiered architectural extravaganza opens to the sky, birds fly freely, and magnificent potted plants and full-sized palm trees create the atmosphere of a modern Polynesian palace. Nooks and crannies abound where you can lounge in kingly wicker

thrones. The walls are adorned with first-class artwork and tapestries, while glass showcases hold priceless ceramics. Peacocks strut their regal stuff amid impeccable Japanese gardens, and ducks and swans are floating alabaster on a symmetry of landscaped ponds. Around the swimming pool, guests luxuriate on huge blue hotel towels. The pool's architecture is inspired by the islands: grottoes, caves, waterfalls, and a huge slide are all built in. A swinging wood bridge connects the sections, and you can have an island drink at a sunken poolside bar. There are two five-star "Travel Holiday" award-winning restaurants, one doubling as a disco for human peacocking, and the "Elephant Walk," a covey of specialty shops and boutiques. The hotel offers half-hour scuba lessons in the pool for $10, beach dives for $59, and a four-day certification course, including all rental equipment and dives, for $395.

Sheraton-Maui
These 505 rooms are built around Kaanapali's most conspicuous natural phenomenon, Puu Kekaa. For reservations, call (800) 325-3535, or on Maui tel. 661-0031. The prices are not as astronomical as the Hyatt's, with a basic room at $190, up to $400 for an oceanside suite. The snorkeling around Black Rock is the best in the area. There are two pools, and the view from the upper-level **Sundowner Bar** is worth the price of a drink. A catamaran is available to guests, and you can rent snorkeling equipment at a poolside kiosk, but the prices are triple what you pay at a dive shop.

The Westin Maui
The newest in luxury hotels to spring up along Kaanapali, at 2365 Kaanapali Pkwy., Lahaina, HI 96761, tel. 667-2525, (800) 228-3000, is actually a phoenix, risen from the old Maui Surf Hotel. True to the second life of that mythical bird, it is a beauty. Westin is known for its fabulous entranceways, lobbies, and quiet nooks, where superb artwork makes you feel as if you're inhabiting a museum. A series of strolling paths take you through resplendent manicured grounds that surround an extensive pool area. Waterfalls, water slides, and natural rock formations all blend to create

civilized paradise. To the left of the main lobby are a collection of exclusive boutiques. The hotel's restaurant, **Cook's at the Beach,** is surprisingly reasonable (see "Food"). Standard rooms begin at $185, $25 extra person, $500-1,600 suites, and $350 Royal Beach Club. The price range, as usual, depends upon the view.

Royal Lahaina Resort
The largest acreage of all in Kaanapali, these 27 idyllic acres surround 514 luxurious rooms. The tropical landscaping leads directly to the sun-soaked beach. The property, one of the first to be developed, is divided into two categories: cottages and towers. Rates range from a standard room at $150 to a deluxe oceanfront at $225. The cottages rent from $175 to $225, with suites from $300 to $1,000. Reservations can be made at tel. (800) 733-7777 through Outrigger Hotels, Hawaii. There are no less than three restaurants and a nightly luau (see following), and three swimming pools on the well-maintained grounds. It's also home to the **Royal Lahaina Tennis Ranch,** boasting 11 courts and a stadium. Special tennis packages are offered.

Maui Marriott
The fifth of the big five hotels on Kaanapali Beach is the Maui Marriott, 100 Nohea Kai Drive, Lahaina 96761, tel. (800) 228-9290 on

the Mainland, tel. (800) 268-8181 in Canada, or (800) 542-6821 in Hawaii. With over 700 rooms, two swimming pools, a beach recreation center, five tennis courts, two dozen shops, a half dozen restaurants and lounges, and indoor and outdoor parking, the Marriott is one of the largest properties on West Maui. Open to the beach and facing the setting sun, the hotel is graced with cooling breezes which waft across its manicured courtyard and through the open atriums of both its buildings. Indoors, the many flowers and potted plants seem to bring the outdoors inside. On the premises are Lokelani, an excellent seafood restaurant, Nikko Japanese Steak House, one of the best spots for Japanese cuisine on the island, and Banana Moon, the only video disco on Maui and a favorite weekend spot for the young dancing crowd. The hospitable staff orchestrates the numerous daily handicraft and recreational activities. Room rates range from $195 to $285 for mountain- and oceanview rooms, and upwards of $400 for suites. Special honeymoon, tennis, and family plans are available, as well as optional meal plans.

Kaanapali Beach Hotel
For Kaanapali, this hotel is a bargain. Standard rooms from $135, suites to $525, a distinctive whale-shaped pool, and tennis privileges at the Royal Lahaina are some of the amenities. This is perhaps the most "Hawaiian" of

Hyatt Kaanapali pool scene (J.D. BISIGNANI)

the hotels in Kaanapali. For reservations, call (800) 367-5170, on Maui tel. 661-0011.

Condos

Generally less expensive than the hotels, condos begin at around $100 per night and offer full kitchens, some maid service, swimming pools, and often convenience stores and laundry facilities. Off-season rates and discounts for longer stays are usually offered. Combinations of the above are too numerous to mention, so it's best to ask all pertinent questions when booking. Not all condos accept credit cards, and a deposit is the norm when making reservations. The following should give you an idea of what to expect.

The Aston Kaanapali Shores

The green tranquility of this created oasis fronting Kaanapali Beach offers an unsurpassed view of sun-baked Lanai just across the channel. You enter a spacious and airy lobby, open, framing a living sculpture of palms and ferns. Water melts over a huge copper painting-sculpture of the moon, creating a smooth and soothing natural music. The grounds are a trimmed garden in large proportions dappled with sunlight and flowers. Soak away your cares in two whirlpools, one tucked away in a quiet corner of the central garden area for midnight romance, the other near the pool. Sundays offer a special warmth at the Kaanapali Shores, where you can enjoy old-fashioned family fun at "Sandcastle Sundays." Kids of all ages get a bucket and shovel, while sand-sculpture artists help you to build the castle of your dreams. Shop at **Beachside Casuals,** a special children's boutique of hand-picked toys, clothing, and games (big people's clothes, too) that will remind the little ones of their fabulous trip to Maui. Enjoy a romantic dinner at **The Beach Club,** a beautifully appointed restaurant serving delectables ranging from *pasta primavera* to the fresh catch-of-the- day (see "Food"). All units have been recently refurbished with new drapes, carpets, and furniture, and include gourmet kitchens, sweeping lanais, TV, and a/c. Prices range from an affordable studio at $129, to $280 for a two-bedroom oceanfront suite. For reservations contact the Aston Kaanapali Shores at 3445 Lower Honoapiilani Hwy., tel. 667-2211, (800) 367-5124.

Mahana: The second that you walk into these reasonably priced condos and look through a large floor-to-ceiling window framing a swimming pool and the wide blue sea, your cares immediately begin to slip away. The condo sits on a point of beach at 110 Kaanapali Shore Pl., Lahaina, HI 96761, tel. 661-8751, (800) 922-7866, which allows all apartments to have an ocean view at no extra cost. Studios begin at $119, to $199 for a huge two-bedroom (up to six people). Enjoy a complete kitchen plus pool, sauna, tennis, maid service, and a money-saving family plan.

Aston Kaanapali Villas: Enjoy the surroundings of 11 sculpted acres at this affordably priced condo at 2805 Honoapiilani Hwy., Lahaina, HI 96761, tel. 661-7791, (800) 922-7866. The extensive grounds of cool swaying palms harbor three pools, a jacuzzi, and expert tennis courts. Rates begin at $149 for a hotel room, studio suites $164-179, and to $215 for one-bedroom with a/c, cable TV, small refrigerator and coffee pot, and maid service. This property, located at the far west end of the Kaanapali development, has an added bonus of peace and quiet along with the best of the Kaanapali beaches, although you remain just minutes from the action. You're just a few minutes' walk from Black Rock, a superb snorkeling area. The units are very large with spacious bedrooms; even a one-bedroom is capable of handling four people.

Across the street from the villas is the **Lahaina Health Club,** tel. 667-6684, a private club that is open to walk-in guests. There is a room full of excercise machines, free weights, bicycle machines, and floor mats; aerobic classes are also given. Rates range from a $10 one-day fee to $300 one-year membership.

Others in Kaanapali include **International Colony Club** on the *mauka* side of Route 30, tel. 661-4070, (800) 526-6284 during weekday business hours. It offers individual cottages: one bedroom at $95, two bedrooms at $110, and three bedrooms at $130, $10 extra person, four-day minimum. **Maui Eldorado,** tel. (800) 367-2967, on Maui tel. 661-0021, is surrounded by the golf course, rates from $124-214. **Kaanapali Plantation,** tel. 661-

The Aston Kaanapali Shores is an oasis of leisure. *(J.D. BISIGNANI)*

4446, offers accommodations from $85 with a $10 discount for 14 days or longer, plus maid service and most amenities. **Kaanapali Royal,** a golfer's dream right on the course, tel. (800) 367-5637, on Maui tel. 661-7133, has rooms from $160 with substantial low-season and long-term discounts. Next to the Whalers Shopping Center is **The Whaler,** tel. 661-4861 or (800) 367-7052 nathionwide. Rates range from $160 to $525 for studio, one-, and two-bedroom units. **Kaanapali Alii,** tel. 667-1400, (800) 642-6284, has one- and two-bedroom suites from $205 to $550.

FOOD

Every hotel in Kaanapali has at least one restaurant, with numerous others scattered throughout the area. Some of the most expensive and exquisite restaurants on Maui are found in these hotels, but surprisingly, at others you can dine very reasonably, even cheaply.

The Beach Club
Guest or not, a quiet and lovely restaurant in which to dine is **The Beach Club** at the Aston Kaanapali Shores. Centered in the garden area, the restaurant opens to the sea. Request a table in the terrace area overlooking the pool for an especially romantic setting. The interior is classy, with wrought-iron tables and chairs and crisp starched linens. Service is formal but friendly, and the prices are not as rich as the menu. A light appetite will be satiated with soup and Caesar salad for under $7. You can move on to sauté and broiler specialties like veal piccata for $16.95, pasta carbonara at $11.95, or the delicious catch-of-the-day for $17.95 *(opakapaka* sautéed in a marsala sauce is a standout). For reservations call 667-2211, ext. 43.

Nanatomi's
This Japanese restaurant is located upstairs in the clubhouse at the Royal Kaanapali Golf Course, tel. 667-7902. Every night a sushi chef from Japan entertains with his dexterous hands at the 15-seat sushi bar, followed by a Karaoke sing-along until 1 a.m. Open for breakfast, lunch, and dinner featuring an early-bird breakfast special from 7 to 8:30 a.m. for $1.99, or eggs Benedict, $5.75, or homemade buttermilk pancakes for $2.75. Lunch is from 11 a.m. to 3 p.m.—a wide selection of sandwiches and burgers under $6, Korean ribs, $5.75, or a chef salad for $5.75. The dinner menu has a wide variety of *don buri,* meaning everything from fish to pork served in a bowl of rice. A holdover from when Nanatomi's was a Mexican restaurant is their happy hour, featuring stiff margaritas. You can come here to drink Mexican style, lounge Hawaiian style, and eat Japanese style.

Luigi's

This is one of three locations for Luigi's, formerly Apple Annie's, located just off Honoapiilani Highway at the entrance to Kaanapali Resort. Pizza prices start at $7.99 for a regular cheese-only item to $29.99 for a large super combination pizza smothered with toppings, or you can nibble a salad for only $2.99. Pasta ranges from $8.99 for a marinara sauce, to $12.99 for bolognese. Full-course meals include scallops Luigi for $16.99, and steak Luigi for $17.99. This is a family-oriented restaurant. Don't expect food like mama used to make, but it's not bad for adopted Italians. For information and reservations call 661-3160.

Of special interest to those vacationing in condos who want to eat in but don't want to cook is **Chicken Express,** downstairs from Luigi's. They offer a takeout service for pizza, barbecued ribs, chicken, and sub sandwiches. Dinners are as little as $5.49 for three pieces of chicken, biscuits, potatoes, slaw, and salad, tel. 661-4500. You can also eat there or have them deliver—free from Kapalua to Puamana.

Cook's At The Beach

You'll be surprised to find how reasonable this open-air restaurant at the deluxe Westin Maui can be, especially their evening barbecue buffet. Regular menu selections include various seafood platters for under $17, and a selection of wok-prepared items for under $12.50. The all-you-can-eat prime rib buffet is the best deal at $19.75. The salad bar is all you can eat, and live music soothes as the sun dips into the sea. The restaurant opens at 6:30 a.m. with a breakfast buffet for $13.75, lunch from 10:30 a.m., and dinner from 5 to 9 p.m. For information call 667-2525, free valet parking.

Royal Lahaina Resort

You have no less than three establishments from which to choose, plus a luau. Follow your nose nightly to the Luau Gardens, where the biggest problem after the Polynesian Review is standing up after eating mountains of traditional food. Adults $39.95, children under 12 $19, reservations, tel. 661-3611. **Moby Dick's** is a seafood restaurant open for dinner only, tel. 661-3611. Entrees are priced at $16-27, or you can opt for an all-you-can-eat ticket for $18.95. **Royal Ocean Terrace,** tel. 661-3611, is open daily for breakfast, lunch, and dinner, offering a breakfast buffet and better-than-average salad bar. Sunday brunch from 9 a.m. until 2 p.m. is a winner. **Chopsticks** is a "dinner-hour only" restaurant that serves a variety of dishes from Asia, almost like *dim sum,* all under $6.95.

Swan Court

Save this one for a very special evening. You don't come here to eat, you come here to dine, peasant! Anyone who has been enraptured by those old movies where couples regally glide down a central staircase to make their grand entrance will have his or her fantasies come true. Although expensive, you get your money's worth with attention to detail; prosciutto is served with papaya, ginger butter with the fresh catch-of-the-day, and pineapple chutney with the oysters. The wine list is a connoisseur's delight. The Swan Court offers a sumptuous breakfast/brunch buffet daily from 6:30 a.m., $13.95 per person, and worth the price for the view alone. Located in the Hyatt Regency, daily breakfast and dinner, tel. 661-1234.

Spats II is also at the Hyatt, tel. 661-1234, dinner only. They specialize in Italian food, with the average entree around $18. At night the place becomes a disco, and fancy duds are in order. **Lahaina Provision Co.** could only survive with a name like that because it's at the Hyatt. Regular broiled fare, but you get a complimentary bowl of ice cream and are free to go hog-wild with chocolate toppings at their famous chocoholic bar. Guaranteed to make you repent all your sins!

Discovery Room

Located at the Sheraton, tel. 661-0031, open daily for breakfast and dinner. Entrees include island fish from $26-31, chicken Kaanapali, $27, and noisettes of lamb, $29.95. Entertainment is offered at dinner. The **Aloha Luau** uncovers its *imu* daily at 5:30 p.m. beachside at the Sheraton, adults $36, children $19. The luau features Chief Faa, a fire/knife dancer, rum punch, Hawaiian arts and games, and a Polynesian review. For reservations call 667-9564.

Lokelani

At the Maui Marriott, tel. 667-1200, dinner only, from 6 p.m. Full seafood dinners such as sautéed catch-of-the-day are served with all trimmings from $21. Also there is **Nikko's Japanese Steak House,** tel. 667-1200, dinner from 6 p.m. No cheap imports here; prices are high, but the Japanese chef works right at your table slicing meats and vegetables quicker than you can say "samurai." An expensive but fun meal.

Mango Jones

At 2550 Kekaa Drive, tel. 667-6847, **Mango Jones** has a location that can't be beat. This elegant restaurant was at one time the Kaanapali Golf Course clubhouse and still looks down over the entire Kaanapali area. Raised louvered windows let in the cool evening breezes, torchlights beyond the windows lend a magical air, and the low lights set off the mango-colored fixtures, white wicker furniture, and light-blue linen—very genteel. The menu is gourmet with mostly Hawaiian and Polynesian spices used. Entrees include shrimp scampi for $21.99, scallops and Chinese black bean sauce, $17.99, and tofu vegetarian curry, $14.99. Don't leave without trying the chilled mango soup—a refreshing and delicately spiced delight. Daily specials are also available. The adjoining Longhouse Bar makes a wonderful spot to watch the setting sun.

Kaanapali Beach Hotel Restaurants

The hotel might be fancy but the restaurants are down to earth. Try the Tiki Terrace restaurant for meat, poultry, and seafood, or the Koffee Shop for their great priced breakfast, lunch, and dinner buffets. Call 661-0011.

Whaler's Village

This shopping mall has a half dozen or so dining establishments. You can find everything from pizza and frozen yogurt to lobster tail. Prices range from bargain to moderate. An up-and-comer is **Leilani's.** Their selections go from surf to turf. They offer famous Azeka ribs for $13.95, a sushi bar, and a daily dinner special from 5 to 6:30 p.m. for $8.50.

This includes entree, and soup or salad. Call 661-4495. **El Crab Catcher** is a well-established restaurant featuring seafood, with a variety of crab dishes, steaks, and chops. They have a sunken bar and swimming pool with the beach only a stride or two away. Hawaiian music nightly. Desserts are special here from $10. Popular, so reserve at tel. 661-4423.

The **Rusty Harpoon,** previously a "do-it-yourself" broiler, has remodeled and changed its image. They offer a completly new menu and pleasing atmosphere. Piano music at night and popular with the younger set. They also have a bar that serves the best daiquiris. Breakfast is from 8 a.m. to 10:45 a.m., lunch from 11:30 a.m. to 3 p.m., and dinner from 5-10 p.m. New to the center is the art deco **Kaanapali Cafe.** Open for breakfast, lunch, and dinner, it has a wide selection of standard entrees at inexpensive prices. **Yami Yogurt** sells wholesome, well-made sandwiches for $3 and under. Salads, too, and yogurt, of course. Seating outside, tel. 661- 8843. **Ricco's Deli** makes hefty sandwiches for under $6. Their pizzas, pasta, or salads make a good inexpensive lunch, tel. 661-4433.

Chico's Cantina, tel. 667-2777, has a special happy hour from 4 to 6 p.m., when deluxe nachos, usually $5.95, are only $1, and all other menu items are $1 off; drinks are the same price. "Cinco de Chico's" is a special offered the fifth of every month, when you get all items at 50% off. Chico's offers a pleasant atmosphere in a cool stucco setting with plenty of cooling breezes to counterbalance the fiery-hot dishes. Chico's is popular with the young crowd, who tend to gather late at night (taco bar goes until 1:30 a.m.). Stop in for reasonably priced, south-of-the-border food.

ENTERTAINMENT

If you're out for a night of fun and frivolity, Kaanapali will keep you hopping. The dinner shows accompanying the luau at the Hyatt Regency feature pure island entertainment. "Drums of the Pacific" is a musical extravaganza that you would expect from the Hyatt.

There are torch-lit processions and excitingly choreographed production numbers, with all the hula-skirted *wahines* and *malo*-clad *kanes* that you could imagine. Flames add drama to the setting and the grand finale is a fire dance. At both shows you're dined and entertained by mid-evening.

Those with dancing feet can boogie the night away at the Hyatt's **Spats II.** There is a dress code and plenty of room for those "big dippers" on this very large dance floor. Practice your waltzes for the outdoor **Pavilion Courtyard** at the Hyatt. The **Banana Moon** at the Marriott offers the best of both worlds— dance music and quiet, candlelit corners for romance. Most hotels, restaurants, and lounges offer some sort of music. Often it's a local combo singing Hawaiian favorites, or a pianist tinkling away in the background.

SHOPPING

Kaanapali provides a varied shopping scene: the **Whaler's Village Mall,** which is affordable; the **Maui Marriott** for some distinctive purchases; and the **Hyatt Regency** and **Westin Maui,** where most people get financial jitters even window-shopping.

Whaler's Village
Shopping Mall And Museum
This **whaling museum** has a few outside displays but most items are in the enclosed section on the top floor the mall (free). The compact display area is full of whaling history, photgraphs, drawings, artifacts from whaling ships, a reconstructed section of a ship, and many informative descriptions and stories about the whaling industry, whaling life, and the whalers themselves.

You can easily find anything at this mall that you might need. Some of the shops are: **Lahaina Scrimshaw Factory,** tel. 661-4034, for fine examples of scrimshaw and other art objects ranging from affordable to expensive. **Liberty House,** tel. 661-4451, for the usual department store items. **Ka Honu Gift Gallery,** tel. 661-0137, for a large selection of arts and crafts inspired by the islands. Selections

are wide and varied at **Waldenbooks** on the lower level of the mall, tel. 661-8638, open daily 9 a.m. to 9:30 p.m. The bookstore has it all, from light mysteries for beach reading to travel books to guide you happily around the island. **The Eyecatcher** will take care of your eyes with shades from $150 Revos to $5 cheapies. There are many other shops tucked away here and there. They come and go with regularity.

A fascinating new shop is **Lahaina Printsellers and Engravings,** tel. 667-7617, open daily 8:30 a.m. to 10:30 p.m. The shop features all original engravings, drawings, maps, charts, and naturalist sketches ranging in age from 150 to 400 years, each with an authenticity label. The collection comes from all over the world, but the Hawaiiana collection is amazing in its depth, with many works featuring a nautical theme; reminiscent of the amazing explorers who opened the Pacific. The Lahaina Printsellers, although new as a store, have been collecting for over 15 years, and are the largest purveyor of material relating to Captain Cook in the entire Pacific Basin. Prices range from $25 for the smallest antique print up to $15,000 for rare museum-quality work.

Every Saturday from 9-11:30 a.m. there is a sand scupIture demonstration at the mall.

The Hyatt Regency Mall
Off the main lobby and surrounding the gardens are a number of exclusive shops. They're high-priced, but their offerings are first class. Call 667-7421 and ask for the store of your choice. **Elephant Walk** specializes in primitive art such as tribal African masks and carved wooden statues. **Gold Point's** name says it all with baubles, trinkets, bracelets, and rings all in gold. **Sandal Tree** has footwear for men and women with the emphasis on sandals. **Mark Christopher** is a series of shops selling jewelry, glassware, fabrics, and beachwear.

Maui Marriott Mall
The main store here is a **Liberty House,** tel. 667-6142, with the emphasis on clothing. The **Maui Sun and Surf,** tel. 667-9302, is a well-stocked dive and swimwear store where you'll

find everything from visors to top-notch snorkeling equipment; **Friendship Store's** art objects, clothing, silks, and goods are all from the Republic of China. There are also women's stores and jewelry shops.

Center Art Galleries

In the Kaanapali area the Center Art Galleries have showrooms at the Hyatt and Marriott. All are definitely worth a visit even if you only intend to browse. The art selections are superb and varied. Usually you'll find works by celebrity artists, like Tony Curtis portraying his fascination with Marilyn Monroe, Red Skelton's collection of the liquid faces of heart-melting clowns, and Anthony Quinn with his bold van Gogh style. Fine artists include original Rembrandt etchings, and a collection of Chagall's work. Some contemporary artists on display include Margaret Keene looking at the world with her distinctive "big eyes," Bill Mack with his bonded epoxy resins creating three-dimensional sculptures, and Maui's Chris Lassen with his fantastic suboceanic views of reality, capturing the emotions of the islands in his amazing use of color. Jan Parker, now living on Kauai, who does beautiful impressionism, almost like a macro-pointillism, is featured at the gallery. Most pieces are quite expensive, ranging from around $300, but you should go just to see the state of the arts in Hawaii.

Westin Maui Mall

Stroll the series of exclusive boutiques just left of the main lobby. Fine women's apparel is available at **Collections,** or you can purchase a superb diamond at **Edward Thomas Jewels.**

Beachside Casuals

You'll find a specialized boutique geared toward children located at the Kaanapali Shore. It's small, but jammed like a 12-year-old's closet. They feature handpicked fashions, resortwear, toys, swimsuits, books, mementos, and even snorkel gear. Big people can choose from a few racks, rent a video, or have those special photos developed in 24 hours. Open daily from 9 a.m. to 9 p.m.

SERVICES AND INFORMATION

Banks

There are no banks in Kaanapali; the closest are in Lahaina. Most larger hotels can help with some banking needs, especially with the purchasing or cashing of traveler's checks.

Medical

Dr. Ben Azman maintains an office at the Whaler's Village, tel. 667-9721, or after hours tel. 244-3728.

Camera Needs

Shops are: **Fox Photo** in the Whaler's Village, or **Island Camera and Gift** shops at the Sheraton and Royal Lahaina hotels.

Laundromat

The Washerette Clinic is located in the Sheraton.

Information

For a complete source of information on all aspects of the Kaanapali area, contact Kaanapali Beach Operators Association, Box 616, Kaanapali, HI 96761, tel. 661-3271.

HONOKOWAI AND KAHANA

You head for Honokowai and Kahana if you want to enjoy Maui's west coast and not spend a bundle of money. They're not quite as pretty as Kaanapali or Kapalua, but proportionate to the money you'll save, you come out ahead. To get there, travel along the Honoapiilani Highway, take Lower Honoapiilani Highway through Honokowai, and continue on it to Kahana.

Beaches

Honokowai Beach Park is right in Honokowai just across from the Food Pantry. Here you have a large lawn with palm trees and picnic tables, but a small beach. The water is shallow and tame—good for tots. The swimming is not as nice as at Kaanapali, but take a dip after shopping. Snorkeling is fair, and you can get through a break in the reef at the west end. **Kahana Beach** is near the Kahana Beach Resort; park across the street. Nothing spectacular, but the protected small beach is good for tots. There's a great view of Molokai and the beach is never crowded.

ACCOMMODATIONS

At last count there were well over three dozen condos and apartment complexes in the three miles encompassing Honokowai and Kahana. There are plenty of private homes out here as well which give you a good cross-section of Hawaiian society. A multimillion-dollar spread may occupy a beach, while out in the bay is a local fisherman with his beat-up old boat trying to make a few bucks for the day. Many of the condos built out here were controversial. Locals refused to work on some because they were on holy ground, and a few actually experienced bad luck jinxes as they were being built. The smarter owners called in kahuna to bless the ground and the disturbances ceased.

Paki Maui Resort

Situated between Kaanapali and Kapalua at 3615 Lower Honoapiilani Hwy., Lahaina, HI 96761, tel. 669-8235, (800) 922-7866 Mainland, (800) 342-1551 Hawaii, this excellent-value condo presents airy and bright rooms with sweeping panoramas of the Lahaina Roads. Well-appointed studios begin at $109, to $160 for a two-bedroom apartment for up to six people, additional guests $10. Amenities include maid service, a/c, cable TV, complete kitchens, pool with spa, and coin laundry facilities. Every unit has a private lanai overlooking a gem of a courtyard or the ocean. You can save money by getting a garden-view studio without sacrificing that delightful feeling that you are in the tropics. Although the Paki Maui

Kahana coast from the Paki Maui Resort
(BOB NILSEN)

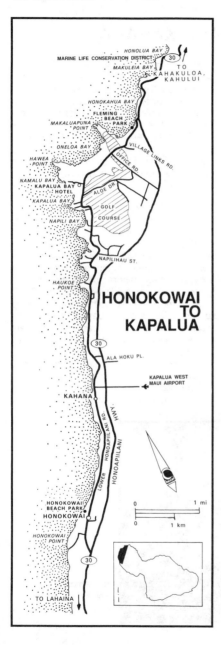

is in town, it feels secluded the moment you walk onto this property, which forms a little oasis of tranquility. There is no sand beach fronting the condo, but the snorkeling along the reef is excellent.

Sands Of Kahana

Your pleasure begins when you spot the distinctive blue tile roofs of this gracious complex, which forms a central courtyard area at 4299 Honoapiilani Hwy., Lahaina, HI 96761, tel. 669-0400, (800) 367-6046 Mainland, (800) 663-1118 Canada. The condo boasts a tennis and pro shop and the poolside **Kahana Terrace Restaurant and Lounge.** The sandy-bottomed beach fronting the property is very safe and perfect for swimming and sunbathing. The Sands of Kahana gives you extraordinarily large units for the money, and to sweeten the pot, they're beautiful and well appointed, mostly in earth tones and colors of the islands. One-bedroom units from $189, two-bedroom units from $245, and three-bedroom units from $310 are massive with two lanais, two baths with a tub built for two, walk-in closets, and great ocean views. Each unit offers a gourmet kitchen, cable TV (free HBO), daily maid service, and washer/drier units. The property, with pool, three tennis courts, putting green, and spa, exudes a sense of peace and quiet, and although there are plenty of guests, you never feel crowded. This is where you come when you want to get away from it all, but still be within reach of the *action*.

Kahana Villa

Across the street from the Sands of Kahana, this modern, five-story condo steps up the hillside and looks out over the channel to Lanai and Molokai. Pleasantly and casually attractive with contemporary designs and Hawaiian artwork, each of the large units features a complete kitchen, color TV and video equipment, washer/dryer, and daily maid service. On the property are a pool, jacuzzi, and sauna, BBQ grills, tennis and volleyball courts, an activities desk, and a sundries store. A complimentary continental breakfast of juice, coffee, and homemade pastries is served daily from 7:30 a.m. to 9 a.m. at the front desk. An added special feature to the condo is the highly acclaimed Erik's Seafood Restaurant, privately operated but located on the property. High-season rates start at $125 for a one-bedroom garden-view unit to $205 for a deluxe ocean-view two-bedroom unit. Located at 4242 Lower Honoapiilani Hwy., tel. 669-5613, or toll-free (800) 367-6046.

Honokawai Palms

At 3666 Lower Honoapiilani Hwy., Lahaina, HI 96761, tel. 669-6130, or toll-free (800) 669-6284, this condo is an old standby for budget travelers. A basic two-story cinder block affair, it was originally used as housing for workers constructing the Sheraton down the road. The manager's office is near the pool. Amenities include ping pong, BBQ grills, book exchange, color TVs. Older but not run-down, with no tinsel and glitter, but neat and clean. A coin laundry is on the premises. Fully furnished with kitchen, full bath, and queen-size hide-a-bed. All units are recently upgraded with new carpets, drapes, bedspreads, and ceiling fans. Forget about the ocean-view rooms, which don't have a great view anyway. Save money by taking the standard rooms. You can get a one-bedroom ocean-view unit with lanai for $65 or without ocean view, $60, two-bedroom with lanai but no view, $65, additional person after two, $6. There are weekly and monthly discounts, $200 deposit required, no credit cards accepted, three-night minimum; maid service is extra. This condo is clean and adequate.

Hale Ono Loa

Hale Ono Loa has peak- and low-season rates with about a $10 or $20 difference. Low-season one-bedroom, one to two days, garden-view is $115, ocean-view, $125, with prices rising as you ascend floors, reduction for longer stays. Offers stay, fly, and drive packages at varying rates; call Real Hawaii Condo vacations at tel. (800) 367-5108. At 3823 Lower Honoapiilani Hwy., Lahaina, HI 96761, tel. 669-6362. Complete kitchens, partial maid service, pool.

Valley Isle

The Valley Isle is located at 4327 Honoapiilani Hwy., Lahaina, HI 96761, tel. (800) 367-6092 Mainland, on Maui 669-4777. Rooms from $128-189 for one to three days (rates go down substantially for longer stays), plus restaurant, cocktails, pool, shop, and weekly maid service.

Noelani

Located at 4095 Lower Honoapiilani Hwy., tel. (800) 367-6030, on Maui tel. 669-8374, it has studios from $77, one-bedroom, $97, two and three bedrrooms for $120 and $145; monthly rates. All ocean-front rooms, two pools, BBQ area, fully equipped kitchens, color TVs, washer/dryer units, and maid service.

Kahana Sunset

Set alone on a small protected bay, the finely sculpted gardens and trellised lanais set off these attractive and privately owned condo units. All units have full kitchens, color televisions, and daily maid service. There is a three-night minimum. Rates for two people are $135 for a one bedroom unit, and two bedrooms run $165-215. A 10% monthly discount is given; no credit cards are accepted. Write P.O. Box 10219, Lahaina, Maui, HI 96761, or call (800) 367-8047, or 669-8011 on Maui.

FOOD AND ENTERTAINMENT

China Boat

This Chinese seafood restaurant at 4474 Lower Honoapiilani Hwy. in Kahana, tel. 669-5089, is open daily 5 to 10 p.m. Since its opening it's been gaining respect from locals and visitors alike. It's tastefully decorated, almost elegant with its highly polished, black lacquer furniture. Reasonably priced from an early-bird special at $8.95 to the deluxe dinners for two at $21.50 per person. House specialties range from *moo shu* pork at $9.50 to a wide assortment of appetizers and soup for under $6.50; with a typically large Chinese menu offering seafood, beef, chicken, vegetables, pork, and noodles, all can be satisfied.

Ricco's

At the **5-A Rent a Space Mall** in Honokowai, tel. 669-6811, Ricco's is a good old-time deli featuring fresh-baked pizza. Large sandwiches for $4 and lunches to go, picnic supplies, spare ribs, beer, wine, and friendly service. A good inexpensive takeout restaurant.

Fat Boy's
If you just want an inexpensive Hawaiian meal try Fat Boy's takeout counter at the Melrose Mall in Honokowai, tel 669-6655. Sandwiches $3.95-5.50 and plate lunches $4.95-5.95 are guaranteed to fill you up.

Dollies
Located at 4310 Honoapiilani Hwy. in the Kahana Monor Shops, tel. 669-0266, open from breakfast to late evening with sandwiches, pizza, and food to go. Deliveries to condos! Good food and fair prices, like turkey and roast beef with Swiss and jack for $5.95. The sandwiches and other entrees are good but the pizza is the best. Wide election of beers and wine. Dollies, one of the few eateries in the area, is usually a laid-back pub/pizzeria but can get hopping on the weekend and is perhaps the most happening place for late night get-togethers in Kahana.

Erik's Seafood Grotto
At 4242 Lower Honoapiilani Hwy., second floor of Kahana Villa, tel. 669-4806. Open daily for dinner 5 to 10 p.m. Their very good fish selection, early-bird special is from 5-6 p.m., $11.95; menu changes daily. Dinners include chowder, bread basket, and potato or rice. Most dinners run $16-19 with a good selection of appetizers. Erik's is known to have *the* best selection of fresh fish on Maui. This is a quality restaurant with fair prices.

Kahana Keyes
Located at the Valley Isle Resort, tel. 669-8071. Dinner only. Music from 7:30 p.m. to 12:30 a.m. seven nights a week. Early-bird specials from 5 to 7 p.m. include whole lobster and prime rib, $13.95, steak and crab, $11.95, prime rib, $9.95, or *mahi mahi* for $9.95. They're well known for their salad bar and fresh fish. The Kahana Keyes Restaurant is the only show in town around here, and luckily it ain't bad! Local bands perform all types of music from rock to Hawaiian, and the intimate dance floor is hardly ever crowded.

SHOPPING AND SERVICES

Honokowai Food Pantry
The only real place west of Lahaina to shop for groceries and sundries. Located on Lower Honoapiilani Hwy. in Honokowai, tel. 669-6208, open daily from 8 a.m. to 9 p.m. The prices are just about right at this supermarket. Condo convenience stores in the area are good in a pinch but charge way too much. Stock up here; it's worth the drive.

The **Honokowai P.O.** is at the Honokowai Food Pantry. Never busy, this full-service post office accepts packages.

Convenience Stores
E-Z store at the Hololani Resort in Kahana, is open 7 a.m. to 11 p.m. A quick-shop store with a good selection of groceries, liquors, and sundries at slightly inflated prices. Valley Isle Resort has the **Kahana Pantry,** a mini-mart and grocery store selling everything from beer to sunglasses. **The Villa** has almost the same items plus fresh fruits and vegetables. The **ABC Store,** in Honokowai, hours 6:30 a.m. to 11 p.m., tel. 669-0271, is a mini-market selling everything from resortwear to wine.

5-A Rent A Space Mall
A new mall has opened in Honokowai called 5-A Rent a Space. Here you'll find **Ricco's Pizza**. The mall also includes **Maui Physicians**, a video store, and a one-hour photo.

The most interesting shop is **Posters Maui**, open 9 to 5 every day, tel. 669-5404, where you can get a vibrant visual memento of Maui, framed and ready for your wall back home. Well-known island artists include Robert Nelson, Anthony Casay, and photographer Robert Talbot, all with an oceanic feel. An upcoming new artist featured by Posters Maui is Richard Field, who has clued into the soul of Maui. He creates paintings turned to posters in the "realistic fantastic" mode, such as *Haleakala Sunrise.*

Kahana Manor Shops
Aside from Dollies pub, there is an E-Z convenience store for food items and sundries, a Videoland and TV store, a one-hour photo

shop, and two clothing stores for resort and beach wear.

Annie And Bob's Rental
Located in Honokowai behind Fat Boy's, tel. 669-0027, they rent everything except scoot-ers on a 24-hour basis. Boogie boards and snorkel gear are $5 ($20 weekly), surfboards $10; scooters for $5 per hour, eight hours $20, or $25 for 24 hours, insurance included. Open daily 9 a.m. to 5 p.m. A mom and pop store with a will to satisfy.

KAPALUA AND NAPILI—THE WEST END

Kapalua sits like a crown atop Maui's head. One of the newest areas on Maui to be devel-oped, it's been nicely done. Out here is the **Kapalua Bay Resort,** golf, horseback riding, and terrific beaches.

BEACHES AND SPORTS

Some of the very best beaches that Maui has to offer are clustered in this area. The following listing proceeds from south to north.

Napili Bay
There are rights of way to this perfect, but condo-lined, beach. Look for beach access signs along Napili Place near the Napili Shores, Napili Surf Beach Resort, and on Hui Drive near the Napili Sunset and Napili Bay condos. They're difficult to spot, but once on the beach there's better-than-average swim-ming, snorkeling, and a good place for begin-ning surfers.

Kapalua Beach
Along Lower Honoapiilani Road look for ac-cess just past the Napili Kai Beach Club. Park in the public lot and follow the path through the tunnel to the beach. It's another beautiful cres-cent beach that's popular, though usually not overcrowded. The well-formed reef here has plenty of fish for snorkeling. Also here are restrooms, showers, and beach concessions.

D.T. Fleming Beach Park
One of Maui's best. Clearly marked just past mile marker 31 on Lower Honoapiilani Hwy. Here you'll find parking, showers, and BBQ grills, and excellent swimming except in win-ter, when there's a pounding surf. Fair snorkel-ing and good surfing.

Oneloa Beach
Located a short mile before Fleming's, Oneloa is a small sandy beach down a steep path. Those who brave it can camp without a hassle from the officials.

Mokuleia Beach
Also known as "Slaughterhouse." You can spot it because the R.V. Deli, a lunch wagon, is usually parked here, about 200-300 yards after mile marker 32. This beach has great bodysurfing, but terribly dangerous currents in the winter when the surf is rough. Be careful. Follow the trail to the left for the beach. The path straight ahead takes you to a rocky lava flow. This entire area, plus all of adjacent Honolua Bay, is a marinelife conservation dis-trict and the underwater life is fabulous.

Honolua Bay
Just past Mokuleia Bay heading north, look for a dirt road, then park. Some can try the road, but it's very rugged. The bay is good for swim-ming, snorkeling, and especially surfing. Many people stay the night without much problem.

Sports
The following are offered in the Kapalua area: **Kapalua Bay Golf Club,** Bay Course, par 72, $75 greens fee and a mandatory $15 cart; Village Course, par 71, $75 fee and a $15 cart. **Tennis** is found at the Napili Kai Beach Club, $9 guests; Kapalua Bay Hotel **Tennis Gar-den,** free to guests, $4 others, dress code, tel. 669-5677. There's **horseback riding** at the

Rainbow Ranch; see "Sports" in the main Introduction for details.

ACCOMMODATIONS

Napili, just south of Kapalua Bay, sports a string of condos and a hotel or two. Almost all front the beach, which is hardly ever crowded in this still largely underdeveloped area of Maui.

Napili Point Condominium

Napili Point is one of the most beautifully situated complexes on Maui. The low-rise complex sits on its own promontory of black lava separating Kahana and Napili, located at 5295 Honoapiilani Hwy., Napili, HI 96761, tel. 669-9222, (800) 922-7866. The reef fronting the condo is home to a colorful display of reef fish and coral, providing some of the best snorkeling on the west end. Not graced with a sand beach (100 yards north along a path), nature, however, was generous in another way. Each room commands an unimpeded panorama with a breathtaking sunset view of Lanai and Molokai. You get a deluxe room for a standard price. Because of the unique setting, little development has occurred in the area, and the condo is very secluded though convenient to shops and stores. The two-story buildings offer fully furnished one- and two-bedroom units from a very affordable $159 to $215, with full kitchens, washers and dryers, walk-in closets, and large dressing and bath areas. Up to four people, rollaway $10, and this includes maid service, two pools, and a family plan. Two-bedroom units on the second floor include a loft with its own sitting area. Floor-to-ceiling windows frame the living still life of sea and surf so you can enjoy the view from every part of the apartment.

Kapalua Bay Hotel And Villas

This, like other grand hotels, is more than a place to stay; it's an experience. The main lobby is partially open and accented with an enormous skylight. Plants trail from the ceiling. Below is a tropical terrace and restaurant and all colors are soothing and subdued. Although relaxing, this hotel is the kind of a place where if you don't wear an evening gown to go to the bathroom, you feel underdressed. In January 1988 renovations were completed to the tune of $20,000 per room which added ultra-luxury details like silk wallpaper in the already beautiful suites. The least expensive room in the hotel itself is one with a garden view at $185. The villas with a mountain view are $275 and climb rapidly to the $375-475 range. You can choose the American plan, consisting of breakfast and dinner, for an extra $40. You must make a three-nights' deposit, refundable only with 14 days' notice. There are five restaurants in the complex, magnificent golf at the Kapalua Village Course, tennis at the Tennis Club, a multitude of daily activities, and a small arcade with plenty of shops. Contact the hotel at One Bay Drive, Kapalua, HI 96761, tel. 669-5656, (800) 367-8000.

Napili Kai Beach Club

At 5900 Honoapiilani Rd., Lahaina, HI 96761, tel. (800) 367-5030, on Maui tel. 669-6271. The Napili Kai Beach Club, the dream-come-true of now deceased Jack Millar, was built before regulations forced properties back from the beach. The setting couldn't be more idyllic, with the beach a crescent moon here with gentle wave action. The bay itself is a swim-only area with no pleasure craft allowed. Jack Millar's ashes are buried near the restaurant under a flagpole bearing the U.S. and Canadian flags. It's expensive at $145 per studio to $475 for a luxury suite, but you do have a kitchenette, complimentary snorkel gear, putting green, jacuzzi, croquet, daily tea party, and all the amenities of home. Several special packages are available. There are four pools, putting greens, tennis courts, and the Kapalua Bay Golf Course just a nine-iron away. All rooms have Japanese touches complete with shoji screens. There's dancing and entertainment at their famous Sea House Restaurant.

Napili Shores

Overlooking Napili Bay from the lava-rock shoreline is Napili Shores condominium. All units surround a tropical garden, fish pond, manicured lawn, and swimming pool. Although not large, each unit is comfortable and contains a full kitchen, color TV, large lanai, and some of the best views on the island. Rates run from $130-170, with an additional $15 for extra persons. There are two restaurants on the premises, including the **Orient Express Thai Restaurant,** and Kalena's Groceries and Gifts for food item, gifts, and sundries. Located at 5315 Honoapiilani Hwy., call tel. 669-8061 or (800) 367-6046 for reservations.

Napili Bay

At 33 Hui Drive, Lahaina, HI 96761, tel. (800) 367-7042, on Maui 669-6044. For this neck of the woods, it's reasonably priced from $85 (four people) for a studio off the ocean. All have queen-size beds, lanai, full kitchens, maid service, and laundromat. No minimum stay.

Napili Surf Beach Resort

Located at 50 Napili Pl., Lahaina, HI 96761, tel. 669-8002 or (800) 541-0638, these are full condo units that operate as a hotel at the south end of Napili Beach. Studios from $84, discount is 12% for 28 days or longer, 15% for 45 days. Preferred views and one-bedroom units from $128, $300 Deposit. Minimum stay is

four nights. The grounds are not luxurious but nicely manicured with plenty of pride put into the property. Very clean rooms with full kitchens have their own lanai and open onto the central grounds area with the sea in the background. Two pools, fantastic beach, maid service, and laundry. Their adjacent Puamala building with its studio apartments are somewhat cheaper.

The Coconut Inn

Although not on the beach this cute 40-unit place has great atmosphere and unbeatable prices. Studio, one-bedroom, and loft units run between $79 and $99 high season, $10 extra person, which includes complimentary continental breakfast, two-night minimum stay. Each unit has a fully equipped kitchen, color TV, and amenities include a pool, spa, daily maid service, and a small but genteel garden. It's only a short walk downhill to the beach. Located at 181 Hui Road F in Napili, tel. 669-5712 or (800) 367-8006.

FOOD

The Grill And Bar

Don't underestimate this excellent restaurant (lunch and dinner), tel. 669- 5653, at the Kapalua Golf Course, which is not nearly as utilitarian as its name suggests. What's more, local people consider it one of the most consistently good and affordable restaurants in the area. The soothing main room is richly appointed with koa wood, and large windows frame a sweeping view of the super-green fairways of the golf course. The lunch menu offers a side of pasta for $8.95, or a large salad for only $3.50. Dinner entrees are tempting, with fettuccine pescatore from $16.95, to filet mignon and lobster for $24.95, and plenty of selections for around $20.95. To relax and soak up the scenery you can order dessert like Amaretto creme caramel at $2.95, or sip wine selected from an extensive list. The best restaurant for the money in the area!

Kapalua Bay Resort Restaurants

There's a complete menu of restaurants, so you can choose from sandwich shops to elegant dining. **Market Cafe,** found in the "shops"

backside Maui (J.D. BISIGNANI)

area, tel. 669-4888, has foods from around the world, including wines, meats, cheeses, and pastries. All kinds of gourmet items, and delicious but expensive sandwiches, cost from $7. **Bay Club,** tel. 669-8008, offers daily lunch from 11:30 a.m. to 2 p.m., dinner 5:30 to 9:30 p.m. on a promontory overlooking the beach and Molokai in the distance. The pool is right here. Dress code; expect to spend $25 for a superbly prepared entree. **Plantation Veranda** offers daily dinner only, with varying hours, tel. 669-5656. The atmosphere is high-lighted by natural woods, flowers everywhere, and original paintings. An extensive wine list compliments magnificent entrees by Chef Randolph Pidd. Formal dining.

Napili Shores Resort
Two restaurants are located at this resort, at 5315 Honoapiilani Hwy. about one mile before Kapalua town. **Orient Express,** tel. 669-8077, is open daily for dinner only from 5:30 to 10 p.m. The restaurant serves Thai and Chinese food with a flair for spices; duck salad and stuffed chicken wings are a specialty. The

early-bird special, served before 7 p.m., is a five-course dinner for $11.95. An extensive menu of finely spiced foods include their well-known curry dishes; takeout available. The **Gazebo,** next to the pool and open 7:30 a.m. to 2 p.m., serves basic American breakfasts for $3-6 and sandwich, burger, and salads at lunch for $4-7.

The Sea House
At the Napili Kai Beach Club, 5900 Honoa-piilani Rd., Lahaina, on Maui tel. 669-6271. The Restaurant of the Maui Moon, perhaps the nicest-sounding name for a restaurant on Maui, has changed to the The Sea House. On Sunday there is a breakfast lunch and you can order eggs Benedict or fresh blueberry pancakes. If you just want to soak up the rays and gorgeous view of Napili Bay, you can wear your swimwear and have a cool drink or light fare on the **Sea Breeze Terrace.** This newly opened addition was a stroke of luck after the federal government redid an old flood project ditch and allowed the hotel to build on the newly reclaimed land.

Inside the semi-open-air restaurant appetizers range from sliced Maui onions and tomatoes from $3.95 or a bucket of little-neck clams for $8.95. Soups and salads range from a reasonable $1.95 to $13.95 for a cold seafood salad stuffed in a papaya with shrimp and scallops. Dinner choices are fresh catch (priced daily), beef teriyaki, $14.95, fillet and lobster, and a special "lite" fare. A full wine list includes selections from California and France. Open daily for breakfast 8 to 11 a.m., lunch 12 to 3 p.m., and dinner 6 to 9 p.m., reservations suggested. There is Hawaiian music nightly and a wonderful show put on by children who have studied their heritage under the guidance of the Napili Kai Foundation.

Others

Two other restuarants to try include **Pineapple Hill,** tel. 669-6129, surrounded by—what else—pineapple fields and overlooking the Kapalua Village Golf Course. It has an extrensive list of seafood and meat selections. A bit on the pricy side but it has a good reputation. **Village Cafe** at the Kapalua Golf Course clubhouse serves light meals, better than you would expect from a small snack shop with outdoor seating.

SHOPPING

Kapalua Resort And Shops

A cluster of exclusive shops service the resort, including **McInerny** with fine women's apparel; **Kapalua Kids** for the younger set; **Kapalua Logo Shop** if you want to show off that you've at least been to the Kapalua Resort, since all items of clothing sport the butterfly logo. **Mandalay Imports** has a potpourri of silks and cottons from the East, especially Thailand. Visit **La Perle** for pearls, diamonds, and other jewels; **Distant Drums** sports an amazing collection of offbeat artifacts from Asia, and **Lahaian Galleries** has a wonderful collection of island artists on display.

Whaler's General Store

At Napili Bay, tel. 669-6773, this well-stocked little store and known landmark is good for last-minute items, with fairly good prices for where it is. You can pick up picnic items and sandwiches. Next door is **Snorkel Bob's,** tel. 669-9603, where you can rent snorkel equipment (prescription masks available) and boogie boards for only $15 per week—one of the best prices on Maui (also in Kihei). **Kalena's Groceries and Gifts** at Napili Shores is mainly a convenience store for last-minute items.

EAST MAUI

KIHEI

Kihei ("Shoulder Cloak") takes it on the chin whenever anti-development groups need an example at which to wag their fingers. For the last two decades, construction along both sides of Kihei Road, which runs the length of town, has continued unabated. Since there was no central planning for the development, mostly high-rise condos and a few hotels were built wherever they could be squeezed in: some are lovely, some are crass. There's hardly a spot left where you can get an unobstructed view of the beach as you drive along. That's the "slam" in a nutshell. The good news is that Kihei has so much to recommend it that if you refrain from fixating on this one regrettable feature, you'll thoroughly enjoy yourself, and save money, too.

The developers went "hyper" here because it's perfect as a tourist area. The weather can be counted on to be the best on all of Maui. Haleakala, looming just behind the town, catches rainclouds before they drench Kihei. Days of blue skies and sunshine are taken for granted. On the other side of the condos and hotels are gorgeous beaches, every one open to the public. Once on the beachside, the condos don't matter anymore. The views out to sea are unobstructed vistas of Lanai, Kahoolawe, Molokini, and West Maui, which gives the illusion of being a separate island. The buildings are even a buffer to the traffic noise! Many islanders make Kihei their home, so there is a feeling of real community here. It's quieter than Lahaina, with fewer restaurants and not as much action, but for sun and surf activities, this place has it all.

Sights

The six-mile stretch bordered by beach and mountain that makes up Kihei has always been an important landing spot on Maui. Hawaiian war canoes moored here many times during countless skirmishes over the years; later, Western navigators such as Capt. George Vancouver found this stretch of beach a congenial anchorage. A totem pole across from the **Maui Lu Hotel** marks the spot where Vancouver landed. During WW II, when a Japa-

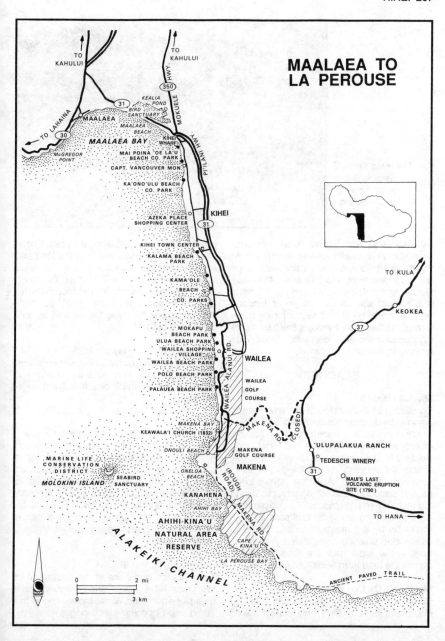

MAALAEA TO
LA PEROUSE

*The broad sands of
Kamaole Beach
beckon for a day
of sunbathing.*
(BOB NILSEN)

nese invasion was feared, Kihei was considered a likely spot for an amphibious attack. Overgrown pillboxes and rusting tank traps are still found along the beaches. Many look like cement porcupines with iron quills. Kihei is a natural site with mountain and ocean vistas. It's also great for beachcombing down toward Maalaea, but try to get there by morning because the afternoon wind is notorious for creating minor sandstorms.

BEACHES

Maalaea Beach
Consisting of three miles of windswept sand partially backed by Kealia Pond and a bird sanctuary, Maalaea Beach has many points of access between Maalaea and Kihei along Route 31. The strong winds make it undesirable for sunning and bathing, but it's a windsurfer's dream. Also the hard-packed sand is a natural track for joggers, profuse in the morning and afternoon. The beachcombing and strolling are quiet and productive. If you're up by 6 a.m. you can see the Kihei canoe club practice here; they put their canoes in the water near the Kihei wharf just across the road from Suda's Store.

Mai Poina Oe Lau Beach Park
On Kihei's western fringe, fronting Maui Lu Hotel, this beach offers only limited paved parking, otherwise just along the road. Showers, tables, and restrooms front the long and narrow white-sand beach, which has good safe swimming but is still plagued by strong winds by early afternoon. A windsurfer's delight, here you can see upwards of 100 sporting enthusiasts out trying the wind when conditions are optimal.

Kaonoulu Beach Park
You'll find parking, picnic tables, showers, and BBQs here, also very safe swimming and lesser winds. A small beach but not overcrowded.

Kalama Park
The park is located about the middle of town. More for looking and outings than beach activities, Kalama has a large lawn ending in a breakwater, little beach in summer, and none in winter. However, there are 36 acres of pavilions, tables, BBQ pits, volleyball, basketball, and tennis courts, a baseball diamond, and a soccer field, plenty of expanse to throw a frisbee. Great views of Molokai and Haleakala.

Kamaole I, II, And III
These beach parks are at the south end of town near Kihei Town Center. All three have beautiful white sand, picnic tables, and all the amenities. Shopping and dining are nearby.

All have lifeguards. The swimming and body-surfing are good. Kamaole III has a kiddies' playground. Snorkeling is good for beginners on the reef between II and III, where much coral and many colorful reef fish abound.

ACCOMMODATIONS

The emphasis in Kihei is on condos. With keen competition among them, you can save some money while having a more homey vacation. Close to 100 condos, plus a smattering of vacation apartments, cottages, and even a few hotel resorts, are all strung along Kihei Road. As always, you pay more for ocean views. Don't shy away from accommodations on the *mauka* side of Kihei Road. You have total access to the beach, some superior views of Haleakala, and you usually pay less money.

Hotels

The Kihei area offers two hotels that are reasonably priced and well appointed. **Maui Lu Resort,** 575 S. Kihei Rd., Kihei, HI 96753, tel. (800) 922-7866, (800) 342-1551 Hawaii, 879-5881 Maui, attempts to preserve the good-vibe feeling of old Hawaii with its Aloha Department and its emphasis on *ohana.* An abundance of activities here include a first-class Saturday evening luau, tennis, a Maui-shaped pool, and tiny private beaches strung along its 28 acres. Rooms from $73, $10 extra person, include refrigerators and hot pot. These are mostly in the new wing toward the mountains, which is also quieter. Cottages start at $93 and are separate units with gourmet kitchens. This full-service hotel pampers you in the old Hawaiian style.

The Wailea Beach Front Hotel (formerly the Surf and Sand Hotel) is at 2980 S. Kihei Rd., Kihei, HI 96753, tel. (800) 367-5004, on Maui 879-7744. This is a very affordable and well-maintained hotel located just before you get to Wailea at the south end of town. At the end of 1990, this hotel went through a complete makeover which included buildings, furnishings, grounds, and the adjacent Italian restaurant. Rates are $77 standard (up to three persons), $85 superior (up to three persons), and $96 deluxe (two people); $15 extra

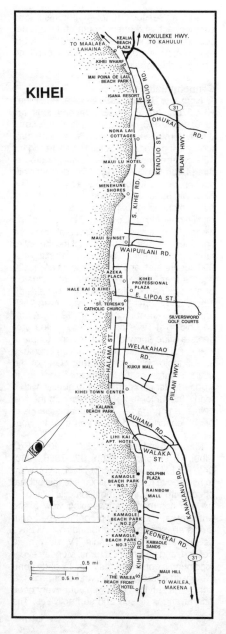

KIHEI

person, off-season $10 lower. It fronts a long sandy beach and offers "room and car" specials. Amenities include air conditioning, room refrigerators, and a jacuzzi. You can't go wrong at this terrific little hotel!

Condominiums

At **Kamaole Sands,** 2695 S. Kihei Rd., Kihei, HI 96753, tel. 879-0666, reservations tel. (800) 922-7866, all apartments come completely furnished with full baths and kitchen, roomy living area, and lanai. Prices are: $110-125 one-bedroom, $145-185 two-bedroom, three-bedroom $205-215; 15% discount off-season, and rental car package available. The Kamaole Sands is a full- service resort offering much more than just a place to stay. It's a family- oriented condo not only because of the wonderful activities, but because all units are spacious and geared toward making the entire family comfortable. One-bedroom units offer 900 square feet, and two bedrooms are 1,300 square feet. **Great Fettucini, Etc.,** situated poolside, serves inexpensive breakfast, lunch, and dinner featuring fresh island fish and pasta—most dinners from $9.95. A marine biologist visits on Wednesday and presents a slide show of the flora and fauna of Maui, and Hawaiian ladies come on Thursday to sell their locally made crafts. One of the main features of the Kamaole Sands is its wonderful tennis courts, free to guests, with a tennis instructor to help you work on the fine points of your game. The Kamaole Sands is bright, cheerful, and gives you a lot for your money.

Maui Hill is located at 2881 S. Kihei Rd., Kihei, HI 96753, tel. (800) 922-7866, (800) 342-1551 Hawaii, 879-6321 Maui. If you want to rise above it all in Kihei come to this upbeat condo with a Spanish motif that sits high on a hill and commands a sweeping view of the entire area. The one-, two-, or three-bedroom suites are spacious, bright, and airy. All have ceiling fans and a/c, cable TV, daily maid service, and gourmet kitchens. Monday evenings bring a complimentary mai tai party complete with games, singing, and door prizes. A concierge service helps with your every need and arranges all sun and surf activities. The

grounds are secluded, beautifully maintained, and offer a pool, tennis courts, and spa. The Maui Hill sits between Kihei and Wailea, so you get a deluxe area at reasonable prices. One-bedroom from $125 (up to four people), two-bedroom from $145 (up to six people), three-bedroom from $165 (up to seven people); $30 higher during high season.

Lihi Kai Cottages, 2121 Ili'ili Rd., Kihei, HI 96753, tel. (800) 544-4524 or 879-2335 on Maui. These nine cottages are such a bargain they're often booked out by returning guests, particularily during winter months. They're not plush, there's no pool, but they're homey and clean, with little touches like banana trees growing on the property; $59 s or d daily, $294 weekly, off-season cheaper, $465 monthly, deposit required (no credit cards), self- service laundromat. For reservations, write well in advance to the managers, Tad and Kimberly Fuller, at the above address.

Nona Lani Cottages, 455 S. Kihei Rd., Kihei, HI 96753, tel. 879-2497, are owned and operated by Dave and Nona Kong. The clean and neat units on the *mauka* side of Kihei Road have full kitchens and baths, queen beds, and daybeds. Laundry facilities, public phones, and BBQs are on the premises. High season $60, discount for weekly rates, $7 additional person. Low season three-night minimum, high season seven-night minimum.

Sunseeker Resort, 551 S. Kihei Rd., tel. 879-1261, write Box 276, Kihei, HI 96753. Rates are: studio with kitchenette $39, one-bedroom $49, two-bedroom $60, $7 additional person. Special rates for off-season and long-term. Deposit required. Not bad at all.

Nani Kai Hale, 73 N. Kihei Rd., Kihei, HI 96753, tel. (800) 367-6032, on Maui tel. 879-9120. Very affordable at $42.50 for a room and bath only, $73.50 for studio with kitchenette, or two-bedroom, two-bath for $125. Substantial savings during off-season, seven-day minimum high season, monthly rates, children under five free. There's a good beach plus sheltered parking, pool, laundry facilities, private lanai, and BBQs on premises. Good views.

Menehune Shores, 760 S. Kihei Rd., tel. (800) 558-9117, or 879-5828 on Maui. For reservations write Menehune Reservations

Kamaole Sands Resort courtyard (BOB NILSEN)

P.O. Box 1327, Kihei, Maui, Hawaii 96753. This huge condo is on the beach overlooking an ancient fishpond. The building is highlighted with Hawaiian petroglyphs. The **Breakers Restaurant** is on the premises. All units have an ocean view; $85-102 one-bedroom, $112 two-bedroom, $122-140 three-bedroom, five-day minimum. No credit cards, but monthly discounts and low-season savings of 30%. Full kitchens with dishwasher, washer and dryer, and disposals. Each unit is individually owned, so furnishings vary, but the majority are well furnished. A lot for the money.

Maui Sunset, 1032 S. Kihei Rd., Kihei, HI 96753, tel. (800) 843-5880. Two large buildings contain over 200 units; some are on a time-share basis and usually have nicer furnishings. High- and low-season rates for the one-, two- and three-bedroom units run from $85-200. Full kitchens. Pitch and putt golf green, pool, jacuzzi, sauna, rec room, beach front, and quality tennis courts are on the premises.

One of the newest resorts in Kihei is the **Maui Isana Resort,** 515 N. Kihei Road, Kihei, HI 96753, tel. (800) 633-3833 or 879-7800 on Maui. These fully equiped condos are located near the popular windsurfing beach, Ma Poina Oe Lau. One-, two-, and three-bedroom units have full kitchens and dining areas, cable TV, and maid service. Room rates for high season run from $130-190 a day with weekly rates

available; three-night minimum stay. A pool, jacuzzi, sports shop, and Japanese restaurant are also on the premises.

Hale Kai O Kihei, 1310 Uluniu Rd., Kihei, HI 96753, tel. 879-2757. Reasonable weekly rates based on double occupancy range from $345-525 (high season) for one-bedroom, $495-695 (high season) for two-bedroom with up to four people, additional person $8.50. Long-stay rates available. No children under six. Pool, shuffleboard, parking, coin-laundry, and maid service on request. Apartment-like cinderblock affair, simple and utilitarian, but clean, well-kept, and cute for what it is.

Kauhale Makai, 930 S. Kihei Rd., write Maui Condo and Home Realty, P.O. Box 1840 Kihei, HI 96753, tel. 879-5445 or call (800) 822-4409 U.S.A. and (800) 648-3301 Canada. Rates from $60 studio, $70 one-bedroom, $85 two-bedroom, $7.50 additional person, five-night minimum. A swimming pool, kiddie pool, BBQs, putting green, and sauna are available.

FOOD

Inexpensive

Azeka's Snacks, Azeka Place, S. Kihei Road, is open daily except Sun., 9:30 a.m. to 4 p.m. Basically takeout, featuring $1 hamburgers and a variety of plate lunches for $4.50. Azeka's is popular with locals and terrific for picnics. A good bargain is the salad bar for only $4.95 (salad bar usually closed by 8 p.m.). Go inside to their bake shop and try a mini-pie for $2.39.

International House of Pancakes is toward the rear of Azeka Place. Open daily from 6 a.m. to midnight, Fri. and Sat. until 2 a.m. Same American standards as on the Mainland with most sandwiches and plate lunches under $7, dinners under $10, and breakfasts anytime around $5. Not exotic, but basic and filling with a good reputation in the area for inexpensive but passable fresh fish and daily specials.

Paradise Fruit Co., 1913 S. Kihei Rd., across from McDonald's. Open 24 hours daily, tel. 879-1723. This fruit and vegetable market has a top-notch snack bar offering hearty, healthy sandwiches (under $4.50), vegetarian dishes, and a good selection of large, filling salads. Try the pita melt for $3.25 and any of the smoothies. There are a few tables out back and a community bulletin board, definitely worth a stop! It's the only place in Kihei open all night.

Moderate

Polli's on the Beach Mexican Restaurant, 101 N. Kihei Rd., tel. 879-5275, is open daily 11 a.m. to midnight. Polli's has a well-deserved reputation for good food at fair prices. Formerly vegetarian, they now serve a variety of meat and chicken dishes, but still use the finest ingredients, cold-pressed oils, and no lard or bacon in preparing their bean dishes. The decor is classical Mexican with white stucco walls and tiled floors. There's an outdoor deck area with a great sunset view. Main dishes are under and up to $14, with a la carte tostadas for $7.75. Imported beers are $3. Polli's is meticulously clean, serves large portions, and has a friendly atmosphere. For a filling and inexpensive meal, try the daily lunch special.

Try **Luigi's Pasta and Pizzeria** at Azeka Place Shopping Center, tel. 879-4446, for live entertainment, pasta, seafood, and pizza plus early-bird specials from 4-6 p.m.; moderately priced but mediocre food. Music nightly with a live band Wed. throung Sat. evenings, $3 cover.

La Familia is an excellent and friendly Mexican restaurant at Kai Nani Village Plaza, 2511 S. Kihei Rd., tel. 879-8824, across from Kamaole Park II. Most dishes are under $8, made with locally grown and organic ingredients when possible, and all soups are homemade. Pleasant waitresses, good service, and personal attention by the owner. Happy hour (2 to 6 p.m., and 10 p.m. to midnight) features traditional margaritas for $1.99, only $.99 on Fridays. Free chips and salsa! Dishes are well prepared and portions large.

Tucked behind La Familia is the new **Greek Bistro,** tel. 879-9330. A wonderful addition to the restaurant scene, the flavors and textures of the Mediterranean dishes served will excite your palate. Breakfast, lunch, and dinner are served 10:30 a.m. to 9:30 p.m. and entrees include two kinds of gyros, spanikopita, $6.95, moussaka, $9.95, and lamb kebob, $10.95. If you're in doubt as to what would be tasty, try the Greek Gods Platter ($10.95) and get a sampling of each homemade entree on the menu. Sandwiches, salads, and island dishes are also served for the less adventurous. This is a family affair. Run by the Arabatzis family, everyone chips in to make your meal enjoyable.

Upstairs is **Kihei Prime Rib House,** open from 5 p.m., tel. 879-1954. A touch expensive with most entrees from $15-20, but this includes a well- stocked salad bar. Scrumptious appetizers like sashimi, lobster, and mushrooms are under $10 and the salad bar is only $9.95. Early-bird specials under $10 are featured from 5 to 6 p.m. and include salad bar. Children's menu. Walls are adorned with carvings by Bruce Turnbull and paintings by Sigrid, two well-known local artists. One of the best choices is rack of lamb for $19.95. There's a good wine list with selections from California to France.

The **Island Fish House,** at 1945 S. Kihei Rd., tel. 879-7771, has a very good reputation and offers early-bird specials, $10.95, from 5 to 6 p.m. that include teri chicken, New York steak, and fresh fish. Entrees include seafood salad for $18.95, shrimp Polynesian at $17.95, and beef and chicken under $19. *Pu pu* range from escargot to a sample platter for two for $15.95, with most around $7. The house specialty is the "king's platter for two," two types of fresh fish, sautéed lobster, deep-fried shrimp and scallops, New York steak, and scampi, all for $64.95.

Fresh Island Fish Co., tel. 244-9633, at Maalaea Harbor is a rare find. Open 10 a.m. to 8 p.m. Mon. through Sat., their fish comes right from the boat. Dinners are served on the lattice-covered outdoor patio, fish (at market prices) and deli counter inside. Dinners include lobster and sea bass combo, Cajun *apuu,* and scampi piccata. Sandwiches and fruit drinks sold throughout the day.

Rainbow Lagoon, at the Rainbow Mall on S. Kihei Rd., open nightly for dinner from 5 to 10 p.m., is a steak, seafood, and prime rib house. Daily early-bird specials from 5 to 7 p.m. include prime rib for $11.95, broiled chicken $9.95, and *mahi mahi,* $8.95. Try the regular selections like broiled lobster tail, $19.95, or teri steak for $16.95. They also have nightly entertainment and serve until 2 a.m., so this is a regular stop for many of the hotel and lounge workers in the area.

At the **Kamaole Shopping Center,** the larger mall just next door to the Rainbow Mall, you'll find three reasonably priced restaurants. **Denny's** serves food just like on the Mainland but with a few more island specialties. **Erik's Seafood Broiler,** tel. 879-8400, has a very good reputation for fresh fish (the biggest selection on Maui) and fair prices. Early-bird specials run $10.95. The **Canton Chef,** open 11 a.m. to 9:30 p.m., tel. 879-1988, is a moderately priced restaurant with the normal Chinese selections and specialties like Szechwan scallops with hot garlic sauce for $8.05, *kung pao* scallops, $8.05, noodles and rice dishes, $5, and chicken dishes from $5-7. Seafood is slightly more expensive, such as fresh fish with black bean sauce for $8.40.

Silversword Golf Course Restaurant has opened at Maui's newest golf course, located at 1345 Piilani Hwy. (above and parallel to Kihei Rd.), daily for lunch 11 a.m. to 3:30 p.m., dinner from 6 to 9 p.m., with sandwiches served all day, tel. 879-0515. From the heights of the course, you get an extraordinary view, not only of the sweeping fairways, but of Kihei's coast below and the islands and mountains in the distance. The best news is that the food is very good, and the prices are unbeatable. You can order a hefty sandwich like pastrami or even lox and bagels for under $5, or a variety of salads from $4. But the best deals are the lunch entrees, like shrimp silversword, beef stroganoff, or hamburger steak for $5-6. The dinner menu is small, but again unbeatable. Choose from chicken cordon bleu, $11, sautéed catfish, $12.50, or choice cuts of beef for under $13. Friday night brings a lobster special, and Saturday night it's rack of lamb, either for only $15 for the full meal. The dining room is basically a portico, and the elegance comes from the panoramic surroundings. A slightly different place to dine, but worth a try.

Expensive

Maui Lu Hotel, 575 S. Kihei Rd., tel. 879-5858. On Mon., Wed., and Fri. a luau and Polynesian review are held in the hotel's Luau Garden, including limitless cocktails and a sumptuous buffet with all the specials—*imu* pork, poi, and a huge assortment of salads, entrees, and side dishes for $38, tax and gratuity included. Also, the **Aloha Mele Luncheon** is a tradition at the hotel. Again, a laden buffet with cocktails from 11 a.m. to 1:30 p.m., Thursday only; $15 includes the luncheon, entertainment, tax, and tip.

The **Waterfront Restaurant,** at the Milowai Condo in Maalaea Harbor, tel. 244-9028, is open daily from 5:30 to 10 p.m. and features whole baked fish in oyster sauce for two, $18.50, or lobster and crab from $20. Scampi is $16.50. Great sunsets, tropical drinks.

Buzz's Wharf, at Maalaea Harbor, tel. 244-5426, is open daily 11 a.m. to 11 p.m. Seafood and fresh fish are the specialties. Most dishes are under $15. The waterfront atmosphere is unbeatable with great views from the second story overlooking the harbor and Haleakala.

Chuck's Steak House, Kihei Town Center, tel. 879-4488. Lunch, Mon. to Sat. 11:30 a.m. to 2:30 p.m., dinner nightly from 5:30 p.m., no reservations necessary but call to see how busy it is. Emphasis on steaks and ribs, most under $15. The children's menu is under $8. Daily and early-bird specials sometimes. Mud pie and sandwiches cost under $5. Salad bar a la carte, $6.95. Standard American, with an island twist.

Isana Shogun, tel. 874-5034 for reservations, is the best Japanese restaurant in the area. Open 5 to 10 p.m. nightly, you can either sit at the sushi bar or have dinner cooked at your table in the teppan style. Upstairs is the Mermaid Bar, which has karaoke sing-along after 10 p.m.

Perhaps the best restaurant location in Kihei is the **Ocean Terrace** at the Mana-Kai Condos which fronts the beach and frames the sunset with palm trees. Emphasis is on fresh fish, but chicken and meat dishes are also on the menu. Entrees range from deep-fried scallops, $16.95, to filet mignon, $20.95, and a special fish, seafood, and meat dinner for two at $64.95

ENTERTAINMENT

Kihei isn't exactly a hotspot when it comes to evening entertainment. There is the **Polynesian Review** at the Maui Lu luau. There's dancing at **Polli's Mexican Restaurant** on weekends, and dancing nightly (Wed. through Sat. to live music) at **Luigi's.** Many of the restaurants offer entertainment on a hit-and-miss basis, usually one artist with a guitar, a small dinner combo, or some Hawaiian music. These are usually listed in the free tourist brochures.

SHOPPING

At the **Azeka Place Shopping Center,** along S. Kihei Rd. in about the center of town, you'll find all the practicalities. **Azeka's Market** is well stocked and features famous Azeka ribs for barbecues. There's also a great community bulletin board listing apartments, yard sales, and odds and ends. In the center are **Ben Franklin** and a small **Liberty House.** A full range of books on Hawaiiana, along with distinctive cards and assorted gifts, are available from the **Silversword Book and Card Store,** tel. 879-4373, open weekdays 8:30 a.m. to 9 p.m., Sat. 8:30 a.m. to 6 p.m., and 10 a.m. to 5 p.m. on Sundays. **Wow! of Hawaii,** tel. 879-1448, operated by Betty Olson, specializes in activewear, sportswear, and bathing suits for the active person—everything

from sea to gymnasium. In winter, selections include more resortwear. Open daily 9 a.m. to 9 p.m. (also in Kahului at the Maui Mall).

Rainbow Connection, tel. 879-5188, open Mon.-Sat. 9 a.m. to 9 p.m., and Sun. 9 a.m. to 6 p.m., features personalized gifts. Look for painted reef fish sculptures, jewelry boxes, earrings, and cups, all with a Polynesian theme. The idea is to "connect" Polynesia and the world through the spirit in its art. **Leilani's** has towels, beachwear, hats, and postcards, and next door is **O'Rourke's Tourist Trap** where the junk ain't bad, and neither are the prices. One of the best shops is **Vagabonds,** stocking resortwear and a wide selection of luggage, especially backpacks, daypacks, and fanny packs, by Caribou Mountaineering. Quality merchandise at affordable prices.

Practicalities And Services

At Azeka Place you'll find **Bank of Hawaii,** tel. 879-5844, **American Savings Bank,** tel. 879-1977, the Kihei **post office** at 1254 S. Kihei Rd., and a gas station. There's also **Kihei Acupuncture Clinic,** tel. 874-0544, with Dr. Nancy Macauley specializing in gentle needling techniques, and a full selection of Chinese herbs. If you're in desperate need of toggle bolts, you'll find **Coast to Coast Hardware,** and the **Fox One Hour Lab** does quick developing and is a good place to buy film. **Maui Dive Shop** has a store here, and **Ocean Activities Center** has a desk. This is where the people do their one-stop shopping. **Azeka Place II,** another shopping center, is going up across the street, next to the two gas stations.

Kihei Town Center

This small shopping center just south of Azeka Place offers a 24-hour **Foodland, Kihei Drug Mart,** a bank, an art gallery, a **Maui Dive Shop,** and a few clothing and gift stores.

Kamaole Shopping Center

This new mall at the east end of town features **Denny's, Erik's Seafood, Canton Chef, Cinnamon Roll Fare,** a takeout pastry shop, and various clothing, souvenir, and sundries stores. From its two floors of shops you can

Opposite page (top left): the restored Wo Hing Temple on Lahaina (ROBERT NILSEN); (top right) cast-bronze Buddha at the Jodo Mission in Lahaina (ROBERT NILSEN); (bottom): The banyon tree at Lahaina covers nearly an acre. (ROBERT NILSEN)

buy a skimpy suit at a skimpy price at **Bikini Discount;** baubles, beads, and some nicer pieces at **Jewels and Gifts of Paradise;** and clothes, luggage, and beachwear at the **Vagabond Trading Co.** O'Rourke's Tourist Trap sells a tangle of novelty items, gifts, sundries, towels, beachwear, and junk. **Lappert's Ice Cream** sells island-made delights, plus fat-free yogurt so that you can bliss out but not balloon out.

Dolphin Shopping Plaza

This small, two-story plaza along S. Kihei Road includes **Miki's** for swimwear and alohawear; **Pro Photo and Gifts,** featuring 40-minute processing; **Baskin-Robbins Ice Cream,** for ice cream treats; and the **Fifth Avenue Mile** for fancy alohawear. You can take care of your sweet tooth by visiting the **Kihei Bakery,** open daily 6 a.m. to 9 p.m., tel. 879-8666, where they make fresh bread, blueberry donuts, and even bagels daily. Here too, the **New York Deli** is nearly as full as any in the Big Apple, and if you have a craving for pizza try **Pizza Fresh**—they make it, you bake it.

Rainbow Mall

Yet another mall just up the road at 2439 S. Kihei Rd., with **Lady Di's** selling eel-skin purses, stained glass, and accouterments for women; **Maui Dive Shop,** a complete diving store with rentals, swimwear, snorkels, cruises, and windsurfing lessons; and **Tropical Trappings,** an aloha store with resortwear.

Kamaole Beach Center

A small group of shops between Dolphin and Rainbow plazas, with the **Sports Page Grill and Bar, Wiki Wiki Pizza, E-Z Discount Store, TCBY Yogurt Shop,** and **Hobie Sports Store.**

Kukui Center

At the new **Kukui Center** along S. Kihei Road are **Waldenbooks, Valley Isle Produce,** a cash-and-carry store, **Kihei Kukui Laundromat, J.R.'s Music Store,** several apparel stores, **Health Spot Natural Foods, Kihei Art Gallery, Wings On The Wind Kites** for all sorts of flying objects, a **Whaler's General Store** for sundries, and **Maui Dive Shop.**

Swap Meet

If you're looking for a bargain on clothes, gifts, craft items, and odds and ends, try the Kihei swap meet every Sat. from 7 a.m. to 4 p.m. across the road from Kalama Beach Park.

North End Shopping

At the very north end of Kihei is the **Sugar Beach General Store,** tel. 879-6224, with a small clutch of shops selling resortwear, snacks, gifts, and jewelry. Nearby at **Ilia Beach Shopping Plaza** are a **Whaler's General Store, Ilia Beach Deli,** several other shops, and the **Pacific Whale Foundation** office. In Maalaea try the **Maalaea Store** (open 8 a.m. to 5 p.m., except Mon.) for sundries, packaged foods, fishing supplies, and gas.

Food/Liquor Stores

Azeka's Market is famous for its ribs and selections of exotic Asian foods and spices; buy health foods and more at **Paradise Fruit Company,** 1913 Kihei Rd., and groceries at **Foodland** at Kihei Town Center and **Star Market** at 1310 S. Kihei Road. **Rainbow Discount Liquor** has a good selection of liquor, imported beers, and wine at the Rainbow Mall along S. Kihei Road.

Sporting Goods And Rentals

Swimwear and sportswear for the entire family are available from **Wow! of Hawaii,** tel. 879-1448, in the Azeka Place Shopping Center. You'll find all you need at **Maui Sailing Center** at 101 N. Kihei Rd., and the **Kealia Beach Center,** open daily 8 a.m. to 5 p.m. They offer windsurfing equipment and lessons, beach equipment, sailboats, snorkeling sets, jet-skis, and tours. **The Dive Shop,** 2411 S. Kihei Rd., tel. 879-5172, owned and operated by John and Marilyn Phipps, is your one-stop dive shop, and more—tours, excursions, snorkel and scuba equipment. **Maui Dive Shop** in Azeka Place has a full range of equipment and rentals. **Snorkel Bob's,** tel. 879-8225, is along S. Kihei Rd. just behind Paradise Fruit Co. The weekly prices can't be beat at $15 for snorkel gear or boogie boards (day rentals too). You also get snorkel tips, a fish I.D. card, and the semi-soggy underwater humor of

Snorkel Bob. **Sea Escape,** tel. 879-3721, offers seagoing motorized rafts that you can use to go to all the snorkel, dive, and picturesque spots of the Lahaina Roads just offshore. The daily special is $135, two-hour minimum $80, and additional hours $25. **Ocean Activities Center,** tel. 879-4485, is at the Kamaole Shopping Center (look for the Denny's sign along S. Kihei); here you can book all fun activities on Maui and purchase anything you'll need for sun and surf at this excellent one-stop store. Both **South Shore Wind and Dive** and **Central Pacific Divers** are located at Maui Isana Resort just down from Suda's Store. Here you can purchase a sailboard and all the gear or arrange for a snorkel trip or lessons.

Medical

For medical emergencies try: **Kihei Physicians,** tel. 879-7781, at 1325 S. Kihei Road, suite 103, open 8 a.m. to 8 p.m. (till 5 p.m. Sat., 1 p.m. Sun); **Kihei-Wailea Medical Center,** tel. 874-8100, at 41 East Lipoa Street, with physicians, a pharmacy, physical therapy, and a clinical laboratory (same hours as Kihei Physicians); or **Kihei Clinic and Wailea Medical Service,** tel. 879-7447, at 1993 S. Kihei Road, open 24-hours a day. Chiropractic services can be had at the **Chiropractic Clinic of Kihei,** tel. 879-7246, at 1819 S. Kihei Road, which specializes in non-force techniques.

WAILEA AND BEYOND

Wailea ("Waters of Lea") isn't for the hoi polloi. It's a deluxe resort area custom-tailored to fit the egos of the upper class like a Bijan original. This section of southeastern Maui was barren and bleak until Alexander and Baldwin Co. decided to landscape it into an emerald 1,450-acre oasis of golf courses and world-class hotels. Every street light, palm tree, and potted plant is a deliberate accessory to the decor so that the overall feeling is soothing, pleasant, and in good taste. To dispel any notions of snootiness, the five sparkling beaches that front the resorts were left open to the public and even improved with better access, parking areas, showers, and picnic tables—a gracious gesture even if state law does require open access! You know when you leave Kihei and enter Wailea. The green, quiet, and wide tree-lined avenues give the impression of an upper-class residential area. Wailea is where you come when you're "puttin' on the ritz," and with the prices you'll encounter it would be helpful if you *owned* the Ritz. At the **Intercontinental Hotel** and **Stouffer's Resort** you'll find five-star dining, and there's exclusive shopping at the Wailea Shopping Center. Hotels are first-rate architecturally and the grounds are exquisite. They're definitely worth a stroll, but remember your Gucci shoes.

Onward And Backward
If you turn your back to the sea and look toward Haleakala, you'll see its cool, green forests and peak wreathed in mysterious clouds. You'll want to run right over, but you can't get there from here! Outrageous as it may sound, you have to double back 18 miles to Kahului and then head down Route 37 for another 20 miles just to get to the exact same spot on Route 37 that you can easily see. On the map there's a neat little road called **Makena Road** that connects the Wailea/Makena area with Upcountry in a mere two mile stretch, but it's closed! An ongoing fight over who's responsible for its maintenance keeps it that way. Once this appalling situation is rectified, you'll be able to travel easily to the **Tedeschi Winery** and continue on the "wrong way" to Hana, or go left to Kula and Upcountry. For now, however, happy motoring!

BEACHES

If you're not fortunate enough to be staying in Wailea, the best reason for coming here are its beaches. These little beauties are crescent moons of white sand that usually end in lava outcroppings on both ends. This makes for sheltered swimmable waters and good snorkeling and scuba. Many of the hotel guests in Wailea seem to hang around the hotel pools, maybe peacocking or just trying to get their money's worth, so the beaches are surprisingly uncrowded. The following beaches are listed from north to south, toward Makena.

Keawakapu

The first Wailea beach, almost a buffer between Kihei and Wailea, is just past the Mana Kai Resort. Turn left onto Kamala Place, or proceed straight on S. Kihei Road until it dead-ends. Plenty of parking at both accesses, but no amenities. Keawakapu is a lovely white-sand beach with a sandy bottom. Good swimming and fair snorkeling. There's also a beginner's dive spot offshore where an underwater junkyard of a few hundred cars forms an artificial reef.

Mokapu And Ulua

These two beaches are shoulder to shoulder, separated only by a rock outcropping. Turn right off Wailea Alanui Drive at the first turn past the Intercontinental Hotel. The beach is clearly marked, and there's a parking area, showers, and restrooms. Being resort beaches, they're both particularly well-kept. Beautiful white sand and protected waters are perfect for swimming. There's good snorkeling at the outcropping separating the beaches, or swim out to the first reef just in front of the rocks for excellent snorkeling.

Wailea Beach

Travel one-half mile past the Wailea town center and turn right onto a clearly marked access road; at the beach there's good parking, also showers and toilets. A short but wide beach of pure white sand, Wailea offers good swimming and bodysurfing, but the snorkeling is only fair.

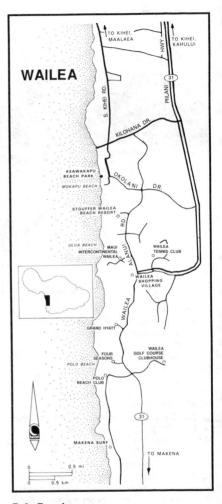

Polo Beach

Follow Wailea Alanui Drive toward Makena. Turn right at the clearly marked sign near Polo Beach condo. Here also are paved parking, showers, and toilets. Polo Beach is good for swimming and sunbathing, with few tourists. There's excellent snorkeling in front of the rocks separating Polo from Wailea Beach—tremendous amounts of fish, and one of the easiest spots to get to.

ACCOMMODATIONS

Stouffer's Wailea Beach Resort

Always a beauty, and destined to be the best, Stouffer's, like a rich red cabernet, has mellowed with age. Under the direction of Donn Takahashi, the general manager, it has not only maintained but surpassed its excellent reputation for service. It's a superbly appointed resort with attention given to the most minute detail of comfort and luxury. When you drive to the main lobby, you're actually on the fifth floor, with the ones below terraced down the mountainside to the white-sand beach. The lobby has huge oak and brass doors, and original artwork adorns the walls, including an intricate tapestry made of natural fibers. The relaxing pool area has been recently renovated and expanded. A bubbling spa fashioned from lava rock is surrounded by vines and flowering trees; another contains three little pools and a gurgling fountain, so that while the therapeutic waters soothe your muscles, the music of the fountain soothes your nerves. The hotel boasts the best beach in the area, long known as an excellent vantage point from which to view cavorting humpback whales in season. The impeccable grounds, originally landscaped to be lush, have grown, and are now an actual botanical garden, with all plants identified. And everywhere there is water, cascading over tiny waterfalls, tumbling in brooks, and reflecting the amazing green canopy in tranquil lagoons.

Stouffer's Wailea Beach Resort has been acclaimed as a Five Diamond Resort by the AAA Motor Club for nine consecutive years, while Raffles Restaurant has not only won official culinary awards but the praise of in-the-know local residents who highly recommend its magnificent Sunday brunch (see description following). There are two other restaurants on the premises, plus a cocktail lounge and dance hall. A luau is held twice weekly. The most amazing feature about the resort is a permeating feeling of peace and tranquility. The rooms, whose color scheme is a soothing rose on blue and gray, are appointed with *koa* and rattan furniture. Thick carpeting meets a spacious lounge area of glazed ceramic flooring, while sliding doors lead to a lanai where you can relax or enjoy a quiet in-room meal. **Ocean Activities Center** maintains a desk at the hotel, and they can book you into every kind of outdoor activity that Maui has to offer. A major renovation of guest rooms was completed at the end of 1990. Room rates are $165-360, with suites to $1200. Varying rates include a family plan, with children under 18 free in their parents' room, and a modified American plan. The hotel features the very private Mokapu Beach Club, a detached low-rise wing complete with its own pool and daily continental breakfast, also a variety of golf and tennis packages. Write Stouffer's Wailea Beach Resort, 3550 Wailea Alanui Dr., Wailea, HI 96753, tel. (800) 992-4532, tel. 879-4900 on Maui.

Maui Intercontinental Hotel

This hotel is a class act. Even the Wrong Way signs on the premises say "*Please*, Do Not Enter." The rooms are lavish with folding screens, original artwork, deep carpets and coordinated bedspreads, full baths, two lanais, refrigerators, and magnificent views no matter which way you're oriented. Rates run $185-350; suites are available from $350. Special family plan, room and car, honeymoon, and golf packages are available. The family plan includes a second room free with a certain class of room or better, and free meals for children 12 and under when accompanied by both parents. There are two lovely pools, a new jacuzzi, a spa and fitness center, four restaurants, and the beach. The Intercontinental has also recently undergone a major renovation, which includes a huge new convention center, an open entrance foyer, Hawaiian and Polynesian artwork, grand staircase to the center pool, and relocation and refurbishing of the dining facilities. For information write 3700 Wailea Alanui Dr., Wailea, Maui, HI 96753, tel. (800) 367-2960 Mainland, 879-1922 on Maui. This is living!

Four Seasons Resort

The second newest resort to open in Wailea is the blue tile-roofed Four Seasons Resort. Situated at the south end of Wailea Beach, it's oriented to the setting sun and opens itself up to the sweet sea breezes. Casually elegant, the open-air lobby is full of cushy chairs and couches, fountains, flowers, fans, and a grand staircase that glides down to the huge pool at beach level. The shape of this pool and the colonnade of lobby pillars above hint at a Romanesque architectural influence, yet the ambience and colors of the hotel say island natural. Original artwork and reproductions hang throughout the lobby and hallways, while huge fossilized sea anemones are displayed on lobby tables for a unique twist, and birds and plants bring the outdoors inside. Countless little details make this resort pleasant and special.

The Four Seasons is a study of cream on cream, and this color scheme runs throughout the resort, offset by coral, almond, beige, pastel salmon and pink, and muted greens, blues, and browns. Each large room has a bedroom and sitting area, a bath with separate shower and deep tub, a well-stocked wet bar, TV and complimentary video, room safe, and private lanai; 85% of the rooms have an ocean view and all have twice-daily room service. While air conditioning is standard, rooms also have sliding screen doors or louvered French doors and overhead fans to give you the option of fresh island air. Double rooms and suites are even more spacious, with the addition of a second bathroom and/or a dining area. Rates run $325-475, and from $600 to $5,000 for a suite. Rates on the Club Floor, which includes on-floor check-in, complimentary continental breakfast, afternoon tea, sunset cocktails and

hors d'oeuvers, and a personal concierge, run an additonal $100 a day. The club lounge on this floor also provides books, newspapers, magazines, and board games to keep you occupied in your idle hours. Golf, family, room and car, and other special packages are also available.

Other amenities include a lounge, a bar that features live music and dancing, meeting rooms for conventions, complimentary valet parking, 24-hour room service, and an early arrival-late departure lounge where you can relax and enjoy the hotel services, store a small bag, or shower off the grit of travel. On site are two tennis courts; lawn croquet; a small but adequate health club with exercise machines, free weights, massage, and a steam room; and organized beach activities. Five shops are also here, including **Viewpoint,** for alohawear, **Hildgund Jewelers,** and **Lamonts,** a gift and sundries shop. A hotel-supervised, full-day (8 a.m. to 5 p.m.) children's activities program is also available for youngsters 5-12 years old.

The Four Seasons' three restaurants are the Seasons, Pacific Grill, and the poolside Cabana Cafe. With table linen, crystal, classical music, and jackets required for men, the **Seasons** is the most elegant, but not stuffy—the decor is weathered bamboo, the windows fully open to let in the sea breeze and moonlight, and the island cuisine is offered in a

Stouffer's Wailea Beach Resort sets the standard of excellence in Wailea. (J.D. BISIGNANI)

garden of the luxurious Four Seasons Resort
(BOB NILSEN)

"homelike" presentation. Dinner is from 6-10 p.m. nightly, and reservations are recommended. Open all day, the Pacific Grill is more casual, with alohawear and activewear the norm. Breakfast offers a choice of buffets. The lunch menu includes sandwiches, salads, and pasta. For dinner, entrees are from Asia and the Pacific, some cooked in view of the guests at the "oriental exhibition kitchen." For a quick bite, try a burger, *pu pu,* or tropical drink at the **Cabana Cafe** from 11 a.m. to 7 p.m.

For hotel reservations and information write 3900 Wailea Alanui, Wailea, Maui, HI 96753, or call (800) 332-3442, 874-8000 on Maui.

Grand Hyatt Wailea Resort And Spa

Completed in the spring of 1991, and located between the Four Seasons and Maui Intercontinental resorts, the Grand Hyatt offers everything on a grand scale. The sprawling buildings house nearly 800 rooms, several pools and interconecting waterways, broad gardens, a spa with everything from massage to aerobic classes, aromatherapy, steam rooms, skin treatment, and exercise rooms. Plenty of shopping is available, along with five restaurants and twelve bars. The Grand Hyatt fronts a long section of Wailea Beach and has a perfect location to watch the setting sun. Room rates range from $350-500, with suites upwards from there. For information and reservations call (800) 233-1234 or 875-1234 on Maui.

Destination Resorts

Located at 3750 Wailea Alanui, Wailea, HI 96753, tel. (800) 367-5246 Mainland, (800) 423-8773 ext. 510 Canada, and 879-1595 collect in Hawaii. This complex is made up of four separate villages: **Ekolu,** from $160, near the golf course; **Ekahi,** the least expensive, from $130 near the tennis courts; **Elua,** the most expensive, from $265 near the sea, and **Grand Champions,** from $175 on the golf links. Additional properties in Makena are the **Polo Beach Club** and **Makena Surf** where rooms are $325. Rates are lower during the off season, and special golf and car packages are available. There is a three-night minimum stay, $20 extra person, and daily housekeeping service. All units are plush and fully furnished, with swimming pools and tennis courts on the premises. The beach, two golf courses, and additional tennis courts are nearby.

FOOD

Raffles Restaurant

At Stouffer's Wailea Beach Resort, tel. 879-4900, reservations a must. Dinner daily from 6:30 to 10:30 p.m. Sunday brunch from 9 a.m. to 2 p.m., a prizewinner! You regally glide down the staircase from the main lobby and walk through enormous oak doors into the classy interior of this first-rate restaurant.

You'd feel comfortable in a sport coat, but tasteful alohawear is fine. Inspired by the famed Raffles of Singapore, this restaurant lives up to the tradition. Sashimi, lobster, and crab cocktails tantalize your taste buds, preparing them for the entrees. Salads galore, including mushroom, spinach, Manoa lettuce —all in savory dressings—complement lobster bisque or Maui onion soup. Roast rack of lamb, *onaga* with baby spinach and caviar, or veal grenadine in whiskey cream are just some of the delights prepared by the chefs. Wines are from the best vineyards around the world, and magnificent desserts make you pray for just a little more room.

The Sunday brunch is legendary. For $25 you choose from the best island fruits and vegetables, and a table laden with rich and creamy desserts. Omelettes made to order are stuffed with seafood, crunchy vegetables, mushrooms, artichokes, or plump Portuguese sausages. The entree table groans with chops, steaks, fresh fish, caviar, prosciutto, crab, lobster, eggs Benedict, and more. Steaming pots of coffee are brought to every table while waiters constantly change all used table settings. Be smart, go slowly, and put only one or two items on your plate at a time. This is gourmet food that demands a gourmet attitude.

The **Palm Court** is Stouffer's main dining room. Walk though the lobby and look over the rail to the beautiful partially open-air restaurant below. It's open for breakfast from 6-11 a.m. and for dinner nightly from 6 p.m. The menu offers sashimi or *carpaccio* to start. Entrees are delightful, with ricotta ravioli and an outstanding selection and preparation of island fish. Sweet loonies can go crazy at the dessert buffet for only $2.50 with a prime rib dinner, or end the meal with dipped ice cream or freshly made yogurt. Besides menu selections, the Palm Court now features prime rib ($18.95 adults, $8.95 children) to order and prepared by chefs before your eyes. The Palm Court is a first-rate restaurant with very reasonable prices, the best in its category in Wailea!

Stouffer's **Sunset Terrace** is a delightful perch on which to have a drink and survey the grounds and beach below. Every evening brings a dramatic torch-lighting ceremony. The drums reverberate and the liquid melancholy of the conch trumpet sends a call for meditation at day's end. Drinks include the full complement of island specialties, and from 5 to 7 p.m. (not every day) you can get wonderful *pu pu* for only $1. These are gourmet quality, more like a mini-buffet with salads, dips, teri beef, Chinese spare ribs, Cajun-style chicken, and beautiful crunchy spring rolls. See **Lost Horizon,** the hotel's bar and disco, below under "Entertainment," and "Luaus" in the main Introduction for Stouffer's traditional Monday-night feast.

The **Maui Onion** is a convenient snack-type restaurant at poolside. Burgers, sandwiches, salads, smoothies, and Maui onion rings (their specialty) are on the limited menu. Prices are a bit steep, but if you don't want to budge from your poolside lounge chair it's worth it. On Wed. and Fri. evenings from 5:30 to 8:30 p.m., relax here next to the pool and dine under the stars. Your choice of three entrees with all the extras costs $19.95.

La Perouse Restaurant

At Maui Intercontinental Hotel, tel. 879-1922. Dinner Tues. to Sun. from 6:30 to 10:30 p.m., reservations recommended. This elegant restaurant is gaining an international reputation. Newly moved to a location in the hotel with superb views over the ocean, the restaurant's surroundings set the theme. A dress code requires collared shirts, and most people dress up; no shorts. The callaloo crabmeat soup is a must. The bouillabaisse is out of this world. Breadfruit vichyssoise is unique. Wines from the private cellar are extremely well chosen but expensive, while the house wine is very palatable and affordable. The best selections are the seafood, but the chicken and lamb are also superb. Save room for dessert, offered on a pastry cart laden with exotic choices. This is no place for will power. Enjoy one of the best meals ever, and don't worry about the second mortgage tonight.

A special **Sunday Champagne Brunch** is offered in the Makani Room from 9 a.m. to 1 p.m., $26. Let the piano accompaniment soothe your soul as you stuff your body with everything from made-to-order omelettes, fresh fruits and pasties, to mouthwatering entrees of fish, poultry, and meat.

The **Kiawe Broiler** offers more moderately priced dinners at the hotel. Daily dinner is served from 5:30 to 10 p.m, basically *kiawe*-broiled seafood, chops, and steaks from $17.50, and a salad bar that's a deal. Informal setting with high-backed rattan decor. Other hotel restaurants include the **Lanai Terrace**, an all-day restuarant that's less formal and a good deal less expensive than La Perouse, the **Sun Spot** snack bar, and **Wet Spot** by the pool if you want to get soaked for an $8 sandwich.

Dance nightly (live bands most nights, with swing-era music on Sunday) at the newly remodeled **Inu Inu Lounge** where there's never a cover, or enjoy **Maui's Merriest Luau** every Tues. and Thurs. from 5:30 p.m. (see "Luaus" in the general Introduction).

Seasons

At the Four Seasons Resort, this elegant restaurant is an experience in fine dinning. Luxuriate in the surroundings of teak and bamboo, or look out over the ocean at the sunset as soft sea breezes waft in through the open terrace. Emphasis is on island seafood such as pan-fried pink snapper with braised fennel, and apple raisin curry sauce, sashimi, gazpacho, and prawns for $25-39. Open 6 to 10 p.m., tel. 874-8000, reservations recommended and proper dress required.

The all-day and casual **Pacific Grill** restaurant combines a large selection of foods from the Orient and the West. Special are the breakfast buffets and Sunday brunch from 10:30 a.m. to 2:30 p.m. For sandwiches and tropical drinks anytime until sundown, try the **Cabana Cafe** at poolside. At dusk, catch the Hawaiian music and hula dancers at the cafe or stroll to the **Sunset Bar** for music, dancing, and live entertainment.

Sandcastle Restaurant

At Wailea Shopping Village, tel. 879-0606, this restaurant is far enough out of the way so you can count on getting a table. Primarily they serve salad and sandwiches at lunch, 11 a.m. to 3 p.m., and dinner from 4 p.m. Early birds can peck from 4 to 6 p.m. for $11.95, which includes *mahi mahi,* prime rib, teriyaki chicken, and deep-fried shrimp, plus soup and salad bar. Most entrees are from $18-25, and they barbecue with mesquite imported from Mexico. The room is comfortable with high-backed cane chairs and even a little patio area.

Golf Ball Soup

The following restaurants are located at the golf links in the area. **Wailea Steak House,** 100 Wailea Ike Dr., on the 15th fairway of Wailea Blue Course, tel. 879-2875, is open daily for dinner from 5:30 p.m. Reasonably priced for this neck of the woods with steaks from $18, chicken from $13, and a decent salad bar for $8. Good sunset views. It holds and deserves one of the best reputations for consistently good food that's well prepared.

Sakura, tel. 879-1577, is open daily from 5:30 p.m. It's surprisingly reasonable, both for being where it is and for serving Japanese fare. The traditional menu presents *yakitori* or *yudo-fu* appetizers for under $4, sashimi plates for under $10, and traditional entrees like sukiyaki, *shabu-shabu,* and *sakura nabe* for under $25. The menu describes all the dishes in English, so this is a good opportunity to sample some delectable Japanese food. Sunset is particularly striking, and small parties can request the tatami rooms (reservations required), $25 per person for the fixed menu for six to ten people. For those who have not experienced one, the sushi bar here is a delight.

Fairway Restaurant, at the Wailea Golf Course clubhouse, tel. 879-4060, is across the street from the entrance to Polo Beach. Open from 7:30 a.m. for a full breakfast, everything from eggs Benedict for $5.95 to a simple omelette for $4.75 or buttermilk pancakes, all you can eat, for $3.50. Lunch offers burgers and sandwiches from $5-7. Dinner selections from $15-20 include filet mignon, New York pepper steak, veal parmigiana, or salad bar for $11.95. Although the dining room isn't ultra fancy, there's a terrace, and the feeling is peaceful in an unhurried romantic setting. A good place to eat in an area not known for budget restaurants.

At the Wailea Tennis Club is the **Set Point Cafe,** tel. 879-3244. Stop here for breakfast or light lunch after a game to invigorate yourself for the rest of the day.

ENTERTAINMENT, SHOPPING, AND SERVICES

Entertainment
If you haven't had enough fun on the Wailea beaches during the day, you can show off your best dance steps at Stouffer's **Lost Horizon.** Rock to the sounds of Hau'ula from 9 p.m. to 1 a.m. Tues.-Thurs., and until 1:30 a.m. on Fri. and Sat. ($5 cover); dress code. The Intercontinental's **Inu Inu Room** swings with live music and disco dancing nightly, and you can dance the night away at Four Season's **Sunset Bar.**

Golf And Tennis
Two of the main attractions in Wailea are the fantastic golf and tennis opportunities. **Wailea Golf Club,** tel 879-2966, has two magnificent golf courses that have been laid out on Haleakala's lower slopes, both open to the public. Tennis is great at the **Wailea Tennis Center,** tel. 879-1958, and many of the hotels and condos have their own championship courts. Please see the Tennis and Golf charts in the Introduction for rates and specifics.

Wailea Shopping Village
The only shopping in this area is **Wailea Shopping Village,** just east past the Intercontinental Hotel off Wailea Alanui Drive. It has the usual collection of boutiques and shops. **Superwhale** offers alohawear for children. **Kiwina's** sells fine jewelry, while **Miki's** has racks of alohawear at very competitive prices that you wouldn't expect in this fancy neck of the woods. More exclusive fashions are at **Chapman's** for fine men's clothing, and **Sea and Shells** has a range of gifts from the islands. **Isle Style** is a fine-arts gallery with works by local artists, and the most remarkable shop is **Lahaina Printsellers,** with their magnificent prints and maps (see p. 71). **Elephant Walk** is a shopping gallery of fine crafted items, and **For Your Eyes Only** sells sunglasses for every eye and lifestyle. Money needs are handled by the **First Hawaiian Bank, Island Camera** has film, accessories, and processing, **Whaler's General Store** offers food items and liquor, and **Ed and Don's** sells fast food, sandwiches, ice cream, beverages, and gift-food items.

Each hotel has an arcade of shops for quick and easy purchases. One of note is the **Coast Gallery, Maui** at the Intercontinental which displays a wide range of mostly island art, including some unique wood and pottery pieces not usually on display at art galleries.

Transportation
The **Wailea Shuttle** is a complimentary jitney which stops at all major hotels and condos, the Wailea Shopping Village, and golf and tennis courts in Wailea about every 20 minutes. It operates 6:30 a.m. to 10:30 p.m. With a little walking, this is a great way to hop from one beach to the next.

MAKENA TO LA PEROUSE

Just a skip south down the road is Makena Beach, but it's a world away from Wailea. This was a hippie enclave during the '60s and early '70s, and the freewheeling spirit of the times is still partially evident in the area even though Makena is becoming more refined, sophisticated, and available to visitors. For one thing, "Little Makena" is a nude beach, but so what? You can skinny-dip in Connecticut. This fact gets too much attention. What's really important is that Makena is *the last* pristine coastal stretch in this part of Maui that hasn't succumbed to undue development . . . yet. As you head down the road you'll notice Hawaii's unofficial bird, the building crane, arching its mechanical neck and lifting girders into place. The Japanese firm

of Seibu Hawaii has built the Maui Prince Hotel, and more luxury accommodations are on the rise. Wailea Point, a promontory of land between Wailea and Makena, is the site of one, and others will be across the road near the golf courses.

In stark contrast, there's unofficial camping at Makena, with a few beach people who live there semi-permanently. Aside from the sundries shop at the Maui Prince Hotel, there's nothing in the way of amenities past Wailea, so make sure to stock up on all supplies. The police come in and sweep the area now and again, but mostly it's mellow. They do arrest the nudists on Little Makena to make the point that Makena "ain't free no more" (see below). Rip-offs can be a problem, so lock your car,

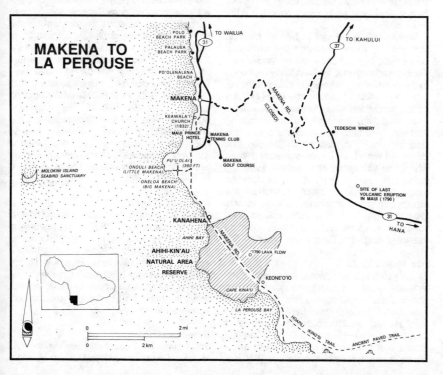

Makena Beach and Red Hill (BOB NILSEN)

hide your camera, and don't leave anything of value in your tent. Be careful of the *kiawe* thorns when you park; they'll puncture a tire like a nail.

Makena is magnificent for bodysurfing and swimming. Whales frequent the area and come quite close to shore during the season. Turtles waddled on to Makena to lay their eggs in the warm sand until early in this century, but too many people gathered the eggs and the turtles scrambled away forever. The sunsets from **Red Hill,** the cinder cone separating Makena from Little Makena, are among the best on Maui; you can watch the sun sink down between Lanai, Kahoolawe, and West Maui. The silhouettes of pastel and gleaming colors are awe-inspiring. Oranges, russets, and every shade of purple reflect off the clouds that are caught here. Makena attracts all kinds: gawkers, burn-outs, adventurers, tourists, free spirits, and a lot of locals. It won't last long, so go and have a look now!

The Naked Truth

Some years ago in an extremely controversial episode the nudists the Maui police came down hard on the nudists. They arrested nine top-free women from various parts of the U.S. and from foreign countries. The police acted in defiance of a recent Hawaii Supreme Court ruling that states that a woman's breasts when uncovered in appropriate circumstances (i.e., iso-

lated beaches) does not violate the state's "open lewdness" statute. The women, defended by attorney Anthony Ranken, sought compensation for malicious prosecution. Some point directly at former Mayor Hannibal Tavares for running a personal crusade against the au naturel sun-worshipers. To show the extent of the conflict, one hare-brained scheme actually proposed was to pave a walkway to Puu Olai ("Red Hill") so that Little Makena is no longer an "isolated beach." The justification was to provide "wheelchair access" to Little Makena although a wheelchair would have to negotiate hundreds of yards of deep sand to get there. Imagine the consternation if the first wheelchair-bound sunbather just happened to be a nudist!

Keawalai Church

In Makena, you'll pass this Congregational church, established in 1832. It was restored in 1952 and services are held every Sunday at 9:30 a.m. Many of the hymns and part of the sermon are still delivered in Hawaiian. Notice the three-foot thick walls and the gravestones, each with a ceramic picture of the deceased. There is a parking lot, restrooms, and showers across the road.

Small Beaches

You'll pass by these beaches, via the Old Makena Road, as you head toward Makena.

There are usually few people and no amenities. **Palauea** and **Poolenalena** are about three-quarters of a mile past Polo. Good swimming and white, sloping sands. **Nahuna** ("Five Graves") **Point** is just over a mile past Polo. An old graveyard marks the entrance. Not good for swimming but great for scuba because of deep underwater caves. Snorkelers can enjoy this area, too. A short distance farther on is the **Makena Boat Landing** (water, restrooms, showers), a launch site for boaters and scuba divers. **Papipi** is along the road 1½ miles past Polo, but its small sand beach is too close to the road. **Oneuli** ("Black Sand Beach") on the north side of Red Crater actually has a salt-and-pepper beach. Turn down a rutted dirt road for a third of a mile. Not good for swimming, but good diving, unofficial camping, and shore fishing. No amenities.

Makena Beach

A short way past the Maui Prince Hotel the road turns to rough asphalt and gravel. Bounce along for about one mile and look for a wide dirt road that two cars can pass on. Turn right and follow the rutted road for a few hundred yards to the parking lot and a few toilets; a second beach access is a few hundred yards farther on. This is **Oneloa Beach,** generally called **Makena Big Beach.** To the left is where most people camp. Right leads you to **Puu Olai** ("Red Hill"), a 360-foot cinder cone. When you cross over the point from Big Makena Beach you'll be on **Little Makena,** a favorite nude beach. You'll know that you're on the right beach by the bare bums and the peace sign outlined in white-painted rocks on the lava outcrop that you just climbed over to get to where you are. Both beaches are excellent for swimming (beware of currents in winter), bodysurfing, and superb snorkeling in front of Red Hill. With families and clothed sunbathers moving in (especially on weekends), Little Makena is no longer so "remote" or isolated. The beginning of the end may be in sight, although there is a movement loosely organized to retain this small sanctuary as a place for those who still wish to swim in the buff.

Ahihi-Kinau Natural Reserve

Look for the sign four miles past Polo Beach. This is the end of the road. Here you'll find a narrow beach, the remnants of a stone wall, and a desolate, tortured lava flow. It's also an underwater reserve, so the scuba and snorkeling are first-rate. The best way to proceed is along the reef toward the left. Beware not to step on the many spiny urchins in the shallow water. If you do, vinegar or urine will help with the stinging. The jutting thumb of lava is **Cape Kinau,** part of Maui's last lava flow which occurred in 1790.

La Perouse Bay

Just shy of six miles from Polo Beach and named after the French navigator Jean de

map of the "Sandwich Isles" by Captain Jean La Perouse, c. 1786 (HAWAII STATE ARCHIVES)

From the Maui Prince Resort you can see Red Hill, Molokini, and Kahoolawe.
(BOB NILSEN)

François La Perouse, first Westerner to land on Maui (in May 1786), the bay is good for snorkelers and divers but beware of the urchins on entry. If you walk left you'll come across a string of pocket-sized beaches. The currents can be tricky along here. Past the bay are remnants of the **Hoapili ("King's") Trail,** still hikable along some of its distance.

PRACTICALITIES

Accommodations And Food

The **Maui Prince Hotel,** 5400 Makena Alanui Rd., Kihei, HI 96753, tel. 874- 1111 on Maui, or (800) 321-6284 elsewhere, is a destination resort. You walk into a gleaming white building and face an enormous central courtyard. The architecture is simple and refined understatement. Lean across the hardwood rails and soak in the visual pleasure of the landscaped artwork below. From the balconies hang flowers and greenery in sympathetic mimic of the waterfalls of Maui. Every evening the water is turned off in the central courtyard. The natural melody is replaced five times a week by **Prince Strings,** a duo that plays classical music that wafts upward for all to enjoy; on Tues. and Fri. evenings an authentic hula show is featured. All rooms have an alcove door so that you can open your front door and still have privacy, but allow the breeze to pass through. The least expensive room is a partial

ocean view beautifully accentuated in earth tones and light pastels. The bathrooms have a separate commode and a separate shower and tub. Ocean-view and oceanfront rooms range from $190-330, while one-bedroom suites are from $400-800, with a giant living room, two lanais, a large- screen TV and VCR, and *yukata* to lounge in. The master bedroom has its own TV, listening center, and king-size bed. A nonsmoking wing is also available. Honeymoon and sports packages and a children's program are available.

The Maui Prince faces a fantastic secluded portion of Maluaka Beach, almost like a little bay, with two points of lava marking it as a safe spot for swimming and snorkeling. Seven sea turtles live on the south point and come up on the beach to nest and lay their eggs. To the left you can see Puu Olai, a red cinder cone that marks Makena. **Ocean Activities Center** comes in the morning with its catamaran, and will take you snorkeling to Molokini or can arrange other activites throughout the island. The pool area is made up of two circular pools, one for adults, the other a wading pool for kids, and a poolside snack bar has recently been added. There's volleyball, a children's program, croquet, six plexi-pave tennis courts with a pro on the staff, and the golf course, the main attraction of the Maui Prince.

With the Prince being one of the newest luxury hotels in the area, head chef Roger

Dikon is building an island-wide reputation for exquisite dining. He's succeeding admirably. The recent addition of low-salt and low-fat items on the menu points to the chef's health-conciousness. The fanciest room is the **Prince Court,** featuring fine dining for dinner only, except for their truly exceptional Sunday brunch. The evening fare is gourmet American cuisine and then some. Start with appetizers like smoked Alaskan salmon with dill cheese-cake and salmon pearls, $11, or any of their copper kettle soups like black bean Creole for $5. Sautéed pink snapper with avocado, arti-choke, and lime is $26, and most chicken, beef, and lamb entrees are under $28. The room is subdued-elegant and highlighted with snow-white tablecloths and sparkling crystal. The view is motionless facing the serene courtyard, or dramatic looking out to sea.

When chefs from the best restaurants on Maui want to impress visiting friends with a brunch, they come to the Maui Prince on Sunday. For only $27 you can surpass most of your dining fantasies. You start with a table laden with exotic fruits and fresh-squeezed juices. Nearby are plump and steaming rolls, croissants, and pastries rich in chocolates and creams. Then comes an omelette gauntlet, where you pick and choose your ingredients and an attendant chef creates it before your eyes. Hot entrees for the gastronomically tim-id are offered, from roast beef to fresh fish. But the real delights are the cornucopia of smoked seafood and shellfish. To the left pate, to the right sushi, and *sashimi* straight ahead, or choose cracked crab to nibble while you de-cide. Fat yellow rounds of imported cheeses squat on huge tables. Waiters and waitresses attend with fresh plates, champagne, and pots of coffee. You couldn't possibly eat like this every day, but *sacrifice* yourself at least once like this while on Maui.

Hakone is a Japanese restaurant and sushi bar with all chefs from Japan. They serve com-plete dinners like *sukiyaki* or tempura for un-der $29, and they also serve sushi and *sash-imi.* Traditional seven- to nine-course *kaiseki* dinners run $42-50 per person. In keeping with the tradition of Japan, the room is sub-dued and simple, with white shoji screens counterpointed by dark open beams. The floor is black slate atop packed sand, a style from old Japan.

The main dining room is **Cafe Kiowai,** which is open for breakfast, lunch, and dinner. It is on the ground level, opening to the court-yard and fish ponds. Lunch choices are almost endless, beginning with appetizers like Dun-geness crab and corn cakes with oven-roast-ed tomatoes coulis, $6.50, or Maui onion soup with jack cheese in a bread bowl, $4.50, and continuing on to seafood curry with mango chutney, coconut flakes, and macadamia nuts, $16, or picatta of veal for $18. Desserts are sinfully rich and delicious. For now, food and accommodations in Makena mean the Maui Prince. The only exceptions are the Ma-kena Golf Course restaurant, which serves breakfast for under $6, and soups, salads, sandwiches, and grilled items for lunch for under $8.

Recreation
As the Maui Prince Hotel is a destination resort, on-site recreation possibilities includes the beach, the swimming pool, and a cata-maran ride to Molokini with Ocean Activities which leaves directly from the beach in front of the hotel. Golf at Makena Golf Course and tennis at Makena Tennis Club are just across the road and offer world-class courts and links. See the "Golf" and "Tennis" charts in the main Introduction for specifics.

Services
Except for phones at the Maui Prince, Makena Golf Course, and Tennis Club, the boutique and sundries shops at the hotel, and the showers and restrooms at Keawalai Church, you won't find any amenities.

UPCOUNTRY

Upcountry is much more than a geographical area to the people who live there: it's a way of life, a frame of mind. You can see Upcountry from anywhere on Maui by lifting your gaze to the slopes of Haleakala. There are no actual boundaries, but this area is usually considered as running from Makawao in the north all the way around to Kahikinui Ranch in the south, and from below the cloud cover up to about the 3,000-foot level. It encircles Haleakala like a large green floral bib patterned by pasture lands and festooned with wild and cultivated flowers. In this rich soil and cool to moderate temperatures, cattle ranching and truck farming thrive. Up here, *paniolo* ride herd on the range of the enormous 20,000-acre **Haleakala Ranch,** spread mostly around Makawao, and the even larger 30,000 acres of the **Ulupalakua Ranch,** which *is* the hills above Wailea. **Pukalani,** the largest town, is

a way station for gas and supplies. **Makawao** is a real cowboy town with saddleries, rodeos, and hitching posts. It's also sophisticated, with some exclusive shops and fine dining.

Kula is Maui's flower basket. This area is one enormous garden producing brilliant blooms and hearty vegetables. **Poli Poli State Park** is a forgotten wonderland of tall forests, a homogenized stand of trees from around the world. **Tedeschi Winery** in the south adds a classy touch to Upcountry; you can taste wine in a historic jailhouse. There are plenty of commercial greenhouses and flower farms to visit all over Upcountry, but the best is a free Sunday drive along the mountain roads and farm lanes, just soaking in the scenery. The purple mists of mountain jacaranda and the heady fragrance of eucalyptus encircling a mountain pasture manicured by herds of cattle portray the soul of Upcountry.

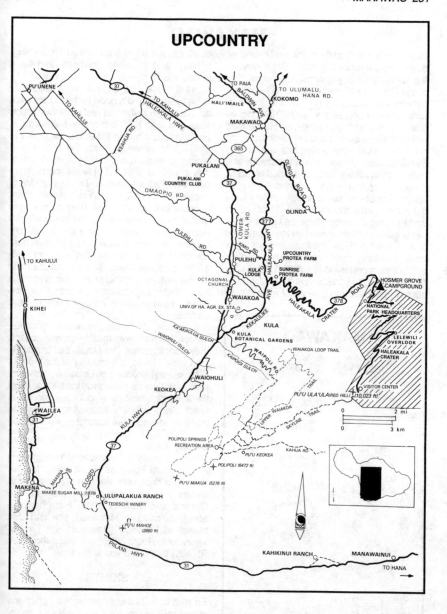

UPCOUNTRY

PU'UNENE

TO KAHULUI

TO KAHULUI

KEAHUA RD.

HALEAKALA HWY.

37

TO PAIA

HALI'IMAILE

BALDWIN AVE.

KOKOMO

TO ULUMALU, HANA RD.

MAKAWAO

365

OLINDA ROAD

PUKALANI

PUKALANI COUNTRY CLUB

37

OMAOPIO RD.

OLINDA

PULEHU RD.

LOWER KULA RD.

377

HALEAKALA HWY.

KIMO RD.

PULEHU

UPCOUNTRY PROTEA FARM

KULA LODGE

SUNRISE PROTEA FARM

OCTAGONAL CHURCH

WAIAKOA

KERAULIKE AVE.

HALEAKALA CRATER ROAD

378

HOSMER GROVE CAMPGROUND

NATIONAL PARK HEADQUARTERS

TO KAHULUI

KIHEI

UNIV. OF HA. AGR. EX. STA.

KULA

LELEWILI OVERLOOK

KA'AKAUKUA GULCH

WAIOHULI GULCH

KULA BOTANICAL GARDENS

WAIPOLI RD.

WAIAKOA LOOP TRAIL

HALEAKALA CRATER

KAIPOLI GULCH

KEOKEA

WAIOHULI

UPPER WAIAKOA TRAIL

VISITOR CENTER

PU'U ULA'ULA (RED HILL) (10,023 ft)

0   2 mi
0   3 km

WAILEA

31

SKYLINE TRAIL

POLIPOLI SPRINGS RECREATION AREA

PU'U KEOKEA

KAHUA RD.

MAKENA

MAENA RD.

CLOSED

KULA HWY.

37

POLIPOLI (6472 ft)

PU'U MAKUA (5276 ft)

MAKEE SUGAR MILL (1878)

ULUPALAKUA RANCH

TEDESCHI WINERY

PU'U MAHOE (2660 ft)

PIILANI HWY.

31

KAHIKINUI RANCH

MANAWAINUI

TO HANA

MAKAWAO

Makawao is proud of itself; it's not *like* a cowboy town, it *is* a cowboy town. Depending on the translation that you consult, it means "Eye of the Dawn" or "Forest Beginning." Both are appropriate. Surrounding lowland fields of cane and pineapples give way to upland pastures rimmed with tall forests, as Haleakala's morning sun shoots lasers of light through the town. Makawao was settled late last century by Portuguese immigrants who started raising cattle on the upland slopes. It loped along as a *paniolo* town until WW II, when it received an infusion of life from a nearby military base in Kokomo. After the war it settled back down and became a sleepy village again, where as many horses were tethered on the main street as cars were parked. The majority of its false-front, one-story buildings are a half century old, but their prototype is strictly "Dodge City, 1850." During the 1950s and '60s, Makawao started to decline into a bunch of worn-out old buildings. It earned a reputation for drinking, fighting, and cavorting cowboys, and for a period was derisively called "Macho-wao."

In the 1970s it began to revive. It had plenty to be proud of and a good history to fall back on. Makawao is *the* last real *paniolo* town on Maui and, with Kamuela on the Big Island, is one of the last two in the entire state. At the Oskie Rice Arena, it hosts the largest and most successful rodeo in Hawaii. Its Fourth of July parade is a marvel of homespun humor, aloha, and an old-fashioned good time. Many people ride their horses to town, leaving them to graze in a public corral. They do business at stores operated by the same families for 50 years. Though much of the dry goods are country-oriented, a new breed of merchant has come to town. You can buy a sack of feed, a rifle, designer jeans, and an imported silk blouse all on one street. At its eateries you can have lobster, vegetarian or Mexican food, or a steamy bowl of saimin, reputed to be the best on Maui.

Everyone, old-timers and newcomers alike, agrees that Makawao must be preserved, and they work together. They know that tourism is a financial lifeline, but shudder at the thought of Makawao becoming an Upcountry Lahaina. It shouldn't. It's far enough off the track to keep the average tourist away, but easy enough to reach and definitely interesting enough to make a side trip there absolutely worthwhile.

Getting There

The main artery to Makawao is through Paia as you travel Route 36 (Hana Hwy.). In Paia town turn right onto Baldwin Avenue at the corner marked by the gaily painted "Ice Creams and Dreams" shop. From here it's about six miles to Makawao. You can also branch off Route 37 (Haleakala Hwy.) in Pukalani, onto Route 365 (some maps show it as Rt. 400) that'll lead you to the town.

MAKAWAO

KEE RD.
BREWER RD.
BALDWIN AVE.
MAKAWAO AVE.
TO ULUMALU, HANA RD.
← TO PAIA
MAHA RD.
AI ST.
390
MINER PL.
OLINDA RD.
TO OLINDA
EDDIE TAM MEMORIAL CENTER
MAHOLA
PAMAKANI PL.
MAKAWAO AVE.
MAKANI RD.
KEALALOA AVE.
MOKUAHI ST.
0   0.2 mi
0   0.2 km
400
TO PUKALANI, HALEAKALA HWY.

SIGHTS

En route on Baldwin Avenue, you pass the **sugar mill,** a real-life Carl Sandburg poem.

It's a green monster trimmed in bare lightbulbs at night, dripping with sounds of turning gears, cranes, and linkbelts, all surrounded by packed, rutted, oil-stained soil. Farther along Baldwin Avenue sits **Holy Rosary Church** and its sculpture of Father Damien. The rendering of Damien is idealized, but the leper, who resembles a Calcutta beggar, has a face that conveys helplessness but at the same time faith and hope. It's worth a few minutes' stop. Coming next is **Makawao Union Church,** and it's a beauty. Like a Tudor mansion made completely of stone with lovely stained-glass windows, the entrance is framed by two tall and stately royal palms. Farther up is **Rainbow State Park,** one of the few non-coastal parks on Maui and one of two set up for tent camping (see p. 112 for camping specifics).

The back way reaches Makawao by branching off Route 36 through Ulumalu and Kokomo. Just where Route 36 turns into Route 360, there's a road to the right. This is Kaupakalua Road, or Route 365. Take it through backcountry Maui, where horses graze around neat little houses. Haleakala looms on the horizon; guavas, mangoes, and bananas grow wild. At the first Y, bear left to Kaupakalua. Pass a large junkyard and continue to Kokomo. There's a general store here. Notice the mixture of old and new houses—Maui's past and future in microcosm. Here, the neat little banana plantation on the outskirts of the diminutive town says it all. Pass St. Joseph's Church and you've arrived through Makawao's back door. This is an excellent off-track route to take on your way to or from Hana. You can also come over Route 365 through Pukalani, incorporating Makawao into your Haleakala trip.

Nearby Attractions

Take Olinda Road out of town. All along it custom-designed houses have been built. **Seabury Hall,** a private boarding school for grades six through twelve, sits amongst trees above Makawao. In May, it hosts an arts and crafts fair, with entertainment, food, and games. Look for **Pookela Church,** a coral-block structure built in 1843. In four miles you pass **Rainbow Acres,** tel. 572-8020. Open Fri. and Sat. 10 a.m. to 4 p.m., they specialize

sculpture of Father Damien at Holy Rosary Church (BOB NILSEN)

in cactus and succulents. At the top of Olinda turn left onto Piiholo Road, which loops back down. Along it is **Aloha O Ka Aina,** a nursery specializing in ferns. Open Wed. and Sun. 10 a.m. to 4 p.m. You'll also pass **Olinda Nursery,** offering general houseplants. Open Fri. and Sat. 10 a.m. to 4 p.m.

PRACTICALITIES

Food

All the following establishments are on Makawao or Baldwin avenues. An excellent place to eat is **Polli's Mexican Restaurant,** open daily 7:30 a.m. to 10:30 p.m., tel. 572-7808. This is the original restaurant; they now have a branch in Kihei. The meals are authentic Mexican, using the finest ingredients. Formerly vegetarian, they still use no lard or animal fat in their bean dishes. You can have a full meal for $8-10. Margaritas are large and tasty for $2.50, pitchers of domestic beer, $6.

The champagne Sunday brunch is particularly good. One unfortunate policy is that they refuse to give free chips and salsa to a person dining alone, even when ordering a full meal, while couples dining get them free! Live entertainment nightly in the bar.

Makawao Steak House, tel. 572-8711, open daily for dinner from 5 p.m. Early-bird special until 6:30, Sunday brunch from 9:30 a.m. to 2 p.m. Casual, with wooden tables, salad bar, and good fish selections, dinners are from $10.95. The steak dishes, especially the prime rib, are the best. The Makawao Steak House has been around a long time and maintains a good, solid reputation. The best all-around restaurant in Makawao! The lounge is open from 9 p.m. until closing.

A surprising and delicious dining experience is found at **Casanova Italian Restaurant and Deli,** tel. 572-0220, located at Makawao Four Corners, open daily for breakfast, lunch, and dinner. The interior is utilitarian. The deli case is loaded with salami, prosciutto, hams, cheeses, smoked salmon, and savory salads. Shelves are stocked with Italian delectables, designer chocolates, and ice cream too. There's a counter for eating, with glossy high-society magazines provided for your reading pleasure. Specials are offered nightly, but the best dishes in the house are the fresh-made lasagna, ravioli, and spaghetti, all smothered in different sauces. Many of the best restaurants on Maui order their pasta from Casanova's. You order at the counter and are given a paper plate and plastic utensils. The best place to sit is on the front porch where you can perch above the street and watch Makawao life go by.

They have recently opened a restaurant in the adjoining section of the building, open for dinner only from 5:30 to 11 p.m., featuring pizza, pasta, and other fine Italian cuisine. While of the same quality as the deli food, most people come for the nightly music and dancing. Having a nightclub atmosphere, and featuring dance bands on the weekends (disco Wed. and Thur.), a large dance floor, and a first-class sound system, it has become one of the hottest night spots, drawing people not only from Upcountry but also Central and West Maui.

Kitada's makes the best saimin on Maui, according to all the locals. It's across from the Makawao Steak House. Open daily 6 a.m. to 1:30 p.m., tel. 572-7241. The 77-year-old owner, Takeshi Kitada, does all the prep work himself. Walk in, pour yourself a glass of water, and take a hardboard- topped table. The saimin is delicious and only $2. There are plate lunches, too. The walls have paintings of Upcountry by local artists; most show more heart than talent. Bus your own table while Kitada-san calculates your bill on an abacus. His birthday, May 26, has become a town event.

Komoda's is a corner general store that has been in business for over 50 years. They sell everything, but their bakery is renowned far and wide. They open at 6:30 a.m. with people already lined up outside to buy their cream buns and homemade cookies—all gone by 9 a.m.

Masa's Kitchen is an inexpensive place to eat along Makawao Avenue (on the rise on the left going toward Pukalani). They serve a variety of plate lunches under $4, Japanese dishes, and sushi. The sushi sells by the roll at $3.10. They offer it pre-made by the piece for only $.50, but if sushi ain't absolutely fresh *pardner san,* it ain't sushi.

At the corner of Makawao and Baldwin avenues is a shop called **Your Just Desserts,** tel. 572-1101, open daily 10:30 a.m. to 9 p.m., Sunday noon to 5 p.m. It's one of those sweet shops where you can satisfy your cravings for goodies and not feel too guilty . . . kind of. Their menu includes frozen yogurt with all the trimmings, honey lemonade, home-baked cookies, and jams and jellies. Light lunch and dinner selections are served Mon. to Saturday. Good stuff! The shelves also hold gift items, housewear, and children's toys. You can browse while you munch.

One of the newest establishments in Makawao is **Circle of the Sun Cafe and Convergence Center.** Open from 7 a.m. for breakfast and lunch, all food items are vegetarian. Taking a holistic approach, the center supports programs that are health conscious, peace oriented, environmentally sound, and financially unexploiting. In esssence, its focus is a campaign for the earth and the uplifting of man. A bulletin board here alerts you to similar happenings throughout the island.

Mountainside Liquor and Deli, tel. 572-0204, can provide all the fixings for a lunch, or a full range of liquid refreshments. **Rodeo General Store** is a one-stop shop with a wide selection of natural foods, pastries, produce, and fresh fish. **Mountain Fresh Market,** open daily 8 a.m. to 7:30 p.m., 10 a.m. to 6 p.m. on Sun., has an excellent community bulletin board out front. Upcountry's health food store, it's small, but jam-packed with juices, grains, vitamins, and organic fruits and vegies. **Upcountry Fishery,** open daily until 7 p.m., until 10 p.m. on Sat. and Sun., is on Makawao Avenue and also houses **Dickey's Healthy Foods** (next to the library and post office). The fish selections are excellent, but the health food store is slightly understocked. However, the prices are good.

One additional place to eat in Upcountry Maui outside Makawao is in Haliimaile. A new establishment, **Haliimaile General Store,** housed in what was this pineapple town's general store, not only serves food but sells gifts, prepared food items, and maintains a full bar. Although the menu changes periodically, entrees include brie and grape quesadillas, roasted chicken halves with pineapple chutney, and fettucini and scallops with sun-dried tomato pesto. Only locally grown and the freshest ingredients are used. Entress in the $11-24 range, appetizers from $6-12. Their desserts alone are what draw many people to eat here. Open Tues. to Sun. 11 a.m. to 3 p.m., then 6 p.m. to 10 p.m., with a Sunday brunch from 10 a.m. to 2 p.m. For reservations call 572-2666.

Shopping

Makawao is changing quickly, and nowhere is this more noticeable than in its local shops. The population is now made up of old-guard *paniolo,* yuppies, and alternative people. What a combo! You can buy a bullwhip, a Gucci purse, a cold Bud, or sushi all within 100 feet of each other. Some unique and fascinating shops here can provide you with distinctive purchases. **Maui Moorea,** at 3639 Baldwin Ave., tel. 572-0801, sells expensive but highly fashionable clothing for women and children. Cindy, the owner, also has shelves of collectibles and handicrafts made on Maui. The rear of the shop is given over to handmade leather and suede clothing made by Carl, Cindy's husband. **Collections Boutique,** tel. 572-0781, open daily till 9 p.m., imports items from throughout Asia: batik from Bali, clothes from India, jewelry and handicrafts from various countries. Operated by Pam Winans.

Silversword Stoves, tel. 572-4569, formerly Outdoor Sports, has the largest line of wood-burning stoves in Hawaii. That's right, stoves! Nights in the high country can get chilly, and on top of Haleakala downright cold. Also here are a good selection of cutlery, and a few residuals left over from when it was a great hardware and tack store. The owner, Gary Moore, is a relative newcomer who helped restore the integrity of Makawao and became a town historian in his own right. For fine art check out **David Warren's Studio,** tel. 572-1864, along Baldwin Avenue. David is one of the featured artists at the prestigious Maui Crafts Guild in Paia, but chose Upcountry for his studio. Two other galleries in Makawao are the **Glassman Galleries,** tel. 572-7132, with a new monthly exhibition of contemporary works by artists living on Maui, and **Crater Galley,** tel. 572-1470, both near Makawao four corners. **Gecko Trading Co.,** tel. 572-0249, a boutique bright with alohawear and T-shirts, is down Baldwin Avenue. **Coconut Classics** tel. 572-7103, features Hawaiian collectibles in their semi-discovery shop, which has old and new merchandise. Close by is **Country Flowers,** tel. 572-1154, for leis or arranged flowers.

Down a narrow alley a few steps from the intersection of Baldwin and Makawao avenues is **The Dragon's Den,** tel. 572-2731, a shop stuffed full of Chinese herbs and medicines, minerals, crystals, teas, gifts, and books on Eastern healing arts. Also in the alley are **Graceland Rejuvenation Center,** tel. 572-6091, for theraputic massage and colonic therapy; and **Grace Clinic,** tel. 572-6091, which specializes in traditional Oriental medicine, new features to the ever-changing face of this Upcountry community.

Hui Noeau ("Club of Skills") Visual Arts Center, tel. 572-6560, is a local organization that features traditional and modern arts.

Their member artisans and craftspeople produce everything from ceramics (created in the workshop on the premises) to *lau hala* (weaving). They are housed at Kaluanui, a mansion built in 1917 by the Baldwin family on their nine-acre estate and located just down the road from Makawao on the way to Paia, at 2841 Baldwin Ave. Throughout the year classes, lectures, and exhibits are offered, and they sponsor an annual Christmas Fair featuring their creations. Worth a stop to visit the gift shop, studio, and gallery.

Events

Makawao has a tremendous rodeo season every year. Most meets are sponsored by the Maui Roping Club. They start in the spring and culminate in a massive rodeo on July 4th, with over $22,000 in prize money. These events attract the best cowboys from around the state. The organization of the event is headed by long-time resident Brendan Balthazar, who welcomes everyone to participate with only one rule, "Have fun, but maintain safety."

KULA

Kula could easily provide all of the ingredients for a full-course meal fit for a king. Its bounty is staggering: vegetables to make a splendid chef's salad, beef for the entree, flowers to brighten the spirits, and wine to set the mood. Up here, soil, sun, and moisture create a garden symphony. Sweet Maui onions, cabbages, potatoes, grapes, apples, pineapples, lettuce, and artichokes grow with abandon. Herefords and black Anguses graze in knee-deep fields of sweet green grass. Flowers are everywhere: beds of proteas, camellias, carnations, roses, hydrangeas, and blooming peach and tangerine trees dot the countryside like daubs from van Gogh's brush. As you gain the heights along Kula's lanes, you look back on West Maui and a perfect view of the isthmus. You'll also enjoy wide-open spaces and rolling green hills fringed with trees like a lion's mane. Above, the sky changes from brooding gray to blazing blue, then back again. Kula is a different Maui—quiet and serene.

Getting There

The fastest way is the same route to Haleakala Crater. Take Route 37 through Pukalani, turn onto Route 377, and when you see Kimo Road on your left and right, you're in Kula country. If you have the time take the following scenic route. Back in Kahului start on Route 36 (Hana Hwy.), but as soon as you cross Dairy Road look for a sign on your left pointing to Pulehu-Omaopio Road. Take it! You'll wade through acres of sugar cane, and in six miles

these two roads will split. You can take either, but Omaopio to the left is better because, at the top, it deposits you in the middle of things to see. Once the roads fork, you'll pass some excellent examples of flower and truck farms. You'll also go by the cooperative **Vacuum Cooling Plant** where many farmers store their produce. Then Omaopio Road comes again to Route 37 (Kula Hwy.). Don't take it yet. Cross and continue until Omaopio dead ends, in a few hundred yards. Turn right onto Lower Kula Road and watch for Kimo (Lower) Drive on your left, and take it straight uphill. This brings you through some absolutely beautiful countryside and in a few miles crosses Route 377, where a right will take you to Haleakala Crater Road.

SIGHTS, FOOD, AND ACCOMMODATIONS

Pukalani

This way-station town is uninteresting but a good place to get gas and supplies. There's a shopping mall and several mini-malls where you can pick up just about anything. **Bullock's** restaurant, just past the T-intersection with Makawao Ave., serves a wide assortment of good-value sandwiches. The Moonburger is a tradition, but a full breakfast here for under $5 will give you all the energy you'll need for the day ahead. They also have plate lunches and some island-flavored shakes. Also at this intersection is the **Pukalani Superette,** a fine

A steer grazes the lush grasses of Upcountry.
(J.D. BISIGNANI)

grocery store. In the Pukalani Terrace Center are **Hua Restaurant** for a wide variety of Chinese foods, a **Subway** sandwich shop, and **Y's Okazu-Ya and Crack Seed Shop.** One of the best restaurants in the area is the **Pukalani Terrace,** open daily 10 a.m. to 9 p.m, tel. 572-1325, at the Pukalani Country Club. They have a salad bar and sandwiches, but specialize in "local" and Hawaiian foods such as *kalua* pig for $8.40 and *lau lau* for $7.85. Most patrons are local people, so you know that they're doing something right. The only Upcountry golf course on Maui, Pukalani Country Club, offers 18 holes of inexpensive golf. In the bargain come spectacular views over the isthmus and up toward Haleakala. See "Golf" in the main Introduction for specifics.

Kula Lodge

The Kula Lodge is on Route 377 just past Kimo Drive and just before Haleakala Crater Road. The address is RR 1, Box 475, Kula, HI 96790, tel. 878-1535, (800) 233-1535. Lodging here is in five $80-140 chalets. Two have fireplaces with wood provided, four have lofts for extra guests, and all have lanais and excellent views of lower Maui. The lobby and dining areas are impressively rustic. The walls are covered with high-quality photos of Maui: windsurfers, silverswords, sunsets, cowboys, and horses. The main dining room has a giant bay window with a superlative view. Breakfast is served daily from 6:30 a.m., lunch 11:30 a.m. to 5 p.m., dinner from 5:30 to 9 p.m. Entertainment in the evenings. Perhaps the only drawback is the noise created from 6:30 to 7:30 a.m. when riders on the Haleakala downhill bike trips arrive in a large group for breakfast. Be up early so as not to be disturbed.

In the basement of the lodge is the **Curtis Wilson Cost Art Gallery.** One of Maui's premier artists, Cost captures scenes reflecting the essence of Upcountry Maui, handles color, light, and shadow to perfection, and portrays the true pastoral nature of the area. Stop in and browse daily from 8:30 a.m to 4:30 p.m.

The Protea Gift Shoppe

An extension of the Hawaii Protea Corporation, it is next door to the Kula Lodge and open Mon. to Fri. 9 a.m. to 4:30 p.m., tel. 878-6464, or (800) 367-8047, ext. 215. Don't miss seeing these amazing flowers. (For a full description see "Flora" in the main Introduction.) Here you can purchase a wide range of protea that can be shipped back home. Live or dried, these flowers are fantastic. Gift boxes starting at $30 are well worth the price. The salespeople are friendly and informative, and it's educational just to visit.

Upper Kimo Road

If you want to be intoxicated by some of the finest examples of Upcountry flower and vegetable farms, come up here. First, head back down Route 377 past the Kula Lodge and turn on **Upper Kimo Road** on your right. One mile up, at the very end, is **Upcountry Protea Farm,** open daily 8 a.m. to 4:30 p.m. Route 1, Box 485F, Kula, HI 96790, tel. 878-2544; for phone orders call (800) 332-8233. They have over 50 varieties of protea and other flowers. You can walk the grounds or visit the gift shop, where they offer gift packs and mail orders. Although harvested all year round, the best time for viewing and sending Protea as gifts is from Sept. through Nov. when they are at their most bountiful.

Sunrise Protea Farm
This farm and gift shop is less than half a mile up Haleakala Hwy. The shop sells gift items, local Maui produce, homemade sweets, and fruit juices. In the flower shop you'll find fresh and dried flowers and arrangements that can be sent anywhere in the country. An easy stop on the way back from Haleakala crater. Open 8 a.m to 4 p.m weekdays, 7 a.m to 5 p.m. weekends, tel. 878-2119 or (800) 222-2797 for phone orders.

Kula Botanical Gardens
Follow Route 377 south (it turns into Kekaulike Ave.) and look for the gardens on your left just before the road meets again with Route 37.

protea (J.D. BISIGNANI)

The gardens are open daily from 7 a.m. to 4 p.m; be sure to start by 3 p.m. to give yourself enough time for a thorough walk-around. Admission is $3, under 12 $.50, tel. 878-1715. Here are five acres of identified plants (mostly trees and flowering bushes—few flowers) on a self-guided tour. There are streams and ponds on the property, and plants include native *koa* and *kukui,* as well as many introduced species. The gardens are educational and will give names to many flowers and plants that you've observed around the island. It makes for a relaxing afternoon, with picnic tables provided.

Poli Poli State Park
If you want quietude and mountain walks, come here, because few others do. Just past the botanical gardens look for the park sign on your left leading up Waipoli Road. This 10-mile stretch is only partially paved, and the second half can be very rutted and muddy. As always, it's worth it. Poli Poli is an established forest of imported trees from around the world: eucalyptus, redwoods, cypress, and *sugi* pines. You can hike the **Redwood Trail** to a shelter at the end. Camping permits are required and are available from the Division of State Parks, Box 1049, Wailuku, HI 96793, tel. 244-4354. The cabin here is a spacious three-bedroom affair with bunks for up to 10 people. It starts at $10 single and goes up about $5 per person. It's rustic, but all camping and cooking essentials are provided, including a wood-burning stove. If you want to get away from it all, this is your spot.

Others
The University of Hawaii maintains an agriculture experimental station of 20 acres of flowers that change with the seasons. Located off Copp Road above Route 37, open Mon. to Fri. 7:30 a.m. to 3:30 p.m. A self-guided tour map is available at the office, which is closed during the lunch hour. **Holy Ghost Church** on Lower Kula Road, in Waiakoa, is an octagonal building raised in 1897 for the many Portuguese who worked the farms and ranches of Upcountry. There's a gas station here, as well as **Morihara Store, Kula Country Store and Deli,** and the **Hawaii Institute of Astronomy.**

At Ulupalakua, four lifelike wood sculptures represent some of the people who shaped Maui's history.
(BOB NILSEN)

Keokea

Continue south on Route 37 through the town of Keokea, where you'll find gas, two general stores, and an excellent park for a picnic. At the far end of the village are two new establishments. **Keokea Gallery** displays works by Maui artists and next door is **Grandma's Maui Coffee.** Grandma's is open every day but closes early on Sunday. You can enjoy fresh pasteries for breakfast, and sandwiches, saimin, and pies for lunch. The real treat, however, is the coffee, grown on the slope below and roasted in an old-fashioned coffee machine in the shop. Stop in for a sip or take a package to go.

Tedeschi Winery

Past Keokea you'll know you're in ranch country. The road narrows and herds of cattle graze in pastures that seem like manicured gardens highlighting *panini* (prickly pear) cactus. You'll pass Ulupalakua Ranch and then come to the Tedeschi Winery tasting room on the left. Open for tasting daily 9 a.m. to 5 p.m., tel. 878-6058, they sell bottles of all their wines and cushioned boxes for transporting it back to the Mainland. Fifteen-minute tours of the winery are offered as well, but as there is no set schedule tours are started whenever enough people ask for one. Here, Emil Tedeschi and his partner Pardee Erdman, who also owns the 30,000-acre Ulupalakua Ranch, offer samples of their wines. This is the only winery in all of Hawaii. When Erdman moved here in 1963 from California and noticed climatic similarities to the Napa Valley, he knew that this country could

grow decent wine grapes. Tedeschi comes from California, where his family has a small winery near Calistoga. The partners have worked on making their dream of Maui wine a reality since 1973.

It takes time and patience to grow grapes and turn out a vintage wine. While they waited for their carnelian grapes (a cabernet hybrid) to mature and be made into a sparkling wine, they fermented pineapple juice, which they call Maui Blanc. If you're expecting this to be a sickeningly sweet syrup, forget it. Maui Blanc is surprisingly dry and palatable. In 1984 the first scheduled release of the winery's carnelian champagne, Maui Brut, celebrated the patience and craftsmanship of the vintners. Maui Blush, a zinfandel-like light dinner wine, and the most recent, Maui Nouveau, a young red wine, round out the line as the two still wines. You can taste the wines at the 100-year-old tasting room, which is a plaster and coral building. It served as the jailhouse of the old Rose Ranch owned by James Makee, a Maui pioneer sugar-cane planter. Look for the 22-acre vineyard one mile before the tasting room on the ocean side of the highway. Tedeschi wines are available in restaurants and stores around the island.

Across the street are remains of the old **Makee Sugar Mill** and down the road across from the Ulupalakua Ranch office, sitting on the front porch of a woodworking shop, are four carved and painted lifelike figues. A cowboy, sea captain, farmhand, and Filipino with his fighting cock represent the varied people who contributed to Maui's history.

HALEAKALA

Haleakala ("House of the Sun") is spellbinding. Like seeing Niagara Falls or the Grand Canyon for the first time, it makes no difference how many people have come before you; it's still an undiminished, powerful, personal experience. The mountain is a power spot, a natural conductor of cosmic energy. *Kahuna* brought their novitiates here to perform final rites of initiation. During the heyday of the *kahuna,* intense power struggles took place between the healing practitioners and "black" sorcerers atop the mountain. The "Bottomless Pit," a natural feature on the crater floor, held tremendous significance for both. Average Hawaiians did not live on Haleakala, but came now and again to quarry toolstones. Only *kahuna* and their apprentices lived here for any length of time, as a sort of spiritual preparation and testing ground. Today, students of higher consciousness from around the world are attracted to this natural cosmic empire because of the rarefied energy. They claim that it accelerates personal growth, and compare it to remote mountain and desert areas in the Holy Lands. Even the U.S. Air Force has a facility here, and their research indicates Haleakala is *the* strongest natural power point in America. Not only is there an energy configuration coming from the earth itself, but there is also a high focus of radiation coming from outside the atmosphere. No one is guaranteed a spiritual experience on Haleakala, but if you're at all sensitive, this is fertile ground.

Natural Features

Haleakala is the world's largest dormant volcano, composed of amazingly dense volcanic rock, almost like poured cement. Its 20,000 feet or so lying under the sea make it one of the tallest mountains on earth. Perhaps this mass accounts for the strange power of Haleakala as it sits like a mighty magnetic pyramid in the center of the North Pacific. The park's boundaries encompass 27,284 variable acres which stretch from Hosmer Grove to Kipahulu, and include dry forests, rainforests, desert, and subtropical beaches. The most impressive feature is the crater itself. It's 3,000 feet deep, 7½ miles long, and 2½ miles wide, accounting for 19 square miles, with a circumference of 21 miles. A mini-mountain range of nine cinder cones marches across the crater floor. They look deceptively tiny from the ob-

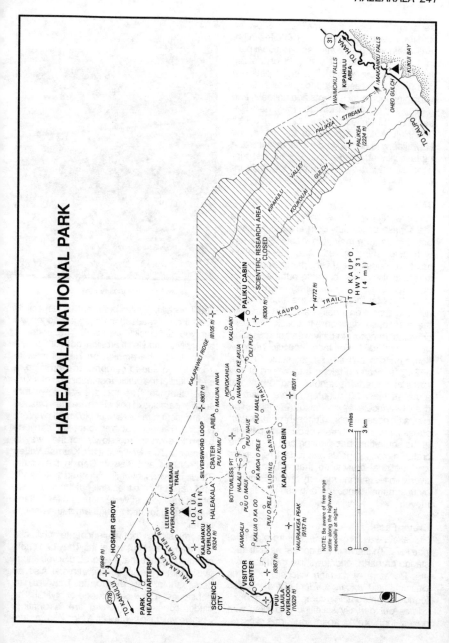

HALEAKALA NATIONAL PARK

NOTE: Be aware of free range cattle along the highway, especially at night.

servation area, but the smallest is 600 feet, and the tallest, Puu O Maui, is 1,000 feet high. Haleakala was designated as a national park in 1961. Before that it was part of the Big Island's Volcanoes Park. The entire park is a nature preserve dedicated to Hawaii's quickly vanishing indigenous plants and animals, and recognized as an International Biosphere Reserve by the United Nations. Only Volcanoes and Haleakala are home to the *nene*, the Hawaiian wild goose, and the **silversword**, a fantastically adapted plant. (For full descriptions, see "Flora And Fauna" in the main Introduction.)

The Experience

If you're after *the* experience, you must see the sunrise or sunset. Both are magnificent, but both perform their stupendous light show with astonishing speed. Also, the weather must be cooperative. Misty, damp clouds can surround the crater, blocking out the sun, or pour into the basin, obscuring even it from view. The *Maui News* prints the hours of sunrise and sunset on a daily basis that vary with the season, so make sure to check. The park provides an accurate daily weather recording at tel. 871-5054. For more specific information, you can call the ranger station at tel. 572-7749. Plan on taking a minimum of 1½ hours to arrive from Kahului, and to be safe, arrive at least 30 minutes before dawn or dusk, because even one minute is critical. The sun, as it rises or sets, infuses the clouds with streaks, puffs, and bursts of dazzling pastels, at the same time backlighting and edging the crater in glorious golds and reds. Prepare for an emotional crescendo that will brim your eyes with tears at the majesty of it all. Engulfed by this magnificence, no one can remain unmoved.

Crater Facts

Haleakala was formed primarily from *pa'hoe-hoe* lava. This lava is the hottest natural substance on earth, and flows like swift fiery rivers. Because of its high viscosity, it forms classic shield volcanos. Plenty of *a'a* is also found in the mountain's composition. This rock comes out partially solidified and filled with gases, then breaks apart and forms clinkers.

nene *(BOB NILSEN)*

You'll be hiking over both, but be especially careful on *a'a*, because its jagged edges will cut you as quickly as coral. The crater is primarily formed from erosion, not from caving in on itself. The erosion on Hawaii is quite accelerated due to carbonic acid build-up, a byproduct of the quick decomposition of abundant plant life. The rocks break down into smaller particles of soil which are then washed off the mountain by rain, or blown off by wind. Natural drainage patterns form, and canyons begin to develop and slowly eat their way to the center. The two largest are **Keanae Valley** in the north and **Kaupo Gap** in the south. These canyons, over time, moved their heads past each other to the center of the mountain, where they took several thousand feet off the summit and formed a huge amphitheater-like crater.

Some stones that you encounter while hiking will be very light in weight. They once held water and gases that evaporated. If you knock two together, they'll sound like crystal. Also, be observant for **Maui diamonds**. They are garnet stones, a type of pyroxene or crystal. The cinder cones in the crater are fascinating. They're volcanic vents with a high iron content and may form electromagnetic lines from the earth's center. Climbing them is not recommended, but many people have, even spending the night within. On top, they are like funnels, transmitters and receivers of energy, natural pyramids. Notice the color of the compacted earth on the trails. It's obvious why you should remain on them. All the plants (silverswords, too) are shallow-rooted and live by condensing moisture on their leaves. Don't walk too close to them because you'll compact the earth around them and damage the roots. The ecosystem on Haleakala is very delicate, so please keep this in mind to preserve its beauty for future generations.

SIGHTS

You'll start enjoying Haleakala long before you reach the top. Don't make the mistake of simply bolting up the mountain without taking time to enjoy what you're passing. Route 37 from Kahului takes you through Pukalani, the last place to buy supplies. Here it branches to clearly marked Route 377; in six miles it becomes the zigzag of Route 378 or **Haleakala Crater Road.** Along the way are forests of indigenous and introduced trees, including eucalyptus, beautifully flowering jacaranda, and stands of cactus. The vistas change rapidly from one vantage point to the next. Sometimes it's the green rolling hills of Ireland, and then instantly it's the tall, yellow grass of the plains. This is also cattle country, so don't

be surprised to see all breeds, from holsteins to Brahmas.

Headquarters

The first stopping point on the Crater Road is **Hosmer Grove Campground** (see below) a short way down a secondary park road on your left. Proceed past here a few minutes and you'll arrive at **park headquarters,** open 7:30 a.m. to 4 p.m. Campers can get their permits here and others will be happy to stop for all manner of brochures and information concerning the park, for water, or to use the toilet. There are some silverswords outside and a cage for *nene* around back. After you pass Park HQ, there's trail parking on your left (see "Hikes," below). Following are two overlooks, **Leleiwi** and **Kalahaku.** Both offer tremendous views and different perspectives on the crater. They shouldn't be missed—especially Kalahaku, where there are silverswords and the remnants of a travelers' lodge from the days when an expedition to Haleakala took two days.

Visitor Center

At road's end is the visitor center, approximately 10 miles up the mountain from headquarters. It's open from sunrise to 3 p.m. and contains a clear and concise display featuring the geology of Haleakala. Maps and books are available, and the ranger talks, given every hour on the hour, are particularly informative (especially those by Ranger Jitsume Kunioke), delving into geology and the leg-

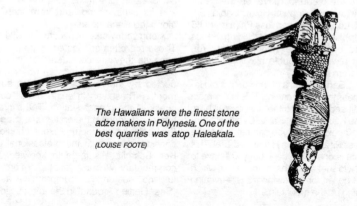

The Hawaiians were the finest stone adze makers in Polynesia. One of the best quarries was atop Haleakala.
(LOUISE FOOTE)

ends surrounding the great mountain. Various ranger-lead hikes are also given, including the crater hike down Sliding Sands Trail, a daily nature walk at the summit, and the Hosmer Grove forest walk. Check with the park headquarters or the visitor center for times and days of programs.

Walks
One of the outside paths leads to **Pakaoao** ("White Hill"). An easy quarter-mile hike will take you to the summit, and along the way you'll pass stone shelters and sleeping platforms from the days when Hawaiians came here to quarry the special tool-stone. It's a type of whitish slate that easily flakes but is so hard that when you strike two pieces together it rings almost like iron. Next comes **Puu'ulaula** ("Red Hill"), the highest point on Maui, at 10,029 feet. Atop is a glass-encased observation area (open 24 hours). This is where many people come to view the sunrise and sunset. From here, if the day is crystal clear, you can see all of the main Hawaiian Islands except Kauai. Behind you on the slope below is **Science City,** a research facility manned by the University of Hawaii and the Department of Defense. It is not open to the public.

Hikes
There are three trails in Haleakala Crater: Halemauu, Sliding Sands, and Kaupo. **Halemauu Trail** starts at the 8,000-foot level along the road about four miles past HQ. It descends quickly to the 6,600-foot level on the crater floor. En route you'll pass Holua Cabin, Silversword Loop, the Bottomless Pit (a mere 65 feet deep), then a portion of Sliding Sands Trail and back to the visitor center. You shouldn't have any trouble hitching back to your car from here.

Sliding Sands begins at the summit of Haleakala near the visitor center. This is the main crater trail and gives you the best overall hike. It joins the Kaupo Trail at Paliku Cabin; alternatively, at Kapaloa Cabin you can turn left to the Bottomless Pit and exit via Halemauu Trial. This last choice is one of the best, but you'll have to hitch back to your car at the visitor center, which shouldn't be left for the dwindling late-evening traffic going up the mountain.

The silversword is one of the world's rarest plants. Don't walk too close when observing them or you could destroy the roots. (J.D. BISIGNANI)

The **Kaupo Trail** is long and tough. It follows the Kaupo Gap to the park boundary at 3,800 feet. It then crosses private land, which is no problem, and after a steep and rocky downhill grade deposits you in the semi-ghost town of Kaupo. This is the rugged part of the Hana loop that is forbidden by the rental car companies. You'll have to hitch west just to get to the scant traffic of Route 31, or head nine miles east to Oheo Gulch and its campground, and from there back along the Hana Road.

Along your walks, expect to see wild goats. These are often eradicated by park rangers, because they are considered an introduced pest. For those inclined, crater walks are conducted by the rangers during the summer months. These vary in length and difficulty, so check at the ranger station. There are also horseback tours of the crater (see "Sports" in the main Introduction). Hikers should also consider a day with the professional guide, Ken Schmitt. His in-depth knowledge and commentary will make your trip not only more fulfilling, but enjoyably informative as well. (See "Getting Around" in the Introduction.)

PRACTICALITIES

Making Do

If you've come to Hawaii for sun and surf and you aren't prepared for alpine temperatures, you can still enjoy Haleakala. For a day-trip, wear your jogging suit or a sweater, if you've brought one. Make sure to wear socks, and even bring an extra pair as makeshift mittens. Use your dry beach towel to wrap around inside your sweater as extra insulation, and even consider taking your hotel blanket, which you can use Indian-fashion. Make raingear from a large plastic garbage bag with holes cut for head and arms; this is also a good wind-breaker. Take your beach hat, too. Don't worry about looking ridiculous in this get-up—you will! But you'll also keep warm! Remember that for every thousand feet you climb, the temperature drops three degrees Fahrenheit, so the summit is about 30° cooler than at sea level. As the sun reaches its zenith, if there are no rain clouds, the crater floor will go from about 50 to 80 degrees. It can flip-flop from blazing hot to dismal and rainy a number of times in the same day. The nights will drop below freezing, with the coldest recorded temperature a bone-chilling 14°. Dawn and dusk are notorious for being bitter. Because of the altitude, be aware that the oxygen level will drop, and those with any impairing conditions should take precautions. The sun is ultra-strong atop the mountain and even those with deep tans are subject to burning. Noses are particularly susceptible.

Trekkers

Serious hikers or campers must have sturdy shoes, good warm clothes, rain gear, can-teens, down bags, and a serviceable tent. Hats and sunglasses are needed. Compasses are useless because of the high magnetism in the rock, but binoculars are particularly re-warding. No cook fires are allowed in the crater, so you'll need a stove. Don't burn any dead wood—the soil needs all the decompos-ing nutrients it can get. Drinking water is avail-able at all of the cabins within the crater but the supply is limited so bring what you will need. This environment is particularly deli-cate. Stay on the established trails so that you don't cause undue erosion. Leave rocks and especially plants alone. Don't walk too close to silverswords or any other plants because you'll compact the soil. Leave your pets at home; ground-nesting birds here are easily disturbed. If nature "calls," dig a very shallow hole, off the trail, and cover your toilet paper and all with the dirt. Urinating on it will hasten the decomposition process.

Camping

Admission to the park is $3, unless you arrive before the ranger at 8 a.m., but camping is free with a necessary camping permit from park headquarters. The Hosmer Grove campground is at the 6,800-foot level, just before park head-quarters; the free camping here is limited to 25 people, but there's generally room for all. There's water, pit toilets, grills, and a pavilion. It was named after Ralph Hosmer, who tried to save the watershed by planting fast-growing foreign trees like cedars, pines, and junipers. He succeeded, but this destroyed any chance of the native Hawaiian trees making a comeback. While here take a stroll along the half-mile forest loop that threads its way through the grove of trees that Hosmer planted.

Oheo Campground is a primitive camping area over at the Seven Pools (a.k.a. Oheo Stream). It's part of the park, but unless you're an intrepid hiker and descend all the way down the Kaupo Trail, you'll come to it via Hana (see "Beyond Hana").

There are campsites in the crater at **Holua, Paliku,** and **Kapalaoa.** All three offer cabins, and tent camping is allowed at the first two. Camping at any of these is extremely popular, and reservations for the cabins must be made months in advance by mail using a special cabin reservation request form only. A lottery of the applicants chosen for sites keeps it fair for all. Environmental impact studies limit the number of campers to 25 per area per day. Camping is limited to a total of three days, with no more than two days at each spot. Rates for cabin use are $5 for adults, and $2.50 for children above age 12. For complete details and reservation form write: Haleakala National Park, Box 369, Makawao, HI 96768, tel. 572-7749.

NORTHEAST MAUI

THE HANA ROAD

On the long and winding road to Hana's door, most people's daydreams of "paradise" come true. A trip to Maui without a visit to Hana is like ordering a sundae without a cherry on top. The 50 miles that it takes to get there from Kahului are some of the most remarkable in the world. The Hana Highway (Rt. 36) starts out innocently enough, passing **Paia.** The inspiration for Paia's gaily painted storefronts looks like it came from a jar of jelly beans. Next come some north-shore surfing beaches where windsurfers fly, doing amazing aquabatics. Soon there are a string of "rooster towns," so named because that's about all that seems to be stirring. Then Route 36 becomes Route 360 and at the 3-mile marker the *real* Hana road begins.

The semi-official count tallies over 600 rollicking turns and more than 50 one-lane bridges, inducing everyone to slow down and soak up the sights of this glorious road. It's like passing through a tunnel cut from trees. The ocean winks with azure blue through sudden openings on your left. To the right, streams, waterfalls, and pools sit wreathed with jungle and wildflowers. Coconuts, guavas, mangoes, and bananas grow everywhere on the mountainside. Fruit stands pop up regularly as you creep along. Then comes **Keanae** with its arboretum, and taro farms indicate that many ethnic Hawaiians still live along the road. There are places to camp, picnic, and swim, both in the ocean and in freshwater streams.

Then you reach **Hana** itself, a remarkable town. The great Queen Kaahumanu was born here, and many celebrities live in the surrounding hills seeking peace and solitude. Past Hana, the road becomes even more rugged and besieged by jungle. It opens up again around **Oheo Stream** (or Seven Pools). Here waterfalls cascade over stupendous cataracts, forming a series of pools until they reach the sea. Beyond is a rental car's no-man's land, where the passable road toughens and Haleakala shows its barren volcanic face scarred by lava flows.

LOWER PAIA

Paia ("Noisy") was a bustling sugar town that took a nap. When it awoke, it had a set of whiskers and its vitality had flown away. At the turn of the century, many groups of ethnic field workers lived here, segregated in housing clusters called "camps" that stretched up Baldwin Avenue. Paia was the main gateway for sugar on East Maui, and even a railroad functioned here until 20 years ago. During the 1930s, its population, at over 10,000, was the largest on the island. Then fortunes shifted toward Kahului and Paia lost its dynamism, until recently. Paia was resuscitated in the 1970s by an influx of paradise-seeking hippies, and then again in the '80s came another shot in the arm from windsurfers. These two groups have metamorphosed into townsfolk and have pumped new life into its old muscles. The practical shops catering to the pragmatic needs of a "plantation town" were replaced. The storefronts were painted and spruced up. A new breed of merchants with their eye on passing tourists has taken over. Now Paia (Lower) focuses on boutiques, crafts, artwork, and food. Since you've got to pass through on your way to Hana, it serves as a great place not only to top off your gas tank, but also to stop for a bite and a browse. The prices are good for just about everything, and it boasts one of the island's best fish restaurants and art shops. Paia, under its heavy makeup, is still a vintage example of what it always was—a homey, serviceable, working town.

Sights

A mile or so before you enter Paia on the left is **Rinzai Buddhist Temple.** Located on Alawai Rd.—reached by going through H. P. Baldwin Park. The grounds are pleasant and worth a look. **Mantokuji Buddhist Temple** on the eastern outskirts of Paia heralds the sun's rising and setting by ringing its huge gong 18 times at dawn and dusk.

H.P. Baldwin Beach County Park is on your left about seven miles past Kahului on Route 36, just past Maui Country Club; this spacious park is good for swimming, shell-collecting, and decent winter surfing. There are tent and trailer camping (county permit required) and full amenities. Unfortunately, Baldwin has a bad reputation. It's one of those places that locals have staked out with the attitude of "us against them." Hassles and robberies have been known to occur. Be nice, calm, and respectful. For the timid, to be on the safe side, be gone.

Hookipa Beach Park is about 10 minutes past Paia. There's a high grassy sand dune along the road and the park is down below, where you'll enjoy full amenities—unofficial camping is done. Swimming is advisable only on calm days, as there are wicked currents. Primarily a surfing beach that is now regarded as one of the best sailboarding areas in Hawaii, this is home to the **O'Neill International Windsurfing Championship,** held yearly during early spring. The world's best sailboarders come here, trying to win the $10,000 prize. A colorful spectacle, often televised. Bring binoculars.

world-class sailboarding at Hookipa (J.D. BISIGNANI)

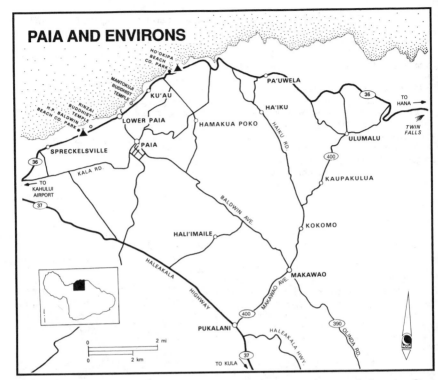

PAIA AND ENVIRONS

HO'OKIPA BEACH CO. PARK
MANTOKUJI BUDDHIST TEMPLE
RINZAI BUDDHIST TEMPLE
H.P. BALDWIN BEACH CO. PARK
KU'AU
LOWER PAIA
PAIA
SPRECKELSVILLE
KALA RD.
36
TO KAHULUI AIRPORT
37
HALEAKALA HIGHWAY
HALI'IMAILE
HAMAKUA POKO
PA'UWELA
HA'IKU
36
TO HANA
TWIN FALLS
ULUMALU
HAIKU RD.
400
KAUPAKULUA
KOKOMO
BALDWIN AVE.
MAKAWAO
MAKAWAO AVE.
PUKALANI
400
37
TO KULA
HALEAKALA HWY.
OLINDA RD.
390

0   2 mi
0   2 km

Accommodations

While there are no hotels or condos in Paia, there is an excellent guest house here for those who want a more home-like stay in a quiet neighborhood at reasonable rates. Located at 237 Baldwin Ave., **Salty Towers** is an unpretentious old cane house that's tastefully filled with the owner's personal collection of artwork, antiques, and craft items, mostly from Hawaii and the Orient—one would expect no less from the proprietor, an extensive traveler and director of an art gallery in one of Maui's major hotels. Light, airy, and comfortable, this house and the proprietor make you feel at home. Two rooms upstairs and two down limit the number of guests and provide an intimate stay. The upstairs rooms have private baths, those downstairs share a bath. All have queen beds, a small refrigerator, and cable television. You are encouraged to use the kitchen for

meals and the garden room for lounging. Storage facilities are available for bicycles and sailboards. A long-time resident of Maui, the owner has good information about what to see, where to go, and how to get there. This is a nonsmoking house so smokers are not accepted. Neither are credit cards, but traveler's checks and cash are. Room rates (two-day minimum) are $50 a night, $275 per week, excluding tax. For more information and reservations write Salty Towers, Drawer E, Old Paia Town, Maui, HI 96779 or call Claire at 579-9669.

Food

Picnic's, along Baldwin Ave., tel. 579-8021, is open daily 7:30 a.m. to 3:30 p.m. Breakfast and lunch offer a great combination of food with everything from roast beef to vegetarian sandwiches like a scrumptious spinach nut burger and cheese or tofu burger, all under $5. The best news are boxed picnic lunches that add a special touch if you're heading to Hana (few restaurants there). They start from the basic "Countryside," which includes sandwiches and sides at $7.95 per person, to the "Executive" with sandwiches, kiawe-broiled chicken, sides, nut bread, condiments, cheeses, and even a tablecloth all in a styrofoam ice chest for $42.50. (Supposedly feeds two, but with extra buns will feed four!) One of the best stops along the Hana Road even for a quick espresso, cappuccino, or frozen yogurt. Or treat yourself with the fresh-baked pastries like macadamia nut sticky buns, and the apple and papaya turnovers: worth the guilt!

Another place for boxed picnic lunches to go is **Peach's and Crumble Cafe and Bakery,** at 2 Baldwin Ave., tel. 579-8612. Try the Hana Bay box for one, $6.95, continental lunch, $6.85, or the Royal Kahuna lunch for two, $25. Open from 6:30 a.m., they also serve sandwiches, smoothies, fresh pasteries and other baked goods, and coffee.

Kihata Restaurant, tel. 579-9035, is a small Japanese restaurant and sushi bar that you can easily pass by. Don't! It's just where Baldwin Avenue meets Route 36 along the main road. Open Tues, Wed., Fri., and Sat. from 11 a.m. to 2 p.m. for lunch and Mon. to Sat. from 5 to 9 p.m. for dinner; closed Sunday. The traditional Japanese menu offers bento and sushi, with all entrees under $8, mostly from $5-6, like donburi, soba, and udon. The best deal is the Kihata teishoku, a full meal of steak, shrimp, vegetables, and miso soup for under $12.

Dillon's, on Hana Rd., Paia, tel. 579-9113, is open daily for breakfast, lunch, and dinner. From the outside you'd expect Marshal Dillon and Kitty to come sashaying through the swinging doors, but inside it's Polynesian with a sort of German beer garden out back. The food is well prepared and the portions large. Mostly steaks, chops, and fish with a Hawaiian twist. Moderate to expensive. Dillon's is famous for it's eggs Benedict special from 7 to 8 a.m. for $5.95. After Mama's (below), the best place in Paia!

Mama's Fish House is just past Paia on the left, but look hard for the turnoffs near the blinking yellow light. At each turnoff, you'll see a vintage car with a sign for Mama's. A ship's flagpole stands out front. Plentiful parking. Lunch from 11 a.m to 2:30 p.m., cocktails and pu pu until dinner at 5 p.m., reservations recommended, tel. 579-9672. Mama's has the best reputation possible—it gets thumbs up from local people. The fish is fresh daily, with some broiled over kiawe. Vegetables come from local gardens and the herbs are Mama's own. Special Hawaiian touches with every meal. Expensive, but worth it. Along with well-prepared food and friendly service, you get a wonderful view of Maui's more active north shore. Make reservations for the evening's return trip from Hana. One of the best restaurants on Maui!

For a quick bite you have **Charlie P. Woofers,** tel. 579-9453, a saloon with pool tables and restaurant specializing in pizza, pasta, subs, and sandwiches. Open 7 a.m. for breakfast, from 11:30 for lunch, and 4 p.m. for dinner. Choices include eggs Benedict, $6.25, huevos rancheros, $5.25, lunch chili burger, $4.75, pasta around $6, and dinner lasagna, $7.50 including salad. **Ice Cream and Dreams** has frosty yummies and sandwiches at the corner of Baldwin Avenue.

On the oposite corner of Baldwin Ave. is **Paia Fish Market Restaurant,** a casual sit-down restaurant with picnic tables inside, specializing in char-broiled fish and chicken and a fresh-fish counter. Most menu items are under $6.

A new and popular eating establishment with those more conscious of what they put into their bodies is the **Vegan Restaurant,** located a short way up Baldwin Ave. at #115. Open Wed. 11:30 a.m. to 5:30 p.m., 11:30 a.m. to 8:30 p.m. Thur. to Sun., closed Mon. and Tuesday. The Vegan serves only vegetarian food made with organic products. Menu items include hummus salad, $4, vegan burger, $3.95, smoothies, $2.75, tofu-vegie lasagna, $6.95, and organic and herbal beverages.

For health food try **Mana Natural Foods,** at 49 Baldwin Ave., tel. 579- 8078, open daily 8 a.m. to 8 p.m., Sun. 9 a.m. to 7 p.m. Much expanded over the old Tradewinds, it's a well-stocked health-food store, maybe the best on Maui. Inside the old building you'll find local

Montokuji Buddhist
Temple (BOB NILSEN)

organic produce, and vitamins, grains, juices, bulk foods, and more. Outside, check out the great community bulletin board for what's selling and happening around Paia.

Shopping

Maui Crafts Guild is on the left just before entering Paia, at 43 Hana Hwy., Box 609, Paia, HI 96779, tel. 579-9697. Open daily from 9 a.m. to 6 p.m. The Crafts Guild is one of the best art outlets in Hawaii. It's owned and operated by the artists themselves, all of whom must pass a thorough "jurying" by present members. All artists must be islanders, and they must use natural materials found in Hawaii to create their work except for some specialized clay, fabrics, and printmaking paper which must be imported. Items are tastefully displayed and it's an experience just to look. You'll find a wide variety of artwork and crafts including pottery, furniture, beadwork, woodcarving, bamboowork, stained glass, batik, and jewelry. Different artists man the shop on different days, but business cards and phone numbers are available if you want to see more of something you like. Prices are reasonable, as there is no middleman, and this is an excellent place to make that one "big" purchase.

In downtown Paia (two blocks along the highway) is **Tropical Emporium** with resortwear, and the **Paia Trading Co.,** a discovery shop, open Mon.-Fri. 9 a.m. to 5 p.m., that has a rack of antique Hawaiian shirts, real collector's items. The **Tee Shirt Factory** sells T-shirts that are more expensive elsewhere. **Paia Gifts and Gallery,** tel. 579-8185, daily 8 a.m. to 7 p.m., displays art by local artists. For boxed and canned goods and picnic items try either of the old-time shops, **Nagata Store** or **Horiuchi.** For the windsurfer, look for boards and gear at **Hi-Tech Sailboards, Paia Sail Company, Sailboards Maui, North Swell Maui,** or **Paia Sports Inc.**

Across the street **Exotic Maui Woods,** tel. 572-2993, open daily 9 a.m. to 6 p.m., is a treasure of amazing wood sculptures from birds on the wing to mermaids emerging from a wooden wave. Displayed are trays with inlaid fish, wooden eggs, and even a beautifully fashioned but practical picnic table is for sale. In the rear is the shop of **Eddie Flotte,** one of the finest and most highly acclaimed artists living on Maui today. His work has been compared with Norman Rockwell's, but he is an artistic genius who has his own style and needs no comparison to elevate his work. Fame has made his simple, sensitive work very expensive, but you can purchase mounted, signed photos of the originals from only $55. Eddie Flotte is able to capture the essence of Maui. His subject matter is the "every day" that everyone else overlooks . . . a rusted-out surfer's VW or some old-timers sitting in the shade of a tree.

If you want to appreciate the soul of Maui on canvas, check out this studio. Next door is **Second Chance,** a discovery shop whose proceeds go to fund a self-help refuge for women and children who are victims of domestic violence. They sell a great selection of old photos, especially of Hawaiiana and classic movie actors like Clark Gable.

Walk along Baldwin Avenue for a half block and you'll find a drawerfull of boutiques and fashion shops. **Nuage Bleu,** a boutique open daily from 10 a.m. to 5 p.m., feaures distinctive fashions and gift items, mostly for women. **Ikeda's** is a tired old department store where locals shop, so the goods are reasonably priced. **Rona Gale,** 27 Baldwin Ave., tel. 579-9984, open daily 10 a.m. to 5 p.m., specializes in natural fabrics and handmade Maui clothing and woodcrafted items from Indonesia along with batik shirts, jackets, and cover-ups. **Yoki's Boutique,** tel. 572-9003, open daily 10 a.m. to 5 p.m., has jewelry, gifts, and apparel from all over the world. Yoki is an artist and she hand-paints the one-of-a-kind fashions that adorn the walls. The **Clothes Addict** has antique aloha shirts, and sexy, new-wave bikinis. Also along Baldwin Ave. are the **Bank of Hawaii,** the **post office,** a washerette, and **Paia 30-minute Photo,** open 8 a.m. to 6 p.m. Mon. to Sat. with shorter hours on Sunday.

Unocal 76 is the last place to fill your tank before reaching Hana. Next door is **Paia General Store** for supplies and sundries, with a takeout snack window called the **Paia Drive Inn.** At the old North Shore Gas station is **Things From the Past** antique shop, open 10 a.m. to 6 p.m. daily. Across the street is the **Paia Mercantile Shopping Complex,** a collection of shops ranging from surfing equipment to **Clementine's,** and for women's clothing, **Tropical Blossoms,** a wholesale outlet for gift items.

Heading down the road to Hana you'll see the **Maui Community Center** on your left, and soon, just past mile marker 12, look for W. Kuiaha Road and make a right heading for the old **Pauwela Cannery,** which is less than five minutes up the road. This huge tin can of a building has been divided into a honeycomb of studios and workshops housing fine artists, woodworkers, cabinetmakers, potters, and sailboard makers. All welcome guests to come and browse, and buy. In the rear is Resta Studio, the workshop of Piero Resta. He, along with his son Luigi, graciously welcomes visitors (call first, 575-2203), and with Italian hospitality makes you feel at home with a cup of cappuccino. To qualify as a real Italian gentleman you must have imagination! Without it you're like pasta with no sauce, or pesto with no basil. You must possess, and be willing to share, opinions on life, politics, religion, philosophy, and moreover you must be a lover . . . of art, women, music, and food, preferably all in the same evening! Piero Resta is an Italian gentleman. His studio with loft (necessary to be a real artist) is a vision of dynamism. His works are bold, colorful, neo-Renaissance personal statements of semi-abstract reality. Broad-hipped women with classical Greek faces pose or stride nonchalantly across a surrealistic collage of vibrant Maui colors. Carved wooden pillars wait to adorn a modern portico, while a mythical yellow tiger on a bold red background opens its mouth in anticipation of eating its own tail. The studio and the artwork surround you like a colorful wave. Soul-surf with Piero. You'll be glad you did!

THE ROAD BEGINS

The road to Hana holds many spectacles and surprises, but one of the best is the road itself . . . it's a marvel! The road was hacked out from the coastline in 1927, every inch by hand using pick and shovel. An ancient Hawaiian trail followed the same route for part of the way, but mostly people moved up and down this coastline by boat. What makes the scenery so special is that the road snakes along Maui's windward side. There's abundant vegetation and countless streams flowing from Haleakala, carving gorgeous valleys. There are a few scattered villages with a house or two that you hardly notice, and the beaches, although few, are empty. Mostly, however, it's the "feeling" that you get along this road. Nature is close and accessible, and it's so incredibly "South Sea island" that it almost seems artificial. But it isn't.

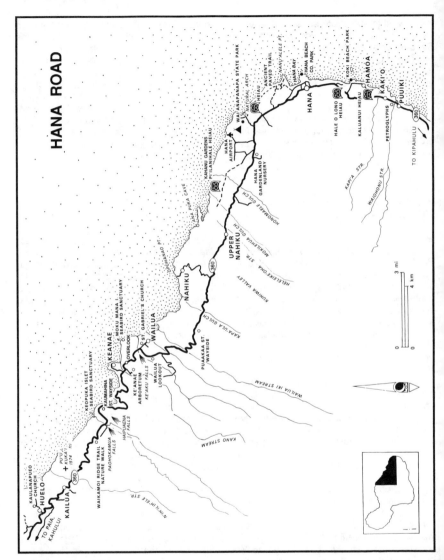

Driving Tips

You've got 30 miles of turns ahead when Route 36 (mile marker 22) becomes Route 360 (mile marker 0) and the fun begins. The Hana Road has the reputation of being a "bad road," but this isn't true. It's narrow, with plenty of hairpin turns, but it's well banked, has clearly marked bridges, and there's always maintenance going on (which can slow you up). Years back, it was a harrowing experience.

When mudslides blocked the road, drivers were known to swap their cars with those on the opposite side and carry on to where they were going. The road's reputation sets people up to expect an ordeal, so they make it one, and unfortunately, drive accordingly. Sometimes it seems as though tourists demand the road to be rugged, so that they can tell the folks back home that they, too, "survived the road to Hana." This popular slogan appears on T-shirts, copyrighted and sold by Hasegawa's famous (though recently burned down)

store in Hana, and perpetuates this belief. You'll have no problem, and you'll see much more if you just take it easy.

Your speed will often drop below 10 miles per hour and will rarely exceed 25. Standard-shift cars are better for the turns. Cloudbursts occur at any time so be ready for slick roads. A heavy fall of fruit from roadside mango trees can also coat the road with slippery slime. Look as far up the road as possible and don't allow yourself to be mesmerized by the 10 feet in front of your hood. If your tire dips off a rough

54 BRIDGES OF HANA, MAUI, HAWAII

1	O'o-pu-ola	life maturing	28	Pu-a-pa-pe	baptismal
2	Ma-ka-na-le	bright vision	29	Ka-ha-wai-ha-pa-pa	extensive valley
3	Ka-ai-ea	breathtaking view	30	Ke-a-a-iki	burning star (sirius)
4	Wai-a-ka-mo'i	waters of the king	31	Wai-oni (Akahi)	first ruffled waters
5	Pu-oho-ka-moa	sudden awakening	32	Wai-oni (Elua)	second ruffled waters
6	Hai-pue-na	glowing hearts	33	Lani-ke-le	heavenly mist
7	Ko-le'a	windborne joy	34	He-lele-i-ke-oha	extending greetings
8	Hono-manu	bird valley	35	Ula-i-no	intense sorrow
9	Nu'a-'ai-lua	large abundance	36	Moku-lehua	solemn feast
10	Pi-na-ao	kind hearted	37	'O-i-lo-wai	first sprouting
11	Pa-lauhulu	leaf sheltered	38	Hono-ma-'e-le	land of deep love
12	Wai-o-ka-milo	whirling waters	39	Ka-wai-pa-pa	the forbidden waters
13	Wai-kani	sounding waters	40	Ko-holo-po	night traveling
14	Wai-lua-nui	increasing waters	41	Ka-ha-wai-'oka-pi-a	frugal valley
15	Wai-lua-iki	diminishing waters	42	Wai-o-honu	water of the turtle
16	Ko-pi-li-ula	sacred ceremony	43	Papa'a-hawa-hawa	stronghold
17	Pu'a-aka-a	open laughter	44	Ala-ala-'ula	reawakening
18	Wai-o-hu-e	deceptive waters	45	Wa-i-ka-ko'i	time of demand
19	Wai-o-hu-e-'lua	second deceptive water	45	Pa-'ihi	place of majesty
20	Pa-akea	spacious enclosure	47	Wai-lua	water spirits
21	Ka-pa-'ula	to hold sacred	48	Wa-'i-lua	scattered spirits
22	Hana-wi (Akahi)	first whistling wind	49	Pu'u-ha-o-a	burning hill
23	Hana-wi (Elua)	second whistling wind	50	Pae-hala	pandanus clusters
24	Ma-ka-pi-pi	desire for blessings	51	Maha-lawa	place of rest
25	Ku-hiwa	precious love	52	Hana-lawe	proud deduction
26	Ku-pu-koi	claiming tribute	53	Pua-a-lu-'u	prayer blossoms
27	Ka-ha-la-o-wa-ka	lightning flash	54	O'he'o	enduring pride

Interpretations Inez MacPhee Ashdown

Inez MacPhee Ashdown's translations of the names of the Hana Road bridges; layout by Sam Eason, a longtime Hana resident and artist

shoulder, don't risk losing control by jerking the wheels back on immediately. Ride it for a while and either stop or wait for an even shoulder to come back on. Local people trying to make time will often ride your rear bumper, but generally they won't honk. Pull over and let them by when possible.

Driving from Kahului to Hana will take three hours, not counting some recommended stops. The greatest traffic flow is from 10 a.m. to noon; returning "car trains" start by 3 p.m. and are heaviest around 5 p.m. Many white-knuckled drivers head for Hana as if it were a prized goal, without stopping along the way. This is ridiculous. The best sights are before and after Hana; the town itself is hardly worth the effort. Expect to spend a long day exploring the Hana Road. To go all the way to Oheo Stream and take in some sights, you'll have to leave your hotel at sunup and won't get back until sundown. If your budget can afford it, plan on staying the night in Hana (reservations definitely) and return the next day. This is a particularly good alternative if you have an afternoon departing flight from Kahului Airport. Also, most tourists seem terrified of driving the road at night. Actually it's easier. There is far less traffic, road reflectors mark the center and sides like a runway, and you're warned of oncoming cars by their headlights. Those in the know make much better time after dark!

SIGHTS

Huelo

This is a quiet "rooster town" famous for **Kaulanapueo Church** built in 1853. The structure is made from coral and is reminiscent of New England architecture. It's still used, and a peek through the door will reveal a stark interior with straight-backed benches and a platform. Few bother to stop, so it's quiet and offers good panoramas of the village and sea below. At the turnoff to Huelo between mile markers 3 and 4, there's a public telephone, in case of emergency.

The next tiny town is **Kailua.** Plenty of mountain apple trees flourish along this stretch. The multicolored trees are rainbow eucalyptus, introduced late last century from Australia and some of the most beautiful trees

in Hawaii. Close by is a cousin, *Eucalyptus robusta,* which produces great timber, especially flooring, from its reddish-brown heartwood. This tree, due to its resins, gets extremely hard once it dries, so it must be milled immediately or you can do nothing with it. A few minutes later, notice a sudden difference in the humidity and in the phenomenal jungle growth that becomes even more pronounced.

Waikamoi Ridge

This nature walk (mosquitos!) is a good place to stretch your legs and learn about native and introduced trees and vegetation. The turnout is not clearly marked along the highway, but look for a metal gate at roadside and picnic tables in a clearing above the road. The trail leads through tall stands of trees. For those never before exposed to a bamboo forest, it's most interesting when the wind rustles the trees so that they knock together like natural percussion instruments. Picnic tables are available at the start and end of the trail. Back on the road, and at the next bridge, is excellent drinking water. There's a stone barrel with a pipe coming out, and local people come to fill jugs with what they call "living water." It doesn't always run in summer but most times can be counted upon.

Following is **Puohokamoa Falls,** where you'll find a nice pool and picnic table. A short stroll will take you to the pool and its 30-foot cliff, from which local kids jump off. You'll also find a trail near the falls, and if you go upstream about 100 yards you'll discover another invigorating pool with yet another waterfall. Swimming is great here, and the small crowd is gone. If you hike downstream about one-half mile *through* the stream (no trail) you come to the top of a 200-foot falls from where you can peer over the edge.

Beach Parks

Less than two miles past Waikamoi Ridge is **Kaumahina State Wayside** along the road, and **Honomanu County Park,** down at Honomanu Bay. Permits are required for camping. There are no amenities at Honomanu, but Kaumahina has them all. Camping here is in a rainforest with splendid views out to sea overlooking the rugged coastline and the

Tidy fields on the Keanae Peninsula are still the pride of Hawaiian farmers.
(BOB NILSEN)

black-sand beach of Honomanu Bay. Puohokamoa Falls are just a short walk away. Honomanu is not good for swimming because of strong currents, but is good for surfing.

Keanae

Honomanu Valley, just before the Kaenae Arboretum, is the largest valley on the north side of Haleakala. Most of the big valleys that once existed, especially on East Maui, were filled in by lava flows, greatly reducing their original size. But Honomanu goes back about five miles toward the center of the mountain, and has 3,000-foot cliffs and 1,000-foot waterfalls. Unfortunately, the trails are both quite difficult to find and to negotiate.

Clearly marked on the right will be **Keanae Arboretum.** A hike through this facility will exemplify Hawaiian plant life in microcosm. There are two sections, one of tropical plants (identified) and the other of Hawaiian domestic plants. Toward the upper end of the arboretum are taro fields, and the hillsides above are covered with the natural rainforest vegetation. You can picnic and swim along Piinaau Stream. Hardier hikers can continue for another mile through the rainforest; at the end of the trail is a pool and waterfall. As there is a gate across the entrance (located at a sharp curve in the road), pull well off the road to park your car and walk in.

Camp Keanae YMCA is just before the arboretum. It looks exactly as its name implies, set in a gorgeous natural pasture. There are various bunkhouses for men and women. Arrival time between 4 and 6 p.m., $8. For more information call the camp at 248-8355. All accommodations are by reservation only. For reservations contact the Kahului YMCA office at 244-3253.

Keanae Peninsula is a thumb-like appendage of land formed by a lava flow that came down the hollowed-out valley from Haleakala crater. A fantastic lookout is here—look for a telephone pole with a tsunami loudspeaker atop, and pull off just there. Below you'll see neat little farms, mostly raising taro. Shortly before this lookout, a public road heads down into the peninsula to a turnaround. Most people living here are native Hawaiians. They still make poi the old-fashioned way: listen for the distinctive thud of poi-pounding in the background. Though *kapu* signs abound, the majority of people are friendly. If you visit, be aware that this is one of the last patches of ground owned by Hawaiians and tended in the old way. Be respectful, please. Notice the lava-rock missionary church. Neat and clean, it has straight-back, hardwood pews and a pleasant altar inside. The cemetery to the side is groomed with tropical flowers while the grounds are rimmed by coconut trees. Next comes the lonely **Wailua Peninsula.** It, too, is covered in taro and is a picturesque spot. Only 3,000 people live along the entire north coast of East Maui leading to and including Hana.

Fruit Stands

Do yourself a favor and look for **Uncle Harry's Fruit Stand,** clearly marked on the left past the Keanae Peninsula just beyond the Keanae school. If he's there stop and talk. He's a medical *kahuna* who knows a great deal of the natural pharmacology of old Hawaii, and is a living encyclopedia on herbs and all their healing properties. Past Kaenae between mile markers 17 and 18 is another roadside stand where you can buy hot dogs, shave ice, and some fruit. Notice the picture-perfect, idyllic watercress farm on your left. Past mile marker 18 on the right is a fruit stand operated by a fellow named Joseph. He not only has coconuts, pineapples, and papayas, but also little-tasted exotic fruits like mountain apples, star fruit, strawberry guavas, and Tahitian lemons. An authentic fruit stand worth a stop. Another one, operated by a Hawaiian woman, is only 50 yards on the left. If you have a hankering for fruit, this is the spot.

Wailua

At mile marker 18, you come to Wailua. Turn left here on Wailua Road, following signs for **Coral Miracle Church.** Here, too, you'll find the **Miracle of Fatima Shrine,** so named because a freak storm in the 1860s washed up enough coral onto Wailua Beach that the church could be constructed by the Hawaiian congregation. Here also are St. Garbriel's Church and St. Augustine's Shrine. There is a lovely and relatively easy-access waterfall nearby. Pass the church, turn right, and park by the large field. Look for a worn path (may be private, but no signs or hassle) that leads down to the falls.

Puaa Kaa State Wayside

This lovely spot is about 14 miles before Hana. There's no camping, but there are picnic tables, grills, and restrooms. Nearby are Kopiliula and Waikani Falls. A stream provides some smaller falls and pools suitable for swimming.

Nahiku

The village, named after the Hawaiian Pleiades, is reached by a steep and bumpy three-mile road and has the dubious distinction of being one of the wettest spots along the coast. The well-preserved and tiny village church has a sign over the door stating that it was constructed in 1867. The turn-around at oceanside is where many locals come to shore-fish and picnic. At one time Nahiku was a thriving Hawaiian village with thousands of inhabitants. Today it's home to only about 70 people, the best-known being George Harrison. A few inhabitants are Hawaiian families, but mostly the people are wealthy Mainlanders seeking isolation. After a few large and attractive homes went up, the real estate agents changed the description from "desolate" to "secluded." What's the difference? About $500,000 per house! At the turn of the century it was the site of the Nahiku Rubber Co., the only commercial rubber plantation in the United States. Many rubber trees still line the road, although the venture collapsed in 1912 because the rubber was poor due to the overabundance of rainfall, and the village once again lost its vitality. Some people have augmented their incomes by growing *pakalolo* in the rainforest of this area. However, the alternative people who first came here and have settled in have discovered that there is just as much money to be made by raising ornamental tropical flowers ($5,000-10,000 per acre), and have become real "flower children." Many have roadside stands (you'll find others along the Hana Highway) where payment for the flowers displayed is on the honor system. Leave what is requested—prices will be marked.

Kahanu Gardens

Continue on the Hana Highway to **Hana Gardenland Nursery,** where you're free to browse and picnic. They have fresh-cut flowers daily, and the prices are some of the best on Maui. Past Gardenland and leading left is Ulaino Road. Here, the pavement soon gives way to a rough track and leads to **Kahanu Gardens,** located just past a shallow stream. Open Tues. to Sat. 10 a.m. to 2 p.m. for self-guided tours, admission $5. The gardens may be closed at any time if, because of heavy rains, the stream (no bridge) is too high or moving too swiftly to cross. For information call 248-8912. This 120-acre tropical garden runs down to the tortured lava coastline. Part of the Pacific Tropical Botanical Garden, the Kahanu Gardens contain a huge variety of domestic and imported tropical plants, including a native pandanus forest and large and varied collections of breadfruit and coconut trees. Also within the gardens is **Piilanihale Heiau**, Hawaii's largest, with massive walls that rise over 50 feet.

Past Kahanu Gardens, Ulaina Road continues to roughen and ends at a parking area. Walking along the coast from there you will arrive at **Venus Pool**, a clothing-optional swimming spot where a waterfall drops fresh water into an oceanside pool.

Hana Airport

Less than a mile past Ulaino Road, on Alalele Road, a sign points left to **Hana Airport**, where **Aloha Island Air**, tel. (800) 323-3345, or 248-8328 in Hana, operates five daily flights to Kahului. All flights to Hana go through Kahului, from where you can get connecting flights to other Hawaiian cities and the Mainland. Hotel Hana Maui operates a shuttle between the airport and the hotel for its guests. There is no public transportation in Hana and only Dollar Rental Car, tel. 248-8237, can arrange wheels for you—make reservations before arriving in Hana.

Even though you're in a remote section of the island, adventure can still be had in Hana. Both Hawaii Helicopters and Soar Maui operate out of the Hana Airport. **Hawaii Helicopters**, tel. 877-3900, has various flight packages over the eastern half of the island, and **Soar Maui**, tel. 248-7433, a sailplane company, can thrill you with an engine-less glide along the mountainside. Its four offerings vary from a 20-minute Introductory Scenic Flight for $75 ($90 for two people) to a 75-minute Haleakala Crater Flight, $225/$250. For the steel-stomach enthusiast, adventure comes by way of the Acrobatic Flight ($175), where you can have your thrills with loops, spins, and gravity-defying stunts. Instruction and rentals available.

Waianapanapa State Park

Only three miles outside Hana, this state park offers not only tent camping but cabins sleeping up to six on a sliding scale, $10 single up to $30 for six. The cabins offer hot water, a full kitchen, electricity, and bedding. A deposit is required. They're very popular so book far in advance by writing Division of State Parks (see "Camping" in the main Introduction). Even for those not camping, Waianapanapa is a "must stop." Pass the office to get to the beach park and its black-sand beach. The swimming is dangerous during heavy surf because the bottom drops off quickly, but on calm days it's mellow. The snorkeling is excellent. Just offshore is a clearly visible natural stone bridge. Write Box 1049, Wailuku, HI 96753, tel. 244-4354.

A short, well-marked trail leads to **Waianapanapa Caves**. The tunnel-like trail passes through a thicket of vines and *hao,* a bush

Mr. Cooper and his grandson (J.D. BISIGNANI)

used by the Hawaiians to mark an area as *kapu*. The two small caves are like huge smooth tubs formed from lava. The water trapped inside is crystal clear. These caves mark the site of a Hawaiian legend, in which a lovely princess named Popoalaea fled from her cruel husband Kakae. He found her hiding here and killed her. During certain times of the year millions of tiny red shrimp invade the caves, turning the waters red, which the Hawaiians say is a reminder of the poor slain princess. Along the coastline here are remnants of the ancient Hawaiian **paved trail** that you can follow for a short distance.

Helani Gardens

Your last stop before Hana town, clearly marked on the right, these gardens are a labor of love begun 30 years ago and opened to the public in 1975. Howard Cooper, founder and longtime Hana resident, still tends them. The gardens are open daily 10 a.m to 4 p.m., adults $2, children and seniors $1, picnic tables and restrooms available. An energetic, talkative, and opinionated man, Mr. Cooper's philosophy on life graces a bulletin board just before you cross the six bridges to heaven. In brief he says, "Don't hurry, don't worry, don't forget to smell the flowers." It's a self-guided driving tour with something for everyone. The "lower gardens" are five acres formally manicured, but the 65 acres of "upper garden" are much more wild and open to anyone wishing to stroll around. The lower gardens have flowering trees and shrubs, vines, fruit trees, flowers, and potted plants everywhere. People see many of these plants in nurseries around the country, and may even have grown some varieties at home, but these specimens are huge. There are baobab trees, ginger plants, carp ponds, even papyrus. The fruit trees alone could supply a supermarket. The upper gardens are actually a nursery where plants from around the world are raised. Some of the most popular are heliconia and ginger, and orchids galore. In one giant tree, Mr. Cooper's grandchildren have built a tree house, complete with picture windows, electricity, and plumbing! The entire operation is family run. In Mr. Cooper's own words, "Helani Garden is where heaven touches the earth." Be one of the saved!

HANA

Hana is about as pretty a town as you'll find anywhere in Hawaii, but if you're expecting anything stupendous you'll be sadly disappointed. For most it will only be a quick stopover at a store or beach en route to Oheo Stream: the townsfolk refer to these people as "rent-a-car tourists." The lucky who stay in Hana, or those not worried about time, will find plenty to explore throughout the area. The town is built on rolling hills that descend to Hana Bay; much of the surrounding lands are given over to pasture, while trim cottages wearing flower corsages line the town's little lanes. Before the white man arrived, Hana was a stronghold that was conquered and reconquered by the kings of Maui and those of the north coast of the Big Island. The most strategic and historically laden spot is Kauiki Hill, the remnant of a cinder cone that dominates Hana Bay. This area is steeped in Hawaiian legend, and old stories relate that it was the demigod Maui's favorite spot. It's said that he transformed his daughter's lover into Kauiki Hill and turned her into the gentle rains that bathe it to this day.

Changing History

Hana was already a plantation town in the mid-1800s when a hard-boiled sea captain named George Wilfong started producing sugar on his 60 acres there. Over the years the laborers came from the standard mixture of Hawaiian, Japanese, Chinese, Portuguese, Filipino, and even Puerto Rican stock. The *luna* were Scottish, German, or American. All have combined to become the people of Hana. Sugar production faded out by the 1940s and Hana began to die, its population dipping below 500. Just then, San Francisco industrialist Paul Fagan purchased 14,000 acres of what was to become the **Hana Ranch**. Realizing that sugar was *pau*, he replanted his lands in *pangola* range grass and imported Hereford cattle from another holding on Molokai. Their white faces staring back at you as you drive past are now a standard part of Hana's scenery.

Fagan loved Hana and felt an obligation to and affection for its people. He also decided to retire here, and with enough money to materialze just about anything, he decided

Panoramic view of Hana from the Fagan Memorial.
(DAVID STANLEY)

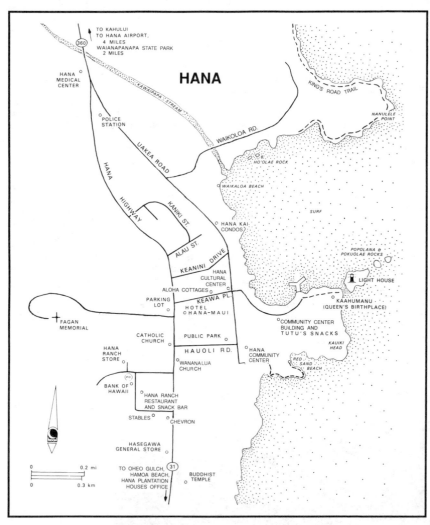

HANA

TO KAHULUI
TO HANA AIRPORT,
4 MILES
WAIANAPANAPA STATE PARK
2 MILES

360

HANA
MEDICAL
CENTER

POLICE
STATION

KAWAIPAPA STREAM

WAIKOLOA RD.

KING'S ROAD TRAIL

NANULELE
POINT

HO'OLAE ROCK

WAIKALOA BEACH

SURF

POPOLANA &
POKUOLAE ROCKS

LIGHT HOUSE

KAAHUMANU
(QUEEN'S BIRTHPLACE)

UAKEA ROAD

HANA
HIGHWAY

KANIKI ST.

ALAU ST.

HANA KAI
CONDOS

KEANINI DRIVE

HANA
CULTURAL
CENTER

ALOHA COTTAGES

PARKING
LOT

KEAWA PL.

HOTEL
OHANA-MAUI

FAGAN
MEMORIAL

CATHOLIC
CHURCH

PUBLIC PARK

HAUOLI RD.

COMMUNITY CENTER
BUILDING AND
TUTU'S SNACKS

KAUIKI
HEAD

HANA
RANCH
STORE

WANANALUA
CHURCH

HANA
COMMUNITY
CENTER

RED
SAND
BEACH

BANK OF
HAWAII

HANA RANCH
RESTAURANT
AND SNACK BAR

STABLES

CHEVRON

HASEGAWA
GENERAL STORE

0   0.2 mi

0   0.3 km

TO OHEO GULCH,
HAMOA BEACH,
HANA PLANTATION
HOUSES OFFICE

31

BUDDHIST
TEMPLE

that Hana could best survive through limited tourism. He built the **Hotel Hana-Maui,** which catered to millionaires, mostly his friends, and began operation in 1946. Fagan owned a baseball team, the San Francisco Seals, and brought them to Hana in 1946 for spring training. This was a brilliant publicity move be-

cause sportswriters came along; becoming enchanted with Hana, they gave it a great deal of copy and were probably the first to publicize the phrase "Heavenly Hana." It wasn't long before tourists began arriving.

Unfortunately, the greatest heartbreak in modern Hana history occurred at just about the same time, on April 1, 1946. An earthquake in Alaska's Aleutian Islands sent huge tidal waves that raked the Hana coast. These destroyed hundreds of homes, wiping out entire villages and tragically sweeping away many people. Hana recovered, but never forgot. Life went on, and the menfolk began working as *paniolo* on Fagan's spread and during round-up would drive the cattle through town and down to Hana Bay where they were forced to swim to waiting barges. Other entire families went to work at the resort, and so Hana lived again. It's this legacy of quietude and old-fashioned aloha that attracted people to Hana over the years. Everyone knows that Hana's future lies in its uniqueness and remoteness, and no one wants it to change. The people as well as the tourists know what they have here. What really makes Hana "heavenly" is similar to what's preached in Sunday school: everyone wants to go there, but not everyone makes it.

SIGHTS

Hana Bay

Dominating the bay is the red-faced **Kauiki Hill.** Fierce battles raged here, especially between Maui chief Kahekili and Kalaniopuu of Hawaii, just before the islands were united under Kamehameha. Kalaniopuu held the natural fortress until Kahekili forced a capitulation by cutting off the water supply. It's believed that Kamehameha himself boarded Capt. James Cook's ship after a lookout spotted it from this hill. More importantly, Queen Kaahumanu, Kamehameha's favorite and the Hawaiian *ali'i* most responsible for ending the old *kapu* system and leading Hawaii into the "new age," was born in a cave here in 1768. Until very recent times fish-spotters sat atop the hill looking for telltale signs of large schools of fish.

To get there, simply follow Uakea Road, when it splits from the Hana Road at the police station at the edge of town, and follow the signs to the bay. Take it right down to the pier and park. Hana Beach has full amenities and the swimming is good. It's been a surfing spot for centuries, although the best breakers oc-

cur in the middle of the bay. To explore Kauiki look for a pathway on your right and follow it. Hana disappears immediately; few tourists come out this way. Walk for a few minutes until the lighthouse comes clearly into view. The footing is slightly difficult but there are plenty of ironwoods to hang onto as the path hugs the mountainside. A few pockets of red-sand beach eroded from the cinder cone are below. A copper plaque erected in 1928 commemorates the spot of Kaahumanu's birth. This entire area is a great spot for a secluded picnic only minutes from town. Proceed straight ahead to the lighthouse sitting on a small island. To cross, you'll have to leap from one jagged rock to another. If this doesn't suit you, take your bathing suit and wade across a narrow sandy-bottomed channel. Stop for a few moments and check the wave action to avoid being hurled against the rocks. When you've got it timed, go for it! The view from up top is great.

Fagan Memorial

Across from the Hotel Hana-Maui, atop Lyon's hill, is a lava-stone cross erected to the memory of Paul I. Fagan, who died in 1960. The land is privately owned, but it's OK to go up there if the gate is open. If not, inquire at the hotel. From atop the hill you get the most panoramic view of the entire Hana area. After a rain, magic mushrooms have been known to pop up in the "cow pies" in the pasture surrounding the cross.

Wananalua Church

Near the hotel is the Wananalua Church, built from coral blocks in 1838. The missionaries deliberately and symbolically built it on top of an old *heiau,* where the pagan gods had been worshipped for centuries. It was the custom of chiefs to build *heiau* before entering battle. Since Hana was always contested ground, dozens of minor *heiau* can be found throughout the region.

Hana Cultural Center

Located along Uakea Road on the right, kitty-corner from the Hana Bay entrance road. Open daily 10 a.m. to 4 p.m., $2 donation. The

Wananalua Church
(J.D. BISIGNANI)

cultural center was founded in 1971 by Babes Hanchett, who is currently on the board of directors. It occupies an unpretentious building (notice the beautifully carved doors, however) on the grounds of the old courthouse and jail. The center houses fine examples of quiltwork: one, entitled "Aloha Kuuhae," was done by Rosaline Kelinoi, a Hana resident and the first woman voted into the State Legislature. There are pre-contact stone implements, tapa cloth, and an extensive shell collection. Your $2 entitles you to visit the courthouse and jail. Simple but functional, with bench and witness stand, it makes "Andy of Mayberry" look like big-time. The jail was used from 1871 to 1978, and the townsfolk knew whenever it held an inmate because he became the groundskeeper and the grass would suddenly be mowed.

BEACHES

Red Sand Beach

This is a fascinating and secluded beach area, but unfortunately the walk down is treacherous. The path, after a while, skirts the side of a cliff, and the footing is made tough because of unstable and crumbly cinders. Grave accidents have occurred, and even locals won't make the trip. Follow Uakea Road past the turnoff to Hana Bay. Proceed ahead until you

pass the public tennis courts on your right and Hana School on your left. The road dead-ends a short way later. Look left for the worn path and follow it around the Hana Ranch property fence. Ahead is a Japanese cemetery with its distinctive headstones. Below are pockets of red sand amidst fingers of black lava washed by sky-blue water. There are many tidepools here. Keep walking around Kauiki Head until you are obviously in the hollowed-out amphitheater of the red cinder cone. Pat the walls to feel how crumbly they are—the red "sand" is eroded cinder. The water in the cove is fantastically blue against the redness.

Across the mouth of the bay are little pillars of stone, like castle parapets from a fairy kingdom, that keep the water safe for swimming. This is a favorite fishing spot for local people and the snorkeling is good, too. The beach is best in the morning before 11 a.m.; afterwards it can get hot if there's no wind and rough if the wind is from the north. The coarse red sand massages your feet, and there's a natural jacuzzi area in foamy pools of water along the shore.

Koki Beach Park

The beach park is a mile or so out of town heading toward the Seven Pools. Look for the first road to your left with a sign directing you to Hamoa Village/Beach. Koki is only a few hundred yards on the left. The riptides are fierce in here so don't swim unless it's absolutely calm. The winds can whip along here, too, even though at Hamoa Beach, less than a mile away, it can be dead calm. Koki is excellent for beachcombing and for a one-night's unofficial bivouac.

A very special person named Smitty lived in a cave on the north side of the beach. Hike left to the end of the beach and you'll find a rope ladder leading up to his platform. A distinguished older man, he "dropped out" a few years back and came here to live a simple monk's existence. He kept the beach clean and saved a number of people from the riptide. He was a long-distance runner who would tack up a "thought for the day" on Hana's public bulletin board. People loved him and he loved them in return. In 1984 the roof of his cave collapsed and he was killed. When his body was recovered, he was in a kneeling position. At his funeral, all felt a loss, but there was no sadness because all were sure that Smitty had gone home.

Hamoa Beach

Follow Hamoa Road a few minutes past Koki Beach until you see the sign for Hamoa. Between Hamoa and Koki are the remnants of an extensive Hawaiian fishpond, part of which is still discernible. This entire area is an eroding cinder cone known as **Kaiwi O Pele** ("The Bones of Pele"). This is the spot where the swinish pig-god, Kama pua'a, ravished her. Pele also fought a bitter battle with her sister here, who dashed Pele on the rocks, giving them their anatomical name. Out to sea is the diminutive Alau Island, a remnant left over by Maui after he fished up the Hawaiian Islands. You can tell that Hamoa is no ordinary beach the minute you start walking down the paved, torch-lined walkway. This is the semiprivate beach of the Hotel Hana-Maui. But don't be intimidated, because no one can own the beach in Hawaii. Hamoa is terrific for swimming and bodysurfing. The hotel guests are shuttled here by buses throughout the day that leave from the hotel on the hour, so if you want this lovely beach to yourself arrive before midmorning and stay after late afternoon. There

is a pavilion that the hotel uses for its Friday night luau, as well as restrooms and showers.

Waioka Pool

Also called Venus Pool, and once used exclusively by Hawaiian royalty. At the bridge near the Hana Planatation Houses office, cross over the fence and hike (public access trail) through the fields above the river to its mouth. There you'll find a spring-fed, freshwater pool scoured out of the solid rock walls of this water course. A refreshing, usually solitary, place for a swim or to sunbathe on the smooth rocks. Be safe and stay out of the ocean—the surf, which is just over the narrow sandbar, is strong. At certain times of the year you may see giant turtles just off the rocks a short way farther down the coast. They are best seen from the road a quarter mile past the river at a sharp turn in the highway. In the fields above Waioka Pool are the remains of an old sugar mill, and part of the King's Highway, a paved pathway that once ran along the coast.

ACCOMMODATIONS

Hotel Hana-Maui

The hotel is the legacy of Paul Fagan, who built it in the late '40s, and operates as close to a family-run hotel as you can get. Most personnel have either been there from the beginning, or their jobs have passed to their family members. Guests love it that way, proven by an astonishing 80% in repeat visitors, most of whom feel like they're staying with old friends. The hotel has had only five managers in the last 45 years. The present manager, Fred Orr, came on board in 1990 when the management of the hotel was taken over by ITT Sheraton Hotels. In 1989 the hotel was sold to the Keola Hana Maui, Inc. company (a group of local Hawaiian, Japanese, and English investors), which has had the good sense to leave well enough alone. What has changed has been for the better. All rooms have been extensively renovated and the hotel can now proudly take its place among the truly luxury hotels of Hawaii. Rooms, all with their own lanai, surround the beautifully appointed grounds where flowers add a splash of color to the green-on-green blanket of ferns and gently sloping lawn. Inside the colors are subdued shades of white and tan. Morning light, with the sun filtering through the louvered windows, is especially tranquil. All suites have a wet bar and large comfortable lounge area with rattan furniture covered in billowy white pillows. A glass-topped table is resplendent with a floral display, and a tray of fresh fruit greets all guests. Refrigerators are stocked with a full choice of drinks, and there's even fresh Kona coffee that you grind and brew yourself. The floors are a deep rich natural wood counterpointed by a light reed mat in the central area. The beds, all queen-size, are covered with a distinctive handmade Hawaiian quilt, while Casablanca fans provide all the cooling necessary. The guest-cottage rooms have large free-standing pine closets; all rooms have two walk-ins. The bathrooms, as large as most sitting rooms, are tiled with earth-tone ceramic. You climb a step to immerse yourself in the huge tub, then open eye-level windows that frame a private mini-garden like an expressionist's still life.

The hotel staff adds an intangible quality of friendliness and aloha that sets the hotel apart from all others. Housekeepers visit twice a day, leaving beige terrycloth robes, and plumeria or orchids on every pillow. There is a library for use by guests, and a few shops for clothes, necessities, and gifts. Other facilities and activities include a wellness center, two heated swimming pools, tennis courts, superb horseback riding, a three-hole practice golf course, free bicycle use by guests, hikes to archaeological sites, and a famous luau held every Fri. at 6 p.m. at the hotel's facilities on Hamoa Beach. All activities are easily arranged by visiting Lovey at the actvities desk, who throughout the day can be counted on to keep family and children happy with Hawaiian language lessons, lei-making, or swaying hula lessons.

Meals become a long-remembered sumptuous event. Follow Francine or Audrey, the hostesses, to your table in the new dining room. Here, breakfasts are all manner of fresh exotic fruits and juices, hot pastries, banana macadamia-nut waffles, eggs poached or herbed into omelettes accompanied with pe-

tite steaks, fresh fish, or Hana Ranch sausages. Lunches, which upon request are prepared as very civilized picnics in wicker baskets with all fine linens and accouterments, include chilled seafood chowder, Oriental sesame chicken salad, smoked turkey-bacon sandwich, *kiawe*-grilled chicken breast, and a potpourri of vegetables. Special dinner menus are prepared daily, but you can begin with a *sashimi* plate, sautéed chicken with peanut sauce, and then move on to an assortment of grilled and roasted fowl, seafood, wild boar, or locally grown beef and lamb, all basted in a variety of gourmet sauces. Vietnamese whole fish for two is especially tantalizing. Desserts are too tempting to resist, and if you can somehow save the room try lime or macadamia-nut pie, banana cream cake, coconut mousse, or a rainbow of rich and creamy ice creams and sherbets.

Rates start at $275 for a garden-view room and progress up to $790 for the sea ranch cottage suites. An option, for an additional $85, includes three meals under the full American plan. Otherwise you can pay as you eat. Write Hotel Hana-Maui, Hana, HI 96713, tel. (800) 325-3535, or 248-8211 on Maui. The entire scene isn't stiff or fancy, but it is a memorable first-class experience!

Heavenly Hana Inn

The second most famous Hana hotel, the Heavenly Hana, resembles a Japanese *ryokan* (inn). Walk through the formal garden and remove your shoes on entering the open-beamed main dining hall. The four suites seem like little apartments broken up into sections by shoji screens. Rates are $65-100 for up to four guests. The present owner is Alfreda Worst, who purchased it from a Japanese family about 16 years ago. The inn is homey and delightful. Two other rental units, a one-bedroom cottage and a family cottage, are also available in town. Write P.O. Box 146, Hana, HI 96713, tel. 248-8442.

Hana Plantation Houses

This is a unique concept where you can rent a private house on the lush, tropical Hana coast. You have five homes to choose from and they range from the "Plantation House," a deluxe cedar one-bedroom, sleeping four and complete with lanai, full kitchen, VCR, BBQ, and your own private waterfall and koi pond, all in a coconut grove for $130, to the "Lanai Makaalae Studio," a Japanese-style studio for two at $75. These units are situated in a quiet compound about four miles past Hana at the 48 mile marker, and the front building is used as check-in for all the units. Several other newly remodeled homes are avialable in town and near Hamoa Beach, like the two-story "Hale Kipa" plantation house ($85/130) that has full amenities as well as an outdoor jacuzzi. There's even a little one-room beach cottage for $45 that can be rented only with the adjoining beach house. They also rent mountain bikes for $10/day. Hana Plantation Houses offer a perfect way to have a no-hassle, no-rush, tranquil vacation. For information contact Hana Plantation Houses, at P.O. Box 489, Hana, HI 96713, tel. 248-7248, or (800) 657-7723 for reservations.

Aloha Cottages
These are owned and operated by Zenzo and Fusae Nakamura and are the best bargain in town. The cottages are meticulously clean, well built, and well appointed. For $55-88 d, $10 per additional guest, you get two bedrooms, a full kitchen, living room, deck, and outdoor grills. Mrs. Nakamura is very friendly and provides daily maid service. The fruit trees on the property provide free fruit to guests. Box 205, Hana, HI 96713, tel. 248-8420.

Hana Kai Maui Resort
These resort apartments directly overlook Hana Bay. All are well maintained and offer a lot for the money. Studios from $103, deluxe one-bedrooms from $125-158. All have private lanai with exemplary views of the bay. Maid service, laundry facilities, and barbecues. Write P.O. Box 38, Hana, HI 96713, tel. 248-8436 or (800) 346-2772.

Hana Bay Vacation Rentals
Stan and Suzanne Collins offer nine private cottages, cabins, two-bedroom houses, and duplexes in and around Hana for rent on a daily and long-term basis. Discounts of 10% are given on stays of seven days or longer.

Rates start at $65 and step up to $170. Their rentals include everything from a rustic cabin to a half-million dollar, beachfront, three-bedroom home with banana and breadfruit trees in the front yard. This small company has an excellent reputation for quality and service. Write Box 318, Hana, HI 96713, tel. 248-7727, or (800) 657-7970. They may be starting a bed and breakfast so ask about it when you call.

Hana Kai Holidays
A second agency in Hana renting everthing from a seaside cottage to large plantation homes scattered throughout the Hana area. Rates vary from $65 to $225 a night. Write P.O. Box 536, Hana, HI 96713 or call (800) 548-0478, or 248-7742 on Maui.

FOOD AND SHOPPING

As far as dining out goes, there's little to choose from in Hana. The **Hotel Hana-Maui** main dining room offers breakfast, lunch, and dinner buffets. Prices vary according to your choice of options, but expect to spend $10 for breakfast, $15 for lunch, and $40 for dinner. Reservations recommended. There's also a self-serve coffee shop at the hotel.

Open for breakfast from 6:30 to 10 a.m., lunch from 1 to 3 p.m., and dinner on Fri. and Sat. nights only from 5 to 9 p.m., the **Hana Ranch Restaurant** serves very tasty family-style meals, but they can be stampeded by ravenous tourists heading up or down the Hana Road. Offerings include a salad bar, $9.95, smoked baby back ribs for $14.50, and fresh-grilled fish of the day, $16.50. About once a month the restaurant presents live music by traveling bands—always a cover. Aside from the nightly Hawaiian music at the hotel bar, this is the only entertainment in town (although you may find the frequent, evening baseball games at the ballpark an alternative). The Ranch Restaurant also has a snack shop (with picnic tables) that serves carry-out, fast food like eggs, french toast, or saimin for breakfast, a variety of sandwiches from $2.75-4.75, plate lunches for $4.75, and side orders.

Tu Tu's Snack Shop is at the community center building at Hana Bay; window service with tables available. Open for breakfast and lunch. Salads $2-3, saimin $2.60, plate lunches about $4, hamburgers, sandwiches, drinks, and ice cream. This building was donated by Mrs. Fagan to the community.

Hasegawa's General Store

In the ranks of "general stores," Hasegawa's, formerly south of town on the Hana Road, would be commander-in-chief. This institution had been in the family for 75 years and before it burned to the ground in the fall of 1990, was run by Harry Hasegawa. While your gas tank was being filled, you could buy anything from a cane knife to a computer disk. There were rows of food items, dry goods, and a hardware and parts store out back. Cold beer, film, blue jeans, and picnic supplies—somehow it all cramned in there. Everybody went to Hasegawa's, and it was a treat just to browse and people-watch.

Hopefully, the store will be rebuilt to again serve the community and visitors that for so long sustained it.

Hana Store

From the Hana Road, make the first right past St. Mary's Catholic Church and go up to the top of the hill. Open daily 7:30 a.m. to 6:30 p.m., tel. 248- 8261. It's a general store with the emphasis on foodstuffs. They carry a supply of imported beers, a wide selection of food items, film, videos, and some gifts. The bulletin board here gives you a good idea of what's currently happening in town.

Wakiu Originals

You'll find this shop along the Hana Road on the right about one mile before entering town. Everything sold here is handmade in Hana; prints, cards, wall hangings, and original T-shirts. Owned and operated by Bill and Anita. Not heavily stocked, but some good choices. If you find them open, stop, because they're frequently not.

SERVICES, INFORMATION, GETTING AROUND

Hana Medical Center

Along the Hana Road, clearly marked on the right just as you enter town, tel. 248-8294. Open Mon. to Fri. 8 a.m. to noon and again from 2 to 5 p.m., Sat. 8-12 only, closed Sunday. For emergencies, use the phone at the hospital entrance.

Police Station

At the Y between Hana and Uakea roads, just as you enter town. For emergencies call 911.

Services

The Bank of Hawaii, tel. 248-8015, is open Mon. to Thurs. 8:30 a.m. to 4:30 p.m., Fri. 3 to 6 p.m.; the **post office** is open weekdays 8 a.m. to 4:30 p.m. Both are next door to the Hana Ranch restaurant. The **library** is at Hana School, open Mon. to Fri. 8 a.m. to 5 p.m., tel. 248-7714.

Gas

Now the only gas available in town is at the Chevron station, next to the horse stables and below the Hana Ranch restaurant.

Rental Cars

Dollar Rental Cars, tel. 248-8237 is the only show in town. It's best to call in advance to assure a reservation. Cars may be available on short notice during low season, but don't count on it.

Hauoli Lio Stable

Open through the day for horseback-riding adventures on the Hana Ranch. Various rides include two-hour trips ($25 per person) through the macadamia nut plantation, tropical rainforest, and near the beach. Book through the activities desk at the Hotel Hana-Maui.

BEYOND HANA

Now you're getting into adventure. The first sign is that the road gets steadily worse after Hana. It begins to narrow, then the twists and turns begin again, and it's potholed. Signs warn Caution: Pig Crossing. There are no phones, no gas, and only a fruit stand or two and one store that can be counted on only to be closed. The fainthearted should turn back, but those with gumption are in for a treat. There are roadside waterfalls, cascading streams filling a series of pools, a hero's grave, and some forgotten towns. If you persevere all the way, you pop out at the Tedeschi Winery, where you can reward yourself with a glass of bubbly before returning to civilization.

Wailua Falls

About seven miles after leaving Hana, Wailua and Kanahualui falls tumble over steep lava *pali,* filling the air with a watery mist and filling their pools below. They're just outside your car door, and a minute's effort will take you to the mossy grotto at the base. There's room to park. If not for Oheo up ahead, this would be a great picnic spot, but wait! Sometimes roadside artists park here. In a few minutes you

pass a little shrine cut into the mountain. This is the **Virgin by the Roadside.** It's usually draped with a fresh lei.

OHEO GULCH

This is where the enormous **Kipahulu Valley** meets the sea. Palikea Stream starts way up on Haleakala and steps its way through the valley, leaving footprints of waterfalls and pools until it spends itself in the sea. The area was named the **Seven Sacred Pools** by white men. They made a mistake, but an honest one. The area should have been held sacred, but it wasn't. Everything was right here. You can feel the tremendous power of nature: bubbling waters, Haleakala red and regal in the background, and the sea pounding away. Hawaiians lived here but the *heiau* that you would surely expect are missing. Besides that there aren't seven pools; there are more like 24!

Getting There

Head straight on Rt. 31 ten miles out of Hana. You'll come to a large cement arched bridge (excellent view) and then a parking area to

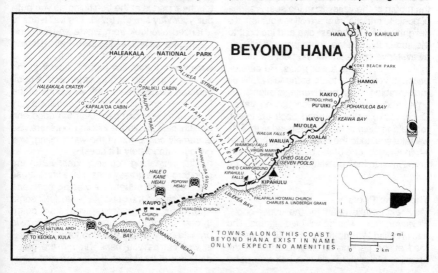

your left with a ranger's station, restrooms, and public telephone. A short way beyond, a dirt trail turns off the highway to the left and leads down to the large grassy camping area.

Warnings And Tips

Before doing any exploring, try to talk to one of the rangers, Eddie Pu and Perry Bednorse, generally found around the parking area. They know a tremendous amount of natural history concerning the area and can inform you about the few dangers in the area, such as the flash flooding that occurs in the pools. Ranger Pu has received a Presidential Citation for risking his life on five occasions to pluck drowning people from the quickly rising streams. For those intending to hike or camp, bring your own water. Don't be put off by the parking area, which looks like a used-car lot for Japanese imports; 99% are gone by sundown. The vast majority of the people go to the easily accessible lower pools, but a stiff hike up the mountain takes you to the upper pools, a bamboo forest, and a fantastic waterfall.

The Lower Pools

Head along the clearly marked path from the parking area to the flat, grass-covered peninsula. The winds are heavy here as they enter the mouth of the valley from the sea. A series of pools to choose from are off to your left. It's delightful to lie in the last one and look out to the sea crunching the shore just a few yards away. Move upstream for the best swimming in the largest of the lower pools. Be careful, because you'll have to do some fairly difficult rock-climbing. The best route is along the right-hand side as you face up the valley. Once you're satiated, head back up to the road along the path on the left-hand side. This will take you up to the bridge that you crossed when arriving, one of the best vantage points from which to look up and down this amazing valley.

The Upper Pools

Very few people head for the upper pools. However, those who do will be delighted. The trail is called **Waimoku Falls Trail.** Cross the road at the parking lot and go through the turnstile. Makahiku Falls is a half-mile uphill

Officer Eddie Pu (J.D. BISIGNANI)

and Waimoku Falls is two miles distant. The toughest part is at the beginning as you huff-puff your way straight uphill. The trail leads to a fenced overlook from where you can see clearly the lace-like Makahiku Falls. Behind you a few paces and to the left will be a waterworn, trench-like path. Follow it to the very lip of the falls and a gorgeous little pool. You can swim safely to the very edge of the falls. The current is gentle here, and if you stay to the right you can peer over the edge and remain safe behind encircling boulders. Be extremely conscious of the water rising, and get out immediately if it does!

After refreshing yourself, continue on the path through a grassy area. Here you'll cross the creek where there's a wading pool, and then zigzag up the opposite bank. After some enormous mango trees, you start going through a high jungle area. Suddenly you're in an extremely dense bamboo forest. The trail is well cut as you pass through the green darkness of this stand. If the wind is blowing, the bamboo will sing a mournful song for you. Emerge into more mangoes and thimbleberries and there's the creek again. Turn left and follow the creek, without crossing yet, and the trail will become distinct again. There's a wooden walkway, and then, eureka! . . . Waimoku Falls. It cascades over the *pali* and is so high that you have to strain your neck back as far as it will go. It's more than a waterfall; it's silver filigree. You can stand in the shallow pool below surrounded by a sheer rock amphitheater. The sunlight dances in this area and tiny rainbows appear and disappear. There is a ranger-led hike to the falls on Saturdays.

Camping

Oheo Gulch is part of Haleakala National Park. It's free to camp for a three-day limit (no one counts too closely) and no permit is necessary. The campgrounds are primitive and mostly empty. From the parking lot follow the sign that says Camping and proceed straight ahead on the dirt track. Bear right to a large grassy area overlooking the sea, where signs warn not to disturb an archaeological area. Notice how spongy the grass seems to be here. You'll see a very strange palm tree that bends and twists up and down from the ground like a serpent. Move to the trees just behind it to escape the wind. Here are clean outhouses and barbecue grills but only a limited supply of water.

BEYOND OHEO

Route 31 beyond Oheo is genuinely rugged and makes the car companies cry. It can be done, and even the tourist vans make it part of their regular route. Be aware, however, that after rough weather that has brought landslides in the past, the road can be closed by a locked gate with access available only for official business and local residents. Check! In 1½ miles you come to **Palapala Hoomau Church** (St. Paul's) and its tiny cemetery where Charles Lindbergh is buried. People, especially those who are old enough to remember the "Lone Eagle's" historic flight, are drawn here like pilgrims. The public is not really encouraged to visit, but the human tide cannot be stopped. If you go, please follow all of the directions posted. Up ahead is Samuel F. Pryor's Kipahulu Ranch. Mr. Pryor was a vice-president of Pan Am and a close chum of Lindbergh's. It was he who encouraged Lindbergh to spend his last years in Hana. Sam Pryor raises gibbons and lives quietly with his wife. Past Sam Pryor's place is B.B. Smith's fruit stand (which isn't always open), and another follows shortly. Here the road really begins to get rugged.

Kipahulu Ranch has seen other amazing men. Last century a Japanese samurai named Sentaro Ishii lived here. He was enormous, especially for a Japanese of that day, over six feet tall. He came in search of work, and at the age of 61 married Kehele, a local girl. He lived in Kipahulu until he died at the age of 102.

Kaupo Store

The vistas open up at the beginning of the Kaupo Gap just when you pass **Huialoha Church,** built in 1859. The village of Kaupo and the Kaupo Store follow Huialoha Church. A sign reads "This store is usually open Mon. to Fri., around 7:30 to 4:30. Don't be surprised if it's not open yet. It soon will be unless otherwise posted. Closed Saturday and Sunday and when necessary." Check out the bulletin board; it's full of business cards from all over the world. Only a few families live in Kaupo, old ones and new ones trying to live independently. Kaupo is the last of a chain of stores that stretched all the way from Keanae and were owned by the Soon Family. Nick Soon was kind of a modern-day wizard. He lived in Kaupo, and among his exploits he assembled a car and truck brought piecemeal on a barge, built the first electric generator in the area, and even made a model airplane from scratch that flew. He was the son of an indentured Chinese laborer.

After Kaupo you'll be in the heart of the Kaupo Gap. Enjoy it because in a few minutes the pavement will pick up again and you'll be back in the civilized world.

KAHOOLAWE

OVERVIEW

The island of Kahoolawe is clearly visible from many points along Maui's south shore, especially when it was lit up like a firecracker during heavy bombardment by the U.S. Navy. Until recently Kahoolawe was a target island, uninhabited except for a band of wild goats that refuse to be killed off. Kahoolawe was a sacred island born to Wakea and Papa, the two great mythical progenitors of Hawaii. The birth went badly and almost killed Papa, and it hasn't been any easier for her ill-omened child ever since. Kahoolawe became synonymous with Kanaloa, the man-god. Kanaloa was especially revered by the *kahuna ana'ana,* the "black sorcerers" of old Hawaii. Kanaloa, much like Lucifer, was driven from heaven by Kane, the god of light. Kanaloa held dominion over all poisonous things and ruled in the land of the dead from his power spot here on Kahoolawe. There are scores of archaeological sites and remnants of *heiau* all over the bomb-cratered face of Kahoolawe. A long, bitter feud has raged between the U.S. Navy,

which wanted to keep the island as a bombing range, and Protect Kahoolawe Ohana, a Hawaiian native-rights organization that wants the sacred island returned to the people. In a recent turn of events, the Navy has agreed to stop bombing, and now the Ohana is one step closer to its goal.

The Land

Kahoolawe is 11 miles long and six miles wide, with 29 miles of coastline. The tallest hill is **Lua Makika** in the northeast section at 1,477 feet. There are no natural lakes or ponds on the island, but it does get some rain and there is a stream running through Ahupu Gulch.

MODERN HISTORY

It's perfectly clear that small families of Hawaiians lived on Kahoolawe for countless generations and that religious rites were carried out by many visiting *kahuna* over the centuries, but mostly Kahoolawe was left alone. In

1917 Angus MacPhee, a cattleman, leased Kahoolawe from the territorial government for $200 per year. The lease would run until 1954 with a renewal option, if by 1921 MacPhee could show reasonable progress in taming the island. Harry Baldwin bought into the **Kahoolawe Ranch** in 1922, and with his money and MacPhee's know-how, Kahoolawe turned a neat profit. The island then supported indigenous vegetation such as *ohia,* mountain apples, and even Hawaiian cotton and tobacco.

MacPhee planted eucalyptus and range grass from Australia, which caught on well and stopped much of the erosion. Gardens were planted around the homestead and the soil proved to be clean and fertile. Within a few years Kahoolawe Ranch cattle were being shipped regularly to markets on Maui.

The Navy Arrives

In 1939, with the threat of war on the horizon, MacPhee and Baldwin, stimulated by patri-

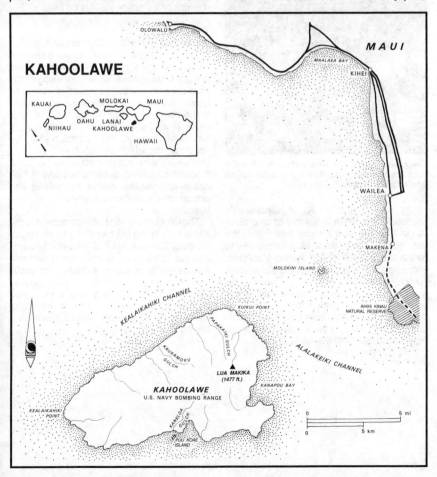

The Protect Kahoolawe Ohana resolutely builds a long house, pitting traditional Hawaiian beliefs against naval artillery. (J.D. BISIGNANI)

otism, offered a small tip of Kahoolawe's southern shore to the U.S. Army as an artillery range. One day after the attack on Pearl Harbor, the U.S. Navy seized all of Kahoolawe to further the "war effort" and evicted MacPhee, immediately disenfranchising the Kahoolawe Ranch. Kahoolawe has since become the most bombarded piece of real estate on the face of the earth. During WW II the Navy praised Kahoolawe as being *the* most important factor in winning the Pacific War, and it held Kahoolawe until the fall of 1990.

The Book On Kahoolawe

Inez MacPhee Ashdown lived on the island with her father and was a driving force in establishing the homestead. She has written a book, *Recollections of Kahoolawe,* available from Topgallant Publishing Co., Honolulu. This book chronicles the events from 1917 until the military takeover and is rife with myths, legends, and historical facts about Kahoolawe. Mrs. Ashdown is in her late eighties, going blind and in failing health, but her mind remains brilliant. She resides on Maui.

The Ohana

The Protect Kahoolawe Ohana is an extended group, favoring traditional values based on *aloha aina* (love of the land), which is the primary binding force for all Hawaiians. They would like the island to return to Hawaiian Lands inventory with the *kahu* (stewardship) to the hands of native Hawaiians. The point driven home by the Ohana is that the military has totally ignored and belittled native Hawaiian values, which are now beginning to be asserted. They maintain that Kahoolawe is not a barren wasteland, but a vibrant part of their history and religion. Indeed, Kahoolawe was placed on the National Register of Historic Sites.

The Ohana currently has legal access to the island for 10 days per month, for 10 months of the year. They have built a *halau* (long house) and use the time on Kahoolawe to dedicate themselves to religious, cultural, and social pursuits. The Ohana look to Kahoolawe as their *pu'uhonua* (refuge), where they gain strength and knowledge from each other and the *aina*. Hopefully Kahoolawe's future as a sacred island is now secure.

LANAI

INTRODUCTION

Lanai, in the long dark past of Hawaiian legend-history, was a sad and desolate place inhabited by man-eating spirits and fiendish bloodcurdling ghouls. It was redeemed by spoiled but tough Prince Kaululaau, exiled there by his kingly father, Kakaalaneo of Maui. Kaululaau proved to be not only brave, but wily too; he cleared Lanai of its spirits through trickery and opened the way for human habitation. Lanai was for many generations a burial ground for the *ali'i* and therefore filled with sacred mana and *kapu* to commoners. Later, reports of its inhospitable shores filled the logs of old sailing vessels. In foul weather, captains navigated desperately to avoid its infamously treacherous waters, whose melancholy whitecaps still outline Shipwreck Beach and give credence to its name.

The vast majority of people visiting the Hawaiian Islands view Lanai from Lahaina on West Maui but never actually set foot upon this lovely quiet island. For two centuries, first hunters and then lovers of the humpback whale have come to peer across the waters of the Auau Channel, better known as the "Lahaina Roads," in search of these magnificent giants. Lanai in Hawaiian means "Hump," and it's as if nature built its own island-shrine to the whale in the exact spot where they are most plentiful. Lanai is a victim of its own reputation. Nicknamed the "Pineapple Island," most visitors are informed by even longtime residents that Lanai is a dull place covered in one large pineapple plantation. It's true that Lanai has the largest pineapple plantation in the world, 12,000 cultivated acres, which account for about 90% of U.S. production. But the island has 74,000 acres that remain untouched and perfect for exceptional outdoor experiences. Besides, the pineapple fields are themselves interesting: endless rows of the porcupine plants, sliced and organized by a labyrinth of roads, contoured and planted by improbable-looking machines, and tended by mostly Filipino workers in wide-brimmed hats and goggles.

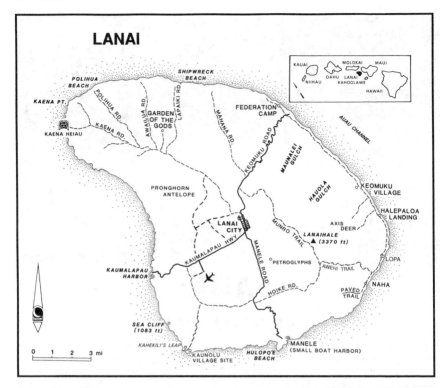

LANAI

Around And About

The people of Lanai live in one of the most fortuitously chosen spots for a working village in the world: Lanai City. All but about two dozen of the island's 2,600 permanent residents make their homes here. (See "Changing Lanai" below.) Nestled near the ridge of mountains in the northeast corner of the Palawai Basin, Lanai City (1,600 feet) is sheltered, cooled, and characterized by a mature and extensive grove of Norfolk pines planted in the early 1900s by the practical New Zealand naturalist, George Munro. This evergreen canopy creates a park-like atmosphere about town while reaching tall green fingers to the clouds. A mountainous spine tickles drizzle from the water-bloated bellies of passing clouds for the thirsty, red, sunburned plains of Lanai below. The trees, like the bristled hair of an annoyed cat, line the **Munro Trail** as it climbs Lanaihale, the high-

est spot on the island (3,370 feet). The Munro Trail's magnificent panoramas encompass sweeping views of no less than five of the eight major islands as it snakes along the mountain ridge, narrowing at times to less than 30 yards across. Here are limitless paths for trekking and four-wheel driving.

Maunalei Gulch, a vast precipitous valley, visible from "The Trail," was the site of a last-ditch effort of Lanai warriors to repel an invasion by the warrior king of the Big Island at the turn of the 18th century. Now its craggy arms provide refuge to mouflon sheep as they execute death-defying leaps from one rocky ripple to the next. On the valley floors roam axis deer, and on the northwest grasslands are the remnants of an experimental herd of pronghorn antelope brought from Montana in 1959. After saturating yourself with the glories of Lanai from the heights, descend and follow a well-paved road from Lanai City to the southern tip of the island. Here, **Manele** and **Hulopoe** bays sit side by side. Manele is a favorite spot of small sailing craft that have braved the channel from Lahaina. Hulopoe Bay, just next door, is as salubrious a spot as you can hope to find. It offers camping and all that's expected of a warm, sandy, palm-lined beach. With its virtually untouched underwater marine park, Hulopoe is regarded as one of the premier snorkeling spots in the entire island chain.

Changing Lanai

Most are amazed that George Munro's pines still shelter a tight-knit community that has remained untouched for so long. But all that's changing, and changing quickly. Two new hideaway luxury hotels are rising, and they're beauties. Both are Rock Resorts! **The Lodge at Koele,** with 102 rooms, is just a five-minute walk from downtown Lanai City. An upland hotel befitting this area of trees and cool summers, it's like a grand country home of the landed gentry, in neo-Victorian style. Amenities include lawn bowling, an orchid house for pure visual pleasure, a swimming pool, tennis courts, golf course, stables and horseback riding, and hunting. The other hotel, **Manele Bay,** houses 250 villas and suites. The architecture is a blend, both classical and island inspired, a *kamaaina* Mediterranean masonry style with tiled roofs. Outdoor features will include the unobstructed natural beauty of Hulope Bay with all rooms having a view, tennis courts, swimming pools, snorkeling, and fishing.

The coming of these resorts will bring the most profound changes to Lanai since James Dole arrived at the turn of the century. Castle and Cooke, practically speaking, owns the island (98%). David Murdoch is the CEO of Castle and Cooke and the hotels are his babies. He's developing them through a newly formed company called Lanai Resort Partners. The hotels will employ a staff of 600 or so, more than all the workers needed to tend the pineapple fields, which today is just over 500 people. This will bring an alternative job market, new life to the downtown area, and a housing spurt. One fact was undeniable concerning Lanai: if you wanted to make a living you either had to work the pineapple fields, or leave. Now that will change. To stop the disenfranchisement of the local people, which was generally the case with rapid development, Castle and Cooke is building several new housing projects, and they come with a promise. Local people, according to seniority with the company and length of residence on Lanai, will have first choice. One group of houses will be multiple-family, geared to the entry-level buyer. The second will be single-family homes, and the third will be for middle-management types. The future also calls for million-dollar homes that will line the fairways of the new golf courses, for people like David Murdoch and his associates. This isn't all *heart* on the part of Castle and Cooke. They want to ensure that the hotels will have a steady and contented workforce to keep them running without a hitch.

Downtown Lanai is inadequate. It couldn't possibly handle the hotel guests and all the new workers and their families who will move to the island. Old buildings will be refurbished, some torn down and replaced, with more upscale businesses taking their place. The tired little shops in town are on Castle and Cooke property, most with month-to-month leases. Castle and Cooke again promises to be fair, but like the rest of Lanai, they'll have a choice: progress or perish. Most islanders are optimistic, keeping an open mind and adopting a "wait and see" attitude concerning the inevitable changes and the promises that have been made for a better life.

Adventure

You can hike or 4WD to Kaunolu Bay, one of the best-preserved ancient Hawaiian village sites. Kamehameha the Great came to this ruggedly masculine shore to fish and frolic his summers away with his favorite cronies. Here, a retainer named Kahekili leaped from a sea cliff to the ice-blue waters below, and challenged all other warriors to prove their loyalty to Kamehameha by following his example and hurtling themselves off of what today is known as **Kahekili's Leap**.

You can quickly span a century by heading for the southeast corner of Lanai and its three

Norfolk pines mark the road to the Garden of the Gods.
(J.D. BISIGNANI)

abandoned villages of **Lopa, Naha,** and **Keomuku.** Here legends abound. *Kahuna* curses still guard a grove of coconut trees which are purported to refuse to let you down if you climb for their nuts without offering the proper prayers. Here also are the remnants of a sugar train believed to have caused its cane enterprise to fail because the rocks of a nearby *heiau* were disturbed and used in its track bed. An enchanting abandoned Hawaiian church in Keomuku insists on being photographed.

You can head north along the east shore to **Shipwreck Beach,** where the rusting hulk of a liberty ship, along with timbers and planks from the great wooden square-riggers of days gone by, lie along the beach, attesting to the authenticity of its name. Shipwreck Beach is a shore stroller's paradise, a real beachcomber's boutique. Also along here are some thought-provoking petroglyphs. Other petroglyphs are found on a hillside overlooking the "pine" fields of the Palawai Basin.

If you hunger for a totally private beach, head north for the Polihua Trail. En route, you'll pass through a fantastic area of ancient cataclysm aptly called **The Garden of The Gods.** This raw, baked area of monolithic rocks and tortured earth turns incredible shades of purple, red, magenta, and yellow as the sun plays upon it from different angles. You have a junction of trails here. You can bear left to lonely **Kaena Point,** where you'll find

Lanai's largest *heiau,* a brooding setting full of weird power vibrations. If you're hot and dusty and aching for a dip, continue due north to trail's end where the desolation of the garden suddenly gives way to the gleaming brightness of virtually unvisited **Polihua Beach.**

After these daily excursions, return to the green serenity of Lanai City. Even if you're only spending a few days, you'll be made to feel like you're staying with old friends. You won't have to worry about bringing your dancing shoes, but if you've had enough hustle and bustle and yearn to stroll in quietude, sit by a crackling fire, and look up at a crystal-clear sky, head for Lanai. Your jangled nerves and ruffled spirit will be glad you did.

THE LAND

The sunburned face of Lanai seems parched but relaxed as it rises in a gentle, steady arc from sea level. When viewed from the air it looks like an irregularly shaped kidney bean. The sixth largest of the eight main islands, Lanai is roughly 140 square miles, measuring 18 miles north to south and 13 miles east to west at its longest points. A classic single-shield volcano, at one time Lanai was probably connected to Maui and Molokai as a single huge island. Marine fossils found at the 1,000-foot mark and even higher in the mountains indicate its slow rise from the sea. Its rounded features appear more benign than the violent creases of its closest island neighbors; this characteristic earned it the unflattering Hawaiian name of "Hump." More lyrical scholars, however, have refuted this translation and claim the real meaning has been lost to the ages, but Lanai does look like a hump when viewed from a distance at sea.

Its topography is simple. A ridge of rugged mountains runs north to south along the eastern half of the island, and their entire length is traversed by the Munro Trail. The highest peak is Lanaihale (3,370 feet). This area is creased by precipitous gulches: the two deepest are Mauanalei and Hauola at more than 2,000 feet. The topography tapers off steadily as it reaches the sea to the east. A variety of beaches stretch from the white sands of Polihua in the north, along the salt-and-pepper sands of Naha on the east, and end with the beautiful rainbow arches of Manele and Hulopoe in the south. Palawai, Lanai's central basin, is completely cultivated in manicured, whorled fields of pineapple. Early this century, Palawai was covered in cactus. The west coast has phenomenal sea cliffs accessible only by boat. Some of the most majestic are the **Kaholo Pali** which runs south from Kaumalapu Harbor, reaching their most amazing ruggedness at Kaunolu Bay. At many spots along this area the sea lies more than 1,500 feet below. Starting at Lanai City in the center, a half-hour of driving in any direction presents a choice of this varied and fascinating geography.

Climate

The daily temperatures are quite balmy, especially at sea level, but it can get blisteringly hot in the basins and on the leeward side, so be sure to carry plenty of water when hiking or four-wheel driving. Lanai City gets refreshingly cool in the evenings and early mornings, but a light jacket or sweater is adequate, although thin-blooded residents bundle up.

Water

Lying in the rain shadow of the West Maui Mountains, even Lanai's windward side receives only 40 inches of rainfall a year. The central basins and leeward shores taper off to a scant 12 inches, not bad for pineapples and sun worshippers. Lanai has always been short of water. Its scruffy vegetation and red-baked earth are responsible for its inhospitable reputation. There are no real rivers; the few year-round streams are found only in the gulches of the windward mountains. Most ventures at colonizing Lanai, both in ancient and modern times, were kept to a minimum because of this water shortage. The famous Norfolk pines of Lanai City, along with other introduced greenery, greatly helped the barrenness of the landscape and provided a watershed. But the rust-red earth remains unchanged, and if you get it onto your clothes, it'll remain there as a permanent souvenir.

FLORA AND FAUNA

Most of Lanai's flora and fauna have been introduced. In fact, the Norfolk pine and the regal mouflon sheep were a manmade attempt to improve the natural, often barren habitat. These species have adapted so well that they now symbolize Lanai, along with, of course, the ubiquitous pineapple. Besides

AVERAGE MAXIMUM/MINIMUM TEMPERATURE AND RAINFALL

Island	Town		Jan.	March	May	June	Sept.	Nov.
Lanai	Lanai City	high	70	71	75	80	80	72
		low	60	60	62	65	65	62
		rain	3	3	2	0	2	4
N.B. Rainfall in inches; temperature in °F								

the mouflon, Lanai boasts pronghorns, axis deer, and a few feral goats. A wide variety of introduced game birds include the Rio Grande turkey, ring-necked pheasant, and an assortment of quail, francolins, and doves. Like the other Hawaiian islands, Lanai, unfortunately, is home to native birds that are headed for extinction. Along the Munro Trail and on the windward coast you pass through forests of Norfolk and Cook Island pines, tall eucalyptus stands, shaggy ironwoods, native koa, and silver oaks. Everywhere, dazzling colors and fragrances are provided by Lanai's flowers.

Flowers

Although Lanai's official flower is the *kaunaoa,* it's not really a flower, but an airplant that grows wild. It's easily found along the beach at Keomuku. It grows in conjunction with *pohuehue,* a pinkish-red, perennial seashore morning glory. Native to Hawaii, the pohuehue grows in large numbers along Lanai's seashore. It's easy to spot, and when you see a yellow-orange vinelike airplant growing with it, you've found Lanai's *kaunaoa,* which is traditionally fashioned into leis. The medicinal *ilima,* used to help asthma sufferers, is found in large numbers in Lanai's open fields. Its flat, open yellow flower is about one inch in diameter and grows on a waist-high shrub. Two other flowers considered by some to be pests are the purple *koali* morning glory and the miniature red and yellow flowering lantana, known for its unpleasant odor. Both are abundant on the trail to the Garden of the Gods.

Norfolk Pines

These pines were discovered by Capt. Cook and named after Norfolk Island in the South Pacific, on which they were found. Imported in great numbers by George Munro, they adapted well to Lanai and helped considerably to attract moisture and provide a firm watershed. Exquisitely ornamental, they can also be grown in containers. Their perfect cone shape makes them a natural Christmas tree, used as such in Hawaii; some are even shipped to the Mainland for this purpose.

Endemic Birds

The list of native birds still found on Lanai gets smaller every year, and those still on the list are rarely seen. The *amakahi* is about five inches long with yellowish-green plumage. The males deliver a high-sounding tweet and a trilling call. Vegetarians, these birds live mostly on grasses and lichens, building their nests in the uppermost branches of tall trees. Some people believe that the *amakahi* is already extinct on Lanai. The *ua'u* or Hawaiian petrel is a large bird with a 36-inch wingspan. Its head and back are shades of black with a white underbelly. This "fisherbird" lives on squid and crustaceans that it regurgitates to its chicks. Unfortunately, the Hawaiian petrel nests on the ground, sometimes laying its eggs under rocks or in burrows, which makes it an easy prey for predators. Its call is reported to sound like a small yapping dog. The *apapane* is abundant on the other main islands, but dwindling rapidly on Lanai. It's a chubby red-bodied bird about five inches long with a black bill, legs, wingtips, and tail feathers. It's quick, flitty, and has a wide variety of calls and songs from beautiful warbles to mechanical buzzes. Its feathers were sought by Hawaiians to produce distinctive ornate featherwork.

Axis Deer

This shy and beautiful creature came to Lanai via Molokai, where the first specimens arrived in 1868 as a gift from the Hawaiian consul in Hong Kong. Its native home is the parkland forests of India and Sri Lanka. The coats of most axis deer are golden tan with rows of round lifetime spots, along with a black stripe down the back and a white belly. They stand three to four feet at the shoulder, with bucks weighing an average of 160 pounds and does about 110. The bucks have an exquisite set of symmetrical antlers that always form a perfect three points. The antlers can stand 30 inches high and more than 20 inches across, making them coveted trophies. Does are antlerless and give birth to one fawn, usually from November to February, but Hawaii's congenial weather makes for good fawn survival anytime of year. Axis deer on Lanai can be spotted anywhere from the lowland *kiawe* forests to

Opposite page (clockwise from top left): plumeria; protea; heliconia; hibiscus; plumeria; bird of paradise (ALL PHOTOS BY ROBERT NILSEN)

the higher rainforests along the Munro Trail. Careful and proper hunting management should keep the population stable for many generations. The meat from axis deer is reported to have a unique flavor, different from Mainland venison—one of the finest tasting of all wild game.

Mouflon Sheep

Another name for these wild mountain sheep is Mediterranean or European bighorn. One of only six species of wild sheep in the world, mouflon are native to the islands of Sardinia and Corsica, whose climates are quite similar to Hawaii's. They have been introduced throughout Europe, Africa, and North America. Although genetically similar to domestic sheep, they are much more shy, lack a woolly coat, and only infrequently give birth to twins. Both rams and ewes are a similar tannish brown, with a snow-white rump which is all that most people get to see of these always-alert creatures as they quickly and expertly head for cover. Rams weigh about 125 pounds (ewes a bit less) and produce a spectacular set of recurved horns. They need little water to survive, going for long periods only on the moisture in green plants. On Lanai they are found along the northwest coast in the grasslands and in the dry *kiawe* forests.

Pronghorns

Not a true antelope, this animal is a native to the Western states of North America. Both males and females produce short black antlers that curve inward at the tip. Males average 125 pounds (females about 90). Pronghorns are a reddish tan with two distinct white bands across the neck and a black patch under the ear. They can also flare the hair on their rumps to produce a white flag when alarmed. In 1959, 38 pronghorn were brought to Lanai in an attempt to introduce another big game animal. Lanai's upper grasslands seemed perfectly suited to the pronghorn, closely resembling the animal's natural habitat in Montana, and hopes ran high for survival. At first the herd increased, but then the numbers began to slowly and irreversibly dwindle. Experts felt that the animals were confused by

pronghorn (LOUISE FOOTE)

the nearby saltwater and those that drank it quickly died. Also, the new grasses of Lanai caused digestion problems. Poaching added even more problems to the troubled pronghorns. It's tough to spot the few that remain, but with good field glasses and perseverance you might catch some browsing on *haole koa* in the northcentral grasslands of Lanai. The fact that even a few pronghorn remain decades after introduction gives some hope that these noble animals can still beat the odds of extinction and make a permanent home for themselves in Hawaii.

HISTORY

Kakaalaneo peered across the mist-shrouded channel between West Maui and Lanai and couldn't believe his eyes. Night after night, the campfire of his son Kaululaau burned, sending its faint but miraculous signal. Could it be that the boy was still alive? Kaululaau had been given every advantage of his noble birth, but still the prince had proved to be unmanageable. King Kakaalaneo had even ordered all children born on the same day as his son to be sent to Lahaina, where they would grow up as his son's friends and playmates. Spoiled rotten, young Kaululaau had terrorized Lahaina with his pranks and one day went too far: he destroyed a new planting of breadfruit.

Opposite page (top): canopy of branches on the Waihee Trail (ROBERT NILSEN); (bottom left): Roots of a banyon tree cascade down a hillside. (ROBERT NILSEN); (bottom right): bamboo (ROBERT NILSEN)

Even the chief's son could not trample the social order and endanger the livelihood of the people. So finally the old *kahuna* had to step in. Justice was hard and swift: Kaululaau must be banished to the terrible island of Lanai, where the man-eating spirits dwelled. There he would meet his fate, and no one expected him to live. But weeks had passed and Kaululaau's nightly fires still burned. Could it be some ghoulish trick? Kakaalaneo sent a canoe of men to investigate. They returned with incredible news. The boy was fine! All the spirits were banished! Kaululaau had cleansed the island of its evil fiends and opened it up for the people to come and settle.

Oral History

In fact, it's recorded in the Hawaiian oral genealogical tradition that a young Kaululaau did open Lanai to significant numbers of inhabitants in approximately A.D. 1400. Lanai passed through the next few hundred years as a satellite of Maui, accepting the larger island's social, religious, and political dictates. During this period, Lanai supported about 3,000 people who lived by growing taro and fishing. Most inhabited the eastern shore facing Maui, but old home sites show that the population became established well enough to homestead the entire island. Lanai was caught up in the Hawaiian wars that raged in the last two decades of the 1700s, and was ravaged and pillaged in 1778 by the warriors of Kalaniopuu, aging king of the Big Island. These hard times marked a decline in Lanai's population; accounts by Western sea captains who passed even a few years later noted that the island looked desolate, with no large villages evident. Lanai began to recover and saw a small boost in population when Kamehameha the Great established his summer residence at Kaunolu on the southern shore. This kept Lanai vibrant for a few years at the beginning of the 19th century but it began to fade soon thereafter. The decline continued until only a handful of Hawaiians remained by the 20th century. The old order ended completely when one of the last traditional *kanaka,* a man named Ohua, hid the traditional fish-god, Hunihi, and died shortly thereafter in his grass hut in the year 1900.

Early Foreign Influences

No one knows his name, but all historians agree that a Chinese man tried his luck at raising sugar cane on Lanai in 1802. He brought boiling pots and rollers to Naha on the east coast, but after a few years of hard luck gave up and moved on. About 100 years later a large commercial sugar enterprise was attempted in the same area. This time the sugar company even built a narrow-gauge railroad to carry the cane. A story goes that after disrupting a local *heiau* to make ballast for the rail line, the water in the area, never in great abundance to begin with, went brackish. Again sugar was foiled.

In 1854 a small band of Mormon elders tried to colonize Lanai by starting a "City of Joseph" at Palawai Basin. This began the career of one of Hawaii's strangest, most unfathomable yet charismatic early leaders. Walter Murray Gibson came to Palawai to start an idyllic settlement for the Latter-day Saints. He energetically set to work improving the land with funds from Utah and hard work of the other Mormon settlers. The only fly in Gibson's grand ointment occurred when the Mormon Church discovered that the acres of Palawai were not registered to the church at all but to Walter Murray Gibson himself! He was excommunicated and the bilked settlers relocated. Gibson went on to have one of the strangest political careers in Hawaiian history, including championing native rights and enjoying unbelievable influence at the royal Hawaiian court. His land at Palawai passed on to his daughter who became possessed by the one evil spirit Kaululaau failed to eradicate: she tried to raise sugar cane, but was fated, like the rest, to fail.

A few attempts proved uneconomical, and Lanai languished. The last big attempt at cattle raising produced The Ranch, part of whose lands make up the Cavendish Golf Course in Lanai City. This enterprise did have one bright note. A New Zealander named George Munro was hired as the manager. He imported all manner of seeds and cuttings in his attempt to foliate the island and create a watershed. The Ranch failed, but Munro's legacy of Norfolk pines stands as a proud testament to this amateur horticulturalist.

The majority of Lanai residents earn their livelihood from the still vibrant pineapple industry. (J.D. BISIGNANI)

The Coming Of Pineapples

The purchase of Lanai in 1922 was one of the niftiest real estate deals in modern history. James D. Dole, the most enterprising of the pineapple pioneers, bought the island—lock, stock, and barrel—from the Baldwins, an old missionary family, for $1.1 million. That comes to only $12 per acre, though many of those acres were fairly scruffy, not to mention Lanai's bad economical track record. Dole had come from Boston at the turn of the century to figure out how to can pineapple profitably. Dole did such a remarkable job of marketing the "golden fruit" on the Mainland that in a few short years, Midwestern Americans who'd never even heard of pineapples before were buying cans of it regularly from the shelves of country grocery stores. In 1922, Jim Dole needed more land for his expanding pineapple fields, and the arid basin of Palawai seemed perfect.

Lanai Plantation was an oligarchy during the early years, with the plantation manager as king. One of the most famous of these characters was H. Broomfield Brown, who ran Lanai Plantation in the '30s. He kept watch over the fields from his house through a telescope. If anyone loafed, he'd ride out into the fields to confront the offender. Mr. Brown personally "eyeballed" every new visitor to Lanai: all prostitutes, gamblers, and deadbeats were turned back at the pier. An anti-litter fanatic, he'd even reprimand anyone who trashed the streets of Lanai City. During the labor strikes of the 1960s, workers' grievances were voiced and Lanai began to function as a more normal enterprise. With pineapple well established on the world market, Lanai finally had a firm economic base. From a few thousand fruits in the early days, the flow today can reach a million fruits per day during the height of the season. They're shipped from the manmade port at Kaumalapau which was specially built to accommodate Lanai's "pines."

ECONOMY

Pineapples! Lanai's 12,000 acres of them make up the largest single pineapple plantation in the world. Virtually the entire island is owned by Castle and Cooke and operated by its subsidary, The Dole Co., whose name has become synonymous with pineapples. A handful of tiny hereditary plots are still held by Hawaiian families and oddly enough, nearly half the working families own their homes, purchased from Dole. In one way or another, everyone on Lanai owes his livelihood to pineapples, from the worker who twists his ankle in a pine field to the technician at the community hospital who X-rays it. Workers come and go all day long from equipment depots in Lanai City. Most field hands are Filipinos, some very recent arrivals to the U.S. Though unskilled workers start at minimum wage, a union member who's worked for Dole for a few years can make a decent living. Japanese and *haole* hold most of the foreman and middle management jobs, although Dole is an equal opportunity employer.

Competition And Technology

Today foreign production, especially in the Philippines, has greatly increased and gives the Hawaiian pineapple industry some competitive headaches—though Dole feels its claim to fame is secure. They are after a premium-pack pineapple, according to Jim Parker, the plantation manager, who states, "Nobody gets more money for their pineapple than Dole does, because nobody ever matches Dole for quality." Pineapple cultivation is as tough as any other business and all competitors are after the very best technology. Dole is a leader in technology, and though they've been cutting down on the number of acres under cultivation, they have at the same time increased yield through intensified methods such as irrigation, which they pioneered. The new hotel development on Lanai will not greatly affect the pineapple industry. Presently there are 12,000 acres under cultivation, but Dole sees a future in which this will be streamlined to 10,000 acres or less. This is in keeping with Dole's view of producing a premium, more expensive pineapple that would reduce its total market share.

A recent furor involved a chemical called heptaclore used to kill ants on pineapples. All the pineapple producers use heptaclore, and though believed to be a carcinogen, it carries a federal label of approval. If guidelines are followed, it's considered safe, and according to testing, no heptaclore is found in the actual fruit itself. But in this case, pineapple stalks and leaves were chopped and sold to dairy farmers as feed. The milk produced had intolerable amounts of heptaclore. Health food stores on Oahu refused to sell this milk outright and the dairies involved recalled their milk until it was once again considered safe. Dole was not involved, but all the producers felt the heat from consumers. Even so, the port at Kaumalapau is very busy sending off the fruits of Lanai's labor. There is work on Lanai for any islander who wants it, and almost all do. The standard of living is working class: decent, hopeful, and proud.

As Dole is slowly taking acreage out of pineapple production and as the population of the island and number of visitors is slowly increasing, there has been a concerted effort on the part of the company to experiment with the raising of various organic vegetables, grains, and cattle in order to diversify the island's economy. This seems to be a pet project of David Murdoch, and the hope is to make the economy of Lanai more locally sustainable and less dependent on imports from the other island and the Mainland.

THE PEOPLE

Lanai is characterized by the incredible mix of racial strains so common in Hawaii—Filipino, Japanese, Hawaiian, Chinese, and Caucasian. It is unique, however, in that 50 to 60 percent of its people are Filipino. The Filipinos, many recent immigrants, were solicited by Castle and Cooke to work as laborers on the pineapple plantation. Mostly 18- to 25-year-old men, the majority speak Ilocano and may have come to join relatives already on Lanai. Most arrive on their own; they learn English and from Lanai they spread out. As workers they're perfect: industrious and quiet. At night you wonder where they all are. Due to the tremendous shortage of eligible women, most

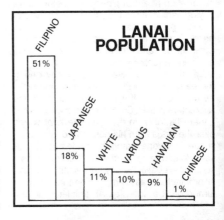

LANAI POPULATION

FILIPINO 51%
JAPANESE 18%
WHITE 11%
VARIOUS 10%
HAWAIIAN 9%
CHINESE 1%

Lorrie, Reggie, and Howard, second and third generation of Lanai's plantation workers
(J.D. BISIGNANI)

workers stay home or fish or have a beer in the back yard with buddies. And on Sundays, there is the illegal (officially nonexistent) cockfight. For high living, everyone heads for Maui or Oahu.

The next largest racial groups are Japanese (18%) and whites (11%). The Japanese started as the field workers before the Filipinos, but now, along with the whites, are Lanai's professionals and middle management. The races coexist, but there are still unseen social strata. There's even a small Chinese population (1%) who fulfill their traditional role as shopkeepers. A good 9% of Lanaians are Hawaiians. Finally, almost 10% fall into the "mixed" category, with many of these Filipino-Hawaiian.

Community
Lanai has a strong sense of community and uniqueness that keeps the people close. For example, during a bitter three-month strike in 1964, the entire community rallied and all suffered equally: laborers, shopkeepers, and management. All who remember say that it brought out the best in the island tradition of aloha. If you really want to meet Lanaians, just sit in the park in the center of Lanai City for an hour or two. You'll notice a lot of old-timers, who seem to be very healthy. You could easily strike up a conversation with some of them.

Other Faces
It should strike you that most of the people you see around Lanai are men. That in itself is a social comment about Lanai. Where are the women? They're in the traditional roles at home, nurturing and trying to add the pleasantries of life. Some are field workers too. You might notice that there are no famous crafts of Lanai and no artists working commercially. This is not to say there is no art on Lanai, but the visitor rarely sees it. One reason that Lanai produces so little commercial art is that it's a workers' island with virtually no unemployment, so everyone is busy making a living. Old-timers are known to make superb fishing poles, nets, and even their own horseshoes. The island ladies are excellent seamstresses and with the rising interest in hula, make lovely leis from the beautiful kaunaoa, Lanai's flower. If you turn your attention to the young people of Lanai, you'll see the statewide problem of babies having babies. Teenage pregnancy is rampant, and teenage parents are common. Young guys customize their 4WDs although there's no place to go. If as a young person you wish to remain on Lanai, then in almost every case your future will be tied to Dole. If you have other aspirations, it's "goodbai to Lanai." These islanders are some of the most easygoing and relaxed people you'll encounter in Hawaii, but with the electronic age extending its long arms of communication, even

Maybe you can hitch a ride with a pleasure boat from Lahaina to Manele Bay.
(BOB NILSEN)

here they're not nearly as "backwater" as you might think.

GETTING THERE

By Air
Hawaiian Air, tel. (800) 367-5320 Mainland and Canada, on Lanai (800) 882-8811 or 565-6977, flies Dash-7 turbo-prop planes to Lanai. They currently have flights only from Honolulu that run twice a week (Fri. and Sat.) every other week, and one on Mon. on the alternate week. Daily flights are available to and from Lanai by **Aloha Island Air,** tel. 833-3219 Oahu, (800) 652-6541 Neighbor Islands, (800) 323-3345 Mainland. They fly to and from Honolulu 10 times daily, with extra flights on Mon. and Fridays. There is also one early morning flight daily from Molokai, two from Kapalua West Maui Airport, and five from Kahului. Flights originating in Princeville go via Honolulu and those from Hana and Kamuela go through Kahului. **Air Molokai,** tel. 521-0090, has recently opened up flights from Lanai and Kahului and Molokai. Call to check schedules and fares.

  Lanai Airport is a practical little strip out in the pineapple fields about four miles southwest of Lanai City. The one-room terminal offers *no* shops, car rental booths, lockers, public transportation, or even access to a toilet, unless there's a scheduled flight. A bulletin board near the waiting-room door has all the practical information and phone numbers you'll need to get to Lanai City, and a courtesy phone outside connects you with City Service/Dollar Rent A Car for those who have not arranged a car before arriving.

By Boat
Expeditions, a new passenger ferry, now plies between Lahaina and Manele Bay. No luxury transportation, this shuttle offers speedy and convenient alternative transportation to the island. The crossing takes one hour and the ferry leaves Manele Bay at 8 a.m., 10:30 a.m., and 4:30 p.m. From Lahaina's public loading pier, ferries leave at 6:45 a.m., 9:15 a.m., and 3:45 p.m. There are late departures from both ends on Thurs., Fri. and Sun. evenings. The adult fare is $25 OW while children under 11 pay $20; luggage is taken free of charge, except for a $10 charge for bicycles. As this shuttle takes only 24 passengers, it's best to reserve a place. For information and reservations call (808) 661-3756 or write P.O. Box 1763, Lahaina, Maui, HI 96767.

  One other possibility for getting to Lanai is going by pleasure boat from Maui. Many Lanai and Maui residents travel by this route and even receive special *kamaaina* rates. These are basically tour boats specializing in snorkeling, dinner cruising, whalewatching, and the like, but they're also willing to drop you off and pick you up at a later date. It's an enjoyable and actually inexpensive way of going. You'll have to make your own arrangements with the boat captains, most berthed at Lahaina Harbor. This alternative is particularly attractive to campers, as they anchor on Lanai at Manele Bay, just a five-minute walk from the campsites at Hulopoe. There are no fixed rates for this service, but *kamaaina* pay about $20. Expect to pay more but use this as a point of reference. One companies to try is Trilogy, tel. 661-4743. Another outfit is Club Lanai, tel. 871-1144, but they anchor at their own private beach on very remote East Lanai, with no way of getting anywhere except by a long and dusty hike. Remember that, in effect, you're going standby with these companies, but there is generally room for one more.

GETTING AROUND

Public Transportation

No public transportation operates on Lanai, but Lanai City Service will pick you up at the airport if you're renting a car/jeep from them. Otherwise their taxi service to the airport is $10 one way and to Manele Bay, $20. Oshiro's Service Station will pick you up at the airport if you're renting a vehicle from them; they'll charge $6 roundtrip. Guests of the Lodge at Koele and the Menele Bay Hotel will be picked up by hotel van free of charge, but be sure to arrange this when making your accommodations reservation. The Hotel Lanai will also pick you up if the van is available and you intend to stay there.

Car Rental

For a car, or better yet, a jeep, try **Lanai City Service,** Lanai City, HI 96763, tel. 565-6780. You'll be outfitted with wheels and given information on where to go and especially about road conditions. Pay heed! Make sure to tell them your plans, especially if you're heading for a remote area. That way, if you have problems and don't return, they'll know where to send the rescue party! Lanai City Service is a subsidiary of Trilogy Excursions and has a franchise with Dollar Rent A Car. It rents compact Nissans for $35-46/day, jeeps $90/day (insurance compulsory). **Oshiro Service and U-Drive,** Box 516, Lanai City, HI 96763, tel. 565-6952, rents modern Japanese compacts for $25-40/day plus gas, and Suzuki jeeps for $85. They're open 8 a.m. to 5:30 p.m., except Sunday, and provide a map and other useful road information.

4WD Rental

With only 22 miles of paved road on Lanai and rental cars firmly restricted to these, there is no real reason to rent one. The *real* adventure spots of Lanai require a 4WD vehicle. Mindboggling spots on Lanai are reachable only on foot or by 4WD. Unfortunately, even the inveterate hiker will have a tough time because the best trailheads are quite a distance from town, and you'll spend as much time getting to them as hiking the actual trails.

Many people who have little or no experience driving 4WDs are under the slap-happy belief that they are unstoppable. Oh, that it were true! They do indeed get stuck, and it's usually miserable getting them unstuck. Both rental agencies will give you up-to-the-minute info on the road conditions, and a fairly accurate map for navigation. They tend to be a bit conservative on where they advise you to take "their" vehicles, but they also live on the island and are accustomed to driving off-road, which balances out their conservative estimates. Also, remember road conditions change rapidly: a hard rain on the Munro Trail can change it from a flower-lined path to a nasty quagmire, or wind might lay a tree across a beach road. Keep your eye on the weather and if in doubt, don't push your luck. If you get stuck, you'll not only ruin your outing and have to hike back to town, but you'll also be charged for a service call which can be astronomical, especially if it's deemed to be due to your negligence. Most of your off-road driving will be in *compound* 4WD, first gear, low range.

Hitchhiking

Like everywhere else in Hawaii, hitching is technically illegal, but the islanders are friendly and quite good about giving you a lift. Lanai, however, is a workers' island and the traffic is really skimpy during the day. You can only reasonably expect to get a ride from Lanai City to the airport or to Manele Bay since both are

the Lodge at Koele
(BOB NILSEN)

on paved roads and frequented by normal island traffic. There is only a very slim chance of picking up a ride out through the pine fields toward the Garden of the Gods or Kaunolu, for example, so definitely don't count on it.

ACCOMMODATIONS

The two new luxury hotels on Lanai will increase Lanai's available rooms three hundredfold. Since these are in the ultra-luxury class and quite expensive, they won't, however, ease the demand for reasonably priced accommodations. If anything, they'll draw the spotlight to Lanai, and will most probably make getting a room tougher. So, if you're contemplating a trip to the island, make doubly sure to book in advance.

The Lodge At Koele
Like a huge country manor set above town in amongst the pine trees, the Lodge at Koele's light exterior and dark metal roof counterpoise the background of green on green. A wide porch fronts the reception building and connects with the two adjoining buildings. Broad lawns surround the lodge front and back. The front holds a bowling green and the back a swimming pool, jacuzzi, fishpond, botanical garden, orchid hothouse, and walking paths. The mural over the front entrance beckons and your first glimpse of the interior is the great

hall. Broad, tall, and open-beamed, this room is filled with overstuffed couches, reading chairs, tables, and desks, all set off by flowers and a cohesive mixture of Western and Oriental antiques and art objects. At both ends are *huge* fireplaces—reputed to be the largest in Hawaii. The skylight above brightens this room and seems to make it more expansive than it is. Off this main hall are the well-equipped music room, old-fashioned trophy room, wood-paneled library where you can spin the globe or browse through one of the world's major newspapers, tea room/cocktail bar, and dining rooms. Many of the paintings that adorn the walls and ceilings of the lodge were done by local and Maui artists, and the numerous antiques and artwork are catalogued—ask the concierge for the listing. Everything about this hotel exudes quality, comfort, and luxury.

You can find sundries at the hotel shop, open 8 a.m. to 9 p.m., and all hotel and island activities, including croquet, tennis, golf, hunting, horseback riding, jeep rides, beach and boating activities can be arranged by the concierge. There is free shuttle service to meet all arriving and departing planes, to and from Lanai City, and to Manele and Hulopoe bays.

Basic rooms have a lanai, sitting area, wet bar, and huge black-and-white tiled bath with separate lavatory room. All necessities are provided: robes, slippers, towels, soap, shampoo, lotion, and blow driers. Furniture is a combination of antique pine and wickerware. The four-poster beds (each post topped with a carved pineapple) are set high off the floor, surrounded by built-in couches, settee, tables and chairs, a writing desk, and artwork on the walls. For security, there is a wall safe, and a walking staff is also provided for your forays into the hills. Even the carpeted hallways are broad and richly paneled, with alcoves for art, lending an air of elegance. The more expensive rooms are even larger and equipped with more comforts. Rates are $275 for a garden room, $290 for a Koele room, and $350 for a plantation room; suites run $425 to 900, most with butler service provided. A modified meal plan (breakfast and dinner) is available for an additional $70 per person per day. For information and reservations contact Rockresorts at tel. (800) 223-7637 or write the Lodge at Koele, P.O. Box 774, Lanai City, Hawaii 96763.

The Manele Bay Hotel

To open in early 1991, this oceanside hotel will overlook Hulopoe Bay and look out onto Kahoolawe. It will sport a combination Mediterranean and island architecture with formal gardens, pools, and courtyards. The lobby will be a place to sit and relax, and the lounge veranda perfect in the late afternoon to see the setting sun. Manele Bay Hotel will also have a library, formal dining room, garden terrace, and shops. As it's located near the ocean, swimming, snorkeling, and scuba will be available, as well as health and fitness facilities, tennis, hunting, golf, and horseback riding. For information and reservations contact Rockresorts (see above).

Hotel Lanai

Being the only hotel on the island (until 1990), you'd think the lack of competition would have made Hotel Lanai arrogant, indifferent, and expensive. Instead, it is a delight. The hotel has gone through very few cosmetic changes since it was built in 1923 as a guest lodge primarily for visiting executives of Dole Pineapple, which still owns it. Its architecture is simple Hawaiiana, and its setting among the tall Norfolk pines fronted by a large lawn is refreshingly rustic. With a corrugated iron roof,

board and batten walls inside and out, and two wings connected by a long enclosed veranda, it looks like the main building at a Boy Scout camp. But don't be fooled. The hotel is managed by Castle and Cooke. The 10 remodeled rooms may not be plush, but they are cozy as can be. All have been painted in lively colors, and are clean with private baths, but no phones or TVs. Room rates are $51 s, $58 d, and $65 for three. The hotel has the only in-town bar on its enclosed veranda, where guests and at times a few islanders have a quiet beer and twilight chat before retiring at the ungodly hour of nine o'clock. The main dining room is large, and lined with hunting trophies. So if you're lured by the quiet simplicity of Lanai and wish to avail yourself of one of the last family-style inns of Hawaii, write for reservations to Hotel Lanai, P.O. Box A-119, Lanai City, HI 96763, tel. 565-7211 or (800) 624-8849. Reservations are a must.

Bed And Breakfast

For a more homey stay on the Pineapple Island, try one of the few bed and breakfasts inns on Lanai. For information and reservations contact any of the bed and breakfast associations listed in the main Introduction (see p. 99).

Lanai Realty

Lanai's first house rental agency recently opened for business. All houses are completely furnished including linens, kitchen utensils, washer/dryer, and TV, and are rented by the day, week, or month. They rent two three-bedroom homes for $95-110/day, one for six and the other seven people; a two-bedroom home with fireplace for $125/day, up to six people; and a four-bedroom home with den and fireplace at $225/day for up to eleven people. Minimum two to three nights. Check-in is at 2 p.m., check-out 11 a.m., 50% deposit required, no credit cards, checks OK. Write Kathy Oshiro, Lanai Realty, Box 67, Lanai City, HI 96763, tel. 565-6597 or 565-6960.

Lanai Bucks Hunting Lodge

This lodge is an anomaly even to longtime island residents, many of whom claim they've never heard of it. It seems impossible on such a small island, but when contacted by mail the lodge does answer. Word is that Bucks Lodge provides small, unadorned, barrack-type rooms with kitchen privileges for $25. If interested write to: Gwendolyn Kaniho, Lanai Bucks Hunting Lodge, Box 879, Lanai City, Lanai, HI 96763. No phone number is available.

Camping

The only official camping permitted to nonresidents is located at Hulopoe Bay, administered by the Lanai Land Company. Reservations for one of the six official campsites here are a must, although unbelievably there's usually a good chance of getting a space. Lanai Land Co. officials state that they try to accommodate any "overflow" unreserved visitors, but don't count on it. Since Lanai is by and large privately owned by Castle and Cooke Inc., the parent company of Koele, you really have no recourse but to play by their rules. It seems they want to hold visitors to a minimum and keep strict tabs on the ones that do arrive.

Nonetheless, the campsites at Hulopoe Bay are great. Lining the idyllic beach, they're far enough apart to afford some privacy. The showers are designed so that the pipes, just below the surface, are solar heated. This means a good hot shower during daylight and early evening. Campsite use is limited to seven nights. The fee includes a one-time $5 group registration and is $5 per person per night. For reservations write to the Lanai Land Co., Box L, Lanai City, Lanai, HI 96763, tel. 565-6661. Permits, if not mailed in advance, are picked up at the Koele office. If visiting on the spur of the moment from a neighboring island, it's advisable to call ahead.

Note

While hiking or four-wheel driving the back roads of Lanai, especially along Naha, Shipwreck, and Polihua beaches, a multitude of picture-perfect camping spots will present themselves, but they can be used only by Lanai residents, although there's little supervision. A one-night bivouac would probably go undetected. No other island allows unofficial camping and unless it can be statistically shown that potential visitors are being turned away, it seems unlikely that the Koele Co. will change its policies. If you're one of the unlucky ones who have been turned down, write your letter of protest to parent company Castle and Cooke, 965 N. Nimitz Hwy., Honolulu, HI 96817, tel. 548-6611.

RESTAURANTS

Aside from the new hotels, Lanai City is the only place on the island where you can dine, shop, and take care of business. The food situation on Lanai is discouraging. Most everything has to be brought in by barge. There's

the Hotel Lanai
(J.D. BISIGNANI)

very little fresh produce, hardly any fresh fish, and even chicken is at a premium, which seems impossible given the huge Filipino population. People surely eat differently at home, but in the two tiny restaurants (Dahang's and S.T. Property) open to the traveler, the fare is restricted to the "two-scoop rice and teri beef" variety, with fried noodles and spam as the *pièce de résistance*. Salad to most islanders means a potato-macaroni combination sure to stick to your ribs and anything else on the way. Vegetables are usually a tablespoon of grated cabbage and soy sauce.

By far the best restaurant in town is at the **Hotel Lanai**, tel. 565-7211. The meals that come out of this kitchen are wholesome home cooking, done under the supervision of the chefs at the Lodge at Koele. The hotel bakes pies, and provides fresh fish and vegetables whenever possible. Budgeters can order a large stuffed potato, salad, soup of the day, and drink for under $8. Restaurant hours are breakfast 7 a.m. to 9 a.m., lunch 11:30 a.m. to 1:30 p.m., dinner 6:30 to 8:30 p.m. The best dish is the fresh fish when available, and all go for under $15 except for a steak dinner.

But if you're looking for a breakfast or snack with a true island flavor, try one of the following. **Dahang's Bakery** has recently remodeled and can even be called chic for Lanai. Their tasty pastries are sold out by early morning, and the breakfasts of eggs, bacon, potatoes, omelettes, and the like cost about $3.50. They also have good plate lunches for about $4.50 and burgers and sandwiches under $2.50. Open every day 5:30 a.m. to 1:30 p.m., closed Sunday. Just up the road is an authentic workers' restaurant and sundries store called **S.T. Property.** No one should visit Lanai without at least stopping in here for morning coffee. It's totally run-down, but it's a pure cultural experience. Arrive before 7 a.m. when the company whistle calls most of the workers to the fields. All you have to do is look around at the faces of the people to see the spirit of Lanai. Breakfast from 6:30 to 10:30 a.m., lunch until 12:30 p.m.

For the best food on the island you must visit the restaurants at the Lodge at Koele. In accordance with the rest of the hotel, the dining rooms are well-furnished, the food is the best quality available, and the selection and presentation what you would expect from a first-class establishment. To give you an idea, breakfast selections include continental breakfast, $7.50, eggs Benedict, $8.50, and sweet rice waffles with lilikoi-coconut chuntey, $7.50. For lunch, try salads and soups, $4 to $9.50, pan-fried Kona crab cakes and grilled banana, $13.50, or other meats and fishes, $10.50 to $18. Some dinner selections include appitizers and soups, $7 to $12.75, Lanai mixed pheasant, quail, and axis deer sausage with Pinot Noir sauce $30, and other entrees, $25 to $34. The Lodge allows for no fainthearted here; your bill will be at least $10 for breakfast, $15 for lunch, and $30 for dinner.

OUTDOOR SPORTS

No question that Lanai's forte is its natural unspoiled setting and great outdoors. Traffic jams, neon lights, blaring discos, shopping boutiques, and all that jazz just don't exist here. The action is swimming, hiking, snorkeling, fishing, horseback riding, and some hunting. Tennis and golf round off the activities. Lanai is the place to revitalize your spirits— you want to get up with the birds, greet the sun, stretch, and soak up the good life.

Snorkeling, Scuba, And Swimming

Lanai, especially around Manele/Hulopoe Bay, has some of the best snorkeling and scuba in Hawaii. If you don't have your own equipment, try renting it from the tour boats that come over from Maui. The *Trilogy,* operated by the Coon family, often does this. Their van is parked at Manele Bay, and if someone is around he might rent you some gear. The hotels can also arrange equipment for their guests. Your other choice is to buy it from Pine Isle or Richards markets, but their prices are quite high. If you're the adventurous sort, you can dive for spiny lobsters off Shipwreck or Polihua, but make absolutely sure to check the surf conditions as it can be super treacherous. It would be best to go with a local.

Lanai City has a brand-new swimming pool. Located in town near the high school, it's open to the public daily during summer, and on a limited schedule during other seasons.

Tennis And Golf

You can play tennis at three (two lighted) courts at the Lanai School. They have rubberized surfaces called "royal duck" and are fairly well maintained—definitely OK for a fun game. The Lodge at Koele has four new "plexipave" courts and the Manele Bay Hotel will have several for their guests; equipment rental and court times arranged by the concierge.

Golfers will be delighted to follow their balls around Cavendish Golf Course on the outskirts of Lanai City. This nine hole, 3,071-yard, par-36 course is set among Norfolk pines. It's free to islanders; guests are requested to pay $5 on the honor system. Just drop your money in the box provided. Come on, pay up! It's definitely worth it! The good news for golf addicts is the new 18-hole, Greg Norman-designed, mountain course being constructed in the hills behind the Lodge at Koele. To be opened in 1991, this will be a championship course with a professional staff, pro shop, and equipment rental. A second, 18-hole, oceanside course near the Manele Bay Hotel, designed by Jack Nicklaus, is on hold for the moment pending further review of land use and water resources.

Hunting

The first cliché you hear about Lanai is that it's one big pineapple plantation. The second is that it's a hunter's paradise. Both are true. The big game action is provided by mouflon sheep and axis deer. Also spotted are the protected yet failing population of pronghorns which, thankfully, can only be shot with a camera. Various days are open for the hunting of game birds, which include ring-necked and green pheasant; Gambel, Japanese, and California quail; wild turkey; and a variety of doves, francolins, and partridges. Hunting of mouflon sheep and axis deer is open to the public only in the northwest of the island, which is leased to the state of Hawaii by the Koele Company. Brochures detailing all necessary information can be obtained free of charge by writing to Dept. of Land and Natural Resources, 1151 Punchbowl St., Honolulu, HI 96813. The Lanai regional office is at 338 8th St., Lanai City, HI 96763. Licenses are required ($10 resident, $20 nonresident) and can be purchased by mail from Dept. of Land and Natural Resources or picked up in person at their office on Lanai.

Public archery hunting of mouflon sheep is restricted to the first and second Sundays of August and rifle season occurs on the third and fourth Sundays, but hunters are restricted by public drawing. Axis deer regular season (rifle, shotgun, and bows) opens on the nine consecutive Sundays up to and including the last Sunday in April; it's also restricted by public drawing. Archery season for axis deer is the two Sundays preceding the regular season. Bag limits are one mouflon ram and one deer.

Axis deer are hunted year-round on the private game reserves of the Koele Co., although the best trophy season is May through

---

LANAI GOLF AND TENNIS

Course	Par	Yards	Fees	Cart
Cavendish Golf Course* • Koele Company, P.O. Box L, Lanai City, HI 96763 tel. 565-9993	36	3071	$5.00 don.	

N.B.* = 9 hole course • = no club rentals

This tennis court is open to the public. Call ahead to check availability.

Location	Name of Court	No. of Courts	Lighted
Near Lanai School	Lanai City	2	Yes
The Lodge at Koele		3	Yes

checking out the pools along rugged Shipwreck Beach, looking for a likely spot to "throw net!"
(J.D. BISIGNANI)

November. The rates are $200 per day for a reguler hunting permit, $50 for an archery hunting permit. Guide service is not officially mandatory, but you must prove that you have hunted Lanai before and are intimately knowledgeable about its terrain, hunting areas, and procedures. If not, you must acquire the services of either Kazu Ohara or Gary Onuma, two excellent rangers on Lanai. Guide service is $750 a day. This service includes all necessities, except lodging and meals, from airport pick-up to shipping the trophy. For full details write to Chief Ranger, Koele Co., Box L, Lanai City, HI 96763, tel. 565-6661.

Fishing

No commercial or charter fishing boats operate out of Lanai, but that's not to say there are no fish. On the contrary, one of the island's greatest pastimes is this relaxing sport. Any day in Lanai City Park, you'll find plenty of old-timers to ask where the fish are biting. If you have the right approach and use the right smile, they just might tell you. Generally, the best fishing and easiest access on the island is at Shipwreck Beach running north toward Polihua. Near the lighthouse ruins is good for *papio* and *ulua,* the latter running to 50 pounds. Many of the local fishermen use throw nets to catch the smaller fish such as *manini,* preferred especially by Lanai's elders. Throw-netting takes skill usually learned from childhood, but don't be afraid

to try even if you throw what the locals call a "banana" or one that looks like Maui (a little head and a big body). They might snicker, but if you laugh too, you'll make a friend.

Mostly you'll fish with rod and reel using frozen squid or crab, available at Lanai's general stores. Bring a net bag or suitable container. This is the best beachcombing on the island and it's also excellent diving for spiny lobster. There is good shore fishing (especially for *awa)* and easy accessibility at Kaumalaupu Harbor, from where the pineapples are shipped. It's best to go after 5 p.m. when wharf activity has slowed down. There is also superb offshore fishing at Kaunolu, Kamehameha's favorite angling spot on the south shore. You can catch *aku* and *kawakawa,* but to be really successful you'll need a boat. Finally, Manele Hulopoe Marine Life Conservation Park has limited fishing, but as the name implies, it's a conservation district so be sure to follow the rules prominently posted at Manele Bay.

PRACTICALITIES

Shopping

The two grocery stores in town are fairly well stocked with basics, but anyone into health foods or vegetarianism should carry supplies and use the markets for staples only. The markets are almost next door to each other: **Pine Isle Market,** run by Kerry Honda, and

Richards Shopping Center, both open Mon. through Sat. 8 a.m. to 5:30 p.m. They supply all your basic camping, fishing, and general merchandise needs, includiung clothing and medicines. Also in town are **Akamai Trading Company,** which sells furniture and gifts, **International Food and Clothing Center,** where you can not only pick up things to eat and wear, but also find hardware and hunting supplies, and **Lanai Family Store** for video tape rentals.

It finally happened even here. An art gallery, **Island Collections,** has opened in Lanai City, just down from Dahang's. Open 9 a.m. to 5 p.m., Mon. to Sat., here you can find art objects from Hawaiian artists on display.

Money

Try full-service **First Hawaiian Bank** in Lanai City for your banking needs. **First Federal Savings** has also established a branch here. All major businesses accept traveler's checks. The *only* credit cards accepted on Lanai are MasterCard and Visa. None of the others, including venerable American Express, is accepted. Banks are open Mon.-Thur., 8:30 a.m. to 3 p.m. (First Federal to 4 p.m.), and until 6 p.m. on Friday.

Post Office

The Lanai P.O., tel. 565-6517, is across the street from the Koele offices on Lanai Avenue. Open daily from 8 a.m. to 4:30 p.m., it's full service, but they do not sell boxes or padded mailers to send home beachcombing treasures; you can get these at the two stores in town.

Laundromat

Open 24-hours a day, the laundromat is located next to the art gallery.

Useful Phone Numbers

Oshiro Service Station, tel. 565-6952; Lanai City Service and Dollar Rent A Car, tel. 565-7227; Hotel Lanai, tel. 565-7211; Lanai Land Co. (camping and hiking info), tel. 565-6661; Dept. of Land and Natural Resources, tel. 565-6688; Lanai Airport, tel. 565-6757; Lanai Community Library, tel. 565-6996; police, tel. 565-6525; and Lanai Community Hospital, tel. 565-6411.

mouflon sheep (LOUISE FOOTE)

EXPLORING LANAI

LANAI CITY

Lanai City (pop. 2,600) would be more aptly described and sound more appealing if it were called Lanai Village. A utilitarian town, it was built in the 1920s by Dole Pineapple Co. The architecture, field-worker plain, has definitely gained "character" in the last 60 years. It's an excellent spot for a town, sitting at 1,600 feet in the shadow of Lanaihale, the island's tallest mountain. George Munro's Norfolk pines have matured and now give the entire town a green, shaded, parklike atmosphere. It's cool and breezy—a great place to launch off from in the morning and a welcome spot to return to at night. Most visitors head out of town to the more spectacular sights and never take the chance to explore the back streets.

Houses

As you'd expect, most houses are square boxes with corrugated roofs, but each has its own personality. Painted every color of the rainbow, they'd be garish in any other place, but here they break the monotony and seem

to work. The people of Lanai make their living from the land and can work wonders with it. Around many homes are colorful flower beds, green gardens bursting with vegetables, fruit trees, and flowering shrubs. When you look down the half-dirt, broken-pavement roads at a line of these houses, you can't help feeling that a certain nobility exists here. The houses are mud-spattered where the rain splashes red earth against them, but inside you know they're sparkling clean. Even some modern suburban homes sprawl on the south end of town. Most of these belong to Lanai's miniature middle class and would fit unnoticed in any up-and-coming neighborhood on the Mainland.

Downtown

If you sit on the steps of Hotel Lanai and peer across its huge front yard, you can scrutinize the heart of downtown Lanai City. Off to your right are the offices of the Dole and Koele companies sitting squat and solid. In front of them, forming a type of town square, is Dole Park where old-timers come to sit and young

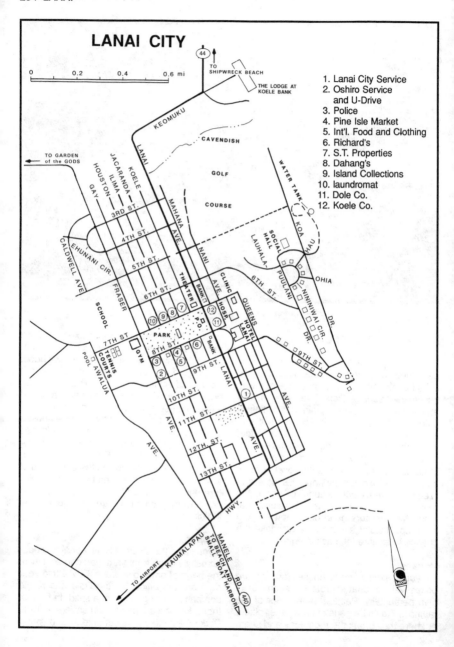

LANAI CITY

0   0.2   0.4   0.6 mi

TO SHIPWRECK BEACH

THE LODGE AT KOELE

TO GARDEN of the GODS

CAVENDISH

GOLF COURSE

KEOMUKU

1. Lanai City Service
2. Oshiro Service and U-Drive
3. Police
4. Pine Isle Market
5. Int'l. Food and Clothing
6. Richard's
7. S.T. Properties
8. Dahang's
9. Island Collections
10. laundromat
11. Dole Co.
12. Koele Co.

GAY
HOUSTON
JACARANDA
ILIMA
KOELE
LANAI
MAHANA
NANI
THEATER
CALDWELL AVE.
EHUNANI CIR.
FRASER
SCHOOL
POOL
AWALUA
AVE.
AVE.
AVE.
KAUMALAPAU

3RD ST.
4TH ST.
5TH ST.
6TH ST.
7TH ST
8TH ST.
9TH ST.
10TH ST.
11TH ST.
12TH ST.
13TH ST.

WATER TANK
SOCIAL HALL
LAUHALA
KOA
HAU
PUULANI
OHIA
DR.
NINIWAI CIR.
DR.
6TH ST.
9TH ST

CLINIC AVE.
BANK
HOSP.
QUEENS
HOTEL LANAI
LANAI
BANK
PARK
GYM
TENNIS COURTS

TO AIRPORT
MANELE RD.
TO BEACH AND SMALL BOAT HARBOR
HWY.

mothers bring their kids for some fresh air. No one in Lanai City rushes to do anything. Look around and you'll discover a real fountain of youth: many octagenarians with a spring in their step. Years of hard work without being hyper or anxious is why they say they're still around. The park is surrounded by commercial Lanai. There's nowhere to *go* except over to the schoolyard to play some tennis or to Cavendish Golf Course for a round of nine holes. Lanai City had a movie theater, but it screened its last picture show a while back. You can plop yourself at Dahang's Pastry Shop or S.T. Properties for coffee, or stay in the park if you're in the mood to strike up a conversation—it won't take long.

Meander down Lanai Avenue past a complex of agricultural buildings and shops. Heavy equipment leaks grease in their rutted dirt lots, where Lanai shows its raw plantation muscle. Just down the street is a complex of log buildings with shake-shingled roofs. These rustic barracks are for the summer help that come to pick the pineapples—often Mormon kids from Utah out to make some money and see a bit of the world. They're known to be clean-living and quiet, and it's ironic that Lanai was once a failed Mormon colony. Do yourself a favor—get out of your rental car and walk around town for at least 30 minutes. You'll experience one of the most unique villages in America.

MUNRO TRAIL

The highlight of visiting Lanai is climbing the Munro Trail to its highest point, Lanaihale (3,370 feet), locally called **The Hale**. As soon as you set foot on Lanai the silhouette of this razor-back ridge with its bristling coat of Norfolk pines demands your attention. Set off for The Hale and you're soon engulfed in its cool stands of pines, eucalyptus, and ironwoods, all colored with ferns and wildflowers. George Munro, a New Zealander hired as the manager of the Lanai Ranch a short time before Jim Dole's arrival, is responsible. With a pouch full of seeds and clippings from his native New Zealand, he trudged all over Lanai planting, in an attempt to foliate the island and create a permanent watershed. Driven by that basic and primordial human desire to see things grow, he climbed The Hale time and again to renew and nurture his leafy progeny. Now, all benefit from his labors.

Getting There

There are two basic ways to go to The Hale, by foot or 4WD. Some local people go on horseback. Head out of town on Route 44 toward Shipwreck Beach. Make sure to start before 8 a.m.; cloud cover is common by early afternoon. After less than two miles, still on the Lanai City side of the mountains, take the first major gravel road to the right, heading for the new upcountry golf course. In about one-quarter mile the road comes to a Y—go left. You immediately start climbing and pass through a forested area past a series of gulches (see below). Continue and the road forks; again bear left. Always stay on the more obviously traveled road. The side roads look muddy and overgrown and it's obvious which is the main one. Robert Frost would be disappointed.

The Trail

As you climb, you pass a profusion of gulches, great red wounds cut into Lanai's windward side. First comes deep and brooding **Maunalei** ("Mountain Lei") **Gulch,** from where Lanai draws its water through a series of tunnels bored through the mountains. It's flanked by **Kuolanai Trail,** a rugged and dangerous footpath leading all the way to the coast. Next is **Hookio Gulch,** a battleground where Lanai's warriors were vanquished in 1778 by Kalaniopuu and his ferocious fighters from the Big Island. All that remains are a few room-sized notches cut into the walls where the warriors slept and piled stones to be hurled at the invaders. After Hookio Gulch, a trail bears left, bringing you to the gaping mouth of **Hauola Gulch,** over 2,000 feet deep. Keep your eyes peeled for axis deer, which seem to defy gravity and manage to cling and forage along the most unlikely and precipitous cliffs. Be very careful of your footing—even skilled Lanai hunters have fallen to their deaths in this area.

The jeep trail narrows on the ridge to little more than 100 feet across. On one side are

The picturesque Munro Trail definitely requires a 4WD. (BOB NILSEN)

the wild gulches, on the other the bucolic green, whorling fingerprints of the pineapple fields. Along the trail you can munch strawberries, common guavas, and as many thimbleberries as you can handle. At the crest of The Hale, let your eyes pan the horizon to see all the main islands of Hawaii (except for Kauai). Rising from the height-caused mirage of a still sea is the hazy specter of Oahu to the north, with Molokai and Maui clearly visible just 10 miles distant. Haleakala, Maui's magical mountain, has a dominant presence viewed from The Hale. Sweep right to see Kahoolawe, bleak and barren, its body shattered by the bombs of the U.S. Navy, a victim of their controversial war games. Eighty miles south of Kahoolawe is the Big Island, its mammoth peaks, Mauna Loa and Mauna Kea, looming like ethereal islands floating in the clouds.

Just past the final lookout is a sign for **Awehi Trail**, which leads left to Naha on the beach. It's extremely rough and you'll definitely need a 4WD in compound low to get down. Most people continue straight ahead and join up with Hoike Road that flattens out and takes you through the pineapple fields until it joins with Route 44 just south of Lanai City. If you have time for only one outing on Lanai or funds budgeted for only one day of 4WD rental, make sure to treat yourself to the unforgettable Munro Trail.

HEADING SOUTH

Joseph Kaliihananui was the last of the free Hawaiian farmers to work the land of Lanai. His great-grandson, Lloyd Cockett, still lives in Lanai City. Joseph made his home in the arid but fertile Palawai Basin that was later bought by Jim Dole and turned into the heart of the pineapple plantation. Just south of Lanai City on Route 440 (Manele Road), the Palawai Basin is the crater of the extinct single volcano of which Lanai is formed. Joseph farmed sweet potatoes, which he traded for fish. He gathered his water in barrels from the dew that formed on his roof and from a trickling spring. His lands supported a few cattle among its now extinct heavy stands of cactus. Here too Walter Murray Gibson attempted to begin a Mormon colony which he later aborted, supposedly because of his outrage over the idea of polygamy. Nothing noteworthy remains of this colony, but high on a hillside overlooking Palawai are the Luahiwa Petroglyphs, considered to be some of the best-preserved rock hieroglyphics in Hawaii.

Luahiwa Petroglyphs

The route through the maze of pineapple roads that lead to the petroglyphs is tough to follow, but the best recipe for success is being pointed in the right direction and adding a large dollop of perseverance. Heading south on Manele Road, look to your left for the back side of a triangular yield sign at Hoike Road, the main pineapple road. Hoike Road was once paved but has now disintegrated into gravel. After turning left onto Hoike, head straight toward a large water tank on the hill. You pass two round-bottomed irrigation ditches, easily spotted as they're always green with grass due to the water they carry. At the second ditch turn left and follow the road, keeping the ditch on your right. Proceed until you come to a silver water pipe about 12 inches in diameter. Follow this pipe as it runs along a hedgerow until you reach the third power pole. At the "No Trespassing" sign, bear left.

Follow this overgrown trail up the hill to the boulders on which appear the petroglyphs. The boulders are brownish-black and covered in lichens. Their natural arrangement resembles an oversized Japanese rock garden. Dotted on the hillside are sisal plants that look like bouquets of giant green swords. As you climb to the rocks be very careful of your footing— the ground is crumbly and the vegetation slippery. The boulders cover a three-acre area; most of the petroglyphs are found on the south faces of the rocks. Some are hieroglyphics of symbolic circles, others are picture stories complete with canoes gliding under unfurled sails. Dogs snarl with their jaws agape, while enigmatic triangular stickmen try to tell their stories from the past. Equestrians gallop, showing that these stone picture-books were done even after the coming of the white man. The Luahiwa Petroglyphs are a very special spot where the ancient Hawaiians still sing their tales across the gulf of time.

Hulopoe And Manele Bays

Proceed south on Route 440 to Lanai's most salubrious spots, the twin bays of Manele and Hulopoe. At the crest of the hill, just past the milepost, you can look down on the white, inviting sands of Hulopoe to the right, and the rockier small boat harbor of Manele on the left. The island straight ahead is Kahoolawe, and on very clear days you might be able to glimpse the peaks of Hawaii's Mauna Loa and Mauna Kea. Manele Bay is a picture-perfect anchorage where a dozen or so small boats

and yachts are tied up on any given day. Tour boats from Maui also tie up here, but according to local sailors the tourists don't seem to come on the weekends. Manele and Hulopoe are a Marine Life Conservation District with the rules for fishing and diving prominently displayed on a large bulletin board at the entrance to Manele. Because of this, the area is superb for snorkeling.

Hulopoe Bay offers very gentle waves and soothing, crystal-clear water. The beach is a beautiful expanse of white sand fringed by palms with a mingling of large boulders that really set it off. This is Lanai's official camping area, and six sites are available. All are well spaced, each with a picnic table and firepit. A series of shower stalls made of brown plywood provides solar-heated water and just enough privacy, allowing your head and legs to protrude. After refreshing yourself you can fish from the rock promontories on both sides of the bay. It's difficult to find a more wholesome and gentle spot anywhere in Hawaii.

Kaumalapau Harbor

A side trip to Kaumalapau Harbor is worth it. This manmade facility, which ships more than a million pineapples a day during peak harvest, is the only one of its kind in the world. Besides, you've probably already rented a vehicle and you might as well cover these few paved miles from Lanai City on Route 44 just to have a quick look. En route you pass Lanai's odoriferous garbage dump, which is a real eyesore. Hold your nose and try not to notice. The harbor facility itself is no-nonsense commercial, but the coastline is reasonably spectacular, with a glimpse of the island's dramatic sea cliffs. Also, this area has supereasy access to some decent fishing, right off the pier area. An added bonus for making the trek to this lonely area is that it is one of the best places on Lanai from which to view the sunset, and you usually have it all to yourself.

KAUNOLU: KAMEHAMEHA'S GETAWAY

At the southwestern tip of Lanai is Kaunolu Bay. At one time, this vibrant fishing village surrounded Halulu Heiau, a sacred refuge where the downtrodden were protected by the temple priests who could intercede with the benevolent gods. Kamehameha the Great would escape Lahaina's blistering summers and come to these very fertile fishing waters with his loyal warriors. Some proved their valor to their great chief by diving from Kahikili's Leap, a manmade opening in the rocks 60 feet above the sea. The remains of over 80 house sites and a smattering of petroglyphs dot the area. The last inhabitant was Ohua, elder brother of Joseph Kaliihananui, who lived in a grass hut just east of Kaunolu in Mamaki Bay. Ohua was entrusted by Kamehameha V to hide the heiau fish-god, Kuniki; old accounts by the area's natives say that he died because of mishandling this stone god. The natural power still emanating from Kaunolu is obvious, and you can't help feeling the energy that drew the Hawaiians to this sacred spot.

Getting There

Proceed south on Manele Road from Lanai City through Palawai Basin until it makes a hard bend to the left. Here, a sign points you to Manele Bay. Do not go left to Manele, but

Archaeological treasures like this stone bell still lie undisturbed at Kaunolu Village site. (J.D. BISIGNANI)

proceed straight and stay on the once-paved pineapple road. At a dip by a huge silver water pipe, go straight through the pineapple fields until another obvious dip at two orange pipes (like fire hydrants) on the left and right. Turn left here onto a rather small road—pineapples on your left and tall grass along the irrigation ditch on your right. Follow the road left to a weatherworn sign that actually says "Kaunolu Road." This dirt track starts off innocently enough as it begins its plunge toward the sea. Only two miles long, the local folks consider it the roughest road on the island. It *is* a bonecruncher, but if you take it super slow, you should have no real problem. Plot your progress against the lighthouse on the coast. This area is excellent for spotting axis deer. The deer are nourished by *haole koa,* a green bush with a brown seed pod that you see growing along the road. This natural feed also supports cattle, but is not good for horses, causing the hair on their tails to fall out.

Kaunolu

The village site lies at the end of a long dry gulch which terminates at a rocky beach, suitable in times past as a canoe anchorage. This entire area is a mecca for archaeologists and anthropologists. The most famous was the eminent Dr. Kenneth Emory of the Bishop Museum; he filed an extensive research report on the area. At its terminus, the road splits left and right. Go right to reach a large *kiawe* tree with a rudimentary picnic table under it. Just in front of you is a large pile of nondescript rocks purported to be the ruined foundation of Kamehameha's house. Unbelievably, this sacred area has been trashed out by disrespectful and ignorant picnickers. Hurricane Iwa also had a hand in changing the face of Kaunolu, as its tremendous force hit this area head on and even drove large boulders from the sea onto the land. As you look around, the ones that have a whitish appearance were washed up on the shore by the fury of Iwa.

The villagers of Kaunolu lived mostly on the east bank and had to keep an ever-watchful eye on nature because the bone-dry gulch could suddenly be engulfed by flash floods. In the center of the gulch, about 100 yards inland, was **Paao,** the area's freshwater well.

Lloyd Cockett at
Kahekili's Leap with
Shark Island framed in
the background
(J.D. BISIGNANI)

Paao was *kapu* to menstruating women, and it was believed that if the *kapu* was broken, the well would dry up. It served the village for centuries. It's totally obliterated now; in 1895 a Mr. Hayselden tried to erect a windmill over it, destroying the native caulking and causing the well to turn brackish—an example of Lanai's precious water being tampered with by outsiders, causing disastrous results.

The Sites
Climb down the east bank and cross the rocky beach. The first well-laid wall close to the beach on the west bank is the remains of a canoe shed. Proceed inland and climb the rocky bank to the remains of Halulu Heiau. Just below in the undergrowth is where the well was located. The *heiau* site has a commanding view of the area, best described by the words of Dr. Emory himself: "The point on which it is located is surrounded on three sides by cliffs and on the north rises the magnificent cliff of Palikaholo, terminating in Kahilikalani crag, a thousand feet above the sea. The ocean swell entering Kolokolo Cave causes a rumbling like thunder, as if under the *heiau*. From every point in the village the *heiau* dominates the landscape." As you climb the west bank, notice that the mortarless walls are laid up for over 30 feet. If you have a keen eye you'll notice a perfectly square firepit right in the center of the *heiau*.

This area still has treasures that have never been catalogued. For example, you might chance upon a Hawaiian lamp, as big and perfectly round as a basketball, with an orange-sized hole in the middle where *kukui* nut oil was burned. Old records indicate that Kuniki, the temple idol itself, is still lying here face down no more than a few hundred yards away. If you happen to discover an artifact, do not remove it under any circumstance. Follow the advice of the late Lloyd Cockett, a *kapuna* of Lanai, who said, "I wouldn't take the rock because we Hawaiians don't steal from the land. Special rocks you don't touch."

Kahekili's Leap
Once you've explored the *heiau*, you'll be drawn toward the sea cliff. **Kaneapua Rock,** a giant tower-like chunk, sits perhaps 100 feet offshore. Below in the tidepool are basin-like depressions in the rock-salt evaporation pools, the bottoms still showing some white residue. Follow the cliff face along the natural wall obstructing your view to the south. You'll see a break in the wall about 15 feet wide with a very flat rock platform. From here, **Shark Island,** which closely resembles a sharkfin, is perfectly framed. This opening is **Kahekili's Leap,** named after a Lanai chief, not the famous chief of Maui. Here, Kamehameha's warriors proved their courage by executing death-defying leaps into only 12 feet of water,

and clearing a 15-foot protruding rock shelf. Scholars also believe that Kamehameha punished his warriors for petty offenses by sentencing them to make the jump. Kahekili's Leap is a perfect background for a photo. Below, the sea surges in unreal aquamarine colors. Off to the right is Kolokolo Cave above which is another, even more daring, leap at 90 feet. Evidence suggests that Kolokolo is linked to Kaunolu Gulch by a lava tube that has been sealed and lost. On the beach below Kahekili's Leap the vacationing chiefs played *konane,* and many stone boards can still be found from this game of Hawaiian checkers.

Petroglyphs

To find them, walk directly inland from Kaneapua Rock, using it as your point of reference. On a large pile of rocks are stick figures, mostly with a bird-head motif. Some heads even look like a mason's hammer. This entire area has a masculine feeling to it. There aren't the usual swaying palms and gentle sandy beaches. With the stones and rugged sea cliffs, you get the feeling that a warrior king would enjoy this spot. Throughout the area is *pili* grass, used by the Hawaiians to thatch their homes. Children would pick one blade and hold it in their fingers while reciting *"E pili e, e pili e, au hea kuu hale."* The *pili* grass would then spin around in their fingers and point in the direction of home. Pick some *pili* and try it yourself before leaving this wondrous, powerful area.

THE EAST COAST: KEOMUKU AND NAHA

Until the turn of this century, most of Lanai's inhabitants lived in the villages of the now-deserted east coast. Before the coming of Westerners, 2,000 or so Hawaiians lived along these shores, fishing and raising taro. It was as if they wanted to keep Maui in sight so that they didn't feel so isolated. Numerous *heiau* from this period still mark the ancient sites. The first white men also tried to make a go of Lanai along this stretch. The Mauanalei Sugar Co. tried to raise sugar cane on the flat plains of Naha but failed and pulled up stakes in 1901—the last time that this entire coastline

ahu, *a traveler's wish for happy trails (J.D. BISIGNANI)*

was populated to any extent. Today, the ancient *heiau* and a decaying church in Keomuku are the last vestiges of habitation, holding out against the ever-encroaching jungle. You can follow a jeep trail along this coast and get a fleeting glimpse of times past.

Getting There

Approach Keomuku and Naha from one of two directions. The most straightforward is from north to south. Follow Route 440 (Keomuku Road) from Lanai City until it turns to dirt and branches right (south) at the coast. This road meanders for about 15 miles all the way to Naha. Though the road is partial gravel and packed sand and not that rugged, you definitely need a 4WD. It's paralleled by a much smoother road that runs along the beach, but it can only be used at low tide. Many small roads connect the two, so you can hop back and forth between them every 200-300 yards.

Consider two tips: first, if you take the beach road, you can make good time and have a smooth ride, but could sail past most of the sights since you won't know when to hop back on the inland road; second, be careful of the *kiawe* trees—the tough, inch-thick thorns can puncture tires as easily as nails. The other alternative is to take Awehi Trail, a rugged jeep track, about halfway between Lopa and Naha. This trail leads up the mountain to the Munro Trail, but because of its ruggedness it's best to take it down from The Hale instead of up. A good long day of rattling in a jeep would take you along the Munro Trail, down Awehi Trail, then north along the coast back to Route 44. If you came south along the coast from Route 44, it would be better to retrace your steps instead of heading up Awehi. When you think you've suffered enough and have been bounced into submission by your jeep, remember that many of these trails were carved out by Juan Torqueza. He trailblazed alone on his bulldozer, unsupervised, and without benefit of survey. Now well into his 70s, he can be found in Dole Park in Lanai City, except when he's out here fishing.

A new island venture based on Maui, called **Club Lanai,** tel. 871-1144, has recently opened the remote east coast of Lanai to visitors. Basically they transport tourists from Maui aboard their boats to their private facility for a day of fun, games, and feasting. For full information see p. 93.

Keomuku Village

There isn't much to see in Keomuku ("Stretch of White") Village other than an abandoned Hawaiian church. Though this was the site of the Mauanalei Sugar Co., almost all the decaying buildings were razed in the early 1970s. A few hundred yards north and south of the town site are examples of some original fishponds. They're tough to see (overgrown with mangrove), but a close observation gives you an idea of how extensive they once were. The **Hawaiian church,** now being refurbished, is definitely worth a stop—it almost pleads to be photographed. From outside, you can see how frail it is, so if you go in tread lightly—both walls of the church are caving in and the floor is humped in the middle. The altar area, a podium with a little bench, remains. A banner on the fading blue-green walls reads *"Ualanaano Jehova Kalanakila Malmalama,* October 4, 1903." Only the soft wind sounds where once strong voices sang vibrant hymns of praise.

A few hundred yards south of the church is a walking trail. Follow it inland to **Kahea Heiau** and a smattering of petroglyphs. This is the *heiau* disturbed by the sugar cane train; its desecration was believed to have caused the sweet water of Keomuku to turn brackish. The people of Keomuku learned to survive on the brackish water and kept a special jug of fresh water for visitors.

Heading South

Farther south a Japanese cemetery and monument were erected for the deceased workers who built **Halepaloa Landing,** from where the cane was shipped. Today, only rotting timbers and stonework remain, but the pier offers an excellent vantage point for viewing Maui, and it's a good spot to fish. The next landmark is a semi-used getaway called "Whale's Tale." A boat sits in the front yard. This is a great place to find a coconut and have a free roadside refreshment. Also, a very fruitful *kamani* nut tree sits right at the entrance. The nut looks like an oversized bean. Place your knife in the center and drive it down. The *kamani,* which tastes like a roasted almond, is 99% husk and 1% nut.

The road continues past **Lopa,** ending at **Naha.** You pass a few coconut groves on the way. Legend says that one of these was cursed by a *kahuna*—if you climb a tree to get a coconut you will not be able to come down. Luckily, most tourists have already been cursed by "midriff bulge" and can't climb the tree in the first place. When you get to Naha check out the remnants of the paved Hawaiian walking trail before slowly heading back from this decaying historical area.

SHIPWRECK BEACH

Heading over the mountains from Lanai City to Shipwreck Beach offers you a rewarding scenario: an intriguing destination point with fantastic scenery and splendid panoramas on

cursed coconuts of Naha (J.D. BISIGNANI)

the way. Head north from Lanai City on Route 440 (Keomuku Road). In less that 10 minutes you crest the mountains, and if you're lucky the sky will be clear and you'll be able to see the phenomenon that guided ancient navigators to land: the halo of dark brooding clouds over Maui and Molokai, a sure sign of landfall. Shorten your gaze and look at the terrain in the immediate vicinity. Here are the famous precipitous gulches of Lanai. The wounded earth bleeds red while offering patches of swaying grass and wildflowers. It looks like the canyons of Arizona have been dragged to the rim of the sea. As you wiggle your way down Keomuku Road, look left to see the rusting hull of a WW II Liberty Ship sitting on the shallow reef almost completely out of the water. For most, this derelict is the destination point on Shipwreck Beach.

The Beach

As you continue down the road, little piles of stones, usually three, sit atop a boulder. Although most are from modern times, these are called *ahu,* a traditional Hawaiian offering to ensure good fortune while traveling. If you have the right feeling in your heart and you're moved to erect your own *ahu* it's OK, but

under no circumstances disturb the ones already there. Farther down, the lush grasses of the mountain slope disappear, and the scrub bush takes over. The pavement ends and the dirt road forks left (north) to Shipwreck Beach, or straight ahead (south) toward the abandoned town of Naha. If you turn left you'll be on an adequate sandy road, flanked on both sides by thorny, tire-puncturing *kiawe* trees. In less than a mile is a large open area to your right. If you're into unofficial camping, this isn't a bad spot for a one-night bivouac—the trees here provide privacy and an excellent windbreak against the constant strong ocean breezes. About two miles down the road is Federation Camp, actually a tiny village of unpretentious beach shacks built by Lanai's workers as "getaways" and fishing cabins. Charming in their humbleness and simplicity, they're made mostly from recycled timbers and boards that have washed ashore. Some have been worked on quite diligently and skillfully and are actual little homes, but somehow the rougher ones are more attractive. You can drive past the cabins for a few hundred yards, but to be on the safe side, park just past them and begin your walk.

Petroglyphs

At the very end of the road is a cabin that a local comedian has named the "Lanai Hilton." Just off to your left *(mauka)* are the ruins of a lighthouse. Look for a cement slab where two graffiti artists of bygone days carved their names: John Kupau and Kam Chee, Nov. 28, 1929. Behind the lighthouse ruins an arrow points you to "The Bird Man of Lanai Petroglyphs." Of all the petroglyphs on Lanai these are the easiest to find; trail-marking rocks have been painted white by Lanai's Boy Scouts. Follow them to a large rock bearing the admonition Do Not Deface. Climb down the path with a keen eye—the rock carvings are small, most only about 10 inches tall. Little childlike stick figures, they have intriguing bird heads whose symbolic meaning has been lost.

Hiking Trail

The trail along the beach goes for eight long hot miles to Polihua Beach. That trip leads

Aptly named Shipwreck Beach is a great place to search for flotsam.
(BOB NILSEN)

through the Garden of the Gods and should be done separately, but at least walk as far as the Liberty Ship, about a mile from the cabins. The area has some of the best beachcombing in Hawaii; no telling what you might find. The most sought-after treasures are glass floats that have bobbed for thousands of miles across the Pacific, strays from Japanese fishnets. You might even see a modern ship washed onto the reef, like the Canadian yacht that went aground in the spring of 1984. Navigational equipment has improved, but Shipwreck Beach can *still* be a nightmare to any captain caught in its turbulent whitecaps and long ragged coral fingers. This area is particularly good for lobsters and shore fishing. And you can swim in shallow sandy-bottom pools to refresh yourself as you hike.

Try to time your return car trip over the mountain for sundown. The tortuous terrain, stark in black and white shadows, is awe-inspiring. The larger rocks are giant sentinels: it's easy to feel the power and attraction they held for the ancient Hawaiians. As you climb the road on the windward side with its barren and beaten terrain, the feelings of mystery and mystique attributed to spiritual Lanai are obvious. You come over the top and suddenly see the valley—manicured, rolling, soft and verdant with pineapples and the few lights of Lanai City beckoning.

THE GARDEN OF THE GODS AND POLIHUA

The most ruggedly beautiful, barren, and inhospitable section of Lanai is out at the north end. After passing through a confusing maze of pineapple fields, you come to the appropriately named Garden of the Gods. Waiting is a fantasia of otherworldly landscapes—barren red earth, convulsed ancient lava flows, tortured pinnacles of stone, and psychedelic striations of vibrating colors, especially moving at sunrise and sunset. Little-traveled trails lead to Kaena Point, a wasteland dominated by sea cliffs where adulterous Hawaiian wives were sent into exile for a short time in 1837. Close by is Lanai's largest *heiau,* dubbed Kaenaiki, so isolated and forgotten that its real name and function were lost even to Hawaiian natives by the middle of the 19th century. After a blistering, sun-baked, 4WD drubbing, you emerge at the coast on Polihau, a totally secluded, pure-white beach where sea turtles once came to bury their eggs in the natural incubator of its soft warm sands.

Getting There

Lanai doesn't hand over its treasures easily, but they're worth pursuing. To get to the Garden of the Gods you have to tangle with the pineapple roads. Head north out of Lanai City on Fraser Avenue. At the fields, it turns to dirt and splits in four directions. Two roads bear right, one goes left, and the main road (which you follow) goes straight ahead. This road proceeds north and then bears left, heading west. Stay on it and ignore all minor pineapple roads. In less than 10 minutes you come to a major crossroad. Turn right heading north again, keeping the ridge of Lanai's mountains on your right. This road gets smaller, then comes to a point where it splits in four again! Two roads bear left, one bears right, and the one you want goes straight ahead, more or less. Follow it, and in five minutes if you pass through an area that is very thick with spindly pine trees on both sides of the road, you know you're heading in the right direction. The road opens up in spots; watch for fields of wildflowers. Shortly, a marker points you off to the right on Lapaiki Road. This is a bit out of the way, but if followed you'll get a good view of the garden, and eventually wind up at Shipwreck Beach. It's better, however, to proceed straight ahead to another marker pointing you down Awailua Trail to the right and Polihua straight ahead. Follow Polihua Trail, and soon you finally come to the garden and another marker for Kaena Road, which leads to magnificent sea cliffs and Kaenaiki Heiau.

Hiking

Anyone wishing to hike this area should drive to the end of the pineapple fields. It's at least half the distance and the scenery is quite ordinary. Make sure to bring plenty of water and a windbreaker because the heavy winds blow almost continuously. Sturdy shoes and a sun hat are also needed. There is no official camping at Polihua Beach, but again, anyone doing so overnight probably wouldn't meet with any hassles. Those with super-keen eyes might even pick out one of the scarce pronghorn that live in the fringe of surrounding grasslands.

The Garden Of The Gods

There, a shocking assault on your senses, is the bleak, red, burnt earth, devoid of vegetation, heralding the beginning of the garden. The flowers here are made of rock, the shrubs are the twisted crusts of lava, and trees are baked minarets of stone, all subtle shades of orange, purple, and sulfurous yellow. The jeep trail has been sucked down by erosion and the garden surrounds you. Stop many times to climb a likely outcropping and get a sweeping view. The wind rakes these badlands and the silence penetrates to your soul. Although eons have passed, you can feel the cataclysmic violence that created this haunting and delicate beauty.

Polihua Beach

Abruptly the road becomes smooth and flat. Straight ahead, like a mirage too bright for your eyes, an arch is cut into the green jungle, framing white sand and moving blue ocean. As you face the beach, to the right it's flat, expansive, and the sands are white, but the winds are heavy; if you hiked eight miles, you'd reach Shipwreck Beach. More interesting is the view to the left, which has a series of lonely little coves. The sand is brown and coarse and large black lava boulders are marbled with purplish-gray rock embedded in long, faulted seams. Polihua is not just a destination point where you come for a quick look. It takes so much effort coming and going that you should plan on having a picnic and a relaxing afternoon before heading back through the Garden of the Gods and its perfectly scheduled sunset light show.

MOLOKAI

INTRODUCTION

Molokai is a sanctuary, a human time capsule where the pendulum swings inexorably forward, but more slowly than in the rest of Hawaii. It has always been so. In ancient times, Molokai was known as *Pule-oo,* "Powerful Prayer," where its supreme chiefs protected their small underpopulated refuge, not through legions of warriors but through the chants of their *kahuna.* This powerful, ancient mysticism, handed down directly from the goddess Pahulu, was known and respected throughout the archipelago. Its mana was the oldest and strongest in Hawaii, and its practitioners were venerated by nobility and commoners alike—they had the ability to "pray you to death." The entire island was a haven, a refuge for the vanquished and *kapu*-breakers of all the islands. It's still so today, beckoning to determined escapees from the rat race!

The blazing lights of super-modern Honolulu can easily be seen from western Molokai, while Molokai as viewed from Oahu is fleeting and ephemeral, appearing and disappearing on the horizon. The island is home to the largest number of Hawaiians. In effect it is a tribal homeland: over 2,500 of the island's 6,000 inhabitants have more than 50% Hawaiian blood and, except for Niihau, it's the only island where they are the majority. The 1920s Hawaiian Homes Act allowed *kuleana* of 40 acres to anyone with more than 50% Hawaiian ancestry. *Kuleana* owners form the grass-roots organizations that fight for Hawaiian rights and battle the colossal forces of rabid developers who have threatened Molokai for decades.

AN OVERVIEW

Kaunakakai And West
Kaunakakai, the island's main town, is like a Hollywood sound stage where Jesse James or Wyatt Earp would feel right at home. The town is flat, treeless, and three blocks long. Ala Malama, its main shopping street, is lined with false-front stores; pickup trucks are

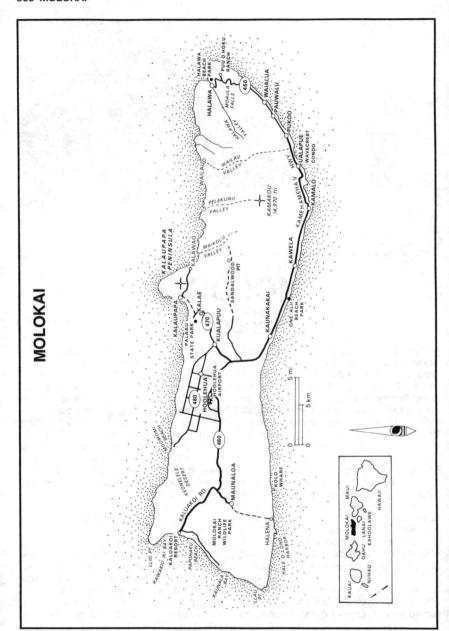

MOLOKAI

parked in front where horses and buggies ought to be. To the west are the prairie-like plains of Molokai. The northern section of the island contains **Pala'au State Park,** where a campsite is always easily found, and **Phallic Rock,** a natural shrine where island women came to pray for fertility. Most of the west end is owned by the mammoth 70,000-acre **Molokai Ranch.** Part of its lands supports 6,000 head of cattle, **Wildlife Safari Park,** and herds of axis deer imported from India in 1867.

The 40-acre *kuleana* are here, as well as abandoned Dole and Del Monte pineapple fields. The once thriving pineapple company towns of **Maunaloa** and **Kualapuu** are now semi-ghost towns since the pineapple companies pulled up stakes in the last few years. Maunaloa is trying to hold on as an embryonic artists' colony, and the Kualapuu area attracts its scattered Filipino workers mostly on weekends, when they come to unofficially test their best cocks in the pit.

On the western shore is the Kaluakoi Resort and a handful of condos perched above the island's best beaches. Here, 7,000 acres sold by the Molokai Ranch to the Louisiana Land and Exploration Company is slated for development. This area, rich with the finest archaeological sites on the island, is a hotbed of contention between developers and preservationists. The Kaluakoi, however, is often pointed to as a well-planned development, a kind of model compromise between the factions. Its first-rate architecture, in low Polynesian style, blends well with the surroundings and is not a high-rise blight on the horizon.

The East Coastal Road

Highway 450 is a magnificent coastal road running east from Kaunakakai to Halawa Valley. A slow drive along this writhing country thoroughfare rewards you with easily accessible beach parks, glimpses of fishponds, *heiau,* wildlife sanctuaries, and small one-room churches strung along the road like rosary beads. Almost every mile has a historical site, like the **Smith and Bronte Landing Site** where two pioneers of trans-Pacific flight ignominiously alighted in a mangrove swamp, and **Paikalani Taro Patch,** the only one from which Kamehameha V would eat poi.

On Molokai's eastern tip is **Halawa Valley,** a real gem accessible by car. This pristine gorge has a just-right walk to a series of invigorating waterfalls and their pools, and a beach park where the valley meets the sea. The majority of the population of Halawa moved out in 1946 when a 30-foot tsunami washed their homes away and mangled their taro fields, leaving a thick salty residue. Today only a handful of mostly alternative lifestylers live in the valley among the overgrown stone walls that once marked the boundaries of manicured and prosperous family gardens. Just south on the grounds of Puu O Hoku Ranch is **Kalanikaula,** the sacred *kukui* grove of Lanikaula, Molokai's most powerful *kahuna* of the classic period. This grove was planted at his death and became the most sacred spot on Molokai. Today the trees are dying.

The Windward Coast

Kalaupapa leper colony, a lonely peninsula completely separated from the world by a hostile pounding surf and a precipitous 1,500-foot *pali,* is a modern story of human dignity. Kalaupapa was a howling charnel house where the unfortunate victims of leprosy were banished to die. Here humanity reached its lowest ebb of hopelessness, violence, and depravity, until one tiny flicker of light arrived in 1873—Joseph de Veuster, a Belgian priest known throughout Hawaii as Father Damien. In the greatest example of pure aloha yet established on Hawaii, he became his brothers' keeper. Tours of Kalaupapa operated by well-informed former patients are enlightening and educational.

East of Kalaupapa along the windward (northeast) coast is a series of amazingly steep and isolated valleys. The inhabitants moved out at the beginning of this century except for one pioneering family that returned a few years ago to carve out a home. Well beyond the farthest reaches of the last road, this emerald-green primeval world awaits. The *pali* here mark the tallest sea cliffs in the world, and diving headfirst is **Kahiwa** ("Sacred One") **Falls,** the highest in Hawaii at 1,750 feet. You get here only by helicopter excursion, by boat in the calmer summer months, or by foot over dangerous and unkempt mountain trails. For now, Molokai remains a sanctuary, reminiscent of the Hawaii of simpler times. Around it the storm of modernity rages, but still the "Friendly Island" awaits those willing to venture off the beaten track.

THE LAND

Molokai is the fifth largest Hawaiian island. Its western tip, at Ilio Point, is a mere 22 miles from Oahu's eastern tip, Makapuu Point. Resembling a jogging shoe, Molokai is about 38 miles from heel to toe and 10 miles from laces to sole, totaling 165,760 acres, with just over 88 miles of coastline. Most of the arable land on the island is owned by the 70,000-acre Molokai Ranch, primarily on the western end, and the 14,000-acre Puu O Hoku Ranch on the eastern end. Molokai was formed by three distinct shield volcanos. Two linked together to form Molokai proper, and a later eruption formed the flat Kalaupapa Peninsula.

Physical Features
Although Molokai is rather small, it has a great deal of geographical diversity. Western Molokai is dry with rolling hills, natural pastures, and a maximum elevation of only 1,381 feet. The eastern sector of the island has heavy rainfall, the tallest sea cliffs in the world, and craggy narrow valleys perpetually covered in a velvet cloak of green mosses. Viewed from the sea it looks like a 2,000-foot vertical wall from surf to clouds, with tortuously deep chasms along the coastline. Mount Kamakou is the highest peak on Molokai, at 4,970 feet. The southcentral area is relatively swampy, while the west and especially northwest coasts around Moomomi have rolling sand dunes. Papohaku Beach, just below the Kaluakoi Resort on western Molokai, is one of the most massive white-sand beaches in Hawaii. A controversy was raised when it was discovered that huge amounts of sand were dredged from this area and hauled to Oahu; the Molokai Ranch was pressured and the dredgings ceased. The newly formed and very political Office of Hawaiian Affairs (OHA) became involved, and a court case on behalf of native Hawaiian rights is pending. A hefty

section of land in the northcentral area is a state forest where new species of trees are planted on an experimental basis. The 240-acre Pala'au State Park is in this cool upland forested area.

Manmade Marvels
Two manmade features on Molokai are engineering marvels. One is the series of ancient fishponds strung along the south shore like pearls on a string—best seen from the air as you approach the island by plane. Dozens still exist, but the most amazing is the enormous **Keawanui Pond,** covering 54 acres and surrounded by a three-foot tall, 2,000-foot long wall. The other is the modern **Kualapuu Reservoir** completed in 1969. The world's largest rubber-lined reservoir, it can hold 1.4 billion gallons of water. Part of its engineering dramatics is the Molokai Tunnel, which feeds it with water from the eastern valleys. The tunnel is eight feet tall, eight feet wide and almost 27,000 feet (five miles) long.

Climate
The average island temperature is 75-85° F (24°C). The yearly average rainfall is 30 inches; the east receives a much greater percentage than the west.

FLORA AND FAUNA

The land animals on Molokai were brought by man. The island is unique in that it offers **Molokai Ranch Wildlife Safari** on the grounds of Molokai Ranch in the western sector, with more than 400 animals mostly imported from the savannahs of Africa (see p. 344). And who knows? Perhaps in a few thousand years after some specimens have escaped there might be such a thing as a "Molokai giraffe" that will look like any other giraffe except that its markings resemble flowers.

Birdlife
A few of Hawaii's endemic birds can be spotted by a determined observer at various locales around Molokai. They include: the Hawaiian petrel (ua'u); Hawaiian coot (alae ke'o-ke'o), prominent in Hawaiian mythology;

AVERAGE MAXIMUM/MINIMUM TEMPERATURE AND RAINFALL

Island	Town		Jan.	March	May	June	Sept.	Nov.
Molokai	Kaunakakai	high	79	79	81	82	82	80
		low	61	63	68	70	68	63
		rain	4	3	0	0	0	2
N.B. Rainfall in inches; temperature in °F								

Hawaiian stilt (ae'o), a wading bird with ridiculous stick legs that protects its young by feigning wing injury and luring predators away from the nest; and the Hawaiian owl (pueo), a bird that helps in its own demise by being easily approached. Molokai has a substantial number of introduced game birds that attract hunters throughout the year (see p. 319).

Flora
The kukui or candlenut tree is common to all the Hawaiian islands; along with being the official state tree, its tiny white blossom is Molokai's flower. The kukui, introduced centuries ago by the early Polynesians, grows on lower mountain slopes and can easily be distinguished by its pale green leaves.

HISTORY

The oral chant "Molokai nui a Hina..." ("Great Molokai, child of Hina") refers to Molokai as the island-child of the goddess Hina and the god Wakea, male progenitor of all the islands; Papa, Wakea's first wife, left him in anger as a result of this unfaithfulness. Hina's cave, just east of Kaluaaha on the southeast coast, can still be visited and has been revered as a sacred spot for countless centuries. Another ancient spot, Halawa Valley, on the eastern tip of Molokai, is considered one of the oldest settlements in Hawaii. As research continues, settlement dates are pushed further back, but for now scholars agree that early wayfarers from the Marquesas Islands settled Halawa in the mid-seventh century.

Molokai, from earliest times, was revered and feared as a center for mysticism and sorcery. Ili'ili'opae Heiau was renowned for its powerful priests whose incantations were mingled with the screams of human sacrifice. Commoners avoided Ili'ili'opae, and even powerful kahuna could not escape its terrible power. One, Kamalo, lost his sons as sacrifices at the heiau for their desecration of the temple drum. Kamalo sought revenge by invoking the help of his personal god, the terrible shark deity, Kauhuhu. After the proper prayers and offerings, Kauhuhu sent a flash flood to wipe out Mapulehu Valley where Ili'ili'opae was located. All perished except for Kamalo and his family, who were protected by a sacred fence around their home.

This tradition of mysticism reached its apex with the famous Lanikaula, "Prophet of Molokai." During the 16th century, Lanikaula lived near Halawa Valley and practiced his arts, handed down by the goddess Pahulu, who even predated Pele. Pahulu was the goddess responsible for the "old ocean highway," which passed between Molokai and Lanai and led to Kahiki, lost homeland of all the islanders. Lanikaula practiced his sorcery in the utmost secrecy and even buried his excrement on an offshore island so that a rival kahuna could not find and burn it, which would surely cause his death. Hawaiian oral history does not say why Kawelo, a sorcerer from Lanai and a friend of Lanikaula, came to spy on Lanikaula and observed him hiding his excrement. Kawelo burned it in the sacred fires, and Lanikaula knew that his end was near. Lanikaula ordered his sons to bury him in a hidden grave so that his enemies could not find his bones and use their mana to control his spirit. To further hide his remains, he had a kukui grove planted over his body. **Kalanikaula** ("Sacred Grove of La-nikaula") is still visible today, though most of the trees appear to be dying.

Western Contacts

Captain James Cook first spotted Molokai on November 26, 1778, but because it looked bleak and uninhabited he decided to bypass it. It wasn't until eight years later that Capt. George Dixon sighted the island and decided to land. Very little was recorded in his ship's log about this first encounter, and Molokai slipped from the attention of the Western world until Protestant missionaries arrived at Kaluaaha in 1832 and reported the native population at approximately 6,000.

In 1790 Kamehameha the Great came from the Big Island as a suitor seeking the hand of Keopuolani, a chieftess of Molokai. Within five years he returned again, but this time there was no merrymaking: he came as a conquering emperor on his thrust westward to Oahu. His war canoes landed at Pakuhiwa Battleground, a bay just a few miles east of Kaunakakai; it's said that warriors lined the shores for more than four miles. The grossly outnumbered warriors of Molokai fought desperately, but even the incantations of their *kahuna* were no match for Kamehameha and his warriors. Inflamed with recent victory and infused with the power of their horrible war-god Ku ("of the Maggot-dripping Mouth"), they slaughtered the Molokai warriors and threw their broken bodies into a sea so filled with sharks that their feeding frenzy made the waters appear to boil. Thus subdued, Molokai slipped into obscurity once again as its people turned to a quiet life of farming and fishing.

Molokai Ranch

Molokai remained almost unchanged until the 1850s. The Great Mahele of 1848 provided for private ownership of land, and giant tracts were formed into the Molokai Ranch. About 1850, German immigrant Rudolph Meyer came to Molokai and married a high chieftess named Dorcas Kalama Waha. Together they had 11 children, with whose aid he turned the vast lands of the Molokai Ranch into productive pastureland. A man of indomitable spirit, Meyer held public office on Molokai and be-came the island's unofficial patriarch. He managed Molokai Ranch for the original owner, Kamehameha V, and remained manager until his death in 1898, by which time the ranch was owned by the Bishop Estate. In 1875, Charles Bishop had bought half of the 70,000 acres of Molokai Ranch and his wife Bernice, a Kamehameha descendant, inherited the remainder. In 1898, the Molokai Ranch was sold to businessmen in Honolulu for $251,000. This consortium formed the American Sugar Co., but after a few plantings the available water on Molokai turned brackish and once again Molokai Ranch was sold. Charles Cooke bought controlling interest from the other businessmen in 1908, and Molokai Ranch remains in the Cooke family to this day.

Changing Times

Very little happened for a decade after Charles Cooke bought the Molokai Ranch from his partners. Molokai did become famous for its honey production, supplying a huge amount to the world up until WW I. During the 1920s, political and economic forces greatly changed Molokai. In 1921, Congress passed the **Hawaiian Homes Act**, which set aside 43,000 acres on the island for people who had at least 50% Hawaiian blood. By this time, however, all agriculturally productive land in Hawaii had already been claimed. The land given to the Hawaiians was very poor and lacked adequate water. Many Hawaiians had long since left the land, and were raised in towns and cities. Now out of touch with the simple life of the taro patch, they found it very difficult to readjust. To prevent the Hawaiians from selling their claims and losing the land forever, the Hawaiian Homes Act provided that the land be leased to them for 99 years. Making a go of these 40-acre parcels *(kuleana)* was so difficult that successful homesteaders were called "Molokai Miracles."

In 1923 Libby Corporation leased land from Molokai Ranch at Kaluakoi and went into pineapple production; Del Monte followed suit in 1927 at Kualapuu. Both built company towns and imported Japanese and Filipino field laborers, swelling Molokai's population and stabilizing the economy. Many of the native Hawaiians subleased their tracts to the pineapple

Opposite page (top): the untouched coast of West Maui's backside (ROBERT NILSEN); (bottom left): on Kalaupapa Peninsula (ROBERT NILSEN); (bottom right): Iao Needle (ROBERT NILSEN)

Hawaiian Homes Lands of northcentral Molokai
(J.D. BISIGNANI)

growers, and the Hawaiian Homes Act seemed to backfire. Instead of the homesteaders working their own farms, they were given monthly checks and lured into a life of complacency. Those who grew little more than family plots became, in effect, permanent tenants on their own property. Much more importantly, they lost the psychological advantage of controlling their own future and regaining their pride as envisioned in the Hawaiian Homes Act.

Modern Times

For the next 50 years life was quiet. The pineapples grew, providing security. Another large ranch, **Puu O Hoku** ("Hill of Stars") was formed on the eastern tip of the island. It was originally owned by Paul Fagan, the amazing San Francisco entrepreneur who also developed Hana on Maui. In 1955, Fagan sold Puu O Hoku to George Murphy, a Canadian industrialist, for a meager $300,000, about 5% of its present worth. The ranch, under Murphy, became famous for beautiful white Charolais cattle, a breed originating in France.

In the late 1960s "things" started quietly happening on Molokai. The Molokai Ranch sold about 7,000 acres to the Kaluakoi Corp., which they controlled along with the Louisiana Land and Exploration Company. In 1969 the long-awaited Molokai reservoir was completed at Kualapuu; finally west Molokai had

plenty of water. Shortly after Molokai's water problem appeared to be finally under control, Dole Corp. bought out Libby in 1972, lost millions in the next few years, and shut down its pineapple production at Maunaloa in 1975. By 1977 the 7,000 acres sold to the Kaluakoi Corp. was developed, and the Molokai Sheraton (now the Kaluakoi Resort) opened along with low-rise condominiums and home sites selling for a minimum of $150,000. Lo and behold, sleepy old Molokai with the tiny Hawaiian Homes farms was now prime real estate and worth a fortune.

To complicate the picture even further, Del Monte shut down its operations in 1982, throwing more people out of work. In 1986 they did resume planting 250-acre tracts, but now all the pineapple is gone. Recently, a Brazilian company has been experimenting with and exploring the possibilities of marketing new varieties of coffee, and a New Zealand interest in the Molokai Company has brought in sheep and cattle to Molokai. These new avenues of diversification are still in their infant stages but might possibly lead to greater economic stength and stability. Today Molokai is in a period of flux in other ways. There is great tension between developers, who are viewed as "carpetbaggers" interested only in a fast buck, and those who consider themselves the last remnants of a lost race holding on desperately to what little they have left.

Opposite page: a memorable sunset from Kaanapali Beach (ROBERT NILSEN)

ECONOMY

If it weren't for a pitifully bad economy, Molokai would have no economy at all. At one time the workers on the pineapple plantations had good steady incomes and the high hopes of the working class. Now with all the jobs gone, Molokai has been transformed from an island with virtually no unemployment to a hard-luck community where a whopping 80-90% of the people are on welfare. Inexplicably, Molokai also has the highest utility rates in Hawaii. Some say this is due to the fact that the utility company built a modern biomass plant, and didn't have enough biomass to keep it operating—the people were stuck with the fuel tab. The present situation is even more ludicrous when you consider that politically Molokai is part of Maui County. It is lumped together with Kaanapali on Maui's southern coast, one of Hawaii's most posh and wealthy areas, where the vast majority of people are recent arrivals from the Mainland. This amounts to almost no political-economic voice for grass-roots Molokai.

Agriculture

The word that is now bandied about is "diversified" agriculture. What this means is not pinning all hope to one crop like the ill-fated pineapple, but planting a potpourri of crops. Attempts at diversification are evident as you travel around Molokai. Fields of corn, wheat, fruits, and nuts are just west of Kaunakakai; many small farmers are trying truck farming by raising a variety of garden vegetables that they hope to sell to the massive hotel food industry in Honolulu. The problem is not in production, but transportation. Molokai raises excellent crops, but little established transport exists for the perishable vegetables. A barge service, running on a loose twice-weekly schedule, is their only link to the market. No storage facilities on Molokai make it tough to compete in the hotel food business which requires the freshest produce. Unfortunately, vegetables don't wait well for late barges.

Development

A debate rages between those in favor of tourist development, which they say will save Molokai, and grass-roots organizations championed by OHA (Office of Hawaiian Affairs), which insist unchecked tourism development will despoil Molokai and give no real benefit to the people. A main character in the debate is the Kaluakoi Corp., which wants to build condos and sell lots for $500,000 each. They claim that this, coupled with a few more resorts, will bring in jobs. The people know that they will be relegated to service jobs (maids and waiters), while all the management jobs go to outsiders. Most islanders feel that only rich people from the Mainland can afford million-dollar condos, and that eventually they will become disenfranchised on their own island. Claims are that outsiders have no feeling for the *aina* (land), and will destroy important cultural sites whenever growth dictates.

A few years back the Kaluakoi Corp. hired an "independent" research team to investigate Kawakiu Iki Bay, known to be an ancient adze quarry. After weeks of study, this Maui-based research team reported that Kawakiu was of "minor importance." Hawaii's academic sector went wild. The Society of Hawaiian Archaeology dispatched it's own team under Dr. Patrick Kirch, who stated that Kawakiu was one of the richest archaeological areas in Hawaii. In one day they discoverd six sites missed by the "independent" research team, and stated that a rank amateur could find artifacts by merely scraping away some of the surface. Reasonable voices call for moderation. Both sides agree Molokai must grow, but the growth must be controlled, and the people of Molokai must be represented and included as beneficiaries.

THE PEOPLE

Molokai is obviously experiencing a class struggle. The social problems hinge on the economy—the collapse of pineapple cultivation and the move toward tourism. The average income on Molokai is quite low and the people are not consumer-oriented. Tourism, especially "getaway condos," brings in the affluent. This creates friction; the "have-nots" don't know their situation until the "haves" come in and remind them. Today, most people hunt a little, fish, and have small gardens.

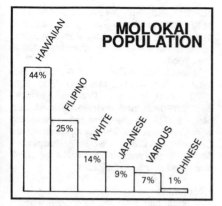

MOLOKAI POPULATION

HAWAIIAN 44%
FILIPINO 25%
WHITE 14%
JAPANESE 9%
VARIOUS 7%
CHINESE 1%

Some are small-time *pakalolo* growers who get over the hard spots by making a few dollars from some back yard plants. There is no organized crime on Molokai. The worst you might run into is a group of local kids drinking on a weekend in one of their favorite spots. It's a territorial thing. If you come into their vicinity they might feel their turf is being invaded, and you could be in for some hassles. All this could add up to a bitter situation except that the true nature of most of the people is to be helpful and friendly. Just be sensitive to smiles and frowns and give people their space.

Ethnic Identity

An underground link exists between Molokai and other Hawaiian communities such as Waianae on Oahu. Molokai is unusual in that it is still Hawaiian in population and influence, with continuing culturally based outlooks which remain unacceptable to Western views. Ethnic Hawaiians are again becoming proud of their culture and heritage, as well as politically aware and sophisticated, and are just now entering the political arena. Few are lawyers, doctors, politicians, or executives; with ethnic identity returning, there is beginning to be a majority backlash against these professions. Among non-Hawaiian residents, it's put down, or unacknowledged as a real occurrence.

Social problems on Molokai relate directly to teenage boredom and hostility in the schools, fueled by a heavy drinking scene. A disproportionate rate of teen pregnancy is a direct byproduct. Teachers unofficially admit that they prefer a student who has smoked *pakalolo* to one who's been drinking. It mellows them out. The traditional educational approach is failing.

Ho'opono'opono is a fascinating family problem-solving technique still very much employed on Molokai. The process is like "peeling the onion" where a mediator, usually a respected *kapuna,* tries to get to the heart of a problem. Similar to group therapy, it's a closed family ordeal, never open to outsiders, and lasts until all emotions are out in the open and all concerned feel "clean."

GETTING THERE

Hawaiian Air, tel. (800) 882-8811, or 567-6510 on Molokai, has regularly scheduled flights throughout the day arriving from all the major islands. Depending on the flight, the planes are either DC-9s or four engine turbo-prop Dashes. There are ten daily 30-min. flights from Honolulu starting at 6:40 a.m. and going until 5:30 p.m. Six of those flights originate in Kauai. The one morning flight from Kahului originates in Hilo on the Big Island.

Aloha Island Air, tel. 833-3219 Oahu, (800) 652-6541 Neighbor Islands, (800) 323-3345 Mainland, offers flights connecting Molokai with Oahu, Kauai, Maui, Lanai, and the Big Island. There are a dozen daily flights from Honolulu from 6:05 a.m. to 5:45 p.m. with five of these originating in Princeville, Kauai. The five daily flights from Hana and Kamuela go through Kahului, from where there are an aditional three daily flights. There are also two direct flights from Kapalua West Maui to Molokai, and two daily from Lanai with an extra on Mon. morning and Fri. evening.

Air Molokai, tel. 553-3636 on Molokai, 877-0026 on Maui, and 556-7217 on Lanai, offers flights connecting Molokai, Kahului, Lanai, and Honolulu. There are twice daily flights between Molokai and Kahului, and four interspersed throughout the day between Molokai and Honolulu. For either trip the fare is $83 roundtrip for adults and $53.25 for children. Having recently opened the connection to Lanai, the frequency of flights between Molokai and the Pineapple Island is still being settled.

Rates are $78 roundtrip for adults and $54.60 for children.

Panorama Air, tel. (800) 352-37321, also runs an extensive commuter schedule between Honolulu, Molokai, Kahului, and Kapalua West Maui airports. There are nine daily flights to Honolulu, four to Kahului, and two to Kapalua. Special *kamaaina* rates are offered.

Molokai Airport
At the Hoolehua Airport you'll find a lounge and lunch counter with not too bad prices, but avoid the hamburgers, which are made from mystery meat. Pick up a loaf of excellent Molokai bread, the best souvenir available, or a lei from the small stand. Tropical, Avis, Dollar, and Budget have rental cars here. If you rent a car make sure to top off in Kaunakakai before returning it. The price is much higher at the car companies' pumps. There is also a state tourist information booth at the terminal where you can pick up brochures, maps, and helpful hints about what to see and do.

By Sea
The only scheduled ferry service to Molokai connects the island to Maui. The *Maui Princess* sails daily from Kaunakakai Wharf at 5:45 a.m. and 3:45 p.m. Roundtrip fares are $42 for adults and $21 for children.

GETTING AROUND

Public Transportation
No public transportation services Molokai. Only one limited shuttle goes between the airport and the Kaluakoi Resort complex on the west end. Operated by Friendly Isle Tours, they run a van throughout the day from 7 a.m. to 5 p.m.; the fare is a stiff $7 per person one way for the 10-mile ride, tel. 567-6177.

Rental Cars
Molokai offers a limited choice of car rental agencies—make reservations to avoid being disappointed. You should arrive before 6 p.m., when most companies close. Special arrangements can be made to pick up your car at a later time. All rental car companies on Molokai are uptight about their cars being used on dirt roads (there are plenty), and strongly warn

against it. No jeeps are available on Molokai at this time, but it's always in the air that one of the car companies will make them available sometime in the future. All companies are at the airport.

Tropical Rent a Car, tel. 567-6118 on Molokai, (800) 367-5140 Mainland, (800) 352-3923 Hawaii, is an island company with the best cars, deals, and reputation for service on Molokai. Ask for their free drive guide and bonus coupons, too. Other companies include **Dollar Rent A Car,** tel. 567-6156; **Budget,** tel. 567-6877; and **Avis,** tel. 567-6814, which offers a free shuttle to their cars.

Hitchhiking
The old thumb gives fair to good results on Molokai. Most islanders say they prefer to pick up hitchers who are making an effort by walking along, instead of lounging by the side of the road. It shows that you don't have a car, but do have some pride. Getting a ride to or from Kaunakakai and the airport is usually easy.

GUIDED TOURS

A few limited tours are offered on Molokai, but they only hit the highlights. If you rent a car, you can get to them just as easily on your own. **Friendly Isle Tours,** tel. 567-6177, runs a "Grand Isle Tour" for $38 that will take you from the Kaluakoi Resort to Maunaloa, a macadamia nut farm, Kalaupapa Lookout, the Halawa Valley, by the fishponds, and to Kaunakakai. A half-day tour runs $18. **Roberts Hawaii,** tel. 552-2988, offers similar tours, but these appeal more to day-trippers from Honolulu. Try to book at least 24 hours in advance.

The newest and one of the most fun-filled cultural experiences that you can have is to spend an afternoon on the **Molokai Wagon Ride,** tel. 558-8380 or 567-6773, cost $33, open daily with rides at noon. The experience starts and ends from a hidden beach just past mile marker 15 on the east end of the island along Route 450. As you drive, look on the right for a sign to Mapulehu Mango Grove; you'll follow the road to a small white house and a picnic area prepared on the beach. The wonderful aspect of this venture is that it is a totally local operation completely devoid of

Larry Helm of Molokai Wagon Ride (J.D. BISIGNANI)

glitz, glamour, and hype. It's run by three local guys: Junior Rawlins the wagonmaster, Kalele Logan who prepares some delicious island dishes and keeps the home fires burning; and Larry Helm, master of ceremonies, guitar player, and all-around funtime merrymaker.

After loading, the wagon leaves the beach and rolls through the **Mapulehu Mango Grove,** one of the largest in the world, with over 2,000 trees. Planted by the Hawaiian Sugar Co. in the 1930s in an attempt to diversify, trees came from all over the world, including Brazil, India, and Formosa. Unfortunately, most of the U.S. was not educated about eating exotic fruits, so the mangos rotted on the tree unpicked, and the grove became overgrown. The ride proceeds down a tree-shrouded lane with Larry Helm playing guitar, singing, and telling anecdotes along the way. In about 20 minutes you arrive at **Ili'Ili'opae Heiau,** among the largest Hawaiian places of worship in the islands (see p. 315). Again Larry takes

over, telling you about the history of the *heiau,* pointing out exotic fruits and plants in the area, and leading you atop the *heiau* for a photo session. You then return to the beach for a demonstration of coconut husking, throw-netting, one of the oldest and most fascinating ways of catching fish, and a hula lesson. You can also count on the Hawaiian tradition of hospitality. After a day in the sun, you won't have to worry about going away hungry. There's always something delicious, like a fish caught from the bay in front of you that Kalele has grilled, along with plenty of fruits and salads, and a fridge full of ice-cold beer and other drinks. The guys know how to treat you, but remember that this is the "real McCoy." It's a day spent hanging out on their turf, so don't expect anything fancy or pretentious.

Helicopter And Airplane Flights

An amazing way to see Molokai is by helicopter. This method is admittedly expensive, but dollar for dollar it is *the* most exciting way of touring and can get you places that no other means can. A handful of companies operate mostly from Maui and include overflights of Molokai. One of the best is **Papillon Helicopters** on Maui, tel. 669-4884. Their 60-min. "West Maui/Molokai" flight costs $185, and the 75-min. "Molokai Odessey," which includes a stop on Kalaupapa, costs $270. Though they'll put a big hole in your budget, most agree they are among the most memorable experiences of their trip.

Scenic Air Tours, tel. 836-0044, has various flights from Maui and Oahu that fly by Molokai, most in combination with other islands and one that takes you to Kalaupapa. These day-long flights are in the $110 range.

SHOPPING

Coming to Molokai in order to shop is like going to Waikiki and hoping to find a grass shack on a deserted beach. Molokai has only a handful of shops where you can buy locally produced crafts and Hawaiiana. Far and away, most of Molokai's shopping is centered along Ala Malama Street in downtown Kaunakakai. All three blocks of it! Here you'll find the island's only health-food store, three very

Halawa Bay (BOB NILSEN)

good food markets, a drugstore that sells just about everything, and a clutch of souvenir shops. Away from Kaunakakai the pickin's get mighty slim. Heading west you'll find the Kualapuu General Store off Route 470 on the way to Kalaupapa, and a sundries store along with a Liberty House at the Kaluakoi Resort on the far west end. The Maunaloa Road (Rt. 460) basically ends in Maunaloa town. Go there! The best and most interesting shop, The Big Wind Kite Factory, is in town and is worth a visit in its own right. Also, in Maunaloa you'll find a market and a small homey restaurant. Heading east from Kaunakakai is another shoppers' wasteland with a few almost dry oases. The Hotel Molokai has one souvenir shop, then comes a convenience store at the Wavecrest Condominium; the last place to spend some money is at the Neighborhood Store, for groceries and snacks, at mile marker 16 on your way to Halawa. That's about it! For a full description see "Shopping" listings in the following travel sections.

BEACHES, OUTDOORS, AND SPORTS

Since Molokai is a great place to get away from it all, you would expect an outdoor extravaganza. In fact, Molokai is a "good news, bad news" island when it comes to sports, especially in the water. Molokai has few excellent beaches with the two best, Halawa and Papohoku, on opposite ends of the island; **Papohoku Beach** on the west end is treacherous during the winter months. Surfers, windsurfers, and Hobie Cat enthusiasts will be disappointed with Molokai except at a few locales at the right time of year, while bathers, sun worshippers, and families will love the small secluded beaches with gentle waves located around the island.

Molokai has a small population and plenty of undeveloped "outback" land. This *should* add up to great trekking and camping, but the land is mostly privately owned and the tough trails are poorly maintained. However, permission is usually granted to trek across private land, and those bold enough to venture into the outback will virtually have it to themselves. Day-hiking trails and lightly used camping areas with good facilities are no problem. Molokai has tame, family-oriented beach parks along its southern shores, superb hunting and fishing, two excellent golf courses, and fine tennis courts. Couple this with clean air, no industrial pollution, no city noise, and a deliciously casual atmosphere, and you wind up with the epitome of relaxation.

Eastern Beaches
The beaches of Molokai have their own temperament, ranging from moody and rebellious to sweet and docile. Heading east from Kau-

nakakai along Route 450 takes you past a string of beaches that varies from poor to excellent. Much of this underbelly of Molokai is fringed by a protective coral reef that keeps the water flat, shallow, and at some spots murky. This area was ideal for fishponds but leaves a lot to be desired as far as beaches are concerned. The farther east you go, the better the beaches become. The first one you come to is at **One Ali'i Park,** about four miles east of Kaunakakai. Here you'll find a picnic area, campsites, good fishing, and family-class swimming where the kids can frolic with no danger from the sea. Next you pass **Kakahaia Beach Park** and **Kumimi Beach,** one of a series of lovely sandy crescents where the swimming is fine. Just before you reach Pukoo, a small dirt road on your right goes to a hidden beach perfect for a secluded swim.

Halawa Bay, on Molokai's far east end, is the best all-around beach on the island. It's swimmable year-round, but be extra careful during the winter months. The bay protects the beach for a good distance; beyond its reach the breakers are excellent for surfing. The snorkeling and fishing are good to very good.

West End Beaches

The people of Molokai favor the beaches on the northwest section of the island. **Moomomi Beach** is one of the best and features good swimming, fair surfing, and pleasurable snorkeling along its sandy, rocky bottom. You have to drive over a dirt road to get there. Although car rental agencies are against it, the only problem is the dust. From Moomomi you can walk west along the beach and find your own secluded spot.

Very few visitors go south from Maunaloa town, but it is possible and rewarding for those seeking a totally secluded area. As you enter Maunaloa town a dirt track goes off to your right. Follow it through the Molokai Ranch gate (make sure to close it behind you). Follow the rugged but passable track down to the coast, the ghost town of Halena, and **Hale O Lono Harbor,** start of the Aloha Week Outrigger Canoe Race. A tough jeep track also proceeds east to collapsing **Kolo Wharf** and very secluded areas. The swimming is only fair because of murky water but the fantasy-feeling of a deserted island is pervasive.

Papohaku and **Kepuhi** beaches just below the Kaluakoi Resort are excellent, renowned for their vast expanses of sand. Unfortunately, they're treacherous in the winter with giant swells and heavy rips which make them a favorite for surfers. Anyone not accustomed to strong sea conditions should limit themselves to sunning and wading only to the ankles. During the rest of the year this area is great for swimming, becoming like a lake in the summer months. North of Kepuhi Bay is an ideal beach named **Kawakiu.** Although it's less than a mile up the coast, it's more than 15 miles away by road. You have to branch off Route 460 and follow the seven-mile dirt track north well before it forks towards the Kaluakoi. This area is well established as an archaeological site and access to the beach was a hard-fought controversy between the people of Molokai and the Molokai Ranch. Good swimming, depending upon tide conditions, and free camping on weekends.

Snorkeling

Some charter fishing boats arrange scuba and snorkeling excursions, but scuba and snorkeling on Molokai is just offshore and you don't need a boat to get to it. **Molokai Fish and Dive** in Kaunakakai, tel. 553-5926, is a full-service snorkel shop. They have very good rental rates, can give you directions to the best spots, and arrange excursions. Beginners will feel safe at **One Ali'i Park,** where the sea conditions are mild, though the snorkeling is mediocre. The best underwater area is the string of beaches heading east past mile marker 18 on Route 450. You'll wind up at Halawa Bay, which is tops. Moomomi Beach on the northwest shore is very good, and Kawakiu Beach out on the west end is good around the rocks, but stay away during winter. Unfortunately, there are no air compressors available on Molokai, so scuba divers will have to bring their full tanks from off island.

Surfing

The best surfing is out on the east end past mile marker 20. Pohakuloa Point has excellent breaks, which continue eastward to Halawa Bay. Moomomi Beach has decent breaks; Kawakiu's huge waves are suitable only for experts during the winter months.

GOLF AND TENNIS

Molokai's two golf courses are as different as custom-made and rental clubs. The **Kaluakoi Golf Course,** tel. 552-2739, is a picture-perfect beauty that would challenge any top pro. Laid out by master links designer Ted Robinson, it's located out at the Kaluakoi Resort. The 6,618-yard, par-72 course winds through an absolutely beautiful setting including five holes strung right along the beach. There's a complete pro shop, driving range, and practice greens. Golf lessons by the hour are also available. Greens fees for 18 holes are $30 for resort guests and $50 for non-guests. The PGA head pro is Marty Keiter, the director Ben Neeley.

Molokai's other golf course is the homey **Ironwood Hills Golf Club.** This rarely used but well-maintained mountain course is nine holes, par 34, and 6,148 yards long. Pay the affordable greens fee, $10 for nine holes and $12 if you want to loop the course twice, to a

groundskeeper who will come around as you play. The course is located up in the hills in Kalae, just before the Meyer Sugar Mill—look for the sign. You can get directions and other information by calling 567-6529 or 567-9097. The Ironwood Golf Course is turning from a frog to a prince. Recent work has concentrated on improving the grounds. Even today there is no building, pro shop, or snack shop, and there are no rental carts available—all these will come in time.

Tennis

The best courts are at the **Kaluakoi Resort**: four lighted Lakloyd courts, free for resort guests and $3/hour for non-guests. They offer a free tennis clinic Fri. at 4 p.m.; call 552-2555, ext. 548, to reserve. Two courts are available at the **Ke Nani Kai Condos,** near the Kaluakoi, which are free to guests. Two courts at the **Wavecrest Condo** east of Kaunakakai on Route 450 are also free to guests. Public courts are available at Molokai High School and at the Community Center in Kaunakakai, but you may have to reserve a spot with the office in the Mitchell Pauole Center next door.

MOLOKAI GOLF AND TENNIS

Course	Par	Yards	Fees	Cart
Ironwood Hills Golf * • Course Del Monte, Molokai, HI 96757 tel. 567-6121	34	6148	$10-9 hole $12-18 hole	—
Kaluakoi Golf Course P.O. Box 26, Mounalo, HI 96770 tel. 552-2739	72	6618	$30	$15

N.B. * = 9 hole course • = no club rentals

These tennis courts are open to the public; call ahead to check availability.

Location	Name of Court	No. of Courts	Lighted
Kepuhi Beach	Kaluakoi Resort	4	Yes
Kaunakakai	Community Center	2	Yes
Molokai High	Hoolehua	2	Yes
Star Route	Wavecrest	2	No

FISHING

The Penguin Banks of Molokai are some of the most fertile waters in Hawaii. Private boats as well as the commercial fishing fleets out of Oahu come here to try their luck. Trolling produces excellent game fish such as marlin, mahi mahi, ahi, a favorite with sashimi lovers, and ono, with its reputation of being the best-tasting fish in Hawaii. Bottom fishing, usually with live bait, yields onaga and uku, a gray snapper favored by local people. Molokai's shoreline, especially along the south and west, offers great bait-casting for ulua and ama ama. Ulua is an excellent eating fish, and with a variance in weight from 15 to 110 pounds, can be a real whopper to catch from shore. Squidding, limu gathering, and torch-fishing are all quite popular and productive along the south shore, especially around the old fishpond sites. These remnants of Hawaii's one-time vibrant aquaculture still produce mullet, the ali'i's favorite, an occasional Samoan crab, the less desirable introduced tilapia, and the better-left-alone barracuda.

Fishing Boats

The Welakaho is a 24-footer specializing in deep-sea fishing, snorkeling, and excursions. Write George Peabody, Box 179, Kaunakakai 96748, tel. 558-8253. The Alyce C. is a 31-foot diesel, fully equipped fishing boat. Captain Joe Reich can take you for full- or half-day charters, and offers whalewatching tours in season; tel. 558-8377. For a larger boat try the Bali Hai, tel. 553-5959. All gear furnished. The **Molokai Fish and Dive Co.** also arranges deep-sea charters as well as excursions and shoreline sailing. Contact them at Box 576, Ala Malama St., Kaunakakai 96748, tel. 553-5926.

Sailing

Molokai is nearly devoid of charter sailboats. However, for those who like to feel the salty sea breeze in their hair, hear the snap of a full-furled sail, or enjoy the sunset from the deck of a sailing ship, try an excursion with **Molokai Charters,** tel. 553-5852, on their 42-foot sloop. Two-hour sunset sails are $30, a half day of sailing is $40, and a full-day trip to Lanai runs $75. Four-person minimum.

HUNTING

The best hunting on Molokai is on the private lands of the 44,000-acre **Molokai Ranch,** open to hunting year-round. However, the enormous fees charged by the Ranch have effectively stopped hunting on their lands to all but the very determined or very wealthy. A permit to hunt game animals (axis deer) costs $400 per day for a guided hunt with an additional fee of $150 per person (up to three). There is an additional $600 preparation fee if you bag a trophy animal. Limited black buck hunting in their Wildlife Park is also permitted, but it's restricted to certain times and locations. Fees are the same, except that the trophy fee here is $1,500! The Molokai Ranch also offers year-round bird hunting for a mere one-time yearly fee of $200. For info contact Molokai ranch, tel. 553-2767.

Public hunting lands on Molokai are open to anyone with a valid state hunting license (see p. 127). Wild goats and pigs can be hunted in various hunting units year-round on weekends and state holidays. Bag limits are two animals per day. Axis deer hunting is limited to licenses drawn on a state public lottery, with a one-buck bag limit per season, which extends for nine consecutive weekends up to and including the last Sunday in April. Hunting game birds (ring-necked pheasants, various quails, wild turkeys, partridges, and francolins) is open on public lands from the first Saturday in November to the third Sunday in January. A special dove season opens in January. For full information, license, and fees (as well as State Park and Forest Service camping permits) contact the Division of Forestry and Wildlife, Puu Kapeelua Ave. near the intersection of Farrington Road (Route 480), Hoolehua, Molokai, HI 96729, tel. 567-5019.

Game Animals

The earliest arrival still extant in the wild is the pua'a (pig). Molokai's pigs live in the upper wetland forests of the northeast, but they can actually thrive anywhere. Hunters say the

axis deer
(LOUISE FOOTE)

meat from pigs that have lived in the lower dry forest is superior to those that acquire the muddy taste of ferns from the wetter upland areas. Pigs on Molokai are hunted mostly with the use of dogs who pin them by the ears and snout while the hunter approaches on foot and skewers them with a long knife.

A pair of **goats** left by Capt. Cook on the island of Niihau spread to all the islands, and were very well adapted to life on Molokai. Originally from the arid Mediterranean, goats could live well without any surface water, a condition quite prevalent over most of Molokai. They're found primarily in the mountainous area of the northeast.

The last free-roaming arrival to Molokai were **axis deer.** Molokai's deer came from the upper reaches of the Ganges River, sent to Kamehameha V by Dr. William Hillebrand while on a botanical trip to India in 1867. Kamehameha V sent some of the first specimens to Molokai, where they prospered. Today they are found mostly on western Molokai, though some travel the south coast to the east.

CAMPING AND HIKING

The best camping on Molokai is at **Pala'au State Park** at the end of Route 470, in the cool mountains overlooking Kalaupapa Peninsula. It's also the site of Molokai's famous Phallic Rock. Here you'll find pavilions, grills, picnic tables, and fresh water. What you won't find are crowds; in fact, most likely you'll have the entire area to yourself. The camping here is free, but you need a permit, good for seven days, from the Dept. of Land and Natural Resouces in Hoolehua, tel. 567-6618. Camping is permitted free of charge at **Waikolu Lookout** in the Molokai Forest Reserve, but you'll have to follow a tough dirt road (Main Forest Road) for 10 miles to get to it. A free permit must be obtained from the Division of Forestry in Hoolehua, tel. 553-5019.

Seaside camping is allowed at **One Ali'i Park** just east of Kaunakakai, and at **Papohaku Beach Park** west of Kaunakakai. These parks have full facilities but due to their beach location and easy access just off the highway they are often crowded, noisy, and bustling. Also, you are a target here for any rip-off artists. A county permit ($3/day) is required and available from County Parks and Recreation in Kaunakakai, tel. 553-3221. The Hawaiian Homelands Dept. in Hoolehua, tel. 567-6104, offers camping at **Kioea Park,** one mile west of Kaunakakai. The permit to this historical coconut grove is $5/day. One of the most amazing royal coconut groves in Hawaii, it's a treat to visit, but camping here, though quiet, can be hazardous. Make sure to pitch your tent away from any coconut-laden trees if possible, and vacate the premises if the winds come up.

Camping is allowed at Halena, Moomomi Beach, Hale O Lono, and Puulakima, for $5 per day for access, and an additional $5 per person for the spot. Contact the Molokai Ranch office. You can also camp free at **Moomomi Beach** on the island's northwest shore on a grassy plot where the pavilion used to be. You can't officially camp at Halawa Bay Beach Park but if you continue along the north side of the bay you'll come to a well-used but unofficial campground fringed by ironwoods and recognizable by old fire pits. This area does attract down-and-outers so don't leave your gear unattended.

Trekking
Molokai should be a hiker's paradise and there are exciting, well-maintained, easily ac-

cessible trails, but others cross private land, skirt guarded *pakololo* patches, are poorly maintained, and tough to follow. This section provides a general overview of the trekking possibilities available on Molokai. Full info is given in the respective "Sights" sections.

One of the most exciting hassle-free trails descends the *pali* to the **Kalaupapa Peninsula.** You follow the well-maintained mule trail down, and except for some "road apples" left by the mules, it's a totally enjoyable experience suitable for an in-shape family. You *must* have a reservation with the guide company to tour the former leper colony (see p. 338).

Another excellent trail is at Halawa Valley, which follows **Halawa Stream** to cascading Moaula Falls, where you can take a refreshing dip if the famous *moo,* a mythical lizard said to live in the pool, is in the right mood. This trail is strenuous enough to be worthwhile and thrilling enough to be memorable.

Molokai Forest Reserve, which you can reach by driving about 10 miles over the rugged Main Forest Road (passable by 4WD only in the dry season), has fine hiking. At road's end you'll find the Sandalwood Measuring Pit. The hale and hearty who push on will find themselves overlooking Waikolu and Pelekunu, two fabulous and enchanted valleys of the north coast.

The most formidable trail on Molokai is the one that completely crosses the island from south to north and leads into **Wailau Valley.** It starts innocently enough at Ili'ili'opae Heiau about 15 miles east of Kaunakakai, but as you gain elevation it gets increasingly tougher to follow. After you've trekked all day, the trail comes to an abrupt halt over Wailau. From here you have to pick your way down an unmarked, slippery, and treacherous 3,000-foot *pali.* Don't attempt this trail alone. It's best to go with the Sierra Club, which organizes a yearly hike, or with a local person who knows the terrain. Wailau Valley is one of the last untouched valleys of bygone days. Here are bananas, papayas, and guavas left over from the last major inhabitants that left early in this century. The local people who summer here, and the one family that lives here year-round, are generous and friendly, but also very aware and rightfully protective of the last of old Hawaii in which they live. If you hike into Wailau Valley remember that in effect you are a guest. Be courteous and respectful and you'll come away with a unique and meaningful island experience.

MOLOKAI: INFORMATION PLEASE

Telephone numbers of service agencies that you might find useful: emergency 911; ambulance 553-5911; police, 553-5355; hospital, 553-5331; County Parks and Recreation, 553-5141; Dept. of Land and Natural Resouces, 567-6618; Division of Forestry, 553-5019; Fire Department, 553-5401; Hawaiian Homelands, 567-6104; library, 553-5483; Office of Hawaiian Affairs (OHA), 553-3611; pharmacy, 553-5790; post office, 553-5845.

KAUNAKAKAI

No matter where you're headed on the island you have to pass through Kaunakakai ("Beach Landing"), the tiny port town that is Molokai's hub. An hour spent walking the three blocks of Ala Malama Street, the main drag, gives you a good feeling for what's happening. As you walk along you might hear a mechanical whir and bump in the background—Molokai's generating plant almost in the middle of town! If you need to do any banking, mailing, or shopping for staples, Kaunakakai's the place. Hikers, campers, and even day-trippers should get all they need here since shops, both east and west, are few and far between, and understocked. Evenings are quiet with no bars or night spots in town, but a cup of coffee or lunch at either the Hop Inn or the Mid-Nite Inn should yield some small talk and camaraderie.

SIGHTS

Head toward the lagoon and you'll see Kaunakakai's wharf stretching out into the shallow harbor for over a half mile. Townsfolk like to drive their cars onto it, but it's much better to walk out. The fishing from the wharf isn't great but it's handy and you never can tell. If you decide to stroll out here, look for the remains of Lot Kamehameha's summer house near the canoe shed on the shore.

Kapuaiwa Coconut Grove
A three-minute drive or a 10-minute walk west brings you to this royal coconut grove planted in the 1860s for Kamehameha V (Lot Kamehameha), or Kapuaiwa to his friends. Kapuaiwa Coconut Grove was originally built because there were seven pools here in which the *ali'i* would bathe, and the grove was planted to provide shade and seclusion. The grove also symbolically provided the king with food for the duration of his life. The grove has diminished from the 1,000 trees originally planted, but more than enough remain to give a sense of grandeur to the spot. Royal coconut palms are some of the tallest of the species, and besides providing nuts, they served as natural beacons pinpointing the spot inhabited by royalty. Now the grove has a parklike atmosphere and mostly you'll have it to yourself. Pay heed to the signs warning of falling coconuts. An aerial bombardment of hefty five pounders will rudely customize the hood of your rental car. Definitely do not walk around under the palms if the wind is up. Just next to the grove is **Kiowea Park,** where camping is

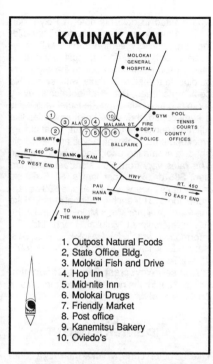

KAUNAKAKAI

MOLOKAI
GENERAL
● HOSPITAL

●GYM POOL
③ ALA ⑨④ MALAMA ST. FIRE TENNIS
⑩ ● DEPT. COURTS
② ⑦⑤⑧⑥ COUNTY
● ● POLICE OFFICES
LIBRARY BALLPARK
RT. 460 GAS● BANK● KAM●
TO WEST END
HWY
RT. 450
PAU TO EAST END
HANA
INN
TO
THE WHARF

1. Outpost Natural Foods
2. State Office Bldg.
3. Molokai Fish and Drive
4. Hop Inn
5. Mid-nite Inn
6. Molokai Drugs
7. Friendly Market
8. Post office
9. Kanemitsu Bakery
10. Oviedo's

Classic Fishponds

Molokai is known for its fishponds, which were a unique and highly advanced form of aquaculture prevalent from at least the early 13th century. Molokai, because of an abundance of shallow, flat waters along its southeastern shore, was able to support a network of these ponds numbering over five dozen during their heyday. Built and tended by the commoners for the royal *ali'i,* they provided succulent fish that could easily be rounded up at any time for a meal or impromptu feast. The ponds were formed in a likely spot by erecting a wall of stone or coral. It was necessary to choose an area that had just the right tides to keep the water circulating, but not so strong as to destroy the encircling walls. Openings were left in the wall for this purpose. **Kalokoeli Pond** is about two miles east of Kaunakakai along Route 450. Easily seen from the road, it's an excellent example of the classic fishpond. You can proceed a few more minutes east until you come to a large coconut grove just a half mile before One Ali'i Beach Park. Stop here for a sweeping view of **Ali'i Fishpond,** another fine example.

ACCOMMODATIONS

Besides camping, Kaunakakai has only three other places to stay. The only other places to lodge on the entire island are way out on the west end at the exclusive Kaluakoi Resort or the three condos that surround it, and at the Wavecrest Condo east of Kaunakakai along the south coast. Head for Kaunakakai and its limited but adequate accommodations if you want to save money. The choices are all along the *makai* side of Route 450 as you head east from town.

Pau Hana Inn

For years the Pau Hana ("Work's Done") Inn had the reputation for being *the* budget place to stay on Molokai. Now all that's left is the reputation, although it's still not too expensive. The new owners are Molokai Beach, Ltd., affiliated with Aston Hotels and Resorts, so many changes have been effected; rooms have been refurbished and the whole place has been spiffed up. Special touches still re-

permitted for $5/day through the Hawaiian Homelands Department (see p. 320).

Church Row

Sin has no chance against this formidable defensive line of churches standing altar to altar along the road across from Kapuaiwa Coconut Grove. A grant from Hawaiian Homelands provides that a church can be built on this stretch of land to any congregation that includes a minimum number of Hawaiian-blooded parishioners. The churches are basically one-room affairs that wait quietly until Sunday morning when worshippers come from all over the island. Let there be no doubt: old Satan would find no customers around here as all spiritual loopholes are covered by one denomination or another. Visitors are always welcome, so come join in. Be wary of this stretch of road—all services seem to let out at the same time on Sunday morning, causing a miniscule traffic jam.

main though, like leaving the windows of the dining room open so that birds can fly in to peck crumbs off the floor. A fireplace is lit in the morning to take the chill off the place; hanging over it is a noble stag with wide perfect antlers and tearful eyes. Outside, in the courtyard bar, a magnificent Bengalese banyan provides the perfect setting to sit back and relax. The waitresses are friendly and go out of their way to make you feel welcome and comfortable. The Pau Hana Bar is a favorite with local people. Friday and Saturday nights feature live music and dancing under the banyan tree. Rates are: Long House, a barracks-type building, clean with newly carpeted floors $45; studio with kitchenette $85; poolside unit $69, oceanfront $85, suite $125, extra person $10, no minimum stay. For reservations write Pau Hana Inn, Box 546, Kaunakakai, Molokai, HI 96748, tel. 553-5342 or (800) 423-6656.

Molokai Shores

This is a relatively new condo with full kitchens, large living rooms, and separate bedrooms, a few minutes east of the Pau Hana. The white walls contrasting with the dark-brown floors are hung with tasteful prints. Plenty of lounge furniture is provided along with a table for outside dining and barbecues. The upper floor of the three-story buildings offers an open-beam ceiling including a full loft. Some units have an extra bedroom built into the loft. The grounds are very well kept, quiet, and restful. The swimming pool fronts the gentle but unswimmable beach, and nearby is a classic fishpond. The only drawback with the Molokai Shores is that the architecture resembles a housing project. It's pragmatic and neat, but not beautiful. Rates are $70-80, one-bedroom deluxe; $100-105 two-bedroom deluxe, two baths; $10 for each additional person. For information write Hawaiian Islands Resorts, Box 212, Honolulu, HI 96810, tel. 531-7595, or (800) 367-7042, or write Molokai Shores, P.O. Box 1037, Kaunakakai, Molokai, HI 96748, tel. 553-5945 or (800) 367-7042.

Hotel Molokai

The hotel was built in 1966 by an architect (Mr. Roberts) enamored with the South Seas, and who wanted to give his hotel a Polynesian village atmosphere. He succeeded. The buildings are two-story, semi-A-frames with sway-backed roofs covered with split wood shingles. Outside staircases lead to the large, airy studios that feature a lanai with swing. No cooking facilities, but a refrigerator in every room is handy. Although the Hotel Molokai is a semi-condo, there are hotel amenities like full maid service, a friendly staff, great dining, weekend entertainment, a well-appointed gift shop, a swimming pool, and a poolside bar. The rates vary from $55 standard, $69 garden, $85 deluxe upper lanais, $115 deluxe family units (sleeps up to six), and $99 oceanfront; add $10 for each additional person. Like the Pau Hana Inn, Motel Molokai is under the new ownership of Molokai Beach, Ltd. For information write Hotel Molokai, Box 546, Kaunakakai, HI 96748, tel. 553-5347 or (800) 423-6656.

Also see **Wavecrest Resort Condominium** (p. 329) for the only other accommodation on this end of the island.

FOOD AND ENTERTAINMENT

Like the hotel scene, Molokai has only a handful of places to eat, but among these are veritable institutions that if missed make your trip to Molokai incomplete. The following are all located on Kaunakakai's main street. Just ask anyone where they are.

Inexpensive

The 50-year-old **Mid-Nite Inn,** tel. 553-5302, was started as a saimin stand by Mrs. Kikukawa, the present owner's mother. People would come here to slurp noodles while waiting for the midnight inter-island steamer to take them to Honolulu. The steamers are gone but the restaurant remains. The Mid-Nite is clean, smells delicious, and looks well-used, which is relative because all of Kaunakakai looks run-down. Large, with Naugahyde atmosphere, it's open for breakfast 5:30 (6 a.m. Sat.) to 10:30 a.m., lunch to 1:30 p.m., dinner 5:30 to 9 p.m., closed Sunday. Breakfasts start at $3.50 for a cheese omelette, and all include hot coffee, tea, or cocoa.

Local families come to socialize at the Mid-Nite Inn.
(J.D. BISIGNANI)

Sandwiches are extremely reasonable, with the Mid-Nite burger, a double two-handed burger with the works and a smile face painted in ketchup, the most expensive at $3. Entrees are inexpensive, like hamburger steak, $4.25, or breaded *mahi mahi*, $7.90. The Mid-Nite has the *only* fresh pizza available on Molokai. Daily specials, like breaded shrimp, cost under $7, and the menu features veal cutlets, teri steak, and flank steak for around $5. No credit cards accepted, but smiles and small talk from travelers are greatly appreciated.

The **Kanemitsu Bakery** has been in business for almost 70 years, and is still run by the same family! The bakery is renowned for its Molokai breads, boasting cheese and onion among the best of its 19 varieties. Small interisland airlines even hold up their planes to get their shipment from the bakery. Mrs. Kanemitsu's cookies are scrumptious, and anyone contemplating a picnic or a day hike should load up. The bakery is open from 5:30 a.m. to 8 p.m., closed Tues., and at the lunch counter in the back you can get eggs, pancakes, and omelettes for breakfast, and local Hawaiian foods for lunch and dinner.

The **Hop-Inn,** tel. 553-5465, is a Chinese restaurant across from the Mid-Nite Inn where you can fill up for $5. The menu is large, but don't let that fool you. Next to many listings is a penciled-in "out," especially the fish dishes. Aside from the usual dishes, lunch plates are

$4.95 and dinner plates $5.95. The funky building at one time housed the Kaunakakai Hotel. The Hop-Inn recently changed hands, but that's about all that changed. They did redecorate, which meant taking down some bad local art that was strung around the place hanging by clothes pins. Some were so dusty that you couldn't make them out. It was better that way. Now the walls have been painted, so there's nothing much of interest to look at while you wait for your chop suey. Open 11 a.m. to 9 p.m.; takeout available.

Oviedo's Filipino Restaurant is the last building on the left along Ala Malama, where every item on the menu is aout $5. Choose from ethnic selections like pork *adobo,* chicken papaya, tripe stew, sweet and sour ribs, pig's feet, mongo beans, and a good selection of ice cream for dessert. Oviedo's is small, run-down, but clean. The decor is worn linoleum floors and Formica tables, and the cooling is provided by breezes that readily pass through large cracks in the walls.

Rabang's Filipino Restaurant looks like a great find, located at the west end of the main drag, but locals say the food is mediocre to awful. A peek through the greasy window reveals an inexpensive ethnic menu thumbtacked to the wall; plate lunches for $3.50. Another tattered sign reads, Rooms for rent, tel. 553-3769, but they're probably no better than the food.

Hotel Restaurants/Entertainment

The **Pau Hana Inn** offers a full menu with most dinners under $15. Start with breakfast for under $5.25, or carbo-load with French toast with meat for $4.75, made from famous Molokai bread dipped in a banana egg batter, coffee and tea included. Lunches are from $5-6, with offerings like chef salad, *mahi mahi*, French dip (sounds contagious!). Full dinners under $15 include chicken or shrimp tempura. The Pau Hana Bar has a daily happy hour with *pu pu* from 4 to 6 p.m., when beer is only $1.75, and well drinks $2.25. Here you can relax under the famous banyan tree for an early evening cocktail. On Fri. and Sat. evenings there is live music and dancing, but there is an annoying cover charge, even for hotel guests who only want a quiet drink.

The **Hotel Molokai** has a salad bar including *soupe du jour* that ranges from mediocre to woeful on any given night. If you hit it lucky, you can combine it with an entree, such as fresh *mahi mahi* (grilled, not deep-fried) for around $16. The best lunch selection is honey-dipped chicken or a French-dipped steak sandwich with cheese and onions. Breakfast from 7 to 10:30 a.m., under $5, and lunch 11:30 a.m. to 2 p.m. The hotel's bar, mostly frequented by local *haole*, has happy hour from 4 to 6 p.m. In the dining room, host Butch Dudoit goes out of his way to make you feel welcome, and island music is provided by the talented Kimo Paleka Thursday through Saturday during the dinner hours. If Kimo looks familiar, you might have seen him at the airport handling bags for Hawaiian Air. With a pair of strong arms by day and gentle guitar fingerings at night, Kimo typifies the Hawaiian man of today.

Grocery Stores And Shopping

For those into wholesome health food, **Outpost Natural Foods** is at 70 Makaena Place near Kalama's Gas Station. It's the only store of its kind on Molokai, but it's excellent. They're open Sun. through Thur. 9 a.m. to 6 p.m., Friday 9 a.m. to 3 p.m., closed Saturday, tel. 553-3377. The fruits and vegetables are locally and organically grown as much as possible. Along with the usual assortment of health foods you'll find bulk grains, granola, nuts, and dried fruits. The jam-packed shelves also hold rennetless cheese, fresh yogurt, non-dairy ice cream, vitamins, minerals, supplements, and a good selection of herbs, oils, and spices. If you can't find what you need, ask Dennis, the general manager. Their Oasis Juice Bar, open 10 a.m to 2 p.m. Mon. to Fri., has huge tofu, avacado, chicken, and cheese sandwiches for up to $3, burritos, $2.50, salad, $3.50, tempeh burger, $3, daily lunch specials for $3.75, and fresh juice and smoothies. There are plans to move the store next door, enlarge the kitchen, and start serving dinner.

For general shopping along Ala Malama Street, the **Friendly Market,** the biggest and best on Molokai, combined with **Takes Variety Store** down the street, and **Misaki's Groceries and Dry Goods** a few steps farther along, sell just about everything in food and general merchandise that you'll require. Across from the Mid-Nite Inn is the mini-mart **C. Paascua Store** for snack items and drinks. For that special evening try **Molokai Wines and Spirits**, which has a small but good selection of vintage wines as well as gourmet treats. Also see **Wavecrest Condo** (p. 329) and the **Neighborhood Store** (p. 330) for shopping at the far east end of Molokai.

Molokai Fish and Dive sounds very practical, and it is, but it has a good selection of souvenirs, T-shirts and fashions, books, and jewelry, along with its fishing equipment. They can give you all the detailed information about fishing and water sports on Molokai, and they rent some water gear like snorkel sets for $7 and boogie boards for $6.

The **Molokai Gallery,** tel. 553-3392, open daily 9 a.m. to 6 p.m., started out as an art shop but has metamorphosed into a clothing store. Inside are millinery, resortwear, T-shirts, jewelry, baubles, and beads.

Molokai Sight and Sound, tel. 553-3600, open daily 9 a.m. to 8:30 p.m, Sunday to 3 p.m., is a video store with records and tapes, camera film, and T-shirts. There is no theater on Molokai, so if you want a movie only the VCR in your condo will serve. They rent camcorders. A few shops up is **Molokai Photo Connection,** tel. 553-9913, open Mon. to Fri. 9 a.m. to 5 p.m., 8 a.m. to noon Sat., closed

Sun., offering film, camera equipment, and one-hour print developing. The **Molokai Hotel Gift Shop** has a good selection of resortwear, sundries, and gift items.

Molokai Drugstore, tel. 553-5790, is open daily 8:45 a.m. to 5:45 p.m., closed Sunday. Don't let the name fool you because they sell much more than potions and drugs. You can buy anything from sunglasses to film, watches, toys, baby food, small appliances, and garden supplies. They have the best selection of film on Molokai, with a very good selection of books, especially on Hawaiiana. Film processing, including slides, takes 48 hours.

For fresh fish check out the Chevron gas station at the light at the crossroads in Kaunakakai. Local fishermen bring their catch here, where it's sold from an ice chest. You'll have to take pot luck on there being any catch that day.

Services And Information

The following phone numbers may be of use in Kaunakakai: Bank of Hawaii, tel. 553-3273; Fire Department, tel. 553-5401; Maui Community College, tel. 553-3605; Molokai Family Health Center, tel. 553-5353; Molokai Drugstore, tel. 553-5790; Molokai General Hospital tel. 553-5331. The Friendly Market has a community bulletin board outside. It might list cars for sale, Hawaiian genealogies, or fund-raising sushi sales. Have a look! There is a laundromat behind the Outpost Natural Food Store.

EAST TO HALAWA VALLEY

The east end of Molokai, from Kaunakakai to Halawa Valley, was at one time the most densely populated area of the island. At almost every milepost is a historical site or point of interest, many dating from pre-contact times. A string of tiny churches attests to the coming of the missionaries in the mid-1800s, and a crash-landing site was an inauspicious harbinger of the deluge of Mainlanders bound for Hawaii in this century. This entire stretch of Route 450 is almost entirely undeveloped, and the classical sites such as *heiau,* listening stones, and old battlegrounds are difficult to find, although just a stone's throw from the road. The local people like it this way, as most would rather see the south shore of Molokai remain unchanged. A determined traveler might locate the sites, but unless you have local help, it will mean hours tramping around in marshes or on hillsides with no guarantee of satisfaction. Some sites such as **Iliilope Heiau** are on private land and require permission to visit. It's as if the spirits of the ancient *kahuna* protect this area.

SIGHTS

It's a toss-up whether the best part about heading out to the east end is the road itself or the reward of Halawa Valley at the end.

Only 30 miles long, it takes 90 minutes to drive. The road slips and slides around corners, bends around huge boulders, and dips down here and there into coves and inlets. The cliff face and protruding stones have been painted white so that you can avoid an accident, especially at night. Sometimes the ocean and road are so close that spray splatters your windshield. Suddenly you'll round a bend to see an idyllic house surrounded by palm trees with a gaily painted boat gently rocking in a protected miniature cove. Behind is a valley or verdant hills with colors so vibrant they shimmer. You negotiate a hairpin curve and there's Lanai and Maui, black on the horizon, contrasted against the waves as they come crashing in foamy white and blue. Down the road chugs a pickup truck full of local people. They wave you a "hang loose" as their sincere smiles light up your already glorious day. Out in one of the innumerable bays are snorkelers, while beyond the reef, surfers glide in exhilarating solitude.

The local people think of the road as "their road." Why not? They use it as a sidewalk, playground, and extension of their back yards. Dogs snooze on it, while the rumps of grazing stock are only inches away from your fender. The speed limit is 35, but go slower and enjoy it more. The mile markers stop at mile 17, then

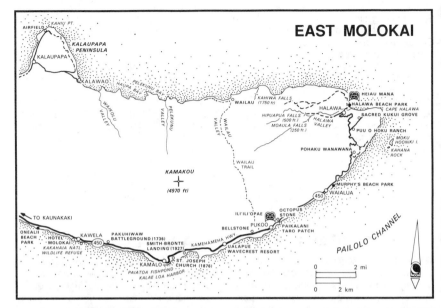

EAST MOLOKAI

four miles farther you come to the best part. Here, the well-tended two-lane highway with the yellow stripe plays out. The road gets old and bumpy, but the scenery gets much more spectacular. It's about nine miles from where the bumpy part begins until you reach the overlook at Halawa Valley. Come with a full tank of gas, plenty of drinking water, a picnic lunch, and your sense of wonder.

One Ali'i Beach Park
Five minutes past the Hotel Molokai brings you to a stand of perhaps 80 coconut palms. Here is a little-used, unnamed beach park with an excellent view of one of the string of fishponds that are famous in this area. One Ali'i Beach Park, only a few minutes farther along, is open for camping. It's too close to the road, not well shaded, and a bit too overused to be comfortable. The swimming here is only fair for those who like a challenging surf, but excellent for families with little children who want calm waters. Clean restrooms and showers are available and the grounds are generally in good shape. Those not camping here would

find it pleasant enough for a day excursion, but it's nothing compared with what's farther east along the road.

About two minutes past One Ali'i, Makanui Road leads up the hillside on the *mauka* side of the road. A two-minute ride up this road exposes the beginnings of a condo development. As you gain the heights (one of the only roads that allows you to do so) you'll have an excellent view of the coastline with a panorama of the fishponds below and Lanai and Maui out to sea. Beyond this road is another just like it, leading into a future subdivision with much the same overview.

Kawela
The Kawela area was a scene of tragedy and triumph in Molokai's history. Here was Pakuhiwa, the battleground where Kamehameha I totally vanquished the warriors of Molokai on his way to conquering Oahu. In nearby Kawela Gulch was Pu'u Kaua, the fortress that Kamehameha overran. The fortress oddly doubled as a *pu'uhonua*, a temple of refuge, where the defeated could find sanctuary. Once the battle

had been joined, and the outcome inevitable, the vanquished could find peace and solace in the very area that they had so recently defended.

Today the area offers refuge as **Kakahai'a County Beach Park and National Wildlife Refuge.** The beach park is not used heavily: it, too, is close to the road. The fishpond here is still used though, and it's not uncommon to see people in it gathering *limu*. This is also an excellent area for coconut trees, with many nuts lying on the ground for the taking. The refuge is an area where birdwatchers can still be captivated by the sight of rare endemic birds.

Wavecrest Resort Condominium
Depending on your point of view the Wavecrest is either a secluded hideaway, or stuck out in the sticks away from all the action. It's east of Kaunakakai on Route 450 just at mile marker 13. You'll find *no* hustle, bustle, anxiety, nightlife, restaurants, or shopping except for a tiny general store that sells the basics for not too much of a mark-up. The Wavecrest sits on five well-tended acres fronting a lovely-to-look-at lagoon which isn't good for swimming. Enjoy a putting green, shuffleboard court, swimming pool, and two lighted tennis courts free to guests. Even if you feel that you're too far from town, remember nothing is going on there anyway. Another attraction is that local

fishermen put in just next to the Wavecrest and sell their fish for unbeatable prices. Guests can barbecue on gas grills provided. Rates: one-bedroom ocean-view $61; car-condo $84; ocean-front $71; car-condo $94, up to two people; two-bedroom oceanview $81, with car $104, two-bedroom oceanfront $91, $114 with car, up to four people; $5 extra person, three-night minimum. Attractive monthly and low-season discounts. For information write Wavecrest Resort, Star Route, Kaunakakai, HI 96748, tel. 558-8101 or (800) 367-2980.

The **Wavecrest Condo Store** is at the entrance of the Wavecrest. They have a small selection of staples and a good selection of beer and wine. More importantly, local fishermen put in at the Wavecrest beach—it's your best chance to get fresh fish at a very reasonable price.

Kamalo To Pukoo
This six-mile stretch is loaded with historical sites. Kamalo is one of Molokai's natural harbors and was used for centuries before most of the island commerce moved to Kaunakakai. **Kamalo Wharf** (turn right down the dirt road at mile marker 10) still occasionally gets large sailboats from throughout the islands. It's a great place to meet local fishermen and inquire about crewing on island-cruising boats. A daily boat for Maui may give you a lift for $20.

picturesque coconut grove and fishpond typical of east Molokai
(J.D. BISIGNANI)

Saint Joseph Church, next in line, was built in 1876 by Father Damien. It's small, no more than 16 by 30 feet, and very basic. Inside is a small wooden altar adorned with flowers in a canning jar. A picture of Father Damien and one of St. Joseph adorn the walls. Outside is a black metal sculpture of Damien.

One mile or so past St. Joseph's is the **Smith and Bronte Landing Site.** These two aviators safely crash-landed their plane here on July 14, 1927, completing the first trans-Pacific civilian flight in just over 25 hours. All you can see is a mangrove swamp, but it's not hard to imagine the relief of the men as they set foot even on soggy land after crossing the Pacific. They started a trend that would bring over four million people a year to the islands. The Wavecrest Condo is nearby at mile marker 13, and if you're not staying there, it's your next-to-last chance to pick up supplies, water, or food before proceeding east.

Before Pukoo are two noteworthy sites. **Kalua'aha Church** looks like a fortress with its tiny slit windows and three-foot-thick plastered walls and buttresses. It was the first Christian church on Molokai, built in 1844 by the Protestant missionaries, Rev. and Mrs. Hitchcock. Used for worship until the 1940s, it has since fallen into disuse. The roof is caving in, but the parishioners have repair plans.

Then comes **Ili'ili'opae Heiau,** one of Hawaii's most famous human-sacrifice temples, and a university of sorcery, as it were, where *kahuna* from other islands were tutored. (For a unique tour of this area, along with nearby Mapulehu Mango Grove, see **Molokai Wagon Ride,** p. 314.) All of the wooden structures on the 267-foot stone platform have long since disappeared. Legend holds that all of the stone was carried across the island from Wai-lau Valley and perfectly fitted in one night of amazing work. Legend also holds that the sorcerers of Ili'ili'opae once sacrificed nine sons of a local *kahuna.* Outraged, he appealed to a powerful shark-god for justice. The god sent a flash flood to wipe out the evil sorcerers, washing them into the sea where the shark-god waited to devour them. The trailhead for Wailau Valley begins at Ili'ili'opae, but since the temple is now on private land it

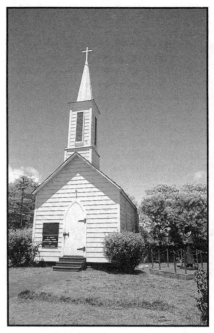

St. Joseph church (BOB NILSEN)

is necessary to receive permission to visit it. The easiest way to go about this is to stop at the "activities desk" of any of the island hotels or condos. They have the right telephone numbers and procedures.

Our Lady of Sorrows Church, another built by Father Damien in 1874 and rebuilt by the parishioners in 1966, is next. Inside are beautiful pen-and-ink drawings of the Stations of the Cross imported from Holland. Just past Our Lady of Sorrows are the **bell stones,** but they're almost impossible to locate.

Before you get to Pukoo, near mile marker 16, is the **Neighborhood Store,** closed Wednesdays. It has changed dramatically from an understocked shack to a modern convenience store. You can buy most picnic items, as well as ice cream, or just pick up a plate lunch at their snack bar for under $6, a bowl of chili for $4, and a full range of burgers for under $2.50. You can even have breakfast for around $3.

Fortunately, Stacy, the young man running the store, is as friendly as ever and will point you in the right direction . . . there's only one: one road in one road out. This is positively the last place to buy anything if you're headed out to the east end.

Across the road is the Manee Canoe Club with its well-tended lawns and tiny inlets. There has recently been a controversy about public access, as there has been for generations, to the beach on the bay across from the canoe club, culminating in public protests and walks to the beach. There is, however, public access to the old wharf area directly west of the canoe club, but it's not good for swimming.

Just past Pukoo is the **octopus stone,** a large stone painted white next to the road. It is believed that this is the remainder of a cave inhabited by a mythical octopus, and that the stone still has magical powers.

On To Halawa Valley

Past Pukoo, the road gets very spectacular. Many blow-your-horn turns pop up as you weedle around the cliff face following the natural roll of the coastline. Coming in rapid succession are incredibly beautiful bays and tiny one-blanket beaches, where solitude and sunbathing are perfect. Be careful of surf conditions! Some of the fruitful valleys behind them are still cultivated in taro, and traditional community life beckons young people from throughout the islands to come and learn the old ways. Offshore is the crescent of **Moku Ho'oniki Island,** and Kanaha Rock in front. The road swerves inland, climbing the hills to the 14,000 acres of **Puu O Hoku** ("Hill of Stars") **Ranch.** People often mistake one of the ranch buildings along the road for a store. It's a print shop, but the people inside can direct you to an overlook where you can see the famous and sacred kukui grove where Lanikaula, one of the most powerful sorcerers of Molokai, is buried. The different-looking cattle grazing these hilly pastures are French Charolais, imported by Puu O Hoku Ranch and now flourishing on these choice pasture lands. The road comes to a hairpin turn where it feels like you'll be airborne. Before you is the magnificent chasm of Halawa Valley with

its famous waterfalls sparkling against the green of the valley's jungle walls. Hundreds of feet below, frothy aquamarine breakers roll into the bay.

Halawa Valley And Bay

This choice valley, rich in soil and watered by Halawa Stream, is believed to be the first permanent settlement on Molokai, dating from the early seventh century. Your first glimpse is from the road's overlook from which you get a spectacular panorama across the half-mile valley to Lamaloa Head forming its north wall, and eastward, deep into its four-mile cleft, where lies Moaula Falls. Many people are so overwhelmed when they gaze from the overlook into Halawa that they don't really look around. Turn to your right and walk only 15 yards directly away from Halawa. This view gives a totally different perspective of a deep V valley and the pounding surf of its rugged beach—so different from the gently arching haven of Halawa Bay. For centuries, Halawa's farmers carved geometric terraces for taro fields until a tidal wave of gigantic proportions inundated the valley in 1946, and left a plant-killing deposit of salt. Most people pulled out and left their homes and gardens to be reclaimed by the jungle.

Follow the paved road into the valley until you see a house that was obviously a church at one time. Cross Halawa Stream and follow the road as far as you can. Here you have a choice of bathing in the cool freshwater stream or in the surf of the protected bay. Don't go out past the mouth of the bay because the currents can be treacherous. This area is great for snorkeling and fishing, one of the only good surfing beaches on Molokai.

Halawa Bay is a beach park, but it's not well maintained. There are toilet facilities and a few dilapidated picnic tables, but no official overnight camping, and the water is not potable. You can bivouac for a night on Puu O Hoku Ranch land at the far north end of Halawa Bay under a canopy of ironwood trees, but be aware that this area attracts rip-offs and it's not safe to leave your gear unattended. Living just near the mouth of the bay is an island fisherman named Glenn and his wife Cathy. Glenn is an expert seaman and knowledgeable about the waters on this side of Molokai. He is willing to take people to Wailau Valley for $30 OW. The only problem is he has no phone, so you'll have to catch him at home or leave a note where he can contact you. Things are less efficient at Halawa Bay, and that's the beauty of it.

Parking

If you're going to Moaula Falls, when you come to the end of the road you'll see a parking lot where a gentleman named Dupre Dudoit sells sodas, chips, etc. He'll promise to watch your car and will give you a map of the walk up the valley for only $5! You can park free, just as long as it's not in his lot. If you have no valuables to lose, forget it. For the $5, this stalwart watchman is just as likely to take a nap or go swimming or fishing as he is to actually watch your car.

Moaula Falls

One of *the* best walks on Molokai (mosquitos!) is to the famous 250- foot Moaula ("Red Chicken") Falls. Depending on recent rainfall it can be very difficult to get there, and although Moaula Falls is quite famous, the trail to it is poorly maintained. Valley residents claim that a full 50% of the people headed for Moaula never get there. They start out wrong! After parking at the turnout at the bottom of the road, follow the dirt road past the little church and the group of houses for about 10 minutes (one-half mile) until it turns into a footpath. Pass a few houses and head toward Halawa Stream, keeping the stone wall on your left. This is where most people go wrong. You must cross the stream to the right-hand bank! If you stay on the left bank, you • get into thick underbrush and miss the falls completely. *Sometimes* an arrow points across the

stream, but it comes and goes at the whim of vandals.

Halawa Stream can be a trickle or torrent, depending upon recent rains. If the stream's hard to cross, Moaula will be spectacular. A minute after crossing, the trail continues under a thick canopy of giant mango trees. The luscious fruits are ripe from early spring to early fall. The trail goes up a rise until it forks at a trail paralleling the stream. Take the left fork and follow the trail on this side of the stream. This entire area shows the remains of countless taro patches and home sites. Groves of *kemani* trees mark the sites where *ali'i* were buried; their tall trunks at one time were used by Hawaiian fishermen and later by sailors as a landmark. Start listening for the falls and let your ears guide you.

Legend recalls that a female lizard, a *moo,* lives in the gorgeous pool at the bottom of the falls. Sometimes she craves a body and will drag a swimmer down to her watery lair. The only way to determine her mood is to place a *ti* leaf (abundant in the area) in the pool. If it floats you're safe, but if it sinks the lady lizard wants company—permanently! Minor gods who live in the rocks above Moaula Falls pool want to get into the act too. They'll drop tiny rocks on your head unless you make an offering (a penny under a *ti* leaf will do).

Before crossing a side stream, a branch trail leads to the right up the cliff where it divides again in about 150 yards. If you take the left fork you come to another pool at the bottom of **Upper Moaula Falls,** but you have to scale the almost vertical cliff face aided only by a wire cable attached to the rock wall. The right fork leads you into heavy brush, but if you persevere for 500 yards or so you come to the cascading brilliance of 500-foot **Hipuapua Falls** and its smaller but totally refreshing swimming hole.

MIDDLE MOLOKAI AND KALAUPAPA

As you head west from Kaunakakai on Route 460 toward Hoolehua Airport you pass fields planted in various crops. These are Molokai's attempt at diversified agriculture since the demise of pineapple a few years ago. Iowa-like corn fields make it obvious that the experiment is working well and has a chance, if the large corporations and the state government get behind it. The cultivated fields give way to hundreds of acres filled with skeletons of dead trees. It's as if some eerie specter stalked the land and devoured their spirits. Farther along and just before a bridge, the **Main Forest Road** intersects, posted for 4WD vehicles but navigable in a standard car during dry weather. This track leads to the Sandalwood Measuring Pit, a depression in the ground which is a permanent reminder of the furious and foolhardy trading of last century. Here too along little-used trails are spectacular views of the lost valleys of Molokai's inaccessible northeast shore.

West on Route 460 another branch road, Route 470, heads due north through Kua-lapuu, Del Monte's diminished pineapple town, to road's end at Palaau State Park, Molokai's best camping area and home to the famous Phallic Rock. Near the State Park entrance is the lookout for Kalaupapa Peninsula and the beginning of the mule trail which switchbacks down over 1,600 feet to the humbling and uplifting experience of Kalaupapa.

Kualapuu

Kualapuu was a vibrant town when pineapples were king and Del Monte was headquartered here, but the vibrancy has flown away. Now, there is Brazilian money and expertise in town trying to grow and market a domestic coffee that would fall somewhere between the aromatic Kona and cheaper South American varieties. Still, it is the only town where you can find basic services on the way to Kalaupapa. Turn left off Route 470 onto Route 480 (Farrington Ave.) and in a minute you'll come to the **Kualapuu Market,** open daily except Sun. from 8:30 a.m. to 6 p.m. Here you'll find a limited selection of food stuffs, fresh produce

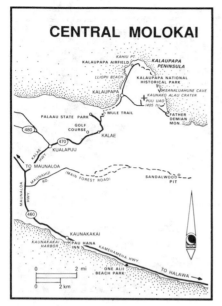

CENTRAL MOLOKAI

and beef, and general merchandise as well as the only gas pump in the area. The post office is located to the rear. Across the street is the **Kualapuu Cookhouse,** tel. 567-6185, serving country-cooked foods of a local variety. The Fri. evening special is pizza, which you can enjoy to live entertainment. Open Mon. to Fri 7 a.m. to 8 p.m., Sat. until 3 p.m., closed Sunday. Notice also the world's largest rubber-lined reservoir across the highway from town. Holding 1.4 billion gallons, its water comes via a five-mile long, eight-foot round tunnel from the water-filled valleys to the east.

Meyer Sugar Mill Museum

Along Route 470, two miles past Kualapuu in the village of Kalae, you'll discover the old R.W. Meyer Sugar Mill (see p. 310), tel. 567-6436. Open daily 10 a.m. to noon, the entrance fee is $2.50 adults, $1 students. Built in 1878, this restored mill, all in functioning order, shows the stages of creating sugar from cane. Within the next few years, a museum and cultural center are in the plans to be added, and they will focus on preserving and demonstrating Hawaiian arts and handicrafts

like quilting, *lau hala* weaving, woodcarving, plus demonstrations of lei-making and hula. The idea is to share and revive the arts of Hawaii, especially those of Molokai, in this interpretive center.

Main Forest Road

After mile marker 3, west on Route 460 from Kaunakakai, is a bridge (just past the Seventh-day Adventist church) with a white fence on both sides. There, heading into the mountains, is a red dirt road called Main Forest or Maunahui Road. Your car rental agency will tell you that this road is impassable except in a 4WD, and they're right—if it's raining! Follow the rutted road up into the hills and you'll soon be in a deep forest of *ohia,* pine, eucalyptus, and giant ferns thriving since their planting early this century. The cool, pleasant air mixes with rich earthy smells of the forest. In just under six miles a sign says Main Forest Road. If you miss this sign look for a Boy Scout camp (also under six miles) that'll let you know that you're on the right road. Ignore many small roads branching off.

After 10 miles, look for the road sign, "Kamiloloa"; park 100 yards past in a turnout and walk five minutes to the **Sandalwood Measuring Pit** *(Lua Na Moku Iliahi).* It's not very spectacular, and this is a long way to go to see a shallow hole in the ground, but the Sandalwood Pit is a permanent reminder of the days of mindless exploitation in Hawaii when money and possessions were more important than the land or the people. Hawaiian chiefs had the pit dug to measure the amount of sandalwood necessary to fill the hold of a ship. They traded the aromatic wood to Yankee captains for baubles, whiskey, guns, manufactured goods, and tools. The traders carried the wood to China where they made huge profits. The trading was so lucrative that the men of entire villages were forced into the hills to collect it, even to the point where the taro fields were neglected and famine gnawed at the door. It only took a few years to denude the mountains of their copious stands of sandalwood, even more incredible when you consider that all the work was done by hand and all the wood was carried to the waiting ships on the coast using the *makaainana* as beasts of burden.

Travel past the Sandalwood Pit for about one mile and you'll come to **Waikolu** ("Three Waters" **Overlook**). From here you can peer down into this pristine valley 3,700 feet below. If rains have been recent, hundreds of waterfalls spread their lace as they fall to the green jungle. The water here seeps into the ground, which soaks it up like a huge dripping sponge. A water tunnel, bored into the valley, collects the water and conducts it for more than five miles until it reaches the 1.4-billion gallon Kualapuu Reservoir. Only drive to this area on a clear day, because the rain will not only get you stuck in mud, but also obscure your view with heavy cloud cover.

Hiking trails through this area are poorly marked, poorly maintained, and strenuous—great qualifications for those who crave solitude and adventure. Up-to-the-minute information and maps are available from the Dept. of Land and Natural Resources in Hoolehua, tel. 567-6618. **Hanalilolilo Trail** begins not far from Waikolu Lookout and winds through high mountain forests of *ohia* until it comes to a breathtaking view of **Pelekunu** ("Foul Smelling, No Sunshine") **Valley**. Don't let the name fool you. Hawaiians lived happily and well in this remote, north shore valley for centuries. Time, aided by wind and rain, has turned the 4,000-foot sea cliffs of Pelekunu into the tallest in the world. Today, Pelekunu is more remote and isolated than ever. No permanent residents, although islanders come sporadically to camp in the summer, when the waters are calm enough to land.

The Hanalilolilo Trail is in the 2,774-acre **Kamakou Preserve**, established by the Nature Conservancy of Hawaii in 1982. It seeks to preserve this unique forest area, home to five species of endangered Hawaiian birds, two of which are endemic only to Molokai. There are 250 species of Hawaiian plants and ferns, 219 of which grow nowhere else in the world. Even a few clusters of sandalwoods tenaciously try to make a comeback. The land was donated by the Molokai Ranch, but they kept control of the water rights. Two officials of the ranch are on the conservancy board, which causes some people to look suspiciously at their motives. The Kamakou Preserve manager is Ed Misaki. Most trails have been mapped and hunting is encouraged throughout most of the area.

Pala'au State Park
Proceed west from Kaunakakai on Route 460 for four miles until it intersects Route 470 heading north to Kualapuu and Pala'au State Park. A few minutes past Kualapuu are the stables for Molokai Mule Rides which take you down to Kalaupapa. Even if you're not planning a mule ride (see below), make sure to stop and check out the beauty of the countryside surrounding the mule stables. Follow the road until it ends at the parking lot for Pala'au State Park.

In the lot, two signs direct you to the Phallic Rock and to the Kalaupapa Overlook (which is not the beginning of the trail down to the peninsula). Pala'au State Park offers the best camping on Molokai although it's quite a distance from the beach (see p. 320). Follow the signs from the parking lot for about 200 yards to **Phallic Rock** ("Kauleomamahoa"). Nanahoa, the male fertility god inhabiting the anatomical rock, has been performing like a champ and hasn't had a "headache" in centuries! Legend says that Nanahoa lived nearby and one day sat to admire a beautiful young girl who was looking at her reflection in a pool. Kawahuna, Nanahoa's wife, became so jealous when she saw her husband leering that she attacked the young girl by yanking on her hair. Nanahoa became outraged in turn, and struck his wife, who rolled over a nearby cliff and turned to stone. Nanahoa also turned to stone in the shape of an erect penis and there he sits pointing skyward to this day. Barren women have come here to spend the night and pray for fertility. At the base of the rock is a tiny pool the size of a small bowl that collects rainwater. The women would sit here hoping to absorb the child-giving mana of the rock. You can still see offerings and of course graffiti. One says Zap—parents thankful for twins maybe.

Return to the parking lot and follow the signs to **Kalaupapa** ("Flat Leaf") **Overlook.** Jutting 1,600 feet below, almost like an afterthought, is the peninsula of Kalaupapa, which was the home of the lost lepers of Hawaii, picked for its remoteness and inaccessibility.

Kalaupapa Peninsula juts out like an appendage from the north coast of Molokai.
(BOB NILSEN)

The almost vertical *pali* served as a natural barrier to the outside world. If you look to your right you'll see the mule trail weedling back and forth down the cliff. Look to the southeast sector of the peninsula to see the almost perfectly round **Kauhako Crater,** the remnant of the separate volcano that formed Kalaupapa.

THE KALAUPAPA EXPERIENCE

No one knew how the dreaded disease came to the Hawaiian Islands, but they did know that if you were contaminated by it your life would be misery. Leprosy has caused fear in the hearts of man since biblical times, and last century King Kamehameha V and his advisors were no exception. All they knew was that lepers had to be isolated. Kalawao Cove, on the southeast shore of Kalaupapa Peninsula, was regarded as the most isolated spot in the entire kingdom. So it was to Kalawao that the lepers of Hawaii were sent to die. Through crude diagnostic testing, anyone who had a suspicious skin discoloration, ulcer, or even bad sunburn was rounded up and sent to Kalawao. The islanders soon learned that once sent, there was no return. So the afflicted hid. Bounty hunters roamed the countryside. Babies, toddlers, teenagers, wives, grandfathers—none were immune to the bounty hunters. They hounded, captured, and sometimes killed anyone that had any sort of skin

ailment. The captives were ripped from their villages and loaded on a ship. No one would come near the suspected lepers on board and they sat open to the elements in a cage. They were allowed only one small tin box of possessions. As the ship anchored in the always choppy bay at Kalawao, the cage was opened and the victims were tossed overboard. Their contaminated cage was followed by a few sealed barrels of food and clothing that had been collected by merciful Christians. Those too weak or sick or young drowned; the unlucky made it to shore. The crew waited nervously with loaded muskets in case any of the howling, walking nightmares on shore attempted in their delirium to board the ship.

Hell On Earth

Waiting for the newcomers were the forsaken. Abandoned by king, country, family, friends, and apparently the Lord himself, they became animals—beasts of prey. Young girls with hardly a blemish were raped by reeking deformed men in rags. Old men were bludgeoned, their tin boxes ripped from their hands. Children and babies cried and begged for food, turning instinctively to the demented women who had lost all motherly feelings. Finally too weak even to whimper, they died of starvation. Those victims that could made rude dwellings of sticks and stones, while others lived in caves or on the beach open to the elements.

Finally, the conscience of the kingdom was stirred in 1866: the old dumping ground of Kalawao was abandoned and the lepers were exiled to the more hospitable Kalaupapa Peninsula, just a few hundred yards to the west.

The Move To Kalaupapa

The people of the sleepy village of Kalaupapa couldn't believe their eyes when they saw the ravaged ones. But these lepers now sent to Kalaupapa were treated more mercifully. Missionary groups and *kokua* ("helpers") provided food and rudimentary clothing. An end was put to the lawlessness and depravity. Still, the lepers were kept separate. For the most part they lived outdoors or in very rude huts. They never could come in direct contact with the *kokua*. If they met a healthy person walking along a path, they had to grovel at the side. Most fell to the ground, hiding their faces and attempting to crawl like beaten dogs under a bush. Many *kokua*, horrified by Kalaupapa, left on the next available boat. With no medical attention, death was still the only release from Kalaupapa.

Light In Hell

It was by accident or miracle that **Joseph Damien de Veuster**, a Catholic priest, came from Belgium to Hawaii. His brother, also a priest, was supposed to come but he became ill and Father Damien came in his place. Damien spent a few years in Hawaii, building churches and learning the language and ways of the people, before he came to Kalaupapa in 1873. What he saw touched his heart. He was different from the rest, having come with a sense of mission to help the lepers and bring them hope and dignity. The other missionaries saw Kalaupapa not as a place to live, but to die. Damien saw the lepers as children of God, who had the right to live and be comforted. When they hid under a bush at his approach, he picked them up and stood them on their feet. He carried water all day long to the sick and dying. He bathed their wounds and built them shelters with his own two hands. When clothes or food or materials ran short, he walked topside and begged for more. Other church groups were against him and the gov-

Father Damien just weeks before his death from Hansen's Disease

ernment gave him little aid, but he persevered. Damien scraped together some lumber and fashioned a flume pipe to carry water to his people, who were still dying mainly from pneumonia and tuberculosis brought on by neglect. Damien worked long days alone, until he dropped exhausted at night.

Father Damien built **St. Philomena Church** and invited the lepers inside. Those grossly afflicted could not control their mouths, so spittle would drip to the floor. They were ashamed to soil the church, so Damien cut squares in the floor through which they could spit onto the ground. Slowly a light began to shine in the hearts of the lepers and the authorities began to take notice. Conditions began to improve, but there were those that resented Damien. Robert Louis Stevenson visited the settlement, and after meeting Damien wrote an open letter that ended " . . . he is my father." Damien contracted leprosy, but by the time he died in 1889 at age 49, he knew his people would be cared for. In 1936, Damien's native Belgium asked that his remains be returned. He was exhumed and his remains sent home, but a memorial still stands where he was interred at Kalaupapa.

The Light Grows Brighter

Mother Mary Ann Cope, a Franciscan nun from Syracuse, New York, arrived in 1888 to carry on Damien's work. In addition, many missionary groups sent volunteers to help at the colony. Thereafter the people of Kalaupapa were treated with dignity and given a sense of hope. In 1873, the same year that Damien arrived at Kalaupapa, Norwegian physician Gerhard Hansen isolated the bacteria that causes leprosy, and shortly thereafter the official name of the malady became Hansen's disease. By the turn of this century, adequate medical care and good living conditions were provided to the patients at Kalaupapa. Still, many died, mostly from complications such as TB or pneumonia. Families could not visit members confined to Kalaupapa unless they were near death, and any children born to the patients—who were now starting to marry—were whisked away at birth and adopted, or given to family members on the outside. Even until the 1940s people were still sent to Kalaupapa because of skin ailments that were never really diagnosed as leprosy. Many of these indeed did show signs of the disease, but there is always the haunting thought that they may have contracted it after arrival at the colony. Jimmy, one of the guides for Damien Tours, was one of these. He had some white spots as a child that his Hawaiian grandmother would treat with herbs. As soon as she stopped applying the herbs, the spots would return. A public health nurse at school saw the spots, and Jimmy was sent

to Kalaupapa. At the time he was given only 10 years to live.

In the mid-1940s sulfa drugs were found to arrest most cases of Hansen's disease, and the prognosis for a normal life improved. By the 1960s further breakthroughs made Hansen's disease noncontagious, and the patients at Kalaupapa were free to leave and return to their homes. No new patients were admitted, but most, already living in the only home they'd ever known, opted to stay. The community of resident patients is less than 100 today, and the average age is about 60. Kalaupapa will be turned into a national park soon, but the residents are assured a lifetime occupancy.

Getting There

It shouldn't be a matter of *if* you go to Kalaupapa, but *how* you go. You have choices. You can fly, ride a mule, walk, or walk and fly. No matter how you go, you *cannot* walk around Kalaupapa unescorted. You must take an official tour, and children under 16 are not allowed. If you're going by mule or air, arrangements are made for you by the companies, but if you're walking you have to call ahead to one of the following, who will make arrangements to meet you at the entrance to the community. Contact **Damien Tours,** tel. 567-6171, or **Ike's Scenic Tours,** tel. 567-6437. Both tour companies charge $17.50 for

A mule ride is one way to get down to Kalaupapa.
(BOB NILSEN)

a fascinating, four-hour tour conducted by one of the residents. Definitely worth the money; the insight you get from the resident tour guide is priceless and unique. No food or beverages, except water, are available to visitors, so make sure to bring your own.

Molokai Mule Rides, tel. 567-6088 or (800) 843-5978, rents mules to take you down the 1,600-foot *pali* for $85 including lunch and the tour of Kalaupapa. The mules are sure-footed, well-trained animals which expertly negotiate 26 hairpin switchbacks on the trail to the bottom. Restrictions say riders must weigh under 225 pounds and be in generally good physical condition. The stables are clearly marked on Route 470.

If you're walking to Kalaupapa, follow the mule trail, cut by Manuel Farinha in 1886. Go abou 200 yards past the stables and look for a road to the right. Follow this track down past pastureland to the trailhead, where there is a small metal building with an odd sign that reads Advance Technology Center Hawaii USA. Here as well there is an overgrown observation point for the peninsula. The mules leave by 9 a.m., so make sure you go ahead of them! The three-mile trail goes down the steep north face of the pali, is well maintained, but is only mildly strenuous. It will be rutted and muddy in spots but you'll notice gravel all the way down that is carried by the bagful and deposited daily by the mules. While on the subject, be careful of other mule deposits as you walk along. Don't expect your feet to stay clean. Wear hiking boots, sneakers, or even zoris if you are used to hiking in them. It takes just about an hour and a half to make the descent. Once down, wait at the grassy clearing. Your tour guide will pick you up there by 10:30 a.m.

You can fly in and out, or out only, which is a good alternative and relatively cheap. Aloha Island Air charges $40 RT, or $20 OW from Hoolehua Airport, topside Molokai to Kalaupapa, operating two flights at 8:50 a.m. and 9:55 a.m. The only return flight out is at 2:40 p.m. They also have a direct flight from Kahului, Maui at 9:05 a.m., $45 each way. When you fly in you must still arrange for the ground tour through Damien or Ike's (see above) before you will be sold a ticket. Ocassionally, Scenic Air Tours runs a trip to Kalaupapa in combination with a Maui fly-by for $109. Papillon Helicopters, tel. 669-4884, flies over Kalaupapa from Maui but doesn't land; they charge $185 per person. If you decide to fly, notice the breakers at the end of the runway sending spray 90 feet into the air. The pilots time their take-off to miss the spray!

MOLOKAI'S WEST END

Long before contact with the Europeans, the west end of Molokai was famous throughout the Hawaiian Islands. The culture centered on Maunaloa, the ancient volcanic mountain that formed the land. On its slopes the goddess Laka learned the hula from her sister and spread its joyous undulations to all the other islands. Not far from the birthplace of the hula is Kaluakoi, one of the two most important adze quarries in old Hawaii. Without these stone tools, no canoes, bowls, or everyday items could have been fashioned. Voyagers came from every major island to trade for this perfect stone of Kaluakoi. With all this coming and going, the always small population of Molokai needed godly protection. Not far away at Kalaipahoa, the "poison wood" sorcery gods of Molokai lived in a grove that supposedly sprouted to maturity in one night. With talismans made from this magical grove, Molokai kept invading warriors at bay for centuries.

Most of the island's arable land is out here. The thrust west began with the founding of the Molokai Ranch, whose 70,000 acres make up 50% of the good farmland on the island. The ranch was owned last century by Kamehameha V, and after his death was sold to private interests who began the successful raising of Santa Gertrudis cattle imported from the famous Texas King Ranch. The ranch still employs *paniolo,* with the life of riding the range and rodeo still strong.

The Northwest

The northwest section of Molokai, centered at **Hoolehua,** is where the Hawaiian Homes parcels are located. The entire area has a feeling of heartland America, and if you ignore the coastline in the background you could easily imagine yourself in the rolling hills of Missouri. Don't expect a town at Hoolehua. All that's there is a little post office and a government office.

The real destination is **Moomomi** ("Jeweled Reptile") **Beach**. Follow Route 460 until it branches north at Route 480 a mile east of the airport. Follow Route 480 until it turns left onto Farrington Ave. in Hoolehua, and contine for about four miles until it turns into a red dirt road. Go for about five minutes, bearing right

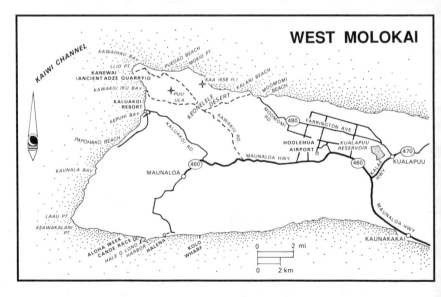

WEST MOLOKAI

at the main intersection until you come to an area where a foundation remains of a burned bathhouse. Below you is Moomomi. This area is a favorite with local people who come here to swim, fish, and surf. The swells are good only in winter, but the beach becomes rocky at this time of year. The tides bring the sand in by April and the swimming until November is good.

Moomomi Beach goes back in Hawaiian legend. Besides the mythical lizards that inhabited this area, a great shark god was born here. The mother was a woman who became impregnated by the gods. Her husband was angry that her child would be from the spirit world, so he directed her to come and sit on a large rock down by the beach. She went into labor and began to cry. A tear, holding a tiny fish, rolled down her cheek and fell into the sea and became the powerful shark-god. The rock upon which his mother sat is the large black one just to the right of the beach.

If you feel adventurous you can head west along the beach. Every 10 minutes or so you come to a tiny beach that you have entirely to yourself. Being so isolated, be extremely careful of surf conditions. About two miles west of Moomomi is **Keonelele,** a miniature desert of sand dunes. The wind whips through this region and carries the sand to the southwest shore. Geologists haunt this area trying to piece together Molokai's geological history. The Hawaiians used Keonelele as a burial site, and strange footprints found in the soft sandstone supposedly foretold the coming of white men. Today, Keonelele is totally deserted; although small, it gives the impression of a vast wasteland. Camping (no permit necessary) is allowed on the grassy area overlooking Moomomi Beach, but since a fire claimed the bathhouse, there are no showers or toilets. Water is available from a tap near the old foundation. You will be personally safe camping here, but if you leave gear unattended it could walk off.

Kawakiu Beach

This secluded and pristine beach on the far northwestern corner of Molokai was an item of controversy between the developers of the Kaluakoi Corporation and the grass-roots ac-

Jonathon displays a hand-crafted kite.
(J.D. BISIGNANI)

tivists of Molokai. For years access to the beach was restricted, and the Kaluakoi Corp. planned to develop the area. It was known that the area was very important during pre-contact times, and rich in unexplored archaeological sites. The Kaluakoi Corp. hired a supposed team of "experts" that studied the site for months, and finally claimed that the area had no significant archaeological importance. Their findings were hooted at by local people and by scholars from various institutions who knew better. This controversy resulted in Kawakiu Beach being opened to the public with plans of turning it into a beach park; the archaeological sites will be preserved.

The swimming at Kawakiu is excellent with the sandy bottom tapering off slowly. To get there, keep your eyes peeled as you follow Route 460 past the airport for about four miles. The seven miles of dirt road from here are dusty and not well maintained, but passable at most times. Just before you reach Kawakiu the road branches—go right to the beach.

Maunaloa

Most people heading east-west between Kaunakakai and the Kaluakoi Resort never make it into Maunaloa town. That's because Route 460 splits just east of Maunaloa, and Kaluakoi Road heads north toward the Kaluakoi Resort and away from the town. With the pineapple gone and few visitors coming, the town is barely hanging on. Maunaloa is a wonderful example of a plantation town. As you pull in, there's a little patch of humble but well-kept workers' houses carved into a field. In front you're likely to see a tethered horse, a boat, or glass fishing floats hanging from the lanai. Overhead you may see a kite flying—that's your beacon that you've arrived in Maunaloa. The townsfolk are friendly and if you're looking for conversation or a taste of Hawaiian history, the old-timers hanging around under the shaded lean-to near the post office are just the ticket.

A good reason to make the trek to Maunaloa is to visit the **Big Wind Kite Factory**, tel. 552-2364, owned and operated by Jonathan Sosher and his wife Daphane. It's amazing to note that the handcrafted kites from this down-home cottage industry are the same ones that sell at Honolulu's slick Ala Moana Mall, the Royal Hawaiian Shopping Arcade, and at the Cannery Shopping Center on Maui. All are made on the premises by Jonathan, Daphane, and a few workers, who come up with designs like panda bears, rainbow stegosauruses, and hula girls in ti-leaf skirts—ask for a free factory tour. Jonathan will give you a lesson in the park next door on any of the kites, including the two string-controllable ones. Prices range from $10 to $200 for a rip-stop nylon kite; they make beautiful, easily transportable gifts that'll last for years.

The shop itself is ablaze with beautiful colors, as if you've walked into the heart of a flower. This is a happy store. Part of it, **The Plantation Gallery**, sells a variety of crafts by local artists—Hawaiian quilt pillow cases, Pacific isle shell jewelry, scrimshaw (on deerhorn), black coral necklaces, earrings, bracelets, boxes, and other wood objects. Island cypress, Japanese *sugi* from a local tree, and *milo* have been carved by a local artist named Robin. **Bali Hale,** part of the boutique, has batiks, Balinese masks, woodcarvings, and sarongs; especially nice are carved mirror frames of storks, birds, and flowers. And if you just can't live without a blow gun from Irian Jaya, this is the place. After you've run through a million tourist shops and are sick of the shell leis, come here to find something truly unique. The Big Wind Kite Factory is *the* most interesting shop on Molokai.

Maunaloa General Store, tel. 552-2868, open daily 9 a.m. to 8 p.m., and Sunday 10 a.m. to 8 p.m., has been taken over by the Hansa family from India via Connecticut. It's well-stocked store where you can pick up anything that you'll need if you'll be staying in one of the condos at Kaunakakai. You can buy liquor, wine, beer, canned goods, meats, and vegetables. The same family has also purchased **Jo Jo's,** tel. 552-2803, the only restaurant in town—have a look at the restaurant menu posted in the general store. Jo Jo's is open for lunch and dinner every day except Wed. and Sun., but these hours may change with the season and influx of tourists so be sure to call ahead to inquire about the current days and hours of business. Most items go for less than $7, like macaroni salad and Korean ribs, $6.99, chopped steak, $4.75, cheeseburgers and hamburgers for around $2.50, teri-plate for $4.75. Every day a special sandwich costs under $3. The cafe is in an old board- and-batten plantation building. The inside was a bar at one time, and it's neat and clean as a pin. Check out the architecture while getting a feeling for a simpler Hawaii.

The South Coast

If wanderlust draws you to the secluded beaches around **Halena** on the south shore, make sure to ask one of the local old-timers hanging around Maunaloa about road conditions (which change with every storm). Before you enter town proper a dirt road is to the right. Follow it for just under three miles to the unlocked gate of the Molokai Ranch. Proceed, closing the gate behind you, and bounce and rattle down the road for just under two miles. At the fork, go right and then almost immediately left. Follow the road to the end and then walk a few hundred yards to Halena. You'll have the entire area and shoreline to yourself. Ask at the ranch office if you want to camp here. Obviously you must bring all the food and water you'll require. If you go west from Halena, you'll come to **Hale O Lono** in about one mile, the launch point for the annual outrigger canoe race to Oahu. There's an old harbor area from which sand from Papohaku Beach was shipped to Oahu for building purposes. If you go east back at the fork to Halena, you'll come to the dilapidated **Kolo Wharf** (two miles), from which Molokai once shipped its pineapples. The road is even more remote and rougher, so getting stuck will mean a long hike out and an astronomical towing charge. It's best to walk from Halena along the coast.

The Kaluakoi Resort And West End

Much of the west end of Molokai is the Kaluakoi Resort, owned by the Louisiana Land and Exploration Company. The complex includes the Kaluakoi Resort, Ke Nai Kai Condominiums, world-famous Kaluakoi Golf Course, private home sites, and Papohaku, Hawaii's largest white-sand beach. (It's illegal even to mention the word "budget" in this area. If you do, you'll be pilloried in stocks made from melted credit cards and lashed with a Gucci whip!)

Accommodations And Restaurants

The **Kaluakoi Hotel and Golf Course,** Box 1977, Maunaloa, HI 96770, tel. 552-2555 or (800) 367-6046, is a showcase hotel and the destination point for most of the people coming to Molokai. The low-rise buildings are made primarily of wood. The architecture is superb and blends harmoniously with the surrounding countryside. The grounds are impeccable and all the trees and shrubbery provide a miniature botanical tour. All rooms have color TVs, refrigerators, and those on the second floor have open-beam construction. Most rooms sit along the fairways of the golf course and have at least a partial ocean view. Because of the constant

cool breezes, no air-conditioning is necessary, but there are ceiling fans.

The rooms, all newly refurbished, are done in light pastels and earth colors, all very harmonious and pleasing to the senses. Dynamic color is provided by the large windows that open onto the fairways and the sea beyond. Actually, for a first-class hotel the rates aren't bad. The least expensive room is $85, and includes greens fee at the Kaluakoi Golf Course. The rates go up to $200 for a one-bedroom ocean cottage suite, but many hotels on the other islands change a lot more for a lot less. The best deal at the Kaluakoi is the **Colony Club.** This package includes rooms, daily cocktails, full American plan, and all activities.

Consult the lobby bulletin board for happenings at the resort, and the activities desk for what's doing around the island. Make sure to avail yourself of the in-house activities. You can have a ball playing volleyball, swimming at the beach or in the freshwater pool, taking nature walks, riding very good bicycles, or taking lei-making and hula lessons. Every Sat. there's a Hawaiian handicrafts and art presentation in the courtyard, with demonstrations on quilting, weaving, woodwork, pottery, and coconut fiber art. On Fri. evenings, a Polynesian revue of music and dance is performed in the garden for $8. And on Tues. a Molokai-style "picnic" with entertainment is given; cost is $22 per person, reservations requested. In the evenings there are free top-rated movies with popcorn. The bar offers daily specials, usually exotic drinks at great prices.

Four lighted tennis courts are free to guests, open 7 a.m. to 10 p.m. The pro shop offers instruction. A small Liberty House provides limited shopping along with a sundries store selling snacks, magazines, and liquor, and a jewelry shop. Past the tenth hole, which would basically be the far north end of the property, you'll overlook a very private beach. No rules or prying eyes here, so if you would like to swim au naturel, this is the place.

The Kaluakoi's **Ohia Lounge** (reservations a must, and long pants and collared shirt required!) is the *best* restaurant on the island. The gourmet food is prepared by Tim and Hillary, a husband-and-wife team who specialize in making all the pastries, jams, and jellies on the premises. You'll be delighted by the range of culinary delights, but don't overlook a simple and light meal of salad bar and bread. The fresh-baked Molokai bread from Kanemitsu's bakery is scrumptious with crisp greens topped with the hot mustard-honey dressing. For a great dining experience, choose the fresh catch cooked to your liking. The most delectable, *opakapaka,* is pan-fried in drawn butter and topped with chopped macadamia nuts. The rack of lamb is so delicious that even in this fancy room people will understand if you run your bread around your plate to soak up the last of the savory juices. You'll pray to have a little extra room for the desserts. Cappuccino Krunch, a light fluffy coffee-flavored pie, is one that will make your taste buds chuckle with glee. The resort's other restaurant, the **Paniolo Broiler,** is only open weekends for dinner; Fri. it serves a seafood buffet and on Sat. a prime rib buffet. The garden-side snack bar is open daily 11 a.m. to 5 p.m. and from 6 to 8 p.m. on Fri. and Sat., and sells sandwiches, burgers, and plate lunches, with most everything under $4.50.

Some of the units at the resort complex, collectively called the **Kaluakoi Villas,** are managed by the Castle Group. Each studio and cottage has been tastefully decorated and includes a color television, lanai, and refrigerator, and guests can use the resort's restaurants and all its recreational facilities. Rates range from $85 for a studio to $185 for a suite. Call (800) 525-1470, or write Kaluakoi Villas, P.O. Box 200, Maunaloa, Molokai, HI 96770.

Ke Nani Kai Condos are *mauka* of the road leading to the Kaluakoi Resort and they charge from $105-115 for one of their fully furnished studios; two bedrooms cost from $125-135. The complex is new so all studios are in excellent condition. Write Ke Nani Kai, Box 126, Molokai, HI 96770, tel. 552-2761 or (800) 888-2791.

Paniolo Hale is another condo complex nearby. Studios start at $75, $95 for one bedroom, $115 two bedroom. Two-bedroom units have a hot tub and enclosed lanai. Guests of the Paniolo Hale can use the Kaluakoi Re-

sort's tennis courts for a small fee. Write Paniolo Hale, Box 146, Molokai, HI 96770, tel. 552-2731 or (800) 367-2984.

Excursions And Attractions

The **Molokai Ranch Wildlife Park** is a one-square-mile preserve on the ranch lands, open to the public, which houses over 800 grazing animals from Africa and India. Among the exotic occupants are giraffes, kudu, ibex, antelopes, and ostrichs that have lost their fear of man and can be seen at very close quarters. Bring your camera! The environment and grazing of west Molokai is almost identical to the animals' home in East Africa; because of this and the exemplary care afforded by the caretaker, Pilipo Solotario, the wildlife park has one of the best reputations in the world. Weather permitting, tours depart from the Kaluakoi Resort, four times daily from 8 a.m. to 3 p.m. The tour costs $25 for adults and $10 for children under 12. Reservations required 24 hours in advance; minimum of four persons, maximum of eight. For information call 552-2555 or 552-2767.

Papohaku Beach, the best attraction in the area, doesn't have a price tag. Papohaku Beach is the giant expanse of white sand running south from the Kaluakoi Resort. The sands here are so expansive that they were dredged and taken to Oahu in the 1950s. During the winter months a great deal of sand is stripped away and large lava boulders and outcroppings are exposed. Every spring and summer the tides carry the sand back and deposit it on the enormous beach. Camping is permitted at the **Papohaku County Beach Park.** Pick up your permit at the Mitchell Pauole Center in Kaunakakai, tel. 553-3221, before you come all the way out here. Here you'll find a large grassy play area, toilets, showers, picnic tables, grills for cooking, and a virtually empty beach. A sign on the road past the park tells you to watch out for wild turkeys! This road runs through a future home development area, with several beach access roads and parking areas that lead to other spots along this huge expanse of beach.

BOOKLIST

INTRODUCTORY

Aloha, The Magazine of Hawaii and the Pacific. Honolulu, Hi.: Davick Publications. This excellent bi-monthly magazine is much more than just slick and glossy photography. Special features may focus on sports, the arts, history, flora and fauna, or just pure island adventure. *Aloha* is equally useful as a "dream book" for those who wish that they could visit Hawaii, and as a current resource for those actually going. One of the best for an overall view of Hawaii, and well worth the subscription price.

Barrow, Terrence. *Incredible Hawaii.* Rutland, Vt.: Tuttle, 1974. Illustrated by Ray Lanternman. A pocket-sized compilation of oddities, little-known facts, trivia, and superlatives regarding the Hawaiian Islands. Fun, easy reading, and informative.

Cohen, David, and Rick Smolan. *A Day in the Life of Hawaii.* New York: Workman, 1984. On December 2, 1983, 50 of the world's top photojournalists were invited to Hawaii to photograph a variety of normal life incidents occurring on that day. The photos are excellently reproduced, and are accompanied by a minimum of text.

Day, A.G., and C. Stroven. *A Hawaiian Reader.* New York: Appleton, Century, Crofts, 1959. A poignant compilation of essays, diary entries, and fictitious writings that takes you from the death of Captain Cook through the "statehood services."

Emphasis International. *On the Hana Coast.* Honolulu: Emphasis International Ltd., 1983. Text by Ron Youngblood. Sketches of the people, land, legends, and history of Maui's northeast coast. Beautifully illustrated with line drawings, vintage photos, and modern color work. Expresses true feeling and insight into people and things Hawaiian by letting them talk for themselves. An excellent book capturing what's different and what's universal about the people of the Hana District.

Friends of the Earth. *Maui, The Last Hawaiian Place.* New York: Friends of the Earth, 1970. A pictorial capturing the spirit of Maui in 61 contemporary color plates along with a handful of historical illustrations. A highly informative as well as beautiful book printed in Italy.

Island Heritage Limited. *The Hawaiians.* Norfolk Island, Australia: Island Heritage Ltd., 1970. Text by Gavan Daws and Ed Sheehan. Primarily a "coffee table" picture book that lets the camera do the talking with limited yet informative text.

Hopkins, Jerry. *The Hula.* Edited by Rebecca Crockett-Hopkins. Hong Kong: APA Productions, 1982. Page after page of this beautifully illustrated book sways with the dynamic vibrancy of ancient Hawaii's surviving artform. Hopkins leads you from dances performed and remembered only through legends to those of past and present masters captured in vintage and classic photos. For anyone interested in the history and the spirit of Hawaii portrayed in its own unique style of expressive motion.

Judd, Gerritt P., comp. *A Hawaiian Anthology.* New York: MacMillan, 1967. A potpourri of observations from literati such as Twain and Stevenson who have visited the islands over the years. Also, excerpts from ordinary people's journals and missionary letters from early times down to a gleeful report of the day that Hawaii became a state.

Krauss, Bob. *Here's Hawaii.* New York: Coward, McCann Inc., 1960. Social commentary in a series of humorous anecdotes excerpted from this newspaperman's column from the late '60s. Dated, but in essence still useful because people and values obviously change very little.

Lueras, Leonard. *Surfing, The Ultimate Pleasure.* New York: Workman Publishing, 1984. An absolutely outstanding pictorial account of Hawaii's own sport—surfing. Vintage and contemporary photos are surrounded by well-researched and written text. Bound to become a classic.

McBride, L.R. *Practical Folk Medicine of Hawaii.* Hilo, Hi.: Petroglyph Press, 1975. An illustrated guide to Hawaii's medicinal plants as used by the *kahuna lapa'au* (medical healers). Includes a thorough section on ailments, diagnosis, and the proper folk remedy to employ. Illustrated by the author, a renowned botanical researcher and former ranger at Volcanoes National Park.

Michener, James A. *Hawaii.* New York: Random House, 1959. Michener's fictionalized historical novel has done more to inform *and* misinform readers about Hawaii than any other book ever written. A great tale with plenty of local color and information that should be read for pleasure and not considered fact.

Piercy, LaRue. *Hawaii, This and That.* Hilo, Hi.: Petroglyph Press, 1981. Illustrated by Scot Ebanez. A 60-page book filled with one-sentence facts and oddities about all manner of things Hawaiian. Informative, amazing, and fun to read.

Rose, Roger G. *Hawaii: The Royal Isles.* Honolulu: Bishop Museum Press, 1980. Photographs, Seth Joel. A pictorial mixture of artifacts and luminaries from Hawaii's past. Includes a mixture of Hawaiian and Western art depicting island ways. Beautifully photographed with highly descriptive accompanying text.

Wilkerson, James A., M.D., ed. *Medicine for Mountaineering.* 3rd ed. Seattle: The Moun-

taineers, 1985. Don't let the title fool you. Although the book focuses on specific health problems that may be encountered while mountaineering, it is the best first-aid and general health guide available today. Written by doctors for the layman to use until help arrives, it is jam-packed with easily understandable techniques and procedures. For those intending extended treks, it is a must.

HISTORY/POLITICAL SCIENCE

Albertini, Jim, et al. *The Dark Side of Paradise, Hawaii in a Nuclear War.* Honolulu: cAtholic Action of Hawaii. Well-documented research outlining Hawaii's role and vulnerability in a nuclear world. This book presents the anti-nuclear and anti-military side of the political issue in Hawaii.

Apple, Russell A. *Trails: From Steppingstones to Kerbstones.* Honolulu: Bishop Museum Press, 1965. This "Special Publication #53" is a special-interest archaeological survey focusing on the trails, roadways, footpaths, and highways and how they were designed and maintained throughout the years. Many "royal highways" from pre-contact Hawaii are cited.

Ashdown, Inez MacPhee. *Old Lahaina.* Honolulu: Hawaiian Service Inc., 1976. A small pamphlet-type book listing most of the historical attractions of Lahaina Town, past and present. Ashdown is a life-long resident of Hawaii and gathered her information firsthand by listening to and recording stories of ethnic Hawaiians and old *kamaaina* families.

————. *Ke Alaloa o Maui.* Wailuku, Hi.: Kamaaina Historians Inc., 1971. A compilation of the history and legends of sites on the island of Maui. Ashdown was at one time a "lady in waiting" for Queen Liliuokalani and has since been proclaimed Maui's "Historian Emeritus."

Bell, Roger. *Last Among Equals: Hawaiian Statehood and American Politics.* Honolulu: University of Hawaii, 1984. Documents Hawaii's long and rocky road to statehood, tracing political partisanship, racism, and social change.

Cameron, Roderick. *The Golden Haze*. New York: World Publishing, 1964. An account of Captain James Cook's voyages of discovery throughout the South Seas. Uses original diaries and journals for an "on the spot" reconstruction of this great seafaring adventure.

Daws, Gavan. *Shoal of Time, A History of the Hawaiian Islands*. Honolulu: University of Hawaii Press, 1968. A highly readable history of Hawaii dating from its "discovery" by the Western world down to its acceptance as the 50th state. Good insight into the psychological makeup of the influential characters that formed Hawaii's past.

Department of Geography, University of Hawaii. *Atlas of Hawaii*. 2nd ed. Honolulu: University of Hawaii Press, 1983. Much more than an atlas filled with reference maps, it also contains commentary on the natural environment, culture, sociology, a gazetteer, and statistical tables. Actually a mini encyclopedia.

Feher, Joseph. *Hawaii: A Pictorial History*. Honolulu: Bishop Museum Press, 1969. Text by Edward Joesting and O.A. Bushnell. An oversized tome laden with annotated historical and contemporary photos, prints, and paintings. Seems like a big "school book," but extremely well done. If you are going to read one survey about Hawaii's historical, social, and cultural past, this is the one.

Fuchs, Lawrence. *Hawaii Pono*. New York: Harcourt, Brace and World, 1961. A detailed, scholarly work presenting an overview of Hawaii's history, based upon psychological and sociological interpretations. Encompasses most socio-ethnological groups from native Hawaiians to modern entrepreneurs. A must for social historical background.

Handy, E.S., and Elizabeth Handy. *Native Planters in Old Hawaii*. Honolulu: Bishop Museum Press, 1972. A superbly written, easily understandable scholarly work on the intimate relationship of pre-contact Hawaiians and the *aina* (land). Much more than its title implies, should be read by anyone seriously interested in Polynesian Hawaii.

The Hawaii Book. Chicago: J.G. Ferguson, 1961. Insightful selections of short stories, essays, and historical and political commentaries by experts specializing in Hawaii. Good choice of photos and illustrations.

Hawaiian Children's Mission Society. *Missionary Album*. Honolulu: Mission Society, 1969. Firsthand accounts of the New England missionaries sent to Hawaii and instrumental in its conversion to Christianity. Down-home stories of daily life's ups and downs.

Heyerdahl, Thor. *American Indians in the Pacific*. London: Allen and Unwin Ltd., 1952. Theoretical and anthropological accounts of the influence on Polynesia of the Indians along the Pacific coast of North and South America. Fascinating reading, with unsubstantiated yet intriguing theories presented.

Ii, John Papa. *Fragments of Hawaiian History*. Honolulu: Bishop Museum, 1959. Hawaii's history under Kamehameha I as told by a Hawaiian who actually experienced it.

Joesting, Edward. *Hawaii: An Uncommon History*. New York: W.W. Norton Co., 1972. A truly uncommon history told in a series of vignettes relating to the lives and personalities of the first white men in Hawaii, Hawaiian nobility, sea captains, writers, and adventurers. Brings history to life. Absolutely excellent!

Lee, William S. *The Islands*. New York: Holt, Rinehart, 1966. A socio-historical set of stories concerning malihini (newcomers) and how they influenced and molded the Hawaii of today.

Liliuokalani. *Hawaii's Story By Hawaii's Queen*. Rutland, Vt.: Tuttle, 1964. A moving personal account of Hawaii's inevitable move from monarchy to U.S. Territory by its last queen, Liliuokalani. The facts can be found in other histories, but none provides the emotion or point of view as expressed by Hawaii's deposed monarch. A "must" read to get the whole picture.

Nickerson, Roy. *Lahaina, Royal Capital of Hawaii.* Honolulu: Hawaiian Service, 1978. The story of Lahaina from whaling days to present, spiced with ample photographs.

Smith, Richard A., et al., eds. *The Frontier States.* New York: Time-Life Books, 1968. Short and concise comparisons of the two newest states: Hawaii and Alaska. Dated information, but good social commentary and an excellent appendix suggesting tours, museums, and local festivals.

Takaki, Ronald. *Plantation Life and Labor in Hawaii, 1835-1920.* Honolulu: University of Hawaii Press, 1983. A perspective of plantation life in Hawaii from a multi-ethnic viewpoint. Written by a nationally known island scholar.

MYTHOLOGY AND LEGENDS

Beckwith, Martha. *Hawaiian Mythology.* Honolulu: University of Hawaii Press, 1970. Forty-five years after its original printing, this work remains the definitive text on Hawaiian mythology. Ms. Beckwith compiled this book from many sources, giving exhaustive cross-references to genealogies and legends expressed in the oral tradition. If you are going to read one book on Hawaii's folklore, this should be it.

Colum, Padraic. *Legends of Hawaii.* New Haven: Yale University Press, 1937. Selected legends of old Hawaii reinterpreted, but closely based upon the originals.

Elbert, S., comp. *Hawaiian Antiquities and Folklore.* Honolulu: Univerity of Hawaii Press, 1959. Illustrated by Jean Charlot. A selection of the main legends from Abraham Fornander's great work, *The Polynesian Race.*

Melville, Leinanai. Children of the Rainbow. Wheaton, Ill.: Theosophical Publishing,

1969. A book on higher spiritual consciousness attuned to nature, which was the basic belief of pre-Christian Hawaii. The appendix contains illustrations of mystical symbols used by the kahuna. An enlightening book in many ways.

Thrum, Thomas. *Hawaiian Folk Tales.* Chicago: McClurg and Co., 1907. A collection of Hawaiian tales from the oral tradition as told to the author from various sources.

Westervelt, W.D. *Hawaiian Legends of Volcanoes.* Boston: Ellis Press, 1916. A small book concerning the volcanic legends of Hawaii and how they related to the fledgling field of volcanism at the turn of the century. The vintage photos alone are worth a look.

NATURAL SCIENCES

Abbott, Agatin, Gordon MacDonald, and Frank Peterson. *Volcanoes in the Sea.* Honolulu: University of Hawaii Press, 1983. A simplified yet comprehensive text covering the geology and volcanism of the Hawaiian Islands. Focuses upon the forces of nature (wind, rain, and surf) that shape the islands.

Boom, Robert. *Hawaiian Seashells.* Honolulu: Waikiki Aquarium, 1972. Photos, Jerry Kringle. A collection of 137 seashells found in Hawaiian waters, featuring many found nowhere else on Earth. Broken into categories with accompanying text including common and scientific names, physical descriptions, and likely habitats. A must for shell collectors.

Brock, Vernon, and W.A. Gosline. *Handbook of Hawaiian Fishes.* Honolulu: University of Hawaii Press, 1960. A detailed guide to most of the fishes occurring in Hawaiian waters.

Carlquist, Sherwin. *Hawaii: A Natural History.* New York: Doubleday, 1970. Definitive account of Hawaii's natural history.

Carpenter, Blyth, and Russell Carpenter. *Fish Watching in Hawaii.* San Mateo, Ca.: Natural World Press, 1981. A color guide to many of the reef fish found in Hawaii and often spotted by snorkelers. If you're interested in the fish that you'll be looking at, this guide will be very helpful.

Fielding, Ann, and Ed Robinson. *An Underwater Guide to Hawaii*. Honolulu: University of Hawaii Press, 1987. If you've ever had a desire to snorkel/scuba the living reef waters of Hawaii and to be familiar with what you're seeing, get this small but fact-packed book. The amazing array of marine life found througout the archipelago is captured in glossy photos with accompaning informative text. Both the scientific and common names of specimens are given. This book will enrich your underwater experience, and serve as an easily understood reference guide for many years.

Hamaishi, Amy, and Doug Wallin. *Flowers of Hawaii*. Honolulu: World Wide Distributors, 1975. Close-up color photos of many of the most common flowers spotted in Hawaii.

Hawaii Audubon Society. *Hawaii's Birds*. Honolulu: Hawaii Audubon Society, 1981. A field guide to Hawaii's birds, listing the endangered indigenous species, migrants, and introduced species that are now quite common. Color photos with text listing distribution, description, voice, and habits. Excellent field guide.

Hosaka, Edward. *Shore Fishing in Hawaii*. Hilo, Hi.: Petroglyph Press, 1984. Known as the best book on Hawaiian fishing since 1944. Receives the highest praise because it has born and bred many Hawaiian fishermen.

Hubbard, Douglass, and Gordon MacDonald. *Volcanoes of the National Parks of Hawaii*. Volcanoes, Hi.: Hawaii Natural History Assoc., 1982. The volcanology of Hawaii, documenting the major lava flows and their geological effect on the state.

Island Heritage Limited. *Hawaii's Flowering Trees*. Honolulu: Island Heritage Press. A concise field guide to many of Hawaii's most common flowering trees. All color photos with accompanying descriptive text.

Kay, E. Alison, comp. *A Natural History of the Hawaiian Islands*. Honolulu: University of Hawaii Press, 1972. A selection of concise articles by experts in the fields of volcanism, oceanography, meteorology, and biology. An excellent reference source.

Kuck, Lorraine, and Richard Togg. Hawaiian Flowers and Flowering Trees. Rutland, Vt.: Tuttle, 1960. A classic field guide to tropical and subtropical flora illustrated in watercolor. A "to the point" description of Hawaiian plants and flowers with a brief history of their places of origin and their introduction to Hawaii.

Merlin, Mark D. *Hawaiian Forest Plants, A Hiker's Guide*. Honolulu: Oriental Publishing, 1980. A companion guide to trekkers into Hawaii's interior. Full-color plates identify and describe the most common forest plants encountered.

————. *Hawaiian Coastal Plants*. Honolulu: Oriental Publishing, 1980. Color photos and botanical descriptions of many of the plants and flowers found growing along Hawaii's varied shorelines.

Merrill, Elmer. *Plant Life of the Pacific World*. Rutland, Vt.: Tuttle, 1983. The definitive book for anyone planning a botanical tour to the entire Pacific Basin. Originally published in the 1930s, it remains a tremendous work.

Nickerson, Roy. Brother Whale, A Pacific Whalewatcher's Log. San Francisco: Chronicle Books, 1977. Introduces the average person to the life of Earth's greatest mammals. Provides historical accounts, photos, and tips on whale-watching. Well written, descriptive, and the best "first time" book on whales.

Sohmer, S. H., and R. Gustafson. *Plants and Flowers of Hawaii*. Honolulu: University of Hawaii Press, 1987. Sohmer and Gustafson range the vegetation zones of Hawaii, from mountains to coast, introducing you to the wide and varied floral biology of the islands. They give a good introduction to the history, and the uniqueness of the evolution of Hawaiian plantlife. Beautiful color plates are accompanied by clear and concise plant descriptions, with the scientific and common Hawaiian names listed.

Stearns, Harold T. *Road Guide to Points of Geological Interest in the Hawaiian Islands.* Palo Alto, Ca.: Pacific Books, 1966. The title is almost as long as this handy little book that lets you know what forces of nature formed the scenery that you see in the islands.

van Riper, Charles, and Sandra van Riper. *A Field Guide to the Mammals of Hawaii.* Honolulu: Oriental Publishing. A guide to the surprising number of mammals introduced into Hawaii. Full-color pages document description, uses, tendencies, and habitat. Small and thin, makes a worthwhile addition to any serious trekker's backpack.

TRAVEL

Birnbaum, Stephen, et al., eds. *Hawaii 1984.* Boston: Houghton Mifflin, 1983. Well-researched, informative writing, with good background material. Focuses primarily on known tourist spots with only perfunctory coverage of out-of-the-way places. Lacking in full-coverage maps.

Bone, Robert W. *The Maverick Guide to Hawaii.* Gretna, La.: Pelican, 1983. Adequate, personalized writing style.

Fodor, Eugene, comp. *Fodor's Hawaii.* New York: Fodor's Guides, 1983. Great coverage on the cliches, but short on out-of-the-way places.

Hammel, Faye, and Sylvan Levy. *Frommer's Hawaii on $35 a Day.* New York: Frommer, Pasmantier, 1984. Hammel and Levy are good writers, but the book is top-heavy with info on Honolulu and Oahu and skimps on the rest.

Riegert, Ray. *Hidden Hawaii.* Berkeley, Ca.: And/Or Press, 1982. Ray offers a "user friendly" guide to the islands.

Rizzuto, Shirley. *Hawaiian Camping.* Berkeley, Ca.: Wilderness Press, 1979. Adequate coverage of the "nuts and bolts" of camping in Hawaii. Slightly conservative in approach and geared toward the family.

Smith, Robert. *Hawaii's Best Hiking Trails.* Also, *Hiking Kauai, Hiking Maui, Hiking Oahu,* and *Hiking Hawaii.* Berkeley: Wilderness Press, 1977 to 1982. Smith's books are specialized, detailed trekker's guides to Hawaii's outdoors. Complete with useful maps, historical references, official procedures, and plants and animals encountered along the way. If you're focused on hiking, these are the best to take along.

Stanley, David. *South Pacific Handbook.* 3rd ed. Chico, Ca.: Moon Publications, 1986. The model upon which all travel guides should be based. Simply the best book in the world for travel throughout the South Pacific.

Sutton, Horace. *Aloha Hawaii.* New York: Doubleday, 1967. A dated but still excellent guide to Hawaii providing sociological, historical, and cultural insight. Horace Sutton's literary style is the best in the travel guide field. Entertaining reading.

Thorne, Chuck. *The Diver's Guide to Maui.* Kahului, Hi.: Maui Dive Guide, 1984. A no-nonsense snorkeler's and diver's guide to Maui waters. Extensive maps, descriptions, and "straight from the shoulder" advice by one of Maui's best and most experienced divers. A must for all levels of divers and snorkelers.

Thorne, Chuck, and Lou Zitnik. *A Divers' Guide to Hawaii.* Kihei, Hi.: Hawaii's Diver's Guide, 1984. An expanded divers' and snorkelers' guide to the waters of the 6 main Hawaiian islands. Complete list of maps with full descriptions, tips, and ability levels. A must for all levels of snorkelers and divers.

Warner, Evie, and Al Davies. *Bed and Breakfast Goes Hawaiian.* Kapaa, Hi.: Island Bed and Breakfast, 1990. A combination bed and breakfast directory and guide to sights, activities, events, and restaurants on the six major islands.

Wurman, Richard. *Hawaii Access.* Los Angeles: Access Press, 1983. The "fast food" publishers of travel guides. The packaging is colorful and bright like a burger in a styrofoam box, but there's little of substance inside.

COOKING

Alexander, Agnes. *How to Use Hawaiian Fruit.* Hilo, Hi.: Petroglyph Press, 1984. A full range of recipes using delicious and different Hawaiian fruits.

Fitzgerald, Donald, et al., eds. *The Pacific House Hawaii Cookbook.* Pacific House, 1968. A full range of Hawaiian cuisine including recipes from traditional Chinese, Japanese, Portuguese, New England, and Filipino dishes.

Gibbons, Euell. *Beachcombers Handbook.* New York: McKay Co., 1967. An autobiographical account of this world-famous naturalist as a young man living "off the land" in Hawaii. Great tips on spotting and gathering naturally occurring foods, survival advice, and recipes. Unfortunately the lifestyle described is long outdated.

Margah, Irish, and Elvira Monroe. *Hawaii, Cooking with Aloha.* San Carlos, Ca.: Wide World, 1984. Island recipes including *kalua* pig, *lomi* salmon, and hints on decor.

LANGUAGE

Boom, Robert, and Chris Christensen. *Important Hawaiian Place Names.* Honolulu: Boom Enterprises, 1978. A handy pocket-sized book listing most of the major island place names and their translations.

Elbert, Samuel. *Spoken Hawaiian.* Honolulu: University of Hawaii Press, 1970. Progressive conversational lessons.

Elbert, Samuel, and Mary Pukui. *Hawaiian Dictionary.* Honolulu: University of Hawaii, 1971. The best dictionary available on the Hawaiian language. The *Pocket Hawaiian Dictionary* is a condensed version of this dictionary which is less expensive and adequate for most travelers with a general interest in the language.

GLOSSARY

Words marked with an asterisk (*) are used commonly throughout the islands.

*a'a**—rough clinker lava. *A'a* has become the correct geological term to describe this type of lava found anywhere in the world.

ahuapua—pie-shaped land divisions running from mountain to sea that were governed by *konohiki,* local *ali'i* who owed their allegiance to a reigning chief

aikane—friend; pal; buddy

aina—land; the binding spirit to all Hawaiians. Love of the land is paramount in traditional Hawaiian beliefs.

akamai—smart; clever; wise

akua—a god, or simply "divine." You'll hear people speak of their family or personal *amakua* (ancestral spirit). A favorite is the shark or the *pueo* (Hawaiian owl).

*ali'i**—a Hawaiian chief or nobleman

*aloha**—the most common greeting in the islands. Can mean both hello or goodbye, welcome or farewell. It also can mean romantic love, affection, or best wishes.

aole—no

auwe—alas; ouch! When a great chief or loved one died, it was a traditional wail of mourning.

halakahiki—pineapple

*hale**—house or building; often combined with other words to name a specific place such as Haleakala ("House of the Sun") or Hale Pai ("printing house").

*hana**—work; combined with *pau* means end of work or quitting time

hanai—literally "to feed." Part of the true aloha spirit. A *hanai* is a permanent guest, or an adopted family member, usually an old person or a child. This is an enduring cultural phenomenon in Hawaii, in which a child from one family (perhaps that of a brother or sister, and quite often one's grandchild) is raised as one's own without formal adoption.

*haole**—a word that at one time meant foreigner, but which now means a white person or Caucasian. Many etymological definitions have been put forth, but none satisfies everyone. Some feel that it signified a person without a background, because the first white men could not chant their genealogies as was common to Hawaiians.

*hapa**—half, as in a mixed-blooded person being referred to as *hapa haole*

*hapai**—pregnant; used by all ethnic groups when a *keiki* is on the way

*haupia**—a coconut custard dessert often served at luau

*heiau**—a traditional Hawaiian temple. A platform made of skillfully fitted rocks, upon which structures were built and offerings made to the gods.

*holomuu**—an ankle-length dress that is much more fitted than a muumuu, and which is often worn on formal occasions

hono—bay, as in Honolulu ("Sheltered Bay")

ho'oilo—traditional Hawaiian winter that began in November

hoolaulea—any happy event, but especially a family outing or picnic

*hoomalimali**—sweet talk; flattery

*huhu**—angry; irritated

*hui**—a group; meeting; society. Often used to refer to Chinese businessmen or family members who pool their money to get businesses started.

hukilau—traditional shoreline fish-gathering in which everyone lends a hand to *huki* (pull) the huge net. Anyone taking part shares in the *lau* (food). It is much more like a party than hard work, and if you're lucky you'll be able to take part in one.

*hula**—a native Hawaiian dance in which the rhythm of the islands is captured by swaying hips and stories told by lyrically moving hands. A *halau* is a group or school of hula.

huli huli—barbecue, as in *huli huli* chicken

i'a—fish in general. *I'a maka* is raw fish.

*imu**—underground oven filled with hot rocks and used for baking. The main cooking feature at luaus, used to steam-bake the pork and other succulent dishes. Traditionally the tending of the *imu* was for men only.

ipo—sweetheart; lover; girlfriend or boyfriend

kahili—a tall pole topped with feathers, resembling a huge feather duster. It was used by an *ali'i* to announce his presence.

kahuna*—priest; sorcerer; doctor; skillful person. *Kahuna* had tremendous power in old Hawaii which they used for both good and evil. The *kahuna 'ana'ana* was a feared individual because he practiced "black magic" and could pray a person to death, while the *kahuna lapa'au* was a medical practitioner bringing aid and comfort to the people.

kai—the sea. Many businesses and hotels employ *kai* as part of their name.

kalua—roasted underground in an *imu*. A favorite island food is *kalua* pork.

kamaaina*—a child of the land; an old-timer; a longtime island resident of any ethnic background; a resident of Hawaii or native son. Oftentimes hotels and airlines offer discounts called "*kamaaina* rates" to anyone who can prove island residency.

kanaka—man or commoner; later used to distinguish a Hawaiian from other races. Tone of voice can make it a derisive expression.

kane*—means man, but actually used to signify a relationship such as husband or boyfriend. Written on a door it means "Men's Room."

kaola*—any food that has been broiled or barbecued

kapu*—forbidden; taboo; keep out; do not touch

kapuna—a grandparent or old-timer; usually means someone who has gained wisdom. The statewide school system now invites *kapuna* to talk to the children about the old ways and methods.

kaukau*—slang word meaning food or chow; grub. Some of the best food in Hawaii comes from the "*kaukau* wagons," trucks that sell plate lunches and other morsels.

kauwa—a landless, untouchable caste that was confined to living on reservations. Members of this caste were often used as human sacrifice at *heiau*. Calling someone *kauwa* is still considered a grave insult.

kava—a mildly intoxicating traditional drink made from the juice of chewed awaroot, spat into a bowl, and used in religious ceremonies.

keiki*—child or children; used by all ethnic groups. "Have you hugged your *keiki* today?"

kiawe*—an algaroba tree from S. America commonly found in Hawaii along the shore. It grows a nasty long thorn that can easily puncture a tire. Legend has it that the trees were introduced to the islands by a misguided missionary who hoped the thorns would coerce natives into wearing shoes. Actually, they are good for fuel, as fodder for hogs and cattle, and for reforestation, none of which you'll appreciate if you step on one of their thorns, or flatten a tire on your rental car!

kokua—help. As in "Your *kokua* is needed to keep Hawaii free from litter."

kona wind*—a muggy subtropical wind that blows from the south and hits the leeward side of the islands. It usually brings sticky hot weather, and is one of the few times when air-conditioning will be appreciated.

konane—a traditional Hawaiian game, similar to checkers, played with pebbles on a large flat stone used as a board

koolau—windward side of the island

kukui—a candlenut tree whose pods are polished and then strung together to make a beautiful lei. Traditionally the oil-rich nuts were strung on the rib of a coconut leaf and used as a candle.

kuleana—homesite; the old homestead; small farms. Especially used to describe the small spreads on Hawaiian Homes Lands on Molokai.

Kumulipo*—ancient Hawaiian genealogical chant that records the pantheon of gods, creation, and the beginning of mankind

la—the sun. Often combined with other words to be more descriptive, such as *La*-haina ("Merciless Sun") or Haleaka*la* ("House of the Sun").

lanai*—veranda or porch. You'll pay more for a hotel room if it has a lanai with an ocean view.

lani—sky or the heavens

*lau hala**—traditional Hawaiian weaving of mats, hats, etc., from the prepared fronds of the pandanus (screw pine)

*lei**—a traditional garland of flowers or vines. One of Hawaii's most beautiful customs. Given at any auspicious occasion, but especially when arriving or leaving Hawaii.

lele—the stone altar at a *heiau*

limu—edible seaweed of various types. Gathered from the shoreline, it makes an excellent salad. It's used to garnish many island dishes and is a favorite at luaus.

lomilomi—traditional Hawaiian massage; also, raw salmon made up into a vinegared salad with chopped onion and spices

*lua**—the toilet; the head; the bathroom

luakini—a human sacrifice temple. Introduced to Hawaii in the 13th C. at Wahaula Heiau on the Big Island.

*luau**—a Hawaiian feast featuring poi, *imu*-baked pork, and other traditional foods. Good ones provide some of the best gastronomical delights in the world.

luna—foreman or overseer in the plantation fields. They were often mounted on horseback and were renowned either for their fairness or cruelty. They represented the middle class, and served as a buffer between the plantation workers and the white plantation owners.

*mahalo**—thank you. *Mahalo nui* means "big thanks" or "thank you very much."

mahele—division. The "Great Mahele" of 1848 changed Hawaii forever when the traditional common lands were broken up into privately owned plots.

*mahi mahi**—a favorite eating fish. Often called a dolphin, but a *mahi mahi* is a true fish, not a cetacean.

mahu—a homosexual; often used derisively like "fag" or "queer"

maile—a fragrant vine used in traditional leis. It looks ordinary but smells delightful.

maka'ainana—a commoner; a person "belonging" to the *aina* (land), who supported the *ali'i* by fishing, farming, and as warriors

*makai**—toward the sea; used by most islanders when giving directions

make—dead; deceased

*malihini**—newcomer; tenderfoot; a recent arrival

malo—the native Hawaiian loincloth. Never worn anymore except at festivals or pageants.

*mana**—power from the spirit world; innate energy of all things animate or inanimate; the grace of god. Mana could be passed on from one person to another, or even stolen. Great care was taken to protect the *ali'i* from having their mana defiled. Commoners were required to lie flat on the ground and cover their faces whenever a great *ali'i* approached. *Kahuna* were often employed in the regaining or transference of mana.

manauahi—free; gratis; extra

manini—stingy; tight. A Hawaiianized word taken from the name of Don Francisco *Marin*, who was instrumental in bringing many fruits and plants to Hawaii. He was known for never sharing any of the bounty from his substantial gardens on Vineyard Street in Honolulu.

*mauka**—toward the mountains; used by most islanders when giving directions

mauna—mountain. Often combined with other words to be more descriptive, such as Mauna Kea ("White Mountain").

mele—a song or chant in the Hawaiian oral tradition that records the history and genealogies of the *ali'i*

menehune—the legendary "little people" of Hawaii. Like leprechauns, they are said to have shunned mankind and possess magical powers. Stone walls said to have been completed in one night are often attributed to them. Some historians argue that they actually existed and were the aboriginals of Hawaii, inhabiting the islands before the coming of the Polynesians.

moa—chicken; fowl

*moana**—the ocean; the sea. Many businesses and hotels as well as places have *moana* as part of their name.

moe—sleep

moolelo—ancient tales kept alive by the oral tradition and recited only by day

*muumuu**—a "Mother Hubbard," an ankle-length dress with a high neckline introduced by the missionaries to cover the nakedness of the Hawaiians. It has become fashionable attire for almost any occasion in Hawaii.

nani—beautiful

nui—big; great; large; as in *mahalo nui* (thank you very much)

ohana—a family; the fundamental social division; extended family. Now used to denote a social organization with grass-roots overtones, as in the "Protect Kahoolawe Ohana."

okolehau—literally "iron bottom"; a traditional booze made from *ti* root; *okole* means your "rear end" and *hau* means "iron," which was descriptive of the huge blubber pots that it was made in. Also, if you drink too much it'll surely knock you on your *okole*.

ono*—delicious; delightful; the best. *Ono ono* means "extra or absolutely delicious."

opihi—a shellfish or limpet that clings to rocks and is gathered as one of the islands' favorite *pu pu*. Custom dictates that you never remove all of the *opihi* from a rock; some are always left to grow for future generations.

opu—belly; stomach

pa'hoehoe*—smooth ropey lava that looks like burnt pancake batter. *Pa'hoehoe* is now the correct geological term used to describe this type of lava found anywhere in the world.

pake—a Chinese person. Can be derisive, depending on tone in which it is used. It is a bastardization of the Chinese word meaning "uncle."

pali*—a cliff; precipice. Hawaii's geology makes them quite common. The most famous are the *pali* of Oahu where a major battle was fought.

paniolo*—a Hawaiian cowboy. Derived from the Spanish *espaniola*. The first cowboys brought to Hawaii during the early 19th century were Mexicans from California.

papale—hat. Except for the feathered helmets of the *ali'i* warriors of old Hawaii, hats were generally not worn. However, once the islanders saw their practical uses and how fashionable they were, they began weaving them from various materials and quickly became experts at manufacture and design.

pau*—finished; done; completed. Often combined into *pau hana*, which means end of work or quitting time.

pa'u—long split skirt often worn by women when horseback riding. Last century, an island treat was when *pa'u* riders would turn out in their beautiful dresses at Kapiolani Park in Honolulu. The tradition is carried on today at many of Hawaii's rodeos.

pilau—stink; bad smell; stench

pilikia—trouble of any kind, big or small; bad times

poi*—a glutinous paste made from the pounded corn of taro which ferments slightly and has a light sour taste. Purplish in color, it's a staple at luaus, where it is called "one-, two-, or three-finger" poi, depending upon its thickness.

pono—righteous or excellent

pua—flower

puka*—a hole of any size. *Puka* is used by all island residents, whether talking about a pinhole in a rubber boat or a tunnel through a mountain.

punalua—the tradition of sharing mates in practice before the missionaries came. Western seamen took advantage of it, and this led to the spreading of contagious diseases and eventually to the ultimate demise of the Hawaiian people.

punee*—bed; narrow couch. Used by all ethnic groups. To recline on a *punee* on a breezy lanai is a true island treat.

pu pu*—an appetizer; a snack; hors d'oeuvres; can be anything from cheese and crackers to sushi. Oftentimes, bars or nightclubs offer them free.

pupule—crazy; nuts; out of your mind

pu'u—hill, as in Pu'u Ulaula ("Red Hill")

tapa*—a traditional paper cloth made from beaten bark. Intricate designs were stamped in using beaters, and natural dyes added color. The tradition was lost for many years, but is now making a comeback, and provides some of the most beautiful folk art in the islands.

taro*—the staple of old Hawaii. A plant with a distinctive broad leaf that produces a starchy root. It was brought by the first Polynesians and was grown on magnificently irrigated plantations. According to the oral tradition, the life-giving properties of taro hold mystical significance for Hawaiians, since it was created by the gods at about the same time as mankind.

ti—a broad green-leafed plant that was used for many purposes, from plates to hula skirts (never grass), and especially used to wrap religious offerings presented at the *heiau*.

tutu*—grandmother; granny; older woman. Used by all as a term of respect and endearment.

ukulele*—*uku* means "flea" and *lele* means "jumping," so literally "jumping flea"—the way the Hawaiians perceived the quick finger movements on the banjo-like Portuguese folk instrument called a *cavaquinho*. The ukulele quickly became synonymous with the islands.

wahine*—young woman; female; girl; wife. Used by all ethnic groups. When written on a door it means "Women's Room."

wai—fresh water; drinking water

wela—hot. *Wela kahao* is a "hot time" or "making whoopee."

wiki*—quickly; fast; in a hurry. Often seen as *wiki wiki* (very fast), as in "Wiki Wiki Messenger Service."

RESTAURANT INDEX

HOTEL INDEX

INDEX

Page numbers in **boldface** indicate the primary reference; numbers in *italics* indicate information in maps, charts, callouts, or illustrations. (M) = Maui (L) = Lanai (Mo) = Molokai

ABOUT THE AUTHORS

Joe Bisignani (PHOTO BY "BIRDS OF PARADISE")

Joe Bisignani is a fortunate man because he makes his living doing the two things that he likes best: traveling and writing. Joe has been with Moon Publications since 1979 and is the author of *Japan Handbook, Kauai Handbook, Hawaii Handbook, Oahu Handbook, Maui Handbook,* and *Big Island Handbook.* When not traveling, he makes his home in Northern California.

Robert Nilsen has been with Moon Publications since 1983, and is the author of *South Korea Handbook.* He has had the pleasant task of selecting, revising, and updating material from *Hawaii Handbook* for this edition of *Maui Handbook.* Born and raised in Minnesota, he now lives in Northern California where he writes, explores, and rides his bicycle with friend and fellow cyclist Joe Bisignani.

Illustrations for chapter heads were done by the following people: Brian C. Bardwell: 111; Sue Strangio Everett: 133, 140, 143, 230; Louise Foote: 69; Diana Lasich Harper: 5, 9, 38, 65, 100, 293, 333; Hawaii State Archives: 43, 60, 82, 96; Keith Perkins: 206, 217; Robert Race: 1, 17, 73, 119, 148, 164, 186, 240, 246, 270, 273, 305.

Robert Nilsen (PHOTO BY DON PURDY)

Pathways.

Over one thousand years ago, Polynesians in outrigger canoes crossed the vast ocean with determination, skill and the strong commitment of the people.

Today, Hawaiian Airlines has pathways to the east and west. East to Los Angeles, San Francisco, Seattle, Portland, Las Vegas and Anchorage. West to American Samoa, Western Samoa and the Kingdom of Tonga. And in Hawaii, we still connect these lovely islands just as we've done for the past 60 years. And our deep Polynesian roots make hospitality second nature and every guest first in our heart.

Our spirit is unique. We are Hawaiian.

HAWAIIAN.
The Colors of Paradise.

U.S. Toll Free 1-800-367-5320, Statewide Toll Free 1-800-882-8811.
Call Hawaiian or your travel agent.

Moon Handbooks—The Ideal Traveling Companions

Open a Moon Handbook and you're opening your eyes and heart to the world. Thoughtful, sensitive, and provocative, Moon Handbooks encourage an intimate understanding of a region, from its culture and history to essential practicalities. Fun to read and packed with valuable information on accommodations, dining, recreation, plus indispensable travel tips, detailed maps, charts, illustrations, photos, glossaries, and indexes, Moon Handbooks are ideal traveling companions: informative, entertaining, and highly practical.

TO ORDER BY PHONE: (800) 345-5473 • Monday-Friday • 9 a.m.-5 p.m. PST

The Pacific/Asia Series

BALI HANDBOOK by Bill Dalton
Detailed travel information on the most famous island in the world. 12 color pages, 29 b/w photos, 68 illustrations, 42 maps, 7 charts, glossary, booklist, index. 428 pages. **$12.95**

INDONESIA HANDBOOK by Bill Dalton
This one-volume encyclopedia explores island by island the many facets of this sprawling, kaleidoscopic island nation. 30 b/w photos, 143 illustrations, 250 maps, 17 charts, booklist, extensive Indonesian vocabulary, index. 1,000 pages. **$19.95**

SOUTH KOREA HANDBOOK by Robert Nilsen
Whether you're visiting on business or searching for adventure, *South Korea Handbook* is an invaluable companion. 8 color pages, 78 b/w photos, 93 illustrations, 109 maps, 10 charts, Korean glossary with useful notes on speaking and reading the language, booklist, index. 548 pages. **$14.95**

SOUTHEAST ASIA HANDBOOK by Carl Parkes
Helps the enlightened traveler discover the real Southeast Asia. 16 color pages, 75 b/w photos, 11 illustrations, 169 maps, 140 charts, vocabulary and suggested reading, index. 873 pages. **$16.95**

HONG KONG HANDBOOK by Laurie Fullerton
This definitive guide introduces the visitor to the many moods of this British colony. Color and b/w photos, illustrations, maps, charts, index. 250 pages. **$10.95**

PHILIPPINES HANDBOOK by Peter Harper and Evelyn Peplow
Crammed with detailed information, *Philippines Handbook* equips the escapist, hedonist, or business traveler with thorough coverage of the Philippines's colorful history, landscapes, and culture. Color and b/w photos, illustrations, maps, charts, index. 587 pages. **$12.95**

HAWAII HANDBOOK by J.D. Bisignani
Winner of the 1989 Hawaii Visitors Bureau's Best Guide Book Award and the Grand Award for Excellence in Travel Journalism, this guide takes you beyond the glitz and high-priced hype and leads you to a genuine Hawaiian experience. 12 color pages, 86 b/w photos, 132 illustrations, 86 maps, 44 graphs and charts, Hawaiian and pidgin glossaries, appendix, booklist, index. 879 pages. **$15.95**

KAUAI HANDBOOK by J.D. Bisignani
Kauai Handbook is the perfect antidote to the workaday world. 8 color pages, 36 b/w photos, 48 illustrations, 19 maps, 10 tables and charts, Hawaiian and pidgin glossaries, booklist, index. 236 pages. **$9.95**

MAUI HANDBOOK: Including Molokai and Lanai by J.D. Bisignani
"No fool-'round" advice on accommodations, eateries, and recreation, plus a comprehensive introduction to island ways, geography, and history. 8 color pages, 60 b/w photos, 72 illustrations, 34 maps, 19 charts, booklist, glossary, index. 350 pages. **$11.95**

OAHU HANDBOOK by J.D. Bisignani
A handy guide to Honolulu, renowned surfing beaches, and Oahu's countless other diversions. Color and b/w photos, illustrations, 18 maps, charts, booklist, glossary, index. 354 pages. **$11.95**

BIG ISLAND OF HAWAII HANDBOOK by J.D. Bisignani
An entertaining yet informative text packed with insider tips on accommodations, dining, sports and outdoor activities, natural attractions, and must-see sights. Color and b/w photos, illustrations, 20 maps, charts, booklist, glossary, index. 347 pages. **$11.95**

SOUTH PACIFIC HANDBOOK by David Stanley
The original comprehensive guide to the 16 territories in the South Pacific. 20 color pages, 195 b/w photos, 121 illustrations, 35 charts, 138 maps, booklist, glossary, index. 740 pages. **$15.95**

MICRONESIA HANDBOOK:
Guide to the Caroline, Gilbert, Mariana, and Marshall Islands by David Stanley
Micronesia Handbook guides you on a real Pacific adventure all your own. 8 color pages, 77 b/w photos, 68 illustrations, 69 maps, 18 tables and charts, index. 287 pages. **$9.95**

FIJI ISLANDS HANDBOOK by David Stanley
The first and still the best source of information on travel around this 322-island archipelago. 8 color pages, 35 b/w photos, 78 illustrations, 26 maps, 3 charts, Fijian glossary, booklist, index. 198 pages. **$8.95**

TAHITI-POLYNESIA HANDBOOK by David Stanley
All five French-Polynesian archipelagoes are covered in this comprehensive guide by Oceania's best-known travel writer. 12 color pages, 45 b/w photos, 64 illustrations, 33 maps, 7 charts, booklist, glossary, index. 225 pages. **$9.95**

NEW ZEALAND HANDBOOK by Jane King
Introduces you to the people, places, history, and culture of this extraordinary land. 8 color pages, 99 b/w photos, 146 illustrations, 82 maps, booklist, index. 546 pages. **$14.95**

BLUEPRINT FOR PARADISE: How to Live on a Tropic Island by Ross Norgrove
This one-of-a-kind guide has everything you need to know about moving to and living comfortably on a tropical island. 8 color pages, 40 b/w photos, 3 maps, 14 charts, appendices, index. 212 pages. **$14.95**

The Americas Series

NORTHERN CALIFORNIA HANDBOOK by Kim Weir
An outstanding companion for imaginative travel in the territory north of the Tehachapis. 12 color pages, b/w photos, 69 maps, illustrations, booklist, index. 759 pages. **$16.95**

NEVADA HANDBOOK by Deke Castleman
Nevada Handbook puts the Silver State into perspective and makes it manageable and affordable. 34 b/w photos, 43 illustrations, 37 maps, 17 charts, booklist, index. 400 pages. **$12.95**

NEW MEXICO HANDBOOK by Stephen Metzger
A close-up and complete look at every aspect of this wondrous state. 8 color pages, 85 b/w photos, 63 illustrations, 50 maps, 10 charts, booklist, index. 375 pages. **$12.95**

TEXAS HANDBOOK by Joe Cummings
Seasoned travel writer Joe Cummings brings an insider's perspective to his home state. 12 color pages, b/w photos, maps, illustrations, charts, booklist, index. 483 pages. **$11.95**

ARIZONA TRAVELER'S HANDBOOK by Bill Weir
This meticulously researched guide contains everything necessary to make Arizona accessible and enjoyable. 8 color pages, 194 b/w photos, 74 illustrations, 53 maps, 6 charts, booklist, index. 505 pages. **$13.95**

UTAH HANDBOOK by Bill Weir
Weir gives you all the carefully researched facts and background to make your visit a success. 8 color pages, 102 b/w photos, 61 illustrations, 30 maps, 9 charts, booklist, index. 452 pages. **$12.95**

ALASKA-YUKON HANDBOOK by Deke Castleman, Don Pitcher, and David Stanley
Get the inside story, with plenty of well-seasoned advice to help you cover more miles on less money. 8 color pages, 26 b/w photos, 92 illustrations, 90 maps, 6 charts, booklist, glossary, index. 384 pages. **$11.95**

WASHINGTON HANDBOOK by Dianne J. Boulerice Lyons
Covers sights, shopping, services, transportation, and outdoor recreation, with complete listings for restaurants and accommodations. 8 color pages, 92 b/w photos, 24 illustrations, 81 maps, 8 charts, booklist, index. 400 pages. **$12.95**

OREGON HANDBOOK by Stuart Warren and Ted Long Ishikawa
Brimming with travel practicalities and insider views on Oregon's history, culture, arts, and activities. Color and b/w photos, illustrations, 28 maps, charts, booklist, index. 422 pages. **$12.95**

WYOMING HANDBOOK by Don Pitcher
All you need to know to open the doors to this wide and wild state. Color and b/w photos, illustrations, over 60 maps, charts, booklist, index. 427 pages. **$12.95**

BRITISH COLUMBIA HANDBOOK by Jane King
With an emphasis on outdoor adventures, this guide covers mainland British Columbia, Vancouver Island, the Queen Charlotte Islands, and the Canadian Rockies. 8 color pages, 56 b/w photos, 45 illustrations, 66 maps, 4 charts, booklist, index. 381 pages. **$11.95**

GUIDE TO CATALINA and California's Channel Islands by Chicki Mallan
A complete guide to these remarkable islands, from the windy solitude of the Channel Islands National Marine Sanctuary to bustling Avalon. 8 color pages, 105 b/w photos, 65 illustrations, 40 maps, 32 charts, booklist, index. 262 pages. **$9.95**

YUCATAN HANDBOOK by Chicki Mallan
All the information you'll need to guide you into every corner of this exotic land. 8 color pages, 154 b/w photos, 55 illustrations, 57 maps, 70 charts, appendix, booklist, Mayan and Spanish glossaries, index. 391 pages. **$12.95**

CANCUN HANDBOOK and Mexico's Caribbean Coast by Chicki Mallan
Covers the city's luxury scene as well as more modest attractions, plus many side trips to unspoiled beaches and Mayan ruins. Color and b/w photos, illustrations, over 30 maps, Spanish glossary, booklist, index. 257 pages. **$10.95**

BELIZE HANDBOOK by Chicki Mallan
Complete with detailed maps, practical information, and an overview of the area's flamboyant history, culture, and geographical features, *Belize Handbook* is the only comprehensive guide of its kind to this spectacular region. Color and b/w photos, illustrations, maps, booklist, index. 212 pages. **$11.95**

JAMAICA HANDBOOK by Karl Luntta
From the sun and surf of Montego Bay and Ocho Rios to the cool slopes of the Blue Mountains, author Karl Luntta offers island-seekers a perceptive, personal view of Jamaica. Color and b/w photos, illustrations, maps, charts, index. 350 pages. **$12.95**

The International Series

EGYPT HANDBOOK by Kathy Hansen
An invaluable resource for intelligent travel in Egypt. 8 color pages, 20 b/w photos, 150 illustrations, 80 detailed maps and plans to museums and archaeological sites, Arabic glossary, booklist, index. 510 pages. **$14.95**

PAKISTAN HANDBOOK by Isobel Shaw
For armchair travelers and trekkers alike, the most detailed and authoritative guide to Pakistan ever published. 28 color pages, 86 maps, appendices, Urdu glossary, booklist, index. 478 pages. **$15.95**

MOSCOW-LENINGRAD HANDBOOK by Masha Nordbye
Provides the visitor with an extensive introduction to the history, culture, and people of these two great cities, as well as practical information on where to stay, eat, and shop. 8 color pages, 36 b/w photos, 20 illustrations, 16 maps, 9 charts, booklist, index. 205 pages. **$12.95**

NEPAL HANDBOOK by Kerry Moran
Whether you're planning a week in Kathmandu or months out on the trail, *Nepal Handbook* will take you into the heart of this Himalayan jewel. Color and b/w pages, illustrations, 50 maps, 6 charts, glossary, index. 450 pages. **$12.95**

NEPALI AAMA by Broughton Coburn
A delightful photo-journey into the life of a Gurung tribeswoman of Central Nepal. Having lived with Aama (translated, "mother") for two years, first as an outsider and later as an adopted member of the family, Coburn presents an intimate glimpse into a culture alive with humor, folklore, religion, and ancient rituals. B/w photos. 165 pages. **$13.95**

IMPORTANT ORDERING INFORMATION

FOR FASTER SERVICE ORDER BY PHONE: (800) 345-5473
Monday-Friday · 9 a.m.-5 p.m. PST

PRICES: All prices are subject to change. We always ship the most current edition. We will let you know if there is a price increase on the book you ordered.

SHIPPING & HANDLING OPTIONS:
  1) Domestic UPS or USPS 1st class (allow 10 working days for delivery):
    $3.50 for the 1st item, 50 cents for each additional item.
Exceptions:
  · **Moonbelt** shipping is $1.50 for one, 50 cents for each additional belt.
  · Add $2.00 for same-day handling.

  2) UPS 2nd Day Air or Printed Airmail requires a special quote.
  3) International Surface Bookrate (8-12 weeks delivery):
    $3.00 for the 1st item, $1.00 for each additional item.

FOREIGN ORDERS: All orders which originate outside the U.S.A. must be paid for with either an International Money Order or a check in U.S. currency drawn on a major U.S. bank based in the U.S.A.

TELEPHONE ORDERS: We accept Visa or MasterCard payments. Minimum order is US $15.00. Call in your order: 1 (800) 345-5473. 9 a.m.-5 p.m. Pacific Standard Time.

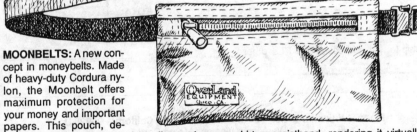

MOONBELTS: A new concept in moneybelts. Made of heavy-duty Cordura nylon, the Moonbelt offers maximum protection for your money and important papers. This pouch, designed for all-weather comfort, slips under your shirt or waistband, rendering it virtually undetectable and inaccessible to pickpockets. Many thoughtful features: 1-inch-wide nylon webbing, heavy-duty zipper, and a 1-inch high-test quick-release buckle. No more fumbling around for the strap or repeated adjustments, this handy plastic buckle opens and closes with a touch, but won't come undone until you want it to. Accommodates traveler's checks, passport, cash, photos. Size 5 x 9 inches. Available in black only.   **$8.95**

ORDER FORM

Be sure to call (800) 345-5473 for current prices and editions · 9 a.m.-5 p.m. PST
(See important ordering information on preceding page)

Name:_____Date:_____

Street:_____

City:_____

State or Country:_____Zip Code:_____

Daytime Phone:_____

Quantity	Title	Price

Taxable Total	
Sales Tax (6%) for California Residents	
Shipping & Handling	
TOTAL	

Ship: ☐ 1st class ☐ UPS (no P.O. Boxes) ☐ International Surface

Ship to: ☐ address above ☐ other_____

_____

_____

Make checks payable to:
Moon Publications Inc., 722 Wall Street, Chico, California 95928 U.S.A.
We Accept Visa and MasterCard
To Order: Call in your Visa or MasterCard number, or send a written order with your Visa or
MasterCard number and expiration date clearly written.

Card Number: ☐ **Visa** ☐ **MasterCard**

☐☐☐☐☐ ☐☐☐☐☐ ☐☐☐☐ ☐☐☐☐

Exact Name on Card: ☐ same as above expiration date:_____

☐ other_____

signature_____